THE VICTORIAN MUSE

Selected Criticism and Parody of the Period

*A thirty-nine-volume facsimile set
essential to the study of one of the most
prolific periods in English literature*

*Edited by
William E. Fredeman, Ira Bruce Nadel, John F. Stasny*

A Garland Series

VICTORIAN POETRY
A Collection of Essays
from the Period

Edited by
John F. Stasny

Garland Publishing, Inc.
New York & London
1986

For a complete list of the titles in this series
see the final pages of this volume.

The facsimile of *An Answer to the Question What is Poetry?* is
from a copy in the British Library; those of *Wordsworth,
Tennyson, and Browning* and *Poetry, Poets, and Poetical Powers* are
from copies in the Library of Congress. The remaining
facsimiles are from copies in the libraries of Yale University.

Introduction © 1986 by John F. Stasny

Library of Congress Cataloging-in-Publication Data

Victorian poetry.

(The Victorian muse)
1. English poetry—19th century—History and
criticism—Theory, etc.   I. Stasny, John F.
II. Series.
PR592.V53   1986   821'.8'09   86-7535
ISBN 0-8240-8630-9 (alk. paper)

Design by Bonnie Goldsmith

The volumes in this series are printed on
acid-free, 250-year-life paper.

Printed in the United States of America

Introduction

Eccentricity is the inevitable hazard of a selection of essays from the mass of Victorian periodical literature on poetry and poetic theory. The problem is exacerbated by an editorial decision to exclude from this selection essays frequently anthologized or essays conveniently available among the collected works, especially of the major authors. Such exclusions might be expected to leave "one vast expanse," a desert "boundless and bare" across which "The lone and level sands stretch far away." The explorer among Victorian periodicals, guided by the long lists of titles in the standard indexes and bibliographies, has, however, riches enough to find and treasures to share, the number of which makes selection necessary and leaves much unretrieved for future explorers with other destinations. The selections included here are simply those that captured this explorer's attention, reveal his private enthusiasms (as seen in the inclusion of the more familiar essays by Newman, Hallam, Mill, Hunt, and Bagehot), or appealed to his eccentric interests.

The chronological arrangement of these essays allows a journey through the critical thought of the nineteenth century from the end of the Romantic period to the fin de siècle. At the beginning of the journey one hears everywhere continuations of the concerns of the Romantics. Echoes of Wordsworth and Coleridge abound in discussions of such issues as the nature of poetry and the poet, the Imagination, poetic Truth, and the role of the poet in society. These early essayists share the exalted Romantic view of the importance of poetry, but they also reveal characteristic early Victorian anxieties for the future of poetry.

In 1825 Macaulay wrote in his essay on "Milton" that "as civilization advances, poetry almost necessarily declines." Also in 1825 Jeremy Bentham wrote, "Prejudice apart, the game of push-pin is of equal value with the arts and sciences of music and poetry." These provocations and denigrations demanded and received response. The Romantics provided the hopes; Macaulay and Bentham expressed the bases of fear for the future of poetry. Among the early essayists in our collection the characteristic Victorian dialogue and debate begins.

Walter Bagehot's 1864 essay "Wordsworth, Tennyson, and Browning; or, Pure, Ornate, and Grotesque Art in English Poetry" offers a convenient compendium of the characteristic concerns for poetry of the mid-Victorian period. Bagehot reminds his readers that "neither English poetry nor English criticism have ever recovered the *eruption* which they both made at the beginning of this century into the fashionable world." He refers, however, specifically to poems of Byron, which "were received with an avidity that resembles our present avidity for sensation novels." He adds, "If now-a-days a dismal poet were, like Byron, to lament the fact of his birth, and to hint that he was too good for the world, the *Saturday Review* would say that 'they doubted if he *was* too good; that a sulky poet was a questionable addition to a tolerable world; that he need not have been born, as far as they were concerned.'" Bagehot indicts Byron's poetry for "the harm which it has done. . . . It fixed upon the minds of a whole generation, it engraved in popular memory and tradition, a vague conviction that poetry is but one of the many *amusements* for the light classes, for the lighter hours of all classes." It is Bagehot's intention to remind a more serious generation and class that "poetry is a deep thing, a teaching thing, the most surely and wisely elevating of human things." Lord Jeffrey and his *Edinburgh Review* influentially pandered to a frivolous taste of an idle class. "For the great and (as time now proves) the *permanent* part of the poetry of his time—for Shelley and for Wordsworth—Lord Jeffrey," declares Bagehot, "had but one word. He said 'It won't do.' And it will not do to amuse a drawing-room." Walter Bagehot and the *National Review* clearly address a more serious and earnest Victorian middle class, a class already addressed by Carlyle, who "most rudely contradicted . . . the doctrine that poetry is a light amusement." "He has denied," Bagehot says of Carlyle, "but he has not disproved. He has contradicted the floating paganism, but he has not founded the deep religion." Bagehot aspires to be a John the Baptist for a future messiah. The messiah's name is Matthew Arnold. The issues in Arnold's literary and social criticism are the issues that dominate the periodical literature on poetry during the 1860s and 70s.

Bagehot's essay is a review article, ostensibly a joint review of the latest publications of Tennyson and Browning. The Victorians had in them practitioners of the high and serious art of poetry. Bagehot observes, however, that "it is singularly characteristic of this age that the poems which rise to the surface, should be examples of ornate art, and grotesque art, not of pure art." He continues, "We live in the realm of the *half* educated. The number of readers grows daily, but the quality of readers does not improve rapidly. The middle class is scattered, headless; it is well-meaning but aimless; wishing to be wise, but ignorant how to be wise." It is clear that Bagehot and his colleagues writing in Victorian periodicals assumed the roles of self-appointed educators to their contemporaries, eager for guidance, who sought a succedaneum for religion and other sources of failing wisdom and who might find in poetry, as Arnold predicted, "an ever surer and surer stay." Taste had to be educated. Contemporary poets and artistic tendencies had to be evaluated, and warnings had to be issued—more frequently as the century progressed. The essays selected from the last two decades of the century concern themselves with various issues. There are reflections of the aesthetic movement in essays on purely aesthetic concerns such as those found in several articles comparing poetry with the other arts. Trends toward skepticism and pessimism are detected and duly analyzed. There are essays on "Poetic Morality" and "Poetry and Politics." There are short essays with only modest pretensions. There are debates and polite dialogues, and there are lengthy essays, such as the final selection in this collection, in which W. H. Mallock, with his characteristic satiric wit and dogmatic assurance, has the "last" word as he assesses, in the last year of the century, not only the poetry but the age itself.

The essays in this collection, with the exception of those by Newman and Mill, are not the work of major Victorian authors. Hallam and Hunt, Bagehot, Palgrave, Mallock, and several others are names familiar to students of the Victorian Age, but the authors of several of the anonymously published articles remain unidentified, and when names can be assigned—Joseph Downes, Alexander Smith, James Bucham Brown, and W. H. Hadow, for example—obscurity remains undispelled. All of the essays are preeminently readable. There are delightful discoveries to be made of shrewd insights and observations, cogent judgments, and passages of various stylistic charms or effectiveness. It is testimony to the high level of Victorian journalism that a selection such as this contains so much that remains undeniably interesting and attractive.

Contents

"Wordsworth, Tennyson, and Browning; or, Pure, Ornate, and Grotesque Art in English Poetry," *The National Review*, 1864
W. B.

"Modern Verse Writers," *Fraser's Magazine*, 1867

"Music in Poetry," *The Dublin University Magazine*, 1868

"Scepticism and Modern Poetry," *Blackwood's Edinburgh Magazine*, 1874

"Culture and Modern Poetry," *The Cornhill Magazine*, 1876
J.B.S.

"Ethics and Aesthetics of Modern Poetry," *The Cornhill Magazine*, 1878
J.B.S.

"A Dialogue on Poetic Morality," *The Contemporary Review*, 1881
Vernon Lee

"Aesthetic Poetry: Dante Gabriel Rossetti," *The Contemporary Review*, 1882
J. C. Shairp

"Poetry and Culture," *The Month*, 1883
C. Cowley Clarke

"Poetry and Politics," *Macmillan's Magazine*, 1885
Andrew Lang

"Poetry and Politics: Form and Subject," *The National Review*, 1886
William John Courthope

"Poetry and Politics," *Macmillan's Magazine*, 1886
Ernest Myers

"The Poetic Imagination," *Macmillan's Magazine*, 1886
Arthur Tilley

"The Musical and the Picturesque Elements in Poetry," *Macmillan's Magazine*, 1886
Thomas Whittaker

"The Province and Study of Poetry," *Macmillan's Magazine*, 1886
[Francis T. Palgrave]

"Poetry Compared with the Other Fine Arts," *The National Review*, 1886
F. T. Palgrave

"Poetry and Pessimism," *The Westminster Review*, 1892
E. K. Chambers

"Poetry and Music," *Macmillan's Magazine*, 1895

"Poetry, Poets, and Poetical Powers," *The Westminster Review*, 1898
"Judius"

"The Philosophy of Poetry," *The Nineteenth Century*, 1899
Martin Morris

"The Conditions of Great Poetry," *The Quarterly Review*, 1900
[W. H. Mallock]

I.

POETRY, WITH REFERENCE TO ARISTOTLE'S POETICS.

W E propose to offer some speculations of our own on Greek Tragedy, and on Poetry in general, as suggested by the doctrine of Aristotle on the subject.

I.

Aristotle considers the excellence of a tragedy to depend upon its plot—and, since a tragedy, as such, is obviously the exhibition of an action, no one can deny his statement to be abstractedly true. Accordingly, he directs his principal attention to the economy of the fable ; determines its range of subjects, delineates its proportions, traces its progress from a complication of incidents to their just and satisfactory settlement, investigates the means of making a train of events striking or affecting, and shows how the exhibition ·of character may be made subservient to the purpose of the action. His treatise is throughout interesting and valuable. It is one thing, however, to form the *beau ideal* of a tragedy on scientific principles ; another to point out the actual beauty of a particular school of dramatic composition. The Greek tragedians are not generally felicitous in the construction of their plots. Aristotle, then, rather tells us what Tragedy should be, than what Greek Tragedy really was. And this doubtless was the intention of the philosopher. Since, however, the Greek drama has obtained so extended and lasting a celebrity, and yet its excellence does not fall under the strict rules of the critical art, we have to inquire in what it consists.

That the charm of Greek Tragedy does not ordinarily arise from scientific correctness of plot, is certain as a matter of fact. Seldom does any great interest arise from the action; which, instead of being progressive and sustained, is commonly either a mere necessary condition of the drama, or a convenience for the introduction of matter more important than itself. It is often stationary —often irregular—sometimes either wants or outlives the catastrophe. In the plays of Æschylus it is always simple and inartificial; in four out of the seven there is hardly any plot at all; and, though it is of more prominent importance in those of Sophocles, yet even here the Œdipus at Colonus is a mere series of incidents, and the Ajax a union of two separate subjects; while in the Philoctetes, which is apparently busy, the circumstances of the action are but slightly connected with the *dénouement.* The carelessness of Euripides in the construction of his plots is well known. The action then will be more justly viewed as the vehicle for introducing the personages of the drama, than as the principal object of the poet's art; it is not in the plot, but in the characters, sentiments, and diction, that the actual merit and poetry of the composition are found. To show this to the satisfaction of the reader, would require a minuter investigation of details than our present purpose admits; yet a few instances in point may suggest others to the memory.

For instance, in neither the Œdipus Coloneus nor the

Philoctetes, the two most beautiful plays of Sophocles, is the plot striking ; but how exquisite is the delineation of the characters of Antigone and Œdipus, in the former tragedy, particularly in their interview with Polynices, and the various descriptions of the scene itself which the Chorus furnishes ! In the Philoctetes, again, it is the contrast between the worldly wisdom of Ulysses, the inexperienced frankness of Neoptolemus, and the simplicity of the afflicted Philoctetes, which constitutes the principal charm of the drama. Or we may instance the spirit and nature displayed in the grouping of the characters in the Prometheus, which is almost without action ; the stubborn enemy of the new dynasty of gods ; Oceanus trimming, as an accomplished politician, with the change of affairs ; the single-hearted and generous Nereids ; and Hermes, the favourite and instrument of the usurping potentate. So again, the beauties of the Thebæ are almost independent of the plot; it is the Chorus which imparts grace and interest to the actionless scene ; and the speech of Antigone at the end, one of the most simply striking in any play, has, scientifically speaking, no place in the tragedy, which should already have been brought to its conclusion. Then again, amid the multitude of the beauties of the irregular Euripides, it would be obvious to notice the character of Alcestis, and of Clytemnestra in the Electra; the soliloquies of Medea ; the picturesque situation of Ion, the minister of the Pythian temple ; the opening scene of the Orestes ; and the dialogues between Phædra and her attendant in the Hippolytus, and the old man and Antigone in the Phœnissæ ;—passages nevertheless which are either unconnected with the development of the plot, or of an importance superior to it.

Thus the Greek drama, as a fact, was modelled on no

scientific principle. It was a pure recreation of the imagination, revelling without object or meaning beyond its own exhibition. Gods, heroes, kings, and dames, enter and retire : they may have a good reason for appearing,—they may have a very poor one ; whatever it is, still we have no right to ask for it ; the question is impertinent. Let us listen to their harmonious and majestic language, to the voices of sorrow, joy, compassion, or religious emotion,—to the animated odes of the chorus. Why interrupt so transcendent a display of poetical genius by inquiries degrading it to the level of every-day events, and implying incompleteness in the action till a catastrophe arrives ? The very spirit of beauty breathes through every part of the composition. We may liken the Greek drama to the music of the Italian school ; in which the wonder is, how so much richness of invention in detail can be accommodated to a style so simple and uniform. Each is the development of grace, fancy, pathos, and taste, in the respective media of representation and sound.

However true then it may be, that one or two of the most celebrated dramas answer to the requisitions of Aristotle's doctrine, still, for the most part, Greek Tragedy has its own distinct and peculiar praise, which must not be lessened by a criticism conducted on principles, whether correct or not, still leading to excellence of another character. This being as we hope shown, we shall be still bolder, and proceed to question even the sufficiency of the rules of Aristotle for the production of dramas of the highest order. These rules, it would appear, require a fable not merely natural and unaffected, as a vehicle of more poetical matter, but one laboured and complicated, as the sole legitimate channel of tragic effect ; and thus tend to withdraw the mind of the poet from the spontaneous exhibition of pathos or imagination to a minute diligence in the formation of a plot.

2.

To explain our views on the subject, we will institute a short comparison between three tragedies, the Agamemnon, the Œdipus, and the Bacchæ, one of each of the tragic poets, as to which, by reference to Aristotle's principles, we think it will be found that the most perfect in plot is not the most poetical.

1. Of these, the action of the Œdipus Tyrannus is frequently instanced by the critic as a specimen of judgment and skill in the selection and combination of the incidents ; and in this point of view it is truly a masterly composition. The clearness, precision, certainty, and vigour with which the line of the action moves on to its termination is admirable. The character of Œdipus, too, is finely drawn, and identified with the development of the action.

2. The Agamemnon of Æschylus presents us with the slow and difficult birth of a portentous secret—an event of old written in the resolves of destiny, a crime long meditated in the bosom of the human agents. The Chorus here has an importance altogether wanting in the Chorus of the Œdipus. They throw a pall of ancestral honour over the bier of the hereditary monarch, which would have been unbecoming in the case of the upstart king of Thebes. Till the arrival of Agamemnon, they occupy our attention, as the prophetic organ, not commissioned indeed, but employed by heaven, to proclaim the impending horrors. Succeeding to the brief intimation of the watcher who opens the play, they seem oppressed with forebodings of woe and crime which

they can neither justify nor analyze. The expression of their anxiety forms the stream in which the plot flows —everything, even news of joy, takes a colouring from the depth of their gloom. On the arrival of the king, they retire before Cassandra, a more regularly commissioned prophetess ; who, speaking first in figure, then in plain terms, only ceases that we may hear the voice of the betrayed monarch himself, informing us of the striking of the fatal blow. Here, then, the very simplicity of the fable constitutes its especial beauty. The death of Agamemnon is intimated at first—it is accomplished at last ; throughout we find but the growing in volume and intensity of one and the same note—it is a working up of one musical ground, by figure and imitation, into the richness of combined harmony. But we look in vain for the progressive and thickening incidents of the Œdipus.

3. The action of the Bacchæ is also simple. It is the history of the reception of the worship of Bacchus in Thebes ; who, first depriving Pentheus of his reason, and thereby drawing him on to his ruin, reveals his own divinity. The interest of the scene arises from the gradual process by which the derangement of the Theban king is effected, which is powerfully and originally described. It would be comic, were it unconnected with religion. As it is, it exhibits the grave irony of a god triumphing over the impotent presumption of man, the sport and terrible mischievousness of an insulted deity. It is an exemplification of the adage, " Quem deus vult perdere, prius dementat." So delicately balanced is the action along the verge of the sublime and grotesque, that it is both solemn and humorous, without violence to the propriety of the composition : the mad fire of the Chorus, the imbecile mirth of old Cadmus and Tiresias,

and the infatuation of Pentheus, who is ultimately induced to dress himself in female garb to gain admit-
tance among the Bacchæ, are made to harmonize
with the terrible catastrophe which concludes the life
of the intruder. Perhaps the victim's first discovery
of the disguised deity is the finest conception in this
splendid drama. His madness enables him to discern the emblematic horns on the head of Bacchus,
which were hid from him when in his sound mind; yet
this discovery, instead of leading him to an acknowledgment of the divinity, provides him only with matter for
a stupid and perplexed astonishment:

> A Bull, thou seem'st to lead us; on thy head
> Horns have grown forth : wast heretofore a beast ?
> For such thy semblance now.

This play is on the whole the most favourable specimen of the genius of Euripides—not breathing the
sweet composure, the melodious fulness, the majesty
and grace of Sophocles; nor rudely and overpoweringly
tragic as Æschylus; but brilliant, versatile, imaginative,
as well as deeply pathetic. Here then are two dramas
of extreme poetical power, but deficient in skilfulness of
plot. Are they on that account to be rated below the
Œdipus, which, in spite of its many beauties, has not
even a share of the richness and sublimity of either?

3.

Aristotle, then, it must be allowed, treats dramatic
composition more as an exhibition of ingenious workmanship, than as a free and unfettered effusion of genius.
The inferior poem may, on his principle, be the better
tragedy. He may indeed have intended solely to delineate the outward framework most suitable to the reception of the spirit of poetry, not to discuss the nature

of poetry itself. If so, it cannot be denied that, the
poetry being given equal in the two cases, the more perfect plot will merit the greater share of praise. And it
may seem to agree with this view of his meaning, that
he pronounces Euripides, in spite of the irregularity of
his plots, to be, after all, the most tragic of the Greek
dramatists, that is, inasmuch as he excels in his appeal
to those passions which the outward form of the drama
merely subserves. Still there is surely too much stress
laid by the philosopher upon the artificial part ; which,
after all, leads to negative, more than to positive excellence ; and should rather be the natural and, so to say,
unintentional result of the poet's feeling and imagination, than be separated from them as the direct object of
his care. Perhaps it is hardly fair to judge of Aristotle's
sentiments by the fragment of his work which has come
down to us. Yet as his natural taste led him to delight
in the explication of systems, and in those connected
views following upon his vigorous talent for thinking
through large subjects, we may be allowed to suspect
him of entertaining too cold and formal conceptions of
the nature of poetical composition, as if its beauties
were less subtile and delicate than they really are. A
word has power to convey a world of information to the
imagination, and to act as a spell upon the feelings ;
there is no need of sustained fiction,—often no room for
it. The sudden inspiration, surely, of the blind Œdipus,
in the second play bearing his name, by which he is
enabled, " without a guide," to lead the way to his place
of death, in our judgment, produces more poetical effect
than all the skilful intricacy of the plot of the Tyrannus.
The latter excites an interest which scarcely lasts beyond
the first reading—the former " decies repetita placebit."
    Some confirmation of the judgment we have ventured

to pass on the greatest of analytical philosophers, is the account he gives of the source of poetical pleasure; which he almost identifies with a gratification of the reasoning faculty, placing it in the satisfaction derived from recognizing in fiction a resemblance to the realities of life—" The spectators are led to recognize and to syllogize what each thing is."

But as we have treated, rather unceremoniously, a deservedly high authority, we will try to compensate for our rudeness by illustrating his general doctrine of the nature of Poetry, which we hold to be most true and philosophical.

4.

Poetry, according to Aristotle, is a representation of the ideal. Biography and history represent individual characters and actual facts ; poetry, on the contrary, generalizing from the phenomenon of nature and life, supplies us with pictures drawn, not after an existing pattern, but after a creation of the mind. Fidelity is the primary merit of biography and history ; the essence of poetry is fiction. " Poesis nihil aliud est," says Bacon, "quam historiæ imitatio ad placitum." It delineates that perfection which the imagination suggests, and to which as a limit the present system of Divine Providence actually tends. Moreover, by confining the attention to one series of events and scene of action, it bounds and finishes off the confused luxuriance of real nature; while, by a skilful adjustment of circumstances, it brings into sight the connexion of cause and effect, completes the dependence of the parts one on another, and harmonizes the proportions of the whole. It is then but the type and model of history or biography, if we may be allowed the comparison, bearing some resemblance to the abstract

mathematical formulæ of physics, before they are modified
by the contingencies of atmosphere and friction.   Hence,
while it recreates the imagination by the superhuman
loveliness of its views, it provides a solace for the mind
broken by the disappointments and sufferings of actual
life ; and becomes, moreover, the utterance of the inward
emotions of a right moral feeling, seeking a purity and a
truth which this world will not give.

It follows that the poetical mind is one full of the
eternal forms of beauty and perfection; these are its
material of thought, its instrument and medium of observation,—these colour each object to which it directs its
view.   It is called imaginative or creative, from the
originality and independence of its modes of thinking,
compared with the commonplace and matter-of-fact
conceptions of ordinary minds, which are fettered down
to the particular and individual.   At the same time it
feels a natural sympathy with everything great and
splendid in the physical and moral world ; and selecting
such from the mass of common phenomena, incorporates
them, as it were, into the substance of its own creations.
From living thus in a world of its own, it speaks the
language of dignity, emotion, and refinement.   Figure
is its necessary medium of communication with man ;
for in the feebleness of ordinary words to express its
ideas, and in the absence of terms of abstract perfection,
the adoption of metaphorical language is the only poor
means allowed it for imparting to others its intense
feelings.   A metrical garb has, in all languages, been
appropriated to poetry—it is but the outward development of the music and harmony within.   The verse, far
from being a restraint on the true poet, is the suitable index
of his sense, and is adopted by his free and deliberate
choice.   We shall presently show the applicability of our

doctrine to the various departments of poetical composition ; first, however, it will be right to volunteer an explanation which may save it from much misconception
and objection. Let not our notion be thought arbitrarily to
limit the number of poets, generally considered such. It
will be found to lower particular works, or parts of works,
rather than the authors themselves ; sometimes to dis-
parage only the vehicle in which the poetry is conveyed.
There is an ambiguity in the word "poetry," which is taken
to signify both the gift itself, and the written composition which is the result of it. Thus there is an apparent, but no real contradiction, in saying a poem may be
but partially poetical ; in some passages more so than
in others ; and sometimes not poetical at all. We only
maintain, not that the writers forfeit the name of poet
who fail at times to answer to our requisitions, but that
they are poets only so far forth, and inasmuch as they do
answer to them. We may grant, for instance, that the
vulgarities of old Phœnix in the ninth Iliad, or of the
nurse of Orestes in the Choephoræ, are in themselves unworthy of their respective authors, and refer them to the
wantonness of exuberant genius ; and yet maintain that
the scenes in question contain much incidental poetry.
Now and then the lustre of the true metal catches the
eye, redeeming whatever is unseemly and worthless in
the rude ore ; still the ore is not the metal. Nay, sometimes, and not unfrequently in Shakspeare, the introduction of unpoetical matter may be necessary for the sake
of relief, or as a vivid expression of recondite conceptions,
and, as it were, to make friends with the reader's imagination. This necessity, however, cannot make the additions in themselves beautiful and pleasing. Sometimes,
on the other hand, while we do not deny the incidental
beauty of a poem, we are ashamed and indignant on

witnessing the unworthy substance in which that beauty is imbedded. This remark applies strongly to the immoral compositions to which Lord Byron devoted his last years.

5.

Now to proceed with our proposed investigation.

1. We will notice *descriptive poetry* first. Empedocles wrote his physics in verse, and Oppian his history of animals. Neither were poets—the one was an historian of nature, the other a sort of biographer of brutes. Yet a poet may make natural history or philosophy the material of his composition. But under his hands they are no longer a bare collection of facts or principles, but are painted with a meaning, beauty, and harmonious order not their own. Thomson has sometimes been commended for the novelty and minuteness of his remarks upon nature. This is not the praise of a poet; whose office rather is to represent known phenomena in a new connection or medium. In L'Allegro and Il Penseroso the poetical magician invests the commonest scenes of a country life with the hues, first of a cheerful, then of a pensive imagination. It is the charm of the descriptive poetry of a religious mind, that nature is viewed in a moral connexion. Ordinary writers, for instance, compare aged men to trees in autumn—a gifted poet will in the fading trees discern the fading men.* Pastoral poetry is a description of rustics, agriculture, and cattle, softened off and corrected from the rude health of nature. Virgil, and much more Pope and others, have run into

---

* Thus :—

> "How quiet shows the woodland scene !
> Each flower and tree, its duty done,
> Reposing in decay serene,
> Like weary men when age is won," etc.

the fault of colouring too highly; instead of drawing generalized and ideal forms of shepherds, they have given us pictures of gentlemen and beaux.

Their composition may be poetry, but it is not pastoral poetry.

2. The difference between poetical and historical *narrative* may be illustrated by the Tales Founded cn Facts, generally of a religious character, so common in the present day, which we must not be thought to approve, because we use them for our purpose. The author finds in the circumstances of the case many particulars too trivial for public notice, or irrelevant to the main story, or partaking perhaps too much of the peculiarity of individual minds: these he omits. He finds connected events separated from each other by time or place, or a course of action distributed among a multitude of agents; he limits the scene or duration of the tale, and dispenses with his host of characters by condensing the mass of incident and action in the history of a few. He compresses long controversies into a concise argument, and exhibits characters by dialogue, and (if such be his object) brings prominently forward the course of Divine Providence by a fit disposition of his materials. (Thus he selects, combines, refines, colours, —in fact, poetizes.) His facts are no longer actual, but ideal; a tale founded on facts is a tale generalized from facts. The authors of Peveril of the Peak, and of Brambletye House, have given us their respective descriptions of the profligate times of Charles II. Both accounts are interesting, but for different reasons. That of the latter writer has the fidelity of history; Walter Scott's picture is the hideous reality, unintentionally softened and decorated by the poetry of his own mind. Miss Edgeworth sometimes apologizes for certain incident in her tales, by

stating they took place " by one of those strange chances which occur in life, but seem incredible when found in writing." Such an excuse evinces (a misconception of the principle of fiction, which, being the perfection of the actual, prohibits the introduction of any such anomalies of experience.) It is by a similar impropriety that painters sometimes introduce unusual sunsets, or other singular phenomena of lights and forms. Yet some of Miss Edgeworth's works contain much poetry of narrative. Manœuvring is perfect in its way,—the plot and characters are natural, without being too real to be pleasing.

3. *Character* is made poetical by a like process. The writer draws indeed from experience; but unnatural peculiarities are laid aside, and harsh contrasts reconciled. If it be said, the fidelity of the imitation is often its greatest merit, we have only to reply, that in such cases the pleasure is not poetical, but consists in the mere recognition. All novels and tales which introduce real characters, are in the same degree unpoetical. Portrait-painting, to be poetical, should furnish an abstract representation of an individual; the abstraction being more rigid, inasmuch as the painting is confined to one point of time. The artist should draw independently of the accidents of attitude, dress, occasional feeling, and transient action. He should depict the general spirit of his subject—as if he were copying from memory, not from a few particular sittings. An ordinary painter will delineate with rigid fidelity, and will make a caricature; but the learned artist contrives so to temper his composition, as to sink all offensive peculiarities and hardnesses of individuality, without diminishing the striking effect of the likeness, or acquainting the casual spectator with the secret of his art. Miss Edgeworth's

representations of the Irish character are actual, and not
poetical—nor were they intended to be so. They are
interesting, because they are faithful. If there is poetry
about them, it exists in the personages themselves, not
in her representation of them. She is only the accurate
reporter in word of what was poetical in fact. Hence,
moreover, when a deed or incident is striking in itself, a
judicious writer is led to describe it in the most simple
and colourless terms, his own being unnecessary; for
instance, if the greatness of the action itself excites the
imagination, or the depth of the suffering interests the
feelings. In the usual phrase, the circumstances are left
"to speak for themselves."

Let it not be said that our doctrine is adverse to that
individuality in the delineation of character, which is a
principal charm of fiction. It is not necessary for the
ideality of a composition to avoid those minuter shades
of difference between man and man, which give to poetry
its plausibility and life; but merely such violation of
general nature, such improbabilities, wanderings, or
coarsenesses, as interfere with the refined and delicate enjoyment of the imagination; which would have the
elements of beauty extracted out of the confused multitude of ordinary actions and habits, and combined with
consistency and ease. Nor does it exclude the introduction of imperfect or odious characters. The original
conception of a weak or guilty mind may have its intrinsic beauty; and much more so, when it is connected
with a tale which finally adjusts whatever is reprehensible
in the personages themselves. Richard and Iago are
subservient to the plot. Moral excellence in some characters may become even a fault. The Clytemnestra of
Euripides is so interesting, that the divine vengeance,
which is the main subject of the drama, seems almost

unjust.   Lady Macbeth, on the contrary, is the conception of one deeply learned in the poetical art.   She is
polluted with the most heinous crimes, and meets the
fate she deserves.   Yet there is nothing in the picture
to offend the taste, and much to feed the imagination.
Romeo and Juliet are too good for the termination to
which the plot leads ; so are Ophelia and the Bride of
Lammermoor.   In these cases there is something inconsistent with correct beauty, and therefore unpoetical.
We do not say the fault could be avoided without sacri-
ficing more than would be gained ; still it is a fault.   It
is scarcely possible for a poet satisfactorily to connect
innocence with ultimate unhappiness, when the notion of
a future life is excluded.   Honours paid to the memory
of the dead are some alleviation of the harshness.   In
his use of the doctrine of a future life, Southey is admirable.   Other writers are content to conduct their
heroes to temporal happiness ;—Southey refuses present
comfort to his Ladurlad, Thalaba, and Roderick, but
carries them on through suffering to another world.   The
death of his hero is the termination of the action ; yet
so little in two of them, at least, does this catastrophe
excite sorrowful feelings, that some readers may be
startled to be reminded of the fact.   If a melancholy is
thrown over the conclusion of the Roderick, it is from
the peculiarities of the hero's previous history.

4. Opinions, feelings, manners, and customs, are made
poetical by the delicacy or splendour with which they
are expressed.   This is seen in the *ode, elegy, sonnet,*
and *ballad ;* in which a single idea, perhaps, or familiar
occurrence, is invested by the poet with pathos or
dignity.   The ballad of Old Robin Gray will serve for
an instance, out of a multitude ; again, Lord Byron's
Hebrew Melody, beginning, " Were my bosom as false,"

etc. ; or Cowper's Lines on his Mother's Picture ; or Milman's Funeral Hymn in the Martyr of Antioch ; or Milton's Sonnet on his Blindness ; or Bernard Barton's Dream. As picturesque specimens, we may name Campbell's Battle of the Baltic ; or Joanna Baillie's Chough and Crow ; and for the more exalted and splendid style, Gray's Bard ; or Milton's Hymn on the Nativity ; in which facts, with which every one is familiar, are made new by the colouring of a poetical imagination. It must all along be observed, that we are not adducing instances for their own sake ; but in order to illustrate our general doctrine, and to show its applicability to those compositions which are, by universal consent, acknowledged to be poetical.

The department of poetry we are now speaking of is of much wider extent than might at first sight appear. It will include such moralizing and philosophical poems as Young's Night Thoughts, and Byron's Childe Harold. There is much bad taste, at present, in the judgment passed on compositions of this kind. It is the fault of the day to mistake mere eloquence for poetry ; whereas, in direct opposition to the conciseness and simplicity of the poet, the talent of the orator consists in making much of a single idea. " Sic dicet ille ut verset sæpe multis modis eandem et unam rem, ut hæreat in eâdem commoreturque sententiâ." This is the great art of Cicero himself, who, whether he is engaged in statement, argument, or raillery, never ceases till he has exhausted the subject ; going round about it, and placing it in every different light, yet without repetition to offend or weary the reader. This faculty seems to consist in the power of throwing off harmonious verses, which, while they have a respectable portion of meaning, yet are especially intended to charm the ear. In popular poems, common ideas are unfolded with copiousness, and set off in polished verse—and this is called poetry. Such is the character of Campbell's Pleasures of Hope; it is in his minor poems that the author's poetical genius rises to its natural elevation. In Childe Harold, too, the writer is carried through his Spenserian stanza with the unweariness and equable fulness of accomplished eloquence; opening, illustrating, and heightening one idea, before he passes on to another. His composition is an extended funeral sermon over buried joys and pleasures. His laments over Greece, Rome, and the fallen in various engagements, have quite the character of panegyrical orations; while by the very attempt to describe the celebrated buildings and sculptures of antiquity, he seems to confess that *they* are the poetical text, his the rhetorical comment. Still it is a work of splendid talent, though, as a whole, not of the highest poetical excellence. Juvenal is perhaps the only ancient author who habitually substitutes declamation for poetry.

5. The *philosophy of mind* may equally be made subservient to poetry, as the philosophy of nature. It is a common fault to mistake a mere knowledge of the heart for poetical talent. Our greatest masters have known better;—they have subjected metaphysics to their art. In Hamlet, Macbeth, Richard, and Othello, the philosophy of mind is but the material of the poet. These personages are ideal; they are effects of the contact of a given internal character with given outward circumstances, the results of combined conditions determining (so to say) a moral curve of original and inimitable properties. Philosophy is exhibited in the same subserviency to poetry in many parts of Crabbe's Tales of the Hall. In the writings of this author there is much to offend a refined taste; but, at

least in the work in question, there is much of a highly poetical cast. It is a representation of the action and reaction of two minds upon each other and upon the world around them. Two brothers of different characters and fortunes, and strangers to each other, meet. Their habits of mind, the formation of those habits by external circumstances, their respective media of judgment, their points of mutual attraction and repulsion, the mental position of each in relation to a variety of trifling phenomena of every-day nature and life, are beautifully developed in a series of tales moulded into a connected narrative. We are tempted to single out the fourth book, which gives an account of the childhood and education of the younger brother, and which for variety of thought as well as fidelity of description is in our judgment beyond praise. The Waverley Novels would afford us specimens of a similar excellence. One striking peculiarity of these tales is the author's practice of describing a group of characters bearing the same general features of mind, and placed in the same general circumstances ; yet so contrasted with each other in minute differences of mental constitution, that each diverges from the common starting-point into a path peculiar to himself. The brotherhood of villains in Kenilworth, of knights in Ivanhoe, and of enthusiasts in Old Mortality, are instances of this. This bearing of character and plot on each other is not often found in Byron's poems. The Corsair is intended for a remarkable personage. We pass by the inconsistencies of his character, considered by itself. The grand fault is, that whether it be natural or not, we are obliged to accept the author's word for the fidelity of his portrait. We are told, not shown, what the hero was. There is nothing in the plot which results from his peculiar formation of mind. An every-

day bravo might equally well have satisfied the requirements of the action. Childe Harold, again, if he is anything, is a being professedly isolated from the world, and
uninfluenced by it. One might as well draw Tityrus's
stags grazing in the air, as a character of this kind;
which yet, with more or less alteration, passes through
successive editions in his other poems. Byron had very
little versatility or elasticity of genius ; he did not know
how to make poetry out of existing materials. He
declaims in his own way, and has the upperhand as long
as he is allowed to go on ; but, if interrogated on principles of nature and good sense, he is at once put out
and brought to a stand.

Yet his conception of Sardanapalus and Myrrha is fine
and ideal, and in the style of excellence which we have
just been admiring in Shakspeare and Scott.

6.

These illustrations of Aristotle's doctrine may suffice.

Now let us proceed to a fresh position ; which, as before, shall first be broadly stated, then modified and
explained. How does originality differ from the poetical
talent ? Without affecting the accuracy of a definition, we
may call the latter the originality of right moral feeling.

Originality may perhaps be defined the power of ab-
stracting for one's self, and is in thought what strength of
mind is in action. Our opinions are commonly derived
from education and society. Common minds transmit
as they receive, good and bad, true and false ; minds of
original talent feel a continual propensity to investigate
subjects, and strike out views for themselves ;—so that
even old and established truths do not escape modification and accidental change when subjected to this process
of mental digestion. Even the style of original writers

is stamped with the peculiarities of their minds. When originality is found apart from good sense, which more or less is frequently the case, it shows itself in paradox and rashness of sentiment, and eccentricity of outward conduct. Poetry, on the other hand, cannot be separated from its good sense, or taste, as it is called ; which is one of its elements. It is originality energizing in the world of beauty ; the originality of grace, purity, refinement, and good feeling. We do not hesitate to say, that poetry is ultimately founded on correct moral perception ; that where there is no sound principle in exercise there will be no poetry ; and that on the whole (originality being granted) in proportion to the standard of a writer's moral character will his compositions vary in poetical excellence. This position, however, requires some explanation.

Of course, then, we do not mean to imply that a poet must necessarily display virtuous and religious feeling ; we are not speaking of the actual material of poetry, but of its sources. A right moral state of heart is the formal and scientific condition of a poetical mind. Nor does it follow from our position that every poet must in fact be a man of consistent and practical principle ; except so far as good feeling commonly produces or results from good practice. Burns was a man of inconsistent life ; still, it is known, of much really sound principle at bottom. Thus his acknowledged poetical talent is in nowise inconsistent with the truth of our doctrine, which will refer the beauty which exists in his compositions to the remains of a virtuous and diviner nature within him. Nay, further than this, our theory holds good, even though it be shown that a depraved man may write a poem. As motives short of the purest lead to actions intrinsically good, so frames of mind short of virtuous will produce a partial and limited poetry. But even where this is instanced, the poetry of a vicious mind will be inconsistent and debased; that is, so far only poetry as the traces and shadows of holy truth still remain upon it. On the other hand, a right moral feeling places the mind in the very centre of that circle from which all the rays have their origin and range; whereas minds otherwise placed command but a portion of the whole circuit of poetry. Allowing for human infirmity and the varieties of opinion, Milton, Spenser, Cowper, Wordsworth, and Southey, may be considered, as far as their writings go, to approximate to this moral centre. The following are added as further illustrations of our meaning. Walter Scott's centre is chivalrous honour; Shakspeare exhibits the characteristics of an unlearned and undisciplined piety; Homer the religion of nature and conscience, at times debased by polytheism. All these poets are religious. The occasional irreligion of Virgil's poetry is painful to the admirers of his general taste and delicacy. Dryden's Alexander's Feast is a magnificent composition, and has high poetical beauties; but to a refined judgment there is something intrinsically unpoetical in the end to which it is devoted, the praises of revel and sensuality. It corresponds to a process of clever reasoning erected on an untrue foundation—the one is a fallacy, the other is out of taste. Lord Byron's Manfred is in parts intensely poetical; yet the delicate mind naturally shrinks from the spirit which here and there reveals itself, and the basis on which the drama is built. From a perusal of it we should infer, according to the above theory, that there was right and fine feeling in the poet's mind, but that the central and consistent character was wanting. From the history of his life we know this to be the fact. The connexion between want of the religious principle and want of poetical feeling, is seen in the instances of Hume and Gibbon, who had radically unpoetical minds. Rousseau, it may be supposed, is an exception to our doctrine. Lucretius, too, had great poetical genius ; but his work evinces that his miserable philosophy was rather the result of a bewildered judgment than a corrupt heart.

According to the above theory, Revealed Religion should be especially poetical—and it is so in fact. While its disclosures have an originality in them to engage the intellect, they have a beauty to satisfy the moral nature. It presents us with those ideal forms of excellence in which a poetical mind delights, and with which all grace and harmony are associated. It brings us into a new world—a world of overpowering interest, of the sublimest views, and the tenderest and purest feelings. The peculiar grace of mind of the New Testament writers is as striking as the actual effect produced upon the hearts of those who have imbibed their spirit. At present we are not concerned with the practical, but the poetical nature of revealed truth. With Christians, a poetical view of things is a duty,—we are bid to colour all things with hues of faith, to see a Divine meaning in every event, and a superhuman tendency. Even our friends around are invested with unearthly brightness— no longer imperfect men, but beings taken into Divine favour, stamped with His seal, and in training for future happiness. It may be added, that the virtues peculiarly Christian are especially poetical—meekness, gentleness, compassion, contentment, modesty, not to mention the devotional virtues ; whereas the ruder and more ordinary feelings are the instruments of rhetoric more justly than of poetry—anger, indignation, emulation, martial spirit, and love of independence.

7.

A few remarks on poetical composition, and we have done. The art of composition is merely accessory to the poetical talent. But where that talent exists, it necessarily gives its own character to the style, and renders it perfectly different from all others. As the poet's habits of mind lead to contemplation rather than to communication with others, he is more or less obscure, according to the particular style of poetry he has adopted, less so in epic, or narrative and dramatic representation, —more so in odes and choruses. He will be obscure, moreover, from the depth of his feelings, which require a congenial reader to enter into them—and from their acuteness, which shrinks from any formal accuracy in the expression of them. And he will be obscure, not only from the carelessness of genius, and from the originality of his conceptions, but it may be from natural deficiency in the power of clear and eloquent expression, which, we must repeat, is a talent distinct from poetry, though often mistaken for it.

However, dexterity in composition, or *eloquence* as it may be called in a contracted sense of the word, is manifestly more or less necessary in every branch of literature, though its elements may be different in each. Poetical eloquence consists, first, in the power of illustration ; which the poet uses, not as the orator, voluntarily, for the sake of clearness or ornament, but almost by constraint, as the sole outlet and expression of intense inward feeling. This spontaneous power of comparison may, in some poetical minds, be very feeble ; these of course cannot show to advantage as poets. Another talent necessary to composition is the power of unfolding the meaning in an orderly manner. A poetical mind is often too impatient to explain itself justly; it is overpowered by a rush of emotions, which sometimes want of power, sometimes the indolence of inward enjoyment, prevents it from describing. Nothing is more difficult than to analyse the feelings of our own minds; and the power of doing so, whether natural or acquired, is clearly distinct from experiencing them. Yet, though distinct from the poetical talent, it is obviously necessary to its exhibition. Hence it is a common praise bestowed upon writers, that they express what we have often felt, but could never describe. The power of arrangement, which is necessary for an extended poem, is a modification of the same talent, being to poetry what method is to logic. Besides these qualifications, poetical composition requires that command of language which is the mere effect of practice. The poet is a compositor; words are his types; he must have them within reach, and in unlimited abundance. Hence the need of careful labour to the accomplished poet,—not in order that his diction may attract, but that the language may be subjected to him. He studies the art of composition as we might learn dancing or elocution; not that we may move or speak according to rule, but that, by the very exercise our voice and carriage may become so unembarrassed as to allow of our doing what we will with them.

A talent for composition, then, is no essential part of poetry, though indispensable to its exhibition. Hence it would seem that attention to the language, for its own sake, evidences not the true poet, but the mere artist. Pope is said to have tuned our tongue. We certainly owe much to him—his diction is rich, musical, and expressive: still he is not on this account a poet; he elaborated his composition for its own sake. If we give him poetical praise on this account, we may as appropriately bestow it on a tasteful cabinet-maker. This does not forbid us to ascribe the grace of his verse to an inward principle of poetry, which supplied him with archetypes of the beautiful and splendid to work by. But a similar gift must direct the skill of every fancy-artist who subserves the luxuries and elegances of life. On the other hand, though Virgil is celebrated as a master of composition, yet his style is so identified with his conceptions, as their outward development, as to preclude the possibility of our viewing the one apart from the other.   In Milton, again, the harmony of the verse is but the echo of the inward music which the thoughts of the poet breathe.   In Moore's style, the ornament continually outstrips the sense.   Cowper and Walter Scott, on the other hand, are slovenly in their versification.   Sophocles writes, on the whole, without studied attention to the style ; but Euripides frequently affected a simplicity and prettiness which exposed him to the ridicule of the comic poets.   Lastly, the style of Homer's poems is perfect in their particular department. It is free, manly, simple, perspicuous, energetic, and varied.   It is the style of one who rhapsodized without deference to hearer or judge, in an age prior to the temptations which more or less prevailed over succeeding writers—before the theatre had degraded poetry into an exhibition, and criticism narrowed it into an art.

January, 1829.

Note on Essay I.

The *London Review*, in the first number of which the foregoing Essay appeared, was started in 1829, under the editorship of Mr. Blanco White. Its history is given in his Life by Mr. Thom (vol. i., p. 448, etc.) : " On Sunday, 27th July, 1828," (Mr. White says in his Journal,) " Dr. Mayo, who came to see Senior and myself from Tunbridge Wells to Hastings, where I was for the benefit of my health, made me the proposal of editing a new Review. The project of this Quarterly had originated in Senior, who, having engaged the support of Dr. Whately and many others, had now only to procure an editor. Dr. Mayo urged me to accept the offer, both as a literary friend and as my medical adviser. . . . The unexpected opening thus made for useful occupation, and the chance of a better provision for my old age than I could make by taking pupils at Oxford, roused me into all the energy of revived hope : I accepted the charge with alacrity."

The time was favourable for a new Quarterly, so far as this, that the long-established Quarterly (if my memory is correct) was in the crisis of a change, or a succession, of editors, and was not at the moment altogether satisfactory to the great political and religious party, which it has ever represented. And in fact its publisher entered into correspondence with Mr. White with a view to an arrangement, which would supersede the projected Review. However, the former had no real cause of apprehension ; the new publication required an editor of more vigorous health and enterprising mind, of more cheerful spirits, and greater power of working, and with larger knowledge of the English public, than Mr. White possessed ; and writers, less bookish and academical than those, able as they were, on whom its fate depended. Southey, by anticipation, hit the blot. As a whole, the Review was dull. "Be of good heart in your new undertaking," he says in a letter to Mr. White, November 11th, 1828, "and it cannot fail. My advice is, that you should have always a considerable proportion of *attractive matter*, for which current literature may always supply abundant subjects. A *good* journal I know you will make it ; *get for it the character of an entertaining one*, and you have hit your own mark as well as the publisher's. Rely upon this, that you have my best word, my best wishes, and shall not want my best aid, when I can with propriety give it."

Also it happened unfortunately for Mr. White, that, having been brought to Oxford mainly by the Tory party on account of his "seasonable," as they called it, witness against Catholicism, during the contest about the Catholic claims, he formed, when settled there, so close a friendship with Dr. Whately and others of opposite political opinions, as to be led in February, 1829, to vote for the re-election of Mr. Peel, on his change in Parliament in favour of the Catholics. This step, which gave great umbrage to the majority of residents, had a proportionate effect upon his wearied and troubled mind. His editorial duties and the Review itself ended with its second number. He writes to a friend, May 20, 1829, "My compact with the evil spirit, the demon of the book-market is almost at an end. . . . . I hope very soon to be entirely free from the nightmare of the *London Review*."

As to my own article, the following reference is made to it in my "*Religious Opinions,*" p. 11 : " I recollect how dissatisfied Dr. Whately was with an article of mine in the *London Review,* which Blanco White goodhumouredly only called ' Platonic ' ; " and indeed it certainly omits one of the essential conditions of the idea of Poetry, its relation to the affections,—and that, in consequence, as it would seem, of confusing the function and aim of Poetry with its formal object. As the aim of civil government is the well-being of the governed, and its object is expediency ; as the aim of oratory is to persuade, and its object is the probable ; as the function of philosophy is to view all things in their mutual relations, and its object is truth ; and as virtue consists in the observance of the moral law, and its object is the right ; so Poetry may be considered to be the gift of moving the affections through the imagination, and its object to be the beautiful.

I should observe that several sentences of this Essay, which in passing through the press were, by virtue of an editor's just prerogative, altered or changed, now stand as I sent them to him.

On Some of the Characteristics of Modern Poetry, and on the Lyrical Poems of Alfred Tennyson

[This review of Tennyson's *Poems, Chiefly Lyrical*, 1830, appeared unsigned in Moxon's *Englishman's Magazine* for August, 1831, pp. 616-628. It was reprinted in part in all editions of the *Remains*, and in full in LeGallienne's edition of 1893. Of it Hallam wrote Edward Spedding under postmark of July 28, 1831: "My general occupations have been of a more grave character; I have read a great deal of Justinian, who is infinitely more entertaining than Miss Edgeworth (*N.B.* I read them at the same time, so ought to know), and I have been writing a review of Alfred's poems in the forthcoming number of the Englishman's Magazine, an affair of my acquaintance Mr. Moxon, who I hope will succeed in it. . . . Perhaps my article will not be in time for the August number." (From a letter owned by Lady Charnwood and printed in her *An Autograph Collection and the Making of It*, New York [1930], pp. 177-179). Since the August issue was announced to appear August 1 (Cf. Leigh Hunt's *Examiner* for July 31, 1831, p. 494) not much time was allowed for typesetting. It is not surprising, therefore to read, in a letter from Hallam to Charles Merivale of August 14, 1831 that the August *Englishman's Magazine* contains "a sonnet of Tennyson's and a review of his book written by your humble servant, but so execrably printed that every line contains an error, and these not always palpable. But this is parenthetical—a little by-play of author-vanity." (*Autobiography of Dean Merivale*, London, 1899, pp. 119-121). A full discussion of the review appears in an unpublished letter from Hallam to Edward Spedding in the possession of the present editor. Writing on August 23, Hallam said: "I am glad you are pleased with my article. I would sooner have the approbation of one such man, as I take you to be, than of a whole generation of fools. . . . You treat what I have written better than it deserves: it was the hasty product of the evenings of one week: I had no time for revision, or that adding & subtracting work, by means of which Good Sense, 'θνητός πες ἐων,' follows up the ἀθανατοις ἱπποιοι,' of Imagination. My article went up to its final audit with all its sins on its head, mortal as well as venial: 'unhouseled and unanealed' the poor child of my brain was hurled into the eternity of Print, which alas! is too often one of damnation. . . ."

The damnation followed tardily in Christopher North's "Tennyson's Poems" in *Blackwood's Edinburgh Magazine* for May, 1832, pp. 721-741. Referring to the fact that Moxon's venture failed with the October, 1831, issue, the critic wrote: "The Englishman's Magazine ought not to have died; for it threatened to be a very pleasant periodical. An Essay 'on the genius of Alfred Tennyson,' sent it to the grave. The superhuman—nay, supernatural—pomposity of that one paper, incapacitated the whole work for living one day longer in this unceremonious world. The solemnity with which the critic approached the object of his adoration, and the sanctity with which he laid his offerings on the shrine, were too much for our irreligious age. The Essay 'on the genius of Alfred Tennyson awoke a general guffaw, and it expired in convulsions. Yet the Essay was exceedingly well-written—as well as if it had been 'on the genius of Sir Isaac Newton.' Therein lay the mistake. Sir Isaac discovered the law of gravitation; Alfred had but written some pretty verses, and mankind were not prepared to set him among the stars. But that he has genius is proved by his being at this moment alive; for had he not, he must have breathed his last under that critique."

The opening paragraphs of the review allude to two exceedingly popular works by a young man named Robert Montgomery, whose deficiencies in breeding and education no less than his lack of poetical power inevitably attracted the furious scorn of all critics of the ruling caste. *Oxford*, which went through at least three editions soon after its publication in 1831, flowered into several additional editions early in that same year with illustrations by one T. Skelton "and other Artists." That Hallam soon realized the unfortunateness of his participation in the general hue and cry after Montgomery is clear when he wrote Spedding (in the letter of August 23): "in parts I endeavored, [sic] as you observe, to put myself in a Magazine humour, and the result was trash that you are very properly ashamed of, and so am I." The references to Montgomery were among the parts eliminated in 1834 by Henry Hallam. (Lounsbury deals illuminatingly with Montgomery in *The Life and Times of Tennyson*, pp. 181-203.)

The text of the review here given is that of its first publication, with corrections as noted.]

So Mr. Montgomery's *Oxford*, by the help of some pretty illustrations, has contrived to prolong its miserable existence to a second edition! But this is slow work, compared to that triumphant progress of the *Omnipresence*, which, we concede to the author's friends, was "truly astonishing." We understand, moreover, that a new light has broken upon this "desolator desolate;" and since the "columns" have begun to follow the example of "men and gods," by whom our poetaster has long been condemned, "it is the fate of genius," he begins to discover, "to be unpopular."

Now, strongly as we protest against Mr. Montgomery's application of this maxim to his own case, we are much disposed to agree with him as to its abstract correctness. Indeed, the truth which it involves seems to afford the only solution of so curious a phenomenon as the success, partial and transient though it be, of himself, and others of his calibre. When Mr. Wordsworth, in his celebrated Preface to the *Lyrical Ballads*, asserted that immediate or rapid popularity was not the test of poetry, great was the consternation and clamour among those farmers of public favour, the established critics. Never had so audacious an attack been made upon their undoubted privileges and hereditary charter of oppression.

"What! *The Edinburgh Review* not infallible!" shrieked the amiable petulance of Mr. Jeffrey.

"*The Gentleman's Magazine* incapable of decision!" faltered the feeble garrulity of Silvanus Urban.

And straightway the whole sciolist herd, men of rank, men of letters, men of wealth, men of business, all the "mob of gentlemen who think with ease," and a terrible number of old ladies and boarding-school misses began to scream in chorus, and prolonged the notes of execration with which they overwhelmed the new doctrine, until their wits and their voices fairly gave in from exhaustion. Much, no doubt, they did, for much persons will do when they fight for their dear selves: but there was one thing they could not do, and unfortunately it was the only one of any importance. They could not put down Mr. Wordsworth by clamour, or prevent his doctrine, once uttered, and enforced by his example, from awakening the minds of men, and giving a fresh impulse to art. It was the truth, and it prevailed; not only against the exasperation of that hydra, the Reading Public, whose vanity was hurt, and the blustering of its keepers, whose delusion was exposed, but even against the false glosses and narrow apprehensions of the Wordsworthians themselves. It is the madness of all who loosen some great principle, long buried under a snow-heap of custom and superstition, to imagine that they can restrain its operation, or circumscribe it by their purposes. But the right of private judgment was stronger than the will of Luther; and even the genius of Wordsworth cannot expand itself to the full periphery of poetic art.

It is not true, as his exclusive admirers would have it, that the highest species of poetry is the reflective; it is a gross fallacy, that because certain opinions are acute or profound, the expression of them by the imagination must be eminently beautiful. Whenever the mind of the artist suffers itself to be occupied, during its periods of creation, by any other predominant motive than the desire of beauty, the result is false in art.

Now there is undoubtedly no reason why he may not find beauty in those moods of emotion, which arise from the combinations of reflective thought; and it is possible that he may delineate these with fidelity, and not be led astray by any suggestions of an unpoetical mood. But though possible, it is hardly probable; for a man whose reveries take a reasoning turn, and who is accustomed to measure his ideas by their logical relations rather than the congruity of the sentiments to which they refer, will be apt to mistake the pleasure he has in knowing a thing to be true, for the pleasure he would have in knowing it to be beautiful, and so will pile his thoughts in a rhetorical battery, that they may convince, instead of letting them flow in a natural course of contemplation, that they may enrapture.

It would not be difficult to shew, by reference to the most admired poems of Wordsworth, that he is frequently chargeable with this error; and that much has been said by him which is good as philosophy, powerful as rhetoric, but false as poetry. Perhaps this very distortion of the truth did more in the peculiar juncture of our literary affairs to enlarge and liberalize the genius of our age, than could have been effected by a less sectarian temper.

However this may be, a new school of reformers soon began to attract attention, who, professing the same independence of immediate favor, took their stand on a different region of Parnassus from that occupied by the Lakers,[1] and one, in our opinion, much less liable to perturbing currents of air from ungenial climates. We shall not hesitate to express our conviction, that the cockney school (as it was termed in derision from a cursory view of its accidental circumstances) contained more genuine inspiration, and adhered more steadily to that portion of truth which it embraced, than any *form* of art that has existed in this country since the days of Milton. Their *caposetta* was Mr. Leigh Hunt, who did little more than point the way, and was diverted from his aim by a thousand personal predilections and political habits of thought.

But he was followed by two men of very superior make; men who were born poets, lived poets, and went poets to their untimely graves. Shelley and Keats were indeed of opposite genius; that of the one was vast, impetuous, and sublime, the other seemed to be "fed with honey-dew," and to have "drunk the milk of Paradise." Even the softness of Shelley comes out in bold, rapid, comprehensive strokes; he has no patience for minute beauties, unless they can be massed into a general effect of grandeur. On the other hand, the tenderness of Keats cannot sustain a lofty flight; he does not generalize or allegorize Nature; his imagination works with few symbols, and reposes willingly on what is given freely.

---

[1] This cant term was justly ridiculed by Mr. Wordsworth's supporters; but it was not so easy to substitute an inoffensive denomination. We are not at all events the first who have used it without a contemptuous intention, for we remember to have heard a disciple quote Aristophanes in its behalf:—'Ουτος ὁυ τῶν ἠθαδων τῶνδ' ῶν ὁρᾶθ' ὑμεῖς ἀεὶ, ἀλλὰ ΛΙΜΝΑΙΟΣ. "This is no common, no barn-door fowl: No, but a *Lakist.*" [H.]

[2] 1831 and 1893 have 'speedily.' But the obvious misprint was corrected in 1834 and all subsequent editions to 1893.

Yet in this formal opposition of character there is, it seems to us, a groundwork of similarity sufficient for the purposes of classification, and constituting a remarkable point in the progress of literature. They are both poets of sensation rather than reflection. Susceptible of the slightest impulse from external nature, their fine organs trembled into emotion at colors, and sounds, and movements, unperceived or unregarded by duller temperaments. Rich and clear were their perceptions of visible forms; full and deep their feelings of music. So vivid was the delight attending the simple exertions of eye and ear, that it became mingled more and more with their trains of active thought, and tended to absorb their whole being into the energy of sense. Other poets seek for images to illustrate their conceptions; these men had no need to seek; they lived in a world of images; for the most important and extensive portion of their life consisted in those emotions which are immediately conversant with the sensation. Like the hero of Goethe's novel, they would hardly have been affected by what is called the pathetic parts of a book; but the *merely beautiful* passages, "those from which the spirit of the author looks clearly and mildly forth," would have melted them to tears. Hence they are not descriptive, they are picturesque. They are not smooth and *negatively* harmonious; they are full of deep and varied melodies.

This powerful tendency of imagination to a life of immediate sympathy with the external universe, is not nearly so liable to false views of art as the opposite disposition of purely intellectual contemplation. For where beauty is constantly passing before "that inward eye, which is the bliss of solitude;" where the soul seeks it as a perpetual and necessary refreshment to the sources of activity and intuition; where all the other sacred ideas of our nature, the idea of good, the idea of perfection, the idea of truth, are habitually contemplated through the medium of this predominant mood, so that they assume its colour, and are subject to its peculiar laws, there is little danger that the ruling passion of the whole mind will cease to direct its creative operations, or the energetic principle of love for the beautiful sink, even for a brief period, to the level of a mere notion in the understanding.

We do not deny that it is, on other accounts, dangerous for frail humanity to linger with fond attachment in the vicinity of sense. Minds of this description are especially liable to moral temptations; and upon them, more than any, it is incumbent to remember, that their mission as men, which they share with their fellow-beings, is of infinitely higher interest than their mission as artists, which they possess by rare and exclusive privilege. But it is obvious that, critically speaking, such temptations are of slight moment. Not the gross and evident passions of our nature, but the elevated and less separable desires, are the dangerous enemies which misguide the poetic spirit in its attempts at self-cultivation. That delicate sense of fitness which grows with the growth of artist feelings, and strengthens with their strength, until it acquires a celerity and weight of decision hardly inferior to the correspondent judgments of conscience, is weakened by every indulgence of heterogeneous aspirations, however pure they may be, however lofty, however suitable to human nature.

We are therefore decidedly of opinion that the heights and depths of art are most within the reach of those who have received from nature the 'fearful and wonderful" constitution we have described, whose poetry is a sort of magic, producing a number of impressions, too multiplied, too minute, and too diversified to allow of our tracing them to their causes, because just such was the effect, even so boundless and so bewildering, produced on their imaginations by the real appearance of Nature.

These things being so, our friends of the new school had evidently much reason to recur to the maxim laid down by Mr. Wordsworth, and to appeal from the immediate judgment of lettered or unlettered contemporaries to the decision of a more equitable posterity. How should they be popular, whose senses told them a richer and ampler tale than most men could understand, and who constantly expressed, because they constantly felt, sentiments of exquisite pleasure or pain, which most men were not permitted to experience? The public very naturally derided them as visionaries, and gibbeted in terrorem those inaccuracies of diction occasioned sometimes by the speed of their conceptions, sometimes by the inadequacy of language to their peculiar conditions of thought.

But it may be asked, does not this line of argument prove too much? Does it not prove that there is a barrier between these poets and all other persons so strong and immovable, that, as has been said of the Supreme Essence, we must be themselves before we can understand them in the least? Not only are they not liable to sudden and vulgar estimation, but the lapse of ages, it seems, will not consolidate their fame, nor the suffrages of the wise few produce any impression, however remote or slow matured, on the judgment of the incapacitated many.

We answer, this is not the import of our argument. Undoubtedly the true poet addresses himself, in all his conceptions, to the common nature of us all. Art is a lofty tree, and may shoot up far beyond our grasp, but its roots are in daily life and experience. Every bosom contains the elements of those complex emotions which the artist feels, and every head can, to a certain extent, go over in itself the process of their combination, so as to understand his expressions and sympathize with his state. But this requires exertion; more or less, indeed, according to the difference of occasion, but always some degree of exertion. For since the emotions of the poet, during composition. follow a regular law of association, it follows that to accompany their progress up to the harmonious prospect of the whole, and to perceive the proper dependence of every step on that which preceded, it is absolutely necessary *to start from the same point,* i.e. clearly to apprehend that leading sentiment of the poet's mind, by their conformity to which the host of suggestions are arranged.

Now this requisite exertion is not willingly made by the large majority of readers. It is so easy to judge capriciously, and according to indolent impulse! For very many, therefore, it has become *morally* impossible to attain the author's point of vision, on account of their habits, or their prejudices, or their circumstances; but it is never *physically* impossible, because nature has placed in every man the simple elements, of which art is the sublimation. Since then this demand on the reader for activity, when he wants to peruse his author in a luxurious passiveness, is the very thing that moves his bile, it is obvious that those writers will be always most popular who require the least degree of exertion. Hence, whatever is mixed up with art, and appears under its semblance, is always more favorably regarded than art free and unalloyed. Hence, half the fashionable poems in the world are mere rhetoric, and half the remainder are, perhaps, not liked by the generality for their substantial merits. Hence, likewise, of the really pure compositions, those are most universally agreeable which take for their primary subject the *usual* passions of the heart, and deal with them in a simple state, without applying the transforming powers of high imagination. Love, friendship, ambition, religion, &c., are matters of daily experience even amongst unimaginative tempers. The forces of association, therefore, are ready to work in these directions, and little effort of will is necessary to follow the artist.

For the same reason, such subjects often excite a partial power of composition, which is no sign of a truly poetic organization. We are very far from wishing to depreciate this class of poems, whose influence is so extensive, and communicates so refined a pleasure. We contend only that the facility with which its impressions are communicated is no proof of its elevation as a form of art, but rather the contrary.

What, then, some may be ready to exclaim, is the pleasure derived by most men, from Shakespeare, or Dante, or Homer, entirely false and factitious? If these are really masters of their art, must not the energy required of the ordinary intelligences that come in contact with their mighty genius, be the greatest possible? How comes it then, that they are popular? Shall we not say, after all, that the difference is in the power of the author, not in the tenor of his meditations? Those eminent spirits find no difficulty in conveying to common apprehensions their lofty sense and profound observation of Nature. They keep no aristocratic state, apart from the sentiments of society at large; they speak to the hearts of all, and by the magnetic force of their conceptions, elevate inferior intellects into a higher and purer atmosphere.

The truth contained in this observation is undoubtedly important; geniuses of the most universal order, and assigned by destiny to the most propitious era of a nation's literary development, have a clearer and a larger access to the minds of their compatriots than can ever open to those who are circumscribed by less fortunate circumstances. In the youthful periods of any literature there is an expansive and communicative tendency in mind which produces unreservedness of communion, and reciprocity of vigor between different orders of intelligence.

Without abandoning the ground which has always been defended by the partizans of Mr. Wordsworth, who declare with perfect truth, that the number of real admirers of what is really admirable in Shakespeare and Milton is much fewer than the number of apparent admirers might lead one to imagine, we may safely assert that the intense thoughts set in circulation by those "orbs of song" and their noble satellites "in great Eliza's golden time," did not fail to awaken a proportionable intensity of the nature of numberless auditors. Some might feel feebly, some strongly; the effect would vary according to the character of the recipient; but upon none was the stirring influence entirely unimpressive. The knowledge and power thus imbibed became a part of national existence; it was ours as Englishmen; and amid the flux of generations and customs we retain unimpaired this privilege of intercourse with greatness.

But the age in which we live comes late in our national progress. That first raciness and juvenile vigor of literature, when nature "wantoned as in her prime, and played at will her virgin fancies" is gone, never to return. Since that day we have undergone a period of degradation. "Every handicraftsman has worn the mask³ of Poesy." It would be tedious to repeat the tale so often related of the French contagion

³ 1831 has 'mark,' as does 1893. All other editions, from 1834 on, correct to 'mask.'

and the heresies of the Popian school.

With the close of the last century came an era of reaction, an era of painful struggle to bring our over-civilised condition of thought into union with the fresh productive spirit that brightened the morning of our literature. But repentance is unlike innocence; the laborious endeavor to restore has more complicated methods of action than the freedom of untainted nature. Those different powers of poetic disposition, the energies of Sensitive,[*] of Reflective, of Passionate Emotion, which in former times were intermingled, and derived from mutual support an extensive empire over the feelings of men, were now restrained within separate spheres of agency. The whole system no longer worked harmoniously, and by intrinsic harmony acquired external freedom; but there arose a violent and unusual action in the several component functions, each for itself, all striving to reproduce the regular power which the whole had once enjoyed.

Hence the melancholy which so evidently characterises the spirit of modern poetry; hence that return of the mind upon itself and the habit of seeking relief in idiosyncrasies rather than community of interest. In the old times the poetic impulse went along with the general impulse of the nation; in these it is a reaction against it, a check acting for conservation against a propulsion towards change.

We have indeed seen it urged in some of our fashionable publications, that the diffusion of poetry must be in the direct ratio of the diffusion of machinery, because a highly civilized people must have new objects of interest, and thus a new field will be open to description. But this notable argument forgets that against this *objective* amelioration may be set the decrease of *subjective* power, arising from a prevalence of social activity, and a continual absorption of the higher feelings into the palpable interests of ordinary life. The French Revolution may be a finer theme than the war of Troy; but it does not so evidently follow that Homer is to find his superior.

Our inference, therefore, from this change in the relative position of artists to the rest of the community is, that modern poetry in proportion to its depth and truth is likely to have little immediate authority over public opinion. Admirers it will have; sects consequently it will form; and these strong under-currents will in time sensibly affect the principal stream. Those writers whose genius, though great, is not

---

[*] We are aware that this is not the right word, being appropriated by common use to a different signification. Those who think the caution given by Caesar should not stand in the way of urgent occasion, may substitute "sensuous;" a word in use amongst our elder divines, and revived by a few bold writers in our own time. [H.]

strictly and essentially poetic, become mediators between the votaries of art and the careless cravers for excitement.[5] Art herself, less manifestly glorious than in her periods of undisputed supremacy, retains her essential prerogatives, and forgets not to raise up chosen spirits who may minister to her state and vindicate her title.

One of the faithful Islâm, a poet in the truest and highest sense, we are anxious to present to our readers. He has yet written little and published less; but in these "preludes of a loftier strain" we recognize the inspiring god. Mr. Tennyson belongs decidedly to the class we have already described as Poets of Sensation. He sees all the forms of nature with the "eruditus oculus," and his ear has a fairy fineness. There is a strange earnestness in his worship of beauty which throws a charm over his impassioned song, more easily felt than described, and not to be escaped by those who have once felt it. We think he has more definiteness and roundness[6] of general conception than the late Mr. Keats, and is much more free from blemishes of diction and hasty capriccios of fancy. He has also this advantage over that poet and his friend Shelley, that he comes before the public unconnected with any political party or peculiar system of opinions. Nevertheless, true to the theory we have stated, we believe his participation in their characteristic excellences is sufficient to secure him a share of their unpopularity.

The volume of "Poems, chiefly Lyrical," does not contain above 154 pages; but it shews us much more of the character of its parent mind, than many books we have known of much larger compass and more boastful pretensions. The features of original genius are clearly and strongly marked. The author imitates nobody; we recognise the spirit of his age, but not the individual form of this or that writer. His thoughts bear no more resemblance to Byron or Scott, Shelley or Coleridge, than to Homer or Calderon, Firdúsí or Calidasa.[7]

We have remarked five distinctive excellencies of his own manner. First, his luxuriance of imagination, and at the same time his control over it. Secondly his power of embodying himself in ideal characters, or rather moods of character, with such extreme accuracy of adjustment, that the circumstances of the narration seem to have a natural correspondence with the predominant feeling, and, as it were, to be

---

[5] May we not compare them to the bright but unsubstantial clouds which, in still evenings, girdle the sides of lofty mountains, and seem to form a natural connexion between the lowly vallies spread out beneath, and those isolated peaks above that hold the "last parley with the setting sun?" [H.]

[6] 1831 and 1893 have 'definiteness and soundness.' 1834 has 'definiteness and roundness.' 1853 and all following editions have 'definitiveness and roundness.'

[7] 1831 and 1893 have "Ferdusi," "Calidas." 1834, "Ferdusi," 1853 and following, as here given.

evolved from it by assimilative force. Thirdly his vivid, picturesque delineation of objects, and the peculiar skill with which he holds all of them *fused*, to borrow a metaphor from science, in a medium of strong emotion. Fourthly, the variety of his lyrical measures, and exquisite modulation of harmonious words and cadences to the swell and fall of the feelings expressed. Fifthly, the elevated habits of thought, implied in these compositions, and imparting a mellow soberness of tone, more impressive, to our minds, than if the author had drawn up a set of opinions in verse, and sought to instruct the understanding rather than to communicate the love of beauty to the heart.

We shall proceed to give our readers some specimens in illustration of these remarks, and, if possible, we will give them entire; for no poet can be fairly judged of by fragments, least of all, a poet like Mr. Tennyson, whose mind conceives nothing isolated, nothing abrupt, but every part with reference to some other part, and in subservience to the idea of the whole.

Recollections of the Arabian Nights!—What a delightful, endearing title! How we pity those to whom it calls up no reminiscence of early enjoyment, no sentiment of kindliness as towards one who sings a song they have loved, or mentions with affection a departed friend! But let nobody expect a multifarious enumeration of Viziers, Barmecides, Fire-worshippers, and Cadis; trees that sing, horses that fly, and Goules that eat rice-pudding!

Our author knows what he is about; he has, with great judgment, selected our old acquaintance, "the good Haroun Alraschid," as the most prominent object of our childish interest, and with him has called up one of those luxurious garden scenes, the account of which, in plain prose, used to make our mouth water for sherbet, since luckily we were too young to think much about Zobeide! We think this poem will be the favourite among Mr. Tennyson's admirers; perhaps upon the whole it is our own; at least we find ourselves recurring to it oftener than to any other, and every time we read it, we feel the freshness of its beauty increase, and are inclined to exclaim with Madame de Sévigné, "*à force d'être ancien, il m'est nouveau.*" But let us draw the curtain.

[The poem is reprinted here]

Criticism will sound but poorly after this; yet we cannot give silent votes. The first stanza, we beg leave to observe, places us at once in the position of feeling, which the poem requires. The scene is before us, around us; we cannot mistake its localities, or blind ourselves to its colours. That happy ductility of childhood returns for the moment;

"true Mussulmans are we, and sworn," and yet there is a latent knowledge, which heightens the pleasure, that to our change from really
childish thought we owe the capacities by which we enjoy the recollection.

As the poem proceeds, all is in perfect keeping. There is a solemn
distinctness in every image, a majesty of slow motion in every cadence,
that aids the illusion of thought, and steadies its contemplation of the
complete picture. Originality of observation seems to cost nothing to
our author's liberal genius; he lavishes images of exquisite accuracy
and elaborate splendour, as a common writer throws about metaphorical truisms, and exhausted tropes. Amidst all the varied luxuriance
of the sensations described, we are never permitted to lose sight of the
idea which gives unity to this variety, and by the recurrence of which,
as a sort of mysterious influence, at the close of every stanza, the mind
is wrought up, with consummate art, to the final disclosure. This poem
is a perfect gallery of pictures; and the concise boldness, with which in
a few words an object is clearly painted, is sometimes (see the 6th
stanza) majestic as Milton, sometimes (see the 12th) sublime as
Aeschylus.

We have not, however, so far forgot our vocation as critics, that we
would leave without notice the slight faults which adhere to this
precious work. In the 8th stanza, we doubt the propriety of using the
bold compound "black-green," at least in such close vicinity to "gold-
green;" nor is it perfectly clear by the term, although indicated by the
context, that "diamond plots" relates to shape rather than colour. We
are perhaps very stupid, but "vivid stars unrayed" does not convey to
us a very precise notion. "Rosaries of scented thorn," in the 10th stanza
is, we believe, an entirely unauthorized use of the word. Would our
author translate "biferique rosaria Paesti"—"And rosaries of Paestum,
twice in bloom?"

To the beautiful 13th stanza we are sorry to find any objection; but
even the bewitching loveliness of that "Persian girl" shall not prevent
our performing the rigid duty we have undertaken, and we must hint
to Mr. Tennyson that "redolent" is no synonyme for "fragrant." Bees
may be redolent of honey; spring may be "redolent of youth and love;"
but the absolute use of the word has, we fear, neither in Latin nor
English any better authority than the monastic epitaph on Fair Rosa-
mond: "Hic jacet in tombâ Rosa Mundi, non Rosa Munda, non redolet,
sed olet, quae redolere solet."

We are disposed to agree with Mr. Coleridge when he says "no
adequate compensation can be made for the mischief a writer does by
confounding the distinct senses of words." At the same time our feelings

in this instance rebel strongly in behalf of "redolent;" for the melody of the passage, as it stands, is beyond the possibility of improvement, and unless he should chance to light upon a word very nearly resembling this in consonants and vowels, we can hardly quarrel with Mr. Tennyson if, in spite of our judgment, he retains the offender in his service.

Our next specimen is of a totally different character, but not less complete, we think, in its kind. Have we among our readers any who delight in the heroic poems of Old England, the inimitable ballads? Any to whom Sir Patrick Spens, and Clym of the Clough, and Glorious Robin are consecrated names? Any who sigh with disgust at the miserable abortions of simpleness mistaken for simplicity, or florid weakness substituted for plain energy which they may often have seen dignified with the title of Modern Ballads?

Let such draw near and read The Ballad of Oriana. We know no more happy seizure of the antique spirit in the whole compass of our literature; yet there is no foolish self-desertion, no attempt at obliterating the present, but everywhere a full discrimination of how much ought to be yielded and how much retained. The author is well aware that the art of one generation cannot become that of another by any will or skill; but the artist may transfer the spirit of the past, making it a temporary form for his own spirit, and so effect, by idealizing power, a new and legitimate combination. If we were asked to name among the real antiques that which bears greatest resemblance to this gem, we should refer to the ballad of Fair Helen of Kirkconnel Lea in the Minstrelsy of the Scottish Border. It is a resemblance of mood, not of execution. They are both highly wrought lyrical expressions of pathos; and it is very remarkable with what intuitive art every expression and cadence in Fair Helen is accorded to the main feeling.

The characters that distinguish the language of our lyrical from that of our epic ballads have never yet been examined with the accuracy they deserve. But, beyond question, the class of poems which in point of harmonious combination Oriana most resembles, is the Italian. Just thus the meditative tenderness of Dante and Petrarch is embodied in the clear, searching notes of Tuscan song. These mighty masters produce two-thirds of their effect by sound. Not that they sacrifice sense to sound, but that sound conveys their meaning where words would not. There are innumerable shades of fine emotion in the human heart, especially when the senses are keen and vigilant, which are too subtle and too rapid to admit of corresponding phrases. The understanding takes no definite note of them; how then can they leave signatures in language? Yet they exist; in plenitude of being and beauty they exist; and in music they find a medium through which they pass from heart to heart. The tone becomes the sign of the feeling; and they reciprocally suggest each other.

Analogous to this suggestive power may be reckoned, perhaps, in a sister art, the effects of Venetian colouring. Titian *explains* by tints, as Petrarch by tones. Words would not have done the business of the one, nor any groupings or *narration by form*, that of the other. But, shame upon us! we are going back to our metaphysics, when that "sweet, meek face" is waiting to be admitted.

[*The poem is reprinted here.*]

We have heard it objected to this poem that the name occurs once too often in every stanza. We have taken the plea into our judicial consideration, and the result is that we overrule it and pronounce that the proportion of the melodious cadences to the pathetic parts of the narration could not be diminished without materially affecting the rich lyrical impression of the ballad.

For what is the author's intention? To gratify our curiosity with a strange adventure? To shake our nerves with a painful story? Very far from it. Tears indeed may "blind our sight" as we read; but they are "blissful tears." The strong musical delight prevails over every painful feeling and mingles them all in its deep swell until they attain a composure of exalted sorrow, a mood in which the latest repose of agitation becomes visible, and the influence of beauty spreads like light over the surface of the mind.

The last line, with its dreamy wildness, reveals the design of the whole. It is transferred, if we mistake not, from an old ballad (a freedom of immemorial usage with ballad-mongers, as our readers doubtless know) but the merit lies in the abrupt application of it to the leading sentiment, so as to flash upon us in a few little words a world of meaning, and to consecrate the passion that was beyond cure or hope by resigning it to the accordance of inanimate Nature, who, like man, has her tempests and occasions of horror, but august in their largeness of operation, awful by their dependence on a fixed and perpetual necessity.

We must give one more extract, and we are almost tempted to choose by lot among many that crowd on our recollection, and solicit our preference with such witchery as it is not easy to withstand. The poems towards the middle of the volume seem to have been written at an earlier period than the rest. They display more unrestrained fancy and are less evidently proportioned to their ruling ideas than those which we think of later date. Yet in the *Ode to Memory*—the only one which we have the poet's authority for referring to early life—there is a majesty of expression, united to a truth of thought, which almost confounds our preconceived distinctions.

The *Confessions of a Second-rate, Sensitive Mind* are full of deep insight into human nature, and into those particular trials which are sure to beset men who think and feel for themselves at this epoch of social development. The title is perhaps ill-chosen. Not only has it an appearance of quaintness which has no sufficient reason, but it seems to us incorrect. The mood portrayed in this poem, unless the admirable skill of delineation has deceived us, is rather the clouded season of a strong mind than the habitual condition of one feeble and "second-rate." Ordinary tempers build up fortresses of opinion on one side or another; they will see only what they choose to see. The distant glimpse of such an agony as is here brought out to view is sufficient to keep them for ever in illusions, voluntarily raised at first, but soon trusted in with full reliance as inseparable parts of self.

Mr. Tennyson's mode of "rating" is different from ours. He may esteem none worthy of the first order who has not attained a complete universality of thought, and such trustful reliance on a principle of repose which lies beyond the war of conflicting opinions, that the grand ideas, "*qui planent sans cesse au dessus de l'humanité*," cease to affect him with bewildering impulses of hope and fear. We have not space to enter further into this topic; but we should not despair of convincing Mr. Tennyson that such a position of intellect would not be the most elevated, nor even the most conducive to perfection of art.

The *"How" and the "Why"* appears to present the reverse of the same picture. It is the same mind still: the sensitive sceptic, whom we have looked upon in his hour of distress, now scoffing at his own state with an earnest mirth that borders on sorrow. It is exquisitely beautiful to see in this, as in the former portrait, how the feeling of art is kept ascendant in our minds over distressful realities, by constant reference to images of tranquil beauty, whether touched pathetically, as the Ox and the Lamb in the first piece, or with fine humour, as the "great bird" and "little bird" in the second.

The *Sea Fairies* is another strange title; but those who turn to it with the very natural curiosity of discovering who these new births of mythology may be, will be unpardonable if they do not linger over it with higher feelings. A stretch of lyrical power is here exhibited which we did not think the English language had possessed. The proud swell of verse as the harp tones "run up the ridged sea," and the soft and melancholy lapse as the sounds die along the widening space of water, are instances of that right imitation which is becoming to art, but which in the hands of the unskilful, or the affecters of easy popularity, is often converted into a degrading mimicry, detrimental to the best interests of the imagination.

A considerable portion of this book is taken up with a very singular and very beautiful class of poems on which the author has evidently bestowed much thought and elaboration. We allude to the female characters, every trait of which presumes an uncommon degree of observation and reflection. Mr. Tennyson's way of proceeding seems to be this. He collects the most striking phenomena of individual minds until he arrives at some leading fact, which allows him to lay down an axiom or law; and then, working on the law thus attained, he clearly discerns the tendency of what new particulars his invention suggests, and is enabled to impress an individual freshness and unity on ideal combinations. These expressions of character are brief and coherent; nothing extraneous to the dominant fact is admitted, nothing illustrative of it, and, as it were, growing out of it, is rejected. They are like summaries of mighty dramas. We do not say this method admits of such large luxuriance of power as that of our real dramatists; but we contend that it is a new species of poetry, a graft of the lyric on the dramatic, and Mr. Tennyson deserves the laurel of an inventor, an enlarger of our modes of knowledge and power.

We must hasten to make our election; so, passing by the "airy, fairy Lilian," who "clasps her hands" in vain to retain us; the "stately flower" of matronly fortitude, "revered Isabel"; Madeline, with her voluptuous alternation of smile and frown; Mariana, last, but oh not least—we swear by the memory of Shakespeare, to whom a monument of observant love has here been raised by simply expanding all the latent meanings and beauties contained in one stray thought of his genius— we shall fix on a lovely, albeit somewhat mysterious lady, who has fairly taken our "heart from out our breast."

[Here follows Adeline]

Is not this beautiful? When this Poet dies, will not the Graces and the Loves mourn over him, "*fortunatâque favilla nascentur violae?*" How original is the imagery, and how delicate! How wonderful the new world thus created for us, the region between real and unreal! The gardens of Armida were but poorly musical compared with the roses and lillies that bloom around thee, thou faint smiler, Adeline, on whom the glory of imagination reposes, endowing all thou lookest on with sudden and mysterious life. We could expatiate on the deep meaning of this poem, but it is time to twitch our critical mantles; and, as our trade is not that of mere enthusiasm, we shall take our leave with an objection (perhaps a cavil) to the language of cowslips, which we think too ambiguously spoken of for a subject on which nobody, except Mr. Tennyson, can have any information. The "ringing bluebell," too, if it be not a pun, suggests one, and might probably be altered to advantage.

One word more before we have done, and it shall be a word of praise. The language of this book, with one or two rare exceptions, is thorough and sterling English. A little more respect, perhaps, was due to the "*jus et norma loquendi*"; but we are inclined to consider as venial a fault arising from generous enthusiasm for the principles of sound analogy, and for that Saxon element, which constituted the intrinsic freedom and nervousness of our native tongue. We see no signs in what Mr. Tennyson has written of the Quixotic spirit which has led some persons to desire the reduction of English to a single form, by excluding nearly the whole of Latin and Roman derivatives. Ours is necessarily a compound language; as such alone it can flourish and increase; nor will the author of the poems we have extracted be likely to barter for a barren appearance of symmetrical structure that fertility of expression and variety of harmony which "the speech that Shakspeare spoke" derived from the sources of southern phraseology.

In presenting this young poet to the public as one not studious of instant popularity, nor likely to obtain it, we may be thought to play the part of a fashionable lady who deludes her refractory mate into doing what she chooses by pretending to wish the exact contrary; or of a cunning pedagogue who practises a similar manoeuvre on some self-willed Flibbertigibbet of the schoolroom. But the supposition would do us wrong. We have spoken in good faith, commending this volume to feeling hearts and imaginative tempers, not to the stupid readers, or the voracious readers, or the malignant readers, or the readers after dinner!

We confess, indeed, we never knew an instance in which the theoretical abjurers of popularity have shewn themselves very reluctant to admit its actual advances. So much virtue is not, perhaps, in human nature; and if the world should take a fancy to buy up these poems, in order to be revenged on the *Englishman's Magazine*, who knows whether even we might not disappoint its malice by a cheerful adaptation of our theory to "existing circumstances?"

THOUGHTS ON POETRY AND ITS VARIETIES.*

1.

IT has often been asked, What is Poetry? And many and various are the answers which have been returned. The vulgarest of all—one with which no person possessed of the faculties to which Poetry addresses itself can ever have been satisfied—is that which confounds poetry with metrical composition: yet to this wretched mockery of a definition, many have been led back, by the failure of all their attempts to find any other that would distinguish what they have been accustomed to call poetry, from much which they have known only under other names.

That, however, the word 'poetry' imports something quite peculiar in its nature, something which may exist in what is called prose as well as in verse, something which does not even require the instrument of words, but can speak through the other audible symbols called musical sounds, and even through the visible ones which are the language of sculpture, painting, and architecture; all this, we believe, is and must be felt, though perhaps indistinctly, by all upon whom poetry in any of its shapes produces any impression beyond that of tickling the ear. The

* *Monthly Repository*, January and October 1833.

distinction between poetry and what is not poetry, whether explained or not, is felt to be fundamental: and where every one feels a difference, a difference there must be. All other appearances may be fallacious, but the appearance of a difference is a real difference. Appearances too, like other things, must have a cause, and that which can cause anything, even an illusion, must be a reality. And hence, while a half-philosophy disdains the classifications and distinctions indicated by popular language, philosophy carried to its highest point frames new ones, but rarely sets aside the old, content with correcting and regularizing them. It cuts fresh channels for thought, but does not fill up such as it finds ready-made; it traces, on the contrary, more deeply, broadly, and distinctly, those into which the current has spontaneously flowed.

Let us then attempt, in the way of modest inquiry, not to coerce and confine nature within the bounds of an arbitrary definition, but rather to find the boundaries which she herself has set, and erect a barrier round them; not calling mankind to account for having misapplied the word 'poetry,' but attempting to clear up the conception which they already attach to it, and to bring forward as a distinct principle that which, as a vague feeling, has really guided them in their employment of the term.

The object of poetry is confessedly to act upon the emotions; and therein is poetry sufficiently distinguished from what Wordsworth affirms to be its logical opposite, namely, not prose, but matter of fact or science. The one addresses itself to the belief, the other to the feelings. The one does its work by convincing or persuading, the other by moving. The one acts by presenting a proposition to the understanding, the other by offering interesting objects of contemplation to the sensibilities.

This, however, leaves us very far from a definition of poetry. This distinguishes it from one thing, but we are bound to distinguish it from everything. To bring thoughts or images before the mind for the purpose of acting upon the emotions, does not belong to poetry alone. It is equally the province (for example) of the novelist: and yet the faculty of the poet and that of the novelist are as distinct as any other two faculties; as the faculties of the novelist and of the orator, or of the poet and the metaphysician. The two characters may be united, as characters the most disparate may; but they have no natural connexion.

Many of the greatest poems are in the form of fictitious narratives, and in almost all good serious fictions there is true poetry. But there is a radical distinction between the interest felt in a story as such, and the interest excited by poetry; for the one is derived from incident, the other from the representation of feeling. In one, the source of the emotion excited is the exhibition of a state or states of human sensibility; in the other, of a series of states of mere outward circumstances. Now, all minds are capable of being affected more or less by representations of the latter kind, and all, or almost all, by those of the former; yet the two sources of interest correspond to two distinct, and (as respects their greatest development) mutually exclusive, characters of mind.

At what age is the passion for a story, for almost

any kind of story, merely as a story, the most intense? In childhood. But that also is the age at which poetry, even of the simplest description, is least relished and least understood; because the feelings with which it is especially conversant are yet undeveloped, and not having been even in the slightest degree experienced, cannot be sympathized with. In what stage of the progress of society, again, is story-telling most valued, and the story-teller in greatest request and honour?—In a rude state like that of the Tartars and Arabs at this day, and of almost all nations in the earliest ages. But in this state of society there is little poetry except ballads, which are mostly narrative, that is, essentially stories, and derive their principal interest from the incidents. Considered as poetry, they are of the lowest and most elementary kind: the feelings depicted, or rather indicated, are the simplest our nature has; such joys and griefs as the immediate pressure of some outward event excites in rude minds, which live wholly immersed in outward things, and have never, either from choice or a force they could not resist, turned themselves to the contemplation of the world within. Passing now from childhood, and from the childhood of society, to the grown-up men and women of this most grown-up and unchildlike age—the minds and hearts of greatest depth and elevation are commonly those which take greatest delight in poetry; the shallowest and emptiest, on the contrary, are, at all events, not those least addicted to novel-reading. This accords, too, with all analogous experience of human nature. The sort of persons whom not merely in books, but in their lives, we find perpetually engaged in hunting for excitement from without, are invariably those who do not possess, either in the vigour of their intellectual powers or in the depth of their sensibilities, that which would enable them to find ample excitement nearer home. The most idle and frivolous persons take a natural delight in fictitious narrative; the excitement it affords is of the kind which comes from without. Such persons are rarely lovers of poetry, though they may fancy themselves so, because they relish novels in verse. But poetry, which is the delineation of the deeper and more secret workings of human emotion, is interesting only to those to whom it recals what they have felt, or whose imagination it stirs up to conceive what they could feel, or what they might have been able to feel, had their outward circumstances been different.

Poetry, when it is really such, is truth; and fiction also, if it is good for anything, is truth: but they are different truths. The truth of poetry is to paint the human soul truly: the truth of fiction is to give a true picture of life. The two kinds of knowledge are different, and come by different ways, come mostly to different persons. Great poets are often proverbially ignorant of life. What they know has come by observation of themselves; they have found within them one highly delicate and sensitive specimen of human nature, on which the laws of emotion are written in large characters, such as can be read off without much study. Other knowledge of mankind, such as comes to men of the world by outward experience, is not indispensable to them as poets: but to the novelist such knowledge is all in all; he has to describe outward things, not the inward man; actions and events, not feelings; and it will not do for him to be numbered among those who, as Madame Roland said of Brissot, know man but not *men.*

All this is no bar to the possibility of combining both elements, poetry and narrative or incident, in the same work, and calling it either a novel or a poem; but so may red and white combine on the same human features, or on the same canvas. There is one order of composition which requires the union of poetry and incident, each in its highest kind—the dramatic. Even there the two elements are perfectly distinguishable, and may exist of unequal quality, and in the most various proportion. The incidents of a dramatic poem may be scanty and ineffective, though the delineation of passion and character may be of the highest order; as in Goethe's admirable Torquato Tasso; or again, the story as a mere story may be well got up for effect, as is the case with some of the most trashy productions of the Minerva press: it may even be, what those are not, a coherent and probable series of events, though there be scarcely a feeling exhibited which is not represented falsely, or in a manner absolutely commonplace. The combination of the two excellencies is what renders Shake-speare so generally acceptable, each sort of readers finding in him what is suitable to their faculties. To the many he is great as a story-teller, to the few as a poet.

In limiting poetry to the delineation of states of feeling, and denying the name where nothing is deli-neated but outward objects, we may be thought to have done what we promised to avoid—to have not found, but made a definition, in opposition to the usage of language, since it is established by common consent that there is a poetry called descriptive. We deny the charge. Description is not poetry because there is descriptive poetry, no more than science is poetry because there is such a thing as a didactic poem. But an object which admits of being described, or a truth which may fill a place in a scientific treatise, may also furnish an occasion for the generation of poetry, which we thereupon choose to call descriptive or didactic. The poetry is not in the object itself, nor in the scientific truth itself, but in the state of mind in which the one and the other may be contemplated. The mere delineation of the dimensions and colours of external objects is not poetry, no more than a geometrical ground-plan of St. Peter's or Westminster Abbey is painting. Descriptive poetry consists, no doubt, in description, but in description of things as they appear, not as they are; and it paints them not in their bare and natural lineaments, but seen through the medium and arrayed in the colours of the imagination set in action by the feelings. If a poet describes a lion, he does not describe him as a naturalist would, nor even as a traveller would, who was intent upon stating the truth, the whole truth, and nothing but the truth. He describes him by imagery, that is, by suggesting the most striking likenesses and contrasts which might occur to a mind contemplating the lion, in the state of awe, wonder, or terror, which the spectacle naturally excites, or is, on the occasion, supposed to excite. Now this is describing the lion professedly, but the state of excitement of the spectator really. The lion may be described falsely or with exaggeration, and the poetry be all the better; but if the human emotion be not painted with scrupulous truth, the poetry is bad poetry, *i.e.* is not poetry at all, but a failure.

Thus far our progress towards a clear view of the essentials of poetry has brought us very close to the last two attempts at a definition of poetry which we happen to have seen in print, both of them by poets and men of genius. The one is by Ebenezer Elliott, the author of Corn-Law Rhymes, and other poems of still greater merit. ' Poetry,' says he, ' is impassioned truth.' The other is by a writer in Blackwood's Magazine, and comes, we think, still nearer the mark. He defines poetry, ' man's thoughts tinged by his feelings.' There is in either definition a near approximation to what we are in search of. Every truth which a human being can enunciate, every thought, even every outward impression, which can enter into his consciousness, may become poetry when shown through any impassioned medium, when invested with the colouring of joy, or grief, or pity, or affection, or admiration, or reverence, or awe, or even hatred or terror : and, unless so coloured, nothing, be it as interesting as it may, is poetry. But both these definitions fail to discriminate between poetry and eloquence. Eloquence, as well as poetry, is impassioned truth; eloquence, as well as poetry, is thoughts coloured by the feelings. Yet common apprehension and philosophic criticism alike recognise a distinction between the two : there is much that every one would call eloquence, which no one would think of classing as poetry. A question will sometimes arise, whether some particular author is a poet; and those who maintain the negative commonly allow, that though not a poet, he is a highly eloquent writer. The distinction between poetry and eloquence appears to us to be equally fundamental with the distinction between poetry and narrative, or between poetry and description, while it is still farther from having been satisfactorily cleared up than either of the others.

Poetry and eloquence are both alike the expression or utterance of feeling. But if we may be excused the antithesis, we should say that eloquence is *heard*, poetry is *over*heard. Eloquence supposes an audience; the peculiarity of poetry appears to us to lie in the poet's utter unconsciousness of a listener. Poetry is feeling confessing itself to itself, in moments of solitude, and embodying itself in symbols which are the nearest possible representations of the feeling in the exact shape in which it exists in the poet's mind. Eloquence is feeling pouring itself out to other minds, courting their sympathy, or endeavouring to influence their belief or move them to passion or to action.

All poetry is of the nature of soliloquy. It may be said that poetry which is printed on hot-pressed paper and sold at a bookseller's shop, is a soliloquy in full dress, and on the stage. It is so; but there is nothing absurd in the idea of such a mode of soliloquizing. What we have said to ourselves, we may tell to others afterwards; what we have said or done in solitude, we may voluntarily reproduce when we know that other eyes are upon us. But no trace of consciousness that any eyes are upon us must be visible in the work itself. The actor knows that there is an audience present; but if he act as though he knew it, he acts ill. A poet may write poetry not only with the intention of printing it, but for the express purpose of being paid for it; that it should *be* poetry, being written under such influences, is less probable; not, however, impossible; but no otherwise possible than if he can succeed in excluding from his work every vestige of such lookings-forth into the outward and every-day world, and can express his emotions exactly as he has felt them in solitude, or as he is conscious that he should feel them though they were to remain for ever unuttered, or (at the lowest) as he knows that others feel them in similar circumstances of solitude. But when he turns round and addresses himself to another person; when the act of utterance is not itself the end, but a means to an end,—viz. by the feelings he himself expresses, to work upon the feelings, or upon the belief, or the will, of another,—when the expression of his emotions, or of his thoughts tinged by his emotions, is tinged also by that purpose, by that desire of making an impression upon another mind, then it ceases to be poetry, and becomes eloquence.

Poetry, accordingly, is the natural fruit of solitude and meditation; eloquence, of intercourse with the world. The persons who have most feeling of their own, if intellectual culture has given them a language in which to express it, have the highest faculty of poetry; those who best understand the feelings of others, are the most eloquent. The persons, and the nations, who commonly excel in poetry, are those whose character and tastes render them least dependent upon the applause, or sympathy, or concurrence of the world in general. Those to whom that applause, that sympathy, that concurrence are most necessary, generally excel most in eloquence. And hence, perhaps, the French, who are the least poetical of all great and intellectual nations, are among the most eloquent: the French, also, being the most sociable, the vainest, and the least self-dependent.

If the above be, as we believe, the true theory of the distinction commonly admitted between eloquence and poetry; or even though it be not so, yet if, as we cannot doubt, the distinction above stated be a real *bonâ fide* distinction, it will be found to hold, not merely in the language of words, but in all other language, and to intersect the whole domain of art.

Take, for example, music: we shall find in that art, so peculiarly the expression of passion, two perfectly distinct stiles; one of which may be called the poetry, the other the oratory of music. This difference, being seized, would put an end to much musical sectarianism. There has been much contention whether the music of the modern Italian school, that of Rossini and his successors, be impassioned or not. Without doubt, the passion it expresses is not the musing, meditative tenderness, or pathos, or grief of Mozart or Beethoven. Yet it is passion, but garrulous passion—the passion which pours itself into other ears; and therein the better calculated for dramatic effect, having a natural adaptation for dialogue. Mozart also is great in musical oratory; but his most touching compositions are in the opposite stile—that of soliloquy. Who can imagine 'Dove sono' *heard?* We imagine it *over*heard.

Purely pathetic music commonly partakes of soliloquy. The soul is absorbed in its distress, and though there may be bystanders, it is not thinking of them. When the mind is looking within, and not without, its state does not often or rapidly vary; and hence the even, uninterrupted flow, approaching almost to monotony, which a good reader, or a good singer, will give to words or music of a pensive or melancholy cast. But grief taking the form of a prayer, or of a complaint, becomes oratorical; no longer low, and even,. and subdued, it assumes a more emphatic rhythm, a more rapidly returning accent; instead of a few slow equal notes, following one after another at regular intervals, it crowds note upon note, and often assumes a hurry and bustle like joy. Those who are familiar with some of the best of Rossini's serious compositions, such as the air 'Tu che i miseri con- forti,' in the opera of 'Tancredi,' or the duet 'Ebben per mia memoria,' in 'La Gazza Ladra,' will at once understand and feel our meaning. Both are highly tragic and passionate; the passion of both is that of oratory, not poetry. The like may be said of that most moving invocation in Beethoven's 'Fidelio'—

> 'Komm, Hoffnung, lass das letzte Stern
> Der Müde nicht erbleichen;'

in which Madame Schröder Devrient exhibited such consummate powers of pathetic expression. How different from Winter's beautiful 'Paga fui,' the very soul of melancholy exhaling itself in solitude; fuller of meaning, and, therefore, more profoundly poetical than the words for which it was composed—for it seems to express not simple melancholy, but the melancholy of remorse.

If, from vocal music, we now pass to instrumental, we may have a specimen of musical oratory in any fine military symphony or march: while the poetry of music seems to have attained its consummation in

Beethoven's Overture to Egmont, so wonderful in its mixed expression of grandeur and melancholy.

In the arts which speak to the eye, the same distinctions will be found to hold, not only between poetry and oratory, but between poetry, oratory, narrative, and simple imitation or description.

Pure description is exemplified in a mere portrait or a mere landscape—productions of art, it is true, but of the mechanical rather than of the fine arts, being works of simple imitation, not creation. We say, a mere portrait, or a mere landscape, because it is possible for a portrait or a landscape, without ceasing to be such, to be also a picture; like Turner's landscapes, and the great portraits by Titian or Vandyke.

Whatever in painting or sculpture expresses human feeling—or character, which is only a certain state of feeling grown habitual—may be called, according to circumstances, the poetry, or the eloquence, of the painter's or the sculptor's art: the poetry, if the feeling declares itself by such signs as escape from us when we are unconscious of being seen; the oratory, if the signs are those we use for the purpose of voluntary communication.

The narrative style answers to what is called historical painting, which it is the fashion among connoisseurs to treat as the climax of the pictorial art. That it is the most difficult branch of the art we do not doubt, because, in its perfection, it includes the perfection of all the other branches: as in like manner an epic poem, though in so far as it is epic (*i.e.* narrative) it is not poetry at all, is yet esteemed the greatest effort of poetic genius, because there is no kind whatever of poetry which may not appropriately find a place in it. But an historical picture as such, that is, as the representation of an incident, must necessarily, as it seems to us, be poor and ineffective. The narrative powers of painting are extremely limited. Scarcely any picture, scarcely even any series of pictures, tells its own story without the aid of an interpreter. But it is the single figures which, to us, are the great charm even of an historical picture. It is in these that the power of the art is really seen. In the attempt to narrate, visible and permanent signs are too far behind the fugitive audible ones, which follow so fast one after another, while the faces and figures in a narrative picture, even though they be Titian's, stand still. Who would not prefer one Virgin and Child of Raphael, to all the pictures which Rubens, with his fat, frouzy Dutch Venuses, ever painted? Though Rubens, besides excelling almost every one in his mastery over the mechanical parts of his art, often shows real genius in *grouping* his figures, the peculiar problem of historical painting. But then, who, except a mere student of drawing and colouring, ever cared to look twice at any of the figures themselves? The power of painting lies in poetry, of which Rubens had not the slightest tincture—not in narrative, wherein he might have excelled.

The single figures, however, in an historical picture, are rather the eloquence of painting than the poetry: they mostly (unless they are quite out of place in the picture) express the feelings of one person as modified by the presence of others. Accordingly the minds whose bent leads them rather to eloquence than to poetry, rush to historical painting. The French painters, for instance, seldom attempt, because they could make nothing of, single heads, like those glorious ones of the Italian masters, with which they might feed themselves day after day in their own Louvre. They must all be historical; and they are, almost to a man, attitudinizers. If we wished to give any young artist the most impressive warning our imagination could devise against that kind of vice in the pictorial, which corresponds to rant in the histrionic art, we would advise him to walk once up and once down the gallery of the Luxembourg. Every figure in French painting or statuary seems to be showing itself off before spectators: they are not poetical, but in the worst style of corrupted eloquence.

II.

NASCITUR POËTA is a maxim of classical antiquity, which has passed to these latter days with less questioning than most of the doctrines of that early age. When it originated, the human faculties were occupied, fortunately for posterity, less in examining how the works of genius are created, than in creating them: and the adage, probably, had no higher source than the tendency common among mankind to consider all power which is not visibly the effect of practice, all skill which is not capable of being reduced to mechanical rules, as the result of a peculiar gift. Yet this aphorism, born in the infancy of psychology, will perhaps be found, now when that science is in its adolescence, to be as true as an epigram ever is, that is, to contain some truth: truth, however, which has been so compressed and bent out of shape, in order to tie it up into so small a knot of only two words that it requires an almost infinite amount of unrolling and laying straight, before it will resume its just proportions.

We are not now intending to remark upon the grosser misapplications of this ancient maxim, which have engendered so many races of poetasters. The days are gone by, when every raw youth whose borrowed phantasies have set themselves to a borrowed tune, mistaking, as Coleridge says, an ardent desire of poetic reputation for poetic genius, while unable to disguise from himself that he had taken no means whereby he might *become* a poet, could fancy himself a born one. Those who would reap without sowing, and gain the victory without fighting the battle, are ambitious now of another sort of distinction, and are born novelists, or public speakers, not poets. And the wiser thinkers understand and acknowledge that poetic excellence is subject to the same necessary conditions with any other mental endowment; and that to no one of the spiritual benefactors of mankind is a higher or a more assiduous intellectual culture needful than to the poet. It is true, he possesses this advantage over others who use the 'instrument of words,' that, of the truths which he utters, a larger proportion are derived from personal consciousness, and a smaller from philosophic investigation. But the power itself of discriminating between what really is consciousness, and what is only a process of inference completed in a single instant—and the capacity of distinguishing whether that of which the mind is conscious be an eternal truth, or but a dream—are among the last results of the most matured and perfect intellect. Not to mention that the poet, no more than any other person who writes, confines himself altogether to intuitive truths, nor has any means of communicating even these but by words, every one of which derives all its power of conveying a meaning, from a whole host of acquired notions, and facts learnt by study and experience.

Nevertheless, it seems undeniable in point of fact, and consistent with the principles of a sound metaphysics, that there are poetic *natures*. There is a mental and physical constitution or temperament, peculiarly fitted for poetry. This temperament will not of itself make a poet, no more than the soil will the fruit; and as good fruit may be raised by culture from indifferent soils, so may good poetry from naturally unpoetical minds. But the poetry of one who is a poet by nature, will be clearly and broadly distinguishable from the poetry of mere culture. It may not be truer; it may not be more useful; but it will be different: fewer will appreciate it, even though many should affect to do so; but in those few it will find a keener sympathy, and will yield them a deeper enjoyment.

One may write genuine poetry, and not be a poet; for whosoever writes out truly any human feeling, writes poetry. All persons, even the most unimaginative, in moments of strong emotion, speak poetry; and hence the drama is poetry, which else were always prose, except when a poet is one of the characters. What *is* poetry, but the thoughts and words in which emotion spontaneously embodies itself? As there are few who are not, at least for some moments and in some situations, capable of some strong feeling, poetry is natural to most persons at some period of their lives. And any one whose feelings are genuine, though but of the average strength,—if he be not diverted by uncongenial thoughts or occupations from the indulgence of them, and if he acquire by culture, as all persons may, the faculty of delineating them correctly,—has it in his power to be a poet, so far as a life passed in writing unquestionable poetry may be considered to confer that title. But *ought* it to do so? Yes, perhaps, in a collection of 'British Poets.' But 'poet' is the name also of a variety of man, not solely of the author of a particular variety of book: now, to have written whole volumes of real poetry is possible to almost all kinds of characters, and implies no greater peculiarity of mental construction, than to be the author of a history, or a novel.

Whom, then, shall we call poets? Those who are so constituted, that emotions are the links of association by which their ideas, both sensuous and spiritual, are connected together. This constitution belongs (within certain limits) to all in whom poetry is a pervading principle. In all others, poetry is something extraneous and superinduced: something out of themselves, foreign to the habitual course of their everyday lives and characters; a world to which they may make occasional visits, but where they are sojourners, not dwellers, and which, when out of it, or even when in it, they think of, peradventure, but as a phantom-world, a place of *ignes fatui* and spectral illusions. Those only who have the peculiarity of association which we have mentioned, and which is a natural

though not an universal consequence of intense sensibility, instead of seeming not themselves when they
are uttering poetry, scarcely seem themselves when
uttering anything to which poetry is foreign. Whatever be the thing which they are contemplating, if it
be capable of connecting itself with their emotions, the
aspect under which it first and most naturally paints
itself to them, is its poetic aspect. The poet of culture
sees his object in prose, and describes it in poetry; the
poet of nature actually sees it in poetry.

This point is perhaps worth some little illustration;
the rather, as metaphysicians (the ultimate arbiters of
all philosophical criticism), while they have busied
themselves for two thousand years, more or less, about
the few *universal* laws of human nature, have strangely
neglected the analysis of its *diversities.* Of these, none
lie deeper or reach further than the varieties which
difference of nature and of education makes in what
may be termed the habitual bond of association. In a
mind entirely uncultivated, which is also without any
strong feelings, objects whether of sense or of intellect
arrange themselves in the mere casual order in which
they have been seen, heard, or otherwise perceived.
Persons of this sort may be said to think chronologi-
cally. If they remember a fact, it is by reason of a
fortuitous coincidence with some trifling incident or
circumstance which took place at the very time. If
they have a story to tell, or testimony to deliver in a
witness-box, their narrative must follow the exact
order in which the events took place: *dodge* them,
and the thread of association is broken; they cannot
go on. Their associations, to use the language of philosophers, are chiefly of the successive, not the syn-

chronous kind, and whether successive or synchronous, are mostly casual.

To the man of science, again, or of business, objects group themselves according to the artificial classifications which the understanding has voluntarily made for the convenience of thought or of practice. But where any of the impressions are vivid and intense, the associations into which these enter are the ruling ones: it being a well-known law of association, that the stronger a feeling is, the more quickly and strongly it associates itself with any other object or feeling. Where, therefore, nature has given strong feelings, and education has not created factitious tendencies stronger than the natural ones, the prevailing associations will be those which connect objects and ideas with emotions, and with each other through the intervention of emotions. Thoughts and images will be linked together, according to the similarity of the feelings which cling to them. A thought will introduce a thought by first introducing a feeling which is allied with it. At the centre of each group of thoughts or images will be found a feeling; and the thoughts or images will be there only because the feeling was there. The combinations which the mind puts together, the pictures which it paints, the wholes which Imagination constructs out of the materials supplied by Fancy, will be indebted to some dominant *feeling*, not as in other natures to a dominant *thought*, for their unity and consistency of character, for what distinguishes them from incoherencies.

The difference, then, between the poetry of a poet, and the poetry of a cultivated but not naturally poetic mind, is, that in the latter, with however bright a halo of feeling the thought may be surrounded and glorified, the thought itself is always the conspicuous object; while the poetry of a poet is Feeling itself, employing Thought only as the medium of its expression. In the one, feeling waits upon thought; in the other, thought upon feeling. The one writer has a distinct aim, common to him with any other didactic author; he desires to convey the thought, and he conveys it clothed in the feelings which it excites in himself, or which he deems most appropriate to it. The other merely pours forth the overflowing of his feelings; and all the thoughts which those feelings suggest are floated promiscuously along the stream.

It may assist in rendering our meaning intelligible, if we illustrate it by a parallel between the two English authors of our own day, who have produced the greatest quantity of true and enduring poetry, Wordsworth and Shelley. Apter instances could not be wished for; the one might be cited as the type, the *exemplar*, of what the poetry of culture may accomplish: the other as perhaps the most striking example ever known of the poetic temperament. How different, accordingly, is the poetry of these two great writers! In Wordsworth, the poetry is almost always the mere setting of a thought. The thought may be more valuable than the setting, or it may be less valuable, but there can be no question as to which was first in his mind: what he is impressed with, and what he is anxious to impress, is some proposition, more or less distinctly conceived; some truth, or something which he deems such. He lets the thought dwell in his mind, till it excites, as is the nature of thought,

G 2

other thoughts, and also such feelings as the measure of his sensibility is adequate to supply. Among these thoughts and feelings, had he chosen a different walk of authorship (and there are many in which he might equally have excelled), he would probably have made a different selection of media for enforcing the parent thought: his habits, however, being those of poetic composition, he selects in preference the strongest feelings, and the thoughts with which most of feeling is naturally or habitually connected. His poetry, therefore, may be defined to be, his thoughts, coloured by, and impressing themselves by means of, emotions. Such poetry, Wordsworth has occupied a long life in producing. And well and wisely has he so done. Criticisms, no doubt, may be made occasionally both upon the thoughts themselves, and upon the skill he has demonstrated in the choice of his media: for, an affair of skill and study, in the most rigorous sense, it evidently was. But he has not laboured in vain: he has exercised, and continues to exercise, a powerful, and mostly a highly beneficial influence over the formation and growth of not a few of the most cultivated and vigorous of the youthful minds of our time, over whose heads poetry of the opposite description would have flown, for want of an original organization, physical or mental, in sympathy with it.

On the other hand, Wordsworth's poetry is never bounding, never ebullient; has little even of the appearance of spontaneousness: the well is never so full that it overflows. There is an air of calm deliberateness about all he writes, which is not characteristic of the poetic temperament: his poetry seems one

thing, himself another; he seems to be poetical because he wills to be so, not because he cannot help it:
did he will to dismiss poetry, he need never again, it
might almost seem, have a poetical thought. He
never seems *possessed* by any feeling; no emotion
seems ever so strong as to have entire sway, for the
time being, over the current of his thoughts. He
never, even for the space of a few stanzas, appears
entirely given up to exultation, or grief, or pity, or
love, or admiration, or devotion, or even animal
spirits. He now and then, though seldom, attempts
to write as if he were; and never, we think, without
leaving an impression of poverty: as the brook which
on nearly level ground quite fills its banks, appears
but a thread when running rapidly down a precipi-
tous declivity. He has feeling enough to form a
decent, graceful, even beautiful decoration to a
thought which is in itself interesting and moving;
but not so much as suffices to stir up the soul by mere
sympathy with itself in its simplest manifestation,
nor enough to summon up that array of 'thoughts of
power' which in a richly stored mind always attends
the call of really intense feeling.   It is for this reason,
doubtless, that the genius of Wordsworth is essentially
unlyrical.   Lyric poetry, as it was the earliest kind,
is also, if the view we are now taking of poetry
be correct, more eminently and peculiarly poetry
than any other: it is the poetry most natural to a
really poetic temperament, and least capable of being
succesfully imitated by one not so endowed by
nature.

Shelley is the very reverse of all this. Where
Wordsworth is strong, he is weak; where Words-

worth is weak, he is strong. Culture, that culture by which Wordsworth has reared from his own inward nature the richest harvest ever brought forth by a soil of so little depth, is precisely what was wanting to Shelley: or let us rather say, he had not, at the period of his deplorably early death, reached sufficiently far in that intellectual progression of which he was capable, and which, if it has done so much for greatly inferior natures, might have made of him the most perfect, as he was already the most gifted of our poets. For him, voluntary mental discipline had done little: the vividness of his emotions and of his sensations had done all. He seldom follows up an idea; it starts into life, summons from the fairy-land of his inexhaustible fancy some three or four bold images, then vanishes, and straight he is off on the wings of some casual association into quite another sphere. He had scarcely yet acquired the consecutiveness of thought necessary for a long poem; his more ambitious compositions too often resemble the scattered fragments of a mirror; colours brilliant as life, single images without end, but no picture. It is only when under the overruling influence of some one state of feeling, either actually experienced, or summoned up in the vividness of reality by a fervid imagination, that he writes as a great poet; unity of feeling being to him the harmonizing principle which a central idea is to minds of another class, and supplying the coherency and consistency which would else have been wanting. Thus it is in many of his smaller, and especially his lyrical poems. They are obviously written to exhale, perhaps to relieve, a state of feeling, or of conception of feeling, almost oppressive from its vividness. The thoughts and imagery are suggested by the feeling, and are such as it finds unsought. The state of feeling may be either of soul or of sense, or oftener (might we not say invariably?) of both: for the poetic temperament is usually, perhaps always, accompanied by exquisite senses. The exciting cause may be either an object or an idea. But whatever of sensation enters into the feeling, must not be local, or consciously organic; it is a condition of the whole frame, not of a part only. Like the state of sensation produced by a fine climate, or indeed like all strongly pleasurable or painful sensations in an impassioned nature, it pervades the entire nervous system. States of feeling, whether sensuous or spiritual, which thus possess the whole being, are the fountains of that which we have called the poetry of poets; and which is little else than a pouring forth of the thoughts and images that pass across the mind while some permanent state of feeling is occupying it.

To the same original fineness of organization, Shelley was doubtless indebted for another of his rarest gifts, that exuberance of imagery, which when unrepressed, as in many of his poems it is, amounts to a fault. The susceptibility of his nervous system, which made his emotions intense, made also the impressions of his external senses deep and clear: and agreeably to the law of association by which, as already remarked, the strongest impressions are those which associate themselves the most easily and strongly, these vivid sensations were readily recalled to mind by all objects or thoughts which had co-existed with them, and by all feelings which in any degree resembled them. Never did a fancy so teem with sensuous imagery as Shelley's. Wordsworth economizes an image, and detains it until he has distilled all the poetry out of it, and it will not yield a drop more: Shelley lavishes his with a profusion which is unconscious because it is inexhaustible.

If, then, the maxim *Nascitur poëta,* mean, either that the power of producing poetical compositions is a peculiar faculty which the poet brings into the world with him, which grows with his growth like any of his bodily powers, and is as independent of culture as his height, and his complexion; or that any natural peculiarity whatever is implied in producing poetry, real poetry, and in any quantity—such poetry too, as, to the majority of educated and intelligent readers, shall appear quite as good as, or even better than, any other; in either sense the doctrine is false. And nevertheless, there *is* poetry which could not emanate but from a mental and physical constitution peculiar, not in the kind, but in the degree of its susceptibility: a constitution which makes its possessor capable of greater happiness than mankind in general, and also of greater unhappiness; and because greater, so also more various. And such poetry, to all who know enough of nature to own it as being in nature, is much more poetry, is poetry in a far higher sense, than any other; since the common element of all poetry, that which constitutes poetry, human feeling, enters far more largely into this than into the poetry of culture. Not only because the natures which we have called poetical, really feel more, and consequently have more feeling to express; but because, the capacity of feeling being so great, feeling, when excited and not voluntarily resisted, seizes the helm of their thoughts, and the succession of ideas and images becomes the mere utterance of an emotion; not, as in other natures, the emotion a mere ornamental colouring of the thought.

Ordinary education and the ordinary course of life are constantly at work counteracting this quality of mind, and substituting habits more suitable to their own ends: if instead of substituting they were content to superadd, there would be nothing to complain of. But when will education consist, not in repressing any mental faculty or power, from the uncontrolled action of which danger is apprehended, but in training up to its proper strength the corrective and antagonist power?

In whomsoever the quality which we have described exists, and is not stifled, that person is a poet. Doubtless he is a greater poet in proportion as the fineness of his perceptions, whether of sense or of internal consciousness, furnishes him with an ampler supply of lovely images—the vigour and richness of his intellect, with a greater abundance of moving thoughts. For it is through these thoughts and images that the feeling speaks, and through their impressiveness that it impresses itself, and finds response in other hearts; and from these media of transmitting it (contrary to the laws of physical nature) increase of intensity is reflected back upon the feeling itself. But all these it is possible to have, and not be a poet; they are mere materials, which the poet shares in common with other people. What constitutes the poet is not the imagery nor the thoughts, nor even the feelings, but the law according to which they are called up. He is a poet, not because he has ideas of any particular kind, but because the succession of his ideas is subordinate to the course of his emotions.

Many who have never acknowledged this in theory, bear testimony to it in their particular judgments. In listening to an oration, or reading a written discourse not professedly poetical, when do we begin to feel that the speaker or author is putting off the character of the orator or the prose writer, and is passing into the poet? Not when he begins to show strong feeling; *then* we merely say, he is in earnest, he feels what he says; still less when he expresses himself in imagery; then, unless illustration be manifestly his sole object, we are apt to say, this is affectation. It is when the feeling (instead of passing away, or, if it continue, letting the train of thoughts run on exactly as they would have done if there were no influence at work but the mere intellect) becomes itself the originator of another train of association, which expels or blends with the former; when (for example) either his words, or the mode of their arrangement, are such as we spontaneously use only when in a state of excitement, proving that the mind is at least as much occupied by a passive state of its own feelings, as by the desire of attaining the premeditated end which the discourse has in view.*

Our judgments of authors who lay actual claim to

* And this, we may remark by the way, seems to point to the true theory of poetic diction; and to suggest the true answer to as much as is erroneous of Wordsworth's celebrated doctrine on that subject. For on the one hand, *all* language which is the natural expression of feeling, is really poetical, and will be felt as such, apart from conventional associa-

the title of poets, follow the same principle. Whenever, after a writer's meaning is fully understood, it is still matter of reasoning and discussion whether he is a poet or not, he will be found to be wanting in the characteristic peculiarity of association so often adverted to. When, on the contrary, after reading or hearing one or two passages, we instinctively and without hesitation cry out, This is a poet, the probability is, that the passages are strongly marked with this peculiar quality. And we may add that in such case, a critic who, not having sufficient feeling to respond to the poetry, is also without sufficient philosophy to understand it though he feel it not, will be apt to pronounce, not 'this is prose,' but 'this is exaggeration,' 'this is mysticism,' or, 'this is nonsense.'

Although a philosopher cannot, by culture, make himself, in the peculiar sense in which we now use the term, a poet, unless at least he have that peculiarity of nature which would probably have made poetry his earliest pursuit; a poet may always, by culture, make himself a philosopher. The poetic laws of association are by no means incompatible with the more ordinary laws; are by no means such as *must* have their course, even though a deliberate purpose require their suspension. If the peculiarities of the poetic temperament were uncontrollable in any poet, they might be supposed so in Shelley; yet how powerfully, in the Cenci, does he coerce and restrain all the characteristic qualities of his genius; what

tions; but on the other, whenever intellectual culture has afforded a choice between several modes of expressing the same emotion, the stronger the feeling is, the more naturally and certainly will it prefer the language which is most peculiarly appropriated to itself, and kept sacred from the contact of more vulgar objects of contemplation.

severe simplicity, in place of his usual barbaric splendour; how rigidly does he keep the feelings and the imagery in subordination to the thought.

The investigation of nature requires no habits or qualities of mind, but such as may always be acquired by industry and mental activity. Because at one time the mind may be so given up to a state of feeling, that the succession of its ideas is determined by the present enjoyment or suffering which pervades it, this is no reason but that in the calm retirement of study, when under no peculiar excitement either of the outward·or of the inward sense, it may form any combinations, or pursue any trains of ideas, which are most conducive to the purposes of philosophic inquiry; and may, while in that state, form deliberate convictions, from which no excitement will afterwards make it swerve. Might we not go even further than this? We shall not pause to ask whether it be not a misunderstanding of the nature of passionate feeling to imagine that it is inconsistent with calmness; whether they who so deem of it, do not mistake passion in the militant or antagonistic state, for the type of passion universally; do not confound passion struggling towards an outward object, with passion brooding over itself. But without entering into this deeper investigation; that capacity of strong feeling, which is supposed necessarily to disturb the judgment, is also the material out of which all *motives* are made; the motives, consequently, which lead human beings to the pursuit of truth. The greater the individual's capability of happiness and of misery, the stronger interest has that individual in arriving at truth; and when once that interest is felt, an impassioned nature is sure to pursue this, as to pursue any other object, with greater ardour; for energy of character is commonly the offspring of strong feeling. If, therefore, the most impassioned natures do not ripen into the most powerful intellects, it is always from defect of culture, or something wrong in the circumstances by which the being has originally or successively been surrounded. Undoubtedly strong feelings require a strong intellect to carry them, as more sail requires more ballast: and when, from neglect, or bad education, that strength is wanting, no wonder if the grandest and swiftest vessels make the most utter wreck.

Where, as in some of our older poets, a poetic nature has been united with logical and scientific culture, the peculiarity of association arising from the finer nature so perpetually alternates with the associations attainable by commoner natures trained to high perfection, that its own particular law is not so conspicuously characteristic of the result produced, as in a poet like Shelley, to whom systematic intellectual culture, in a measure proportioned to the intensity of his own nature, has been wanting. Whether the superiority will naturally be on the side of the philosopher-poet or of the mere poet—whether the writings of the one ought, as a whole, to be truer, and their influence more beneficent, than those of the other—is too obvious in principle to need statement: it would be absurd to doubt whether two endowments are better than one; whether truth is more certainly arrived at by two processes, verifying and correcting each other, than by one alone. Unfortunately, in practice the matter is not quite so simple;

there the question often is, which is least prejudicial
to the intellect, uncultivation or malcultivation. For,
as long as education consists chiefly of the mere inculcation of traditional opinions, many of which, from
the mere fact that the human intellect has not yet
reached perfection, must necessarily be false; so long
as even those who are best taught, are rather taught
to know the thoughts of others than to think, it is
not always clear that the poet of acquired ideas has
the advantage over him whose feeling has been his
sole teacher.   For, the depth and durability of wrong
as well as of right impressions, is proportional to the
fineness of the material; and they who have the
greatest capacity of natural feeling are generally
those whose artificial feelings are the strongest.
Hence, doubtless, among other reasons, it is, that in
an age of revolutions in opinion, the cotemporary
poets, those at least who deserve the name, those who
have any individuality of character, if they are not
before their age, are almost sure to be behind it.   An
observation curiously verified all over Europe in the
present century.   Nor let it be thought disparaging.
However urgent may be the necessity for a breaking
up of old modes of belief, the most strong-minded
and discerning, next to those who head the movement, are generally those who bring up the rear
of it.

A CAMBRIAN COLLOQUY ON THE DECLINE AND FALL OF POETRY.

WALES, if no longer the land of poets, is still the land of poetry. What happy truant from the great " Babel " and its " stir " but has felt the poetic influence of pastoral mountains, the bluer air of their wild white heights of cliff, the sunset languishing glory of the valley opening westward, its flowering cottage roofs, and its tinkling sheepcote on the sheltered greensward by the river of rocks? That pensive vacancy which merely rural scenes so lullingly diffuse over the mind, rather disposes it to receive the impression of the poetic influence than creates it. The addition of the sublime to the beautiful is required to produce that high-raised tone of natural feeling, that impassioned or refined turn of sentiment, which, whether developed in truth or in fiction, in metre or prose, ever or never finding vent beyond the bosom it dilates and warms, is equally poetry. Bishop Heber, after exploring the " gorgeous east," with its pictorial scenery, still gave the palm of romantic beauty to Wales, as we are informed by his biographer; and Heber was a poet. The right place, then, for a talk about poetry is not the place of its embodied mechanical coming forth in hot-press and letter-press, for trial before the critical press, but the place of its nativity—not only " under the shade of melancholy boughs," but of mighty mountains; or, at least, in their glorious presence, if not their shadow. A critical colloquy about poets, their fates and present prospects, will not therefore, it is hoped, be deemed out of place, though far, and very far out of London, which, with all deference to its classic ground, boasts more of its superiority to enthusiasm, than of inspiration from it.

The spot where the three interlocutors of the ensuing dialogue fell into these " pribbles and prabbles " is one in Merionethshire, North Wales, which, though quite " unknown to fame," commands an unrivalled prospect of combined maritime, mountain, and pastoral scenery. The parties, perhaps poets themselves (whether " still-born," or known or " unknown," great or small, we beg to keep to ourselves, letting the " dear sacred names rest ever unrevealed "), then performing a tour of the principality, were, *imprimis*, a long-

retired officer of the army, who has renewed on the banks of our Welsh rivers his old college acquaintance with Theocritus and Virgil by the Isis— exchanging the sword for the angling rod, and his *bivouac* in the " tented " field for one in the green or hay-field, under an oak or in a hollow one, when benighted in his piscatory campaign ; secondly, a romantic Doctor Medicinæ, as fond of " babbling of green fields " as his brother-traveller of the babbling of a river-shallow inviting his rod and fly ; thirdly, a reader of our old dramatists, partial to summer vagrancy, the leader of the party (whose mode of travelling was truly Egyptian), and whom we may call the " Amateur Gipsy." The days were just about at the longest, the evening a golden one :

" The world was all before them, where
       to choose
Their place of "—tea !

So they chose it on a little island (the spot above-mentioned), situated in the estuary of the river Dyrrwhyd, where it disembogues about four miles from Harlech. It was now accessible by the sands, which are here called the Traeth Bach (little sand-bank), the river channel being about two miles across. All round was a shelly marbled expanse of finest sand, diversified by pink sea-weeds and crystal-hued gellies. On one hand was all Snowdon's chaotic region, always rolled in blackness of mist ; on the other, the sunny sea, sending its soft, solemn, yet immense sound, as it broke broad on the distant beach, round all those mountains, and answered by their echoes. The noble ruin of Harlech Castle towered dark on its promontory. Sea-birds fishing over the shallow pools, and figures in the mid-channel, where ran a fresh stream, appeared in their blue and red colours of Welsh woollen dress, their giant shadows stretching almost to the island, and our party sitting on its purply heath, each watching for fish, made visible in their slow motions by the level sun, hung over the broad expanse of sea beyond them, which heaved and sparkled boundlessly, like molten silver. The little isle itself was a perfect epitome of the principality. Though in extent but a very few acres, there is height and dell—ruinous rock, ivy-mantled, fit for an artist's study—wild shrubbery, tasseled with honeysuckle—patches of greenest meadow—and *one* human home, overtopped by green crags, from the brink of which the hermit-owner's few sheep look down on the flowering house-roof. It is a fairy Wales.

They who in such scenes feel irresistibly rising in their bosoms, rather than minds, a something, an agitating emotion, which would fain vent itself in they know not what harmonious, rapturous, lofty language, or soliloquy suitable to the " height of that great argument" which Nature seems dumbly to invite them to hold with her—they, I say, may be called *poets*, albeit they never spoiled paper with a sonnet. And such persons will acutely feel that sort of self-imprisonment, if I may use the term, which the decline and fall of poetry seems threatening to inflict on the true-born bard. For what is poetry but the living language of communion between sensitive minds? To all others it is a dead language. Many a well-educated man can no more read poetry than he can Chinese. The neglect, not to say contempt, of the muses, now a fashion, bids fair to render this Parnassian *illiteracy* universal ; nay, to make the very tongue in which Milton enshrined his soul, mute, a worse than dead, a forgotten, an unintelligible one.

As the gorgeous horizon glowed like a mighty bed of flowers after the last ring of the round disc had disappeared, while the floor of the sea, into which those colours melted, yet retained a silver gloss like that of the dewy leaves of lilies—and a wild purple haze came floating over the black headland-tower of Harlech, and shut it in to that landscape of a sky, so softly and sublimely painted, yet fading, that an enthusiast might dream he saw the closing curtains of the paradise of souls, the *real* heaven within the nominal—and the sea itself seemed lulled into a moaning sleep,—the scene imposed its own peace, with somewhat of its grandeur, on the minds of all.

The nights being warm and beautiful, more like a shaded day than night, their tents stood pitched to receive them under a rock, while they partook the mental beverage—tea, with fire, cross sticks, kettle, and all true Egyptian vagrancy " appliances to boot "—the

old Roman love of flowers seeming to survive in the party—cowslips (they grow late there), which beautify the warm dingles, lying amongst their cups, and hanging in their button-holes, &c. like the *orders* of some great hero of the field,—these the bloodless trophies of nature, they the heroes of happier, purer fields.

After a long admiring pause, one of the peripatetics — the D. M. before mentioned—broke forth in the words of Cowley, as appeareth in the following record of their discourse : —

D.M. " What shall I do to be for ever known,
And make the world to come my own ?"

Major. Any thing but write poetry now-a-days.

D. M. Pooh, pooh ! I was not cogitating how to live for ever, or how to " put a girdle round about the world in twenty minutes " or twenty years — but thinking of poor Cowley when he breathed this high aspiration after fame. What a melancholy despairing kind of question would it be now, were he alive in this day, and under the reverse of fortune the English muse has met with of late.

Amateur Gipsy. Sir, I wish Cowley were living now, notwithstanding, were it only to come and see the Traeth Brach and Traeth Mawr ; he had such a true poet's passion for rural peace and beauty, whatever that city-heretic to the true faith of poets in nature's supremacy of charms, old Johnson, may please to insinuate to the contrary. Poor Cowley was a victim to the Civil War, like his friend the Lord Falkland, whose pensive peace-loving cast of mind he seems to have shared. He did not fall in battle indeed, but he may almost as truly be said to have lost his life in the troubles of the times as the other. The poetical life, the life he so desired, that of rural and studious retirement, was denied him during all his prime by the state of his country, his exile abroad, imprisonment and danger on return — added to a bad state of health. And when at last the Restoration seemed to shed a placid gleam to light up his evening of life, life itself was snatched from him at the first moment when he might be said to begin to live. For what is the " poet's ever gentle mind "—what a poet in the stormy atmosphere of revolution ? The fate of the " gentle Cowley " was that of a

dove doomed to the mode of existence
which belongs to the " stormy petrel,"
that makes a home of the sea in storms.
His spirit languished for the brooks,
and the voice of the nightingale, and
old " ancestral woods," and peace :
his fate was to " rove a banished man "
after the steps of a fugitive king — to
toil in a hopeless, though honourable
diplomacy, in aid of his fallen fortunes
— to hide, like a guilty alien, in his
own country, when he ventured home.
And as soon as that peace, for which,
like the noble royalist in his fine humanity, he seems to have groaned from
the bottom of his heart, as Clarendon
tells us the ill-fated Falkland did audi-
bly, sighing, " Peace, peace !" — as soon,
I say, as that peace smiled on our poet,
death interposed, and divorced his heart
from his old first love for ever.

D. M. Do you remember his little
essay, entitled, *Of Myself* ? So little
is now ever said or thought of Cowley,
that it is quite a surprise to me to find
you cherishing his memory. That pretty
bit of egotism is a good specimen of his
prose, to which at least Dr. Johnson did
justice. After telling us that " from his
earliest life, even before he knew or was
capable of guessing what the world or
its glories, or business of it, were, the
natural affections of his soul gave a
secret bent of aversion from them, even
as some plants are said to turn away
from others by an antipathy imperceptible to 'themselves," — he goes on
to say : " With these affections of mind,
and my heart wholly set upon letters,
I went to the university ; but was soon
torn thence by that public violent storm,
which would suffer nothing to stand
where it came, but rooted up every
plant, even from the princely cedar to
me, the hyssop. Yet I had as good
fortune as could have befallen me in
such a tempest, being thrown by it into
the family of one of the best of persons,
and into the court of one of the best
princesses in the world." After describing his mode of life and conve-
niences as the " best that could be
hoped by a man in banishment and
public distresses ; yet I could not,"
says he, " abstain from renewing my
old schoolboy's wish in a copy of verses :

Well, then, I now do plainly see
This busy world and I shall ne'er agree.

And I never then proposed any other
advantage to myself from his majesty's
happy restoration, than the getting into

some moderately convenient retreat in
the country." This he at last obtained ;
and his remarks on his late good fortune
are affecting — a mournful comment on
the text, "All is vanity." " But God
laughs at man who says to his soul
take thy ease : I met not only with
many incumbrances and impediments,
but with so much sickness as would
have spoiled the happiness of an emperor as well as mine. Yet I do
neither repent nor alter my course.
Nothing shall separate me from a mistress which I have loved so long, and
have now at last married.

' Nec vos, dulcissima mundi
Nomina, vos musæ, libertas, otia, libri,
Hortique, sylvæque, animâ remanente
relinquam.'

' Nor by me e'er shall you,
You of all names the sweetest and the
best !
You, muses, books, and liberty, and rest —
You, gardens, fields, and woods — for-
saken be,
As long as life itself forsakes not me.' "

But life did forsake him not very long
after thus renewing his ardent vow of
devotion to the " mistress he had loved
so long " — the spirit of poetry in rural
solitude. I have just been reading his
prose, and have been struck with its
simplicity of ornament, justifying Johnson's remarks on its contrast to his
poetry. Poor forgotten Cowley ! his
hope of immortality failed him, like his
desire of mortal life, for the sake of the
country and muse.

Major. I have read him in a hollow
tree by the brook when it has rained
desperately, and really think he deserves to be forgotten as a poet. Such
abstruse conceits in a lover of nature !

D. M. The fate of the poet was as
perversely luckless as that of the man.
Like Milton, " blinded by excess of
light," Cowley has perished through
excess of genius. Half or a quarter of
that imaginative faculty which made
him famous for his day, might have
made him so for ever. What Plato
says of the passions, that they are the
" horses of the soul run away with her,"
may be applied to the unbridled imagination of the poet-mind. In his day,
hyperbole and fantastic flights of fancy
were the fashion, so that there was no
check to his besetting sin. Where the
needful check was applied, as by his
own sense of what was becoming the
modesty of prose, we perceive the
beauty of his fancy undistorted and at

ease, and there it becomes really beautiful without alloy. Prose seems to his genius like the restraining trappings of a Roman triumphal car to the fiery steeds which drew it, adding to their beauty of attitude and spirit by the measured step and straight course to which they restrained them. His excursive fancy, like those steeds unharnessed, was ever ready to scour, with flying manes and heels, out of the way. It required the guiding coercion of prose.

Amateur Gipsy. It is a pity, then, that the fashion of his time did not, as it does now, drive poets into the shackles, and tame and tie his rampant genius fast to drag the car of the historical novel or romance, as the revolution in our taste has done by most of our new and some of our elder living poets. To him, according to you and the major's theory, it would have been a step toward immortality, instead of a fall from it, as a genuine poet is apt to conceive of thus hiding his "talent" under the bushel of a three volumes octavo prose work.

Major. Ay, this war of the giants, with the Briareus of the north at their head, against the divinities of the earthly Olympus—poor deserted Parnassus, has driven the muses to assume some rather grotesque disguises; it has "brought them acquainted with strange bedfellows." Nor can one imagine the delicate, the ethereal beauty of a muse, creeping into a shape of such familiar homeliness as the novel, without many qualms, and sighs, and "lingering looks behind" to her own sweet hill, with its diamond-sparkling spring, and "airs from heaven." But what is to be done? When the Pelion of political economy is piled upon the Ossa of scientific research, surmounted with a pagoda of four-volumed fashionable novel, it's time for the invaded deities to betake them to earth, and become (or appear) as "of the earth, earthy," or perish utterly.

D. M. Yes, a great change is "come over the spirit of every young poet's dream" in this decline and fall of the muse's empire. Our Cowley, probably, when he said, "What shall I do to be for ever known?" feeling the "immortal longings" within him so natural to a real poet, knew very well what he would do—write a noble poem, and throw himself and his genius on his country's justice, to live

or die—eternally. But our Cowleys and Miltons—if such indeed be born in our days, use the same self-interrogatory in a very different spirit—a perplexed, a despondent spirit. They see too clearly there is no longer a high court sitting, no arena in which to engage, no tribunal to listen to their appeal. If they enter the old deserted place of trial and triumph, the real poem, they are laughed at for indulging so obsolete an ambition; they are in the ridiculous predicament of a tragic actor, who, in his death-scene, the climax of his efforts, should be left without an audience, "superfluous lagging on the stage," and acting away to his brother-actor solus; whose fine tragic emotion is thus, as it were, shut up within him instantly; the heart of his genius seared, in his highest exertion of art he is become ridiculous to himself. A poet in like manner deserted, owing to the caprice of the public, his expected audience, and left but to the notice of a few rival poets or poetasters, must feel all his poetry turn cold upon his heart, which had so long lain warm at its very core, while expectation and conscious merit buoyed him with the prospect of at least a fair trial. Supposing a real genius to arise in our day, and to "feel the god within," his first question must be with himself, "*Cui bono?* What am I to do with my *genius?*"

Major. Why you said just now what he must do with it; he must begin *prosing*, like others.

D. M. I'm not sure that such a genius as I have imagined would submit to such a prostitution of the divine spirit of poesy. Can we imagine a prose *Paradise Lost?*

Amateur Gipsy. No; for though the measure were taken away, it would still be poetry; the very cadence would remain. The force of Milton's fancy, his affluence of language, his gigantic thought, and delicacy of ear, would act like Midas's touch; the coarsest common vehicle he could stoop to use would turn to a car all gold, burnished, with wheels of fire. Why, sir, Milton's whole prose is poetry. Even his controversial writings glow with imagery and sentimental painting. Why do you speak of this transfusion of poetry through the grosser body of prose—this subtle instilling of the animal spirits of the muses into the veins of that aged monarch of our tongue, to vivify and beautify with new life, like another Æson, as a new experiment, and a forlorn resource?

D. M. Why, to confess the truth, I have the same opinion as you hold of the practicability of thus making prose the preserving amber for those precious pearls of poetry, which else our Swinish multitude—I beg pardon!—our new-fangled muse-haters, the *Radicals* of poetry, would otherwise leave at the bottom of the hog-trough. But really there is something so revolting in this coxcombical scorn of a dialect in which Milton himself, nay Virgil and Homer, enshrined their fames, and eternised their perishable thoughts, that one cannot, without doggedness, bow to this unjust necessity of stamping on pure gold the impress that bespeaks an alloy, or an inferior metal, to gain it currency,— in other words, *smuggling* in poetry under the colour of prose.

Major. You know I'm a bit of a botanist. The expedient you are discussing, or rather this constrained obliquity of development in poor poetry (left in the dark to shoot how it can, like a weed, instead of being cherished like a glorious flower, as it always has been), reminds me of a phenomenon in plants, whose instinctive seeming effort to reach the sun's influence is like that of your poet to get a bask in the sunshine of fame. If you place a plant in a flower-pot in a dark room, with but *one hole admitting light,* you shall see it contorting its shoots, and pointing them in a surprising manner to attain that hole, which having passed through, up they spring again, and no more creep or writhe, but flourish upright in the sun's eye, which they had languished for.

Amateur Gipsy. No bad fancy of the Major's that! And his image of his flower in the dark, methinks suggests a cheering answer to your despairing poet's question. May he not stoop, writhe, wriggle his pride of genius *through* the humble, dark, narrow avenue of prose, till it meet the sun (the sun of popular favour),—then, disclaiming its unworthy task and perverted growth, soar in its own shape and gorgeousness?

D. M. No. The taste of this age will not bear the strong impregnation of that fine spirit which so sparkles through the prose of our noble old English classics. The modern taste is most extremely delicate! there must be no body in its potations. The modern mind is a water-drinker; even if the pure element effervesce at all, there is great chance of a nausea; consequently such an outbreak of prose-poetry, or poetry-prose, as you suggest for an experiment, would be called prose run mad; and all that poetry struggling for life would thus be strangled in the birth, or after it for a monster; so that the axiom *Mors janua vitæ* would be reversed, and it would be the fate of its beauty to find *Vita janua mortis.*

Major. But what, after all, is the proof of this decline of Poetry you reason about? The general supply of " the article" is of rather improved quality; and we read the names of new poems advertised as forthcoming often enough quite. Do you mean the failure of genius in poetry, or decline of that favour which it used to enjoy? Certainly we do hear much said of its being in bad odour with the reading public, but still much is said of poetry. But lately the old *quæstio vexata* has been brought up of, What is poetry? as if it had never been started before.

D. M. To answer your query, I should say that the decline of poetry from its highest style of excellence must as certainly follow the withdrawing of the popular countenance from its authors, as a poor and sickly harvest is sure to succeed a cold summer, and almost total absence of the sun's rays upon the stem that is to produce the crop. Like such blighted field, there may be still a good show of a poetical crop; but is there a full, rich, heavy ear among them all? It is not the question whether the art shall be wholly disused, but whether any truly high and gifted artist is likely to arise under that distaste towards his productions, which I suppose it cannot be denied has been manifested for several years by the English public.

Major. Why, as the poet's mind at least must be allowed to be born, not wholly raised by culture to the height of excellence, I do not see how prejudice can operate to prevent the rise of such minds thus armed by nature herself for the fight.

Amateur Gipsy. I shall side with my friend, the doctor, there, and speak for him, for he's too busy with his quart of tea and his stone bottle of cream to answer you. For my part, I don't believe a word of poetic genius being born with a man, but only genius — the convertible ductile ore which may receive any impress whatever at the hand of culture, and in the mint of whatever asylum chance may present for its final form and figure.

Perhaps, had poetry and not arms been the vogue in Napoleon's youth, we should now be reading some sublime epic poem of the great Corsican poet Napoleon Buonaparte, instead of a still sublimer didactic one on the vanity of mortal glory, written not with hands, nor on paper, nor on marble, but a tablet *ære perennius* — the universal heart of man,— though its theatre be but the little round shadow of a weeping willow, and its hero a skeleton of a prisoner in the rock-floor of his prison.

When the stage was rising in popular estimation — the Reformation and the revival of learning having stamped new characters on life and society, which men loved to view in its mirror, however rude — the dramatic taste speedily raised dramatists of high excellence : Marlow, Shakespeare, Ford, Webster, Chapman, and a host of that rank, leaped to life at once. The English drama rose at once (in all that marks lofty genius) to its greatest glory with the suddenness of a Lapland meadow's spring, which, almost as soon as the warmth of the returned sun disrobes it of its sheet of iced snow which sepulchred it in the long night, waves a very galaxy of glorious flowers, born and blossoming almost together, to the intense blue sky ! In France, the taste for blood instead of books having arisen under the republic, a crop of warriors was the produce, as in England one of dramatists.

Major. Stop there. How happened it, then, that the great rage for poetry about Byron's time did not foster a crop of Byrons ?

D. M. Fashion and a mystery had as much to do in founding his fame as his genius had, great as that was. Accordingly we saw a whole host of spurious poets and mock - Byrons swarming in the glow of his glory, warming their feeble vitality with a little of the reflected lustre. I would say the taste then prevalent was not for poetry, but for Byron, who happened to write in verse. Neither Scott, who

preceded him, nor he, based their claims on the eternal truth of nature. Was *Marmion* or the *Corsair* a creation of the same flesh and blood reality with *Macbeth* or *Othello*, or with Penthea, her of the " broken heart," in the tragedy of Ford ?

Byron, by his nerve and depth of feeling, though morbid and masked, drove from the field the feebler ballad-style, which had played strange antics on the very throne of taste, with its cloud of retainers. But the evil was not much abated by the success of the new hero, strong as he was. He drove off, and slew, indeed, the dragon of the mock-chivalry school—the ballad-epic, that mighty monstrosity obedient to the great enchanter; but having banished one nuisance he gave rise to another. The sacred " well-head of poesy," which the dragon had defiled while it pretended to guard, like that by the fountain of Mars, was no more free of approach than before. The all-imitated Byron was the Cadmus who undesignedly reared such a crop of earthly warriors, that had they not killed each other very fast, after a few heavy hits from their creator's own hand (who fitted them well, like his prototype), God knows what would have become of the sacred spring, or who would have borne to have tasted it, defiled and discoloured with blood of knights, and by " glamour " of wizard and fay, and hung round with bagpipes instead of harps, before; and afterwards made the head-quarters of pirates, murderers, and moping gentlemen, peeping through masks " wonderous melancholy."

Major. Ay; perhaps Byron was the greatest foe to poetry and its reign in England that ever was. In fact, the glut in the market which his servile followers produced gave the public a surfeit that has turned it against poetry ever since : the tone of its stomach will come round again after awhile.

D. M. Doubtless the world was grown truly sick of the breed of Byrons. The island was peopled with misanthropes, " looking unutterable things "— in foolscap. But, perhaps, the rise of the historical novel had much to do with the fall of the poem. Scott, you know, after his discomfiture and flight from Parnassus, came back with his reinforcement from the realms of history, re-appearing in the field, ten thousand strong, after being given up for lost. *Waverley* avenged his former defeat on Byron himself, casting some of even his later poems into the background; and as for his raggamuffin regiment of followers, they were returned "missing," for nobody found even their *disjecta membra* from that day to this. *Amateur Gipsy. Requiescant in pace!* Yes, looking back to that time — *eheu fugaces! et cætera*—we are struck with that revolution in taste we are talking of very forcibly. I remember, some seventeen years since, on the *début* of *Waverley*, an Edinburgh reviewer began a critique on that work by saying that it was already read and sought after rather like an admired poem than a novel. The same critic, now writing in the same work, should he wish to express the sudden success of a new poem, would or might properly give us the converse of this comparison,— so versatile is popular taste, at least in our days! *D. M.* Rather say to-day! It was not thus in my boyhood, and you see I am not yet quite a human antiquity. I remember when the title-page of an admired poem would keep its place as a fixture in a bookseller's window, shewing its honest front to my devouring eyes month after month, with only the change of the second, third edition, and so forth. Then the names of a very few true sons of genius and just fame maintained a sort of regal solitariness of state, and became to the young muse-smitten (such I was then) august as that of the laurelled head on a coin, yet familiar as a brother's; then a man might remember and even admire a work "six months after date." He was not deemed a Goth himself for discussing the beauties of *Roderick the last of the Goths.* The *Wanderer of Switzerland* ceased his wanderings for a long sojourn in the public mind ; the *World before the Flood* was not become antediluvian even at three months' end ; the *Pleasures of Hope* might hope to please a second season ; so might the *Ancient Mariner* and his philosophical poet-creator. Southey, Montgomery, Crabbe, Coleridge, Campbell! These names and a few more were then to a few ardent readers of verse like a pleasant and well-known ring of bells ; any one of them conjured up sweet associations of ideas that rapt us out of our world-weary selves. But now number, not merit, seems the grand desideratum as regards the productions of

mind. A perpetual new supply of food for the hunger of the reading public must be got up; and in the intellectual, as in any other feast, the hurried feeding and hurried cookery promises not much delicacy in the guests or perfection in the viands. This only regards prose works. As to poetry, he is a bold man who publishes it now; we may say of him as has been said of the man who enjoys solitude,— he must be either below or above humanity ; he must either have the besotted conceit to hope to stem the tide of opinion thus set in against poetry by the charm of his single voice, or be really the destined hero of that achievement which it was almost madness to hope for.

Amateur Gipsy. Why, truly, the poem which should effect a revulsion in the present course of the public mind, would scarcely effect a stranger miracle than was wrought by that fiery sign which of a sudden came forth on the front of heaven full before the army of Constantine, and led back whole hosts to the true faith and way. It becomes matter for curious speculation (to folks idle as we are, thus babbling of poetry in this extra-mundane island by a rising moon) whether John Milton, had his fate thrown him on our evil days (far more so than his own), would have accomplished this conversion, would have stood up this restorer of true taste, would have erected the "Paradise" aloft and alone in the poetical hemisphere, like that sign and standard of the one God (his the ensign of the one divine poet); or have indeed died, like you or me, a "mute inglorious Milton?" What say you, and you — ay or no ? Would he print or burn his twelve books? Would he wreak some of that fatal fury which burned so fiercely against his erring more than sinning king against this usurpation of sole dominion by our prose cavaliers? Seeing fame thus "at one entrance quite shut out," would he stoop to the apostasy we were talking of, and seek her under the banners of prose ? Then, perhaps, we should see published by Fraser, 215 Regent Street, "A Tale of the Fall ;" or else, "Some Passages in the Life of our Father Adam," 3 vols. 8vo. But, as I understand the publisher of REGINA never puffs his publications, we should, I fear, lose some neat puffs oblique which might otherwise meet our eye in a paragraph or two in this wise, thrust in for those few country simple souls who yet survive to enjoy the happiness of being "well deceived," and take it for a bit of "News."

"We understand the reading world is still on the cold scent, yet eager as ever, in the pursuit of the unknown author of the 'Romance of the Paradise.' Many lordly, ducal, and even one illustrious name, have been confidently assigned: the mystery, however, is yet uncleared. As one proof of the eagerness, as well as wildness, of conjecture, we may repeat one rumour, for the reader's diversion. Some wiseacres have found out this great unknown in an *old blind schoolmaster*, lodging somewhere about Wilderness Row!!!"

Major. Or perhaps something like this, now, would be edged in among accidents, or "*on dits* of the day:" "Many fashionables expressed great disappointment to find that the great new novelist, whom they had heard spoken of at the drawing-room the last levee day as having a touch at Pandemonium and its inmates, has no occult discoverable allusion to the 'hells' of St. James's Street, &c. Satan and Crockford do not tally in every particular to sustain the allegory."

D. M. Well done our major! he deserves a penny per line. But let us follow the fate of our Milton redivivus. We shall suppose him to have gone through all the requisite process of fostering and feeding that genius he has discovered in himself, agreeably to his own beautiful description of his actual studies. "From the laureate fraternity of poets," I remember he says, "riper years, and *the ceaseless round of study and reading*, led me to the shady spaces of philosophy." This done, we see him in that justifiable mood of self-promise (not then self-flattery) which such labours and such a mind gave rise to; he has "found that whatever task of composition he undertook, whether imposed, or betaken to of his own choice, in English or other tongue, prosing or versing, but chiefly the latter, *the style, by certain vital signs it had, was likely to live.*" He says that at last, thus prepared, he "began to assent to an inward prompting, which grew daily upon him, that by labour and intense study, joined to the strong propensity of nature, he might perhaps leave something so writ-

ten to after-times, as they *should not willingly let it die.*" "Then," says he, "I applied myself to the *resolution to fix all the industry and art I could unite* to the adorning of my native tongue. That what the greatest and choicest wits of Athens, Rome, or modern Italy, and those Hebrews of old did for their country, I, in my proportion, with this over and above of being a Christian, might do for mine. Not caring to be once named abroad, though perhaps I could attain to that, but *content with these British islands as my world.*" Was not this as truly English, as noble a resolve, of so eagle-winged a spirit, to bound its flight to our own white walls of rock, and though strong and beautiful enough to mount the empyrean, skim the world of waters, and become visible to many climes, to content itself with home and home-born gazers, — and even those little in a frame of mind to do justice to its glory?

Amateur Gipsy. It was at least a fortunate resolve. Milton would otherwise, to this day, have been a ponderous Latin author, chained in the dusty corner of some few old libraries, instead of the heroic poet of England.

D. M. Ay, what would our "ever-gentle" critical court of judicature say to such a burst of poetry in a plain treatise on the "Reason of Church Government?" &c. The words just quoted are not, of course, applied to his own future works by himself, but me.

Now I think you'll both allow, that our Milton of to-day having gone through this course of mental training, as we may call it — having endured that sort of death to the world — that abandonment of its ordinary hopes — that estrangement from its ties — that midnight sapping of life's foundation, the denial of nature's rightful rest — the anxiety and the solitude which must in a degree be endured by every lofty aspirant of fame, — I say, you will allow that it would no longer be an optional question with the scrivener's son (or even the secretary of Cromwell), whether he should or should not become, or try to become, a poet. No; that athletic state of his mental constitution which he has thus painfully produced — those sweet and gentle solicitings of his fancy to be received into the service of that towering mind — the one must be employed, and strenuously — the other must be obeyed, or

life past has passed in vain — life to
come is bitterness and a curse. Life
immortal, or no life, would certainly
be the secret irresistible *ultimatum* of
Milton's decision on his own fate and
fortunes. A man with this plethoric
condition of mind if I may so call it,
has no hope of its prolonged health, or
even life—no escape from the sickness
of dire hypochondriacism, or the mental
death of madness, but in severe exercise, that exercise fed by the richest
meed of fame ; for however vanity in
inferior geniuses may soothe its little
sorrows by coquetting with that great
unknown, Posterity, nothing but a
present, full, overpowering majority of
voices assenting to its claims will satisfy a legitimate genius. A hundred
pretenders to a crown may " strut
their hour" on the stage of mock royalty, and slink back to the plebeian
sphere that claims them, quietly enough,
content to keep their life alone ; but
the true claimant, if confounded and
spurned from his high place among
those, would have fierce pangs, and
furious regrets to gnaw and agonise his
heart, unshared and unconceivable by
them.

Major. But surely, Doctor, you
don't seriously think that a Milton
born in our times, of high literary pretension and boasted patronage of literature, would be born in vain — toil
out life in hearing little boys their
lessons—and enjoy no wider world of
fame than his school-room ?

D. M. Why, no ; for my solitary
opinion (if worth giving) is, that our
times politically promise a field for the
fury of his spirit to fight in, if not for
its softer sublimity to disport itself in
Eden. We have a large part of our
population imbued with all the fierce
obduracy, the pampered self-conceit
of their own infallibility, the bitter
scorn and hate of all dissenting from
their dictatorship, which ever marked
the puritanical rebels ; without that
religious impression, however fanatical,
which did render the outbreak of that
age not quite so bloody as that of
France in ours.

Intolerant *fanatics* in politics, without religion to make them merciful by
fear of God's judgment, if not by brotherly pity, threaten, of all revolution-
ists, the most anarchical revolution.
Hence I conceive, that while the poet
of *Comus* and the *Paradises* and *Il
Penseroso* would, in our day, sleep in
the faintly-stirring chrysalis of a book
that falls still-born from the press, just
perceived to be quick by the contemptuous touch of some fashionable critic,
bound by his office to ascertain the
fact of life or no life in the lumpy form
of a twelve-booked sacred poem, with
its ill-defined wings in moveless em-
bryo—to all but him a lifeless lump —
still Milton might live. The regicide
Milton — the revolutionary Milton —
the bitter controversialist—the glorious
rebel-spirit of Milton (glorious for its
indomitable strength only), might find
its fit element in the whirlwind of our
" coming events," and hereafter be the
idol of some " public " revelling in the
bloody streets of republican London—
hover an eagle-winged vampire over
the nameless, stoneless, lime-filled
grave-hole of some " Grey-discrowned
head ;" as did that of Milton, clapping
its wings over the unknown sepulture
of the " great Barabbas at Windsor,"
when he wrote that unworthy libel on
a dead monarch (mild and suffering,
if not a martyr), the work on the *Eikon
Basilike* : thus raging against even his
posthumous groans in " his solitudes
and his sufferings!"

What, in all likelihood, would now
be the blind bard's fate, supposing the
stormy air of revolution or the rage of
anti-prelacy to leave him like a crip-
pled eagle on the earth, and without a
chance of soaring, except from the wing
of his own Urania ? Can we imagine
a man of his stern elevation of soul to
conceive the slightest pleasure from the
fullest fruition of such literary triumph
as the present state of poetry and its
readers promises, to even the *highest*
candidate ? To be read a little, be
praised much, run the titillating gaunt-
let of approving reviews, and " then
be seen no more,"— could this satisfy
the yearnings of the man who felt
" immortal longings" in his soul ?

Amateur Gipsy. That is rating low
indeed the critical acumen of our times.

D. M. By no means. I conceive
something more than the cool-minded
judgment of even accomplished men
goes to poetical justice of award ; for
there is that in high flights of genius
which defies all canons. *Mediocrity of
excellence* — will you allow that term ?
—may be gauged, weighed, pronounced
upon in any cultivated age ; but that
more violent intense flame of imagination, which turns all to fire whereon it
alights—that giant reach of mind which

spurns the planet on which it lives, and exists more in heaven than on earth; that burns with a desire like that of the mad, to drag up all minds along with it above our clouds and our miseries, to the uttermost heaven of all those dim yet glorious stars which gem the night, in which such high imagination dwells apart, and knows no human day or human society during more than half the existence of the animal man;—that arch-genius, which burned as a fixed star in Milton, as a comet in Lucan, and in Chapman, Homer's translator (to select a few)—that, I say, only an enthusiastic age can judge. There was much enthusiasm afloat in the public mind at the period of the rise of *Paradise Lost.* Inspiration was the fashion in the high places, in the parliament, in the army, in the conventicle; great and terrible events and changes of society bring along with them a grand dreaminess of thought—a looking-for of the fearful future, which disposes the general mind to receive the kindred excitement of the poetic character. The poet comes to the bar of opinion in his old awful guise of the *vates*, and is listened to as if Apollo were invisibly touching his harp, or his strain were the anthem of the eve of the day of judgment. Certainly an excitable, delicately-sensitive state of the recipient mind, is as necessary to the due appreciation of a " muse of fire " as the same state is in the creative mind, whose wealth is to be poured into it. Now what I conceive is, that this is not the age to inspirit, to bring forth a divine poet; much less to acknowledge such a poet, if by some chance cast on its evil days, like a wind-sown tree the pride of the orchard, shot up green alone on a cliff of the sea, blossoming there unseen with the rosy beauty of the east in a May morning, and shedding its fruit untasted on a savage solitude of beach below, to be washed away for ever by the next tide. Hence I think our poet would have either betaken himself to Italy, there to have written in a dead language, soon to have been ranked with the learned *living dead* himself, or else——

Amateur Gipsy. Or else his dark spirit—darkened by disgust, and by misanthropy not groundless, to tenfold darkness—would of itself fight the half-lost battle of Genius, and triumph at last by dint of the mere fury of failure;

which, by the way, I suspect was half the secret of Byron's "dark bosom," and his wonderful seizure of men's minds all at once. Read what nobody reads, Milton's prose works, and you will find the genius of the poet of the lake of penal fire at work darkly, like a roaring underground volcano, yet as palpably as when painting the pains immortal of the blessed become the damned. There is something terrible in his wrath, and its outpourings are no less noisome and foul than the sooty and sulphureous breath of the eternal prison-house.

Major. You having both had your " or else," let me put in my *aliter* also, though one of you thought it before, when we began this prabble — *or else* he would, by his main strength, have stopped the silken-reined steeds that amble with our car of prose literature; have stowed into it his whole freight of poetry, made it roll with a due solemnity and ponderosity becoming its cargo, and — and ——

Amateur Gipsy. Given the sleek lady-steeds a double feed of fire, and a little of Diomedes' provender—blood and muscle and nerve, which they lack so wofully, and lashed them with one of the snakes of one of the furies for a whip, and away!

D. M. And whither, I pray you? To the mud of Lethe's black-tide river, there to stick fast for ever? No! the same inaptitude of taste which would, I think, shut him up with all his genius within himself, by the living burial of neglect, would pursue that genius, broken into the pale of prose, like a wolf leaped into the fold, and a rabid one. Much of the prose-poetry which charmed an age of more vigorous taste than this, would now be deemed rank madness in a modern work.

Amateur Gipsy. I think quite differently from you in your idea of his failing in this resource of his homeless muse, and falling like Phaeton at last. Who knows what new taste, or rather, what sudden return to that true one— to the fine old nervous style of the " throned Vestal's" reign, an Elizabethan prose Milton might have produced? For surely Milton's spirit was of an age gone by. We trace in it all that fervid glow of imagination which marked the elder dramatists — their high and unworldly modes of thought, without their eccentric and often unnatural ecstasies, in him joined to a fine dark solemnity all his own. If we might compare them to the wildly-beautiful *aurora borealis* of a polar region's night, illuminating with their bursts and coruscations of glory the lingering shades of the night of ages, him we may liken to that settled lustre shed over all by the moon's red orb, rising upon their sublime play, which, though heavenly of place, was not of heaven; he, on the contrary, that lofty region's own denizen, "paleing their fires."

For, to say truth, though it were profane to name Milton and barbarism in the same breath, his own predilections for the old Italian writers have diffused an air over his work of a monkish era; and Dante's mantle descended on him. Hence, though the dark ages no longer shadowed the world of his mind, a light very different from that of contemporary minds, and even long antecedent ones, prevails there.

Perhaps, even to this day, the irruption of such a tide of poetry into English prose, had it occurred, would have been mighty in its effects, and prevented that too-subdued current I conceive it to flow with now, approaching to the character of the canal nearer than to that of the noble river.

D. M. It did occur. As you have yourself remarked, Milton's prose teems with poetry; but then his prose works are deemed unreadable from their temporary topics, as well as their virulence of controversial zeal or by-gone questions. Hence we have no work of his which professedly enshrines his poetic genius in prose like the *Telemachus* of Fenelon. I remember many a passage like that I recited before, proving that Milton could, when he pleased, lay his hand on the mane of our old British lion (if I may so designate the genius of our prose tongue), and make a Pegasus of it, to transport him, "an earthly guest, into the heaven of heavens." Apologising for some bitterness of angry zeal objected to his writings, he has this passage (he is supposing "the cool, impassionate mildness of positive wisdom, to have failed in its opposition to corrupt falsehoods," &c.): "Then Zeal, whose substance is ethereal, arming in complete diamond, ascends his fiery chariot, drawn with two blazing meteors figured like beasts, but of a higher breed than any the zodiac yields; like those four seen by Ezekiel and St. John.

With these the invincible warrior, Zeal, shaking loosely the slack reins, drives over the heads of scarlet prelates, bruising their stiff necks under his flaming wheels," &c. There we have again the Bard of Paradise suddenly uplifting himself, as he says elsewhere, and "soaring in the high region of his fancies, with his garland and singing-robes about him," even while "sitting here below in the cool element of prose." For this high-raised style he had the example of the great Bacon, of Raleigh, and most great men of their age; as well as Jeremy Taylor's, the most richly poetical mind of his own. I cannot think our style has gained any thing by that divorce between Prose and Poetry which has been effected since his day. Certain it is, that now all strenuous writing that bespeaks an impassioned soul, seeking in a reader a kindred soul, is sneered at under the term of striving after *effect*: figurative language is too ornate for the age of the steam-engine, and perhaps for the capacities of the operative world; which is to constitute, possibly ere long, the parliament of taste and letters as of legislation. *Sic transit gloria mundi!*

Major. I am no enthusiast in the "olden times," I confess; yet I cannot but think we arrogate a little too much to our intellectual selves in exalting our own age above that which produced Bacon, Burleigh, Raleigh, Sir P. Sidney, and all that host you could name better than I, in the court, camp, senate, and even in science; and a Shakespeare with his host; and a Massinger and a Milton even in its passing away! Indeed it is curious to imagine with what severe scorn our poet would have heard poetry — the mother-tongue of his soul — poetry, that sanctuary of his highest hope, where ne had garnered up his heart, where either he must live or know no life — flippantly decried as the "barbarous amusement of a half-civilised age," as void of pleasure to our scientific minds, by the very beings who devour fashionable novels of vile grammar and worse morals — all sorts of idle gossiping scandal in print — who visit the theatre to see a beast or witness a melodrame, not the drama of Shakespeare — who shake the empire to its foundations to purify the senate-house, and then fill it with demagogues, prize-fighters, sedition-mongers, and venders of blacking. Oh, for the march of intellect, and a Milton to arise and sing his admiration !

Amateur Gipsy. I confess, when I consider the character of our times, thus frivolous, yet vain, I am half a convert to your despair, Doctor, of even a Milton regenerating the popular taste, supposing him now on the eve of publication, as we say.

D. M. Rely upon it, that his highest beauties would be the stumbling-blocks in his road to fame. The sublime and the ridiculous, we say, meet. Though no two things can be more opposite to each other than the writing which awakens and fills the soul, and that which merely surprises the attention and fills the ear—than noble sentiment and painting in language, and the mock-heroic endeavour at those perfections—the distinction is by no means palpably drawn to all mental optics. That astonishing, exhaustless flow of fancy, applied to the illustration (by beautiful images) of exalted sentiment, and even the gravest argument, which is so striking in Jeremy Taylor and even in Bacon, while treating on experimental philosophy, has not the least shadow of a copy in any writing that I recollect since their time.

Amateur Gipsy. Yes, one writer; Dryden, although not a copyist, gives a beautiful example in his prose style of those charms of their genius, without the quaintness and constraint visible, often, in their language and its construction, never in the ideas. Dr. Johnson extols *Comus*, as exhibiting " the dawn or twilight of *Paradise Lost.*" In Dryden's style, I would say, may be seen the evening twilight of the *Paradise.* Clarendon threw off the Latin idiom and perplexed inversions of his great precursors' styles, but wanted or despised their imaginative wealth ; the glory was reserved for Dryden of combining freedom and ease with their poetical luxury of imagery and loftiness of style.

D. M. That's one of the main points on which I build my prediction of our phantom Milton, of this present year 1834, being *burked* by *us*, the " march-of-intellect" men. Johnson has passed the highest eulogium on Dryden's prose style ; critics of our own day have very recently declared, that it has " not been equalled since his time." Five minutes' reading at random, of any part of his prose writings, will satisfy any

judicious reader of the justice of these plaudits. And what do we find the character of this style, which draws forth this concurrent testimony to its excellence ? Why, its poetry. Not only is the language choice, apposite, and, as it were, instinctively springing to the idea—the very word or words to the very thought precise, which no others would have suited so well, like one particle of steel, in a promiscuous heap of atoms of other metals, leaping to the magnet, and clinging there alone ; but the flow of images is perpetual. However grave the topic, however dry — whether a dedication of condolence before some elegiac tribute, or one of self-condolence, touching on his own troubles, and angling by the fulsomest praise for a small tribute to the relief of them, still he is full of sentimental painting. Nature and art, the city and the country, alike afford figures for it ; often elaborate, yet always beautiful. Hence it is that, for my part, I can read the poet Dryden, as well through the shaded glass of his prose as in his poems. The dullest subject ceases to tire, so enlivened is it by this flush of the blossoms of fancy blushing every where through its blank. To steal his " trick " of play with the reader, one might compare the flow of his writing, thus unpromising yet thus delightful, to a mountain-river, which art has for a space converted into a dull canal of traffic ; yet in an under-current of which (below the surface bearing barges and bales of goods) mountain-flowers come floating down from the higher land, and aquatic plants of beauty may still be seen growing in its channel, and flowing with its flow, like emerald-green streamers on the wind.

Major. To the point, Doctor! to the point ! Still, I don't see what you build on all this about Dryden.

D. M. You military men are so fond of battle-fields, you have no patience to " babble of green fields." Then this I infer: first, with all this praise and acknowledgment of its beauty and excellence, *who does ever now adopt such a style?* To see and approve the better genius of our prose tongue, and follow the worse, seems the mode at present. Hence, I conceive, should a writer start up, imbued by nature with the same *plethora* of poetry, farther confirmed in that his literary constitution by day and night feasting on the fruits of those kindred minds left to our age in those fine *cornua copiæ* — their teeming volumes — it would avail him nothing in attaining the only fame he would think worth the anxiety of its pursuit. If he could bear to "waste their sweetness on the desert air," he might strew those exotic flowers of his heated mind through periodicals, annuals, or other temporary garden-pots of literature — perennial plants in a soil which must be devoted speedily to other plants. What no author thinks worthy of imitation, will any critic deem worthy of immortality? Without a steady prospect of that meed of fame his self-conscious mightiness of genius would know to be his right, would Milton stoop to become a claimant for it? And in the present universality of pseudo-fame, the present tame content in mellifluous sentences and maudlin pathos, and the mummy of History's defunct body served up for the *vera et viva effigies* of its fresh and unshrivelled form, how doubtful must be the prospect of the temple of Fame! how unworthy of a great mind's strivings—even that meed, if attained, to be shared with a thousand usurpers flaunting their mock laurels (fac-similes of the true), bestowed by the false priests of the false divinity Fashion, throned on the high altar-place of the true, the earthly-immortal Fame!

Amateur Gipsy. "*Fuit Fama !*" Thus, then, you consign *our* Milton to oblivion — "earth to earth." But what say you to the stage, as a forlorn hope to his smothered genius? 'Twere strange too, methinks, that so mighty a genius should perish from want of an opening to break out at—the whole English mind *calloused* against its efforts to make an impression — perish like a leviathan, with all its enormity of strength, under a north-sea frozen for mere want of a vent—beating itself to death against the floor of its own element, become its prison and its grave, while mere man walks over the back of him who could, by one lash of his tail, whelm a man-of-war! Would he have sought the stage for his muse's transport to posterity?

D. M. Milton, tremblingly awaiting the pleasure of the pit or the gallery-gods, after the ordeal of trial before managers at rehearsals, the chances of stage-effect, &c.! — Milton thus enslaved, first to fashion and next to the mob, would be indeed like Ariel ministering to Caliban. To "do *his* bidding featly," would better become a fairy genius than an angel one. Nor does his spirit seem to have been essentially dramatic.

Major. According to you, then, Gray's conjectural "mute" Milton is not only possible but certain. For as there have been "giants in those days," how can it be but the same stature of mind must be occasionally attained in ours, only kept invisible by the foul fog of ignorance, or deformed, or fallen to the fate of him, "wet with the dews of heaven," who fed with the beasts of the field, through the malign influence of their evil star?

D. M. I regard Gray's idea as literally true. It is my opinion, that not only may Miltons and Cromwells sleep under these white-tiled graves, with sprigs of evergreen stuck over them, coffin-shaped, in this very country, but men to whom Milton himself might have yielded up his harp in despair, and Cromwell the helm of state on compulsion. Why should we conclude that the perfection of man has yet been born? Who shall set bounds to God's mysteries or almightiness—his sublime reserving of creative strength? And why, since mightier minds than we know of on earth may in future be created, may they not have been created and gone to the earth whence they came, without a record or even man's consciousness? Millions of seeds perish, yet each containing the germ of the oak; which, if planted, might outlive not only the British, but yet unfounded empires, and shade the shepherd or herdsman, and roost the night-hooting owl, rooted in the heart of the ruins of London. A Roman under the later empire would have deemed this as wild a fancy as you do by your smiling, yet it would have been true.

The telescope reveals new wonders and worlds in the infinity of greatness, as does the microscope in the infinity of littleness. The kraken, more than rumoured, now and then half reveals the living acres of his island body to the deceived seaman anchoring by it. The earth, in like manner, darkly half reveals its old secrets of God's undreamed-of sublimities of creation, when the osseous ruins of the ante-diluvian mammoth, or megatherium, peep through the disturbed mould or rent rock that has veiled them, and shew us, for the first time, that the elephant is not the hugest of the creatures of the earth. Were minds like planets or animals, composed of matter to be objects of sense, the grave, too, might unfold as wonderful secrets of gigantic proportions as the earth, the heavens, and the great deep.

Major. And what a world might we have been rejoicing in now, had those glorious abortions of minds but come to maturity! This moral world, now so chaotic, so dark with clouds, so hideous of features, and ever stormy, might under their influence have attained to something of that celestial purity, and calm and harmonious order, which we see in the material; where the clouds fructify, the darkness brings us rest, the very comets keep their appointed road, and all is beauty, all intelligible!

D. M. Traversing the lonelier parts of this wildly-beautiful but melancholy country of Wales, as I sometimes do in the middle of night, I love to ruminate awhile under the half-arch of some one of the many ruinous castles we find here by moonlight; to scramble down into its dry and weedy moat, once brimming with defensive water often bloodied; or seat myself in its grand court full of stones, tumbled from the top so long ago that trees have grown up among them, and watch, perhaps, the yellow glistering of the sea through its skeleton walls, by which a fisher's solitary sail glides in soundless distance. The wonderful defences which have been made by a handful against a host, in many sieges recorded of these towers, then pass in review as History has arranged them in her pages, but left the human histories—the lives and deaths of besiegers and besieged—in the blank of oblivion; retaining but a name or two of the leaders, perhaps the least worthy record of them all. Who shall say what Curtii what Mutii may have there suffered torture or death, self-inflicted for their little native nook disdained by the muse of history? No more self-devotion, even to the death, was displayed by the heroes of Thermopylæ, than has been by many of these poor Welshmen in many a hopeless field, fighting but for a barren land or a nameless grave in its bosom; while the Greeks have their apotheosis in the eternal memory of mankind. A skeleton upturned within the castle precincts (or many in some green mound's neighbourhood)—a dark hint of tradi-

tion—a name of a spot—" The Bloody Spring," " The Stone of Lamentation and Weeping," " The Grave of the Men of Ardaddwy"—*vox et præterea nihil*—such the poor immortality of heroes, between whom and those true immortals of Grecian or Roman fame the accidents of time and place have made the only difference; the Creator none.

As warriors lie thus unhonoured beneath our feet, why not poets? There is a noble vein of poetry in the older Welsh authors, which bespeaks a very high degree of poetic civilisation in the popular mind, and which shines through all the obscurement of translation; yet the names that have survived, even in Cambrian fame, are so few, that it is impossible but that a host of poets still-born must sleep " without their fames" in such a region, where one may almost say of the churchyards —

> " Every sod beneath our feet
> Shall be a *poet's* sepulchre."

Amateur Gipsy. The extreme beauty of them will at least excuse the fancy, and make us walk beneath the black and gilded fretwork roof of their enormous yews, glittered through by a full moon, as a cathedral cloister with its stained window, and a " poet's corner" of the " unknown poets."

D. M. I must take you to my favourite churchyard in the neighbourhood of Builth, that of Abereddw; the village where Llewellyn the Last had a castle, his last hold in his own country. In such a night as this—for I think we have talked down the very last of that fine orange glow of light in the west sea, without seeing it overcome by the confirmed moonlight, " so still, so soft, so bright"—I always wish myself in Abereddw churchyard, listening to the tumbling Eddw far down in its rock bed; its feathered cliffs and embosoming mountains shutting me in with the dead beneath its most ancient of yews.

Amateur Gipsy. At least in this *our* isle, with the tide making music against its banks, with that low patter more like a lake than an ocean estuary — that low roar of the main sea, washing the cape of the little promontory of Gest—this shiver of a wood of ivy overhead, and that low white building shining dim and white on the shore, like a church—these mighty mountains rolled in blackness all behind, and that wide-flashing sea all before,—you must be unreasonably romantic to form a wish beyond.

D. M. True: the mountains and the sea are a conjunction of the sublime in natural objects, which leaves but one sublimity more to be desired —a moral one—the terrible mysterious presence of death. A sea-side mountain churchyard, of which we have many in Wales, is, methinks, the *ne plus ultra* of the moral picturesque. There are Salvator Rosas in the art of thinking as well as painting : let all such haunt Wales and her wild coasts.

Major. For my part, I shall take up with "Death's twin-brother Sleep," for want of the "real presence" of the grisly king; though I confess this silvery light, and the fragrance of the wild thyme (drenched in dew already) of this short turf, and of the wild roses overhead festooning our rock-chamber, would keep me out of my tent longer than that presence you regret, and invite me more temptingly than a grave, or even a whole charnel, to sit here all night. Thus I think our "little senate" has debated long and decided nothing, about the present state and prospects of English poetry.

D. M. Therein following the laudable example of some great senates, which, after wasting session after session in debating a point, and "sitting attentive to its own applause," hand it over at last to the sovereign people to decide ; as we must do our question, Whether or not a great poet would find "audience meet" in our day ?

Amateur Gipsy. Leaving the question, then, of the chances of life to Miltonic genius, which is not in much danger of being brought to the test, what shall we say to the prospects of authors in this era of authorship; which, if Brazen or Iron be objected to, may fitly be named the Publishing Age? It is indeed marvellous, that whereas literary ambition — the public trial of which has always been a lottery with but a few capitals—did formerly tempt to his fate or fame one, it now drives with a sort of fury a hundred ; yet now, as you have observed, one may almost deny that there is any great prize at all. Such a fame as that of Scott and. Byron, and a few precursors, is hardly to be supposed left in the wheel now. The new fashion is to make all prizes — of twopence

sterling ! every blank being beautifully got up as fac-similes of prizes, like the flash-notes of the swindling world.

D. M. Cui bono? If ever that soul-damping question may justly be asked on the eve of any human undertaking, surely it may by him who is about to bless his enemy with his wish, according to Solomon; that is, to publish a book. I mean, on the presumption that the author is fired with ambition—not of fashionable brief notice, not of praise deserved or not, but of that station and rank in the estimation of refined and thinking men which Justice herself has, up to our time, assigned to intellectual birthright, almost as steadily as his rightful inheritance of title or tower to the legal heir. It is easy to say to the querulous gifted man in his indignant dumbness, " Why then write ?" Nor would it be easy to make one who can ask that question comprehend, how a man may reasonably write much and publish nothing. The necessity of the pen, the fierce craving for fame, can no more be made intelligible to them than the need of sight can be explained to those born blind, or of speech to those who have never spoken. To the multitude of modern writers, writing is a craft and the pen a tool. Now to all those elder writers we have been talking of, composition was the outpouring of a mind filled with sentiment to repletion, and the pen did the office of a tongue. Whereas, the minds of the publishing multitude seem now for ever tasked to concocting some *somethings*, hard-sought and far, as the *matériel* of a book, on purpose that they may publish, publish, publish ! It seems to me, that those finer old English minds were vacantly at their ease when their genius revealed herself to each, surprising them like an angel: they were the wooed of Nature, not the wooers ; or, as our bard said, " sitting calm in the cool element" of unworldly contemplative feeling, " with their garlands and singing-robes about them." When her beauties were thus unveiled to their eyes, her riches strewn at their feet, the social spirit, strong in all lofty intellects, then and not till then prompted, importuned, and at last, with gentle violence, forced them to the presence of their brethren ; that is, to seeking the sympathy of the public in their delight ; as one who finds a treasure, or has a fortune devolved to him, never rests till he has run to tell his whole family what has befallen him.

There are minds which extract out of every thing in nature food for sentiment. From the silvery and blush-coloured shell, and the living crystal of the gelly on the sea-shore, to the mountainous and thundering sea itself in a storm; from the cottage-child singing, hid in deep grass flowering in the blue and sweet noonday, accompanied by the humming-bee on the clover flower, to the blue and bloated body of its sailor-father, that moment thrown up ghastly on a solitary sand-bank, there to lie like a polypus, rolled over by the tide, and torn by birds of prey;—all is food for sentiment, in terror, in pity, or in beauty. The paragon of such minds was Shakespeare's; such a mind was Webster's, a humble parish-clerk of St. Andrew's, Holborn; that sombre, solemn, truly-tragical one, which created the terrible scenes of the dying Duchess of Malfy, kept from that rest in death she seeks by a whole band of involuntary tormentors, a dance of madmen;—such was Marlow's, he who depicted *before* Shakespeare the agonies of reluctant royalty discrowning its own head—the horrors of the same majesty knee-deep in the castle-filth of an underground dungeon, watched by murderers and afraid to sleep, though half-dead for want of sleep, lest they should seize the opportunity of his falling eyelids to make that sleep eternal. With such men, to feel, to think, to write, were almost as one act. It was the natural tendency of such habits of the mind to seclude, in a degree, their possessor from the worldlings round him; however his wants or even sociability might intimately connect him bodily with them in their busiest resorts. Still the most frequent abode of such a spirit must be in the lofty solitude of its own philosophic melancholy. From that still vantage ground, not only does the solitary look down on the whole human species with all-different eyes from those jostling in the crowd—not only does he regard the living mass, instead of individually hurrying on each to some proud and happy bourn of his own, as rolling on to a universal grave in one motley tide, like a leaf-strewn river to its fall—but his solemn vision turns inward; his own mind, in all its shadows and its few gleams of vivid sunlight, lies exposed like a

map before him; or, to speak as poets write, like the disk of the moon seen through a night-telescope — dusky, doubtful, yet grand, with conjectures of volcanic ruin. Now in this withdrawal to the watch-tower of supramundane thought, consists the peculiarity of the intense literary character —of that only I speak. From this arises that dramatic excellence which those minds attained; that keen relish (by contrast of utter abstraction, for the most part) which a return to humanity, as it were, afforded them, made them intuitive masters of human passions, and vivid painters of that scenic procession and pomp of many-coloured life in detail, which, from their habitual lone stand, ever looked in the mass to them but a vast procession of mourners, and a pomp of death. I am so habituated to soliloquy, that I am apt to talk as one reads—on and on. The Major I hear asleep in his tent; my two boys look fast also, half in and half out of mine; the sea comes in brimming, and gurgles no more in the hollow banks of our prison — all's asleep but that fern-owl, and a sea-mew at a distance. Are you awake yet?

Amateur Gipsy. Awake and attentive.

D. M. Narcotics, then, have no power over you. Now one can well imagine that some cause may arise to make constant, perpetual to the mind which I have described its dreary dreamy insulation. Solitude, melancholy — not that finer kind, but the offspring of worldly disgust, or blighted passions, or remorse — death of friends, or its own fiery over-sensitive character, formed to cause, but not to well endure, that cutting off — for ever repulsing sympathetic human approach, like a never-sleeping volcano, yet for ever needing that sympathy,—one or all these causes may shut up such a jarring mind and heart, with all their thoughts and all their pains, like two creatures of hostile natures, each with its whole mutual-hating progeny inclosed in a cage, to beat each other and themselves to death against its bars. Writing, in this hermit of my imagining, would be as necessary as the systole of the heart filled with blood to life. The mind overcharged with its contents, like that heart with the tide of life, must find vent or perish. Such a being, in the midst of his eternal civil war within, would have said, or might, not many years ago, reflecting on his own forlornness at gaze on his own desolation of mind—" True, 'tis sad, 'tis terrible! a dismal prospect! I am alone in a world that seems not *my* world, but the bald round of some planet peopled with aliens to my nature, my heart, my feelings, though bearing my form. This immense of stirring life I look upon daily is to me but as a restless sea, and this raging human multitude as its waves, from whose approach I shrink up to my desert rock —this rock of an unexplored, unregarded mind. Yet I know—I *do* know—that there is a sentient power, a mind, even sympathy in that vast body, though my own fate has made it thus unkindred to mine. What then? With *this*—this poor feather—I will command those sympathies which personally I forego! With *this* I am not voiceless in my desert, nor will die dumb. With *this* I may possibly cause my voice to be heard above all the uproar of that living war of waves— heard to that hazy shore beyond, even to dim and far posterity! With *this* I will yet talk, lone and lost man though I be—mind to mind, with the unseen, unknown, unborn!" Thus he might have soothed himself, while there remained for him an open court, a fair trial, and elbow-room, unjostled by impudent pretenders. Such I think was the sort of social soothing Rousseau found in the praise and listening of a world he did not love—keeping a sort of perpetual levee of fine minds round him, in his deepest solitude, writing out music for bread in his garret, or floating face upward at his length on the lake, between the blue of the clear depth and that of heaven in all its summer; like a sleeping spirit poised in the mid air of the cerulean concave.

Amateur Gipsy. Yet is there no joy in the pen apart from all ambition? Hunger of praise,—is that all which stimulates genius?

D. M. To me it seems that it is not the mere desire of being praised that actuates writers, as is generally imagined. Communion with the minds of their species is perhaps the strongest incentive to publication. The pain of failure is not so much mortified *vanity*, as baffled, repulsed, disappointed *sociability*. What is an author without readers? An orator without an audience. Demosthenes himself,

without auditors, and admiring ones too, were no more than a gibbering man of the woods. It is hard for the writer of ambition, even if not just ambition, after enduring that solitariness of study and preparation for the grand trial, when at last the eventful step is taken, to come forth only to endure the sadder solitude of neglect, the living burial of obscurity. But supposing his aspirings well founded, that he has stored his mind with images, exercised himself in combining and refining them, forced acquaintance by dint of lonely labour with the illustrious dead of antiquity in their disused tongues—that, above all, he feels that *viridis vis animi*, or whatever genius is, within him (although we no longer speak of Miltonic genius)—I say what dethronement—even Napoleon's, or the Swede's, or Bajazet's, I had almost said or Belshazzar's—what imprisonment or what prostration of the whole man, body and soul, can exceed the fall of the heaven-born hope of genius? Would not the fate of such a man be like that of Demosthenes, had the orator been doomed to spend all life in that cave where he immured himself—to ever listen to its melancholy drip, or declaim for ever to those deaf waves on that solitary shore where he painfully learned to declaim, there to waste all his impassioned eloquence against its senseless thunder? Yes— Genius, at this day addressing the reading world, is in that predicament.

Amateur Gipsy. But all successful authors have not had their ordeal of the cave, or the sea-shore, or even that of the midnight lamp which cost Milton his eyes. Moore and Scott are examples—when was their living burial?

D. M. Exceptions do not destroy the truth established by experience. Abundant evidence exists of the lonely and melancholy habits of poets; enough to authorise our calling such their fate. Perhaps the spirit which impels them to solitude and gloom is inseparable from the poetic temperament. If not, still that frequent converse with the famous dead, rather than living, is necessary to the formation of their character; and to this much seclusion is necessary. There was a time when this intense devotion to the hope of literary fame fulfilled its own promise; for there was a time when this our island was not peopled with authors. In the really Augustan age of English literature (the Elizabethan), this long preparation for authorship was not deemed any thing romantic. But in our age such a pains-taking personage, I suspect, would reap ridicule instead of respect for his pains.

Amateur Gipsy. But you don't mean to say that classical and polite attainments are actually deemed superfluous to our professed writers by this fastidious age?

D. M. What I would say is, that a certain frame of mind, produced by long contemplation of the best models in composition, as well as the noblest objects in nature, is essential to future grandeur of literary effort; and this preparative course demands that temporary mental farewell to the world I spoke of, the pains of which the public (as not desiring any high effort, or valuing it if made) is not disposed to compensate by one smile more than it bestows on every smart and agreeable scribbler of fashion. A writer, therefore, thus to come blinking abroad from the dusk of his study, among the gay authors of " the day," would resemble an owl among canary-birds, all singing together in a golden-wired aviary, full in the sun. As I have sketched the mind of such an anchoret, let us, before we retire, take a peep at the man, as he sits wasting life's taper as vainly as that which is dying out before him in the socket, long after midnight. The muse (as we may designate his passion for letters, whether poetical or no) has been to him a sort of fatal Egeria. Nothing more pure, gentle, or harmonious than her first whispered invitation to his sanguine youth — to turn from the turmoil of the world and its ways — turn to the solemn wood with her, the silent, shaded, still, sunshiny wood of pensive thoughtfulness! to return to the full glare of sun and world when he would — only to disport for awhile and away. But what young enthusiast has not experienced the strange and sweet spell which bound him to the soft sod and labyrinthine glades of that wood, as soon as entered — how hard to return, how irksome, how wearisome return, when by force accomplished? Once become a fame-smit student, thenceforth study and fame are the only sun and moon of the enthusiast. Thither, then, our invited goes, and stays; and regards every whisper of the siren as the oracle of a true Egeria, tenfold dearer

for the sweet secret of her call, pent in his own bosom like a sin from his nearest kindred, though prompting nothing but the noblest aims, the utmost benevolence to his brother man, and down to the very worm. Then comes a sort of moonlight dimness, and a dulled soundlessness, on that glare and tumult of the world in all its glories, to *his* mind's eye and ear, which grows and grows into a dusk, and almost a silence — still not dreadful, though solemn. And though friends wonder at the apathy with which a youth can look and listen to those worldly temptations of every sense, in which even palsied age finds music and strong attraction — he has his joy! Let them wonder! Little they know what a green, glorious, more delicious world he has in prospect, his secret own! — on what a bank of lilies and without spot he is reposing himself, in readiness for the ascent of that paradise of the mountain before him, which has become to him *the* world, shining glorified by the purple morning, in the (not long) perspective of the tangled vista of his wood — which he will disentangle, and clear, and penetrate — how soon! And then! No wonder that every moment devoted to the every-day tasks of common life seems a moment stolen from life. His new birth is finished. He walks this wearisome world still, but is the creature of another. No, as yet there is no other. Clouds and shadows still hover round that fine hill's narrow path. Fame is still but a hope, a doubt — meanwhile the change in his actual existence is become a certainty. Thus he begins to feel, in his intellectual life, a fear and failing of heart, and in that outward diurnal scene the natural sadness of a world without hope. An aimless hopeless world who can endure? Voluntarily, who would return to such? Especially, seeing that every step taken in it is one lost to the path of his only aim and hope. Perhaps he is of ardent passions. If he withhold himself from tender ties, he lives loveless, unloved, and is miserable. If he venture on them, he pines for the sweet society of his little ones, whose prattle no music less sweet than that of hope-fed learning, no jealous mistress less divine than Urania herself, should have forced him to even partially renounce. Oh, but he will come forth (so whispers vanity) a glorified being, and they too shall share that glory by reflection! Though he live friendless, it is that he may make " mankind his friend," and by consequence theirs. Behold him emerge at last—alas! to the unromantic world which laughs at enthusiasm—he is a child for its ignorance of it, and a madman for his claim upon it. Had he become a gay and worldly man, he would have better qualified himself for obtaining its applause, than by all that martyrdom of his heart and social feelings. He is indeed like a child which has wandered into a wood at earliest dawn, tempted by the peeping rubies of wood-strawberries in the ground-ivy and mosses, and insects in their emerald and golden armours, the gilding streaks of sunrise, the moving mosaic of the summer green leaves' shadows, flickering—whatever can charm a young eye, as does Parnassus seen by sunrise a young poet. He is like such a child, who wanders there lost—yet so delighted that he forgets that he is lost; till coming out, with his little childish harvest of treasure, he finds the sun he left mounting, low—the landscape he left brilliant, dull, with a cloudy afternoon. The child may find his home, and rest, and mother's smile again—the man never. He is transfigured to himself and to others. After that sweeter voice of the Muse, and her low and sweet duet with Hope, still ringing in his ears, the voice of man sounds—oh, how harsh it sounds! There is no music after theirs—no light after that delicious twilight of his Egerian grove of contemplation; the sun itself is grown a gorgeous impertinent—it looks reproach at his listless distaste of worldly tasks; the very smoothest highway of life seems rugged as a rock after his soundless foot-fall on the moss velvet of its labyrinthine walks, in all their dew and silence. His nerves shrink from the impressions even of common life's demands, like the flesh abraded of its skin, that will ache at the very air that is our life. He shivers and pines after his solitude; but that also is now transformed, with the silencing of its sweet oracle, by the stern new faith—the ascendancy of fashion over fame, of mock science over poetry. Dumb is his lifelong haunt, dumb the every day scene around him—all dumb and joyless. Thus become an outcast, and sad looker-on of the great family of man, instead of an actor, he has time and

tact to pry disconsolately severe into their characters. He is conscious of a sort of perpetual imprisonment within himself; having much, perhaps, worthy of living in other men's minds, which he knows he must carry to his grave. Hence secret wrath and disgust. And now his too keen sense of the self-tormenting madness of man wakes his sorrowful anger; and this is called misanthropy. Excess of feeling makes him impatient of many things unfelt by the gross and self-absorbed man of the world; and this is called selfishness and want of feeling, if it find vent in fury. He is full of misery; therefore fiercely intolerant of the least unjust and wanton addition to it. In short, loving children, he has lived childless—not uncourted by fortune, he has lived unfortunate—the extravagance of his eager genius has classed him with fools in the vulgar estimation—of a hopeful, aspiring, social man, he is become a hopeless, sunken-hearted, savage, solitary one. He feels that he is no longer fit for the world, nor has he any longer delight in his wood (the dumb, the hope-deserted!); and loiters and languishes out the remnant of his blasted life, a nondescript, all shunned, misunderstood outcast of both. Petty minds, whose possessors are ever children, delight to call him mad, in that spirit of half play, half malice, which prompts vulgar and ill-taught children to persecute a madman. Perhaps, after all, they speak truth without knowing it, and so are more bitterly injurious than they mean to be; for in this case, at least, " the greater the truth the greater the libel."

Amateur Gipsy. Let us hope your picture of blighted ambition in literature over-coloured. But do you design the prototype of your copy or caricature to be viewed as an author disappointed after trial or before?

D. M. Oh, assuredly before! A man who could deliberately get up a work, submit it to the modern critical court, and thus limit his ambition to that ephemeral reward which the highest genius can now expect, would neither have devoted himself to such an ambition with that kind of fury from his earliest age, nor suffer that intense pain and dark conversion of character from its failure. Assuredly before. Such a man would be (and for ever be) one of the " unknown poets." A volume of mournful interest might

perhaps be written on the fates of
the *little* " unknowns," explored and
dragged to light from the shepherds'
haunts of the mountain-side and sheep-
fold in the dingle, and even from the
city purlieus.—But see! the moon is
near its set—or else that thick haze
we see rolled immense along that dim
magnificent coast, to beyond Barmouth,
gives that appearance to it of a beam-
less globe of fire.

Amateur Gipsy. What a fine background its disc just now gives to that
promontory rock not far off—isn't it
a dark rock?

D. M. It towers, indeed, like a rock
upon a rock; but that black bulk you
see as it were hanging in air, cut off
by the moonlight fog from the level
below, is the ruinous castle of Harlech,
once overhanging that sea, now a mile
of sand-hills distant from it. You can
see through it now: the red moon
behind shews trees branching across
the clefts time has made in its round
towers. Good night. By day, perhaps,
we'll have a talk of our prose.

Amateur Gipsy. Peace be with you!
[*Exeunt into respective tents.*

THE PHILOSOPHY OF POETRY.

Few questions have more frequently been asked, than that—" wherein does *poetry* differ from *prose ?*" and few questions have been less satisfactorily answered. Those who have little taste for poetry, have seldom troubled themselves about this matter at all, while those who regard the art with enthusiasm, have seemed to shrink from too narrow an examination of the object of their adoration, as if they felt that they might thereby dissipate a charming illusion, and increase their knowledge at the expense of their enjoyment. For my own part, I confess myself one of those who are not so much dazzled with the charms of poetry, as to be unable to examine them steadily, or describe them coolly. My interest in it is such as to

incline me to speculate upon the nature of its attractions, while I am yet sufficiently *insensible* to those attractions to be able to pursue my speculations with the most philosophical composure.

The term *prose*, is used in two significations; in one of which it stands opposed to *poetry*—in the other, to *verse*. It being admitted, however, that verse is not essential to poetry, it follows that *prose*, in the sense in which it is merely opposed to *verse*, may be *poetry*—and, in the sense in which it is merely opposed to *poetry*, may be *verse*. What is to be inquired here, is, what is the nature, not of *verse*, but of *poetry*, as opposed to prose. So strong, however, is the connexion between poetry and verse, that this

subject would be but very indifferently treated should that connexion
fail to be properly accounted for;
and I shall, in the sequel, have occasion to point out how it happens that
verse must, generally speaking, always be *poetry.*

It seems to me that a clear line of
demarcation exists between poetry
and prose, and one which admits of
being plainly and accurately pointed
out.

No distinction is more familiarly
apprehended by those who have considered the different states in which
the mind exists, or acts which it performs, than that which subsists between acts or states of *intelligence,*
and acts or states of *emotion.* Acts
or states of intelligence are those in
which the mind perceives, believes,
comprehends, infers, remembers.
Acts or states of emotion are those in
which it hopes, fears, rejoices, sorrows, loves, hates, admires, or dislikes. The essential distinction between poetry and prose is this :—
prose is the language of *intelligence,*
poetry of *emotion.* In prose, we communicate our *knowledge* of the objects
of sense or thought—in poetry,
we express how these objects *affect*
us.

In order, however, to appreciate
the justice of the definition of poetry
now given, the term *feeling,* or *emotion,* must be taken in a somewhat
wider, but more logical or philosophical, sense, than its ordinary ac-
ceptation warrants. In common
discourse, if I mistake not, we apply
the word *emotion* more exclusively
to mental affections of a more violent
kind, or at least only to high degrees
of mental affection in general. Except in philosophical writings, the
perception of the *beautiful* is not designated as a state of emotion. A
man who is tranquilly admiring a
soft and pleasing landscape, is not,
in common language, said to be in a
state of emotion; neither are curiosity, cheerfulness, elation, reckoned
emotions. A man is said to be under
emotion, who is strongly agitated
with grief, anger, fear. At present,
however, we include, in the term
emotion, every species of mental (as
distinct from bodily) pleasure or
pain, desire or aversion, and all degrees of these states.

It will be asked, does every expression of emotion then constitute

poetry? I answer it does, as regards
the specific character of poetry, and
that which distinguishes it from
prose. Every expression of emotion
is poetry, in the same way, but only
in the same way, as every succession
of sounds, at musical intervals, every
single chord, is *music.* In one sense,
we call such successions or harmonies *music,* only when they are
combined into rhythmical pieces of
a certain length ; so we only call the
expression of emotion *poetry,* when
it expands itself to a certain extent,
and assumes a peculiar defined form
—of which more afterwards. But
as even two or three notes, succeeding one another, or struck together
at certain intervals, are *music,* as distinct from any other succession or
combinations of sounds—such as the
noise of machinery, of water, of fire-
arms, so is the shortest exclamation
expressive of emotion *poetry,* as distinct from the expression of any
intellectual act, such as that of belief, comprehension, knowledge. To
which it is to be added, that though
looking to the specific essence of poetry, every expression of feeling is poetry, yet that expression may always be
more or less true and successful ;
and, as we sometimes say of a dull
or insipid air, that there is *no music*
in it—so we say, that a composition,
in its essential character poetical, is
not *poetry*—as meaning, that it is not
good poetry—*i. e.* though an expression of feeling, yet not of a refined
feeling, or not a faithful, an affecting,
or a striking expression of it.

By the *language of emotion,* however, I mean the language in which
that emotion vents itself—not the
description of the emotion, or the
affirmation that it is felt. Such description or affirmation is the mere
communication of a fact—the affirmation that I feel something. This
is prose. Between such and the expression of emotion, there is much
the same difference as that which
exists between the information a
person might give us of his feeling
bodily pain, and the exclamations or
groans which his suffering might
extort from him.

But by expressions of feeling or
emotion, it is not, of course, to be
supposed that I mean mere *exclamation.* Feeling can only be expressed
so as to excite the sympathy of
others—(being the end for which it

is expressed)—with reference to a cause or object moving that feeling. Such cause or object, in order to be comprehended, may require to be stated in the form of a proposition or propositions (whether general or particular), as in a narrative, a description or a series of moral truths. The essential character, however, of a poetical narrative or description, and that which distinguishes it from a merely prosaic one, is this—that its direct object is not to convey information, but to intimate a subject of feeling, and transmit that feeling from one mind to another. In prose, the main purpose of the writer or speaker is to inform, or exhibit truth. The information may excite emotion, but this is only an accidental effect. In poetry, on the other hand, the information furnished is merely subsidiary to the conveyance of the emotion. The particulars of the information are not so properly stated or told, as appealed or referred to by the speaker for the purpose of discovering and justifying his emotion, and creating a sympathetic participation of it in the mind of the hearer.

The description of a scene or an incident may be highly picturesque, striking, or even affecting, and yet not in the slightest degree poetical, merely because it is communicated as information, not referred to as an object creating emotion; because the writer states the fact accurately and distinctly as it is, but does not exhibit himself as affected or moved by it. Take the following extract, for instance:—

"The Torch was lying at anchor in Bluefields' Bay. It was between eight and nine in the morning. The land wind had died away, and the sea breeze had not set in—there was not a breath stirring. The pennant from the masthead fell sluggishly down, and clung amongst the rigging like a dead snake; whilst the folds of the St George's ensign that hung from the mizen peak were as motionless, as if they had been carved in marble.

"The anchorage was one unbroken mirror, except where its glass-like surface was shivered into sparkling ripples by the gambols of a skip jack, or the flashing stoop of his

enemy the pelican; and the reflection of the vessel was so clear and steady, that at the distance of a cable's length you could not distinguish the water line, nor tell where the substance ended and shadow began, until the casual dashing of a bucket overboard for a few moments broke up the phantom ship; but the wavering fragments soon re-united, and she again floated double, like the swan of the poet. The heat was so intense, that the iron stancheons of the awning could not be grasped with the hand; and where the decks were not screened by it, the pitch boiled out from the seams. The swell rolled in from the offing, in long shining undulations, like a sea of quicksilver, whilst every now and then a flying fish would spark out from the unruffled bosom of the heaving water, and shoot away like a silver arrow, until it dropped with a flash into the sea again. There was not a cloud in the heavens; but a quivering blue haze hung over the land, through which the white sugar works and overseers' houses on the distant estates appeared to twinkle like objects seen through a thin smoke, whilst each of the tall stems of the cocoa-nut trees on the beach, when looked at steadfastly, seemed to be turning round with a small spiral motion, like so many endless screws. There was a dreamy indistinctness about the outlines of the hills, even in the immediate vicinity, which increased as they receded, until the blue mountains in the horizon melted into sky." *

It would seem to me impossible for words to convey a more vivid picture than is here presented; yet there is not, I think, more *poetry* in it than in the specification of a patent.

To illustrate the distinction between poetry and prose, we may remark, that words of precisely the same grammatical and verbal import, nay, the *same words*, may be either prose or poetry, according as they are pronounced without, or with *feeling;* according as they are uttered, merely to inform or to express and communicate emotion. "The sun is set," merely taken as stating a fact, and uttered with the

* From "Heat and Thirst—A Scene in Jamaica."—*Blackwood's Mag.* Vol. XXVII. p. 861.

enunciation, and in the tone in which we communicate a fact, is just as truly prose, as " it is a quarter past nine o'clock." " The sun is set," uttered as an expression of the emotions which the contemplation of that event excites in a mind of sensibility, is poetry; and, simple as are the words, would, with unexceptionable propriety, find place in a poetical composition. " My son Absalom " is an expression of precisely similar import to " my brother Dick," or " my uncle Toby," not a whit more poetical than either of these, in which there is assuredly no poetry. It would be difficult to say that " oh ! Absalom, my son, my son," is not poetry; yet the grammatical and verbal import of the words is exactly the same in both cases. The interjection " oh," and the repetition of the words " my son," add nothing whatever to the meaning; but they have the effect of making words which are otherwise but the intimation of a fact, the expression of an *emotion* of exceeding depth and interest, and thus render them eminently poetical. *

The poem of *Unimore*, published sometime ago by Professor Wilson in Blackwood's Magazine, commences with these words :

" Morven, and morn, and spring, and solitude. "

Suppose these to be the explanatory words at the beginning of a dramatic piece, and stated thus : " Scene, Morven, a solitary tract in the Highlands—season, spring— time, the morning," it would be absurd to say that the import conveyed is not precisely the same. Why is the second mode of expression prose? Simply because it informs. Why is the first poetry ? (and who, in entering on the perusal of the composition, the commencement of which it forms, would deny it to be poetry ?) because it conveys not information, but emotion; or at least

what information it contains is not offered as such, being only an indirect intimation of the objects in regard to which the emotion is felt. The words, pronounced in a certain rhythm and tone, are those of a person placed in the situation described, and in the state of feeling which that situation would excite, the feeling, namely, of *sublimity*, inspired by solitude and mountainous or romantic scenery; of *beauty*,† by the brilliant hues of the morning sky, the splendour of the rising sun, and the bright green of the new leaves yet sparkling with dew; the feeling of *tenderness*, which we experience in regard to the infancy, not less of the vegetable, than of the animal world; the feeling, lastly, of complacent delight with which we compare the now passed desolation and coldness of winter, with the warmth and animation of the present and the approaching period. These are the feelings, joined perhaps with various legendary associations connected with the scene, that would be conveyed by the words we are considering. Pronouncing these words in the tone and manner which disposes us to sympathize with the feelings with which they were uttered, and exerting our imagination to promote that sympathy, we experience a peculiar delight which no words, conveying mere information, could create; we attribute that delight to the poetical character of the composition.

So much for what may be called the soul of poetry. Let us next consider the peculiarities of its bodily form, and outward appearance. It is well known that emotions express themselves in different *tones* and *inflections* of voice from those that are used to communicate mere processes of thought, properly so called ; and also that, in the former case, the words of the speaker fall into more smooth and rythmical combinations than in the latter. Our

---

* See an instance of a singular effect produced by the passionate repetition of a name in the ballad of " Oriana, " by Alfred Tennyson.

† The philosophical reader will sufficiently understand what I mean by the *feelings* of sublimity and beauty, taken as distinct from certain *qualities* in outward objects supposed to be the cause of those feelings; to which qualities, however, and not the feelings, the terms *sublimity* and *beauty* are, in common discourse, more exclusively applied. The word *heat* either means something in the fire, or something in the sentient body affected by the fire. It is in a sense resembling the latter, that I here use sublimity and beauty.

feelings are conveyed in a melodious succession of tones, and in a measured flow of words; our thoughts (and in a greater degree the less they are accompanied with feeling) are conveyed in irregular periods, and at harsh intervals of tone. Blank verse and rhyme are *but more artificial dispositions of the natural expressions of feeling.* They are adapted to the expression of feeling, *i. e.,* suitable for poetry—but not necessary to it. They do not constitute poetry when they do not express feeling. The propositions of Euclid, the laws of Justinian, the narratives of Hume, might be thrown into as elaborate verse as ever Pope or Darwin composed; but they would never, even in that shape, be taken for poetry, unless so far as a certain structure of words is a natural indication of *feeling.* Indeed, when there is a possibility, from the nature of the subject, that feeling may be excited, the use of a measured structure of words, and a harmonious inflection of tones, implies that the speaker is in a *state of feeling;* and hence what he utters we should denominate poetry.

And in this behold the true reason why verse and poetry pass in common discourse for synonymous terms—verse, especially when recited in the modulations of voice requisite to give it its proper effect, possessing *necessarily* the peculiar qualities which distinguish an *expression of feeling.* Hence it may perhaps be truly said, that though all poetry is not verse, all serious verse is poetry —poetry in its kind, at least, if not of the degree of excellence to which we may choose to limit the designation. I say, all *serious* verse—because a great part of the amusement we find in humorous and burlesque poetry, arises from the incongruity observed between the language — that of feeling — and the subject, which may not only have no tendency to excite such feeling, but to excite a feeling of an opposite kind. But that—although verse, generally speaking, is poetry—poetry may ex-

ist without verse (although never without rhythmical language), is evident from a reference, for example, to the compositions ascribed to Ossian, which none would deny to be poetry.

These considerations explain how that which, in its original language, is poetry, becomes, in a translation, however exactly and properly conveying the meaning, the merest prose. The following translation of Horace, by Smart, conveys the exact meaning of the original. Why, then, is it not poetry? (For who would ever take it for poetry?) Simply, because it is not formed into the rhythmical periods, and thence does not suggest the melodious inflections in which we convey emotion. And it is yet in our power, by speaking it in a feeling manner, to give it the character of poetry:—

" The royal edifices will, in a short time, leave but a few acres for the plough. Ponds of wider extent than the Lucrine lake, will be every where to be seen; and the barren planetree will supplant the elms. Then banks of violets, and myrtle groves, and all the tribe of nosegays, shall diffuse their odours in the olive plantations, which were fruitful to their preceding master. Then the dense boughs of the laurel shall exclude the burning beams. It was not so prescribed by the institutes of Romulus, and the unshaven Cato, and ancient custom. Their private revenue was contracted, while that of the community was great. No private men were then possessed of ten-foot galleries, which collected the shady northern breezes ; nor did the laws permit them to reject the casual turf for their own huts, though at the same time they obliged them to ornament, in the most sumptuous manner, with new stone, the buildings of the public, and the temples of the gods, at a common expense.*"

But although verse, however highly adapted to poetry, is not essential to it, it is found very materially to heighten the intrinsic charms of poetical composition.

---

* I have said that no one would take this for poetry, which is true generally ; yet there is as much even here as would indicate it to be a translation from poetry. Thus the second and third sentences—the epithet, " unshaven "—the expression, " reject the casual turf." These parts are distinguished from the rest (which might be taken to convey mere information), as intimating that the speaker is affected or moved by the subject of his statement.

There is a pleasure derived from the reading of harmonious * verse, whether blank or rhymed, altogether distinct from any that is conveyed by the mere sense or meaning of a composition, and which indeed is capable of being excited by the verse of an unknown language. Of the cause of this pleasure we can (so far as I am aware) give no other account than that such is our constitution; although there is no doubt that our perception of contrivance and ingenuity—of difficulty overcome (and apparently no slight difficulty) —enters largely into the delight which we feel; a delight too which admits of receiving great increase from the infinite varieties of form and combination which verses and rhymes are capable of assuming. The same observation holds with regard to music; the pleasure derived from the different varieties of musical rhythm being distinct from— though eminently auxiliary to—that excited by the melody and harmony. Music, however, is far more dependent for its full effect upon rhythmical division, than poetry is upon verse. In the former, as well as in the latter, the observation of contrivance adds very materially to the gratification. Hence the use of musical fugues, canons, &c. And I would observe, by the way, that a censure frequently passed in regard to musical compositions of a more elaborate cast, by persons whose ear is not sufficiently exercised to discern the merits of such—namely, that a taste for such composition is an unnatural and false taste—is by no means a reasonable one; or at least it is no more reasonable than a similar censure would be on our permitting ourselves to be gratified by the varieties of verse and rhyme

in poetry. I am not sure, indeed, but there have been persons of so etherealized a taste, as even to profess a squeamishness in regard to the use of rhyme.

Nor is verse merely adapted, in a general way, to the expression of emotion. The infinite variety of particular measures and rhymes—some swift and lively, some slow and melancholy—are available by the poet for the purpose of heightening every expression of sentiment. Hence, while he ministers to the physical delight of the ear, and gratifies us by the perception of the art displayed in his easy and correct versification, he humours the character or the caprices of his subject, by causing his verses sometimes to glide on in a smooth unmurmuring stream—sometimes to dash away with a noisy and startling vehemence.

But farther—the language of *emotion* is generally *figurative* or *imaginative* language. It is of the nature of emotion to express itself in the most forcible manner—in the manner most adapted to justify itself, and light up a kindred flame in the breast of the auditor. Hence the poet flies from the use of literal phraseology as unfit for his purpose; and the eye of his fancy darts hither and thither, until it lights on the figures or images that will most vividly and rapidly convey the sentiment that fills his soul. The mind, anxious to convey not the truth or fact with regard to the object of its contemplation, but its own feelings as excited by the object, pours forth the stream of its associations as they rise from their source. Our perceptions of external events and objects are distinct, fixed, and particular. The feelings which such objects excite are dim, fluctuating, ge-

---

* It may not be superfluous to observe, that such words as *melodious, harmonious*, or *musical*, applied to verse, are purely figurative, possessing nothing whatever of the kind to which these terms are applied in music. The only thing that verse and music possess in common, is rhythmical measure. The musical qualities applied to verse have regard to mere articulations of sound, not to intervals or combinations of it. In the audible reading of verse, however, and even of poetical prose, there is room for the introduction of musical intervals; and, so far as my own observation goes, the inflections of a good speaker are not, as is usually stated, performed by chromatic or imperceptible slides, but by real diatonic intervals, and these generally of the larger kinds, such as fifths, sixths, and octaves— bearing a considerable resemblance, in fact, to the movements of a fundamental bass—the difference, if I mistake not, being mostly in the nature of the rhythm and the cadences. So intimate is the connexion between a musical sound and its concords (3d, 5th, and 8th), so natural and easy the transition, that any but a practised ear is apt to take for an imperceptible slide what is in reality a *large* interval.

neral. Our language is correspondent in each case. Hence many expressions highly poetical, that is, eminently fitted for conveying a *feeling* from one mind to another, would be, if taken in reference to the object, and considered in their grammatical meaning, absolutely nonsensical. Washington Irving speaks of the " dusty splendour " of Westminster Abbey—an expression deservedly admired for the vividness of the impression it conveys. Taken as conveying a specific matter of information, it is absolute nonsense. *Splendour* is not a subject of which *dusty* could be an attribute; a space or a body might be dusty; but the splendour of an object might, in strict propriety of language, as well be spoken of as long, or loud, or square. So in the line,

" The starry Galileo and his woes,"

the literal inapplicability of the epithet " starry " to an astronomer is obvious. The expression is one, not of a truth that is *perceived*, but of an association that is *felt*. No epithet, signifying the mere addiction of Galileo to astronomical pursuits, could have struck us like that which thus suggests the visible glories that belong to the field of his speculations. From the consideration now illustrated, it results also, that the imagery, having often no essential connexion with the object, but merely an accidental connexion in the mind of the poet, strikes one class of readers in the most forcible manner, and fails of all effect with others. The expression of Milton—" smoothing the raven plume of darkness till it smiled," is greatly admired, or at least often quoted. I must confess, that, to my mind, it is like a parcel of words set down at random. I may observe, indeed, that many persons of an imaginative frame of mind, and who, in consequence, take a great delight in the mere exercise of imagination (and who at the same time possess a delicate ear for verse), find any poetry exquisite, however destitute of meaning, which merely suggests ideas or images that may serve as the germs of fancy in their own minds. There are many passages in Byron — Wordsworth — Young—and these enthusiastically admired, which, I must confess, are to me utterly unintelligible; or at

least, the understanding of which (where that is possible) I find to require as great an exercise of thought as would be required by so much of Butler's Analogy, or Euclid's Demonstrations.

Lastly—as regards the peculiar character of the *language* of poetry —it is important to observe, that a principal cause of the boldness and variety that may be remarked to belong to poetical expression, is one which would, at first sight, seem to produce an effect directly the reverse ; this is—*the fetters imposed by the verse.* The expression which would be the most obvious, and even the most exact (if exactitude were what was most required), is often not the one that will suit the verse. The consequence is, that a new one must be coined for the purpose ; and I believe every poet would admit that some of his happiest epithets and most adorned expressions have been lighted upon in the course of a search for terms of a certain *metrical dimension.* The necessity of obeying the laws of the verse, leads also to a peculiar latitude in the application of terms ; and as the impression of this necessity is also present to the mind of the reader, he readily grants the poetical license to the composer, and admits of verbal combinations, which, in prose, would seem far-fetched and affected. Thus the verse, then, instead of contracting, extends the choice of expression. The aptitude of a term or an epithet to fill the verse, becomes part of its aptitude in general ; and what is first tolerated from its necessity, is next applauded for its novelty.

Behold now the whole character of poetry. It is *essentially* the *expression of emotion ;* but the expression of emotion *takes place* by measured language (it may be verse, or it may not)—harmonious tones— and figurative phraseology. And it will, I think, invariably be found, that wherever a passage, line, or phrase of a poetical composition, is censured as being of a *prosaic* character, it is from its conveying some matter of mere *information*, not subsidiary to the prevailing emotion, and breaking the continuity of that emotion.

It might perhaps be thought a more accurate statement, if, instead of defining poetry to be in its essence the *language of emotion*, and representing the imaginative character of poetry as merely resulting from its essential nature as thus defined, I had included its imaginative character in the definition, and made that character part of the essence of poetry. It will seem that the "*language of imagination*" would be to the full as just a definition of poetry as the "*language of emotion;*" or, at least, that these are respectively the definitions of two different species of poetry, each alike entitled to the denomination. I shall assign the reasons why I consider the statement I have adopted to be a more true and philosophical one than that now supposed.

In the first place, the conveyance, by language, of an imaginative mental process, needs not be in the slightest degree poetical. A novel is entirely a work of imagination—it is not therefore a poem. The description of an imagined scene or event, needs not indeed differ in the least from that of a real one; it may therefore be purely prosaical. It is not the imaginative process by itself, and merely as such, but the feelings that attend it, the expression of which constitutes poetry. So much as regards the subject of a composition. As regards style, in like manner, there may be a great deal of imagery or figurative phraseology in a composition, without entitling it to be reckoned poetical; or, so far as entitled to be called poetical, it will be found to be expressive of emotion. On the other hand, the expression of emotion, even in relation to an actual scene or event (if it is merely the language of emotion and not that of persuasion—which, as elsewhere remarked, is the definition of eloquence) is, in every case, poetical, and notwithstanding that the style may be perfectly free from imagery or figure; nor again, without implying emotion on the part of the writer or speaker, will any language, or any subject, be poetical. It is then essential to poetry to be of an emotive—not essential to it to be of an imaginative character. But this imaginative character, though not of the essence of poetry, results from that essence. It is in a moved or excited state of mind, and only, I might say, in a moved or excited

state, that we resort to the use of figure or imagery. The exercise of imagination is pleasurable chiefly as an indulgence of emotion. Do we usually exercise imagination on uninteresting subjects?—or what does *interesting* or *uninteresting* mean, but exciting or not exciting emotion? What else is it but our craving desire to admire—to be awed—to sympathize—to love—to regret—to hope; in one word, to feel or to be moved, that leads us to picture to the mind, scenes, or forms, or characters of beauty or grandeur; or states of enjoyment or distress; or situations of agony or rapture; or incidents of horror or delight; or deeds of heroism, or tenderness, or mercy, or cruelty? Why do we recall the joys or the sorrows that are past? why do we dwell on hopes that have been blighted—affections that have been crushed—delusions that have been dispelled? Why do we summon up the scenes and the companions of our childhood and youth? It is because such images or pictures *move* us—and poetry is the expression of our emotions.

So intimate is the connexion between *emotion* and *fancy*, that it is often not very easy to say whether the feeling is the parent of the image by which it expresses itself, or whether, on the contrary, the image is the parent of the feeling. The truth seems to be, that they produce and reproduce one another. Feeling generates fancy; and fancy, in its turn, upholds and nourishes feeling. If, as Mr Alison has maintained, and as most people seem disposed to grant, the pleasures of taste are resolvable in a great measure into a certain delight which we experience in pursuing a train of images and associations—the intimate connexion between emotion and fancy, and the consequent tendency to express emotion (or at least the emotions of taste) by figures and imagery, will be at once apparent. It is however sufficient for my present purpose to exhibit the fact of the connexion.

We may, in one or two familiar instances, exemplify the nature of the poetical character, and the intimacy of the union that subsists between fancy and emotion.

"The curfew tolls the knell of parting day."

The vital character of this line, as constituting it poetry, is, that it is not the mere *fact* or *truth*—(namely, that the tolling of the bell is a sign of the ending of the day)—that the words of the poet aim at communicating, but his *emotion* in regard to the fact; and, filled as his mind is with this emotion, his fancy first flies away to the origin of the evening bell, and, as we may imagine, rapidly wanders amid the associations of antiquity and romance, which link themselves to the name of the *curfew.* The sound of the bell, intimating the close of day, he invests, for the moment, with the import of the death knell summoning a soul from life; and the epithet " parting," bespeaks the similitude of his present frame of mind to that excited by the interruption of a cherished intercourse with an animated being—with a companion, a friend, a lover.

" How sweet the moonlight sleeps upon this bank."

The obvious purpose of these words is to express a feeling, not to furnish a matter of information; and the feeling cannot be adequately expressed by literal, or without figurative phraseology. " To represent the tranquillity of moonlight is the object of this line; and the *sleep* is beautiful, because it gives *a more intense and living form of the same idea ;* the rhythm falls beautifully in with this, and just lets the cadence of the emphasis dwell upon the sound and sense of the sweet word ' sleep,' and the alliteration assimilates the rest of the line into one harmonious symmetry."*

And here I may distinguish two different exercises of the imagination in poetry. The first of these is where a figure of speech—a trope or metaphor—is used for the mere purpose of giving strength or illustration to some expression of feeling.† The other—and what is more properly called imagery in poetry— is where the recollection or imagi-

nation of a sensible impression is that itself which moves the feeling. In many cases—as in the instance just quoted—the two operations are blended. And as sensible objects are so often the exciting causes of feeling, the happy conveyance of the impressions they create is one of the chief arts of the poet. Hence the *picturesque* character of poetical language—its aptitude to present a picture or image of an actual object calculated to affect us.

We may now see that a poetical genius—a poetical taste—may be said to consist essentially of *sensibility* (or aptitude to feel emotion), and, by consequence, of *imagination* (or aptitude to place ourselves in situations exciting emotion). The poet—the reader of poetry—seeks not to know truth as distinct from falsehood or error—to reason or draw inferences—to generalize—to classify—to distinguish; he seeks for what may move his awe—admiration — pity — tenderness ; scenes of sublimity and beauty ; incidents exciting fear, suspense, grief—joy — surprise — cheerfulness — regret. Whether these scenes or these incidents are real or fictitious, he cares not. It is enough to him that he can imagine them. Behold the compressed lips—the knitted brows—the fixed and sharpened eye of the philosophical enquirer—whose aim it is to *know*—to discover and communicate truth. The character of his countenance is that of keen penetration, as if he would dart his glances into the innermost recesses of science. Compare with this the open forehead—the rolling eye—the flexible mouth—the changing features of the poet, whose aim it is to feel, and convey his feeling. His countenance has been moulded to the expression of feeling, and is a constant record of that succession of emotions which passes through his breast.

Let us not suppose, however, that the pleasure derived from poetical composition is simply a pleasure

---

* New Monthly Mag. vol. xxix. p. 331—Art. " Byron and Shelley in the character of Hamlet." I had adopted, as an illustration of my remarks, the line here referred to, when I just chanced to find what I wanted to express in regard to it, exactly provided for me.

† And it is because a figure may also be used to strengthen or illustrate a mere truth or the expression of an intellectual process, that *figurative* language is not necessarily *poetical.*

arising from being in a state of emotion. Many emotions are themselves far from pleasant; but we take pleasure in the skilful expression of these emotions, for the same reason that we are often delighted with the picture of an object which would itself attract no notice, or be positively offensive or painful.

A survey of the different species of poetical composition will serve to illustrate and strengthen the preceding statements.

In an epic or narrative poem, some event, or connected chain of events, is narrated with the various feelings which arise from the view of such event or events, and in a manner calculated to excite a sympathetic participation of these feelings in the mind of the hearer or reader. The historian of such transactions merely speaks for our information. He arranges his subjects so as to give us the clearest understanding of the dates, course, and connexion of the incidents. The poet seeks not to inform us, or, at least, this is not his ultimate or principal object, but merely subsidiary to the expression of his own emotions, and the excitement of similar emotions in the breasts of others. Hence, instead of a methodical introduction such as a historian would adopt, he plunges at once *in medias res*—places before us some scene, strongly calculated, both from its own character and the apparent feelings with which he describes it, to excite our interest. Our curiosity once raised, he continues at once to gratify and keep alive, by the presentation of a succession of circumstances, or rather the indirect intimation of a succession of circumstances, filling, as his language testifies, his own mind with grief, joy, indignation, pity, tenderness, fear, hope, awe, admiration, and all the other passions of the soul, and awakening the like passions in ours. From the nature and ends of epic poetry arises the necessity of preserving what is called the *unity* of the poem; which means the presenting of one object to the mind of the reader of sufficient interest to absorb his continued attention, and in reference to which the subordinate incidents may acquire a degree of importance not perhaps intrinsically belonging to such incidents themselves.

Similar remarks will apply to the tragic drama—with only this difference, that here the actors of the scene are made to express directly the emotions which their several situations excite.

Descriptive poetry conveys an expression of the feelings excited by *the view of the scenes and operations of nature and the works of art*, whether grand, or simply beautiful. The rugged precipice, the vast mountain, the fierce torrent, the sombre forest, the hurricane, the thunder, the earthquake, the storm ; or, on the other hand, the variegated plain, the glittering stream, the gracefully undulating surface, the luxuriant foliage, the hedge-row, the shrub, the flower, the rising and setting sun, the refreshing shower, the lively breeze, the glowing stars; or, again, the proud feudal fortress, the melancholy abbey, the splendid villa, the awful cathedral, with the associations connected with each ; or, lastly, the appearance of animated nature, the peaceful labours of the husbandmen, the groups of flocks and herds, the bright plumage, the exhilarating song of the feathered tribes, or the mazy dance and mingled hum of the fluttering insects : —all these objects excite, in the mind of sensibility, the emotions of sublimity, or beauty, or tenderness, or melancholy, or cheerfulness; and the aim of descriptive poetry is the expression and communication of these feelings.

Didactic or sentimental poetry expresses the emotions produced by the *contemplation of general truths regarding subjects of human interest*, the shortness of life, the vanity of youthful expectations, the ravages of the passions, the miseries of human existence, the passage of time, the terrors of death, the hopes and fears of immortality.

Satirical and humorous poetry is the expression of emotions which arise at *the view of human vice, folly, and weakness;* the expression, namely, of indignation, scorn, contempt, derision.

Of all the emotions which arise in the human breast, none are either so universally and intensely felt, or so readily sympathized with, as the *affections which take place between the sexes ;* nor perhaps are there any which are capable of being so much varied and modified by the situations in which they are excited, and the individual character of the parties. Hence the innumerable aspects of the passion—its hopes and fears — its headlong ardour, and moving tenderness—its ebbs, and flows, and changes, and caprices— the torments of jealousy—the bitterness of absence, the exultation of success—" the pang of despised love"—constitute a class of subjects which has ever, above all others, been consecrated to poetry. To be a lover, indeed, is a part of the poet's profession ; not to have loved is never to have been truly inspired with the poetical flame.

The difference between *eloquence* and *poetry* seems to me to consist in this, that, while the sole object of poetry is to transmit the *feelings* of the speaker or writer, that of eloquence is to convey the *persuasion* of some *truth*—whether with a view to excite to action or not. And in proportion as the writer, in enforcing any particular truth, exhibits himself as affected by such truth, i. e. as feeling emotion at the contemplation of it ; or, which is the index of emotion, expresses himself in a figurative or imaginative style—in such proportion the composition, though in a prose form, becomes in reality, and is felt to be, poetical. Hence poetry may be eloquent, and eloquence poetical—which is only saying, in other words, that the expression of emotion may contain an impressive statement of some truth which excites the emotion ; or, *vice versa*, that the enforcement of a truth may be attended with a striking display of emotion excited by the contemplation of that truth. The line that separates poetry and eloquence, then, is sometimes altogether imperceptible. Indeed, for reasons which we have seen, the same proposition

which *not* in verse, will be *prose*—*in* verse will be *poetry*.

The reasons already assigned to show why verse must generally possess the poetical character, have occasioned the term poetry to be almost exclusively confined to verse : so that though a composition, not in verse, may be essentially poetical, as being the expression of emotion, we do not call it poetical unless eminently so— that is, distinguished by a peculiarly imaginative and refined cast of thought.*

And now, having attempted to assign the *essential distinction* that subsists between poetical and prosaic composition, I cannot help expressing my opinion that compositions in *verse* are, *as such*, and as distinct from the degree of merit they may individually possess, usually rated at a value far disproportionate to their real importance.

The expression of an *emotive* does not seem to possess any intrinsic superiority over that of an *intellectual* mental process. The interest attending it is different, but not necessarily greater. In one important respect it is inferior. Feelings associate among themselves, and are capable of being presented in connexion ; but they will generally connect in one order as well, or nearly so, as in another. Hence the want in poetry (that is, in what is *nothing but poetry*) † of progressive interest—of that sort of interest which belongs to chains of fact or reasoning—interest kept alive by the expectation of, and gratified by the arrival at, a result. The mathematician's famous query in regard to the Æneid, " What does all this prove ?" is more faulty in regard to its applicability to the particular case, and to the narrowness of the idea it expresses, than as being destitute of a general foundation in

---

* A prayer to the Deity is essentially poetical, as being the expression of awe, admiration, gratitude, contrition, entreaty. Hence good taste, as well as just religious feeling, is shocked by the introduction, in a prayer, of any mere *proposition* (such as the affirmation of a doctrine) not in its nature exciting emotion. But *verse*, however generally suitable to the expression of emotion, would be inconsistent with the simplicity that ought to belong to prayer.

† I say *what is nothing but poetry*, because the interest derived from story, incident, and character, can be equally well conveyed in prose composition, nay, infinitely better, from a variety of causes, and chiefly from the inadmissibility, in poetry, of the mention of any fact not calculated to be spoken of *with emotion*. Hence, at once, the comparative meagreness and obscurity of poetical narratives.

truth. Take up any sentimental poem, that is, a composition which is poetry alone, poetry left to its own resources, " the Seasons," " the Pleasures of Hope"—your enjoyment in reading will be much the same whether you dip into a page here and there, or go directly on from the commencement. Here then is one essential inferiority attaching to the poetical as compared with the prosaic character—to the expression of *emotive*, as compared with that of *intellectual* processes. But, waving this comparison, *verse* is not indispensable to the expression of feeling. What is prose in form, is often poetry in substance. Our question regards the value generally attached to verse, as verse. Is verse then never employed but in the conveyance of sentiments of a *more valuable* kind than are ever to be found in the prose form ? In answer, I take upon me to affirm, that in any ordinary book of serious or tasteful reflection, there are sentiments to be found, which, extracted from the connexion in which they are presented, no one would think of looking at twice, which are to the full as important, as striking, as touching, as vividly and elegantly expressed, as any thing which one may please to signify the value of a sentiment by, as are the subjects of many a "sonnet," or set of "stanzas," or " verses" which will yet be copied, translated, criticised, and the date and occasion of its composition settled with as much precision as if it were the commencement of an era. Is it the mere versification then that confers the value? Now without doubt there is a peculiar pleasure in verse as such, a pleasure which is the effect of positive constitution, and about which, therefore, there can be no dispute. But the pleasure arising from versification merely, will only, I think, be ranked among the more insignificant of our gratifications. It is not an enjoyment of a vivid, considerable kind. It is at most agreeable. But so is elegant penmanship—so may be the pattern of a carpet, a room paper, or a chimney ornament. There is that trifling sort of gratification which one will rather meet than the contrary, but not what we should go far out of our way to find. Then, again, the perception of ingenuity and contri-

vance, is no doubt pleasing; but a pleasure of that kind which inevitably loses its value as we become familiarized to it. We give our tribute to the talent and ingenuity of the workman, but we derive little pleasure from the work. It is trite to observe that many things which cost a vast deal of skill and labour to do, are felt of very little value when done. But farther, I must allow, in addition to the sort of pleasure which we take in verse, as such, the additional intensity which it is capable of giving to the expression of the sentiment. But here the difference between verse and prose is but in degree, and the degree sometimes but very slight. *A sentiment, which expressed in prose would be of little value, cannot be of much when expressed in verse.* Is there not, then, I again ask, a degree of interest and importance generally attached to " verses," " lines," " stanzas," utterly disproportionate to what is in justice due ?

One will be apt to say here, all this is disputing about a matter of *taste*, which is universally allowed to be idle. To a person destitute of a taste for poetry, it is as impossible to prove its value, as to prove the value of music to one who has no musical ear. Now all this would be very well if verse were something essentially different from any thing else, and, in its distinctive nature, the object of a *specific taste*, distinguishable from other tastes. This cannot be pretended to be the case. The difference between a thought expressed in prose, and the same thought expressed in verse, is obviously too trifling to make the former the object of a distinct constitutional faculty. The musician can, *with mathematical precision*, state the intervals, and the chords, and the successions of sounds, which, and which alone, delight his ear. Musical successions or harmonies can never be mixed or confounded with other species of sounds, nor with any thing else whatever, as poetry may be mixed or confounded with prose. Again, there is no one who fails of receiving a strong delight from music who has the mere organic perception of musical intervals (who has an ear). To every man who can merely take up or remember an air —who can hum, whistle, or sing it, *in tune,* music is not merely pleasing, but a substantial, material enjoyment. The love of music, then, is universal among those who have merely a certain physical capacity, and whoever does not relish it, can be shown to want a physical capacity. Not so with poetry. A man who is extremely callous to its charms shall detect a flaw in versification as accurately as the keenest poetical enthusiast—shall do verse as much justice in the reading (in proportion to what he could do to prose composition)—shall even (I do not say he could do so without difficulty) compose faultless verses. He shall be—with the reservation we are supposing, if a reservation it must be—a man of sense, feeling, taste; nay, generally addicted to literary pursuits. Here, then, is one having all the physical and mental requisites for enjoying poetry, and who, though without in any considerable degree enjoying, may even be able to distinguish its beauties. If such a person fails in deriving any lively enjoyment from poetry—and numerous cases of this kind I believe exist—must not the fair inference be, not that he wants a peculiar faculty, but that, to the object of this supposed faculty there is attached a somewhat fictitious and imaginary value?

The comparison now made between poetry and music may not, it is true, seem a fair one, inasmuch as a love of music is so indisputably dependent on a certain physical organization. There are many cases, it will be urged, in which *taste* is allowed to be the *sole arbiter,* without appeal to any other tribunal, where yet there is no particular independent faculty such as an ear for music, and where yet the degree of taste for particular species of beauty differs remarkably in different individuals—as taste for painting, sculpture, architecture, natural scenery. Now I say, in the first place, that each of these objects of taste differ from every other thing in a way that *poetry* does not differ from *prose,* and may claim to be amenable to taste in a way that poetry, *simply as distinguished from prose,* cannot; and,

next, that I believe there is no person of cultivated mind who is so indifferent to the objects of taste now enumerated, as many persons of cultivated mind are to poetry.

What then do I aim at showing? That all poetry is worthless? that the pleasure derived from poetry is altogether factitious and imaginary? no more than I should aim at showing that prose is worthless; that the pleasure derived from prose is factitious and imaginary. But I contend that poetry, *as poetry,* has no more claim to have value attached to it than prose has *as prose.* I object not to the estimation that is made of numerous individuals of the species, but to that mode of the species itself. I complain, not that many compositions that are poetical are placed in the highest rank of literary merit; not even that their being poetical is conceived greatly to heighten their value, and to display a peculiar and additional talent in the authors of them; but that many others have this value assigned to them, *simply because they are poetical, and for nothing else.* But, after all, what is there here, it will be asked, that any body disputes? Who desires, on the one hand, that worthless poetry should be preserved or valued? Who would deny, on the other, that worthless poetry is, in fact, despised and allowed to perish?

Now I acknowledge the difficulty, without specific proofs, which my present limits would not admit, of satisfying any one who should object to the justice of the opinions now offered. These opinions undoubtedly relate to a question of degree. I do not affirm that all poetry is rated above its value. I do not deny that some poetry is rejected. But I affirm, that much of what is allowed a place as poetry *of value,* poetry worth preserving and reading, is intrinsically worthless, worthless at least as regards any *pleasure to be derived from the perusal of it.* The truth of this position, with merely the general reasons on which it is founded, I must leave to be determined by the experience and reflection of individual readers.

S.

AN ANSWER TO THE QUESTION

WHAT IS POETRY?

INCLUDING

REMARKS ON VERSIFICATION.

POETRY, strictly and artistically so called, that is to say, considered not merely as poetic feeling, which is more or less shared by all the world, but as the operation of that feeling, such as we see it in the poet's book, is the utterance of a passion for truth, beauty, and power, embodying and illustrating its conceptions by imagination and fancy, and modulating its language on the principle of variety in uniformity. Its means are whatever the universe contains ; and its ends, pleasure and exaltation. Poetry stands between nature and convention, keeping alive among us the enjoyment of the external and the spiritual world : it has constituted the most enduring fame of nations ; and, next to Love and Beauty, which are its parents, is the greatest proof to man of the pleasure to be found in all things, and of the probable riches of infinitude.

B

Poetry is a passion,* because it seeks the deepest impressions ; and because it must undergo, in order to convey, them.

It is a passion for truth, because without truth the impression would be false or defective.

It is a passion for beauty, because its office is to exalt and refine by means of pleasure, and because beauty is nothing but the loveliest form of pleasure.

It is a passion for power, because power is impression triumphant, whether over the poet, as desired by himself, or over the reader, as affected by the poet.

It embodies and illustrates its impressions by imagination, or images of the objects of which it treats, and other images brought in to throw light on those objects, in order that it may enjoy and impart the feeling of their truth in its utmost conviction and affluence.

It illustrates them by fancy, which is a lighter play of imagination, or the feeling of analogy coming short of seriousness, in order that it may laugh with what it loves, and show how it can decorate it with fairy ornament.

It modulates what it utters, because in running the whole round of beauty it must needs include beauty of sound ; and because, in the height of its enjoyment, it must show the perfection of its

* *Passio*, suffering in a good sense,—ardent subjection of one's-self to emotion.

triumph, and make difficulty itself become part of its facility and joy.

And lastly, Poetry shapes this modulation into uniformity for its outline, and variety for its parts, because it thus realizes the last idea of beauty itself, which includes the charm of diversity within the flowing round of habit and ease.

Poetry is imaginative passion. The quickest and subtlest test of the possession of its essence is in expression; the variety of things to be expressed shows the amount of its resources; and the continuity of the song completes the evidence of its strength and greatness. He who has thought, feeling, expression, imagination, action, character, and continuity, all in the largest amount and highest degree, is the greatest poet.

Poetry includes whatsoever of painting can be made visible to the mind's eye, and whatsoever of music can be conveyed by sound and proportion without singing or instrumentation. But it far surpasses those divine arts in suggestiveness, range, and intellectual wealth ;—the first, in expression of thought, combination of images, and the triumph over space and time ; the second, in all that can be done by speech, apart from the tones and modulations of pure sound. Painting and music, however include all those portions of the gift of poetry that can be expressed and heightened by the visible and melodious. Painting, in a certain apparent manner, is things themselves ; music, in a certain audible manner, is their very emotion and grace. Music and painting are proud to be related to poetry, and poetry loves and is proud of them.

Poetry begins where matter of fact or of science ceases to be merely such, and to exhibit a further truth ; that is to say, the connexion it has with the world of emotion, and its power to produce imaginative pleasure. Inquiring of a gardener, for instance, what flower it is we see yonder, he answers, "a lily." This is matter of fact. The botanist pronounces it to be of the order of "Hexandria Monogynia." This is matter of science. It is the "lady" of the garden, says Spenser; and here we begin to have a poetical sense of its fairness and grace. It is

The plant and flower of *light*,

says Ben Jonson ; and poetry then shows us the beauty of the flower in all its mystery and splendour.

If it be asked, how we know perceptions like these to be true, the answer is, by the fact of their existence,—by the consent and delight of poetic readers. And as feeling is the earliest teacher, and perception the only final proof, of things the most demonstrable by science, so the remotest imaginations of the poets may often be found to have the closest connexion with matter of fact ; perhaps might always be so, if the subtlety of our perceptions were a match for the causes of them. Consider this image of Ben Jonson's — of a lily being the flower of light. Light, undecomposed is white; and as the lily is white, and light is white and whiteness itself is nothing *but* light, the two things, so far, are not merely similar, but identical. A poet might add, by an analogy drawn from the connexion of light and colour, that there is a "golden dawn" issuing out of the white lily in the yellow of the stamens. I have no desire to push this similarity farther than it may be worth. Enough has been stated to show that, in poetical as in other analogies, " the same feet of Nature," as Bacon says, may be seen " treading in different paths; " and that the most scornful, that is to say, dullest disciple of fact, should be cautious how he betrays the shallowness of his philosophy by discerning no poetry in its depths.

But the poet is far from dealing only with these subtle and analogical truths. Truth of every kind belongs to him, provided it can bud into any kind of beauty, or is capable of being illustrated and impressed by the poetic faculty. Nay, the simplest truth is often so beautiful and impressive of itself, that one of the greatest proofs of his genius consists in his leaving it to stand alone, illustrated by nothing but the light of its own tears or smiles, its own wonder, might, or playfulness. Hence the

complete effect of many a simple passage in our
old English ballads and romances, and of the passionate sincerity in general of the greatest early poets,
such as Homer and Chaucer, who flourished before
the existence of a " literary world," and were not
perplexed by a heap of notions and opinions, or by
doubts how emotion ought to be expressed.   The
greatest of their successors never write equally to
the purpose, except when they can dismiss every
thing from their minds but the like simple truth.
In the beautiful poem of " Sir Eger, Sir Graham
and Sir Gray-Steel" (see it in Ellis's Specimens, or
Laing's Early Metrical Tales), a knight thinks him
self disgraced in the eyes of his mistress :—

> Sir Eger said, " If it be so,
> Then wot I well I must forego
> Love-liking, and manhood, all clean !"
> *The water rush'd out of his een !*

Sir Gray-Steel is killed :—

> Gray-Steel into his death thus thraws (throes ?)
> He *walters* (welters,—throws himself about) *and the*
>   *grass up draws ;*
> *   *   *   *   *
> *A little while then lay he still*
> (*Friends that him saw, liked full ill*)
> *And bled into his armour bright.*

The abode of Chaucer's *Reve*, or Steward, in the
Canterbury Tales, is painted in two lines, which
nobody ever wished longer :—

His wonning (dwelling) was full fair upon an heath,
With greeny trees yshadowed was his place.

Every one knows the words of Lear, "most
matter-of-fact, most melancholy."

Pray do not mock me ;
I am a very foolish fond old man
Fourscore and upwards :
Not an hour more, nor less ; and to deal plainly
I fear I am not in my perfect mind.

It is thus, by exquisite pertinence, melody, and
the implied power of writing with exuberance, if
need be, that beauty and truth become identical in
poetry, and that pleasure, or at the very worst, a
balm in our tears, is drawn out of pain.

It is a great and rare thing, and shows a lovely
imagination, when the poet can write a commentary, as it were, of his own, on such sufficing passages of nature, and be thanked for the addition.
There is an instance of this kind in Warner, an old
Elizabethan poet, than which I know nothing
sweeter in the world. He is speaking of Fair Rosa-
mond, and of a blow given her by Queen Eleanor.

With that she dash'd her on the lips,
So dyèd double red :
Hard was the heart that gave the blow,
Soft were those lips that bled.

There are different kinds and degrees of imagination, some of them necessary to the formation of

every true poet, and all of them possessed by the
greatest. Perhaps they may be enumerated as follows :—First, that which presents to the mind any
object or circumstance in every-day life ; as when we
imagine a man holding a sword, or looking out of a
window ;—Second, that which presents real, but not
every-day circumstances; as King Alfred tending
the loaves, or Sir Philip Sidney giving up the
water to the dying soldier ;—Third, that which combines character and events directly imitated from
real life, with imitative realities of its own invention ;
as the probable parts of the histories of Priam and
Macbeth, or what may be called natural fiction as distinguished from supernatural ;—Fourth, that which
conjures up things and events not to be found in
nature ; as Homer's gods, and Shakspeare's witches,
enchanted horses and spears, Ariosto's hippogriff,
&c. ;—Fifth, that which, in order to illustrate or ag-
gravate one image, introduces another ; sometimes in
simile, as when Homer compares Apollo descending in his wrath at noon-day to the coming of
night-time : sometimes in metaphor, or simile comprised in a word, as in Milton's "motes that
people the sunbeams;" sometimes in concentratirg
into a word the main history of any person or
thing, past or even future, as in the "starry
Galileo" of Byron, and that ghastly foregone conclusion of the epithet "murdered" applied to the
yet living victim in Keats's story from Boccaccio,—

So the two brothers and their *murder'd* man
Rode towards fair Florence ;—

sometimes in the attribution of a certain representative quality which makes one circumstance stand for others; as in Milton's grey-fly winding its " *sultry horn*," which epithet contains the heat of a summer's day ;—Sixth, that which reverses this process, and makes a variety of circumstances take colour from one, like nature seen with jaundiced or glad eyes, or under the influence of storm or sunshine; as when in Lycidas, or the Greek pastoral poets, the flowers and the flocks are made to sympathize with a man's death ; or, in the Italian poet, the river flowing by the sleeping Angelica seems talking of love—

Parea che l' erba le fiorisse intorno,
E d' amor ragionasse quella riva!—
Orlando Innamorato, Canto iii.

or in the voluptuous homage paid to the sleeping Imogen by the very light in the chamber and the reaction of her own beauty upon itself; or in the " witch element" of the tragedy of Macbeth and the May-day night of Faust;—Seventh, and last, that which by a single expression, apparently of the vaguest kind, not only meets but surpasses in its effect the extremest force of the most particular description; as in that exquisite passage of Coleridge's Christabel, where the unsuspecting object of the witch's malignity is bidden to go to bed:—

B 5

> Quoth Christabel, So let it be!
> And as the lady bade, did she.
> Her gentle limbs did she undress,
> *And lay down in her loveliness ;—*

a perfect verse surely, both for feeling and music. The very smoothness and gentleness of the limbs is in the series of the letter *l's.*

I am aware of nothing of the kind surpassing that most lovely inclusion of physical beauty in moral, neither can I call to mind any instances of the imagination that turns accompaniments into accessories, superior to those I have alluded to. Of the class of comparison, one of the most touching (many a tear must it have drawn from parents and lovers) is in a stanza which has been copied into the "Friar of Orders Grey," out of Beaumont and Fletcher:—

> Weep no more, lady, weep no more,
>   Thy sorrow is in vain ;
> *For violets pluck'd the sweetest showers*
>   *Will ne'er make grow again.*

And Shakspeare and Milton abound in the very grandest; such as Antony's likening his changing fortunes to the cloud-rack; Lear's appeal to the old age of the heavens ; Satan's appearance in the horizon, like a fleet " hanging in the clouds ;" and the comparisons of him with the comet and the eclipse. Nor unworthy of this glorious company, for its extraordinary combination of delicacy and

vastness, is that enchanting one of Shelley's in the
Adonais :—

Life, like a dome of many-coloured glass,
Stains the white radiance of eternity.

I multiply these particulars in order to impress
upon the reader's mind the great importance of
imagination in all its phases, as a constituent part of
the highest poetic faculty.

The happiest instance I remember of imaginative
metaphor, is Shakspeare's moonlight "sleeping" on
a bank; but half his poetry may be said to be made
up of it, metaphor indeed being the common coin
of discourse. Of imaginary creatures, none out of
the pale of mythology and the East, are equal,
perhaps, in point of invention, to Shakspeare's
Ariel and Caliban; though poetry may grudge to
prose the discovery of a Winged Woman, especially
such as she has been described by her inventor in
the story of Peter Wilkins; and in point of treatment, the Mammon and Jealousy of Spenser, some
of the monsters in Dante, particularly his Nimrod,
his interchangements of creatures into one another,
and (if I am not presumptuous in anticipating what
I think will be the verdict of posterity) the Witch
in Coleridge's Christabel, may rank even with the
creations of Shakspeare. It may be doubted, indeed,
whether Shakspeare had bile and nightmare enough
in him to have thought of such detestable horrors

as those of the interchanging adversaries (now serpent, now man), or even of the huge, half-blockish enormity of Nimrod,—in Scripture, the "mighty hunter" and builder of the tower of Babel,—in Dante, a tower of a man in his own person, standing with some of his brother giants up to the middle in a pit in hell, blowing a horn to which a thunderclap is a whisper, and hallooing after Dante and his guide in the jargon of a lost tongue! The transformations are too odious to quote: but of the towering giant we cannot refuse ourselves the "fearful joy". of a specimen. It was twilight, Dante tells us, and he and his guide Virgil were silently pacing through one of the dreariest regions of hell, when the sound of a tremendous horn made him turn all his attention to the spot from which it came. He there discovered through the dusk, what seemed to be the towers of a city. Those are no towers, said his guide; they are giants, standing up to the middle in one of these circular pits.

> Come quando la nibbia si dissipa,
>   Lo sguardo a poco a poco raffigura
>   Ciò che cela 'l vapor che l' aere stipa ;
> Così forando l' aer grossa e scura
>   Più e più appressando in ver la sponda,
>   Fuggémi errore, e giugnémi paura :
> Perocchè come in su la cerchia tonda
>   Montereggion di torri si corona,
>   Così la proda che 'l pozzo circonda

Torreggiavan di mezza la persona
　Gli orribili giganti, cui minaccia
　Giove del cielo ancora, quando tuona :
Ed io scorgeva già' d'alcun la faccia,
　Le spalle e 'l petto, e del ventre gran parte,
　E per le coste giù ambo le braccia.
　　　　＊　　＊　　＊　　＊
La faccia sua mi parea lunga e grossa
　Come la pina di san Pietro a Roma :
　E a sua proporzion eran l'altr' ossa.
　　　　＊　　＊　　＊　　＊
Rafel mai amech zabì almi
　Cominciò a gridar la fiera bocca,
　Cui non si convenien più dolci salmi.
E 'l duca mio ver lui : anima sciocca,
　Tienti col corno, e con quel ti disfoga,
　Quand' ira o altra passion ti tocca.
Cercati al collo, e troverai la soga
　Che 'l tien legato, o anima confusa,
　E vedi lui che 'l gran petto ti doga.
Poi disse a me : egli stesso s' accusa :
　Questi è Nembrotto, per lo cui mal coto
　Pure un linguaggio nel mondo non s' usa.
Lasciamlo stare, e non parliamo a voto :
　Che così è a lui ciascun linguaggio,
　Come 'l suo ad altrui ch' a nullo è noto.
　　　　　　　　　　Inferno, Canto xxxi. ver. 34.

I look'd again ; and as the eye makes out,
By little and little, what the mist conceal'd
In which, till clearing up, the sky was steep'd ;
So, looming through the gross and darksome air,
As we drew nigh, those mighty bulks grew plain,
And error quitted me, and terror join'd :
For in like manner as all round its height
Montereggione crowns itself with towers,
So tower'd above the circuit of that pit,

Though but half out of it, and half within,
The horrible giants that fought Jove, and still
Are threaten'd when he thunders. As we near'd
The foremost, I discern'd his mighty face,
His shoulders, breast, and more than half his trunk,
With both the arms down hanging by the sides.
His face appear'd to me, in length and breadth,
Huge as St. Peter's pinnacle at Rome,
And of a like proportion all his bones.
He open'd, as we went, his dreadful mouth,
Fit for no sweeter psalmody ; and shouted
After us, in the words of some strange tongue,
Ràfel ma-èe amech zabèe almee!—
" Dull wretch !" my leader cried, " keep to thine horn,
And so vent better whatsoever rage
Or other passion stuff thee. Feel thy throat
And find the chain upon thee, thou confusion!
Lo! what a hoop is clench'd about thy gorge."
Then turning to myself, he said, " His howl
Is its own mockery. This is Nimrod, he
Through whose ill thought it was that humankind
Were tongue-confounded. Pass him, and say nought :
For as he speaketh language known of none,
So none can speak save jargon to himself."

Assuredly it could not have been easy to find a
fiction so uncouthly terrible as this in the hypochondria of Hamlet. Even his father had evidently
seen no such ghost in the other world. All his
phantoms were in the world he had left. Timon,
Lear, Richard, Brutus, Prospero, Macbeth himself,
none of Shakspeare's men had, in fact, any thought
but of the earth they lived on, whatever supernatural fancy crossed them. The thing fancied was

still a thing of this world, "in its habit as it lived,"
or no remoter acquaintance than a witch or a fairy.
Its lowest depths (unless Dante suggested them)
were the cellars under the stage. Caliban himself
is a cross-breed between a witch and a clown. No
offence to Shakspeare; who was not bound to be
the greatest of healthy poets, and to have every
morbid inspiration besides. What he might have
done, had he set his wits to compete with Dante, I
know not : all I know is, that in the infernal line
he did nothing like him ; and it is not to be wished he
had. It is far better that, as a higher, more universal, and more beneficent variety of the genus Poet,
he should have been the happier man he was, and
left us the plump cheeks on his monument, instead
of the carking visage of the great, but over-serious,
and comparatively one-sided Florentine. Even the
imagination of Spenser, whom we take to have been
a "nervous gentleman" compared with Shakspeare,
was visited with no such dreams as Dante. Or, if it
was, he did not choose to make himself thinner (as
Dante says *he* did) with dwelling upon them. He
had twenty visions of nymphs and bowers, to one of
the mud of Tartarus. Chaucer, for all he was
"a man of this world" as well as the poets' world,
and as great, perhaps a greater enemy of oppression
than Dante, besides being one of the profoundest
masters of pathos that ever lived, had not the heart
to conclude the story of the famished father and his

children, as finished by the inexorable anti-Pisan.
But enough of Dante in this place. Hobbes, in
order to daunt the reader from objecting to his
friend Davenant's want of invention, says of these
fabulous creations in general, in his letter prefixed
to the poem of Gondibert, that " impenetrable
armours, enchanted castles, invulnerable bodies, iron
men, flying horses, and a thousand other such
things, are easily feigned by them that dare." These
are girds at Spenser and Ariosto. But, with leave
of Hobbes (who translated Homer as if on purpose
to show what execrable verses could be written by a
philosopher), enchanted castles and flying horses
are not easily feigned, as Ariosto and Spenser
feigned them; and that just makes all the difference. For proof, see the accounts of Spenser's
enchanted castle in Book the Third, Canto Twelfth,
of the Fairy Queen; and let the reader of Italian
open the Orlando Furioso at its first introduction
of the Hippogriff (Canto iii. st. 4), where Brada-
mante, coming to an inn, hears a great noise,
and sees all the people looking up at something
in the air; upon which, looking up herself, she
sees a knight in shining armour riding towards
the sunset upon a creature with variegated wings,
and then dipping and disappearing among the hills.
Chaucer's steed of brass, that was

So horsly and so quick of eye,

is copied from the life. You might pat him and

feel his brazen muscles. Hobbes, in objecting to what he thought childish, made a childish mistake. His criticism is just such as a boy might pique himself upon, who was educated on mechanical principles, and thought he had outgrown his Goody Two-shoes. With a wonderful dimness of discernment in poetic matters, considering his acuteness in others, he fancies he has settled the question by pronouncing such creations " impossible!" To the brazier they are impossible, no doubt; but not to the poet. Their possibility, if the poet wills it, is to be conceded; the problem is, the creature being given, how to square its actions with probability, according to the nature assumed of it. Hobbes did not see, that the skill and beauty of these fictions lay in bringing them within those very regions of truth and likelihood in which he thought they could not exist. Hence the serpent Python of Chaucer,

Sleeping against the sun upon a day,

when Apollo slew him. Hence the chariot-drawing dolphins of Spenser, softly swimming along the shore lest they should hurt themselves against the stones and gravel. Hence Shakspeare's Ariel, living under blossoms, and riding at evening on the bat; and his domestic namesake in the " Rape of the Lock" (the imagination of the drawing-room) saving a lady's petticoat from the coffee with his plumes, and directing atoms of snuff into a coxcomb's nose.

In the " Orlando Furioso" (Canto xv. st. 65) is a
wild story of a cannibal necromancer, who laughs at
being cut to pieces, coming together again like
quicksilver, and picking up his head when it is cut
off, sometimes by the hair, sometimes by the nose!
This, which would be purely childish and ridiculous
in the hands of an inferior poet, becomes interesting,
nay grand, in Ariosto's, from the beauties of his
style, and its conditional truth to nature. The
monster has a fated hair on his head,—a single
hair,—which must be taken from it before he can be
killed. Decapitation itself is of no consequence,
without that proviso. The Paladin Astolfo, who
has fought this phenomenon on horseback, and
succeeded in getting the head and galloping off
with it, is therefore still at a loss what to be at.
How is he to discover such a needle in such a
bottle of hay? The trunk is spurring after him to
recover it, and he seeks for some evidence of the
hair in vain. At length he bethinks him of scalp-
ing the head. He does so; and the moment the
operation arrives at the place of the hair, *the face of
the head becomes pale, the eyes turn in their sockets,* and
the lifeless pursuer tumbles from his horse.

Si fece il viso allor pallido e brutto,
Travolse gli occhi, e dimostrò a l' occaso
Per manifesti segni esser condutto.
E 'l busto che seguia troncato al collo,
Di sella cadde, e diè l' ultimo crollo.

Then grew the visage pale, and deadly wet;
The eyes turn'd in their sockets, drearily;
And all things show'd the villain's sun was set.
His trunk that was in chace, fell from its horse,
And giving the last shudder, was a corse.

It is thus, and thus only, by making Nature his
companion wherever he goes, even in the most
supernatural region, that the poet, in the words of
a very instructive phrase, takes the world along with
him. It is true, he must not (as the Platonists
would say) humanize weakly or mistakenly in that
region; otherwise he runs the chance of forgetting
to be true to the supernatural itself, and so betray-
ing a want of imagination from that quarter. His
nymphs will have no taste of their woods and
waters; his gods and goddesses be only so many
fair or frowning ladies and gentlemen, such as we
see in ordinary paintings; he will be in no danger
of having his angels likened to a sort of wild-fowl,
as Rembrandt has made them in his Jacob's
Dream. His Bacchuses will never remind us, like
Titian's, of the force and fury, as well as of the
graces, of wine. His Jupiter will reduce no females
to ashes; his fairies be nothing fantastical; his
gnomes not " of the earth, earthy." And this again
will be wanting to Nature; for it will be wanting to
the supernatural, as Nature would have made it,
working in a supernatural direction. Nevertheless,
he poet, even for imagination's sake, must not

become a bigot to imaginative truth, dragging it down into the region of the mechanical and the limited, and losing sight of its paramount privilege, which is to make beauty, in a human sense, the lady and queen of the universe. He would gain nothing by making his ocean-nymphs mere fishy creatures, upon the plea that such only could live in the water : his wood-nymphs with faces of knotted oak ; his angels without breath and song, because no lungs could exist between the earth's atmosphere and the empyrean. The Grecian tendency in this respect is safer than the Gothic ; nay, more imaginative ; for it enables us to imagine *beyond* imagination, and to bring all things healthily round to their only present final ground of sympathy,—the human. When we go to heaven, we may idealize in a superhuman mode, and have altogether different notions of the beautiful ; but till then we must be content with the loveliest capabilities of earth. The sea-nymphs of Greece were still beautiful women, though they lived in the water. The gills and fins of the ocean's natural inhabitants were confined to their lowest semi-human attendants ; or if Triton himself was not quite human, it was because he represented the fiercer part of the vitality of the seas, as they did the fairer.

To conclude this part of my subject, I will quote from the greatest of all narrative writers two passages ;—one exemplifying the imagination which brings supernatural things to bear on earthly, without confounding them; the other, that which paints events and circumstances after real life. The first is where Achilles, who has long absented himself from the conflict between his countrymen and the Trojans, has had a message from heaven bidding him reappear in the enemy's sight, standing outside the camp-wall upon the trench, but doing nothing more; that is to say, taking no part in the fight. He is simply to be seen. The two armies down by the sea-side are contending which shall possess the body of Patroclus; and the mere sight of the dreadful Grecian chief—supernaturally indeed impressed upon them, in order that nothing may be wanting to the full effect of his courage and conduct upon courageous men—is to determine the question. We are to imagine a slope of ground towards the sea, in order to elevate the trench; the camp is solitary; the battle ("a dreadful roar of ▄▄▄▄▄s Homer calls it) is raging on the sea-shore; ▄▄▄ ▄▄ goddess Iris has just delivered her message ▄▄▄ ▄▄ disappeared.

▄▄▄▄ Αχιλλευς ωρτο Δυ φιλος· αμφι δ' Αθηνη
Ωμοις ιφθιμοισι βαλ' αιγιδα θυσσανοισσαν·
Αμφι δι δι κεφαλη νεφος εστεφε δια θεαων
Χρυσιον, εκ δ' αυτου δαιε φλογα παμφανοωσαν.
'Ως δ' οτε καπνος ιων εξ αστεος αιθερ' ικηται
Τηλοθεν εκ νησου, την δηιοι αμφιμαχονται,
'Οιτε πανημεριοι στυγερω κρινονται αρηι
Αστεος εκ σφετερου, αμα δ' ηελιω καταδυντι

Πυρσοι τε φλεγεθουσιν επητριμοι, ὑψοσε δ' αυγη
Γιγνεται αισσουσα, περικτιονεσσιν ιδεσθαι,
Αικεν πως συν νηυσιν αρεως αλκτηρες ικωνται,
'Ως απ' Αχιλληος κεφαλης σελας αιθερ' ικανε.

Στη δ' επι ταφρον ιων απο τειχεος· ουδ' ες Αχαιους
Μισγετο· μητρος γαρ πυκινην ωπιζετ' εφετμην.
Ενθα στας ηυσ', απατερθε δε Παλλας Αθηνη
Φθεγξατ'· αταρ Τρωεσσιν εν ασπετον ωρσε κυδοιμον.
'Ως δ' ότ αριζηλη φωνη, ότετ' ιαχε σαλπιγξ
Αστυ περιπλομενων δηιων ὑπο θυμοραιστεων,
'Ως τοτ' αριζηλη φωνη γενετ' Αιακιδαο.
'Οι δ' ως ουν αιον οπα χαλκεον Αιακιδαο,
Πασιν ορινθη θυμος· αταρ καλλιτριχες ιπποι
Αψ οχεα τροπεον· οσσοντο γαρ αλγεα θυμω.
'Ηνιοχοι δ' εκπληγεν, επει ιδον ακαματον πυρ
Δεινον ὑπερ κεφαλης μεγαθυμου Πηλειωνος
Δαιομενον· το δ' εδαιε θεα γλαυκωπις Αθηνη.
Τρις μεν ὑπερ ταφρου μεγαλ' ιαχε διος Αχιλλευς,
Τρις δ' εκυκηθησαν Τρωες κλειτοι τ' επικουροι.
Ενθα δε και τοτ' ολοντο δυωδεκα φωτες αριστοι
Αμφι σφοις οχεεσσι και εγχεσιν.

Iliad, Lib. xviii. v. 203.

But up Achilles rose, the lov'd of heaven ;
And Pallas on his mighty shoulders cast
The shield of Jove ; and round about his head
She put the glory of a golden mist,
From which there burnt a fiery-flaming light.
And as, when smoke goes heaven-ward from a town,
In some far island which its foes besiege,
Who all day long with dreadful martialness
Have pour'd from their own town ; soon as the sun
Has set, thick lifted fires are visible,
Which, rushing upward, make a light in the sky,
And let the neighbours know, who may perhaps

Bring help across the sea : so from the head
Of great Achilles went up an effulgence.

Upon the trench he stood, without the wall,
But mix'd not with the Greeks, for he rever'd
His mother's word ; and so, thus standing there,
He shouted ; and Minerva, to his shout,
Added a dreadful cry ; and there arose
Among the Trojans an unspeakable tumult.
And as the clear voice of a trumpet, blown
Against a town by spirit-withering foes,
So sprang the clear voice of Æacides.
And when they heard the brazen cry, their hearts
All leap'd within them; and the proud-maned horses
Ran with the chariots round, for they foresaw
Calamity ; and the charioteers were smitten,
When they beheld the ever-active fire
Upon the dreadful head of the great-minded one
Burning ; for bright-eyed Pallas made it burn.
Thrice o'er the trench divine Achilles shouted ;
And thrice the Trojans and their great allies
Roll'd back ; and twelve of all their noblest men
Then perish'd, crush'd by their own arms and chariots.

Of course there is no further question about the
body of Patroclus. It is drawn out of the press,
and received by the awful hero with tears.

The other passage is where Priam, kneeling
before Achilles, and imploring him to give up the
dead body of Hector, reminds him of his own
father; who, whatever (says the poor old king) may
be his troubles with his enemies, has the blessing of
knowing that his son is still alive, and may daily
hope to see him return. Achilles, in accordance

with the strength and noble honesty of the passions
in those times; weeps aloud himself at this appeal,
feeling, says Homer, " desire" for his father in his
very " limbs." He joins in grief with the venerable
sufferer, and can no longer withstand the look of
" his grey head and his grey *chin*." Observe the
exquisite introduction of this last word. It paints
the touching fact of the chin's being imploringly
thrown upward by the kneeling old man, and the
very motion of his beard as he speaks.

Ὡς αρα φονησας απιβη προς μακρον Ολυμπον
Ἑρμειας· Πριαμος δ᾿ εξ ἱππων αλτο χαμαζε,
Ιδαιον δε κατ᾿ αυθι λιπεν· ὁ δε μιμνεν ερυκων
Ἱππους ἡμιονους τε γερων δ᾿ ιθυς κιεν οικου,
Τῃ ῥ᾿ Αχιλευς ιζεσκε, Δια φιλος· εν δε μιν αυτον
Ευρ᾿ ἑταροι δ᾿ απανευθε καθειατο· τω δε δυ᾿ οιω
Ἡρως Αυτομεδων τε, και Αλκιμος οζος Αρηος,
Ποιπνυον παριοντε· νεον δ᾿ απελήγεν εδωδης
Εσθων και πινων, ετι και παρεκειτο τραπεζα.
Τους δ᾿ ελαθ᾿ εισελθων Πριαμος μεγας, αγχι δ᾿ αρα στας,
Χερσιν Αχιλληος λαβε γουνατα, και κυσε χειρας
Δεινας, ανδροφονους, δι δε πολεας εκτανον νιας·
Ὡς δ᾿ ὁταν ανδρ᾿ ατη πυκινη λαβῃ, ὁστ᾿ ενι πατρῃ
Φωτα κατακτεινας, αλλον εξικετο δημον,
Ανδρος ες αφνειον, θαμβος δ᾿ εχει εισοροωντας,
Ὡς Αχιλευς θαμβησεν, ιδων Πριαμον θεοειδεα·
Θαμβησαν δε και αλλοι, ες αλληλους δε ιδοντο.
Τον και λισσομενος Πριαμος προς μυθον εειπε·

Μνησαι πατρος σειο, θεοις επιεικελ᾿ Αχιλλευ,
Τηλικου, ὡσπερ εγων, ολοω επι γηραος ουδω.
Και μεν που κεινον περιναιεται αμφις εοντες
Τειρουσ᾿, ουδε τις εστιν, αρην και λοιγον αμυναι,

Αλλ' ητοι κεινος γε, σεθεν ζωοντος ακουων,
Χαιρει τ' εν θυμω, επι τ' ελπεται ηματα παντα
Οψεσθαι φιλον υιον απο Τροιηθεν ιοντα·
Αυταρ εγω παναποτμος, επει τεκον υιας αριστους
Τροιη εν ευρειη, των δ' ουτινα φημι λελειφθαι.
Πεντηκοντα μοι ησαν, οτ' ηλυθον υιες Αχαιων·
Εννεακαιδεκα μεν μοι ιης εκ νηδυος ησαν,
Τους δ' αλλους μοι ετικτον ενι μεγαροισι γυναικες.
Των μεν πολλον θουρος Αρης υπο γουνατ' ελυσεν·
῾Ος δε μοι οιος εην, ειρυτο δε αστυ και αυτους,
Τον συ πρωην ετεινας, αμυνομενον περι πατρης,
῾Εκτορα· του νυν εινεχ᾽ ικανω νηας Αχαιων,
Λυσομενος παρα σειο, φερω δ' απερεισι' αποινα.
Αλλ' αιδειο θεους, Αχιλευ, αυτον τ' ελεησον,
Μνησαμενος σου πατρος· εγω δ' ελεεινοτερος περ,
Ετλην δ', ὁ ουπω τις επιχθονιος βροτος αλλος,
Ανδρος παιδοφονοιο ποτι στομα χειρ' ορεγεσθαι.
῾Ως φατο· τω δ' αρα πατρος υφ' ιμερον ωρσε γοοιο,
Αψαμενος δ' αρα χειρος, απωσατο ηκα γεροντα.
Τω δε μνησαμενω, ὁ μεν ῾Εκτορος ανδροφονοιο,
Κλαι' αδινα, προπαροιθε ποδων Αχιληος ελυσθεις·
Αυταρ Αχιλλευς ελαιεν ιον πατερ', αλλοτε δ' αυτε
Πατροκλον· των δε στοναχη κατα δωματ᾽ ορωρει.
Αυταρ επει ρα γοοιο τεταρπετο διος Αχιλλευς,
Και δε απο πραπιδων ηλθ' ιμερος, ηδ' απο γυιων,
Αντισ' απο θρονου ωρτο, γεροντα δε χειρος ανιστη,
Οικτειρων πολιον τε καρη, πολιόν τε γενειον·

Iliad, Lib. xxiv. v. 468.

So saying, Mercury vanished up to heaven :
And Priam then alighted from his chariot,
Leaving Idœus with it, who remain'd
Holding the mules and horses ; and the old man
Went straight in doors, where the belov'd of Jove
Achilles sat, and found him.   In the room

C

Were others, but apart; and two alone,
The hero Automedon, and Alcimus,
A branch of Mars, stood by him. They had been
At meals, and had not yet remov'd the board.
Great Priam came, without their seeing him,
And kneeling down, he clasp'd Achilles' knees,
And kiss'd those terrible, homicidal hands,
Which had deprived him of so many sons.
And as a man who is press'd heavily
For having slain another, flies away
To foreign lands, and comes into the house
Of some great man, and is beheld with wonder,
So did Achilles wonder to see Priam;
And the rest wonder'd, looking at each other.
But Priam, praying to him, spoke these words :—
" God-like Achilles, think of thine own father!
To the same age have we both come, the same
Weak pass; and though the neighbouring chiefs may vex
Him also, and his borders, find no help,
Yet when he hears that thou art still alive,
He gladdens inwardly, and daily hopes
To see his dear son coming back from Troy.
But I, bereav'd old Priam! I had once
Brave sons in Troy, and now I cannot say
That one is left me. Fifty children had I,
When the Greeks came; nineteen were of one womb;
The rest my women bore me in my house.
The knees of many of these fierce Mars has loosen'd;
And he who had no peer, Troy's prop and theirs,
Him hast thou kill'd now, fighting for his country,
Hector; and for his sake am I come here
To ransom him, bringing a countless ransom.
But thou, Achilles, fear the gods, and think
Of thine own father, and have mercy on me:
For I am much more wretched, and have borne

What never mortal bore, I think, on earth,
To lift unto my lips the hand of him
Who slew my boys."

　　　　　　　He ceased ; and there arose
Sharp longing in Achilles for his father ;
And taking Priam by the hand, he gently
Put him away ; for both shed tears to think
Of other times ; the one, most bitter ones
For Hector, and with wilful wretchedness
Lay right before Achilles : and the other,
For his own father now, and now his friend ;
And the whole house might hear them as they moan'd.
But when divine Achilles had refresh'd
His soul with tears, and sharp desire had left
His heart and limbs, he got up from his throne,
And rais'd the old man by the hand, and took
Pity on his grey head and his grey chin.

O lovely and immortal privilege of genius! that can stretch its hand out of the wastes of time, thousands of years back, and touch our eyelids with tears. In these passages there is not a word which a man of the most matter-of-fact understanding might not have written, *if he had thought of it.* But in poetry, feeling and imagination are necessary to the perception and presentation even of matters of fact. They, and they only, see what is proper to be told, and what to be kept back ; what is pertinent, affecting, and essential. Without feeling, there is a want of delicacy and distinction ; without imagination, there is no true embodiment. In poets, even good of their kind, but without a genius for narra-

c 2

tion, the action would have been encumbered or diverted with ingenious mistakes. The over-contemplative would have given us too many remarks ; the over-lyrical, a style too much carried away ; the over-fanciful, conceits and too many similes ; the unimaginative, the facts without the feeling, and not even those. We should have been told nothing of the " grey chin," of the house hearing them as they moaned, or of Achilles gently putting the old man aside; much less of that yearning for his father, which made the hero tremble in every limb. Writers without the greatest passion and power do not feel in this way, nor are capable of expressing the feeling ; though there is enough sensibility and imagination all over the world to enable mankind to be moved by it, when the poet strikes his truth into their hearts.

The reverse of imagination is exhibited in pure absence of ideas, in commonplaces, and, above all, in conventional metaphor, or such images and their phraseology as have become the common property of discourse and writing. Addison's Cato is full of them.

> Passion unpitied and successless love
> *Plant daggers in my breast.*

> I've sounded my Numidians, man by man,
> And find them *ripe for a revolt.*

> The virtuous Marcia *towers above her sex.*

Of the same kind is his "courting the yoke"—
"distracting my very heart"—"calling up all"
one's "father" in one's soul — "working every
nerve"—"copying a bright example;" in short,
the whole play, relieved now and then with a smart
sentence or turn of words. The following is a
pregnant example of plagiarism and weak writing.
It is from another tragedy of Addison's time,—the
Mariamne of Fenton :—

> Mariamne, *with superior charms,*
> *Triumphs o'er reason :* in her look she *bears*
> A paradise of ever-blooming sweets ;
> Fair as the first idea beauty *prints*
> In the young lover's soul ; a winning grace
> Guides every gesture, and obsequious love
> *Attends* on all her steps.

"Triumphing o'er reason" is an old acquaintance
of every body's. "Paradise in her look" is from
the Italian poets through Dryden. "Fair as the
first idea," &c. is from Milton, spoilt;—"winning
grace" and "steps" from Milton and Tibullus, both
spoilt. Whenever beauties are stolen by such a
writer, they are sure to be spoilt: just as when a
great writer borrows, he improves.

To come now to Fancy,—she is a younger sister
of Imagination, without the other's weight of thought
and feeling. Imagination indeed, purely so called,
is all feeling; the feeling of the subtlest and most
affecting analogies; the perception of sympathies

in the natures of things, or in their popular attributes.   Fancy is a sporting with their resemblance,
real or supposed, and with airy and fantastical
creations.

> — Rouse yourself; and the weak wanton Cupid
> Shall from your neck unloose his amorous fold,
> *And, like a dew-drop from the lion's mane,*
> *Be shook to air.*
>> *Troilus and Cressida*, Act III. sc. 2.

That is imagination;—the strong mind sympathizing with the strong beast, and the weak love
identified with the weak dew-drop.

> Oh!—and I forsooth
> In love! I that have been love's whip!
> *A very beadle to a humorous sigh!—*
> A domineering pedant o'er the boy,—
> This whimpled, whining, purblind, wayward boy,
> This senior-junior, giant-dwarf, Dan Cupid,
> *Regent of love-rhymes, lord of folded arms,*
> *The anointed sovereign of sighs and groans, &c.*
>> *Love's Labour Lost*, Act III. sc. 1.

That is fancy;—a combination of images not in
their nature connected, or brought together by the
feeling, but by the will and pleasure; and having
just enough hold of analogy to betray it into the
hands of its smiling subjector.

> Silent icicles
> *Quietly shining to the quiet moon.*
>> Coleridge's *Frost at Midnight*.

That, again, is imagination;—analogical sympathy;
and exquisite of its kind it is.

" You are now sailed *into the north of my lady's opinion ;* where
you will hang *like an icicle on a Dutchman's beard,* unless you do
redeem it by some laudable attempt."

Twelfth Night, Act III. sc. 2.

And that is fancy ;—one image capriciously suggested by another, and but half connected with the
subject of discourse ; nay, half opposed to it ; for
in the gaiety of the speaker's animal spirits, the
" Dutchman's beard" is made to represent the lady !
Imagination belongs to Tragedy, or the serious
muse ; Fancy to the comic.   Macbeth, Lear, Paradise Lost, the poem of Dante, are full of imagination : the Midsummer Night's Dream and the
Rape of the Lock, of fancy : Romeo and Juliet,
the Tempest, the Fairy Queen, and the Orlando
Furioso, of both.   The terms were formerly identical, or used as such ; and neither is the best that
might be found.   The term Imagination is too confined : often too material.   It presents too invariably
the idea of a solid body ;—of " images" in the sense
of the plaster-cast cry about the streets.   Fancy, on
the other hand, while it means nothing but a spiritual image or apparition (Φαντασμα, appearance,
phantom), has rarely that freedom from visibility
which is one of the highest privileges of imagination.   Viola, in Twelfth Night, speaking of some
beautiful music, says :—

> It gives a very echo to the seat,
> Where Love is throned.

In this charming thought, fancy and imagination
are combined; yet the fancy, the assumption of
Love's sitting on a throne, is the image of a solid
body; while the imagination, the sense of sympathy
between the passion of love and impassioned music,
presents us no image at all. Some new term is
wanting to express the more spiritual sympathies of
what is called Imagination.

One of the teachers of Imagination is Melancholy;
and like Melancholy, as Albert Durer has painted her,
she looks out among the stars, and is busied with
spiritual affinities and the mysteries of the universe.
Fancy turns her sister's wizard instruments into toys.
She takes a telescope in her hand, and puts a mimic
star on her forehead, and sallies forth as an emblem
of astronomy. Her tendency is to the child-like
and sportive. She chases butterflies, while her
sister takes flight with angels. She is the genius of
fairies, of gallantries, of fashions; of whatever is
quaint and light, showy and capricious; of the
poetical part of wit. She adds wings and feelings to
the images of wit; and delights as much to people
nature with smiling ideal sympathies, as wit does to
bring antipathies together, and make them strike
light on absurdity. Fancy, however, is not incapable of sympathy with Imagination. She is
often found in her company; always, in the case of
the greatest poets; often in that of less, though
with them she is the greater favourite. Spenser has

great imagination and fancy too, but more of
the latter ; Milton both also, the very greatest,
but with imagination predominant ; Chaucer, the
strongest imagination of real life, beyond any
writers but Homer, Dante, and Shakspeare, and
in comic painting inferior to none ; Pope has
hardly any imagination, but he has a great deal
of fancy ;·Coleridge little fancy, but imagination
exquisite. Shakspeare alone, of all poets that ever
lived, enjoyed the regard of both in equal perfection.
A whole fairy poem of his writing will be found in
the present volume. See also his famous description of Queen Mab and her equipage, in Romeo and
Juliet :—

> Her waggon-spokes made of long spinners' legs ;
> The cover, of the wings of grasshoppers :
> Her traces of the smallest spider's web ;
> Her collars of the moonshine's watery beams, &c.

That is Fancy, in its playful creativeness. As a
small but pretty rival specimen, less known, take
the description of a fairy palace from Drayton's
Nymphidia :—

> This palace standeth in the air,
> By necromancy placèd there,
> That it no tempest needs to fear,
>   Which way soe'er it blow it :
> And somewhat southward tow'rd the noon,
> Whence lies a way up to the moon,
> And thence the Fairy can as soon
>   Pass to the earth below it.

c 5

> The walls of spiders' legs are made,
> Well morticèd and finely laid :
> He was the master of his trade,
>   It curiously that builded :
> *The windows of the eyes of cats :*

(because they see best at night)

> And for the roof instead of slats
> Is cover'd with the skins of bats
> *With moonshine that are gilded.*

Here also is a fairy bed, very delicate, from the same poet's Muse's Elysium.

> Of leaves of roses, *white and red,*
> Shall be the covering of the bed ;
> The curtains, vallens, tester all,
> Shall be the flower imperial ;
> And for the fringe it all along
> *With azure hare-bells shall be hung.*
> *Of lilies shall the pillows be*
> *With down stuft of the butterfly.*

Of fancy, so full of gusto as to border on imagination, Sir John Suckling, in his " Ballad on a Wedding," has given some of the most playful and charming specimens in the language. They glance like twinkles of the eye, or cherries bedewed :

> *Her feet beneath her petticoat,*
> *Like little mice stole in and out,*
>   *As if they fear'd the light :*
> But oh ! she dances such a way !
> *No sun upon an Easter day*
>   Is half so fine a sight.

It is very daring, and has a sort of playful grandeur,

to compare a lady's dancing with the sun. But as
the sun has it all to himself in the heavens, so she,
in the blaze of her beauty, on earth. This is imagination fairly displacing fancy. The following has
enchanted every body :—

> Her lips were red, *and one was thin*
> *Compared with that was next her chin,*
> *Some bee had stung it newly.*

Every reader has stolen a kiss at that lip, gay or
grave.

With regard to the principle of Variety in Uniformity by which verse ought to be modulated, and
one-ness of impression diversely produced, it has been
contended by some, that Poetry need not be written
in verse at all; that prose is as good a medium, provided poetry be conveyed through it; and that to
think otherwise is to confound letter with spirit, or
form with essence. But the opinion is a prosaical
mistake. Fitness and unfitness for *song*, or metrical
excitement, just make all the difference between a
poetical and prosaical subject; and the reason why
verse is necessary to the form of poetry, is, that
the perfection of poetical spirit demands it ; —
that the circle of its enthusiasm, beauty and
power, is incomplete without it. I do not mean
to say that a poet can never show himself a
poet in prose; but that, being one, his desire and
necessity will be to write in verse; and that, if he

were unable to do so, he would not, and could not,
deserve his title. Verse to the true poet is no clog.
It is idly called a trammel and a difficulty. It is a
help. It springs from the same enthusiasm as the
rest of his impulses, and is necessary to their satisfaction and effect. Verse is no more a clog than
the condition of rushing upward is a clog to fire,
or than the roundness and order of the globe we
live on is a clog to the freedom and variety that
abound within its sphere. Verse is no dominator
over the poet, except inasmuch as the bond is reci-
procal, and the poet dominates over the verse. They
are lovers, playfully challenging each other's rule,
and delighted equally to rule and to obey. Verse
is the final proof to the poet that his mastery over
his art is complete. It is the shutting up of his
powers in "*measureful* content;" the answer of form
to his spirit; of strength and ease to his guidance.
It is the willing action, the proud and fiery happiness, of the winged steed on whose back he has
vaulted,

> To witch the world with wondrous horsemanship.

Verse, in short, is that finishing, and rounding, and
"tuneful planetting" of the poet's creations, which
is produced of necessity by the smooth tendencies
of their energy or inward working, and the harmonious dance into which they are attracted round

the orb of the beautiful. Poetry, in its complete
sympathy with beauty, must, of necessity, leave no
sense of the beautiful, and no power over its forms,
unmanifested; and verse flows as inevitably from
this condition of its integrity, as other laws of proportion do from any other kind of embodiment of
beauty (say that of the human figure), however
free and various the movements may be that play
within their limits. What great poet ever wrote his
poems in prose? or where is a good prose poem, of
any length, to be found? The poetry of the Bible
is understood to be in verse, in the original. Mr.
Hazlitt has said a good word for those prose en-
largements of some fine old song, which are known
by the name of Ossian; and in passages they deserve what he said; but he judiciously abstained
from saying anything about the form. Is Gesner's
Death of Abel a poem? or Hervey's Meditations?
The Pilgrim's Progress has been called one; and,
undoubtedly, Bunyan had a genius which tended to
make him a poet, and one of no mean order: and
yet it was of as ungenerous and low a sort as was
compatible with so lofty an affinity; and this is the
reason why it stopped where it did. He had a
craving after the beautiful, but not enough of it in
himself to echo to its music. On the other hand,
the possession of the beautiful will not be sufficient
without force to utter it. The author of Telemachus had a soul full of beauty and tenderness.

He was not a man who, if he had had a wife and
children, would have run away from them, as Bunyan's hero did, to get a place by himself in heaven.
He was "a little lower than the angels," like our
own Bishop Jewells and Berkeleys; and yet he was
no poet. He was too delicately, not to say feebly,
absorbed in his devotions, to join in the energies of
the seraphic choir.

Every poet, then, is a versifier; every fine poet
an excellent one; and he is the best whose verse
exhibits the greatest amount of strength, sweetness,
straightforwardness, unsuperfluousness, *variety*, and
one-ness;—one-ness, that is to say, consistency, in
the general impression, metrical and moral; and
variety, or every pertinent diversity of tone and
rhythm, in the process. *Strength* is the muscle
of verse, and shows itself in the number and force
of the marked syllables; as,

Sonòrous mètal blòwing màrtial sòunds.

Paradise Lost.

Behèmoth, bìggest born of eàrth, ùphèav'd
His vàstness.

Id.

Blòw winds and cràck your chèeks! ràge! blòw!
You càtàràcts and hurricànoes, spòut,
Till you have drènch'd our stèeples, dròwn'd the còcks!
You sùlphurous and thoùght-èxecuting fìres,
Vaùnt coùriers of òak clèaving thùnderbòlts,

Singe my whìte hèad ! and thòu, àll-shàking thùnder,
Strìke flàt the thìck rotùndity o' the wòrld !

Lear.

Unexpected locations of the accent double this
force, and render it characteristic of passion and
abruptness. And here comes into play the reader's
corresponding fineness of ear, and his retardations and
accelerations in accordance with those of the poet :—

> Then in the kcyhole turns
> The intrìcàte wards, and every bolt and bar
> Unfastens.—On à sùddĕn òpen fly
> Wìth ìmpètuous recoil and jarring sound
> The infernal doors, and on their hinges grate
> Harsh thunder.
>
> *Par. Lost,* Book II.
>
> Abòmìnàblĕ—unùttĕràblĕ—and worse
> Than fables yet have feigned.
>
> *Id.*
>
> Wàllòwìng ùnwìĕldy̆—ĕnòrmous in their gait.
>
> *Id.*

Of unusual passionate accent, there is an exquisite
specimen in the Fairy Queen, where Una is lamenting her desertion by the Red-Cross Knight :—

> But he, my lion, and my noble lord,
> How does he find in cruel heart to hate
> Her that him lov'd, and ever most ador'd
> *As the gòd of my lìfe ?* Why hath he me abhorr'd ?

See the whole stanza, with a note upon it, in the
present volume.

The abuse of strength is harshness and heaviness; the reverse of it is weakness. There is a

noble sentiment,—it appears both in Daniel's and
Sir John Beaumont's works, but is most probably
the latter's,—which is a perfect outrage of strength
in the sound of the words :—

> Only the firmest and the *constant'st* hearts
> God sets to act the *stout'st* and hardest parts.

Stout'st and *constant'st* for "stoutest" and "most
constant!" It is as bad as the intentional crabbed-
ness of the line in Hudibras;

> He that hangs or *beats out's* brains,
> The devil's in him if *he* feigns.

Beats out's brains, for "beats out his brains." Of
heaviness, Davenant's "Gondibert" is a formidable
specimen, almost throughout :—

> With silence (òrder's help, and màrk of câre)
> They chìde thàt nòise which hèedless yòuth affèct ;
> Still coùrse for ùse, for heàlth thèy clèanness wèar,
> And sàve in wèll-fìx'd àrms, all nìceness chèck'd.
> Thèy thoùght, thòse that, unàrm'd, expòs'd fràil lìfe,
> But nàked nàture vàliantly betrày'd ;
> Whò wàs, thoùgh nàked, sàfe, till prìde màde strìfe,
> But màde defènce must ùse, nòw dànger's màde.

And so he goes digging and lumbering on, like a
heavy preacher thumping the pulpit in italics, and
spoiling many ingenious reflections.

Weakness in versification is want of accent and
emphasis. It generally accompanies prosaicalness,
and is the consequence of weak thoughts, and of the
affectation of a certain well-bred enthusiasm. The

writings of the late Mr. Hayley were remarkable
for it; and it abounds among the lyrical imitators of
Cowley, and the whole of what is called our French
school of poetry, when it aspired above its wit and
"sense." It sometimes breaks down in a horrible,
hopeless manner, as if giving way at the first step.
The following ludicrous passage in Congreve, intended to be particularly fine, contains an instance:—

> And lo! Silence himself is here;
> Methinks I see the midnight god appear.
> In all his downy pomp array'd,
> Behold the reverend shade.
> *An ancient sigh he sits upon!!!*
> *Whose memory of sound is long since gone,*
> *And purposely annihilated for his throne!!!*
> *Ode on the singing of Mrs. Arabella Hunt.*

See also the would-be enthusiasm of Addison
about music:

> For ever consecrate the *day*
> To music and *Cecilia;*
> Music, the greatest good that mortals know,
> And all of heaven we have below,
> Music can noble HINTS *impart!!!*

It is observable that the unpoetic masters of ridicule are apt to make the most ridiculous mistakes,
when they come to affect a strain higher than the
one they are accustomed to. But no wonder.
Their habits neutralize the enthusiasm it requires.

Sweetness, though not identical with smoothness,

any more than feeling is with sound, always includes it ; and smoothness is a thing so little to be
regarded for its own sake, and indeed so worthless
in poetry but for some taste of sweetness, that I
have not thought necessary to mention it by itself;
though such an all-in-all in versification was it regarded not a hundred years back, that Thomas
Warton himself, an idolator of Spenser, ventured to
wish the following line in the Fairy Queen,

And was admirèd much of fools, *women*, and boys—

altered to

And was admirèd much of women, fools, and boys—

thus destroying the fine scornful emphasis on the
first syllable of "women !" (an ungallant intimation, by the way, against the fair sex, very
startling in this no less woman-loving than great
poet.) Any poetaster can be smooth. Smoothness
abounds in all small poets, as sweetness does in the
greater. Sweetness is the smoothness of grace and
delicacy,—of the sympathy with the pleasing and
lovely. Spenser is full of it,—Shakspeare—Beaumont and Fletcher—Coleridge. Of Spenser's and
Coleridge's versification it is the prevailing characteristic. Its main secrets are a smooth progression
between variety and sameness, and a voluptuous
sense of the continuous,—"linked sweetness long
drawn out." Observe the first and last lines of the
stanza in the Fairy Queen, describing a shepherd

brushing away the gnats;—the open and the close
e's in the one,

As gèntle shèpherd in swēēt ēventide—

and the repetition of the word *oft*, and the fall from
the vowel *a*, into the two *u's* in the other,—

She brusheth *oft*, and *oft* doth màr their mùrmùrings.

So in his description of two substances in the handling, both equally smooth ;—

*Each smoother seems than each, and each than each seems
smoother.*

An abundance of examples from his poetry will
be found in the volume before us. His beauty re-
volves on itself with conscious loveliness. And
Coleridge is worthy to be named with him, as the
reader will see also, and has seen already. Let him
take a sample meanwhile from the poem called the
Day-Dream! Observe both the variety and sameness of the vowels, and the repetition of the soft
consonants :—

My eyes make pictures when they're shut :—
I see a fountain, large and fair,
A willow and a ruin'd hut,
And *thee* and *me* and Mary there.
O *Mary!* make *thy gentle lap our pillow;*
Bend o'er us, like a bower, my beautiful green willow.

By *Straightforwardess* is meant the flow of words
in their natural order, free alike from mere prose,
and from those inversions to which bad poets recur

in order to escape the charge of prose, but chiefly to
accommodate their rhymes. In Shadwell's play of
Psyche, Venus gives the sisters of the heroine an
answer, of which the following is the *entire* substance, literally, in so many words. The author
had nothing better for her to say :—

"I receive your prayers with kindness, and will give success to
your hopes. I have seen, with anger, mankind adore your sister's
beauty and deplore her scorn : which they shall do no more. For
I'll so resent their idolatry, as shall content your wishes to the full."

Now in default of all imagination, fancy, and expression, how was the writer to turn these words
into poetry or rhyme? Simply by diverting them
from their natural order, and twisting the halves of
the sentences each before the other.

> With kindness I your prayers receive,
> And to your hopes success will give.
> I have, with anger, seen mankind adore
> Your sister's beauty and her scorn deplore;
> Which they shall do no more.
> For their idolatry I'll so resent,
> As shall your wishes to the full content !!

This is just as if a man were to allow that there
was no poetry in the words, "How do you find
yourself?" "Very well, I thank you;" but to hold
them inspired, if altered into

> Yourself how do you find?
> Very well, you I thank.

It is true, the best writers in Shadwell's age were

addicted to these inversions, partly for their own
reasons, as far as rhyme was concerned, and partly
because they held it to be writing in the classical
and Virgilian manner. What has since been called
Artificial Poetry was then flourishing, in contradis-
tinction to Natural; or Poetry seen chiefly through
art and books, and not in its first sources. But
when the artificial poet partook of the natural, or, in
other words, was a true poet after his kind, his best
was always written in his most natural and straightforward manner. Hear Shadwell's antagonist Dryden. Not a particle of inversion, beyond what is
used for the sake of emphasis in common discourse,
and this only in one line (the last but three), is to be
found in his immortal character of the Duke of
Buckingham :—

A man so various, that he seemed to be
Not one, but all mankind's epitome :
Stiff in opinions, *always in the wrong,*
Was everything by starts, and nothing long ;
But in the course of one revolving moon
Was chemist, fiddler, statesman, and buffoon :
Then all for women, rhyming, dancing, drinking,
Besides ten thousand freaks that died in thinking.
Blest madman ! who could every hour employ
With something new to wish or to enjoy !
Railing and praising were his usual themes ;
And both, to-show his judgment, in extremes :
So over violent, or over civil,
That every man with him was god or devil.

In squandering wealth was his peculiar art;
Nothing went unrewarded, but desert.
Beggar'd by fools, whom still he found too late,
He had his jest, and they had his estate.

Inversion itself was often turned into a grace in these poets, and may be in others, by the power of being superior to it; using it only with a classical air, and as a help lying next to them, instead of a salvation which they are obliged to seek. In jesting passages also it sometimes gave the rhyme a turn agreeably wilful, or an appearance of choosing what lay in its way; as if a man should pick up a stone to throw at another's head, where a less confident foot would have stumbled over it. Such is Dryden's use of the word *might*—the mere sign of a tense— in his pretended ridicule of the monkish practice of rising to sing psalms in the night.

And much they griev'd to see so nigh their hall
The bird that warn'd St. Peter of his fall;
That he should raise his mitred crest on high,
And clap his wings and call his family
To sacred rites; and vex th' ethereal powers
With midnight matins at uncivil hours;
Nay more, his quiet neighbours should molest
Just in the sweetness of their morning rest.

(What a line full of " another doze" is that!)

Beast of a bird! supinely, when he *might*
Lie snug and sleep, to rise before the light!
What if his dull forefathers used that cry?
Could he not let a bad example die?

I the more gladly quote instances like those of
Dryden, to illustrate the points in question, because
they are specimens of the very highest kind of writing in the heroic couplet upon subjects not heroical.
As to prosaicalness in general, it is sometimes in-
lulged in by young writers on the plea of its being
natural; but this is a mere confusion of triviality
with propriety, and is usually the result of indolence.

Unsuperfluousness is rather a matter of style in
general, than of the sound and order of words: and
yet versification is so much strengthened by it, and so
much weakened by its opposite, that it could not
but come within the category of its requisites.
When superfluousness of words is not occasioned
by overflowing animal spirits, as in Beaumont and
Fletcher, or by the very genius of luxury, as in
Spenser (in which cases it is enrichment as well as
overflow), there is no worse sign for a poet altogether, except pure barrenness. Every word that
could be taken away from a poem, unreferable to
either of the above reasons for it, is a damage; and
many such are death ; for there is nothing that
posterity seems so determined to resent as this want
of respect for its time and trouble. The world is
too rich in books to endure it. Even true poets have
died of this Writer's Evil. Trifling ones have survived, with scarcely any pretensions but the terseness of their trifles. What hope can remain for

wordy mediocrity? Let the discerning reader take
up any poem, pen in hand, for the purpose of discovering how many words he can strike out of it
that give him no requisite ideas, no relevant ones
that he cares for, and no reasons for the rhyme beyond its necessity, and he will see what blot and
havoc he will make in many an admired production
of its day,—what marks of its inevitable fate.
Bulky authors in particular, however safe they may
think themselves, would do well to consider what
parts of their cargo they might dispense with in
their proposed voyage down the gulfs of time; for
many a gallant vessel, thought indestructible in its
age, has perished;—many a load of words, expected
to be in eternal demand, gone to join the wrecks of
self-love, or rotted in the warehouses of change and
vicissitude. I have said the more on this point, because in an age when the true inspiration has undoubtedly been re-awakened by Coleridge and his
fellows, and we have so many new poets coming forward, it may be as well to give a general warning
against that tendency to an accumulation and osten-
tation of *thoughts*, which is meant to be a refutation in
full of the pretensions of all poetry less cogitabund,
whatever may be the requirements of its class.
Young writers should bear in mind, that even some
of the very best materials for poetry are not poetry
built; and that the smallest marble shrine, of exquisite workmanship, outvalues all that architect ever

chipped away. Whatever can be so dispensed with is rubbish.

Variety in versification consists in whatsoever can be done for the prevention of monotony, by diversity of stops and cadences, distribution of emphasis, and retardation and acceleration of time; for the whole real secret of versification is a musical secret, and is not attainable to any vital effect, save by the ear of genius. All the mere knowledge of feet and numbers, of accent and quantity, will no more impart it, than a knowledge of the "Guide to Music" will make a Beethoven or a Paisiello. It is a matter of sensibility and imagination; of the beautiful in poetical passion, accompanied by musical; of the imperative necessity for a pause here, and a cadence there, and a quicker or slower utterance in this or that place, created by analogies of sound with sense, by the fluctuations of feeling, by the demands of the gods and graces that visit the poet's harp, as the winds visit that of Æolus. The same time and quantity which are occasioned by the spiritual part of this secret, thus become its formal ones,—not feet and syllables, long and short, iambics or trochees; which are the reduction of it to its *less* than dry bones. You might get, for instance, not only ten and eleven, but thirteen or fourteen syllables into a rhyming, as well as blank, heroical verse, if time and the feeling permitted; and in irregular measure this is often done; just as

D

musicians put twenty notes in a bar instead of two,
quavers instead of minims, according as the feeling
they are expressing impels them to fill up the time
with short and hurried notes, or with long; or as
the choristers in a cathedral retard or precipitate
the words of the chaunt, according as the quantity
of its notes, and the colon which divides the verse
of the psalm, conspire to demand it.   Had the moderns borne this principle in mind when they settled the prevailing systems of verse, instead of
learning them, as they appear to have done, from
the first drawling and one-syllabled notation of the
church hymns, we should have retained all the advantages of the more numerous versification of the
ancients, without being compelled to fancy that
there was no alternative for us between our sylla-
bical uniformity and the hexameters or other special
forms unsuited to our tongues.   But to leave this
question alone, we will present the reader with a
few sufficing specimens of the difference between
monotony and variety in versification, first from
Pope, Dryden, and Milton, and next from Gay and
Coleridge.   The following is the boasted melody of
the nevertheless exquisite poet of the " Rape of the
Lock,"—exquisite in his wit and fancy, though not
in his numbers.   The reader will observe that it is
literally *see-saw*, like the rising and falling of a
plank, with a light person at one end who is jerked
up in the briefer time, and a heavier one who is set

down more leisurely at the other. It is in the otherwise charming description of the heroine of that poem :—

> On her white breast—a sparkling cross she wore,
> Which Jews might kiss—and infidels adore;
> Her lively looks—a sprightly mind disclose,
> Quick as her eyes—and as unfix'd as those;
> Favours to none—to all she smiles extends,
> Oft she rejects—but never once offends;
> Bright as the sun—her eyes the gazers strike,
> And like the sun—they shine on all alike;
> Yet graceful ease—and sweetness void of pride,
> Might hide her faults—if belles had faults to hide;
> If to her share—some female errors fall,
> Look on her face—and you'll forget them all.

Compare with this the description of Iphigenia in one of Dryden's stories from Boccaccio :—

> It happen'd—on a summer's holiday,
> That to the greenwood shade—he took his way,
> For Cymon shunn'd the church—and used not much to pray.
> His quarter-staff—which he could ne'er forsake,
> Hung half before—and half behind his back :
> He trudg'd along—not knowing what he sought,
> And whistled as he went—for want of thought.
>
> By chance conducted—or by thirst constrain'd,
> The deep recesses of a grove he gain'd :—
> Where—in a plain defended by a wood,
> Crept through the matted grass—a crystal flood,
> By which—an alabaster fountain stood;
> And on the margent of the fount was laid—
> Attended by her slaves—a sleeping maid;
> Like Dian and her nymphs—when, tir'd with sport,

To rest by cool Eurotas they resort.—
The dame herself—the goddess well express'd,
Not more distinguished by her purple vest—
Than by the charming features of the face—
And e'en in slumber—a superior grace :
Her comely limbs—compos'd with decent care,⎫
Her body shaded—by a light cymarr,   ⎬
Her bosom to the view—was only bare;   ⎭
Where two beginning paps were scarcely spied—
For yet their places were but signified.—
The fanning wind upon her bosom blows—
To meet the fanning wind—the bosom rose ;   ⎫
The fanning wind—and purling stream—continue her repose.⎬

For a further variety take, from the same author's
Theodore and Honoria, a passage in which the couplets are run one into the other, and all of it modulated, like the former, according to the feeling demanded by the occasion :—

Whilst listening to the murmuring leaves he stood—
More than a mile immers'd within the wood—
At once the wind was laid.|—The whispering sound
Was dumb.|—A rising earthquake rock'd the ground.
With deeper brown the grove was overspread—⎫
A sudden horror seiz'd his giddy head—   ⎬
And his ears tinkled—and his colour fled.   ⎭

Nature was in alarm.—Some danger nigh
Seem'd threaten'd—though unseen to mortal eye.
Unus'd to fear—he summon'd all his soul,
And stood collected in himself—and whole :
Not long.—

But for a crowning specimen of variety of pause
and accent, apart from emotion, nothing can surpass

the account, in Paradise Lost, of the Devil's search
for an accomplice:—

> There was a plàce,
> Nòw nòt—though Sìn—not Time—first wroùght the chànge,
> Where Tìgris—at the foot of Pàradise,
> Into a gùlf—shòt under ground—till pàrt
> Ròse up a foùntain by the Trèe of Lìfe.
> *In* with the river sunk—and *with* it *ròse*
> Sàtan—invòlv'd in rìsing mìst—then soùght
> Whère to lie hìd.—Sèa he had search'd—and lànd
> From Eden over Pòntus—and the pòol
> Mæòtis—*àp* beyond the river *Ob;*
> Dòwnward as fàr antàrctic;—and in lèngth
> Wèst from Oròntes—to the òcean bàrr'd
> At Dàriën—thènce to the lànd whère flòws
> Gànges and Indus.—Thùs the òrb he ròam'd
> With nàrrow sèarch;—and with inspèction dèep
> Consìder'd èvery crèature—which of àll
> Mòst opportùne might sèrve his wìles—and foùnd
> The sèrpent—sùbtlest bèast of all the fìeld:

If the reader cast his eye again over this passage,
he will not find a verse in it which is not varied and
harmonized in the most remarkable manner. Let
him notice in particular that curious balancing of
the lines in the sixth and tenth verses:—

> *In* with the river sunk, &c.

and

> *Up* beyond the river *Ob.*

It might, indeed, be objected to the versification
of Milton, that it exhibits too constant a perfection

of this kind. It sometimes forces upon us too great a sense of consciousness on the part of the composer. We miss the first sprightly runnings of verse,—the ease and sweetness of spontaneity. Milton, I think, also too often condenses weight into heaviness.

Thus much concerning the chief of our two most popular measures. The other, called octosyllabic, or the measure of eight syllables, offered such facilities for *namby-pamby*, that it had become a jest as early as the time of Shakspeare, who makes Touchstone call it the " butterwoman's rate to market," and the " very false gallop of verses." It has been advocated, in opposition to the heroic measure, upon the ground that ten syllables lead a man into epithets and other superfluities, while eight syllables compress him into a sensible and pithy gentleman. But the heroic measure laughs at it. So far from compressing, it converts one line into two, and sacrifices every thing to the quick and importunate return of the rhyme. With Dryden, compare Gay, even in the strength of Gay,—

> The wind was high, the window shakes ;
> With sudden start the miser wakes ;
> Along the silent room he stalks,

(A miser never " stalks;" but a rhyme was desired for " walks")

Looks back, and trembles as he walks :
Each lock and every bolt he tries,
In every creek and corner pries ;
Then opes the chest with treasure stor'd,
And stands in rapture o'er his hoard ;

("Hoard" and "treasure stor'd" are just made
for one another)

But now, with sudden qualms possess'd,
He wrings his hands, he beats his breast ;
By conscience stung, he wildly stares,
And thus his guilty soul declares.

And so he denounces his gold, as miser never
denounced it; and sighs, because

Virtue resides on earth no more !

Coleridge saw the mistake which had been made
with regard to this measure, and restored it to the
beautiful freedom of which it was capable, by calling to mind the liberties allowed its old musical
professors the minstrels, and dividing it by *time* instead of *syllables;*—by the *beat of four* into which
you might get as many syllables as you could, instead of allotting eight syllables to the poor time,
whatever it might have to say. He varied it further
with alternate rhymes and stanzas, with rests and
omissions precisely analogous to those in music, and
rendered it altogether worthy to utter the manifold
thoughts and feelings of himself and his lady
Christabel. He even ventures, with an exquisite
sense of solemn strangeness and license (for there is

witchcraft going forward), to introduce a couplet of
blank verse, itself as mystically and beautifully modulated as anything in the music of Gluck or
Weber.

> 'Tis the middle of night by the castle clock,
> And the owls have awaken'd the crowing cock ;
> Tu-whit !—Tu-whoo !
> And hark, again ! the crowing cock,
> *How drowsily he crew.*
> Sir Leoline, the baron rich,
> Hath a toothless mastiff bitch ;
> From her kennel beneath the rock
> She maketh answer to the clock,
> *Fòur fòr thĕ quàrtĕrs ănd twĕlve fŏr thĕ hoùr ;*
> Ever and aye, by shine and shower,
> Sixteen short howls, not over loud :
> Some say, she sees my lady's shroud.
>
> *Is the nĭght chĭlly and dàrk?*
> *The nĭght is chĭlly, but nŏt dàrk.*
> The thin grey cloud is spread on high,
> It covers, but not hides, the sky.
> The moon is behind, and at the full,
> And yet she looks both small and dull.
> The night is chilly, the cloud is grey ;

(These are not superfluities, but mysterious returns of importunate feeling)

> *'Tis a month before the month of May,*
> *And the spring comes slowly up this way.*
> The lovely lady, Christabel,
> Whom her father loves so well,
> What makes her in the wood so late,
> A furlong from the castle-gate ?

She had dreams all yesternight
Of her own betrothèd knight ;
And shè In thĕ midnight wood will pray
For the wèal ŏf hĕr lover that's far away.

She stole along, she nothing spoke,
The sighs she heav'd were soft and low,
And nought was green upon the oak,
But moss and rarest misletoe ;
She kneels beneath the huge oak tree,
And in silence prayeth she.

The lady sprang up suddenly,
The lovely lady, Christabel !
It moan'd as near as near can be,
But what it is, she cannot tell.
On the other side it seems to be
Of thĕ hùge, broàd-breàsted, òld oàk trèe.

The night is chill, the forest bare ;
Is it the wind that moaneth bleak ?

(This " bleak moaning" is a witch's)

There is not wind enough in the air
To move away the ringlet curl
From the lovely lady's cheek—
There is not wind enough to twirl
The òne rĕd lĕaf, the làst ŏf ĭts clan,
That dàncĕs ăs ŏftĕn ăs dànce ĭt căn,
Hàngĭng sŏ light and hànging sŏ hìgh,
On thĕ tòpmost twìg thăt lòŏks ŭp ăt thĕ sky.

Hush, beating heart of Christabel !
Jesu Maria, shield her well !
She folded her arms beneath her cloak,
And stole to the other side of the oak.
What sees she there ?

There she sees a damsel bright,
Drest in a robe of silken white,
That shadowy in the moonlight shone:
The neck that made that white robe wan,
Her stately neck and arms were bare :
Her blue-vein'd feet unsandall'd were ;
And wildly glitter'd, here and there,
The gems entangled in her hair.
I guess 'twas *frightful* there to see
A lady so richly clad as she —
Beautiful exceedingly.

The principle of Variety in Uniformity is here worked out in a style " beyond the reach of art." Every thing is diversified according to the demand of the moment, of the sounds, the sights, the emotions; the very uniformity of the outline is gently varied; and yet we feel that *the whole is one and of the same character*, the single and sweet unconsciousness of the heroine making all the rest seem more conscious, and ghastly, and expectant. It is thus that *versification itself becomes part of the sentiment of a poem*, and vindicates the pains that have been taken to show its importance. I know of no very fine versification unaccompanied with fine poetry; no poetry of a mean order accompanied with verse of the highest.

As to Rhyme, which might be thought too insignificant to mention, it is not at all so. The universal consent of modern Europe, and of the East in all ages, has made it one of the musical beauties of

verse for all poetry but epic and dramatic, and even
for the former with Southern Europe,—a sustain-
ment for the enthusiasm, and a demand to enjoy.
The mastery of it consists in never writing it for its
own sake, or at least never appearing to do so ; in
knowing how to vary it, to give it novelty, to render
it more or less strong, to divide it (when not in
couplets) at the proper intervals, to repeat it many
times where luxury or animal spirits demand it (see
an instance in Titania's speech to the Fairies), to impress an affecting or startling remark with it, and to
make it, in comic poetry, a new and surprising addition to the jest.

Large was his bounty and his soul sincere,
    Heav'n did a recompense as largely send ;
He gave to misery all he had, *a tear ;*
    He gain'd from heav'n ('twas all he wish'd) *a friend.*
                                        Gray's Elegy.

The fops are proud of scandal ; for they cry
At every lewd, low character, " That's *I.*"
                        Dryden's Prologue to the Pilgrim.

What makes all doctrines plain and clear ?
About two hundred pounds a-year.
And that which was proved true before,
Prove false again ! *Two hundred more.*
                                        Hudibras.

Compound for sins they are *inclin'd to,*
By damning those they have *no mind to.*
                                        Id.

———— Stor'd with deletery *med'cines,*
Which whosoever took is *dead since.*
                                        Id.

Sometimes it is a grace in a master like Butler to force his rhyme, thus showing a laughing wilful power over the most stubborn materials:—

> Win
> The women, and make them draw in
> The men, as Indians with a *female*
> Tame elephant inveigle *the* male.
>
> *Hudibras.*
>
> He made an instrument to know
> If the moon shines at full or no;
> That would, as soon as e'er she *shone, straight*
> Whether 'twere day or night *demonstrate;*
> Tell what her diameter to an *inch is,*
> And prove that she's not made of *green cheese.*
>
> *Id.*

Pronounce it, by all means, *grinches*, to make the joke more wilful.   The happiest triple rhyme, perhaps, that ever was written, is in Don Juan:—

> But oh! ye lords of ladies *intellectual,*
> Inform us truly,—haven't they *hen-peck'd you all?*

The sweepingness of the assumption completes the flowing breadth of effect.

Dryden confessed that a rhyme often gave him a thought.   Probably the happy word "sprung" in the following passage from Ben Jonson was suggested by it; but then the poet must have had the feeling in him.

> —Let our trumpets sound,
> And cleave both air and ground
> With beating of our drums.

Let every lyre be strung,
Harp, lute, theorbo, *sprung*
With touch of dainty thumbs.

Boileau's trick for appearing to rhyme naturally
was to compose the second line of his couplet first!
which gives one the crowning idea of the "artificial
school of poetry." Perhaps the most perfect master
of rhyme, the easiest and most abundant, was the
greatest writer of comedy that the world has
seen,—Molière.

Mr. Tennyson's 'Princess' affords us, of continuing our sketch of modern poetry and poets.

If a man were to scrutinise the external features of our time, for the purpose of characterising it compendiously, he would be tempted, we suspect, to give up the task before long, and to pronounce the age a Medley. It would be hard to specify the character of our Philosophy, including as it does fragments of all systems, sometimes at open war, and sometimes eclectically combined. Not less various is the texture of Society among us, in which time-honoured traditions are blended with innovations which a few months make antiquated. The Political condition of our day is a war of great principles. As heterogeneous in its character is Art among us. Here we have an imitation of the antique, there a revival of the middle ages; while sculpture itself is sometimes compelled to relax its severity, and copy the rude attire of our northern yeomen. By what term could we describe the architecture of the day? In our rising cities we find a Gothic church close to a Byzantine fane or an Italian basilica; and in their immediate neighbourhood a town-hall like a Greek temple, a mansion like a Roman palace, and a club-house after the fashion of Louis XIV. The age in which we live may have a character of its own; but that character is not written in its face.

In this respect Mr. Tennyson's poem ' The Princess,' not without design if we may judge by the title, resembles the age. 'A Medley' he calls it; and a medley, so far as its materials are concerned, it assuredly is. We find in it classical allusions, a tournament of the middle ages, and the scientific and political associations of modern times. It is only on a repeated perusal that a certain unity of purpose which methodises its variegated exterior discloses itself. It professes but to weave together a chaplet of gay devices, such as might amuse the idleness of a young party on a summer's day: and the reader will perhaps be disposed to regret this —if his experience be not sufficient to warn him that grand undertakings are apt to turn out tedious performances, and that often where least is promised most is accomplished.

The ' Prologue ' of the poem explains its drift, and is indeed one of its most graphic and graceful portions. A rural festival is celebrated in the grounds of Sir Walter Vivian, a ' good old country gentleman,' fond of sports and of the poor. His son, with several young college friends, is passing the vacation at his house; and some ladies from the neighbouring country-seats are of the party. The morning is spent in looking

---

Art. III.—1. *The Princess: a Medley.* Poems by Alfred Tennyson. Fifth Edition. London: 1848.

2. *The Poetical Works of Percy Bysshe Shelley.* Edited by Mrs. Shelley. 3 vols. London: 1847.

3. *Life, Letters, and Literary Remains of John Keats.* Edited by R. Monckton Milnes. 2 vols. London: 1848.

In our recent notices of Mr. Taylor's ' Eve of the Conquest' and of the ' King Arthur' of Sir E. B. Lytton, we ventured to deal with these remarkable productions as representatives of those forms of the poetical character to which they seemed severally to belong. On the present occasion we propose, though somewhat late, to take the opportunity which

over those curiosities of art and antiquity with which an old country-house may be supposed to abound : the guests inspect the rusty armour of times gone by, and dive into old family records, including a chronicle which celebrates a knight without fear and without reproach, Sir Ralph, who fought at Ascalon, and a certain lady who had herself borne helmet and sword, and driven the foe from her walls. Leaving the house they then mingle with the crowd; after witnessing whose revels for a time, they make their retreat at last within the walls of a Gothic ruin, where they sit down to tell college tales, criticise Masters, Proctors, and Tutors, and compare old things with new. A broken statue of the good knight Ralph which Lilia, the daughter of Sir Walter, has in a childish caprice mantled with a scarf of crimson silk, recalls the family legend ; and where, asks Walter, is a true heroine now to be found ? His young sister affirms that the land is still rich in such, but that their heroic qualities are undeveloped in consequence of their being deprived of a befitting education. Catching at this idea, half in ridicule and half in sympathy, the young men agree to recount a tale of which the heroine is to be a Princess who devotes herself to the exaltation of her sex, bringing up the maidens of her land in all manly knowledge and training. The narrators who are seven in number engage to take up the story in succession. The character of the tale is thus announced (p. 12) :—

' But one that really suited time and place
Were such a medley! we should have *him* back
Who told the Winter's Tale to do it for us !
A Gothic ruin, and a Grecian house,
A talk of college and of ladies' rights,
A feudal knight in silken masquerade,
And there, with shrieks and strange experiments,
For which the good Sir Ralph had burnt them all,
The nineteenth century gambols on the grass.'

With this intimation the tale corresponds. The poem begins as an English Decameron of the nineteenth century ; but it swells as it proceeds into a wider continuity of interests, and deepens in pathos. A vein of kindly irony runs through no small portion of it ; but, by insensible gradations, the serious and the tender first, then the pathetic and the profound, supervene upon the gamesome. Any but the most delicate execution in this respect would have produced a very coarse, not to say grotesque, effect. The humorous and the serious are, however, seldom here found antithetically opposed to each other ; but blend rather, like the different shades of some fine material shifted in

the light. In this respect the poem is in harmony with nature ; who so intertwines the grave with the gay, in her passages of sadness or promise, that the colour of the web is dark or bright according to the humour of him who handles it. There is room both for Democritus and Heraclitus in the world ; and their dispute is one in which neither can have the last word.

The narrative is but a slender thread ; perhaps too slender compared with the gems of precious poetry with which it is strung. A certain Prince, of whom we know no more than that he was ' blue-eyed and fair in face,' and that ' on his cradle shone the Northern Star,' had been betrothed and proxy-wedded while a child, to a Princess in the south not more than eight years old. The boy wears next his heart her picture, and one dark tress of southern hair ; and around these relics, as boyhood changes into youth,

' Sweet thoughts would swarm as bees about their queen.'

Ida, the Princess, has had her ideal also ; but to her young lover she has been faithless before she has had the opportunity of being faithful. She admits, indeed, that

' We had our dreams—perhaps he mingled with them ;'

but she has been the spoilt child of a doting father, and she has had her way in all things. The motherless girl had fallen moreover under the influence of two widows, Lady Psyche and Lady Blanche : and they have taught her, how

' Knaves are men
That lute and flute fantastic tenderness,
And dress the victim to the offering up,
And paint the gates of Hell with Paradise,
And play the slave to gain the tyranny.' (P. 71.)

Among her own companions the Princess has seen also an instance of ill-requited truth. These circumstances have strengthened an early aspiration into a fixed resolve. It is thus that the king, her father, describes it to the young Prince who has sought his court, and in vain demanded the fulfilment of the early contract. He speaks of her two widow friends (pp. 18, 19.) :—

' They fed her theories, in and out of place
Maintaining that with equal husbandry
The woman were an equal to the man.
They harp'd on this ; with this our banquets rang ;
Our dances broke and buzz'd in knots of talk ;
Nothing but this : my very ears were hot
To hear them. Last, my daughter begged a boon,

A certain summer-palace which I have
Hard by your father's frontier : I said no,
Yet being an easy man, gave it ; and there,
All wild to found an University
For maidens, on the spur she fled.'

The utmost that the Prince can obtain is permission to seek her out, and use his own powers of persuasion. Accompanied by two faithful friends, Florian and Cyril, he returns northward to the neighbourhood of the Princess' university, which no man is allowed to enter on pain of death. The three adventurers however effect an entrance, disguised as students. The Princess is thus presented (p. 25.) :—

' There at a board, by tome and paper, sat,
　With two tame leopards couch'd beside her
　　throne,
All beauty compass'd in a female form,
The Princess liker to the inhabitant
Of some clear planet close upon the Sun,
Than our man's earth : such eyes were in her
　head,
And so much grace and power, breathing down
From over her arch'd brows, with every turn
Lived thro' her, to the tips of her long hands,
And to her feet.'

It would be difficult to exceed the skill with which this female university is described. Even the colleges of our native land, though devoted to manly studies, once held in them a certain feminine element of seclusion, decorous observance, innocence, sanctity, and obedience—of which the gown survives as the symbol. In early times, indeed, they were households on a larger scale, collected round the hearths of the church. Mr. Tennyson has availed himself of the points of analogy, touching more rarely those of contrast, and treating them in a spirit rather of friendly raillery than of satire. In his management of a theme so perilous as the adventures of three young men in a secular nunnery, there is no offence against good taste or good manners. He does all honour to the purity of a high though erring intention ; sees only what is worthiest to be seen, and turns even the aberrations of female wilfulness into the graceful, the winning, and the womanly. The first thing that the disguised youths do is to attend lecture. The Lady Blanche and the Lady Psyche are the most famous of the professors. They enrol themselves among Psyche's pupils. (P. 28.)

　　　　　　　' As we enter'd in,
There sat along the forms, like morning doves
That sun their milky bosoms on the thatch,
A patient range of pupils.'

Her lecture begins with science, and ends

in something more like song. Psyche, though she had been married to a nobleman of the southern land, is the sister of Florian ; nor can his disguise protect him long from her recognition. After much pleading, however, the young men prevail upon her to keep their secret, on condition of their speedy departure. The next evening the Princess heads a riding party, to take the dip of certain strata in the base of the neighbouring hills. All the evening they climb the precipices, and after their repast sing songs. The following, rather a suspicious one, is that sung by the Northern Prince (pp. 69, 70.) :—

' O Swallow, Swallow, flying, flying South,
Fly to her, and fall upon her gilded eaves,
And tell her, tell her what I tell to thee.

' O tell her, Swallow, thou that knowest each,
That bright and fierce and fickle is the South,
And dark and true and tender is the North.

' O Swallow, Swallow, if I could follow, and
　light
Upon her lattice, I would pipe and trill,
And cheep and twitter twenty million loves.

' O were I thou that she might take me in,
And lay me on her bosom, and her heart
Would rock the snowy cradle, till I died !

' Why lingereth she to clothe her heart with
　love,
Delaying as the tender ash delays
To clothe herself, when all the woods are green ?

' O tell her, Swallow, that thy brood is flown :
Say to her, I do but wanton in the South,
But in the North long since my nest is made.

' O tell her, brief is life but love is long,
And brief the sun of summer in the North,
And brief the moon of beauty in the South.

' O Swallow, flying from the golden woods,
Fly to her, and pipe and woo her, and make her
　mine,
And tell her, tell her, that I follow thee.'

Before the evening is over, Cyril breaks in with some wild boisterous catch, and quite forgets the necessity of mimicking the female voice. The strangers are consequently discovered : and a sudden flight ensues. As the Princess gallops away in indignation, her horse stumbles upon the bridge, and she is precipitated into the river just above the falls. While her maidens clap their hands and scream upon the bank, the Prince plunges into the flood, and after a hard struggle brings her safe to land. Again she mounts, and with her train reaches the university. Downcast and with a slower pace the discovered youths follow. They are brought before the judgment-seat of the incensed Princess, who is not in the most placable of moods. (P. 78.)

' They haled us to the Princess, where she sat
High in the hall: above her droop'd a lamp,
And made the single jewel on her brow
Burn like the mystic fire on a mast-head,
Prophet of storm: a handmaid on each side
Bow'd toward her, combing out her long black
    hair
Damp from the river: and close behind her
    stood
Eight daughters of the plough,—stronger than
    men!
Huge women blowzed with health, and wind,
    and rain
And labour. Each was like a Druid rock;
Or like a spire of land that stands apart
Cleft from the main, and clang'd about with
    mews.'

It is in vain that the Prince boldly pleads his love, and urges his contract. At this critical moment the college is suddenly beleaguered by an armed host. The father of the Prince, a rough fierce old man with hoary hair and a fiery eye flashing beneath it, had thought from the first that an appeal to arms was the orthodox mode of settling the question of the repudiated contract. From that scheme he had been dissuaded; but hearing that his son had made his way into the forbidden precinct, and jealous lest mischance should befall him there, he has hastily collected his army, surprised the little priggish king, the father of our formidable heroine, and surrounded the university. The Princess is equal to the emergency; and her native character, which is heroic and self-devoted, asserts itself. She refuses to surrender, and quells the tumult. (Pp. 88, 89.)

       ' From the illumin'd hall
Long lanes of splendour slanted o'er a press
Of snowy shoulders, thick as herded ewes,
And rainbow robes, and gems and gemlike
    eyes,
And gold, and golden heads; they to and fro
Fluctuated, as flowers in storm, some red, some
    pale,
All open-mouth'd, all gazing to the light,
Some crying there was an army in the land,
And some that men were in the very walls,
And some they cared not; till a clamour grew
As of a new-world Babel, woman-built,
And worse-confounded: high above them stood
The placid marble Muses, looking peace.

' Not peace, She look'd, the Head: but raising
    up
Robed in the long night of her deep hair, so
To the open window moved, remaining there
Fixed like a beacon-tower above the waves
Of tempest, when the crimson-rolling eye

Glares ruin, and the sea-birds on the light
Dash themselves dead. She stretch'd her arms
    and call'd
Across the tumult—and the tumult fell !'

The Prince is expelled by the eight ' daughters of the plough.'

From this moment the story gradually becomes more serious. The Princess has been from her infancy the delight of three warlike brothers; they too collect an army, and the rival hosts meet ere long beneath the walls of the maiden college. The Prince rides forth to the hostile camp, and has an interview with the brothers of the Princess. He challenges them to submit the dispute to the arbitrament of a combat, to be fought by fifty chosen knights on each side. The combat takes place, in the presence of both courts; and the Prince, with his two friends, after a terrible conflict, is left on the plain among the dying and the dead.

The next book begins with the Princess' song of triumph—but ends with her defeat. This scene has a greatness of character beyond perhaps any other part of the poem. In it more than anywhere else, the large performance breaks through the narrow limits of the unambitious design; and we recognise, as we glance around on its manifold sources of interest—the wounded Prince, the unhappy father, the mother pleading for her child, the indignant warrior, and the Princess slow to yield—an epic breadth of effect as well as style of handling. Accompanied by her maidens, and holding in her arms the infant child of Psyche, whom she had taken to herself on its mother's flight, Ida descends to the battlefield. An enemy more formidable than armed hosts there assails her—Pity. It is not by physical suffering alone that she is confronted. Psyche pleads hard for the restoration of her child. Cyril forgets his own wounds while vindicating her claims. The memory of old friendship comes to their aid,—and Psyche is forgiven. Old Gama bitterly reproaches his daughter. The Prince's father refuses her aid. Reality comes suddenly home to one whose life has been a dream; and nature will have her way. ' Let the wounded be carried into the university,' she exclaims, overwhelmed by the passion of sudden grief; ' Psyche shall be Cyril's nurse; she will herself tend her chief enemy.' She speaks, and it is done. The Prince gains, unconsciously and in defeat, the privilege after which in health and strength he had in vain aspired.

The conclusion need hardly be narrated —unless we too could tell it as it is told by the poet. The wounded knights, after a struggle discreetly prolonged, recover. The remedial process was apparently rather empirical in character, consisting, in a large measure, of transfusion and counter-irritation. By degrees renovated strength glided, from the touch of their youthful nurses and very friendly physicians, into the veins of the wounded warriors: by degrees fever left the wearied head; but a kindred unrest was transferred into the hearts (how recently occupied only by learned cares) of those who were piously grateful for the work of their own hands. The knights live; and the ladies indulgently favour their devotion. In ice itself there are different degrees of coldness. Psyche is already betrothed to Cyril, and Melissa, the daughter of the spiteful Blanche, to Florian; while the Princess still holds out, ' like Teneriffe or Atlas unremoved.' Example, however, is dangerous; idleness is more so; and Ida's great design has been brought by compulsion to a stand still. Remorse, also, as well as compassion, has been dealing with her; and Spring-tide falls at last upon Ida's heart. One evening the Prince awakens from a long trance, and for the first time is conscious of outward things. Seldom has love been so described. (Pp. 148—150.)

' I saw the forms: I knew not where I was:
Sad phantoms conjured out of circumstance,
Ghosts of the fading brain, they seem'd; nor more
Sweet Ida. Palm to palm she sat: the dew
Dwelt in her eyes, and softer all her shape
And rounder show'd: I moved: I sign'd: a touch
Came round my wrist, and tears upon my hand!
Then, all for languor and self-pity, ran
Mine, down my face; and with what life I had,
And like a flower that cannot all unfold,
So drench'd it is with tempest, to the sun,
Yet, as it may, turns toward him, I on her
Fixt my faint eyes, and utter'd whisperingly:

' "If you be, what I think you, some sweet dream,
I would but ask you to fulfil yourself:
But if you be that Ida whom I knew,
I ask you nothing: only, if a dream,
Sweet dream, be perfect. I shall die to-night!
Stoop down and seem to kiss me ere I die."

' I could no more, but lay like one in trance,
That hears his burial talk'd of by his friends,
And cannot speak, nor move, nor make one sign,
But lies and dreads his doom. She turn'd; she paused;
She stoop'd; and with a great shock of the heart

Our mouths met! out of languor leapt a cry,
Crown'd Passion from the brinks of death, and up
Along the shuddering senses struck the soul,
And closed on fire with Ida's at the lips;
Till back I fell, and from mine arms she rose,
Glowing all over noble shame; and all
Her falser self slipt from her like a robe,
And left her woman, lovelier in her mood
Than in her mould that other, when she came
From barren deeps to conquer all with love,
And down the streaming crystal dropt, and she
Far-fleeted by the purple island sides,
Naked, a double light in air and wave,
To meet her Graces, where they deck'd her out
For worship without end! Nor end of mine,
Stateliest, for thee! but mute she glided forth,
Nor glanced behind her, and I sank and slept,
Fill'd thro' and thro' with Love, a happy sleep.'

Again, in the middle of the night, the Prince wakes: Ida sits beside him, and holds (pp. 150, 151.)—

' A volume of the Poets of her land:
There to herself, all in low tones, she read.

"Now sleeps the crimson petal, now the white;
Nor waves the cypress in the palace walk;
Nor winks the gold fin in the porphyry font:
The fire-fly wakens: waken thou with me!

"Now droops the milkwhite peacock like a ghost,
And like a ghost she glimmers on to me.

"Now lies the Earth all Danaë to the stars,
And all thy heart lies open unto me.

"Now slides the silent meteor on, and leaves
A shining furrow—as thy thoughts in me.

"Now folds the lily all her sweetness up,
And slips into the bosom of the lake:
So fold thyself, my dearest, thou, and slip
Into my bosom and be lost in me." '

There is silence. Again she opens the volume, and reads the following Idyl (pp. 151—153.):—

' " Come down, O maid, from yonder mountain height:
What pleasure lives in height (the shepherd sang),
In height and cold, the splendour of the hills?
But cease to move so near the Heavens, and cease
To glide a sunbeam by the blasted Pine,
To sit a star upon the sparkling spire;
And come, for Love is of the valley, come,
For Love is of the valley, come thou down
And find him! by the happy threshold, he,

Or hand in hand with Plenty in the maize,
Or red with spirited purple of the vats,
Or foxlike in the vine ; nor cares to walk
With Death and Morning on the Silver Horns,
Nor wilt thou snare him in the white ravine,
Nor find him dropt upon the firths of ice,
That huddling slant in furrow-cloven falls,
To roll the torrent out of dusky doors :
But follow ; let the torrent dance thee down
To find him in the valley ; let the wild
Lean-headed Eagles yelp alone, and leave
The monstrous ledges there to slope, and spill
Their thousand wreaths of dangling water-
       smoke,
That like a broken purpose waste in air.
So waste not thou ! but come ! for all the vales
Await thee ; azure pillars of the hearth
Arise to thee ; the children call and I
Thy shepherd pipe, and sweet is every sound !
Sweeter thy voice, but every sound is sweet ;
Myriads of rivulets hurrying through the lawn,
The moan of doves in immemorial elms,
And murmuring of innumerable bees."

' So she, low-toned ; while with shut eyes I lay
Listening ; then look'd. Pale was the perfect
       face ;
The bosom with long sighs labour'd ; and
       meek
Seem'd the full lips, and mild the luminous
       eyes,
And the voice trembled and the hand. She
       said
Brokenly, that she knew it, she had fail'd,
In sweet humility ; had fail'd in all ;
That all her labour was but as a block
Left in the quarry.'

In surrendering herself Ida surrenders
all. Her lover, however, restores to her the
substance of her early hope, now purified
from presumption and ambition ; and, learning as well as teaching through the sympathies, assures her that there had been a
heart of truth in her aspiring creed. (Pp.
156, 157.)

' For woman is not undevelopt man
But diverse : could we make her as the man,
Sweet love were slain, whose dearest bond is
       this
Not like to like, but like in difference :
Yet in the long years liker must they grow ;
The man be more of woman, she of man ;
He gain in sweetness and in moral height,
Nor lose the wrestling thews that throw the
       world ;
She mental breadth, nor fail in childward care :
More as the double-natured Poet, each ;
Till at the last she set herself to man,
Like perfect music unto noble words ;
And so these twain, upon the skirts of Time,
Sit side by side, full-summ'd in all their powers,
Dispensing harvest, sowing the To-be,
Self-reverent each and reverencing each,
Distinct in individualities,
But like each other ev'n as those who love.
Then comes the statelier Eden back to men :

Then reign the world's great bridals, chaste
       and calm :
Then springs the crowning race of humankind !'

The reader will have been enabled, by
our analysis of the story, and still more by
our extracts, to form a judgment of Mr.
Tennyson's poem. He will perceive that,
although the discordant materials of the tale
are put together with much skill, it does not
propose to itself the highest objects of narrative poetry. He will discover, also, that it
is equally far from being a burlesque. The
work, which is eminently original in its conception, is in narrative poetry much what
the comedy of poetry and character, as distinguished from that of wit and manners, is
in dramatic. The ' Midsummer Night's
Dream ' and the ' Tempest ' include a serious
meaning, although the tragic element enters
not into them. They contemplate human
life in the main from the sunny side ; but,
even from faery-land, it is still human life
which they regard. So it is with Mr. Tennyson's ' Princess.' The abundant grace
and descriptive beauty which meet the superficial eye, constitute but its external
charm. Studying his work with that attention which the labour of a true poet
should always command, we soon discover
that, while fantastic in its subject, it is eminently human in sentiment, and that the
human gradually rises higher and higher
into the moral. The poem plays with the
arbitrary and the theoretical ; but it plays
with them only to make them their own
confuters. Such is the lore which we learn
from human life. Our follies are our most
effectual instructors ; and the strongest re-
solutions of manhood flourish best in that soil
in which the extravagances of youthful hopes
have found a grave.

The deep and rich humanity with which
this poem, notwithstanding its fanciful plot,
is replete, can hardly be illustrated by quotations. That its tendency is not to depreciate womanhood, but to exalt it, we have
already remarked ; and our observation is
amply borne out by the passage, one of the
most deeply touching in the poem, in which
the Prince speaks of his mother. The same
reverence for what is holiest in the affections is shown in the delineation of the
Princess' late and reluctant love. Poets of
a different class from Mr. Tennyson are
always more successful in painting love
than any of the other affections. One reason of this may be that in that passion there
is often less of the humanities than in any
other. If the love be very immature or
very egotistical,—if it float in the imagination only, or be rooted in the exclusive de-

mands of a narrow nature, and still more if it be mainly a matter of temperament,—in any of these cases it admits of being easily described, because it is little modified by the more complex sympathies of our nature. Such love-poetry, accordingly, is very easily written,—or rather such love is poetry ready made ; and it will find acceptance with the least poetical readers. The love-poetry of the 'Princess' is of another sort. In Ida the personal love rises out of that human love from which caprice and a wild enterprise had long estranged her. There is nothing new in the philosophy that 'pity is akin to love ;' but the pity which exists only for a lover, is too like the charity which begins, and ends, at home. Ida has first pitied the deserted infant :—

'We took it for an hour this morning to us
In our own bed : the tender orphan hands
Felt at our heart, and seemed to charm from thence
The wrath we nursed against the world.'

She also pities the bereft mother, the estranged friend, the grey old father : and it is thus that at last she requires no formal refutation of that which had been the favourite object of her youthful aspirations. It drops away unshaken. She has been humanised ; and all the great human relations assume at once their due place. Loyalty is the basis of them all. She loves ; and feminine subjection appears to her no longer a tyranny, but a something beautiful, befitting, and worthy :—'Thy *desire* shall be to thy husband, and he shall have the *rule* over thee.' The scientific eminence which she has wished her sex to share becomes at once a trifling as well as a visionary thing. For this development we are prepared by many artistic touches in the progress of the poem.

It has been remarked, among the distinguishing attributes of high poetry, that such contains ever, whether intentionally or not, a number of subordinate meanings, besides that which lies on the surface. Indeed we know not how it should be otherwise : the stream will make mention of its bed ; the river will report of those shores which, sweeping through many regions and climes, it has washed ; and those currents of thought whose sources lie afar off must needs be enriched with a various and precious store. The results of large generalisations must ever, though undesignedly, be symbolical— a fact which in itself proves how needless is the labour of a poet who, with a didactic purpose, devises a formal allegory, and models his work on such a framework. Suggestiveness we should class among the chief characteristics of Mr. Tennyson's poetry.

Among the lesser meanings of his most recent work, that vindication of the natural ties against the arbitrary and the theoretical, is not the least significant. · Many passages in it have a remarkable reference to children. They sound like a perpetual child-protest against Ida's Amazonian philosophy, which, if realised, would cast the whole of the child-like element out of the female character, and at the same time extirpate from the soul of man those feminine qualities which the masculine nature, if complete, must include. Human society can only be a perfect thing when it is the matured exponent of man's nature fully developed in it ; and such development can only take place when, with due distinction and division, the contrasted parts of it, whether brought out by diversity of sex, age, rank, power, or other circumstance, are allowed an independent and separate expansion. We dare not, however, undertake the exposition of all Mr. Tennyson's hidden meanings. In these cases every reader is best contented with his own discoveries.

The faults of 'the Princess' are, in the main, faults of detail. Here and there the heroine seems to us a little too metaphysical in her discourse, as in p. 62. ; and the distinction between her real character and the unnatural one which she has chosen to assume is, in one or two instances, not so carefully maintained as is usually the case. In the college hall, for instance, we would have been better pleased to hear of her 'grave professors' having scattered 'gems of art and science,' than of the Princess herself having riveted admiring eyes by her skill in so idle a pastime. We do not know whether the general effect of the poem is the worse for the fact that its hero, like Keats's Endymion, is rather an embodiment of youthful impulses than a special and individual character. It strikes us, however, that its classical allusions are put too often into his mouth, —considering that he belongs to the fair academy in pretence alone. The diction of the poem, too, though scarcely ever quite simple or natural, seems to us occasionally too familiar. In the main it is graceful and terse, and in the more important parts it is richly expressive ; but, notwithstanding its uniformly elaborate and *recherché* tone, there are places in which its aversion to the stilted makes it colloquial to a degree hardly consistent with the dignity of poetry ;—the language of which, when most homely, should still be a 'lingua communis,' unconnected with trivial, as well as with stately associations. Occasionally also we meet with periods which in their ample sweep appear to us deficient in compactness. These faults are, however, minute in character, and interfere but little with the interest of the poem.

Many characteristic qualities of 'the Princess' will have been illustrated by our quotations: we shall remark on but a few in addition. There is a peculiar sweetness in Mr. Tennyson's vein of tenderness and pathos as exhibited in this poem. He is not one of those writers who think that the heart can never lawfully surrender till it has undergone a battery of exaggerated phrases, and who drive nails into us by way of touching our feelings. He knows that the odour from the flower-bed wafted to us in the casual gust is sure to please, but that the flower which is pressed too hard or held too near will smell of the stalk. The scene in which Psyche, who has discovered the secret of the intruders, promises at last not to betray them, is a remarkable specimen of the tender united with the playful. Equally tender, in a pathetic vein, is the description of Psyche, when, driven in disgrace from the university and wearied with wandering in the dark, she laments her child (pp. 98, 99.):—

' Ah me, my babe, my blossom, ah my child,
My one sweet child, whom I shall see no more!
For now will cruel Ida keep her back;
And either she will die from want of care,
Or sicken with ill usage, when they say
The child is hers!—for every little fault,
The child is hers; and they will beat my girl
Remembering her mother: O my flower!
Or they will take her, they will make her hard,
And she will pass me by in after-life
With some cold reverence worse than were she
    dead.
Ill mother that I was to leave her there,
To lag behind, scared by the cry they made,
The horror of the shame among them all:
But I will go and sit beside the doors,
And make a wild petition night and day,
Until they hate to hear me like a wind
Wailing for ever, till they open to me,
And lay my little blossom at my feet,
My babe, my sweet Aglaïa, my one child!
And I will take her up and go my way,
And satisfy my soul with kissing her:
Ah! what might that man not deserve of me,
Who gave me back my child?" " Be comforted,"
Said Cyril, " you shall have it:" but again
She veil'd her brows, and prone she sank, and so,
Like tender things that being caught feign death,
Spoke not, nor stirr'd.'

The descriptive power exhibited throughout the whole of 'the Princess' is of the highest order. As an example we will quote the following sketch of the female university (pp. 45, 46.):—

' At last a solemn grace
Concluded, and we sought the gardens: there
One walk'd reciting by herself, and one
In this hand held a volume as to read,
And smoothed a petted peacock down with that:

Some to a low song oar'd a shallop by,
Or under arches of the marble bridge
Hung shadow'd from the heat: some hid and
    sought
In the orange thickets: others tossed a ball
Above the fountain-jets, and back again
With laughter: others lay about the lawns,
Of the older sort, and murmur'd that their May
Was passing: what was learning unto them?
They wished to marry: they could rule a house;
Men hated learned women! and to us came
Melissa, hitting all we saw with shafts
Of gentle satire, kin to charity,
That harm'd not: so we sat; and now when day
Droop'd, and the chapel tinkled, mixt with those
Six hundred maidens clad in purest white,
Before two streams of light from wall to wall,
While the great organ almost burst his pipes,
Groaning for power, and rolling thro' the court
A long melodious thunder, to the sound
Of solemn psalms, and silver litanies,
The work of Ida, to call down from Heaven
A blessing on her labours for the world.'

Had we space we would add the description of the Princess descending with her train to the battle-field, and the picture of Florian's love, Melissa.

If extending our regard from the work before us to the body of Mr. Tennyson's poetry, we endeavour to ascertain the peculiar character of his genius, we are at once impressed by the Versatility of his imagination. In his earlier efforts he was fond of exploring new forms of beings; and sang us songs of mermen and sea fairies,—wild themes treated with no lack of verisimilitude. In his more recent efforts he has exercised the same rare faculty, by embodying the most dissimilar forms of poetic thought and sentiment. In his ' Ænone ' we have a thoroughly classic Idyl; in his ' Dora,' while the associations are English, the handling of the narrative reminds us, by its brevity, force, and rugged simplicity, of the old Hebrew legends. The spirit of the chivalrous romance meets us in his ' Morte d'Arthur :' in his ' Dream of Fair Women ' we are reminded of Dante's sharp outline, keen intensity, and definite imagery; while in his ' Recollections of the Arabian Nights,' and ' Day Dream,' we are led back to the East, and lodged in a garden of delights, where the splendour is never a mere glitter without taste or congruity,—a thing too commonly the case in that gilded furniture-poetry which takes its name from the East, and lies, amid more honest trinketry and perfumery, in the boudoir and on the dressing-table. Of all our recent poets Mr. Tennyson, we think, is the most versatile. Versatility is sometimes indeed in poetry as in life, only the exercise of that imitative power which betrays a want of individuality, original conception, and tenacity of purpose.

In such cases it proceeds from quick and volatile sympathies vividly open to external impressions, and from that clear unwrinkled mind, which, being all surface, apprehends and reflects all forms of thought, but is incapable of receiving a principle or resting in a conclusion. Poetry thus produced is the result neither of genius nor of high ability; but of that cleverness which bears often more resemblance to the former than to the latter.

Before examining into the character of Mr. Tennyson's poetry, considered relatively to that of our other recent poets, it may be well to make a few observations on that high poetic attribute, versatility, which it so strikingly exemplifies; for the purpose, first of removing some popular misapprehensions, and, secondly, of illustrating the importance of a faculty which gives to poetry its earliest impulse, and supplies it to the end with fresh materials. Genuine versatility like Mr. Tennyson's must ever be numbered among the chief poetical gifts. It consists in mobility of temperament united to a large mind, and an imagination that diffuses or concentrates itself at will. It is only when the 'various talents' are united with 'the single mind,' that they give their possessors 'moral might and mastery o'er mankind.' The Hebrew Poet says 'my heart is fixed,' and then proceeds, 'I will sing.' And it is truly when the heart is most fixed that the imagination can afford to be most flexible. It may wave like a pine tree in the breeze, if, like the pine, it sends its roots deep into the rocky soil. On these conditions, the more versatile the genius is, the ampler will be its sweep, and the mightier its resilient power. It is such versatility that enables the poet to apply his own experience, analogically and by imaginative induction, to regions unknown and forms of life untried,—at once passing into the being of others and retaining his own. The characters delineated by the greatest poets have accordingly been always remarked to possess the two great attributes of universality and individuality. But they could never unite these, if the corresponding faculties were not united in the versatile imagination and profound moral sense of the poet. For want of the former faculty there are men who can produce but a single work of value. And such writers are plagiarists even when they borrow from life itself, for they add nothing to that which they borrow. Beyond the limit of their individual experience there is for them 'nil nisi pontus et aer,' and within that narrow pasture their faculties grow lean. On the other hand how many are there who, for want of moral depth and tenacity in conjunction with versatility, remain for ever but imitators, and wholly

fail to fulfil the promise of their earlier and happier efforts.

We cannot better corroborate these opinions than by observing that the greatest of dramatists not only exhibits the faculty of versatility in its perfection, but proves to us, at the same time, that other and converse faculties are consistent with it. Shakspeare, it has been said, is but a voice. If so, it is a voice direct from nature's heart—and far indeed from the voice of a mocking bird. The *affection* which we feel for him is in itself a proof of this. In poetry, as elsewhere, those who forget themselves are the last to be forgotten by others. Shakspeare is everywhere present in his poetry, though he may be nowhere distinctly or completely seen. As the spirit of poetry tacitly pervades all nature,—refreshing, consoling, renewing,—so Shakspeare himself accompanies us through all his works, a potent and friendly genius. In all his thoughts we recognise one method of thought; his own sweet and large nature ever mediates between the natures that he describes, even when they are most discordant; his manner is familiar to us, and throughout his ample domain we recognise his genial laugh or his doubtful smile—like that of the Dryad evanescent in the branches, or the Nereid descending in the wave. Does any one need a biography to tell him whether Shakspeare was a kindly man or cold, liberal or niggardly, humble or proud? whether his faults were faults of infirmity or of malice? whether there were weeds amid his abundance, or whether his heart was a soil protected by its barrenness? whether he was a patriot, or had secluded himself from national sympathies? whether his disposition was to believe or to scoff? *These* questions, at all events, have hitherto furnished no materials for critical battles.

It is of course in dramatic poetry that versatility is most needed; but all genuine poetry is in its spirit dramatic. It would be a truism to remark, that in narrative poetry there is a dramatic element,—it being in fact the soil out of which the drama (but a more concentrated form of narration) grew. Even in idyllic, nay, in descriptive poetry, the dramatic, and therefore the versatile faculty, is also necessary; nay, the humblest object which includes the beautiful, or has ever inspired song, cannot be poetically appreciated by one who is unwilling to forget himself, or unable to pass into other forms of being. In many an orderly and compact tragedy, there is less of dramatic versatility than in Burns's allusion to a worn-out horse, or Dante's description of the bird

' who midst the leafy bower
Has in her nest sat darkling through the night,
With her sweet brood; *impatient to descry*
Their wished looks, and to bring home their food.'
(Cary's translation.)

Such things, it is obvious, cannot be thus described unless they are known—nor thus known except through the imaginative insight of the affections. Sympathy is, in truth, but versatility of heart; and large sympathies are, therefore, the most powerful auxiliaries of poetic genius. For the same reason egotism, prejudice, a habit of dogmatism, and whatever else locks up our nature, are impediments to poetry. On the other hand, among many supposed to be removed from literary influences—among the poor, and especially among children—the very essence of poetry is to be found in the form of prompt and extended sympathies. A versatile imagination is indeed the chief faculty of children. Having as yet hardly realised a self-conscious being of their own, they have the less difficulty in passing into that of others. The consequence is that their life is almost wholly poetical; all that goes on around them is a long drama; a piece of stick with a ribbon tied to it represents a king or a queen; and they can hold delighted and truly dramatic colloquy with men and women impersonated by their fancy alone. Hans Andersen's genius consists mainly in his being so far still a child. It has been often remarked, that with nations also the poetical period is that of early youth. And the reason is, that when men have ceased to be pressed down by the selfish wants of savage life, and not yet hardened and made selfish by the conventions of over civilization, the imagination has a versatility, and sympathy a vital power, which at other periods is unknown. It is then that the emotions are fresh; in other words, that a man has a power of *moving out of himself;* it is then that the most ordinary objects appear to him wonderful, and that nothing wonderful is either extraordinary or incredible; it is then that religion is natural to him, and that nature is invested with supernatural attributes, and regarded with religious awe. A lively sensibility to grief and joy, to love and to hate, is that through which all outward things acquire for us a real existence, and become objects of affection. In the absence of these, our nearest domestic interests would have for us as remote and visionary an · existence as spiritual truths possess for the merely secular intelligence; and in the presence of these, not only the animal races are brought home to our human sympathies—the brooding bird, or the faithful hound—but the inanimate elements be-

come humanized; waves and clouds live in our life; if they swell, it is in wrath; if they fly, it is in fear; if they pursue, it is in love. In other words, nature itself, and all its powers, are dramatised; and the faculty which makes them rehearse their several parts is that of a versatile imagination.

That Mr. Tennyson's versatility is the result of a high poetic mind, and not merely that of a pliable temperament, we have abundant evidence. It is associated, in the first place, with those powers of imagination and passion which belong only to original genius. However he may vary his strain, there always remains behind an identity which cannot be overlooked; and the most dissimilar of his poems are more like to each other than any of them is to the school of which it most reminds us. Lastly, we observe, that, in all his later works, his own peculiar character of poetry has become more and more pronounced, and that his poems have proportionally increased in power. The versatility of a very young poet is indeed but a part of his docility. He will listen, with the susceptive faith of youth, successively to each of the great masters of song; and the echo which remains in his ear will in some degree modulate his tone. He will trace every path which the Muse has trod, in the hope of reaching that point from which they diverge; and it is well that he should try all things, provided he hold fast to that which is best. The infancy of the life poetic, like that of all life, learns much by unconscious imitation; but it can only so learn when the poet possesses those high faculties which seek, through imitation, only to work out their own development. True genius will soon cast aside whatever is alien to its individual nature; while, on the other hand, incorporating into its proper substance all poetic elements that are truly congenial, it will blend them also with each other, and stamp upon them a unity of its own. The poet will be original when he wields collectively the powers that once were his only alternately; and versatility will then have been exalted into a higher gift,—that of comprehensiveness.

It is not in the instance of Mr. Tennyson alone that the faculty of versatility has recently shown itself, not only in a dramatic illustration of character, nature, and life, but also in the manifold power with which the same poet has produced the most dissimilar species of poetry. We need hardly name Byron, Shelley, and Keats. In these cases, and especially in the latter two, the character of the poetry produced by the same person was wholly different at different times. But in cases too numerous to be named, poetic versatility has also shown itself in a very different manner. All regions of the earth have been ransacked for the materials of poetry—Persia, Arabia, Hindostan, Iceland : it has been the ambition of the poet to reproduce the forms and manners, if not the mind, of the remotest lands ; and even where his imagination has been content to tread on English soil, it has commonly taken refuge in some remote period of our history, and recounted the Saxon legend, the chivalrous exploit, or the feuds of border warfare. Our poets may have been impelled to this practice, in part by the fact that the age in which we live is not eminently poetical, and that the unknown has always a charm. This circumstance, however, can but have supplied the external occasion for their course. Its cause is to be found within, and may be referred to the versatile powers and instincts of the imagination. Indeed, it is only in a qualified sense that we can admit our age to be unpoetical.

That any age not too late for virtue, too late for religion, and too late for the human affections, should be really too late for poetry we cannot believe,—though it may easily be unpoetical in its outward features. The Roman Empire during its decline was probably unable to produce any better poetry than those snatches of sacred song, in which, protesting against the illusive vision of corrupt sense that surrounded it, the early Christian intelligence expressed its aspirations after the realities of the world unseen. The Greek empire, during its long and mummied existence, was as incapable as modern China is of producing anything great in poetry or in the kindred arts. Surrounded by the noblest monuments of ancient genius, the best of her degenerate children could do little more than lecture on them ; and gratify with them, not a generous pride, but a narrow and sectarian vanity. In neither of these cases was it tyranny which had subdued the human mind, however tyranny may have assisted in keeping it prostrate. The positive and negative evil proceeded from the same cause. That decay of all rational and manly sentiment which connived at a despotism unsupported by the moral sense, and sustained only by arms and the superstition of custom, was inconsistent with the instincts and aspirations which incite to poetry.

Except, however, at periods of barbarism, of thoroughly corrupt morals, or of utter effeminacy, the poetic instinct will ever assert itself. For the imagination at all times pervades the whole of our nature ; and is sure to work its way up into the light, no matter through what obstructions. If the

age be a poetical one, the imagination will embody its sentiment, and illustrate its tendencies. If it be unpoetical, the imagination will not therefore be repressed. It will then create a world for itself—or revert to some historic period, the memorials of which it will invest with a radiance not their own. Unquestionably those ages are the most favourable to poetry in which the imagination can pluck the ears of corn as it passes through the field, and is not obliged to seek its food afar. At those periods in which life retains much of the adventurous, in which no political conventions can supply the place of valour and wisdom in rulers and of a generous loyalty in subjects, in which moral refinement coexists with an imperfect civilisation, in which the first great triumphs of patriotism are won, and in which temples rise from the ground at the bidding of a zeal which has not learned to measure itself or its efforts ;—at such periods it is that poetry is most genial, most real, and most authentic. Such were the periods at which Homer, Dante, and Shakspeare wrote. The heroic age of Greece, the theology and philosophy of mediæval Europe, and the manners and history of his country furnished these men respectively with the main materials of their verse. These are the great *National* poets of the world. They belong indeed to all ages ; but they belonged especially each to his own. The materials of each were supplied by the objects surrounding him, or the traditions which had descended to him by inheritance.

It would, however, be a grave error to suppose that the national is alone the great poet. On the contrary, it is among the results of poetic versatility, as well as of the instincts of the human heart, that there has ever existed in our literature, and, to no small degree, in that of other countries, two great schools of poetry, one only of which can properly be called national. It does not depend on the circumstances of the age alone whether the poet find his materials in the circle of surrounding things, or seek them elsewhere : this will in the main be determined by the constitution of his own moral nature, and the preponderance in it of a vivid sympathy with reality on the one hand, or, on the other, of an ardent aspiration after the ideal. In either case the imagination will lend to him its high mediating powers ; in the former interpreting the outward world to him, in the latter interpreting him to his fellow men. Even in the best and healthiest periods of national development the human mind will aspire after a region more exalted and pure than it can ever find on earth ; even in the most prosaic it will be able to detect something noble in the world of common things. From this double power arise two converse schools of poetry; the one characterised by its plastic power and its function of embodying the abstractedly great and the ideally beautiful; the other by its reality, its homebred sympathies, its affinities with national history, character, and manners. To expound the philosophy of these two schools would be to write a treatise on poetical versatility and imagination. On such an enterprise we cannot now adventure. We must content ourselves with some slight historical notices of the two schools among ourselves,—schools which have existed from the beginning of our literature, and which have been reproduced in our own day. The merest outline will illustrate the momentous truth that neither in nations nor individuals has poetry an isolated existence, but that it flourishes or declines in conjunction with that moral, political, and spiritual well-being which it helps to sustain. We shall conclude with some remarks on two poets of the ideal school, Shelley and Keats; with whom Mr. Tennyson has been sometimes compared —although, as we shall endeavour to show, the points of resemblance between him and them are not more marked than those of dissimilarity.

The imagination then, as we have observed, has ever recognised two great offices, distinct though allied—the one, that of representing the actual world; the other, that of creating an ideal region, into which spirits whom this world has wearied may retire. The former function, which is chiefly discharged by the 'historia spectabilis' of dramatic poetry, is that to which Bacon refers when he speaks of poetry as 'submitting the shows of things to the desires of the mind.' The latter belongs for the most part to poets lyrical or mythic, who, in the 'enchanted islands' or 'snowy cloisters' of ideal poetry have provided retreats in which spirits

' Assoiled from all encumbrance of the time,'

might rest and be thankful. Mr. Keats boasts that 'a thing of beauty is a joy for ever,' assigning as a reason that

' it still will keep
A bower quiet for us, and a sleep
Full of sweet dreams, and health, and happy breathing.'

A perfect Poet ought to unite both the great attributes of poetry. To a limited extent the greatest have done so; but even in their case the balance has ever preponderated in one direction or the other. In Greece, as in England, those two spe-

cies of poetry co-existed; but in the former neither of them connected itself with the associations of any foreign country. No region more beautiful or sacred than Greece could then be conceived of; and the Greek poet could only forsake the company of his heroes for that of his Gods. But in our northern regions, which on emerging from barbarism found the ancient literature a perfect work imperfectly explored, the South has always been regarded with feelings akin to those entertained by the Greek for the fabled Hesperia of the west. It was a region of beauty and delight on which the imagination might rest half way to heaven,—an asylum which combined the solidities of this earth with the ideal perfection of the worlds beyond. The beauty of the southern countries, their remoteness, and their ancient fame, favoured the illusion; and the imagination of England was further drawn to them by the indirect attraction of those other arts, sympathetic with poetry, which have been carried to perfection in the South alone. The southern mind moreover is more inventive than that of the North, though less thoughtful and imaginative; and as a consequence, Italian and Spanish 'Novelle' supplied the plot to half our British Dramas,—a circumstance too commonly ascribed to the single fact that on the revival of letters the literature of the South had sprung first into existence. All these influences imparted a character distinctly southern to that school of English Poetry, which was inspired rather by the love of the beautiful than by national associations, as both advanced to their development.

It was in Shakspeare and Milton that the two great schools found their chief representatives. The former is the greatest of national poets, although he occasionally forsook the national for the ideal department of song; and Milton is not a national poet, although (his ideal resulting as much from his moral sense as his imagination,) his poetry derives from his religion a reality and a solidity which seldom belongs to the ideal school. This distinction between the character of the two poets is illustrated by the different reception their works have met with. Shakspeare's sympathies were keenly native; and he has therefore ever been a favourite with the people. He is above their appreciation, indeed, but not beyond their love. His dramas have many planes of interest, which underlie each other like the concentric layers of bark produced by the annual growth of a tree; and while the most philosophic eye cannot penetrate the inmost, the most superficial is pleased with that which lies outside. Where any love of the drama remains, Shakspeare is enjoyed even by the most homely audience. But if any one were to submit to such an audience a page or two of the Paradise Lost, far from being received like the Rhapsodist of old, the Ballad-singer, or the Methodist Preacher, he would effectually disperse the crowd. The audience which Milton demanded was 'fit though few:' Shakspeare demanded none; but if people came, he probably thought 'the more the merrier.' The latter wrote for the stage, but never was at the trouble of publishing his works: the former prescribed for himself a choral audience consisting of grave divines, sage patriots, and virtuous citizens; and when this selected audience hissed him, as occasionally happened, he cursed them to their faces in Hebrew and in Greek—as 'asses, apes, and dogs,' whose portion ought to be with the schismatics who had 'railed at Latona's twin-born progeny!'

It is not, however, its deficient popularity so much as its subject and its form which proves that Milton's great work is not a national poem, high as it ranks among our national triumphs. If that mind had remained with him, which was his when English landscape supplied the scenery of his 'Allegro,' and Anglican theology inspired the moral teaching of his 'Comus,' he would probably have fulfilled his youthful intention, and celebrated Britain's mythic hero. But, instead of the great romance of the North, he wrote the religious epic of the World. Some will affirm that he illustrated, in that work, his age if not his country. His age, however, gave him hints rather than materials. Puritanism became transmuted, as it passed through his capacious and ardent mind, into a faith, Hebraic in its austere and simple spirit,—a faith that sympathised indeed with the Iconoclastic zeal which distinguished the anti-papal and anti-patristic theology of the day, but held little consent with any of the complex definitions at that time insisted on as the symbols of Protestant orthodoxy. Had the Puritan spirit been as genuine a thing as the spirit of liberty which accompanied it; had it been such as their reverence for Milton makes many persons still suppose it to have been, the mood would not so soon have yielded to the licentiousness that followed the Restoration. Milton laboured as a patriot while a field of labour was open to him: he then turned again to his true greatness, and once more confronted the mighty works of ancient genius. They pleased him still, from their severity and their simplicity: But they did not satisfy him—because they wanted elevation. When some one pointed in admiration to the dome of the Pantheon, Michael Angelo, who was already engaged on his studies for St. Peter's, rejoined, 'but I will lift it up, and plant it in heaven.' It was thus that Milton regarded the ancient Epic! And thus that in his Paradise Lost he elevated and endeavoured to spiritualise that majestic form of composition. There are many who will always regard St. Peter's temple in the air as the first of architectural monuments. The admirers of the classic will, however, feel that its amplitude and elevation are no sufficient substitute for that massive simplicity and breadth of effect which belong to the Parthenon; while those who revere our cathedrals will maintain that it lacks the variety, the mystery, the aspiration and the infinitude which characterise the Christian architecture of the North. On analogous grounds the more devoted admirers of Homer and Shakspeare will ever be dissatisfied with Milton's work—however they may venerate his genius. It is undoubtedly composite in its character—the necessary result of its uniting a Hebraic spirit with a classic form. Dante, like Milton, uses the Greek mythology freely; considering it, no doubt, as part of that inheritance of the Heathen, into possession of which Christendom had right to enter; but he uses it as a subordinate ornament, and in matters of mere detail. His poem is a Vision not an Epic, the vision of supernatural truth—of Hell, Purgatory, and Paradise—that passed before the eyes of the mediæval Church as she looked up in nocturnal vigil; not the mundane circle of life and experience, of action and of passion, exhibited in its completeness, and contemplated with calm satisfaction by a Muse that looks down from heaven. But a mystic subject, open rather to apprehension than comprehension, would not have contented Milton; who, with his classical predilections, had early laid it down as a canon that poetry should be 'simple, sensuous, and impassioned,' a statement of the utmost importance where applicable, but by no means embracing the whole truth. To him the classic model supplied, not the adornment of his poem, but its structure and form. The soul that inhabited that mould was, if we cannot say the spirit of Christianity, at least a religious spirit—profound, zealous, austere, and self-reverent—as analogous perhaps to the warlike religion of the Eastern world, as to the traditional Faith of the second Dispensation. Such was the mighty fabric which, aloof and in his native land an exile, Milton raised; not perfect, not homogeneous, not in any sense a national work,—but the greatest of all those works which prove that a noble poem may be produced with little aid from local sympathies, or national traditions.

From the earliest period of our literature, as we have observed, we have possessed the two schools, which culminated in Shakspeare and in Milton. In Chaucer the national element greatly preponderated: it reigns almost alone in many of the Canterbury Tales, especially in the humorous; but in several, of which the moral tone is higher and the execution more delicate, a southern spirit prevails. Of these his 'Second Nonne's Tale,' including the legend of St. Cecilia, is a beautiful example; illustrating, as it does, that moral influence of which the origin eluded the eye, like the invisible garland of the saint,—that influence which was exhaled from the life and manners of the first Christians, and through which, in part, their religion was diffused. The national element of our poetry, too, has always asserted itself almost exclusively in our historical ballads; that exquisite series, the musical echo of so much of our history. Surrey and Wyatt, in no slight degree, represented that Italian-Gothic school of which Spenser may be considered as the great representative. In him the spirit of chivalry elevated the love of the beautiful; and both, while ennobled by a meditative piety, were enriched by all the gentler associations of classical song. He was a man of graver mind than belonged to any of his models; and we miss in him that buoyant gaiety which animates the poets of the South: But such deficiencies were amply atoned for by that tenderly contemplative spirit which pervades his poetry. His Hymns on 'Heavenly Love' and 'Heavenly Beauty' are noble specimens of the Platonic moral philosophy: and it is probable that we can nowhere meet an exposition of the Christian Religion in its completeness and proportions, doctrinal, devotional, and practical, so searching and so large as exists in the Tenth Canto of his First Book, describing the visit of the Red Cross Knight to the 'House of Holiness.' In the Faery Queen, indeed, we find the essence of the prose Romances of the Middle Ages—as we find the essence of their theologians in Dante. Ariosto is neither more various nor more picturesque: nor is that imaginative love-sentiment which, rather than the passion itself, was the theme of the ideal poets, celebrated with more purity, refinement, and sweetness, in the sonnets of Petrarca than in those of Spenser. Spenser's faery-land will never be much frequented by those whose sympathies are exclusively with Action, Passion, and Character. But with poetic students of another class, who, if they have advanced less in the lore of life, have wandered less

from the breast of the Muses; with those by whom ideal beauty, refined sentiment, rich imagery, 'fancies chaste and noble,' harmonious numbers, and a temperament of poetry steeped in the fountains of pleasure, but irradiating them with its own purity;—with those by whom such qualities are cherished, the poetry of Spenser must ever remain a favourite haunt. It is not, indeed, a classic temple, which charms and rests the eye by the perfection of its finite proportions. Yet to it also belongs, in its several parts, that definiteness without which organic beauty cannot exist. It is a forest palace.—half natural, half artificial: we wander through groves as regular as galleries; and catch glimpses of openings like stately halls dismantled:—but our foot is ever upon flowers; and the moonlight of the allegory helps to sustain the illusion.

From the chivalrous paradise of Spenser's 'Faery Queen' to Milton's 'Paradise Lost,' the two schools of English poetry maintained a friendly rivalry. Both sources of inspiration contended at times in the same author, even when a dramatist. Marlow, in his beautiful narrative poem 'Hero and Leander'; Shakspeare, in his 'Rape of Lucrece' and his 'Venus and Adonis'; Fletcher, in his 'Faithful Shepherdess'; Shirley, in his 'Narcissus and Echo,' are southern, not only in their subject but in their mode of treating it. In Brown's 'Britannia's Pastorals,'—a poem full of beauty, and which, we are glad to see, has recently been republished in a cheap form,—the classic spirit reigns almost alone. The scenery itself is classical, though the author was probably never out of England: and its 'silver streams' and 'pleasant meads' are never depressed by the shade of northern mountains or clouds. The Sonnets of Drummond abound in an Italian beauty; as indeed do many of Daniel's, whose other writings are characterised by an English robustness and thoughtfulness. The exquisite fragments which, in his swift and brief career, were carelessly shaken from Sidney's affluent genius, are as full of the southern inspiration as the dew-drops of dawn are of light: and in Lovelace, Suckling, Carew, as well as other lyric poets of their time, we find a terseness and light-hearted grace which are not of northern origin. In Herrick the southern spirit becomes again the spirit of the antique. In the very constitution of his imagination he was a Greek: Yet he sang in no falsetto key: his thoughts were instinct with the true classical spirit; and it was, as it were, by a process of translation that he recast them in English words. It is to this circumstance that we are to attribute his occasional licence. His poetry hardly lay in the same plane with the conventional part of our Protestant morality; but his genius never stagnates near the marsh. In his poetry we

'Recognise that Idyl scene
　Where all mild creatures *without awe,*
　Amid field-flowers and pastures green
　Fulfil their being's gentle law.'*

With the exception of Milton, the period that succeeded the Restoration was as fatal to the ideal as to the national school of English poetry. The religious sentiment had bled well nigh to death, through the wounds of a society cut up with sects and with schisms. The political enthusiasm had also burned out. The sublime had been changed into the ridiculous; the performance had mocked the conception; and if Milton's majestic prose treatises had sounded the Prologue, the Epilogue of this literary drama was furnished by the shrewd and thoroughly English comment of Butler's Hudibras. The Gothic church was pulled down indeed; but the 'second temple' remained unbuilt. Cromwell passed away; and the grand and gloomy world his shoulders had supported, fell with him. As if the Puritan prophets had but prophesied in somnambulism, as if the nation had but in hypochondria fancied itself a Levitical community, as if their lofty Hebraic aspirations had been but an ethical 'renaissance' or 'the nympholepsy of some fond despair,' the work of their hands melted strangely away before the eyes, and with the seeming consent of the English people! The cavaliers had again their day; but their success turned out likewise a failure. The king had been brought back; but he could not believe in himself—and the ancient loyalty was no more. A less imaginative age had succeeded, and the pleasures of sense were called in, to supply the place of spiritual illusions dispelled. The degradations of society infected literature. The national riot, to be sure, in time subsided; but the debauch of the night left the head giddy and the stomach weak in the morning; and the epicurean had soured into the cynic. That period was succeeded by a still colder one. Its chief political work, the Revolution, was effected in business-like fashion,— but with little on either side of that faith or hope which had elevated the earlier struggle. Its theology held equally in suspicion whatever was passionate and whatever was traditional; its philosophy repudiated abstractions and *à priori* views; and its arts lacked the fervour alike of ideal conceptions and of home-bred affections. At such a time poetry

necessarily became imitative; and the Anglo-Gallican school grew up. The silver age of English poetry was adorned with writers of admirable abilities; of whom Dryden was the greatest in mental power, while Pope has left behind him the most perfect works. Conventional manners, satire, and if not moral philosophy at least moral disquisition, supplied their chief materials to that school; and in the absence of a creative spirit or a shaping art, its chief attractions were found in its executive skill, and a style accomplished, masculine, and pointed. It died out soon, however, for it had no root. Its classical allusions, taken at second hand, had never breathed a genuine classical spirit; and its disquisitions gradually degenerated into metrical treatises on botany, hunting, or medicine!

In conjunction with stronger political interests and deeper feelings on moral and religious subjects, Poetry gradually revived. It exhibited, from the first, a native origin that attested its authenticity, and in time it developed an ideal aim. The former was marked by its fidelity to nature, and its frequent reference to the rural manners of England. The nature which Thomson describes is living nature, and the blood flows freely in her veins. A refined appreciation of the graceful and the poetical he lacked; and the deficiency which makes itself ridiculous in the clumsy handling of his 'Musidora' and other narratives, exists also in his delineations of scenery. The landscapes of Thomson, like those of Rubens, are sensual, though in each case we remark that quality less than when the subject treated is higher; and in each the want of refinement and spirituality is compensated by a rich combination of less exalted merits. The poet and the painter alike present us, in their landscapes, with the 'fat of the land;' their substantial plains and well-watered meads remind us that they were intended to be meat for man and for beast; but whatever they may lack they are not deficient in reality. With an idyllic a moral poetry rose up. The moral meditations of Young had comprised much original thought of native English growth. Cowper, a kindred, though far greater poet, expressed in purer and simpler language thoughts with more of depth and of substantial worth, as well as a strain of sentiment, manly, religious, and gravely affectionate. In him, too, we find an admirable fidelity to outward nature in detail; although with her grander forms, unendeared by association, he had little sympathy; while ideal representations of scenery are no more to be found in his poetry than ideal conceptions of character.

---

* R. M Milnes.

If the poetry of Cowper belongs to our national school, that of Burns is yet more racy of the soil. He was, on the whole, more fortunately circumstanced for poetry, though he had more to contend with. The period at which he lived furnished materials sufficiently poetical, when presented to his keen insight and searching sensibilities; and Burns was luckily without that smattering of learning which often leads men from what surrounds them, without enabling them truly to appreciate the spirit of another age. He felt deeply; and he affected nothing foreign to his genius. Song and ballad, and light tale and humorous dialogue, the forms of composition with which the neighbourhood was familiar,—with these, while he ' unlocked his heart' he also interpreted that of his country. Most of those qualities which were distributed among his countrymen were concentratéd in his larger being, or embraced by his ardent sympathies. As a thousand rivulets are blended in one broad river, so the countless instincts, energies, and faculties, as well as associations, traditions, and other social influences which constitute national life, are reconciled in him whom future ages are to recognise as the poet of the nation. It is not merely the romantic side of the Scotch character which was represented in Burns,—its imagination, its patriotism, its zealous affectionateness, its love of the legendary, the marvellous and the ancient; that part, in fact, which belongs chiefly to the highlands. As amply was he furnished with the better lowland qualities, —sense, independence, courageous perseverance, shrewdness and humour; a retentive heart, and a mind truthful even when reserved. These qualities were united in his abundant nature; and his poetic temperament freed them from the limitations, which belong to every character formed upon a local type. The consequence has been that his songs are sung at the hearth and on the mountain side; his pathos is felt and his humour applauded by the village circle; his sharp descriptions and shrewd questions on grave matters are treated as indulgently by ministers of the ' National Assembly,' the ' Free Kirk,' and ' orthodox dissenters,' as Boccaccio's stories have been by the Italian clergy: and for the lonely traveller from the south the one small volume which contains his works is the best of guide-books,— not indeed to noted spots and the best inns— but to the manners, the moral soul, and the heart of the Scotch people. In other words, Burns is emphatically a national poet.

We have now brought down nearly to our own times our imperfect sketch of the two main schools into which our poetic literature may be divided: and we have already remarked that both these schools have their origin in the nature of poetry and the instincts of man. This statement derives a historical confirmation from the fact that both became extinct together, when English poetry had declined into mere imitation; and that whenever the poetic genius of England has been most powerfully developed, both have flourished together—united like the Latin and Saxon elements of our compound language. The poetic mind of England, on its revival towards the end of the last century, again as of old, manifested itself in the form of two schools which, with much in common, still represented, notwithstanding, the northern and southern hemispheres of our literature. Wordsworth and Coleridge were the chief examples of our national school; though in Coleridge the national frequently passed into a mystical inspiration; Shelley and Keats of the ideal. These were not perhaps the most popular poets of their time; but they were the most characteristic, and they have exercised the most enduring influence. We have referred to but a few of the names most generally known: but to each school belonged many writers whose works will long be remembered.

The word School, we are aware, is an inadequate one; and we use it but for the convenience of classification. The growths of the same region, however diverse in detail, have yet characteristic features in common: and it is thus also with the growths of the mind. In Mr. Coleridge's poetry the reasoning faculty is chiefly that of contemplation and intuition; in Mr. Wordsworth's, the meditative and the discursive prevails; but to both a predominance of the thoughtful is common; and in that respect both poets not only illustrate the peculiar genius of their country, but are also fit interpreters of the *spirit* of their age, as distinguished from the fashion of the moment or the sentiment of the hour. In both, too, there is a remarkable absence of the versatile faculty, as exhibited in one of the modes to which we have alluded;—and accordingly, in the poetry of both, little change has taken place except that of growth. Till their genius had found out its own nature and scope it would rehearse no other part. The ' Laodamia' of the latter shows at once what he might have done, and what it was foreign to him to do; nor does any great poet, mediæval or classical, seem to have ever drawn either of them into the sphere of his separate attraction, and detained him there. In the drama, also, neither of them had versatility enough to avoid a certain psychological effect—the result of a knowledge of character which was metaphysical rather than dramatic. In both, however, we find a deep-seated patriotism, a reverence for the hearth, a love of local traditions, an English enjoyment of nature, a humanity, mournful not seldom, and even in its cheerfulness grave—as though cheerfulness were less an instinct than a virtue or a duty. Most of these qualities exist also in the poetry of Mr. Southey, in which, with less both of thought and imagination, and a style less pregnant and felicitous, there is more of invention, and a more determined purpose. It is thus that with many and important differences poets whose individuality is complete, yet admit of being classed together. The same fact is true with respect to Shelley and Keats, and Mr. Landor and others who might be named,—poets in whom a southern temperament and more classical ideal prevails.

It was in temperament chiefly that Mr. Shelley belonged to the classical school. In intellect he was metaphysical and abstract, to a degree scarcely compatible with the sensuous character of Greek poetry. His imagination likewise, admirable as it was, differed essentially from that of the classic models. It was figurative rather than plastic. In place of moulding the subject of a poem as a whole, it scattered itself abroad in the splendour of countless metaphors, seen sometimes one through another, like a taper discerned through a taper. A beautiful image had for him an attraction independently of the thought with which it was allied ; and, once brought within the sphere of its attraction, his fancy fluttered around it, bewildered and intoxicated. A thought had for him also a value irrespectively of the place which it held in his argument : he prized it as truth ; he prized it yet more as knowledge ; and with such thoughts his poetry, at once subtly and expansively intellectual, is charged to a degree almost unprecedented. The lamentable errors which lurked in the first principles upon which he had so recklessly precipitated himself, (errors, however, hardly worse than lurk in many grave treatises welcomed with little mistrust at the present day,) of course infected his results. The conclusions, however, at which he arrived, were logical ; and those who can learn from errors as well as truths, will find a sad instruction in the coherency of his reasonings, and a comparative safety in the audacity with which they are expressed. If, for instance, we adopt the opinion—which is a suppressed premise in all his speculations, —namely, that there exists no moral evil in the nature of man except that which finds its way there accidentally,—it will be hard to avoid conclusions analogous to his, respect-

ing both religion and government. The seed at least of such principles will be planted, and their growth will depend on the ardour of the climate, and the fertility of the soil. It is only with his poetry, however, that we are now concerned. Its abstruse as well as imaginative character would have rendered it almost unintelligible, if he had not possessed, though apparently by nature rather than by study, a singular gift of language. His diction, which was searching, vigorous, various, arranged itself into periods, scholastic in the skill that joined clause on to clause, and the sustained melody of which at once discriminated the meaning and enforced the sentiment. The same dialectical precision gave dignity to his style, whether he wrote in verse or in prose ; and imparted to both the utmost clearness which the subject matter, the involved thought, and the redundant imagery allowed of. This faculty was eminently Grecian ; and the very sound of that noble language, which was not so much a study to him as a delight, will often be found in his verse. He reminds us of the Greek inspiration chiefly by the skill with which he illustrated the ancient mythology. In his ' Prometheus Unbound,' his classical vein is too often checked by political or metaphysical disquisitions most inappropriately introduced ; but in it, and in the chorusses of his ' Hellas,' there is an Æschilean energy ; and many of the classical touches in his ' Adonais' are admirably true. It is, however, in his minor poems that he most belongs to the South. His ' Hymn of Apollo' and ' Hymn of Pan' are full of the musical hilarity of the Greeks ; his ' Ode to Naples' is a true ode of compact structure and concentrated purpose ; and his ' Arethusa,' the metre of which sweeps along like a vernal torrent, and in which the nymph and the element she presides over are with such skill blended and alternated, proves that Shelley's versatile temperament included that Protean power by which the Greeks dramatised Nature and humanised all her forms.

In few writers are we more instructively reminded than in Shelley, of that analogy between the Poet and the Man, without which poetry would include little inward significance and moral power. His temperament was of the highest order. All temperaments, to be sure, except the phlegmatic, can lend themselves to poetic purposes ; but while that one which unites the saturnine with the impassioned produces poetry often, as it were, by disease, poetry is the natural expression of one like his,—sanguine and organised with the utmost of nervous sensibility. The former quality is marked by that soaring hope with which he watches the destinies of man, heralding the promise of a Future on which he—the professed enemy of Faith—had too credulous a dependence. The second we trace in the childlike wonder with which he regards the daily face of Nature ; all objects, from the far off peak to the flower at the mountain's base, wearing for him a radiance, as if the glorious apparition of the earth had but just started into existence. His disposition also, as it is described by his friends, cordial and full of sweetness, though threatening if assailed,—impetuous, yet shy at intervals, and when shy, opening no more,—makes itself felt throughout his poetry in many a passage, the sentiment of which, if deficient in robustness, is alive with pathetic tenderness. His character, too, affected as it was by outward accidents, stands up in his works conspicuous, for evil and for good. His poetry, in truth, is the embodiment of a social creed, not only dogmatic and exclusive but aggressive. His song is no voice from Nature's recesses, sent forth to indicate the whereabout of sweet and secret passion ; still less is it the orderly array of thought with which the ambitious scholar studiously adorns his theme and commends his name to posterity. It is the chaunt of the bard, or rather the war-note of the prophet-chief. In the solitudes of the soul, and when most ' hidden in the light of thought,' Shelley was a public man—bent on political designs, such designs as even now convulse the world. His spirit did not, indeed, like Milton's, ' sit in the pomp of singing robes,' but to use his own expression, ' hovered in verse o'er his accustomed prey.' Nor, in so estimating himself, did he mistake, we think, either his vocation or his abilities ; but he greatly mistook the subject and himself. He taught when he had but begun to think, and before he had begun to learn ; and the perverse error which blinded his eyes was a snare also to his feet, and made void one half of the work of his hands. Seldom have such gifts been so abused. He was strong in zeal, but weak through self-confidence : he rushed into the fight without armour, though with boundless courage ; and with the weapon of an idle and ignorant scorn he struck, not only at abuses and corruptions, which such as he are sent to plague and to destroy, but at truths older than either science or song, and higher than his highest hopes for man.

The errors of Mr. Shelley were not such as a true charity either conceals or palliates ; but as little do we deem it our duty to enlarge on them here. The infidelity of the mind has its root oftentimes in the will. The gravity and the danger of such error cannot be exaggerated ; but neither its origin, its character, nor its effects, admit of being treated of in a few words. Infidelity and blasphemy need no epithets to characterise them. Partly to account for his opinions, and partly in the passion of the hour, vices were imputed to Shelley from which we believe him to have been exempt. We should believe this (were there no other reason) because we believe that a high moral sense, and a nature, however darkened, neither corrupt nor insincere, must be the basis of all elevated poetry. One of the lessons which we have to learn from Shelley is the insufficiency of the highest moral aspirations alone to guard us against lurking evil in our spiritual nature ; and especially against that of pride—the root of infidelity, and the weakness that borders most nearly on insanity. Our theme, however, is a humbler one than that of theology, and we shall allude to Mr. Shelley's errors only as they affect him as a poet.

With great moral energies he had great moral deficiencies. Few men possessed more than he that high faculty of admiration, through which men learn so much and become so much. He gazed in admiration at all things, whether the triumphs of the human mind or the commonest achievements of mechanic skill ; yet in all his poetry we find no trace of his having possessed the kindred, but nobler habit—that of veneration : And yet, to be without veneration is to be shut out from a complete world,—the world moreover which *contains* that in which we live. The spirit of his poetry often looks up in wonder and glances around in love, and flings its gaze far forward in anger or in scorn ; but its eyes are never cast reverently downwards, —and therefore, even in its zeal for truth it overruns the ground in which truth lies. He had an intellectual defect also which corresponded with this moral one. He had no power of suspending his judgment. He could not doubt ; and his infidelity itself was in part a passionate faith in certain moral principles with which he rashly assumed Christianity to be at war ; and in part that undiscriminating hatred of priestcraft to which the fanatics of liberty are subject. His mind was extraordinarily keen, but deficient in breadth. Such minds, especially when irradiated by an imagination addicted to metaphors, admit no twilight of intelligence. All their thoughts stand out like realities, until eclipsed by rival thoughts. This one-sidedness of mind accounts in part for the fact, otherwise inexplicable, of his having denied, at an age when others at most but doubt—and obtruded rather than confessed his infidelity. His temper also was impetuous, to a degree that while it misapplied his reasonings, deprived his poetry of that perfect sanity which we find in the great masters. He was aware that it lacked self-possession and serenity. It lacked it because his whole nature,—constitutional, intellectual, and moral,—was deficient in gravity. He wrote moreover ambitiously, and with too much effort: And his genius was to a slight degree sophisticated by egotism. The ideal of every poet includes something of himself; and Shelley's nature, in its militant capacity, is indicated in his two most important works, his 'Prometheus' and his 'Revolt of Islam:' but his 'Alastor,' 'Prince of Athanase,' and many of his minor poems, prove that he was fond of dwelling upon it in other relations, and in a spirit of anatomical scrutiny. We should err, however, in our estimate of Shelley's genius if we did not allow for the degree in which its products were modified by circumstance. Ill health had preyed on him till his natural sensibility had been heightened into nervous irritability. This circumstance, together with the belief that his time in this world was short, made him over-task his faculties, which were thus ever in a hectic state of excitement. The abstract habit of his mind gave an additional daring to his conclusions; and that habit was increased by the fact that between him and his countrymen there was war. Isolation indeed always intensifies, for good or for evil, the energies of speculative men; whose powers are at once tamed down and enriched when merged in friendly communion with other minds. In the case of Shelley it also left his poetic education incomplete. He had carefully fed his mind on all things, beautiful and sublime; nor had the influences of study, philosophical, scientific, and political, been wanting to him: But living remote from practical life his genius lacked one species of nourishment, the knowledge that comes by experience. It had never been disciplined.

To estimate justly the faults as well as the merits of the truly great is a duty which we owe not only to truth and to ourselves, but to them. It is only when we know what hinderances were opposed to their greatness by the forfeits exacted from their weakness, that we can know to what that greatness might, without such obstacles, have amounted. We can but guess, therefore, what would have been the mature works of such a mind as Shelley's, when the soil had cooled down sufficiently to produce healthy growths. The manhood of human life is still but the boyhood of genius: yet how much has he not done in his brief span! There is not one of his larger works which is not a storehouse of condensed thought and beauty—

whatever may be its faults in the way of unreality or exaggeration. His 'Hymn on Intellectual Beauty,' his odes to 'Liberty,' to 'Naples,' to 'the West Wind,' his 'Cloud,' his 'Skylark,' and many a choral ode in his Lyrical Dramas, are in themselves a conclusive answer to a charge frequently brought against English Poetry, namely, that it has seldom soared into the highest region of lyrical inspiration: and in his shorter pieces there are numerous snatches of song to which the term 'essential poetry' would not be misapplied,—poems not only of magnetic power, but as flawless as the diamond, and in their minuteness as perfect as the berry on the tree or the bubble on the fountain. Great indeed is the bequest which Shelley has left us: and it is not without somewhat of remorseful sorrow that we remember what life gave him in return. Looking on what is past and gone through the serene medium of distance, all petty details vanish from our view, and a few great realities stand bare. In sad retrospection we look forth—and we see a man and a life! A young man, noble in genius, in heart ardent, full of love, his whole being expanded to all genial and cheering influences as 'a vine-leaf in the sun:'—such an one we behold, endowed richly with the treasured stores of old learning and cherished hopes for future man. With the joy of a strong swimmer he flings himself upon the stream of life—and finds himself bleeding and broken on the rocks it covers! To say 'it was his own fault' is a mode of disposing of the matter rather compendious than (to us) satisfactory. For his errors he is answerable at another tribunal than ours. The age which partakes of and fosters such errors may find time to remember his sufferings as well. Through trials not the less severe because not unprovoked, he fought his way if not in peace of conscience, yet certainly with high courage and heroic hope. He deemed that he had lived long. But he was only in his twenty-ninth year when the Mediterranean waves closed above his head. A sad career was his:—He had his intellectual resources, and he had friends; yet his was a sad career; and worthy of deeper thoughts than belong either to the region of adulation or of anger.

The genius of Keats was Grecian to a far higher degree than that of Shelley. His sense of beauty was profounder still; and was accompanied by that in which Shelley's poetry was deficient—Repose. Tranquillity is no high merit if it be attained at the expense of ardour; but the two qualities are not incompatible. The ardour of Shelley's nature shows itself in a strong evolution of thought and succession of imagery ;—that of Keats in a still intensity. The former was a fiery enthusiasm, the latter was a profound passion. Rushing through regions of unlimited thought, Shelley could but throw out hints which are often suggestive only. His designs are always outline sketches, and the lines of light in which they are drawn remind us of that 'temple of a spirit' described by him, the walls of which revealed

'A tale of passionate change divinely taught,
 Which in their winged dance unconscious genii wrought.'

Truth and action may be thus emblemed ; but beauty is a thing of shape and of colour, not of light merely, and rest is essential to it. That mystic rapidity of interwoven thought, in which Shelley exulted, was foreign to the deeper temperament of Keats. One of his canons of poetry was, that 'its touches of beauty should never be half-way, thereby making the reader breathless, instead of content. The rise, the progress, the setting of imagery, should, like the sun, come naturally to the poet, shine over him, and set soberly, although in magnificence, leaving him in the luxury of twilight.' He disliked all poetical surprises, and affirmed that poetry 'should strike the reader as a wording of his own highest thoughts, and appear almost a remembrance.' Shelley's genius, like the eagle he describes,

'*Runs down* the slanted sunlight of the dawn.'

But, beauty moves ever in curved lines, like the celestial bodies, and even in movement stimulates rest. Beauty was the adornment of Shelley's poetry ; it was the very essence of Keats's. There is in his poetry not only a constant enjoyment of the beautiful,—there is a thirst for it never to be satisfied, of which we are reminded by his portrait. Shelley admired the beautiful, Keats was absorbed in it ; and admired it no more than an infant admires the mother at whose breast he feeds. That deep absorption excluded all consciousness of self,—nay, every intrusion of alien thought ; and while the genius of others, too often like a double-reflecting crystal, returns a twofold image, that poetic vision which day by day grew clearer before Keats was an image of beauty only, whole and unbroken. There is a peculiar significance in the expression, 'a child of song,' as applied to him. Not only his outward susceptibilities retained throughout the freshness of infancy, but his whole nature possessed that integrity which belongs but to childhood, or to the purest and most energetic genius. When the poetic mood was not on him, though his heart was full of manly courage, there was much of a child's way-

wardness, want of self-command, and inexperienced weakness in his nature. His poetry is never *juvenile*. It is either the stammer of the child or the 'large utterance of the early gods.'

Keats possessed eminently the rare gift of invention—as is proved by the narrative poems he has left behind. He had also, though without Shelley's constructive skill as to the architecture of sentences, a depth, significance, and power of diction, which even the imitational affectation to be found in his earliest productions, could not disguise. He instinctively selects the words which exhibit the more characteristic qualities of the objects described. The most remarkable property of his poetry, however, is the degree in which it combines the sensuous with the ideal. The sensuousness of Keats's poetry might have degenerated into the sensual, but for the ideality that exalted it, —a union which existed in consequence of a connexion not less intimate between his sensitive temperament and his wide imagination. Perhaps we have had no other instance of a bodily constitution so poetical. With him all things were more or less sensational ; his mental faculties being, as it were, extended throughout the sensitive part of his nature—as the sense of sight, according to the theory of the Mesmerists, is diffused throughout the body on some occasions of unusual excitement. His body seemed to think ; and, on the other hand, he sometimes appears hardly to have known whether he possessed aught but body. His whole nature partook of a sensational character in this respect, namely, that every thought and sentiment came upon him with the suddenness, and appealed to him with the reality of a sensation. It is not the lowest only, but also the loftiest part of our being to which this character of unconsciousness and immediateness belongs. Intuitions and aspirations are spiritual sensations ; while the physical perceptions and appetites are bodily intuitions. Instinct itself is but a lower form of inspiration ; and the highest virtue becomes a spiritual instinct. It was in the intermediate part of our nature that Keats had but a small part. His mind had little affinity with whatever belonged to the region of the merely probable. To his heart, kindly as he was, everything in the outer world seemed foreign, except that which for the time engrossed it. His nature was Epicurean at one side, Platonist at the other—and both by irresistible instinct. The Aristotelian definition, the Stoical dogma, the Academical disputation, were to him all alike unmeaning. His poetic gift was not a separate faculty which he could exercise or restrain as he pleased, and direct to what-

ever object he chose. It was when 'by predominance of thought oppressed' that there
fell on him that still, poetic vision of truth
and beauty which only thus truly comes.
The 'burden' of his inspiration came to him
'in leni aurâ,' like the visits of the gods; yet
his fragile nature bent before it like a reed;
it was not shaken or disturbed, but wielded
by it wholly.

To the sluggish temperaments of ordinary
men excitement is pleasure. The fervour
of Keats preyed upon him with a pain from
which Shelley was protected by a mercurial
mobility; and it was with the languor of
rest that Keats associated the idea of enjoyment. How much is implied in this description of exhaustion! 'Pleasure has no
show of enticement, and Pain no unbearable
frown; neither Poetry, nor Ambition, nor
Love have any alertness of countenance; as
they pass me by they seem rather like three
figures on a Greek vase—two men and a
woman, whom no one but myself could distinguish in their disguisement. This is the
only happiness; and is a rare instance of
advantage in the body overcoming the mind.'
(P. 264. vol. i.) A nobler relief was afforded to him by that versatility which made
him live in the objects around him. It is
thus that he writes:—'I scarcely remember
counting on any happiness. I look not for
it, if it be not in the present hour. Nothing
startles me beyond the moment. The setting sun will always set me to rights; or if a
sparrow were before my window, I take part
in its existence, and pick with it, about the
gravel.' (P. 67. vol. i.) Elsewhere he
speaks thus of that form of poetic genius
which belonged to him, and which he con-
tradistinguishes from the 'egotistical sublime.' 'It has no self. It is every thing
and nothing—it has no character—it enjoys
light and shade—it lives in gusts, be it foul
or fair, high or low, rich or poor, mean
or elevated—it has as much delight in conceiving an Iago as an Imogen.' (P. 221.
vol. i.) In this passage, as elsewhere, he
seems to confound versatility with the absence of personal character. That versatility of imagination is however by no means
incompatible with depth of nature and
tenacity of purpose we have already observed; and our opinion is confirmed by a
remark of Mr. Milnes, whose life of Keats,
from which we have so largely quoted, is
enriched with many pieces of admirable
criticism. Keats's versatility showed itself,
like Mr. Tennyson's, not only in the dramatic skill with which he realised various and
alien forms of existence, but also, though to
a lesser degree, in the fact that the character of his poetry varied according to the

model he had been studying. In 'Endymion' he reminds us of Chaucer and
Spenser; in 'Hyperion' of Milton; in his
'Cap and Bells' of Ariosto; and in his
drama, the last act of which is very fine, of
Ford. Mr. Milnes remarks, with reference
to the last two works, that Keats's occasional
resemblance to other poets, though it proves
that his genius was still in a growing state,
in no degree detracts from his originality.
He did not imitate others, Mr. Milnes observes, so much as emulate them; and no
matter whom he may resemble, he is still
always himself.

The character of Keats's intellect corresponded well with his large imagination and
versatile temperament. He had not Mr.
Shelley's various and sleepless faculties, but
he had the larger mind. Keats could
neither form systems nor dispute about them;
though germs of deep and original thought
are to be found scattered in his most
careless letters. The two friends used
sometimes to contend as to the relative
worth of truth and of beauty. Beauty is the
visible embodiment of a certain species of
truth; and it was with that species that the
mind of Keats, which always worked in and
through the sensibilities, held *conscious* relations. He fancied that he had no access
to philosophy, because he was averse to definitions and dogmas, and sometimes saw
glimpses of truth in adverse systems. His
mind had itself much of that 'negative capability' which he remarked on as a large part
of Shakspeare's greatness, and which he
described as a power 'of being in uncertainties, mysteries, doubts, without any irritable
reaching after fact and reason.' (P. 93.
vol. i.) There is assuredly such a thing as
philosophical doubt, as well as philosophical belief: it is the doubt which belongs to the
mind, not to the will; to which we are not
drawn by love of singularity, and from
which we are not scared by nervous tre-
mours; the doubt which is not the denial of
anything, so much as the proving of all
things; the doubt of one who would rather
walk in mystery than in false lights, who
waits that he may win, and who prefers the
broken fragments of truth to the imposing
completeness of a delusion. Such is that
uncertainty of a large mind, which a small
mind cannot understand; and such no doubt
was, in part, that of Keats, who was fond of
saying that 'every point of thought is the
centre of an intellectual world.' The passive part of intellect, the powers of susceptibility and appreciation, Keats possessed to
an almost infinite degree: but in this respect
his mind appears to have been cast in a
feminine mould; and that masculine energy

which Shakspeare combined with a susceptive temperament unfathomably deep, in him either existed deficiently, or had not had time for its development.

If we turn from the poet to the man, from the works to the life, the retrospect is less painful in the case of Keats than of Shelley. He also suffered from ill-health, and from a temperament which, when its fine edge had to encounter the jars of life, was subject to a morbid despondency: but he had many sources of enjoyment, and his power of enjoyment was extraordinary. His disposition, which was not only sweet and simple, but tolerant and kindly, procured and preserved for him many friends. It has been commonly supposed that adverse criticism had wounded him deeply: but the charge receives a complete refutation from a letter written on the occasion referred to. In it he says, 'Praise or blame has but a momentary effect on the man whose love of beauty in the abstract makes him a severe critic on his own works. . . . I will write independently. I have written independently *without judgment*. I may write independently, and *with judgment*, hereafter. The Genius of Poetry must work out its own salvation in a man. . . . I was never afraid of failure.'

There are, however, trials in the world from which the most imaginative cannot escape; and which are more real than those which self-love alone can make important to us. Keats's sensibility amounted to disease. 'I would reject,' he writes, 'a Petrarchal coronation—on account of my dying day—and because women have cancers!' A few months later, after visiting the house of Burns, he wrote thus,—'His misery is a dead weight on the nimbleness of one's quill: I tried to forget it . . . it won't do . . . We can see, horribly clear, in the works of such a man, his whole life, as if we were God's spies.' (P. 171.) It was this extreme sensibility, not less than his ideal tendencies, which made him shrink with prescient fear from the world of actual things. Reality frowned above him like a cliff seen by a man in a nightmare dream. It fell on him at last! The most interesting of all his letters is that to his brother (p. 224. vol. i.), in which he, with little anticipation of results, describes his first meeting with the Oriental beauty who soon after became the object of his passion. In love he had always been, in one sense: and personal love was but the devotion to that in a concentrated form which he had previously and more safely loved as a thing scattered and diffused. He loved and he won; but death cheated him of the prize. Tragical indeed were his sufferings during the months of his decline. In leaving

life he lost what can never be known by the multitudes who but half live: and poetry at least could assuredly have presented him but in scant measure with the consolations which the Epicurean can dispense with most easily, but which are needed most by those whose natures are most spiritual, and whose thirst after immortality is strongest. Let us not, however, intrude into what we know not. In many things we are allowed to rejoice with him. His life had been one long revel. 'The open sky,' he writes to a friend, 'sits upon our senses like a sapphire crown: the air is our robe of state; the earth is our throne; and the sea a mighty minstrel playing before it!' Less a human being than an Imagination embodied, he passed 'like a new-born spirit,' over a world that for him ever retained the dew of the morning; and bathing in all its freshest joys he partook but little of its stain.

Shelley and Keats remained with us only long enough to let us know how much we have lost—

'We have beheld these lights but not possessed them.'

The genius of the poet whose latest work we have discussed at the beginning of this paper has been more justly appreciated than that of either of them: But it will now probably be asked to which of the two great schools of English poetry illustrated by us *he* is to be referred? The answer to that question is not easy, for in truth he has much in common with both. His earlier poems might sometimes be classed in the same category with those of Shelley and Keats: For, the three have in common an ardent temperament, a versatile imagination, and an admirable power of embodying the classical; but in other respects they differ widely. Tennyson has indeed, like Keats, with whom he has most in common, a profound sense of the beautiful, a calm and often soft intensity, a certain voluptuousness in style, that reminds us of the Venetian school of painting, and a marvellous depth and affluence of diction—but here the resemblance ends. We do not yet observe in his works, to the same degree, that union of strength with lightness and freedom of touch, which, like the unerring but unlaboured handling of a great master, characterised Keats's latest works. On the other hand, Tennyson has greater variety. Wide indeed is his domain—extending as it does from that of Keats, whose chief characteristic was ideal beauty, to that of Burns, whose songs, native to the soil, gush out as spontaneously as the warbling of the bird or the murmuring of the brook. Even in their delineation of beauty, how different are the two poets. In Keats that beauty is chiefly beauty of form; in Tennyson that of colour has at least an equal place; one consequence of which is, that while Keats, in his descriptions of nature, contents himself with embodying separate objects with a luxurious vividness, Tennyson's gallery abounds with cool far-stretching landscapes, in which the fair green plain and winding river, and violet mountain ridge and peaks of remotest snow, are harmonised through all the gradations of aerial distance. Yet his is not to be classed with that recent poetry which has been noted for a devotion, almost religious, to mere outward nature. His landscapes, like those of Titian, are for the most part but a beautiful background to the figures. Men and manners are more his theme than nature. His genius seems to tend as naturally to the idyllic as that of Shelley did to the lyrical, or that of Keats to the epic.

The moral range of Mr. Tennyson's poetry, too, is as wide as the imaginative. It is remarkable how little place, notwithstanding the ardour of Shelley and of Keats, is given in their works, to the affections properly so called. They abound in emotion and passion : in which respect Mr. Tennyson resembles them; but he is not less happy in the delineation of those human affections which depend not on instinct or imagination alone, but which, growing out of the heart, are modified by circumstance and association, and constitute the varied texture of social existence. His poetry is steeped in the charities of life, which he accompanies from the cradle to the grave. He has a Shakspearean enjoyment in whatever is human, and a Shakspearean indulgence for the frailties of humanity; the life which his verse illustrates with a genial cheer or a forlorn pathos, is life in its homely honesty, life with its old familiar associations and accidents, its 'merry quips' remembered sadly at the death of the old year, its 'flowing can' and its 'empty cup.' The truth of this statement will at once be recognised by all who have read his 'Miller's Daughter,' his 'May Queen,' and 'New Year's Eve,' with their beautiful 'Conclusion;' his 'Dora,' 'Audley Court,' 'Talking Oak,' or his 'Lyrical Monologue.'

Nor is his intellectual region less ample. Many of his poems are the embodiment of deep philosophical speculations on the problem of life. We allude to such pieces as the 'Palace of Art,' 'The Two Voices,' the 'Vision of Sin,' and those brief but admirable political poems, 'You ask me why

though ill at ease,' and 'Of old sat Freedom on the Heights.' In these poems, whether metaphysical or ethical, there is a characteristic difference between the style of Mr. Tennyson and Shelley ; the latter of whom was essentially dogmatic in the corresponding part of his works, while the former, with an interest not less deep in the intellectual and political progress of the human race, speaks only in the way of suggestion, and in his significant hints reminds us of Mr. Keats's expression, ' Man should not dispute or assert, but whisper results to his neighbour.' In this department of Mr. Tennyson's poetry we can, perhaps, trace the influences of German literature, modified by an English mind, and, we are glad to observe, by English traditions.

Mr. Tennyson's genius, so far as we can pretend to judge of what is so large and manifold, is, perhaps, on the whole, most strikingly characterised by that peculiar species of versatility which, as we have already observed, is the application of the dramatic faculty to other subjects instead of the drama. All his important poems are complete embodiments, not merely illustrations of the subject treated. Each is evidently the result of long musings, meditative and imaginative; and each represents, in its integrity and distinctness, an entire system of thought, sentiment, manners, and imagery. Each is a window from which we have a vista of a new and distinct world. In each, too, we come to know far more of the characters than is explicitly stated ; we know their past as well as their present, and speculate about their associates. How much, for instance, of our time and country do we find in ' Locksley-Hall,' that admirable delineation of the modern Outlaw, the over-developed and undisciplined youth, the spoilt child and cast-away son of the nineteenth century ! How many tracts against asceticism are condensed in his St. Simeon ! Whether idyllic or philosophic in form, not a few of these poems are at heart dramas. If it were true, which we cannot believe, that the drama is amongst us but an anachronism, such poems would be perhaps the most appropriate substitute for it. They are remarkable also as works of art. Mr. Tennyson is a great artist; nor would it have been possible without much study, as well as a singular plastic power, to have given his poems that perfection of shape which enables a slender mould to sustain a various interest.

It is frequently asked whether Mr. Tennyson is capable of producing a great and national work. Hitherto such has obviously not been his ambition; nor can we think any man wise who, instead of keeping such a design steadily before him, and making all his labours a preparation for it, embarks on the execution of it at a period earlier than that at which his faculties and his experience approach their maturity. A great poem is a great action; and requires the assiduous exercise of those high moral powers with which criticism has no concern, and action much;—courage, prudence, enterprise, patience, self-reliance founded on self-knowledge, a magnanimous superiority to petty obstacles, a disinterested devotion to art for its own sake, and for that of all which it interprets and communicates. Should Mr. Tennyson devote himself to a great work, he has already exhibited the faculties necessary for his success: But, whether he writes it or not, he has taken his place among the true poets of his country. With reference to a national poem, and to our previous observations concerning the ideal and the national in poetry, we may remark, that Mr. Tennyson's progress has constantly been towards the latter, while he has carried along with him many attributes of the former. His early poems, steeped as they were in a certain fruit-like richness, and illumined by gleams of an imagination at once radiant and pathetic, like the lights of an evening horizon, were deficient, as all young poetry is, in subject and substance. They had then also a defect, which they shared with much of Shelley's and some of Keats's—that of appearing poetry, distilled from poetry, rather than drawn from the living sources of life and of truth. But that defect has long since been corrected; and it is observable, that in proportion as his poetry has become more robust and characteristic, it has also become more home-bred. He has given us admirably characteristic landscapes from almost all countries; but it is plainly among the meads and lawns of his native land that his imagination finds a home. Nor is it English scenery only that he illustrates with such truth and power, but English manners likewise; indeed, when we say that his poetry does not shrink from the interests and accidents of daily life, it is especially English life to which we refer. It is not merely the romantic tale that he records, as in ' Godiva' and ' The Lord of Burleigh,' but many a modern trait from the village green, the corn-field, the manor-house, many a recollection from college life, or the social circle. The tale which we have reviewed, though not English in subject, is yet eminently English in its setting. That modern England does not contain the materials of poetry we cannot believe, as long as we find that it produces the faculties that tend to poetry;

but those materials unquestionably are obscured by the rubbish that now overlays them; and to extricate and exhibit them requires, therefore, unusual poetic discernment. The difficulty of illustrating our modern manners is increased by the fact that they include much from which poetic sympathies recoil. A deep interest in national manners and history is the best imaginative preparation for a national poem. In what way the poetical side of modern life might be seized and set forth on a large scale, is a problem well worth consideration; but our limits deter us from even an attempt at the solution of it. Assuredly that life will not be poetically exhibited merely by allusions to its outward accidents,—its railways, and its steamboats, or by the application of poetry, in the spirit of a partisan, to the disputes of the hour. To delineate modern life, the first thing must be to understand human life; and the second to trace its permanent relations as they are modified by the more essential characteristics of modern society. In this process the poet will be assisted in proportion as his sympathies are vivid, as his habits are thoughtful, and as his versatile imagination unites itself to fixed principles. The sympathies which give power to those who feel them, are such as help their immediate objects likewise. The man must feel himself a part of that life which he would illustrate (though the poet in the man, must ever preserve his isolation); the hand must inform the heart, and the heart direct the mind; for it is through the neighbourly duties alone that the universal relations of society become understood vitally. Scanned in speculation alone, they are a theme for the philosopher, not the poet.

———

V.

THEORIES OF POETRY.[1]

THERE have been hundreds of disquisitions on poetry in all ages, long and short, good, bad, and indifferent; and, now-a-days, we cannot open a magazine or a review without finding something new said about our friend " *The* Poet," as distinguished from our other friend " *The* Prophet " and the rest. But cant cannot be helped; and, if we are to abandon good phrases because they have been used a great many times, there is an end to all reviewing.

Much, however, as has been spoken about poetry and poets, it may be doubted whether the world, in its meditations on this subject, has got far beyond the antithesis suggested by what Aristotle said about it two thousand years ago, on the one hand, and what Bacon advanced two hundred and fifty years ago, on

---

[1] *North British Review*, August 1853.—" Poetics : an Essay on Poetry." By E. S. Dallas. London, 1852.

the other. At least, acquainted as we are with a good
deal that Wordsworth, and Coleridge, and Goethe, and
Leigh Hunt, and now Mr. Dallas, have written about
poetry by way of more subtle and insinuating investigation, we still feel that the best notion of the thing,
for any manageable purpose, is to be beaten out of
the rough-hewn definitions of it, from opposite sides,
supplied by Aristotle and Bacon. In his *Poetics,*
Aristotle writes as follows :—

"Epic poetry and the poetry of tragedy, as well as
comedy and dithyrambic poetry, and most flute and
lyre music, all are, in their nature, viewed generally,
imitations (μιμήσεις) ; differing from each other, however, in three things—either in that they imitate by
different means, or in that they imitate different things,
or in that they imitate differently and not in the same
manner. For, as some artists, either from technical
training or from mere habit, imitate various objects by
colours and forms, and other artists by vocal sound,
so, of the arts mentioned above, all effect their imitation by rhythm, and words, and melody, employed
either severally or in combination. For example, in
flute and lyre music, and in any other kind of music
having similar effect, such as pipe music, melody and
rhythm are alone used. In the dance, again, the imitation is accomplished by rhythm by itself, without
melody ; there being dancers who, by means of rhythmical gesticulations, imitate even manners, passions, and
acts. Lastly, epic poetry produces its imitations either
by mere articulate words, or by metre superadded. . . .

Since, in the second place, those who imitate copy living characters, it behoves imitations either to be of serious and lofty, or of mean and trivial objects. The imitation must, in fact, either be of characters and actions better than they are found among ourselves, or worse, or much the same; just as, among painters, Polygnotus represented people better-looking than they were, Pauson worse-looking, and Dionysius exactly as they were. Now, it is evident that each of the arts above mentioned will have these differences, the difference arising from their imitating different things. In the dance, and in flute and lyre music, these diversities are visible; as also in word-imitations and simple metre. Homer, for example, really made men better than they are; Cleophon made them such as they are; whereas Hegemon, the first writer of parodies, and Nicochares, made them worse. So also, in dithyrambics and lyrics, one might, with Timotheus and Philoxenus, imitate even Persians and Cyclopes. By this very difference, too, is tragedy distinguished from comedy. The one even now strives in its imitations to exhibit men better than they are, the other worse. . . . Still the third difference remains : namely, as to the manner or form of the imitation. For, even though the means of imitation, and the things imitated, should be the same, there might be this difference, that the imitation might be made either in the form of a narration (and that either through an alien narrator, as Homer does, or in one's own person without changing) or by representing the imitators as all active and taking part. So that, though in one respect Homer and Sophocles would go together as imitators, as both having earnest subjects, in another Sophocles and Aristophanes would go together, as both imitating dramatically. . . . Two causes, both of them natural, seem to have operated together to originate the poetic art. The first is that the tendency to imitate is innate in men from childhood (the difference between man and other animals being that he is the most imitative of all, acquiring even his first lessons in knowledge through imitation) and that all take pleasure in imitation. . . . . In the second place, just as the tendency to imitate is natural to us, so also is the love of melody and of rhythm ; and metre is evidently a variety of rhythm. Those, therefore, who from the first were most strongly inclined to these things by nature, proceeding by little and little, originated poetry out of their impromptu fancies. Poetry, thus originated, was broken into departments corresponding to the peculiar characters of its producers, the more serious imitating only beautiful actions and their issues, while the more thoughtless natures imitated mean incidents, inventing lampoons, as others had invented hymns and eulogies. Before Homer we have no poem of this kind to be mentioned, though doubtless many existed."

Such, as indicated in those sentences of the treatise which seem to be of most essential import, is the general doctrine of Aristotle as to the nature of Poetry. With this contrast Bacon's theory, as stated, cursorily but profoundly, in the following sentences from the *Advancement of Learning* :—

" The parts of Human Learning have reference to the three parts of man's understanding, which is the seat of learning—History to his Memory; Poesy to his Imagination; and Philosophy to his Reason. . . . Poesy is a part of learning, in measure of words for the most part restrained, but in all other points extremely licensed, and doth truly refer to the imagination; which, being not tied to the laws of matter, may at pleasure join that which Nature hath severed, and sever that which Nature hath joined, and so make unlawful matches and divorces of things. *Pictoribus atque Poetis*, &c. It [Poetry] is taken in two senses— in respect of words, or matter. In the first sense, it is but a character of style, and belongeth to the arts of speech, and is not pertinent for the present; in the latter, it is, as hath been said, one of the principal portions of learning, and is nothing else but Feigned History, which may be styled as well in prose as in verse. The use of this Feigned History hath been to give some shadow of satisfaction to the mind of man in the points wherein the nature of things doth deny it— the world being in proportion inferior to the soul; by reason whereof there is agreeable to the spirit of man a more ample greatness, a more exact goodness, and a more absolute variety than can be found in the nature of things. Therefore, because the acts or events of true history have not that magnitude which satisfieth the mind of man, Poesy feigneth acts and events greater and more heroical; because true history propoundeth the successes and the issues of actions not so agree-able to the merits of virtue and vice, therefore Poesy feigneth them more just in retribution, and more according to revealed Providence; because true his-tory representeth actions and events more ordinary and less interchanged, therefore Poesy endueth them

with more rareness : so as it appeareth that Poesy
serveth and conferreth to magnanimity, morality, and
delectation. And, therefore, it was ever thought to
have some participation of divineness, because it
doth raise and erect the mind, by submitting the shows
of things to the desires of the mind, whereas Reason
doth buckle and bow the mind unto the nature of
things. . . . In this third part of learning, which is
Poesy, I can report no deficience. For, being as a
plant that cometh of the lust of the earth without a
formal seed, it hath sprung up and spread abroad more
than any other kind."

Now, though it would be possible so to stretch and
comment upon Aristotle's theory of poetry as to make
it correspond with Bacon's, yet, *primâ facie*, the two
theories are different, and even antithetical. If both
are true, it is because the theorists tilt at opposite
sides of the shield. Aristotle makes the essence of
Poetry to consist in its being imitative and truthful ;
Bacon, in its being creative and fantastical. According
to Aristotle, there is a natural tendency in men to the
imitation of what they see in nature ; the various arts
are nothing more than imitations, so to speak, with different kinds of imitating substance ; and poetry is that
art which imitates in articulate language, or, at most,
in language elevated and rendered more rich and exquisite by the addition of metre. According to Bacon,
on the other hand, there is a natural tendency, and

a natural prerogative, in the mind of man to condition
the universe anew for its own intellectual satisfaction.
It may brood over the sea of actual existences, carrying on the work of creation, with these existences for
the material, and its own phantasies and longings for
the informing spirit; it may be ever on the wing
among nature's sounds and appearances, not merely
for the purpose of observing and co-ordinating them,
but also that it may delight itself with new ideal combinations, severing what nature has joined, and joining
what nature has put asunder. Poetry, in accordance
with this view, might perhaps be defined as the art of
producing, by means of articulate language, metrical
or unmetrical, a *fictitious concrete*, either like to something existing in nature, or, if unlike anything there
existing, justifying that unlikeness by the charm of its
own impressiveness.

Amid all the discussions of all the critics as to the
nature of poetry, this antagonism, if such it is, between the Aristotelian and the Baconian theories, will
be found eternally reproducing itself.

When Wordsworth defined poetry to be "emotion
recollected in tranquillity," and declared it to be the
business of the poet to represent out of real life, and
as nearly as possible in the language of real life, scenes
and events of an affecting or exciting character, he
reverted, and with good effect, to the imitation-theory

of Aristotle. All Coleridge's disquisitions, on the other
hand, even when his friend Wordsworth is the theme
and exemplar, are subtle developments of the imagina-
tion-theory of Bacon. His famous remark that the
true antithesis is not Poetry and Prose, but Poetry and
Science, is but another form of Bacon's remark, that,
whereas it is the part of Reason "to buckle and bow
the mind to the nature of things," it is the part of
Imagination, as the poetical faculty, "to raise the mind
by submitting the shows of things to its desires." And
so with the definitions, more or less formal, of other
writers. Thus Leigh Hunt: "Poetry is the utterance
of a passion for truth, beauty, and power, embodying
and illustrating its conceptions by imagination and
fancy, and modulating its language on the principle
of variety in uniformity." That this definition, notwithstanding that it is constructed on the principle of
omitting nothing that any one would like to see included, is yet essentially a glimpse from the Baconian
side of the shield, is obvious from the fact that its
author afterwards uses as synonymous with it the
abbreviations "Imaginative passion," "Passion for imaginative pleasure." Lastly, Mr. Dallas, with all his
ingenuity, does not really get much farther in the end.
Beginning with an expression of dissatisfaction with all
existing definitions of poetry, Aristotle's and Bacon's
included, as being definitions of the thing not in itself,

but in its accidents, he proceeds first, very properly, to make a distinction between poetical feeling, which all men have, and the art of poetical expression, which is the prerogative of those who are called poets. Both are usually included under the term Poetry; but, to avoid confusion, Mr. Dallas proposes to use the general term Poetry for the poetical feeling, and to call the art which caters for that feeling Poesy. Then, taking for his guide the fact that all have agreed that, whatever poetry is, it has *pleasure* for its end, he seeks to work his way to the required definition through a prior analysis of the nature of pleasure. Having, as the result of this analysis, defined pleasure to be "the harmonious and unconscious activity of the soul," he finds his way then clear. For there are various kinds of pleasure, and poetry is one of these. It is "imaginative pleasure;" or, if we write the thing more fully out, it is the "imaginative harmonious and unconscious activity of the soul," or that kind of harmonious and unconscious activity of the soul which consists in the exercise of the imagination. Poesy, of course, is the corresponding art, the art of producing what will give imaginative pleasure. Now, with all our respect for the ability with which Mr. Dallas conducts his investigation, and our relish for the many lucid and deep remarks which drop from his pen in the course of it, we must say that, as respects the main matter

in discussion, his investigation does not leave us fully
satisfied. "Poetry is imaginative pleasure": very
well; but Bacon had said substantially the same
thing when he described poetry as a kind of literature
having reference to the imagination; and Leigh Hunt
had, as we have seen, anticipated the exact phrase,
defining poetry to be "imaginative passion," and the
faculty of the poet to be the faculty of "producing
imaginative pleasure." In short, the whole difficulty,
the very essence of the question, consists not in the
word *pleasure*, but in the word *imaginative*. Had Mr.
Dallas bestowed half the pains on the illustration of
what is meant by imagination that he has bestowed
on the analysis of what is meant by pleasure, he would
have done the science of poetry more service. This—
the nature of the imaginative faculty—is "the vapor-
ous drop profound that hangs upon the corner of the
moon," and Mr. Dallas has not endeavoured to catch it.
His chapter upon the Law of Imagination is one of the
most cursory in the book; and the total result, as
far as a fit definition of poetry is concerned, is that
he ends in finding himself in the same hut with
Bacon, after having refused its shelter.

The antagonism between the Aristotelian theory,
which makes poetry to consist in imitative passion,
and the Baconian theory, which makes it to consist in
imaginative passion, is curiously reproducing itself at

present [1853] in the kindred art of painting. Pre-Raphaelitism is in painting very much what the reform led by Wordsworth was in poetical literature. Imitate nature; reproduce her exact and literal forms; do not paint ideal trees or vague recollections of trees, ideal brick-walls or vague recollections of brick-walls, but actual trees and actual brick-walls; dismiss from your minds the trash of Sir Joshua Reynolds about "correcting nature," "improving nature," and the like;—such are the maxims addressed by the Pre-Raphaelites, both with brush and with pen, to their fellow-artists. All this is, we say, a return to the theory of Aristotle, which makes the essence of art to consist in Imitation, and a protest against that of Bacon, which makes the essence of art to consist in Ideali-zation. Poor Sir Joshua Reynolds ought to fall back upon Bacon, so that, when he is next attacked for his phrases "improving nature" and the like, the Pre-Raphaelites may see looming behind him the more formidable figure of a man whose words no one dares to call trash, and whose very definition of art was couched in expressions like these: "There is, agree-able to the spirit of man, a more ample greatness, a more exact goodness, and a more absolute variety than can be found in the nature of things " "The use of feigned history is to give to the mind of man some shadow of satisfaction in those points wherein the

nature of things doth deny it." The battle, we say,
must be fought with these phrases. Nor is the battle
confined to the art of painting. There is a more
restricted kind of Pre-Raphaelitism now making its
way in the department of fictitious literature. Admiring the reality, the truthfulness, of Thackeray's delineations of life and society, there are men who will
have nothing to do with what they call the phantasies and caricatures of the Dickens school. The
business of the novelist, they say, is to represent men
as they are, with all their foibles as well as their
virtues; in other words, to imitate real life. Here
again comes in the Baconian thunder. "Because the
acts or events of true history have not that magnitude
which satisfieth the mind of man, poesy (and Bacon's
definition of poesy includes prose fiction) feigneth
acts and events greater and more heroical." Whether
Dickens can take the benefit of this authority, in
those cases where he is charged with unreality, we
need not inquire; it evidently points, however, to a
possible style of prose fiction different from that of
Fielding and Thackeray, and yet as legitimate in the
view of art.

For ourselves, we hold the imitation-theory as
applied to poetry or art to be so inadequate in
essential respects that it would be time lost to try
to mend it; and we find no suitable statement of

what seems to be the very idea of poetry, except in some definition like that of Bacon.

Only consider the matter for a moment. Take any piece of verse from any poet, and in what single respect can that piece of verse be said to be an imitation of nature? In the first place, that it is verse at all is a huge deviation in itself from what is, in any ordinary sense, natural. Men do not talk in good literary prose, much less in blank verse or rhyme. Macbeth, in his utmost strait and horror—Lear, when the lightnings scathed his white head—did not actually talk in metre. Even Bruce at Bannockburn did not address his army in trochees. Here, then, at the very outset, there is a break-down in the theory of Imitation, or literal truth to nature. And all prose literature shares in this break-down. Not a single personage in Scott's novels would have spoken precisely as Scott makes them speak; nay, nor is there a single character in Thackeray himself strictly and in every respect a fac-simile of what is real. Correct grammar, sentences of varied lengths and of various cadences, much more octosyllabic or pentameter verse, and still more rhymed stanzas, are all artificialities. Literature has them, but in real life they are not to be found. It is as truly a deviation from nature to represent a king talking in blank verse, or a lover plaining in rhyme, as it is, in an opera, to make a martyr sing a song and be encored

before being thrown into the flames. So far as truth
to nature is concerned, an opera, or even a ballet, is
hardly more artificial than a drama. Suppose, however, that, in order to escape from this difficulty, it
should be said that metre, rhyme, rhetorical consecutiveness, and the like, are conditions previously and
for other reasons existing in the material in which
the imitation is to take place: would the theory of
imitation or truth to nature even then hold good? Let
it be granted that grammatical and rhythmical prose is
a kind of marble, that blank verse is a kind of jasper,
and that rhymed verse is a kind of amethyst or
opaline; that the selection of those substances as the
materials in which the imitation is to be effected is
a thing already and independently determined on; and
that it is only in so far as imitation can be achieved
consistently with the nature of those substances that
imitation and art are held to be synonymous. Will the
theory even then look the facts in the face? It will
not. In the time of Aristotle, indeed, when most
Greek poetry was, to a greater degree than poetry is
now, either directly descriptive or directly narrative,
the theory might have seemed less astray than it must
to us. Even then, however, it was necessarily at fault.
The Achilles and the Ajax of Homer, the Œdipus and
the Antigone of Sophocles, were, in no sense, imitations
from nature; they were ideal beings, never seen on

any Ægæan coast, and dwelling nowhere save in the halls of imagination. Aristotle himself felt this; and hence, at the risk of cracking into pieces his own fundamental theory, he indulges occasionally in a strain like that of Bacon when he maintains that poetry "representeth actions and events less ordinary and interchanged, and endueth them with more rareness," than is found in nature. "The poet's business," says Aristotle, "is not to tell events as they have actually happened, but as they possibly might happen." And again: "Poetry is more philosophical and more sublime than history." Very true: but what then becomes of the imitation? In what possible sense can there be imitation unless there is something to be imitated? If that something is ideal, if it exists not actually and outwardly, but only in the mind of the artist, then imitation is the wrong word to use.

All this will be much more obvious if we refer to modern poetry. Here is a stanza from Spenser—part of his description of the access to Mammon's cave He has just described Revenge, Jealousy, Fear, Shame and other entities.

"And over them sad Horror with grim hue
Did always soar, beating his iron wings;
And after him owls and night-ravens flew,
The hateful messengers of heavy things,
Of death and dolour telling sad tidings

P

While sad Celeno, sitting on a clift,
A song of bale and bitter sorrow sings,
That heart of flint asunder could have rift ;
Which having ended, after him she flieth swift."

This is true poetry; and yet, by no possible ingenuity, short of that which identified King Jeremiah with pickled cucumbers, could it be shown to consist of imitation. If it be said that it is mimic creation, and that this is the sense in which Aristotle meant his imitation, or μίμησις, to be understood, we shall be very glad to accept the explanation; but then we shall have to reply that, as the essence of the business lies in the word "creation" as the substantive of the phrase, it is a pity the brunt of the disquisition should have been borne so long by the adjective. Aristotle, we believe, did mean that poetry was, in the main, fiction, or invention of fables in imitation of nature; but, unfortunately, even then he misleads by making imitation, which is but the jackal in the treatise, seem the lion in the definition. Nor even then will his theory be faultless and complete. Spenser's grim-hued Horror, soaring aloft, beating his iron wings, and with owls and night-ravens after him, is certainly a creation ; but in what sense it is a *mimic* creation, or a creation in imitation of nature, it would take a critic, lost to all reasonable use of words, to show.

In short, and to close this discussion with a phrase

which seems to us to fall like a block of stone through all our reasonings about art imitating nature, being true to nature, and the like, "Art is *called* art," said Goethe, "simply because it is *not* nature." This, it will be seen, is identical with Bacon's poesy "submitting the shows of things to the desires of the mind." Only in one sense can it be said that the art itself comes under the denomination of nature. Thus, Shakespeare—

> "E'en that art,
> Which, you say, adds to nature, is an art
> That nature makes."

True, as Goethe would have been the first to admit! In this sense, Spenser's grim-hued Horror beating his iron wings *was* a part of nature, because, in this sense, the poet's own soul, with that very imagination starting out of it, was involved and contained in the universal round. But in any sense in which the words art and nature are available for the purposes of critical exposition, Goethe's saying is irrefragable: "Art is *called* art simply because it is *not* nature." Dissolve the poet through nature, regard the creative act itself as a part of nature, and then, of course, poetry or art is truth to nature. But keep them distinct, as you must do if you talk of imitation, and then the poet is nature's master, changer, tyrant, lover, watcher, slave, and mimic, all in one, his head now low

in her lap and again, a moment after, she scared and
weeping because, though he is with her, he minds
her not.

All this, we believe, it is very necessary to say.
Pre-Raphaelitism in painting, like Wordsworth's reform in poetical literature (which reform consisted
in the precept and example of what may be called
Pre-Drydenism), we regard, so far as it is a recall of
art to truth and observation, as an unmixed good. But
it is essentially, in this particular respect, a reform only
in the *language* of art; and art itself is not language,
but the creative use of it. We believe the Pre-
Raphaelites know this ; for, though, in theorizing, they
naturally put forward their favourite idea of imitation
or truthfulness, yet in their practice they are as much
imaginative artists as imitative. While in any of the
higher Pre-Raphaelite paintings the *language* of the
painting—that is, the flowers, grasses, foliage, brick-
walls, and costumes—may be more real and true to
fact than elsewhere, yet the *thought* which this language
is used to convey is as ideal, as much a supposition,
imagination, or recombination, as much a mere wish or
utinam, as in the majority of other pictures. Still, in
our theory of art at the present day, or at least in our
theory of literary art, the notion of imitation is beginning to exist in excess. The very power of that most
admirable novelist, Thackeray, is beginning to spoil us.

We will have nothing but reality, nothing but true renderings of men and women as they are ; no giants or demigods any more, but persons of ordinary stature, and the black and the white in character so mixed that people shall neither seem crows nor white doves, but all more or less magpies. Good, certainly, all this ; but, had the rule always been peremptory, where had been our Achilleses, our Prometheuses, our Tancreds, our Lears, our Hamlets, our Fausts, our Egmonts ; these men that never were, these idealizations of what might be—not copied from nature, but imagined and full-fashioned by the soul of man, and thence disenchained into nature, magnificent phantasms, to roam amid its vacancies ? Nor will it do to exempt the epic and the tragic muses, and to subject to the rule only the muse of prose fiction. Where, in that case, had been our Quixotes, our Pantagruels and Panurges, our Ivanhoes and Rebeccas, our Fixleins and Siebenkaeses ? These were sublimations of nature, not imitations ; suggestions to history by genius and an inspired philosophy. The muse of prose literature is very hardly dealt with. Why in prose may there not be much of that license in the fantastic, that measured riot, that right of whimsy, that unabashed dalliance with the extreme and beautiful, which the world allows by prescription to verse ? Why may not prose chase forest-nymphs, and see little green-eyed elves, and delight in

peonies and musk-roses, and invoke the stars, and roll
mists about the hills, and watch the seas thundering
through caverns and dashing against promontories?
Why, in prose, quail from the grand or ghastly on the
one hand, or blush with shame at too much of the
exquisite on the other? Is prose made of iron? Must
it never weep, never laugh, never linger to look at a
buttercup, never ride at a gallop over the downs?
Always at a steady trot, transacting only such business
as may be done within the limits of a soft sigh on the
one hand and a thin smile on the other, must it leave
all finer and higher work of imagination to the care
of Verse? Partly so, perhaps; for prose soon becomes
ashamed, and, when highly inspired, lifts itself into
metre. Yet it is well for literature that there should
be among us such prose-poets as Richter was to the
Germans: men avoiding nothing as too fantastic for
their element, but free and daring in it as the verse-
poet in his. All honour to Thackeray and the prose-
fiction of social reality; but let us not so theorize as to
exclude from prose-fiction the boundless imagination of
another Richter, or even the lawless zanyism of another
Rabelais.

Poetry, then, we must, after all, define in terms
tantamount to those of Bacon. With Bacon himself
we may define it vaguely as having reference to the

imagination, " which faculty submitteth the shows of
things to the desires of the mind, whereas reason doth
buckle and bow the mind unto the nature of things."
Or we may vary the phrase, and, with Coleridge, call it
" the vision and faculty divine ; " or, with Leigh Hunt,
" imaginative passion," the passion for " imaginative
pleasure ; " or, with Mr. Dallas, more analytically, " the
imaginative, harmonious, and unconscious activity of
the soul." In any case, IMAGINATION is the main word,
the main idea. Upon this Shakespeare himself has put
his seal :

> " The lunatic, the lover, and the poet,
> Are of *imagination* all compact."

In short, poesy is what the Greek language recognised
it to be—ποίησις, or creation. The antithesis, therefore, *is* between Poetry and Science—ποίησις and
νόησις. Let the universe of all accumulated existence, inner and outer, material and mental, up to the
present moment, lie under one like a sea, and there
are two ways in which it may be intellectually dealt
with and brooded over. On the one hand, the intellect of man may brood over it inquiringly, striving to
penetrate it through and through, to understand the
system of laws by which its multitudinous atoms are
held together, to master the mystery of its pulsations
and sequences. This is the mood of the man of
science. On the other hand, the man of intellect may

brood over it creatively, careless how it is held together, or whether it is held together at all, and
regarding it only as material to be submitted farther
to the operation of a combining energy, and lashed and
beaten up into new existences. This is the mood of
the poet. The poet is emphatically the man who continues the work of creation; who forms, fashions, combines, imagines; who breathes his own spirit into
things; who conditions the universe anew according
to his whim and pleasure; who bestows heads of brass
on men when he likes, and sees beautiful women with
arms of azure; who walks amid Nature's appearances, divorcing them, rematching them, interweaving
them, starting at every step flocks of white-winged
phantasies that fly and flutter into the ether of the
future.

All very well; but, in plain English, what is meant
by this imagination, this creative faculty, which is
allowed by all to be the characteristic of the poet?
Mr. Dallas tells us that psychologists differ in their
definitions of imagination. Dugald Stewart, and others,
he says, have regarded it solely as the faculty which
looks to the possible and unknown, which invents hip-
pogriffs and the like ideal beasts—in short, the creative
faculty proper. Mr. Dallas maintains that this is not
sufficient, and that the faculty unphilosophically called
Conception, the faculty which mirrors or reproduces the

real, must also be included in the poetic imagination.
And this is nearly all that he says on the subject.

Now, if we were to venture on a closer definition,
such as might be found applicable over the whole
domain of poetry, we should perhaps affirm something
to the following effect:—The poetic or imaginative
faculty is *the power of intellectually producing a new or
artificial concrete;* and the poetic genius or temperament is *that disposition of mind which leads habitually,
or by preference, to this kind of intellectual exercise.*

There is much in this statement that might need
explanation. In the first place, we would call attention
to the words " intellectually producing," " intellectual
exercise." These words are not needlessly inserted.
It seems to us that the distinct recognition of what is
implied in them would save a great deal of confusion.
The phrases "poetic fire," "poetic passion," and the
like, true and useful as they are on proper occasion,
are calculated sometimes to mislead. There may be
fire, there may be passion in the poet ; but that which
is peculiar to the poet, that which constitutes the poetic
tendency as such, is a special *intellectual* habit, distinct
from the intellectual habit of the man of science. The
poetic process may be set in operation by, and accompanied by, any amount of passion or feeling; but
the poetic process itself, so far as distinctions are of
any value, is an *intellectual* process. Farther, as to its

kind, it is the intellectual process of producing a new or artificial concrete. This distinguishes poetry at once, in all its varieties, and whether in verse or in prose, from the other forms of literature. In scientific or expository literature the tendency is to the abstract, to the translation of the facts and appearances of nature into general intellectual conceptions and forms of language. In oratorical literature, or the literature of moral stimulation, the aim is to urge the mind in a certain direction, or to induce upon it a certain state. There remains, distinct from either of these, the literature of the concrete, the aim of which is to represent the facts and appearances of nature and life, or to form out of them new concrete combinations. There are men who delight in things simply because they have happened, or because they can imagine them to happen: men, for example, to whom it is a real pleasure to know that at such and such a time a knight in armour rode along that way and across that bridge; who dwell with relish on such a fact as that Sulla had a face mottled white and red, so that an Athenian wit compared it to a mulberry dipped in meal; who can go back to that moment, and re-arrest time there, as in a picture, when Manlius hung half-way from the top of the Tarpeian rock, and had his death of blood yet beneath him, or when Marie Antoinette lay under the axe and it had not fallen; to whom also the mere em-

bodiments of their own fancy or of the fancy of others
are visions they never tire to gaze on. These are the
votaries of the concrete. Now, so far as that literature of
the concrete whose business it is to gratify such feelings
deals merely with the actual facts of the past as delivered
to it by memory, it resolves itself into the department
of *History;* but, so far as it remains unexhausted by
such a subduction, it is *Poetry* or *Creative Literature.*
In practice, as we all know, the two shade into each
other, the historian often requiring and displaying the
imagination of the poet, and the poet, on the other hand,
often relapsing into the describer and the historian.
And here a part of our definition may be found fault
with. Inasmuch as the poet does not necessarily, in
every case, invent scenes and incidents totally ideal,
but often treats poetically the actual fields and landscapes of the earth and the real incidents of life—
so that, in fact, much of our best and most genuine
poetry is descriptive and historical—why define poesy
to be the production of a new or artificial concrete?
Why not call it either the reproduction of an old or
the production of a new concrete? The objection is
that the division which would be thus established is
not fundamental. In every piece of poetry, even the
most descriptive and historical, that which makes it
poetical is not the concrete as furnished by sheer recollection, but the concrete as shaped and bodied forth

anew by the poet's thought—that is, as factitious and artificial. Shelley, indeed, very sweetly calls poetry "the record of the best and happiest moments of the best and happiest minds;" but then this only refers us farther back in time for the poetry, which certainly does not consist in the act of recording, if it *be* only recording, but already lay in the good and happy moments that are recorded. Thus, if it be said that the beautiful passage in Wordsworth describing a winter landscape, with the lake on which he skated with his companions in his boyhood, is a mere transcript of a scene from recollection, it may be replied that, if this is the case (which we do not admit), then the poetry of the passage was transacted along with the skating, and the critic, instead of watching the man at his writing-table, must keep by the side of the boy on the ice. In short, in every case whatever, poetry is the production of an artificial concrete—artificial either in *toto,* or in so far as it is matter of sense or memory worked into form by the infusion of a meaning. The word "artificial" has bad associations connected with it; but, as Hazlitt said of Allegory, it is really a harmless word, and "won't bite you." It is only necessary to see what it means here to like it well enough.

The poetical tendency, then, is the tendency to that kind of mental activity which consists in the production (one might almost say secretion) by the mind of an artificial concrete; and the poetic genius is that kind or condition of mind to which this kind of activity is constitutionally most delightful and easy. Of the legitimacy of such a mode of activity what need to say anything? With some theorists, indeed, poets are little better than privileged liars, and poetry is little better than the art of lying so as to give plea- sure. Even Bacon, with his synonyms of "feigned history" and the like, evidently means to insinuate a kind of contempt for poetry as compared with philo- sophy. The one he calls "the theatre," where it is not good to stay long; the other is the "judicial place or palace of the mind." This is natural enough in a man the tenor of whose own intellectual work must have inclined him, apart even from the original constitu- tional bias which determined *that*, to prefer the exercise which "buckled and bowed the mind to the nature of things" to the exercise which "elevates the mind by submitting the shows of things to its desires." But recognising, as he did, that the one exercise is, equally with the other, the exercise of a faculty which is part and parcel of the human con- stitution, he was not the man to go very far with the joke about poets being a species of liars. That, we believe, was Bentham's fun. One can see what a good thing might be made of it. "Why was that poor fellow transported? Why, the fact is, at last assizes, he originated a piece of new concrete, which the law calls perjury." But the joke may be taken by the other end. When that deity of the Grecian mythology (if the Grecian mythology had such a deity) whose function it was to create trees, walked one sultry day over the yet treeless earth, and when, chancing to lie down in a green spot, the creative phrenzy came upon him, his thought rushed forth, and, with a whirr of earthy atoms all round and a tearing of turf, the first of oaks sprang up completed, that also was the origination of a new piece of concrete, but one could hardly say that it was telling a lie. Had his godship been a philosopher instead of a poet, had he buckled and bowed his mind to the nature of things instead of accommodating the shows of things to his desires, the world might have been without oaks to this very day.

Poetical activity being defined generally to be that kind of intellectual activity which results in the production of new matter of the concrete, it follows that there are as many varieties in the exercise of this activity as there are possible forms of an intellectual concrete. To attempt a complete enumeration of the various ways in which imaginative activity may show itself would be tedious; but an instance or two may bring some of the more common of them before the mind.

" The sun had just sunk below the tops of the mountains, whose long shadows stretched athwart the valley;
but his sloping rays, shooting through an opening of
the cliffs, touched with a yellow gleam the summits of
the forest that hung upon the opposite steeps, and
streamed in full splendour upon the towers and battlements of a castle that spread its extensive ramparts
along the brow of a precipice above. The splendour
of these illuminated objects was heightened by the contrasted shade which involved the valley below."

MRS. RADCLIFFE.

" Almost at the root
Of that tall pine, the shadow of whose bare
And slender stem, while here I sit at eve,
Oft stretches towards me, like a long straight path,
Traced faintly on the greensward—there, beneath
A plain blue stone, a gentle dalesman lies."

WORDSWORTH.

These are plain instances of that kind of imaginative
exercise which consists in the imagination of *scenes* or
objects. A large proportion of the imaginative activity
of men generally, and of authors in particular, is of
this kind. It includes pictures and descriptions of all
varieties, from the most literal reproductions of the
real, whether in country or town, to the most absolute
phantasies in form and colour, and from the scale of a
single object, such as the moon or a bank of violets,
to the scale of a Wordsworthian landscape, or of a
Milton's universe with its orbs and interspaces. It
may be called descriptive imagination.

" And Priam then alighted from his chariot,
Leaving Idæus with it, who remained
Holding the mules and horses; and the old man
Went straight in-doors, where the beloved of Jove,
Achilles sat, and found him. In the room
Were others, but apart; and two alone—
The hero Automedon and Alcinous,
A branch of Mars—stood by him. They had been
At meals, and had not yet removed the board.
Great Priam came, without their seeing him,
And, kneeling down, he clasped Achilles' knees,
And kissed those terrible homicidal hands
Which had deprived him of so many sons."

HOMER.

This is the imagination of *incident,* or narrative imagination. The instance is plain even to baldness; it is direct Homeric narration: but for this very reason it will better stand as a type of that department of imaginative activity to which it belongs. In this department are included all narrations of incidents, whether historical and real, or fictitious and supernatural, from the scale of a single incident as told in a ballad, up to the sustained unity of the epos cr drama, as in *Crusoe, Don Quixote,* the *Iliad,* the *Divine Comedy,* the *Faery Queene, Macbeth,* or *Paradise Lost.* It is hardly necessary to point out that the narration of incident always involves a certain amount of description of scenery.

"The Reve was a slender colerike man,
His beard was a shave as nigh as ever he can,
His hair was by his eares round yshorn,
His top was docked like a priest beforne.
Full longe were his legges and full lean,
Ylike a staff; there was no calf yseen."

CHAUCER.

This may stand as a specimen of what is in reality a sub-variety of the imaginative exercise first mentioned, but is important enough to be adverted to apart. It may be called the imagination of *physiognomy* and *costume;* under which head might be collected an immense number of passages from all quarters of our literature. This department, too, will include both the real and ideal—the real, as in Chaucer's and Scott's portraits of men and women; the ideal, as in Spenser's personifications, in Ariosto's hippogriff, or in Dante's Nimrod in a pit in hell, with his face as large as the dome of St. Peter's, and his body in proportion, blowing a horn, and yelling gibberish.

Connected with this in practice, but distinguishable from it, is another variety of imaginative exercise, which may be called the imagination of *states of feeling.* Here is an example:—

"A fig for those by law protected!
Liberty 's a glorious feast;
Courts for cowards were erected;
Churches built to please the priest."

BURNS'S *Jolly Beggars.*

Q

This stanza, it will be observed (and we have chosen it on purpose), is, in itself, as little poetical as may be; it is mere harsh Chartist prose. But, in so far as it is an imagined piece of concrete—that is, in so far as it is an imagination by the poet of the state of feeling of another mind, or of his own mind in certain circumstances—it is poetical. This is an important consideration, for it links the poet not only with what is poetical in itself, but with a whole, much larger, world of what is unpoetical in itself. The poet may imagine opinions, doctrines, heresies, cogitations, debates, expositions; there is no limit to his traffic with the moral any more than with the sensuous appearances of the universe : only, as a poet, he deals with all these as concrete things, existing in the objective air, and from which his own mind stands disentangled, as a spade stands loose from the sand it digs, whether sand of gold or sand of silex. The moment any of the doctrines he is dealing with melts into his own personal state of being (which is happening continually), at that moment the poet ceases to be a poet pure, and becomes so far a thinker or moralist in union with the poet. As regards the literary range of this kind of imaginative exercise,—the imagination of states of feeling,—it is only necessary to remember what a large proportion it includes of our lyric poetry, and how far it extends into the epic and the drama, where (and especially in the drama) it forms, together with the imagination of physiognomy and costume, the greater part of what is called invention of *character.*

The foregoing is but a slight enumeration of some of the various modes of imaginative exercise as they are popularly distinguishable; and, in transferring them into creative literature at large, they must be conceived as incessantly interblended, and as existing in all varieties and degrees of association with personal thought, personal purpose, and personal calm or storm of feeling. It is matter of common observation, however, that some writers excel more in one and some more in another of the kinds of imagination enumerated. One writer is said to excel in descriptions, but to be deficient in plot and incident; nay, to excel in that kind of description which consists in the imagination of form, but to be deficient in that which consists in the imagination of colour. Another is said to excel in plot, but to be poor in the invention of character, and in other particulars. In short, the imagination, though in one sense it acts loose and apart from the personality, flying freely round and round it, like a seabird round a rock, seems, in a deeper sense, restricted by the same law as the personality in its choice and apprehension of the concrete. The organ of ideality, as the phrenologist would say, is the organ by which man freely bodies forth an ideal objective; and yet, were

Q 2

ideality never so large in a man's head, it would be of
no use to apply it, after Keats or Milton, in the direction of white pinks, pansies freaked with jet, sapphire
battlements, and crimson-lipped shells, unless there
were also a little knot on the eyebrow over the organ
of colour.

The poetical tendency of the human mind being this
tendency to the ideal concrete, to the imagination of
scenes, incidents, physiognomies, states of feeling, and
so on—and all men having more or less of this tendency, catering for them in the ideal concrete, very
much in the same way as their senses cater for them
in the real (so that the imagination of a man might
be said to be nothing more than the ghosts of his
senses wandering in an unseen world)—it follows that
the poet, *par excellence,* is simply the man whose intellectual activity is consumed in this kind of exercise.
All men have imagination; but the poet is " of imagination all compact." He lives and moves in the ideal
concrete. He teems with imaginations of forms,
colours, incidents, physiognomies, feelings, and characters. The ghosts of his senses are as busy in an
unseen world of sky, sea, vegetation, cities, highways,
thronged markets of men, and mysterious beings belonging even to the horizon of *that* existence, as his
real senses are with all the nearer world of nature and

life. But the notable peculiarity lies in this, that every thought of his in the interest of *this* world is an excursion into *that.* In this respect, the theory which has been applied to the exposition of the Grecian mythology applies equally to poetic genius in general. The essence of the mythical process, it is said, lay in this, that, the earlier children of the earth having no abstract language, every thought of theirs, of whatever kind, and about whatever matter, was necessarily a new act of imagination, a new excursion in the ideal concrete. If they thought of the wind, they did not think of a fluid rushing about, but of a deity blowing from a cave; if they thought of virtue rewarded, they saw the idea in the shape of a visible transaction, in some lone place, between beings human and divine. And so with the poetical mode of thought to this day. Every thought of the poet, about whatever subject, is transacted not mainly in propositional language, but for the most part in a kind of phantasmagoric or representative language, of imaginary scenes, objects, incidents, and circumstances. To clothe his feelings with *circumstance;* to weave forth whatever arises in his mind into an objective tissue of imagery and incident that shall substantiate it and make it visible : such is the constant aim and art of the poet. Take an example. The idea of life occurs to the poet Keats, and how does he express it ?

" Stop and consider !   Life is but a day ;
 A fragile dew-drop on its perilous way.
 From a tree's summit ; a poor Indian's sleep,
 While his boat hastens to the monstrous steep
 Of Montmorenci.   Why so sad a moan ?
 Life is the rose's hope while yet unblown ;
 The reading of an ever-changing tale ;
 The light uplifting of a maiden's veil ;
 A pigeon tumbling in clear summer air ;
 A laughing school-boy, without grief or care,
 Riding the springy branches of an elm."

This is true ποίησις.   What with the power of innate
analogy, what with the occult suasion of the rhyme,
there arose first in the poet's mind, contemporaneous
with the idea of life, nay, as incorporate with that
idea, the imaginary object or vision of the dew-drop
falling through foliage.   That imagined circumstance
is, therefore, flung forth as representative of the idea.
But even this does not exhaust the creative force.   The
idea bodies itself again in the new imaginary circumstance of the Indian in his boat ; and that, too, is flung
forth.   Then there is a rest.   But the idea still buds,
still seeks to express itself in new circumstance ; and
five other translations of it follow.   And these seven
pictures, these seven morsels of imagined concrete,
if we suppose them all to be intellectually genuine,
are as truly the poet's *thoughts* about life as any seven
scientific definitions would be the thoughts of the

physiologist or the metaphysician. And so in other instances. Tennyson's *Vision of Sin* is a continued phantasmagory of scene and incident representative of a meaning; and, if the meaning is not plain throughout, it is because it would be impossible for the poet himself to translate every portion of it out of that language of phantasmagory in which alone it came into existence. Again, Spenser's personifications—his grim-hued Horror soaring on iron wings, his Jealousy seated apart and biting his lips, and the rest—are all thoughts expressed in circumstance, the circumstance in this case being that of costume and physiognomy. In short, every thought of the poet is an imagination of concrete circumstance of some kind or other—circumstance of visual scenery, of incident, of physiognomy, of feeling, or of character. The poet's thought, let the subject be what it may, brings him to

"Visions of all places : a bowery nook
Will be elysium—an eternal book
Whence he may copy many a lovely saying'
About the leaves and flowers—about the playing
Of nymphs in woods and fountains, and the shade
Keeping a silence round a sleeping maid ;
And many a verse from so strange influence
That we must ever wonder how and whence
It came."

Regarding the poet, then, considered in his nature, we may sum up by saying that the act of cogitation

with him is nothing else than the *intellectual secretion
of fictitious circumstance*—the nature of the circumstance in each case depending on the operation of
those mysterious affinities which relate thought to the
world of sense. In regarding the poet more expressly
as a literary artist, all that we have to do is to
vary the phrase, and say—the intellectual *invention*
of fictitious circumstance. This will apply to all that
is truly poetical in literature, whether on the large
scale or on the small. In every case what is poetical
in literature consists of the embodiment of some notion
or feeling, or some aggregate of notions and feelings, in
appropriate imagined circumstances. Thus, in historical
or biographical writing, the poetic faculty is shown by
the skill, sometimes conscious and sometimes unconscious, with which the figures are not only portrayed
in themselves, but set against imagined visible backgrounds, and made to move amid circumstances having
a pre-arranged harmony with what they do. The
achievement of this, in consistency with the truth of
record, is the triumph of the descriptive historian. In
fictitious prose-narrative the same poetic art has still
freer scope. That a lover should be leaning over a stile
at one moment, and sitting under a tree at another;
that it should be clear, pure moonlight when Henry
is happy, and that the moon should be bowling through
clouds, and a dog be heard howling at a farmhouse

near, when the same Henry means to commit suicide—
are artifices of which every ordinary novelist is master
who knows his trade. The giant Grangousier, in Rabelais, sitting by the fire, very intent upon the broiling of
some chestnuts, drawing scratches on the hearth with
the end of a burnt stick, and telling to his wife and
children pleasant stories of the days of old, is an instance of a higher kind, paralleled by many in Scott
and Cervantes. And, then, in the epic and the
drama! Hamlet with the skull in his hand, and
Homer's heroes walking by the πολυφλοίσβοιο! It is
the same throughout the whole literature of fiction:
always thought expressed and thrown off in the language of representative circumstance. Indeed, Goethe's
theory of poetical or creative literature was that it is
nothing else than the moods of its practitioners objec-
tivized as they rise. A man feels himself oppressed
and agitated by feelings and longings, now of one kind,
now of another, that have gathered upon him till they
have assumed the form of definite moral uneasiness.
If he is not a literary man, he contrives to work off the
burden, in some way or other, by the ordinary activity
of life—which, indeed, is the great preventive established by nature; but, if he is a literary man, then
the uneasiness is but the motive to creation, and the
result is a song, a drama, an epic, or a novel. Scheming
out some plan or story, which is in itself a kind of

allegory of his mood as a whole, he fills up the sketch
with minor incidents, scenes, and characters, which are
nothing more than the breaking up of the mood into
its minutiæ, and the elaboration of these minutiæ, one
by one, into the concrete. This done, the mood has
passed into the objective; it may be looked at as something external to the mind, which is therefore from
that moment rid of it, and ready for another. Such,
at least, was Goethe's theory; which, he said, would
apply most rigidly to all that he had himself written.
Nor would it be difficult, with due explanation, to
apply the theory to the works of all other masters of
creative or poetical literature. Dante may be said to
have slowly translated his whole life into one representative performance.

Several supplementary considerations must be now
adduced. The form of the poet's cogitation, we have
said, is the evolution not of *abstract propositions* but of
representative concrete circumstances. But in this, too,
there may be degrees of better and worse, of greater
and less. Precisely as, of two writers thinking in the
language of abstract speculation, we can say, without
hesitation, which has the more powerful mind, so of
two writers thinking in the other language of concrete
circumstance, one may be evidently superior to the
other. There is room, in short, for all varieties of
greater and less among poets as among other people.

Hence the folly of the attempts to exalt poetical genius, merely as such, above other kinds of intellectual manifestation. A man may be constitutionally formed so that he thinks his thoughts in the language of concrete circumstance; and still his thoughts may be very little thoughts, hardly worth having in any language. Both poets and men of science must be tried among their peers. Whether there is a common measure, and what it is; whether there is an intrinsic superiority in the mode of cogitation of the poet over that of the philosopher, or the reverse; and whether and how far we may then institute a comparison of absolute greatness between Aristotle and Homer, between Milton and Kant: these are questions of a high calculus, which most men may leave alone. There is no difficulty, however, when the question is between a Kirke White and a Kant; and when a poor poet, never so genuine in a small way, tells people that his intellect is " genius," while theirs is " talent," he runs a risk of being very unceremoniously treated.

> " This palace standeth in the air,
> By necromancy placèd there,
> That it no tempest needs to fear,
>   Which way soe'er it blow it:
> And somewhat southward toward the noon
> There lies a way up to the moon,
> And thence the fairy can as soon
>   Pass to the Earth below it."

This is very sweet, and nice, and poetical (it is by
Drayton, *not* a small poet, but a considerable one);
and yet surely, call it genius or what you will, there
was less commotion of the elements when it was
produced than when Newton excogitated one of his
physical theories.

We may pass to another point. The imagination
following the law of the personality, some imaginations
are strong where others are weak, and weak where
others are strong. In other words, though all poets,
as such, express themselves in the language of concrete
circumstance, some are greater adepts in one kind
of circumstance, others in another. Some are great in
the circumstance of form, which is the sculptor's
favourite circumstance ; others can produce admirable
compositions in *chiaroscuro ;* others have the whole rainbow on their pallet. And so, some express themselves
better in incident, others better in physiognomy and
character. All this is recognised in daily criticism.
Now, the consequence of the diversity is that it is very
difficult to compare poets even amongst themselves.
It is not every poet that exhibits an imagination
absolutely universal, using with equal ease the language of form, of colour, of character, and of incident.
Shakespeare himself, if we may infer anything from his
minor poems, and from the carelessness with which he
took ready-made plots for his dramas from any quarter,

was not so great a master of incident as of other kinds
of circumstance, and could hardly have rivalled Homer,
or Scott, purely as a narrative poet. How, then,
establish a comparative measure, assigning a relative
value to each kind of circumstance? How balance
what Chaucer has and has not against what Milton
has and has not—Chaucer, so skilful in physiognomy,
against Milton, who has so little of it, but who
has so much else; or how estimate the *chiaroscuro*
of Byron as against the richly coloured vegetation of
Keats? Here, too, a scientific rule is undiscoverable,
and a judgment is only possible in very decided cases,
or by the peremptory verdict of private taste.

"Many a night I saw the Pleiads, rising thro' the
     mellow shade,
 Glitter like a swarm of fire-flies tangled in a silver
     braid."

Who will venture to institute a sure comparison of
merit between this exquisite bit of colour from Tennyson and the following simple narrative lines from the
same poet?

"All the man was broken with remorse;
 And all his love came back a hundredfold;
 And for three hours he sobbed o'er William's child,
 Thinking of William."

There is yet a *third* thing that has to be taken into
consideration. Be a man as truly a poet as it is

possible to be, and be the kind of circumstance in which his imagination excels as accurately known as possible, it is not always that he can do his best. The poet, like other men, is subject to inequalities of mood and feeling. Now he is excited and perturbed, because the occasion is one to rouse his being from its depths; now he is placid, calm, and commonplace. Hence variations in the interest of the poetical efforts of one and the same poet. As he cannot choose but think poetically, whether roused or not, even the leisurely babble of his poorest hours, if he chooses to put it forth, will be poetical. But he is not to be measured by this, any more than the philosopher by his casual trifles, or the orator by his speeches on questions that are insignificant. It is even important to remark that it is only at a certain pitch of feeling that some men become poets. Though the essence of poetry consists in a particular mode of *intellectual* exercise, yet the emotional moment at which different minds adopt this mode of exercise may not be the same. The language of concrete circumstance is natural to *all* men when they are very highly excited : all joy, all sorrow, all rage, expresses itself in imaginations. The question then not unfrequently ought to be : At what level of feeling does a man become or profess to be a poet? On this may depend, not the verdict as to the genuineness of his poetry, but the disposition to spare time to listen to it. The most assiduous members of Parliament do not feel bound to be in the House, even when a leader is speaking, unless it is on a Cabinet question or a question of some considerable interest. Some orators know this and reserve themselves; others, delighting in their profession, speak on every question. It is the same with poets, and with the same result. A Keats, though always poetical, may often be poetical with so small a stimulus that only lovers of poetry for its own sake feel themselves sufficiently interested. Why are Milton's minor poems, exquisite as they are, not cited as measures of his genius? Because they are not his speeches on Cabinet questions. Why is Spenser the favourite poet of poets, rather than a popular favourite like Byron? For the same reason that a court of law is crowded during a trial for life or death, but attended only by barristers during the trial of an intricate civil case. The subject chosen by a poetical writer is a kind of allegory of the whole state of his mental being at the moment; but some writers are not moved to allegorize so easily as others, and it is a question with readers what states of mind they care most to see allegorized. This, then, is to be taken into account, in comparing poet with poet. Precisely as an orator is remembered by his speeches on great questions, and as the position of a painter among painters is determined in part by the interest of his subjects, so in a comparison of poets, or of the same poet with himself, the seriousness of the occasion always goes for something. Shakespeare's *Venus and Adonis,* though fine as a poetical study, does not affect one with the same human interest as his plays; and there is a gradation of interest in advancing from leisurely compositions of the sweet sensuous order, such as Keats's *Endymion* and Spenser's *Faery Queene,* to the severe splendour of a *Divina Commedia* or a *Prometheus Vinctus.* True, on the one hand, poets choose their own subjects, so that these themselves are to be taken into the estimate; and, on the other, the very practice of the art of poetical expression on any subject, like the glow of the orator when he begins to speak, leads into unexpected regions. Yet, after all, in weighing a poem against others, this consideration of the emotional level at which it was produced, and of its interest in connexion with the general work and sentiment of the world, is a cause of much perplexity.

> " Sweet bird, that shunn'st the noise of folly,
> Most musical, most melancholy !
> Thee, chantress, oft the woods among
> I woo, to hear thy even-song;
> And, missing thee, I walk unseen
> On the dry, smooth-shaven green,
> To behold the wandering moon
> Riding near her highest noon,
> Like one that hath been led astray

Through the heaven's wide pathless way,
And oft, as if her head she bowed,
Stooping through a fleecy cloud.
Oft, on a plat of rising ground,
I hear the far-off curfew sound,
Over some wide-watered shore,
Swinging slow with sullen roar."

How decide between this from Milton's *Penseroso* and this, in so different a key, from Shakespeare's *Lear?*—

"Blow, winds, and crack your cheeks! rage! blow!
You cataracts and hurricanoes, spout
Till you have drenched our steeples, drowned the
    cocks!
You sulphurous and thought-executing fires,
Vaunt-couriers to oak-cleaving thunderbolts,
Singe my white head! and thou, all-shaking thunder,
Strike flat the thick rotundity o' the world."

A *fourth* consideration, which intrudes itself into the question of our appreciation of actual poetry, and which is not sufficiently borne in mind, is that in almost every poem there is much present besides the pure poetry. Poetry, as such, is cogitation in the language of concrete circumstance. Some poets excel constitutionally in one kind of circumstance, some in another; some are moved to this mode of cogitation on a less, others on a greater, emotional occasion; but, over and above all this, it is to be noted that no poet always and invariably cogitates in the poetical manner. Specu-

R

lation, information, mental produce and mental activity
of all kinds, may be exhibited in the course of a work
which is properly called a poem on account of its
general character; and, as men are liable to be impressed by greatness in every form wherever they
meet it, all that is thus precious in the extra-poetical
contents of a poem is included in the estimate of
the greatness of the poet. One example will suffice.
Shakespeare is as astonishing for the exuberance of
his genius in abstract notions, and for the depth of
his analytic and philosophic insight, as for the scope
and minuteness of his poetic imagination. It is as if
into a mind poetical in *form* there had been poured all
the *matter* that existed in the mind of his contemporary Bacon. In Shakespeare's plays we have thought,
history, exposition, and philosophy, all within the
round of the poet. The only difference between him
and Bacon sometimes is that Bacon writes an essay
and calls it his own, while Shakespeare writes a
similar essay and puts it into the mouth of a Ulysses
or a Polonius. It is only this fiction of a speaker
and an audience that retains many of Shakespeare's
noblest passages within the pale of strict poetry.

Hitherto we have made no formal distinction between the poet, specifically so called, and the general
practitioners of creative literature, of whatever variety.

Our examples, indeed, have been taken in the main from those whom the world recognises as poets ; but, as far as our remarks have gone, poetry still stands synonymous with the whole literature of imagination. All who express their meaning by the literary representation of scenes, incidents, physiognomies, and characters, whether suggested by the real world or wholly imaginary, are poets. All who, doing this, do it grandly, and manifest a rich and powerful nature, are great poets. Those who excel more in the language of one kind of circumstance are poets more especially of that kind of circumstance—poets of visual scenery, poets of incident and narration, poets of physiognomy, or poets of character and sentiment, as the case may be. Those who are poetical only at a high key, and in the contemplation of themes of large human interest, are the poets who take the deepest hold on the memory of the human race. Finally, those who, having the largest amount of poetic genius, and of the best kind, associate therewith the most extensive array of other intellectual qualities, are the poets of the strongest momentum and the greatest universal chance.

Not a word in all this to exclude imaginative prose-writers. So far, Homer, Plato, Sophocles, Aristophanes, Virgil, Dante, Boccaccio, Chaucer, Cervantes, Spenser, Shakespeare, Milton, Tasso, Molière, Goethe, Richter, Scott, Defoe, and a host of others, are all huddled to-

R 2

gether, the principal figures of a great crowd, including alike poets and prose-writers. These indeed may, in accordance with considerations already suggested, be distributed into groups, and that either by reference to degree or by reference to kind. But no considerations have yet been adduced that would separate the imaginative prose-writers, as such, from the imaginative verse-writers, as such. Now, though this is good provisionally—though it is well to keep together for a while in the same field of view all writers of imagination, whether bards or prose-writers—yet the universal instinct, not to say the prejudice of association and custom, demands that the poets, as a brotherhood, shall be more accurately defined. How, then, lead out the poets, in the supreme sense, from the general throng where they yet stand waiting? By what device call the poets by themselves into the foreground, and leave the prose-writers behind? By a union of two devices! Go in front of the general crowd, you two: you, flag-bearer, with your richly-painted flag, and you, fluter, with your silver flute! Flap the flag, and let them see it; sound the flute, and let them hear! Lo! already the crowd wavers: it sways to and fro; some figures seem to be pressing forward from the midst; and at last one silver-headed old serjeant steps out in front of all, and begins to march to the sound of the flute. Who is it but old Homer? He is blind and cannot see the flag; but he knows it is there, and the flute guides him. Others and others follow the patriarch, some looking to the flag, and others listening to the flute, but all marching in one direction. Shakespeare comes with the rest, stepping lightly, as if but half in earnest. And thus at last, lured by the flag and by the flute, all the poets are brought out into the foreground. The flag is *Imagery;* the flute is *Verse.* In other words, poets proper are distinguished from the general crowd of imaginative writers by a peculiar richness of language, which is called imagery, and by the use, along with that language, of a measured arrangement of words known as verse.

It is, as Mr. Dallas observes, a disputed point whether Imagery or Verse is to be regarded as the more essential element of poetry. It has been usual, of late, to give the palm to imagery. Thus, it was a remark of Lord Jeffrey—and the remark has almost passed into a proverb—that a want of relish for such rich sensuous poetry as that of Keats would argue a want of true poetical taste. The same would probably be said of Spenser. Mr. Dallas, on the other hand, thinks Verse more essential than Imagery, and in this Leigh Hunt would probably agree with him. The importance attached to a sensuous richness of language as part of poetry is, Mr. Dallas thinks, too great at present; and in opposition to Lord Jeffrey, or at least by way of

corrective to his remark about Keats, he proposes that
a power of appreciating such severe literary beauty as
that of Sophocles shall, more than anything else, be
reckoned to the credit of a man's poetical taste. Mr.
Dallas, on the whole, is in the right; and this will
appear more clearly if we consider what Imagery and
Verse respectively are, in relation to poetry.

Imagery in poetry is secondary concrete adduced by
the imagination in the expression of prior concrete.
Thus, in the *simile*,—

> " The superior Fiend
> Was moving toward the shore, his ponderous shield,
> Ethereal temper, massy, large, and round,
> Behind him cast: the broad circumference
> Hung on his shoulders like the moon, whose orb
> Through optic glass the Tuscan artist views
> At evening from the top of Fesole."

Here the primary object in the imagination of the
poet is Satan with his shield hung on his shoulders.
While imagining this, however, the poet strikes upon
a totally distinct visual appearance, that of the moon
seen through a telescope, and his imagination, enamoured with the likeness, imparts the new picture to
the reader as something additional to the first. Again,
take the *metaphor* :—

> " Sky lowered, and, muttering thunder, some sad drops
> Wept at completing of the mortal sin
> Original."

Here the process is the same as in the simile, but more unconscious and complete. The concrete object first in the mind (so far at least as these lines are concerned) is the sky dropping rain : in the imagination of this another imagined object, that of a being shedding tears, intrudes itself; the two objects are combined by a kind of identifying flash; and the double concrete is presented to the reader. So, again, with that highest species of metaphor, the *personification* or *vivification*, of which, indeed, the metaphor quoted is an example.

Almost all so-called images may be reduced under one or other of the foregoing heads ; and, in any case, all imagery will be found to consist in the use of concrete to help out concrete. Now, as the very essence of the poet consists in the incessant imagination of concrete circumstance, a language rich in imagery is in itself a proof of the possession of poetical faculty in a high degree. *Cæteris paribus*, the more of subsidiary circumstance evolved in intellectual connexion with the main one the higher the evidence of poetical power. There is a likeness, in this respect, between poetical and scientific writers. Some scientific writers, *e.g.* Locke, attend so rigorously to the main thought they are pursuing as to give their style a kind of nakedness and iron straightness ; others, *e.g.* Bacon, without being indifferent to the main thought, are so full of intel-

lectual matter of all kinds that they enrich every
sentence with a *detritus* of smaller propositions related
to the one immediately on hand. So with poets.
Some poets—as Keats, Shakespeare, and Milton in
much of his poetry—so teem with concrete circumstance, or generate it so fast, as their imagination works,
that every imagined circumstance as it is put forth
from them takes with it an accompaniment of parasitic
fancies. Others, as the Greek dramatists and Dante,
sculpture their thoughts massively in severe outline.
It seems probable that the tendency to excess of imagery is natural to the Gothic or Romantic as distinct
from the Hellenic or Classical imagination; but it is
not unlikely that the fact that poetry is now read
instead of being merely heard, as it once was, has
something to do with it. As regards the question
when imagery is excessive, *when* the richness of a poet's
language is to be called extravagance, no general principle can be laid down. The judgment on this point
in each case must depend on the particular state of
the case. A useful distinction, under this head, might
possibly be drawn between the liberty of the poet and
the duty of the artist. Keats's *Endymion* one might
safely, with reference to such a distinction, pronounce
to be too rich; for in that poem there is no proportion
between the imagery, or accessory concrete, and the
main stem of the imagined circumstance from which

the poem derives its name. In the *Eve of St. Agnes,* on the other hand, there is no such fault.

Of Verse, as connected with poetry, various theories have been given. Wordsworth, whose theory is always more narrow than his practice, makes the *rationale* of verse to consist in this, that it provides for the mind a succession of minute pleasurable surprises in addition to the mere pleasure communicated by the meaning. Others regard it as a voluntary homage of the mind to law as law, repaid by the usual rewards of dis- interested obedience. Mr. Dallas sets these and other theories aside, and puts the matter on its right basis. Verse *is* an artificial source of pleasure; it *is* an incen- tive to attention, or a device for economizing attention; and it *is* an act of obedience to law, if you choose so to regard it. All these, however, are merely statements respecting verse as something already found out and existing; not one of them is a theory of verse in its origin and nature. Such a theory, if it is to be sought for at all, must clearly consist in the assertion of this, as a fundamental fact of nature—that, when the mind of man is either excited to a certain pitch, or engaged in a certain kind of exercise, its actions adjust them- selves, in a more express manner than usual, to time as meted out in beats or intervals. Mr. Dallas, giving to the statement its most transcendental form, says that the *rationale* of metre is to be deduced from the fact that, inasmuch as Time, according to Kant, is but a leading form of Sense, it must fall under the law of Imagination, the faculty representative of Sense. Quite independent of this philosophic generalization, which it would at least require much time to work down to the ordinary apprehension, there are many facts, some of which Mr. Dallas very acutely points out, all tending to indicate the existence of such a law as we have described. The swinging of a student to and fro in his chair during a fit of meditation, the oratorical see-saw, the evident connexion of mental states with the breathings and the pulse-beats, the power of the tick-tick of a clock to induce reverie, and of the clink-clank of a bell to make the fool think words to it, are all instances of the existence of such a law. Nay, the beginnings of poetical metre itself are to be traced in speech far on this side of what is accounted poetry. There is a visible tendency to metre in every articulate expression of strong feeling; and the ancient Greeks, we are told, used to amuse themselves with scanning passages in the speeches of their great orators.

Without trying to investigate this question farther, we would refer to a consideration connected with it which seems important for our present purpose. The law, as stated hypothetically, is that the mind, *either* when excited to a certain pitch, *or* when engaged in a particular kind of exercise, takes on a marked con-

cordance with time as measured by beats. Now,
whether is it the first or the second mental condition that necessitates this concordance ? Poetry
we have all along defined as a special mode of
intellectual exercise, possible under all degrees of
emotional excitement—the exercise of the mind *ima-*
ginatively, or in the figuring forth of concrete circumstance. Is it, then, poetry as such that requires metre,
or only poetry by virtue of the emotion with which
it is in general accompanied—that emotion either
preceding and stimulating the imaginative action, or
being generated by it, as heat is evolved by friction ?
The question is not an easy one. On the whole, however, one might incline to the belief that, though poetry
and passion have metre for their common servant, it is
on passion, and not on poetry, that metre holds by
original tenure. Is not metre found in its highest and
most decided form in lyrical poetry, narrative poetry
having less, and dramatic poetry still less of it? and
wherever, in the course of a poem, there is an unusual
metrical boom, is not the passage so characterized
always found to be one not so much of pure concrete
richness as of strong accompanying passion? What,
then, if song, instead of being, as common language
makes it, the complete and developed form of poetry,
should have to be scientifically defined as the complete
and developed form of oratory, passing into poetry only

in as far as passion, in its utterance, always seizes and whirls with it shreds and atoms of imagined circumstance? If this is the true theory, Verse belongs, by historical origin, to Oratory, and lingers with Poetry only as an entailed inheritance.

Prose, then, *may*, as we have said, make inroads upon that region of the literature of the concrete which has hitherto been under the dominion of verse. But, on the other hand, verse, whatever it may have been in its origin, exists now, like many other sovereignties, by right of expediency, constitutional guarantee, and the voluntary submission of those who are its subjects. And here it is that the theories of Wordsworth and others have their proper place. They are theories of verse, not in its origin, but in its character as an existing institution in the literature of the concrete. They tell us what we can now do intellectually by means of verse which we could not do if her royalty were abolished. They point to the fact that in literature, as in other departments of activity, law and order, and even the etiquette of artificial ceremonial, though they may impose intolerable burdens on the disaffected and the boorish, are but conditions of liberty and development to all higher, and finer, and more cultured natures. In short (and this is the important fact), metre, rhyme, and the like, are not only devices for the sweet and pleasant conveyance of the poet's meaning after it is formed; they are devices assisting beforehand in the creation of that meaning. They are devices so spurring and delighting the imagination, while they chafe and restrain it, that its thoughts and combinations in the world of concrete circumstance are more rich, more rare, more occult, more beautiful, than they would otherwise be. Like the effect of the music on the fountain and the company of Bacchanals in Tennyson's strange vision is the effect of verse on poetical thought:

> "Then methought I heard a mellow sound,
> Gathering up from all the lower ground;
> Narrowing in to where they sat assembled,
> Low, voluptuous music winding trembled,
> Wov'n in circles: they that heard it sigh'd,
> Panted hand in hand with faces pale,
> Swung themselves, and in low tones replied,
> Till the fountain spouted, showering wide
> Sleet of diamond-drift and pearly hail."

Here we must stop our discussion of the Theory of Poetry. For much that we have left undiscussed, and especially for a philosophical division of poetry according to its kinds, we must refer to Mr. Dallas. We recommend his book highly and cordially. There is perhaps a stronger dash of what may be called Okenism in his style of speculation than some readers may like: as, for example, in his systematic laying out of everything into corresponding threes or triads. Poetry

figures throughout this treatise as a compound result
of three laws—the laws of unconsciousness, the law of
harmony, and the law of imagination; which laws are
supreme respectively in three kinds of poetry—lyrical
poetry, epic poetry, and dramatic poetry; which three
kinds of poetry, again, correspond historically with
Eastern, primitive, or divine art, Grecian, antique, or
classical art, and Western, modern, or romantic art;
which historical division, again, corresponds philosophically with such trinities as these—I, he, thou; time
future, time past, time present; immortality, God,
freedom; the good, the true, the beautiful. All this,
stated thus abruptly and without explanation, may
seem hopeless matter to some; but even they will find
in the book much that will please them, in the shape
of shrewd observation and lucid and deep criticism,
valuable on its own account, and very different from
what used to be supplied to the last age by *its*
critics.

DE RE POETICA.

Dr. WHEWELL recently delivered, before the Royal Institution of Great Britain, a lecture " On the Influence of the History of Science upon Intellectual Education," which might be fairly described as a discourse upon the text—" We, the heirs of all the ages." The education of an accomplished man of the nineteenth century is an aggregation of elements which have been formed by the intellectual movements of all preceding time. To this aggregate the Greek has supplied geometry, and the geometric spirit ; the Roman, jurisprudence,* and the jural spirit, breathed into all the moral sciences ; while the post-Baconian centuries have

crowned these great inheritances of deductive reasoning with the inductive sciences and the inductive spirit. And the moral of the whole is, that no man can be considered thoroughly educated who has not appropriated the Greek, the Roman, and the modern contributions to the culture of the mind. Even with our pre-scientific bringing-up, we are ready to maintain that the exact and solid study of any of the natural sciences is a most valuable discipline. But we fear that some persons in this age are falling into the delusion that a knowledge of those facts that are *objectively* most useful, is also *subjectively* most improving, as the organ of mental

---

* Dr. Whewell might have quoted Gibbon. " I am pleased with the epithet *legiferi*, applied to the Roman triumphs ; laws were produced by those triumphs, and were their ordinary fruits."—Journal (speaking of Claudian, Rutil. iter.)

cultivation. The modern element of culture is the Aaron's rod, which swallows up the Grecian and the Roman. Hence the slipshod and illogical character of the sermons and essays of the day; hence (which most concerns us now) the shallow and fluctuating criticism, which we are so often doomed to read and to hear.

There are two principles everywhere manfested in the external world — the principle of *utility* and the principle of *beauty* — unless, with some modern philosophers in sight of certain animal and vegetable formations, we wish to add a third, analogous to *humour* or grotesqueness. These two principles should inform the inward, as they do the outward creation. There is some danger just now that the latter of these may be too completely sacrificed to the former, even in the seats of liberal education, and much more by those who are endeavouring to improve their own minds. An attempt to show that *poetry*—the sublimate and quintessence of the *beautiful* — is a real means of intellectual and moral culture, may, perhaps, be neither uninteresting nor unprofitable. We set out by asking — Is poetry popular?

We might assert that poetry is the deathless instinct of our intellectual being—that man is a poetical, almost as characteristically as he is a rational creature, if we take the word poetical to indicate the love of poetry when produced by others, as well as the faculty of producing it ourselves. There is hardly any mental constitution whose original draught utterly wants a poetical projection. And if some of our readers, having in their minds' eye a matter-of-fact young lady, or an elderly M.P., affirm in our teeth that some of their own acquaintances are not *poetical* in either of these senses, they must suffer us to remind them that there are probably others whom it requires a sort of charitable hypothesis to designate as *rational*. But we will only ask our readers to recall what they may see for themselves any day of the week. Go, and make a morning call upon any one of your acquaintance. Occupy the time until the lady of the house makes her appearance, in turning over those books lying upon the rosewood table. What are they? Tennyson's "Princess," the sixth edition; "In Memoriam," ditto; "The Chris-

tian Year," exquisitely got up in morocco, the thirty-seventh edition. Is there any respectable house in the United Kingdom which has not a copy of Milton and Shakspeare?— Shelley and Byron are reprinted by thousands, at so low a price as to bring them in reach of all who can read. Only last year a young Ayrshire man, by profession originally a drawer of muslin patterns, Mr. Alexander Smith, published a volume of poems, which has gone through three or four impressions in these islands, while 20,000 copies were disposed of on the other side of the Atlantic in a few weeks. In throwing our eye accidentally down the columns of a newspaper, we see that in the Marylebone Free Library (to which the working men of London come in their working dress, but which is said to be as quiet and orderly as the British Museum), out of 687 books, 289 are set down under the head of literature and poetry.

Such indications as these justify us in asserting, that poetry is popular; and this leads us to a momentous question. We cannot put down poetry by placing it on a Protestant *Index Expurgatorius*. In this land of liberty—in this age of the march of intellect, we can no more check the circulation of any set of popular books, than the spring-tide of the Atlantic. If the teeming press of this land be like the Nile, and volumes of poetry like the frogs, that come up into our very bedchambers, assuredly there is at present no Moses who can remove them from us. We may preach against poetry, but we are not to suppose that because we are virtuous, there shall be no more cakes and ale.

Poetry is popular, and all the tribes of staid gentlemen, and men of business, and useful-knowledge enthusiasts, cannot put it down. How are we to interpret the fact? Men who desire, above all things, the progress and improvement of their fellow-men, but who believe that there is no improvement without a purer morality, no progress away from that narrow road of which the Truth hath spoken—men who value every study which has a tendency to refine feeling, and to elevate thought, because it makes a more precious incense to offer with the sacrifice of ourselves upon the altar of God — how shall they take the fact? Shall they make lamentation over it, as another proof of the corruption of our nature, or shall they accept it as it is, and strive to neutralise the accidental evil, and to increase the essential good that there is in it ? This question deserves to be considered by all readers of poetry, and especially by the young. Is poetry, indeed, as it was called of old, " the wine of devils" ? Is it, at best, the confectionary of literature ? If the influence of poetry is against God and goodness — if it intoxicate our better nature, may the glass which contains it be shivered, however delicately textured or rarely cut ; may the wine be spilled, though its ebullient foam toss the sunlight into scented wavelets! If it be not so actively malignant as this, but merely a sweetmeat, we had better have as little to say to it as possible. Life is an earnest and an awful thing. It has battles, and its warriors want wrestling sinews. That is bad food for them which makes flesh, and not thews and muscles. But apart from the abuses to which every human faculty may be wrested, we believe poetry to be an instrument, not simply of *pleasure*, but of improvement *through* *pleasure*. When John Wesley made hymns, and set them to tunes which were known in the tavern and the theatre, he said, " it was pity so much good music should be given up to the devil." We would apply this to poetry. John Milton (who, though a poet, and likely to be biassed by the nothing - like - leather fallacy, knew something of the theory of education) maintained that a study of great poets and good critics would soon make youth " perceive what despicable creatures our common rhymers and play-writers be ; and show them what *religious*, what glorious and magnificent use might be made of poetry." We propose, then, to give some account of what seems to us to constitute poetry. We shall endeavour to vindicate it by a reference to the constitution of our own nature, and the structure of Scripture ; we shall then point out how readings in poetry—

" Haply may requite
Studious regard with opportune delight ;"

may be made subservient to the improvement of our minds, and in some degree to the purification of our hearts.
 I. We account for poetry, then, in this way — we believe it, with Schiller,

to be " the longing for a lost ideal." We believe it to be the sweet expressions of the not unhopeful melancholy which is inseparable from a being like man, who, in the midst of his fall, retains a longing for that which he once was, and looks dimly forward, half smiling through his tears, to what he yet may be. We are so constituted that the present cannot satisfy us, and we desire to relieve ourselves by *making*, *creating*, some better things out of such materials as we have. This longing more or less exists in *every* reasonable being, and is *poetic feeling*. But take some man in whom this feeling is predominant. In the mood of mingled emotions which we have described, the most beautiful objects of the universe, observed or remembered, occur to the mind, which is gifted with an almost miraculous delicacy and fertility of the associative faculty — become fashioned after its likeness, and steep it in a sweet pleasure akin to melancholy ; for the known beauty only awakes a longing for a beauty beyond itself. In his elegy on " Mrs. Anne Killigrew, excellent in the two sister arts of poesy and painting," Dryden says—

" To the next realm she stretch'd her sway,
    For Painture near adjoining lay."

Yet how much more contracted a province than " the spacious empire of the Nine !" Stand upon some hill that " fronts the falling sun," and from which you can behold the ocean ; that vessel, which seems to be steering away to some harbour beyond the golden sunset, may form the point of division for the eye and for the imagination. Up to that vessel there is a realm of beauty — hills that seem glowing in a mighty crucible — trees that are silently falling into that burning orange — ocean for some glorious leagues tinting his waters with a fire that we know not whether to call purple, or rosy, or golden, for it is all at once. So far there is a realm common to poetry and painting ; but *beyond* the vessel there is a bridge, brighter than that which the genius of Tasso flung over Kedron for the passage of Rinaldo ; and beyond those clouds that shine with horned rays like the face of him who came down from the Mount — beyond the furthest isle that floats like a burning ship in that sea of glory, like the seer of the Apocalypse, the poet beholds a door opened in heaven ; and *his* realm stretches outward from that ! The painter fixes on his canvas the finest lights that are possible to his materials—those which are so fine that they defy his skill, are but the beginning of the poet's work. Wordsworth expresses this in four lines on a landscape, the *third* of which we conceive to be the most wonderful in our language :—

" Ah ! then, if mine had been the Painter's hand,
To express what there I saw, and add the gleam,
The light that never was on sea or land—
The consecration, and the Poet's dream."

So far we have had the primary conditions of poetry. Another follows. To be a poet, a man must be enriched with utterance. He must have words; but these words must not only be weighty, passionate, suggestive ; they must not want any element of beauty. As they are a something finer than painting, so they must be a something subtler than music. The poet creates a temple; and a temple has not only graceful pillars, and storied windows, and clouds of incense ; it must have a chant—a measured and ordered voice, as all around it is measured and ordered—of longing and melancholy, but not of grief, so subtly is it blended with *pleasure*. Therefore no man is a poet unless his utterances are in measure.

This account of the *genesis* of poetry excludes such compositions as satires, or copies of verses, like Pope's epistle on criticism. A very able man with a good ear, who never wrote a line of genuine poetry, might be eminently successful in such essays ; so, much more might a real poet (and Pope, after all, pace Wordsworth and Keats, was such), who applied the mechanism of the skill which he had acquired in loftier composition, to rounding off clever thoughts in sharp lines.

" Men's judgments are like watches—none
Goes quite aright, yet each admires his own,"

says Mr. Pope ; and a true sentiment it is, ingeniously expressed, but we instinctively deny its claim to be *poetical*.

" Thirty days hath September," &c.,

is a very *useful* distich — more so than any in Dryden or Spencer, but it is not of the highest order of poetry.

The human faculty " most concerned in poetry " is *imagination* rather than *fancy*. We use *imagination* in the sense which had long been floating down the current of our best writers, but was first grasped and fixed by Wordsworth. The word might suggest to us the idea of a power of recalling *images* from objects once seen.* But it seems to express that faculty by which the finite is connected with, perhaps, we might say, retaining an etymological reference, made a type or *image* of the infinite and super-sensuous. Wordsworth gives us a very happy illustration of the distinction between *fancy* and *imagination,* set to work upon the same material. Lord Chesterfield says—

" The dews of the evening most carefully shun,
They're the tears of the sky for the loss of the sun."

Here is a wretched piece of *fancy*. Milton says of Adam after the fall :—

" Sky lowered, and, muttering thunder, some sad drops
Wept at completion of the mortal sin."—

There is a sublime touch of *imagination*. Wordsworth himself affords some beautiful illustrations of this faculty. He did not overrate himself when he wrote thus :—

"Justified by recollection of the insults which the ignorant, the incapable, and the presumptuous have heaped upon my writings, I shall declare (censurable, I grant, if the notoriety of the fact above stated does not justify me), that I have given evidence of the exertion of this faculty upon its worthiest objects ; which have the same ennobling tendency as the productions of men in this kind, worthy to be holden in undying remembrance."

Thus he says of a beetle seen through a microscope :—

" Like a mail'd angel on a battle day."

Again, in some verses on a vase of gold and silver fishes, the vase is made a "type of a sunny human heart."

---

* " Every one by his own experience knows, that the absence or destruction of things once imagined, doth not cause the absence or destruction of the *imagination* itself. This *imagery* and representation of the qualities of the things without, is that which we call our imagination, ideas, or knowledge of them." — *Hobbes, Human Nature,* 1. sec. 7. Perhaps this sentence has escaped Sir William Hamilton's observations when he says, in his wonderfully learned and acute history of the word *idea*—" Hobbes employs it, and that *historically,* only once or twice."—*Disc.* p. 66.

But mark what the poet says of the fish seen in the twilight :—

> " **Fays,** genii of gigantic size,
> And now in twilight dim,
> Clustering, like constellated eyes
> In wings of cherubim,
> When the fierce orbs abate their glare."

Here is imagination's most glorious work. The beetle and the gold-fish are made the means of linking our thoughts to the sublimest majesty of created strength. Were the order inverted—were angels likened to insects or to fish, it would be the *miniaturing* handiwork of *fancy.*

A Persian poet says — " Night comes on, when the inkbottle of heaven is overturned." Another calls the evening dew " The perspiration of the moon."

Glorious John Dryden says of a noblenian sick of the small-pox :—

> " **Blisters with pride swell'd,** which through's flesh did sprout
> Like rosebuds stuck i' the lily skin about,
> Each little pimple had a tear in it,
> To wail the fault it rising did commit."

We hope none of our readers will attribute these flowers to the stock of *imagination.*

But let us not be unfair to *fancy.* Her work is elegant and pretty, and done with a smiling face — she braids roses and finishes lace-work ; but that which is grand is also serious ; and *fancy,* except under rarely realised conditions, diminishes the impression of seriousness. *Imagination* rears up the pillars before the temple, whose names are Jachin and Boaz, *establishment* and *strength*—*fancy* wreathes them with lily-work. (1 Kings, vii. 15, 20.) One more instance illustrative of the distinction—we do not quite remember whether we are again debtors to Wordsworth. Shakspeare describes Queen Mab as coming—

> " In shape no bigger than an agate stone
> On the forefinger of an alderman."

Here is *fancy ;* see how archly she does her playful work, and how *defined* she makes it. But *imagination* connects us with an *indefinite* vastness :—

> " His spear, to equal which, the tallest pine,
> Hewn on Norwegian hills, to be the mast
> Of some great ammiral, were but a wand
> He walk'd* with, to support uneasy steps,
> Over the burning marl."

So sings Milton of the fallen archangel. Mark, it is not said, " His spear was as high as a pine," or " as high as a mast." The altitude is not measured by anything that is notched on the carpenter's rule. The way to take it is not set down in Bonnycastle or Hutton. But our great poet connects the two : the pine hewn on the hills—the tallest pine, too, there, and that pine the mast of some giant man-of-war ; and he tells you that that tallest pine, which hears the wind shouting over its head on the everlasting hills, which you picture to yourself as nearer than any tree of the forest to the frost-flushed sky, when its fiery roses are beginning to roll in cloudy flakes before the storm—that mast, whose top-sail makes you giddy as you look up to it, are but a wand to his spear ! There is *imagination* of the highest order.

Poetry proper, then, is a longing for a more excellent beauty than " the things which are seen" can supply ; an upward and an onward instinct uttered by gifted persons in musical and modulated words, and gently delighting itself and others by its creations. And the faculty most immediately concerned in this process is *imagination.*[†] Let us here remark (and we make no pretension to originality) that imagination, in the highest sense (what we have termed the *super-naturalising,* in the note), has never been manifested by heathen writers, because imagination points to the infinite and supersensuous.[‡] The heart which is used to give itself up to gods of flesh cannot ascend so high. Accustomed to rest upon the block of marble, the

---

* Is Spencer's description of Orgolio the original of this ?—
> " His stalking steps are stay'd
> Upon a snaggy oak."—*Fuery* Q. b. i. c. 7.

† Perhaps we have drawn the line rather too sharply. After all, there are creations of Shakspeare, in which fancy grows so nearly serious that the acutest critic might be perplexed. May we say that there are two kinds of imagination—the *super-naturalising* of the Hebrew prophets, and of the Hebrew-souled Milton, and the human of Homer and Shakspeare ?

‡ We do not forget that there are anthropopathic and apparently anthropomorphic expressions in the Old Testament. We have known Exodus, xxxiii. appealed to by a Mormon ; but the whole tone of Scripture, and the known principle, *lex loquitur linguam filiorum hominis,* obviate any possible mistake.

dove-like wings of the human spirit become afraid to try the impalpable air. Thus "God is a spirit," becomes a condition of the highest poetry, as well as of the truest religion. But we are apt to think (and this has never been noticed that we know of) that this observation may be extended to that form of Christianity which includes certain transmuted and co-ordinated elements of Paganism. Its ritual supplies abundant food for the fancy. But how is it that Italy has not produced one poem distinguished by this highest kind of imagination? The traditions of her glorious past, compared with her degenerate present, have given her poets a gentle tenderness. Her blue sky and sunny climate have steeped their minds in a congenial hue; but her creed has fastened their souls to the things that are seen. It needs no acute physiognomist to discover a devout Roman Catholic by his look; the induction is generalised from no particular race like the Celtic — it is much more extensive. We have remarked the mysterious expression on the brow of one Roman Catholic member of a family whose other members were Protestants. And we believe that that darkening and contracting frown arises from constantly *gazing* at outward objects of worship — from perpetually *localising*, where it is considered irreverent to *gaze at* the Holy Eucharist — from a straining to recall what Cudworth terms "sensible ideas," when the prototypes are absent. The shadow is thrown upon the brow from the cloud of a materialising religion. Such a shadow is analogously thrown over the pages of poets of that creed. They lack "a muse of fire that would ascend the highest heaven of invention," because they have not learned to worship God in spirit and in truth.

The observations which we have made will give us the best and most intelligible principles by which to decide what compositions we are to accept as *poetry*. It at once rejects prose, however lofty and impassioned, as wanting the musical characteristic. Passages there are in Jeremy Taylor, and exquisite sentences in Bacon, which are, as it were, poetry in ore; but they have not been melted in the furnace, which gives them their perfect form; and divisions of poetry, based upon a different principle, have always been arbitrary and defective. Thus Hobbes will have poetry arranged according to the places in which men have their local habitations. The *court* and the palace, with their heroic faults, magnificent virtues, and darkly majestic passions, cast in a grander mould than those of ordinary mortals, have for their own the princely epic: for them—

"*Gorgeous* Tragedy, in sceptr'd pall, comes sweeping by;"

the tears of kings flow from a fountain too august to be unsealed save by a crowned and kingly sorrow. The *city*, with its teeming population, "insincere, inconstant, and of troublesome humour," laughs at the vices of its betters, and the follies of itself and others, as it reads them in satire (scommatic narrative), or witnesses them in the living caricature of comedy (scommatic dramatic). The third region — *the country*, which has a "plainness, and, though dull, a nutritive faculty in rural people, that endures a comparison with the earth they labour" (so much for the British farmer), has the pastoral narrative, or *bucolic*, where simple swains pipe to silly sheep and sillier shepherdesses; and the *pastoral comedy*, where labour frolics with elephantine gambol, in its clouted shoes, and the perception of some ancient and not very edifying joke, begins to dawn upon the chaos of the rosy and stupid face. Now, where does such a division as this leave room for some of the finest poetry that has charmed the ear of time? The jewelled fingers of "Childe Harold" may knock long enough before he will find admission into this enchanted castle, while "English Bards" may pass through with a savage scowl, and "Don Juan" with an odious sneer. The sonnet, too — the key with which Shakspeare unlocked his heart — the lute on which Petrarch wailed forth the sweet sorrow of his love-wound, whose exquisite music imposed upon succeeding poets the soft necessity of finding a Laura, and singing a love-song, before they could be made "free of their company" * — the pipe that Tasso loved

---

* Cowley's expression, see Johnson's "Lives," p. 8.

to sound, and which soothed Camoens in his exile — the single bright leaf in the funeral cypress that crowns the visionary brow of Dante — the sonnet that glittered like a glowworm before Spencer—

"Called from faery land to struggle through dark ways"—

that became a trumpet in the hand of Milton* — that under the finger of Wordsworth could play all the melodies of the Duddon, or swell out into organ notes that fill the temple of the Lord;— the sonnet can find no room in Hobbes' poet's corner. He quietly eviscerates the problem of its difficulty, by telling us that it is no poetry !

Lord Bacon again divides poetry into *narrative*, which is *history imitated ; dramatic*, which is *history made visible ;* and *parabolic*, which is *history with a type.* Our great Lord Chancellor, here as elsewhere, falls a victim to his exaggerated love of smart, short-clipped, symmetric-looking divisions. It is plain that he excludes about as much poetry as he includes. But give us any mould — narrative, dramatic, lyric, idyllic, didactic, philosopho-satiric, or composite—and we can recognise poetry, under whatever shape — we recognise the ingot, however variously it may be stamped.

II. We now proceed to vindicate Poetry thus understood. We do so by a reference to our own nature. The word *nature* is an ambiguous one. sometimes taken *in bono*, sometimes *in malo sensu*, sometimes indifferently for the total existent sum of our being, intellectual and moral. Of our nature, in the last sense, mingled as it is with alien elements, which had no part in the glory of its original, the thoughtful and philosophic Hamlet exclaims— "What a piece of workmanship is man !" If there be a point of view in which an insect is more beautiful and more wonderful than the sun,† with what comparison shall we compare man ?* And so when David, the poet of God, calls upon " All His works, in all places of His dominions, to bless the Lord," he feels that there is a richer

and more surpassing voice than any other, when he adds, " Bless the Lord, *O my soul.*" And every faculty of that soul must be given—"and all that is within me, bless His holy name." Now, if every faculty of our nature is to be given to God, it should be given to Him, improved and disciplined. What are the leading faculties of man ? We will not appeal to the difficult masters of mental analysis, to the modern Plato and Aristotle— Cousin and Sir William Hamilton, of Edinburgh (or rather, of Oxford). We will take the bold and rough outline-map, dashed on the first page of modern psychology, by the master-hand of Bacon. We answer — *will*, *reason, memory, imagination.* The religious obligation of educating the *reason* is now universally admitted. The delusion can nowhere now obtain an audience that ignorance is an acceptable sacrifice to God. "If you offer the blind for sacrifice, is it not evil ?" But it is not sufficiently attended to, that *imagination* (meaning thereby, not creative imagination, of which we spoke so much, but a kindred though lower faculty, by which the distant, the absent, and the future, are represented to the mind under combinations, and aspects, imposed by the mind itself,"‡ and which is the very condition of poetry subjective) is a veritable constituent, not an adventitious weakness, of human nature. Butler's hard saying about "that forward delusive faculty, ever obtruding beyond its sphere, of some assistance to apprehension, but the author of all error," must be applied to its abuse ; and is nearly equally true of the abuse of reason. We appeal with reverence to the archetype of our humanity—in Him we may best learn ourselves.§

Of this view of imagination we seem to have undeniable evidence in the contexture even of our Lord's perfect humanity. Let His temptation be considered. Be it remembered that that temptation is not an episode in a drama, but a reality, and that its reality consisted in this — that objects, naturally

---

* We must remind the reader that much of this panegyric is but a prose transcription of Wordsworth's " Sonnet on the Sonnet," as it may be called, beginning—

" Scorn not the Sonnet—Critic !"

† St. Augustine's thought.

‡ Whewell's " Elements of Morality," book i. chap. 6, on the Mental Desires.

§ " Apprenons de la verité incarne notre veritable nature."—*Pascal.*

and sinlessly objects of desire, and which only became sin by being chosen against God's will, were presented for His acceptance. " The devil taketh Him up into an *exceeding high mountain.*" What force is there in this circumstance, viewed as an appeal to the imaginative part of that exalted nature ! We are so constituted that the ascent of a mountain, the colours that ever and anon steep its barren sides, the clouds that sail their shadows on its sea of sunshine, the roaring cataract, the screaming wild bird, the brooding mists, the cold blue sky overhead, like the dome of eternity, impart an unusual elevation to the spirit. The sickness of terror, the suicidal impulse felt to the moistened palm of the hand, are succeeded by delighted amazement. Our dwarfishness seems to expand with the gigantic objects around, above, and beneath us. On the mountain-top exaltation borrows for a moment the office of humility, and ends in a speechless worship. Then come other thoughts. We associate ourselves with ideas of power and magnificence.* And if the scenery below us be fruitful in historical recollections, imagination works with these recollections, and tinges them as fitfully as the sunlight paints the clouds. It is not the weak, the narrow-minded, and the ignorant, who are thus affected ; these things are felt most deeply by the noblest spirits and the most refined intellects. When, then, we consider the theatre on which that glorious scene was unfolded, and remember that the magnificence of the offer was not frittered away by being presented in successive parcels, but that, as St. Luke tells us, all those kingdoms were exhibited to the Saviour " in a moment of time," and remember that the temptation was addressed to, and formed a point of contact with the imagination, we begin to see the reality of the trial. Whence we conclude that imagination is an integral part of our nature, and that the poetical, as well as the rational in us, requires its education and proportionate development.

Authority is on our side. The ancient tradition of classical education has always included a large list of poets. It cannot be supposed that the collective wisdom of Christendom has allowed such prominence to poetry simply to crust the style with a superficial polish, or enable the reason to hang some poetic jewel on the naked arm of argument.† Lord Bacon, the philosopher of progress and practical improvement, who considered classical literature much better adapted to be the instruction and delight of mature age, than the educational organ of adolescence, and who sometimes professes not to think very highly of poetry, yet bestows upon it the most satisfactory of testimonies. When he classifies human studies relatively to human faculties, he feels himself constrained to give to reason, philosophy—will, ethics—memory, history —imagination, poetry. Need we do more than refer to the structure of Scripture ? If we look for the representative of *reason* in the Bible, we find the solid and argumentative St. Paul. If we search for that which may elevate, while it sanctifies the imagination, we turn to Ruth in the corn-field (and our simple *Bibelfest* man will not think a whit higher of the book of Ruth, even for a Goethe's pronouncing it the most exquisite of idyls !)—we turn to the burning words of the song of songs— to the Psalter, after all its cries of penitence, and passionate longing, running out in a Hallelujah, to that which, since the researches of Lowth, we may venture to call the sublime poetry of Isaiah. The reader of Milton will hardly need to be reminded of that remarkable passage in the fourth book of Paradise Regained, in which the Saviour compares the songs of Sion with the poetry of Greece ; but he may pos-

---

* We have been pleased to recollect a similarity between our own thought and some beautiful lines of Wordsworth's, which did not occur to us when writing the above :—

" Blue ether's arms flung round thee
  Stilled the pantings of dismay.

" Maiden ! now take flight—inherit
  Alps or Andes, they are thine ;
  With the morning's roseate spirit
  Sweep their length of snowy line.

" Thine are all the coral fountains
    Warbling in each sparry vault
  Of the untrodden lunar mountains ;
    Listen to their songs—or halt.

" To Niphate's top invited
    Whither spiteful Satan steered."
  To —— on her first ascent of Helvellyn.

† Poetarum sententiæ non tantum habent pondus. Nos saepe iis utimur, ut his quæ dicere voluimus ab ipsorum dictis aliquid ornamenti accedat."—*Grotius, De Jure, B. et P. Prolegom.* 47.

sibly thank us for directing his attention to the expression of the same sentiment in majestic prose. " The Scripture also affords us a divine pastoral drama in the song of Solomon, consisting of two persons, and a double chorus, as Origen rightly judges. And the Apocalypse of St. John is the majestic image of a high and stately tragedy, shutting up and intermingling her solemn scenes and acts with a sevenfold chorus of hallelujahs and harping symphonies ; or, if occasion shall lead to imitate those magnific odes and hymns, wherein Pindarus and Callimachus are, in most things, worthy, some others in their frame judicious, in their matter most an end faulty. But these frequent songs throughout the law and prophets, beyond all these, not in their divine argument alone, but in the very critical art of composition, may be easily made to appear, over all the kinds of lyric poesy, to be incomparable."*

It is interesting to contrast the sacred literature of the elder dispensation with the most precious of its other possessions. Contrast, for instance, Solomon's glorious pastoral poem with his Temple. It was built of marble, majestical exceedingly, the interior blazed with gold, and its walls were written over with a charactery of flowers, or sparkled " like starlight hid with jewels." Far away, beneath the shadow of those trees which Ezekiel has described in his 31st chapter (with a tone of colouring richer, more picturesque, and more analogous to modern feeling, than was ever laid on by any classical artist†), " the workmen hewed the cedar for the House of God." The same wild bees who still twinkle like golden motes in that scented air came humming round their toil. The same waterfalls made music in the forest, roaring in the green abysses of the chest-

nut and the algum, but filling the dark recesses of the fir-groves with an eternal, sleepy, melancholy measure. The same broken rainbow fragments hung over the woods, and steeped them in that peculiar purple light which the traveller of our own day describes.‡ The patriarchal trees have been reduced to a scanty number ; perhaps some are still standing, under whose progenitors' shadow the foresters of Hiram looked forth upon the flotes that were carrying materials for the edifice which was growing on Moriah. How proudly, too, for those seven long years must the people of Jerusalem have gazed upon the structure as it advanced to its completion ! What thoughts of duration must they have connected with its walls ! Yet, if the fire of the enemy had never leaped from pinnacle to pinnacle—if the storms of successive centuries had beaten themselves in vain against its marble battlements, the experience of ages tells us that the mightiest building bears necessarily within itself the seed and elements of its own decay. The root of the wild flower insinuates itself into the solid stone. The tiny insect multiplies himself into an innumerable host, and gradually effaces the delicate tracery, rives the granite block, and crumbles away the marble shaft. Even so must it have been with Solomon's Temple, if it had been spared by the hostile fury of the Chaldean. How long has it been survived by the divine poetry of the same date, whose duration shall only be measured by that of the world !

III. Having thus attempted to vindicate poetry, we shall proceed to show how the study of it may be made intellectually profitable. We do not assert, then, that the mind should never be permitted to be passive in reading poetry; that we can in no case surrender ourselves to an unreasoning

---

* " Reason of Ch. Govern." Pref. to b. ii.

† It may interest some of our readers to contrast with the colouring of this passage, that of Lucan, in the famous lines—*Phar.* lib. iii. 339, 447.
  There is no single touch which shows us that the heathen writer loved trees, or entwined delightful associations with their " fair branches, and shadowing shrouds." Plato, however, had such a feeling. " Haec tua platanus non minus quam illa quæ mihi videtur, non tam ipsa aquula, quæ describitur quam platonis oratione crevisse.—*Cic. De Orat.* i. 7.

‡ Lord Lindsay's account of Lebanon adds a second psychological marvel to Coleridge's Kubla Khan. Every one knows that the few lines of that exquisite vision are but a fragment of a poem which rose before the author in his sleep, without conscious effort ; but every one does not know that the scenery of the vision is so exactly that of Lebanon, that the poet minutely painted a landscape of which he had never read a description, which with the eyes of the flesh he had never seen.

pleasure without injury. But, to speak generally, we believe that this passive surrender to admiration of poetry *tends* to affect the intellectual part of our nature something, as the passive surrender to emotion acts upon its moral part. We should learn to catechise ourselves in presence of what is beautiful in poetry, to decompose our delight by reflection, to refer our pleasure to some fixed principles of the human mind. Between the remotest regions of thought lines of communication may be drawn. Each portion of knowledge seems, like a tree in the forest, to stand out in perfect distinctness from its fellows, though serving to make up a common shade, and having some external contiguity in the remotest branches; but he who digs below the surface finds that the roots are inseparably connected, and interlaced by a thousand ramifications. Thus poetry is interlaced with philosophy,* and while we seem to be merely idlers listening to the poet's reed in the pleasant shade, we are unconsciously becoming graduates in the school of abstract thought. The adequate development of these remarks would be a volume rather than a review. We can only, on the present occasion, state, by way of example, a few principles of the refined pleasure which beautiful poetry is capable of affording, not attempting to trace them out *a priori* by any exhaustive process, but, as Bentham says of a rough classification, "picking up, and hanging together some of the principal articles in the catalogue, by way of specimen." We shall not speak much here of *simple unmixed descriptions* — of what is beautiful in external nature. We will admit, or rather assert, that the severity of the Roman poet's criticism —

——" Properantis aquæ per amenos ambitus agros,
Aut flumen Rhemen, aut pluvius describitur arcus,"

would have been unjust and tasteless had he not added—

" Sed nunc non erat his locus."

Still this is too obvious a source of pleasure to require an elaborate analysis; and we must here say that though description is a most delicate

adjunct of true poetry, we cannot consider a chiefly, or merely descriptive poem to stand very high on the list of the Muses. When a description, however rich and gorgeous, is wrought out in an immense expanse, even of pretty and melodious verses, we are apt to ask whether an accomplished rhetorician could not have effected the same more masterfully, without the incumbrance of rhythm. Thus, putting aside moral considerations, and admitting the splendour of many passages in Childe Harold, we do not place it in a high class of poetry, though probably the first of its class. In the preface to the first canto, the author sets out by saying:— " The poem was written, for the most part, amongst the scenes that it attempts to describe." Thus much for the correctness of the descriptions, while in that to the last canto he confesses that "there will be found even less of the pilgrim than in any of the preceding." And it is even so; the gloomy human figure vanishes, and the composition is reduced to landscape. But by contrasting such descriptions the reader may set himself an exercise of no ordinary interest. The *objective* is rarely viewed in the dry light of reason—it is steeped in the *subjective*.

We all know that when the most honest and least imaginative of men suppose themselves to be recording *facts*, they are often but recording their own impressions and unverified hypotheses, and the facts are dressed in the livery of their wishes; so, when the poet seems to be most unmixedly descriptive, he steeps the landscape in the light of his own individual character. Let the reader then, without fail, compare such descriptions of similar objects, as are to be found in different poets. Thus Southey and Byron have each described a waterfall. Byron speaks of Velino :—

" The hell of waters where they howl and hiss,
　And boil in endless torture, while the sweat
Of their great agony, wrung from out this
　Their Phlegethon, curls round the rocks of jet,
That gird the gulf around, in pitiless horror set.—
　—— A matchless cataract,
Horribly beautiful ! but on the verge,
　From side to side, beneath the glittering morn,
An Iris sits, admidst the infernal surge,
　Like Hope upon a death-bed, and unworn

---

* Aristotle profoundly remarks, that poetry is truer than history, because it represents universal truth. When poets enter upon other fields they are apt to exceed other men, from their habits of generalisation. Coleridge in ethics; Goethe in botany and the theory of colours; Milman and Schiller in history, are instances in point.

Its steady dyes, while all around is torn
   By the distracted waters;
Resembling, mid the torture of the scene,
Love watching madness with unalterable mien."

Southey thus paints the birth of the Ganges on the top of Meru :—

" From rock to rock, with shivering force re-
      bounding,
The mighty cataract rushes.
Wide spreads the snowy foam, the sparkling spray
Dances aloft; and ever there at morning
The earliest sunbeams haste to wing their way,
With rainbow-wreaths the holy stream adorning;
And duly the adoring moon at night
Sheds her white glory there,
And in the watery air
Suspends her halo-crown of silver light.
A mountain valley in its blessed breast
   Receives the stream, which there delights to lie
Untroubled, and at rest
Beneath th' untainted sky."

Add a third description of a water-fall by the author of the " Christian Year ":—

" Go where the waters fall,
   Sheer from the mountain's height.

" Mark how a thousand streams in one,
   One in a thousand on they fare—
Now flashing to the sun,
   Now still as beast in lair.

" We that with eye too daring seek
   To scan their course, all giddy turn;
Not so the flowret meek,
   Harebell or nodding fern.

" They from the rocky wall's steep side
   Lean without fear, and drink the spray;
The torrent's foaming pride,
   But keeps them green and gay.

" And Christ has lowly hearts that rest
   Mid fallen Salem's rush and strife;
The pure peace-loving breast
   Even here can find her life.

" What though in harsh and angry note
   The broken flood chafe high? They muse
On mists that lightly float
   On heaven-descending dews :

" On virgin snows, the feeders pure
   Of the bright river's mountain springs;
And still their prayers endure,
   And Hope sweet answer brings ! "

Now, in these *three* cases, the raw material of the verse is the same—*a waterfall.* But the cataract in Byron is a troubled hell of waters howling in agony; the rainbow that glitters in the Italian sunshine, spanning the waterfall from side to side, resembles love watching madness. The cataract in Southey, for all its greatness, is a lovely and rejoicing thing : where the earliest sunlight hastens to come, and the haunting moonlight wreathes silver crowns of spray, and the waters at last sleep quietly beneath the quiet sky. Keble, with his gentle and timid spirit — his love of minute beauty (so natural in a short-sighted poet), and his prevailing religious spirit, turns from the roar and flash of the mighty waters to the hare-bell and fern, nodding over the rocky wall, and drinking life from the awful torrent — as the just man lives by faith, in a troubled world and a disordered Church.

One of the finest opportunities of contrasting the genius of two great poets in this way, is afforded by Dryden's " Tales from Chaucer." But the development of this contrast must be left for another occasion.

GROTE'S GREECE. [*]

Though this remarkable production has now been some time before the public, we doubt much whether beyond the world of universities and professed scholars its contents are so generally known as they deserve to be. The price puts it beyond the reach of one class of readers, and the length to which it runs makes too heavy a demand upon the time and attention of another. Besides it is an encyclopædia of Grecian historical learning, rather than an epitome of Grecian history. Accounts of outlying colonies, minute details of ancient jurisprudence, adjustments of contending authorities, criticisms on disputed texts, disquisitions archæological, chro-

nological and philological, which possess no interest whatsoever for the general reader, occupy no inconsiderable portion of the work. Even to the professed classic it is sometimes heavy reading. We do not mean to insinuate that it is like Sir Michael Scott's " Historie "—

" Which historie was never yet read through,
Nor never will, for no man dare it do;"—

but we are inclined to think that, as in the case of the wondrous wizard's Book of Might, it is mostly—

" Young scholars that have picked out something
   From the contents. '

We think, therefore, that we shall not be performing a task unacceptable

DE RE POETICA.—PART II.

WHEN our last paper was interrupted by the exigencies of the press, we had completed our definition and vindication of poetry. We purposed to preface an enumeration of certain critical principles by a brief comparison of the genius of two great poets, Chaucer and Dryden, as illustrated by the "Tales from Chaucer." Of these, one is especially graceful, and written in a strain of severe and masculine morality — "The Flower and the Leaf." Dryden does not merely translate Chaucer into modern English — he fills up an outline supplied by Chaucer, with a free pencil of his own treatment. It is singular to remark how the picturesque and natural touches of old Geoffry are almost always botched in the transfusion, while the moral and declamatory passages swell into a grander rhetoric. Thus—

!" The braunches brode, laden with leaves new,
That sprungen out agen the sonne sheen,
Some very red, and some a glad light green,"

are marred by this rendering—

" And the new leaves on every bough were seen,
Some ruddy coloured, some of lighter green."

And similarly in "Palamon and Arcite," the Temple of Mars is described by both poets with a savage and terrific grandeur. Nothing can be finer than Dryden's—

" In through that door a northern light there shone—
'Twas all it had, for windows there were none ;
The gate was adamant, eternal frame,
Which, hew'd by Mars himself, from Indian quarries came—
The labour of a god !"

Within the pillars, which, though clenched by iron plates, are brighter than a polished mirror, every form of sin, and treachery, and violence is visible. Chaucer's brief, awful picturesqueness is poorly rendered. Thus—

"The dark imaginings of secret felony,"

is weakened into—

" Then saw I how the secret felon wrought."

That fine line, "The treason of the murdering in the bed," is omitted altogether. The terrible description of the suicide—

" His heart-blood hath bathed all his hair,"

is represented by the commonplace—

" The gore congealed was clotting in his hair."

" The cold death with mouth gaping upright,"

becomes—

"With eyes half closed and gaping mouth, he lay."

Chaucer had by heart every feature of the king of terrors. Thus, further on in the poem, the death of Palamon is thus painted:—

" With that word his speeche faille began—
*For from his feet up to his breast was come
The cold of death !* *
Only the intellect withouten more,
That dwelled in his heart sike and sore,
'Gan faillen when the herte felte deth,
Dusked his eyen two,* and failled his brethe."

What could glorious John have been thinking about when he wrote?—

" This was his last, for death came on amain,
And exercised below his iron reign ;
Then upward to the seat of life he goes—
Sense fled before him ; what he touch'd he froze."

But to return to the "Flower and the Leaf." The knights distinguished by the recognizance of the leaf — less showy, but more lasting than the flower — are eulogised in these massy and majestic lines, which deserve to be written with a pen of gold in the album of youth, but which can scarcely be traced in the earlier poet:—

" No room for cowardice or dull delay—
From good to better they should urge their way ;
For this with golden spurs the chiefs are graced,
With pointed rowels armed to mend their haste ;
For this with lasting leaves their brows are bound,
For laurel is the sign of labour crowned,
Which bears the bitter blast, nor shaken falls to
      ground.
From winter winds it suffers no decay,
For ever fresh and fair—and every month is May ;
E'en when the vital sap retreats below,
E'en when the hoary head is hid in snow,
The life is in the leaf, and still between
The fits of fallen snow appears the streaky green ;
Not so the flower, which lasts for little space.
A short-lived good, and an uncertain grace."

We can at present consider only what may be called the pictorial aspect

---

* It is common among the Irish to say, "The cowld's creeping up from the feet to the heart of him ; he'll soon be done."

of poetry. Just as truly has it its musical aspect ; for music (the golden bridge between sense and intellect), which we know not whether to term etherialised sense, or intellect after a certain beautiful fashion sensualised, lies along it like light upon an upturned countenance ; and its philosophical aspect, for the feud outstanding between poetry and philosophy in Plato's time has long since been composed, and we have learned to recognise poetry " in the passionate expression which there is upon the face of all science." But we now take only the pictorial aspect (eliminating therefrom the mere accurate rendering of nature, which is common to painting, and the mere copiousness of gorgeous verbal colouring, which is common to rhetoric), and we proceed to enumerate certain principles constitutive of the refined pleasure which, in this kind, is consciously recognised.

I. We are so constituted, then, as to find especial pleasure when the scenery is toned into harmony with the predominant sentiment or passion of the human agent with which the poet would tinge our minds and feelings. Thomson's " Castle of Indolence " is, in this respect, the finest specimen in our language. Shenstone, a writer, except for one poem now deservedly forgotten, makes one of God's fallen creatures exclaim, when walking in a garden— with what pathos let our hearts bear witness—

" When through the garden's flowery paths I stray,
  Where bloom the jasmines that could once allure,
  Hope not to find delight in us, they say,
  For *we* are spotless, Jessy—*we* are pure !"

Our " sage and serious" Spencer pre-eminently understood this. When Prince Arthur relates to Una that strange and visionary meeting with the Fairy Queen, how is the external world made to sympathise with the golden glee, the delicious intoxication of knightly youth—

" On a day, prick't forth with jollity,
  Of looser life, and heat of hardiment,
  Ranging the forest wide on courser free :
  The fields, the floods, the heavens, with one consent,
  Did seem to laugh on me, and favour mine intent.
  . . . .
  She seemed by my side a royall maid :
  Her daintie limbs full softly down did lay,
  So fayre a creature yet saw never sunny day."*

This may be termed *keeping*, and we are to be thankful for it, and to admire it when we find it. But we must take care not to turn this admiration into a prosaic and tyrannical astriction of the muse to a particular locality. The caution can scarcely be considered superfluous when Dr. Thomas Browne thinks fit to gird at Gray's—

" Full many a gem of purest ray serene"—

affirming that " to a person moralising in a village churchyard, there is no object that would not sooner have occurred than this piece of minute jewelry." To which we need only reply, by quoting one of the most admirable distinctions in his clever, but ostentatious, and awfully prolix lecture on the philosophy of the human mind : — " The inventions of poetic genius are the suggestions of analogy ; the prevailing suggestions of common minds are those of mere contiguity."†

II. Another source of refined pleasure is when the poet interprets, as it were, the parable of natural beauty into his divine and musical, but most human speech—when external things are made types of our feelings, or illustrate the dark workings of the inner world, or become melodious homilists of virtue and holiness, making pleasure an instrument of purifying and of exalting. Let our first example be from the volume of a young poet, whose name is a high guarantee—Mr. Matthew Arnold. We have especial pleasure in giving this exquisite *morceau*, because it is free from the writer's besetting sins, affectation and versified pschycologising, only just tolerable in Tennyson— because, also, it is in a measure which we can recognise as verse.‡

---

* F. Q. b. i. c. ix. 13, 14.
† Lect. xxxvii. Of the Phenomena of Simple Suggestion.
‡ We strip a short passage from Mr. Arnold's poems of the division addressed to the eye, and challenge any reader to divide it into verse as it stands :—" They see the Indian drifting, knife in hand, his frail boat moored to a floating island, thick matted with large-leafed low creeping melon plants, and the dark cucumber. They see the Scythian ; he tethers his beast down and makes his meal, mare's milk and bread baked in the embers ; he makes his meal !" Mr. Arnold is strangely fond of this expression, and of quaint delicacies for man and beast, such as corn soaked in wine for horses, and sugared mulberries for mortals.—*The Strayed Reveller*, p. 78.

" TO MARGUERITE.

" Yes, in the sea of life enisl'd,
With echoing straits between us thrown,
Dotting the shoreless watery wild,
We mortal millions live alone;
The islands feel the enclasping flow,
And then their endless bounds they know.

" But when the moon their hollows lights,
And they are swept by balms of spring,
And in their glens on starry nights
The nightingales divinely sing;
And lovely notes from shore to shore
Across the sounds and channels pour :

" Oh ! then, a longing, like despair,
Is to their furthest caverns sent ;
For surely once they feel, we were
Parts of a single continent :
Now round us spreads the watery plain.
Oh ! might our marges meet again !

" Who or ler'd that their *longing's* fire
Should be, as soon as kindled, cool'd ?
Who renders vain their deep desire ?
A God—a God the severance rul'd,
And bade betwixt their shores to be
The unplumb'd, salt, estranging sea."
                              pp. 187, 188.

If Mr. Arnold, always or often, wrote
like this, he could afford to dispense
with the praise, and to defy the censure of critics.* We hope that the tone
of his poetry may not evince that *non-
chalant* indolence which is fatal to poetic
as to all other excellence; and which
his illustrious father declares to have
been native to his own moral constitution, and conquered only by an iron
discipline. Again hear Wordsworth :

" As the ample moon
In the deep stillness of a summer night,
Rising behind a thick, and lofty grove,
Burns like an unconsuming fire of light
In the green trees, and, kindling on all sides
Their leafy umbrage, turns the dusky veil
Into a substance glorious as her own—
Like power abides . . . .
In man's celestial spirit : virtue thus
Sets forth and magnifies herself—thus feeds
A calm, a beautiful, and silent fire
From the *encumbrances* of mortal life."

How much more glorious than simple, pictorial description this implica-
tion of the moral fibres of the human
heart with the picture is, may not
unaptly be exemplified by a comparison of the same great poet with the
author of " Queen Mab," singing of
one and the same theme. The admirers of Shelley and Wordsworth re-
pectively would quote their verses to
the skylark, as peculiarly happy specimens of their best manner. But Shelley's poem — running as it does the
round of all beauty, that charms by

being half hidden, from the glowworm,
golden, in a dell of dew, and the rose
embowered in its own green leaves, to
the poet hidden in the light of thought,
and the high-born maiden solacing her
secret soul with music ; sphering the
bird like a spirit in the glory of the
sunken sun, the pale purple of the
even, or the arrows of the silver-
moon ; matching his song with drops
from a rain cloud, sounds of vernal
showers upon the grass, hymeneal
chorus, or triumphal chant — ends in
tones half of lamentation, half of bitter
complaint against our nature and
condition, and dies away in an aspiration after fame. The muse of Shelley
indeed, like Duessa, is outwardly exceedingly fair ; but when the glamour
is touched by the potent spell of truth,
the silken mantle falls off, and we behold the hideousness that it covers.
But Wordsworth concentrates and
compresses where Shelley dilates and
perhaps dilutes, and intensifies by
compression. Where Shelley, " without a conscience or an aim," idly displays beauty after beauty, as a boy
might shift the colours of a kaleidos-
cope, Wordsworth with strong hand
smites upon the anvil of thought, and
welds beauty and holiness into one
glowing mass. Only contrast with
Shelley's diffuse, and evanescent splendours, that soon die away, and leave
the memory in clouds, the bright and
burning spot which Wordsworth's
poem leaves enlamped and enskied in
the heaven of thought. Read Wordsworth " To the Skylark," and say
whether (to add abruptly a new figure
to those which we have employed)
there be not within the compass of a
lady's ring as much stuff as might be
beaten out into a mile of wire :—

" Leave to the nightingale her shady wood ;
A *privacy of glorious light is thine :*
Whence thou dost pour upon the world a flood
Of harmony, with instinct more divine—
Type of *the wise, who soar, but never roam—*
True to the kindred points of Heaven and home."

The wonderful suggestiveness of the
second line — the implicit analogy of
relation between the shady wood to
the nightingale, and the glorious light
to the lark, exceed, we think, Shelley's random gorgeousness. But the

---

* We heartily wish that we had space to do justice to Mr. Arnold, by quoting the description of the huntsman and his pack wrought on the arras, and of the sleeping children in
Tristram and Iseult, pp. 110, 122 ; and of the Church of Brou, pp. 139 to 152.

two concluding lines affect us with the
purest of all delights, with a pleasure
which has a tendency to make us
better. They contain no sermonising,
pinned liked a moveable ornament
upon the poem; they are chiselled
deeply into its very substance. They
are indeed a more appropriate sermon
than will probably be preached in the
British Isles next Ascension Day; but
they have no languor, no tedium, no
monotony—fresh as the air, and delightful as the face of heaven. We
are happy to adduce yet another instance from Mr. Keble's " Lyra Inno-
centium" :—

> " ——— Admire
> How linger yet the showers of fire
> Deep in each fold, high on each spire
> Of yonder mountain proud.
>
> " Thou see'st it not—an envious screen,
> A fluttering leaflet hangs between
> Thee and that fair, mysterious scene—
> A veil too near thine eye.
> One finger's breadth at hand will mar
> A world of light in heaven afar—
> A mote eclipse a glorious star,
> An eylid hide the sky."

Here Mr. Keble is himself. He
does not twist words into any uncouth
and unmusical measure. He does not
mistake obscurity for depth. He does
not perplex the grammarian, and pro-
voke the critic, by breaking away from
metaphor to metaphor,* with no thread
of connexion palpable to the eyes of
ordinary mortals. He is no longer
our Sunday riddler, but our every-day
teacher. Let these instances suffice to
show how the *interpretative* and *para-
bolising* element works out an exalting
delight. By it " a thing of beauty"
becomes indeed " a thing for ever," in
a sense beyond the poet's thought.
Beautiful, but otherwise evanescent
objects, the materials of pleasing but
temporary impressions, tossed on the
flux and mutation of outward things,
and the busy heavings of inward associations, become attached, as it were, to
a sure and steadfast anchor of the soul.
We glide in a boat between some
green island and the mainland, while
the summer sea sobs silverly on the
shore, and the nightingale's long golden
gurgle throbs upon the air. The
heritage of memory is one of many
indistinct impressions, like a child re-

calling at night the wonders of a ma-
gic-lantern. But learn we to make
that island, divided from the mainland
by some former convulsion, the type of
our own heart, divided by some providential necessity from that other heart
which was once so near to it ; then the
scattered fragments of our impressions
are bound up by a presiding unity,
and what otherwise would have been a
pretty but shifting *scene* melts into the
texture of our mind, and lives with
the eternity of our thought. A hundred
times have we seen the moon rising
behind a wood, and turning it into a
mass of white and silent fire; when
we have learned that this is a type of
virtue transfiguring the very *encumbrances* of mortal life, the moon and
the grove become exalted, from the adjuncts of an exquisite picture, into a
light of the spirit and an ornament of
the soul. The music of the lark warbling at heaven-gate does not die away
with a brief delight when the little
bird composes his quivering wings;
the leaf that shut out some golden
spot of heaven from our view does not
redden, and fall, and rot ; they attach
themselves to the most permanent associations of our moral nature, and
transient impressions of pleasure, reflected from minute and transitory objects, become abiding and delightful
monitors of truth and holiness.

III. The power of glorifying that
which in itself is revolting—of exalting
that which in itself is commonplace
is a peculiar source of pleasure.
Thus drunkenness surely is most hideous and revolting ; yet the poet, like
the chemist, can extract rare perfume
from filth.

> " Sweeping by,
> As in a fit of Thespian jollity,
> Beneath her vine-leaf crown, the green earth reels,"

sings Wordsworth, on the banks of the
Rhine, in the vintage season. Not
only is drunkenness odious, but *tipsy*
is the most vulgar word to express
the odious thing. Yet listen to Coleridge describing a number of nightingales in a grove—

> " Those wakeful birds
> Have all burst forth in choral minstrelsy,
> As if some sudden gale had swept at once]

---

* " In serious poetry I am inclined to think that it is improper in the course of the same
allusion to include more than one of these analogies ; as by doing so, an author discovers
an affectation of wit, or a desire of tracing analogies, instead of illustrating the subject of
his composition."—*E. of P. of the Human Mind,* cv. part i. sec. 3 ; *D. Stewart's.*

A hundred airy harps.
Many a nightingale, perched giddily
On blossom twig, still swinging to the breeze,
And to the motion tuning his wanton song,
Like tipsy joy that reels with tossing head."

Under the condition that Sophocles, Æschylus,* and Milton have misinterpreted the meaning of the nightingale's song — granting that it is the very quintessence, and, as it were, agony of joy — the last line will thrill any competent reader with an irresistible delight, heightened at least, if not created, by a sympathy with the poet's mastery over such unpromising material. Or turn to the poetry of Scripture. How picturesque the description of seamen in a storm. "They reel to and fro, and stagger like drunken men." How awful Isaiah's image of the earth under her Maker's wrath! — "The earth shall reel to and fro like a drunkard."

Most of our readers must have seen a captive eagle, chained among Cockney imitations of Switzerland, in a certain exhibition that delighted our boyhood. The poor draggle-feathered bird is infinitely more unlike the glorious thing which rode the winds of heaven, or lit upon the Alpine crag, in the glory of its golden wings, than a fat goose — and however Gibbon may make *anser*† the butt of his pleasantry, said *anser* looks very pretty upon a blue mountain lake—is unlike a swan. When the prisoned eagle is sick, he is positively loathsome to more senses than one. Yet, from one of his feathers, Mr. Alexander Smith extracts a new and fine comparison for a morbid state of an originally powerful mind—

" Oft an unhappy thought,
Telling all is not well, falls from his soul,
Like a diseased feather from the wing
Of a sick eagle."

And if the poet has the power of hitting off the revolting, in some aspect which, either by contrast or suggestion, renders it beautiful, much more has he the power of doing so with that which is merely *common-*

place. This is one characteristic privilege of poetic genius, to arrest the new and the beautiful masquerading in the disguise of the familiar and the ordinary — as *inductive* genius apprehends the universal, the law latent in the particular fact, and disengages it from its coarse, concrete envelope. Shakspeare's sonnets present us with two apt illustrations. Doubtless a long, flowing, Oriental beard is poetical, especially if it be covered with white blossoms of old age, as the Irish have it. But what—one would think—more unpoetical than the short, grizzled bristles of an old man among ourselves? Before deciding too peremptorily, recall Shakspeare's lines—

" When I behold
The summer's green all girded up in sheaves,
Borne on the bier with white and bristly beard ;"

and still more remarkably in a cognate subject-matter. There may be sermons in stones, and good in everything; is there poetry in a wig? What shall we say of the sweetly simple and pathetic image rising into the superb and almost terrible declamation against the artificial beauty of the age, contained in these few lines :—

" *When beauty lived and died as flowers do now*,
Before the *golden tresses* of the dead,
The *right of sepulchres*, were shorn away,
To live a second life on second head,
Ere beauty's dead fleece made another gay."

Eating and drinking are decidedly commonplace : yet they have been a favourite topic with all poets, from Homer down to Keats. The classical poets *intensified* eating into a poetical aspect, by the rude strength of heroic hunger, with a few concomitants of golden beakers and lusty wines. Our tastes are less healthy ;‡ and such banquet-pictures as have been most appreciated are made odorous by the introduction of delicate wines and fruits, which, coming from countries far away from our colder regions, by the trick of some melodious Oriental name steep us in a sort of sunny haze

---

* Yet Æschylus makes Cassandra envy the nightingale's
" God-given wings, and sweet and wailless life ;"
while the chorus compares her to the same bird—
" Wailing out Itys, Itys evermore."—*Agam.* 1144, *sqq.*

† " Decline and Fall," c. xxiii.

‡ We cannot approve of Mr. Arnold's side of roasted sheep and melons. As the footman says of his master's boiled mutton and apple-pudding in *Punch*, " He and the other gentlemen isn't used to this *cuissine.* Wholesome enough, but coarse—very."

of suggestion. This beautiful art of giving *remoteness*,* by the introduction of a name,† depending upon laws of infinite subtlety and complication, is pre-eminently Miltonic. Of its application to banquet-pieces, two happy specimens may be cited. Before the tournament between the Redcross Knight and the Saracen Sansloy, they partake of a banquet in the common hall. Spencer thus sings :—

" They bring them wines of *Greece and Araby,*
And *dainty spices fetcht from furthest Ind ;*
And in the wine a solemn oath they bind
T' observe the sacred laws of arms that are assign'd."
                      Book i. c. 5.

What thinks the reader of the banquet that tempted the virtue of the youthful Thalaba ?—

" The very light came cool'd through silvering panes
Of pearly shell, like the pale moonbeam tinged ;
Or where the wine-vase fill'd the aperture,
Rosy as rising moon, or softer gleam
Of saffron, like the sunny evening mist.
From golden goblets there
The guests sat quaffing the delicious juice
Of *Shiraz' golden grape.*
All rich fruits were there :
Pistachios from the heavy cluster'd trees
Of *Malavert* or *Haleb's fertile soil ;*
And Cashin's luscious grapes, of amber hue.
Here cased in ice the apricot,
A topaz crystal-set ;
Here, on a plate of snow
The sunny orange rests ;
And still the aloes and the sandal-wood,
From golden censers, o'er the banquet-room
Diffuse their dying sweets." ‡
                Thalaba, b. iv. 24, 25.

We need only just hint at Keats' " Eve of St. Agnes" :—

" Manna and dates, in argosy transferr'd
From *Fez*, and spiced dainties, every one
From silken Samarcand to cedar'd Lebanon."

IV. From this *transformative* or *amplicative* element, we hurry on to what may be called the *centralising* power. We are affected with an exquisite delight when the poet, as it were, lays a sunbeam under some object or circumstance, which thus becomes the luminous centre of an entire landscape ; when a picture is compressed into a pregnant epithet, or suggested by the light touch of a happy attribute. Unless the poet possess this faculty, he is, at least as a painter, inferior to the accomplished rhetorician, who is untrammelled by verse, and possesses a larger canvas, which he can cover with the profusest masses of colouring. Ælian's description of Tempe — Gibbon's of Daphne, near Antioch — Bayard Taylor's of the tropic foliage on the Chagres River, in his " Dorado," would lose by being translated into verse. We have seen Mr. Keble's *interpretative* power exercised on a leaf ; Keats has also made a leaf a memorable instance of the *centralising* power :—

" Deep in the shady sadness of a vale
Sat grey-hair'd Saturn, quiet as a stone ;
Forest on forest hung about his head,
Like cloud on cloud. No stir of air was there,
Not so much life as on a summer's day
Robs not one light seed from the feather'd grass,
But *where the dead leaf fell, there did it rest.*"

What a landscape of calm centres in that leaf! How much would be marred, in the following four lines, by the substitute of *down* for *up ;* the whole picture centring in that little word—

---

* It may further be added, that remoteness in all table articles implies another poetic element—preciousness. Dr. Newman has remarked this in his strange and spiteful story " Loss and gain." " A luxury in its very idea is a something *recherché.* Thus Horace speaks of the *perigrina lagois.* What nature yields *sponte sue* around you, however delicious, is no luxury."—p. 265. So Spencer—
            " And precious odours fetched from far away."—F. Q. b. i. c. 12.
† Every one recollects Shakspeare's " furthest steep of India ;" and Milton's
            " Utmost Indian isle, Taprobane."
Comp. Spencer's exquisitely melodious lines, where Una tells her story to Prince Arthur.— F. Q. b. i. c. 7.
‡ Aristotle shows that we should not consider a men ἀκόλαστος for enjoying the smell of roses or incense, though we should do so for excessive pleasure in those smells which are more directly associated with the taste. The former classes of smell give no pleasure to brutes.—(*Ethic. Nic.* iii. 13.) Thus flowers and scents in the poetic banquet take off from the heavy animal impression, and connect us with a more refined and intellectual sense than taste. We have heard of a certain London diner-out, who always used to stand by the door of a confectioner's shop, near his house, for half an hour before dinner, that the ἀνάμνησις supplied by the scent of raspberry tartlets might whet his jaded appetite. Hobbes maintains that the pleasures and displeasures of odours are, for the most part, not organical ; referring to the fact that smells, when they seem to proceed from others, are displeasing, though in reality our own. There are curious observations on smells in Fitzgerald's " Arist. Ethic." p. 166, and in " Loss and Gain."

" But see, the tall elm-shadows reach
  Athwart the field ; the rooks fly home ;
The light streams gorgeous *up* the o'erarching beech,
With the calm hour soft weary fancies come."
                Lyra Innocentum.

Or let us remark how much magnificent description may be compressed into one or two words, by two instances, in both of which an imagined touch of the finger is the vehicle of the magic. As long as England has autumnal woods, there shall be lips to quiver with delight, as they repeat from Tennyson's " In Memoriam" :—

" Autumn, *laying here and there,*
A fiery finger on the leaves."

As long as there are stormy nights succeeded by radiant mornings, he will not be forgotten who sings :—

" Thus pass'd the night so foul, till morning fair
Came forth with pilgrim steps in amice grey,
Who with her radiant finger still'd the roar
Of thunder." *

To this head belongs all the fine beauty of pregnant and suggestive epithets. *The Doctor,* we are sorry to say, singles out three lines of Milton for especial blame; one of which is—

" What time the grey fly winds her *sultry horn.*"

The grey fly is the chaffer, which begins its flight in the evening. What a landscape have we in that one word, *sultry,* of a warm summer evening, whose brooding quiet is only broken by insects, by the happy transference of the epithet from the weather to that one of its concomitants which, at such a season, makes most impression upon the languid attention. A throng of orientals are described by Milton:—

" *Dusk* faces in *white* silken turbans wreath'd."

The most picturesque line in our language. Cowper personifies the East, as—

" The jewelled and turban'd East."

Mr. Leigh Hunt has justly remarked, the exquisite suggestiveness with which Homer makes Achilles reverence " the grey chin" of Priam, showing, as it does, the old father's sharp and worn face upturned in the agony of supplication.

V. *Aggregation* is another peculiar source of pleasure, by which we mean, not a vague, dim, meaningless profusion of colours and images, in themselves beautiful, with or without pretext, the " *dulce vitium*" of Shelley, of Gerald Massie, and Mr. Edwin Arnold, and in degree of Keats,' and Tennyson ; but a " scattering from the pictured urn" round a beautiful object such cognate and congruous beauties *heaped together* as fill the imagination with delight. Hobbes seems to us to have penetrated the secret of this power as an intellectual phenomenon, though not so completely as he would have done had he lived to see his doctrine of the " coherence or consequence of one conception to another, from their first coherence or consequence at that time when they are produced† originally," developed (by Dr. Thomas Brown especially) into the phenomena of association and suggestion. Hobbes tells us that by memory " the fancy, when any work of art is to be performed, finds her materials prepared, and needs no more than a swift motion over them. So that when she seems to fly from one Indies to another, and from heaven to earth, and all this in a point of time, the voyage is not very great, herself being all she seeks, and her wonderful celerity consisteth *not so much in motion as in copious imagery, discreetly ordered and perfectly registered in the memory.*"‡ Of this aggregative power of accumulating beautiful objects round some *one,* not with a random splendour, but with a living and guiding principle of harmony, Burns may afford us an illustration :—

" Alas ! it's not *thy neighbour sweet,*
  The bonnie *lark,* companion meet,
  Bending thee 'mang the *dewy weet*
  Wi' speckled breast,
When upward springing blithe to greet
  The *purpling east.*"

Did any rational being ever read or hear these lines without pleasure ? and if he proceeded to analyse his pleasure, would he not find that it arose from the life given to the daisy by the word *neighbour,* and then from the *aggregation* round it of the dew, the lark,

---

* " Paradise Regained," iv. 426. The expression, " horns coming out of his hand " (Habakkuk, iii. 4), seems to be just equivalent to " radiant hand."
  † " Human Nature," chap. iv. 2.
  ‡ Letter concerning Sir W. Davenant's Preface.

and the purpling east, all exquisitely pertinent to the picture in hand?

VI. The poet illuminates, emblazons narrative as rarely and delicately as some old artist coloured a favourite chronicler. Among the assistants of memory, Bacon places the *deductio intellectualis ad sensibile;* among the glories of poetry we may place the "clothing upon" of narrative with beauty, the translation of the *factual* into the imaginative equivalent, without the sacrifice of literal truth. Every proposition boiled down to its bones, logically may be resolved into subject, predicate, and copula; every proposition robed and diademed imperially by poetry arrays the subject in the purple garment of the loveliest attribute which it possesses, and sets upon the predicate a crown all starred with subtly-wrought jewelry of selected words, whose multilateral cutting catches the finest lights of its happiest associations. In prose we might say, "a nice, pretty child, with blue eyes, seven years old;" an ordinary rhymer might exchange years for summers, "A blue-eyed thing, seven summers old." But Campbell says immortally—

"In her young eyes the *seventh blue summer shone.*"

In prose we should say, "Such a thing happened two years ago." The poet dates not by an almanac, but by successive eras of beauty. Mr. Alexander Smith very daintily sings—

"Twice hath the windy *summer made a noise Of leaves o'er all the land* from sea to sea."

The lover sighs out to his intended, "In four days I shall be happy." Edmund Spencer in his "Epithalamium," and Alfred Tennyson, *passim,* are the most golden interpreters of the poetry of the betrothal and the espousal; but it is no reproach to the memory of Spencer, it will not be felt as a disparagement by our great living poet, to say that Shakspeare is the most honourable of these three mighty men. Let us remember how the *Midsummer Night's Dream* opens:—

THESEUS.

"Now, fair Hippolyta, our nuptial hour
Draws on apace. Four happy days bring on
Another moon; but O! methinks how slow
This old moon wanes; she lingers my desires
Like to a step-dame, or a dowager,
Long withering out a young man's revenue.

HIP.

"Four days will quickly steep themselves in nights,
Four nights will quickly dream away the time;
And then the moon, like to a silver bow
New bent in heaven, shall behold the night
Of our solemnities."

Many other subordinate sources of pleasure might of course be named—for instance, the transference of beautiful effects by analogy from one sense to another. Bacon,[*] speaking of that yet unnamed Philosophia Prima, the receptacle of axioms which cannot be exclusively appropriated by particular sciences, gives as an analogous example, the following—"The tremulous sound of music affords the same species of pleasure to the ear which the scintillating light upon water or a jewel affords to the eye." "*Splendet tremulo sub lumine pontus.*"

And he elsewhere speaks of a *scent* "warbling in the air." So Virgil sings—

"*Claro* cernes *sylvas Aquilone moveri;*"

And Æschylus has his λαμπρὸς ἄνεμος; and Shelley—

"All the earth and air
With thy voice is *loud,*
As, when night is bare,
From one lonely cloud
The moon rains out her beams, and heaven is overflowed.
From rainbow clouds there flow not
Drops so bright to see,
As from thy presence *showers* a rain of melody."

One more topic we cannot refrain from introducing under the present head.

Is absolute originality necessary to the pleasure which poetry is fitted to produce? if so, of the three classes under which Gibbon arranges the images of the creation—man, art, and nature — the latter is completely exhausted, and the poetry of this age, beyond that of every other, is hollow and unreal. "Nature," says that critic, "vast as it is, has furnished the poets with but few ideas. Restricted to its mere outside shell, they have been able to depict only the successive variations of the seasons, a sea wrought up by tempests, or the zephyrs of spring breathing pleasure and love. A small number of geniuses quickly exhausted these subjects." That this criticism dislimns the entire pictorial aspect of all poetry, save that of remote antiquity, is sufficiently

---

[*] "De Augn. Scient." lib. iii. c. 5.

clear. But as well might we accuse Nature of sameness, because her ever fresh and ever lovely effects are produced by a limited number of constantly-recurring materials — wood, hill, and water; sunlight and moonlight; an apparatus of cloud and shadow, of stars above and flowers below; such are the elements from which she evokes the glory and the loveliness which covers this ancient earth with a youth that is perpetually renewed. Of this salient freshness, of this sempiternal youth, poetry is a partaker. Shakspeare, for instance, seems to have exhausted the poetry of clouds, when the doomed Anthony speaks so wonderfully of—

" Black vesper's pageant."

Yet Wordsworth sings " To the clouds" a strain as new as if the imperial fancy of Shakspeare had never collated imagery from cloudland; nay, in his " Sky prospect from the plain of France," concluding in that majestically imaginative moral—

" Meek nature's evening comment on the shows,
That for oblivion take their daily birth,
From all the fuming vanities of earth,"

he takes the same canopy of clouds, and moulds it not less beautifully than Shakspeare, yet as diversely from him as if they were two designers kneading the ductile clay for different purposes. Or, again, in our own day, Wordsworth has described the sunset in his most glorious colours. Does this diminish our delight in hearing Mr. Keble sing, in his exquisite poem, "Looking Westward"?—

" Wide be the western casement thrown
At sultry evening's fall—
The gorgeous lines be duly shown,
That weave heaven's wondrous pall!"

But let us illustrate our view of the distinction between the genius which exalts what it has, perhaps unconsciously, borrowed, toning it into a finer music, and touching it with the colours of its proper thought, and the plagiarism which wears another's splendours, as Braggadocio wore the armour of Sir Guyon, worthy of the literary whip and treadmill.

Our illustration may take the form of a legal apologue.

Ourselves sitting in judgment, there are cited before us William Wordsworth, Esq., and the Rev. W. E. Green, of Worcester College, Oxford, accused of misdemeanour, each, and severally — to wit, of stealing certain thoughts. And first the indictment runs against Mr. Wordsworth, " For that he, in a poem, entitled ' Laodamia,' did, in a covert and secret manner, filch from one Abraham Tucker, commonly called Edward Search, one of his most ingenious thoughts." We listen with patience to the case, of which we can only give the counsel's speech for defence :— " That there exists similarity between thoughts in Mr. Tucker's forgotten work and Mr. Wordsworth's exquisite poem, cannot be denied. Thus Mr. Tucker describes himself as a disembodied spirit, conducted into the presence of a beloved wife. John Locke, his companion and guide, warns him, ' She is not a woman here, so you must consider her a friend, and not a wife. Let us have no kissings nor embracings, no raptures nor transports; remember that we are here all *Isangeloi*, therefore your love must be pure, sedate, and angelical.' After much talk, the husband at last says, ' The laws of this place lay a severe restraint upon the fondness of love—a love pure and innocent. My rigid tutor here has forbid me one civil salute ; am I not allowed to take your hand ?' At this the dear eyes seemed ready to overflow with tears; there came out a taper arm, and pretty hand, having on one of the fingers the semblance of our wedding-ring. I shot forth an eager arm to take hold of it, and now, perhaps, had grasped it fast, had not that severe, relentless pedagogue, who never knew the tenderness of love, been too nimble for me."[*] Similarly Laodamia exclaims to the ghost of her loved and lost Protesilaus, and with a similar result—

" ' Redundant are thy locks, thy lips as fair
As when their breath enrich'd Thessalian air.

" No spectre greets me ; no vain shadow this.
Come, blooming hero, place thee by my side,
Give, on this well-known couch, one nuptial kiss
To me, this day a second time thy bride !'
Jove frowned in heaven, the conscious Parcæ threw
Upon those roseate lips a Stygian hue.

[*] Tucker's " Light of Nature Pursued," c. xxiii.—The Vision.

' Be taught, O faithful consort, to control
Rebellious pass one, for the gods approve
The depth, and not the tumult of the soul;
A fervent, not ungovernable love.'

Aloud she shrieks, for Hermes reappears.
Round the dear shade she would have clung—'tis vain,
The hours are past—too brief, had they been years,
And him no mortal effort can detain.''
                                  pp. 164, 165.

Those who can " without a hound
fine footing trace," may please themselves with the keenness of their scent.
There is something agreeable to
geniuses of the smaller kind in reduc-
ing mighty intellects somewhat nearer
to their own level. There are a sort
of literary American Indians, who love
to trace great poets in the snow, and
over the dead leaves of other men's
thoughts. But this honourable court
will assuredly judge, that admitting the
suggestion to have been another's, Mr.
Wordsworth rather deserves another
circlet of laurel to be wreathed round
his brow. The prose of Tucker was at
best merely like the coloured earth
which is laid at the root of some gor-
geous-blossomed plant. The genius
of the poet assimilated its hues to the
form of his own mind, and stained
every leaf of the unfolded flower with
a richness that belonged to its proper
juices, and glorified, and transele-
mented the comparatively worthless
substance on which it fed. Such, indeed, is the character of my client's
muse. She often finds a cloud-bank
of prose, and, like the sunset, tinges it
with a heavenly transfiguration of song.
I willingly refer to other instances :—

" The discerning intellect of man,
When wedded to this goodly universe
In love and holy passion, shall find these
A simple produce of the common day.
   I, long before the blissful hour arrives,
Would chant in lonely peace the spousal verse
Of this great consummation."

Thought and expression here are
nobly Baconian — " existimamus nos
thalamum mentis et universi, pronubâ
divinâ bonitate, stravisse et ornâsse."
One very dear to Mr. Wordsworth,
beautifully describes the rafters and
beams of a Highland cottage, tarnished
with perpetual smoke, as crossing each
other in almost as intricate and fantastic a manner as the underboughs of
a large beech-tree " withered by the
depth of shade above." These expressions he afterwards produces in
two fine lines, and in a context which
heightens their impressiveness.

We forthwith direct the jury to find
a verdict of acquittal. Next, the
Rev. W. E. Green, author of the
"Dedication of Solomon's Temple," the
successful competitor for the prize
poem on a sacred subject at Oxford,
unlimitedly open to graduates, tri-
ennially awarded, and restricted in
length, thus realising three probable
conditions of a fine poem, is cited
before us, accused for having stolen
two lines from the Right Rev. Reginald
Heber, D.D., sometime Lord Bishop
of Calcutta :—

" No workmen's steel, no ponderous axes rung ;
   Like some tall palm the noiseless fabric sprung."

The stolen property reproduced by
Mr. Green, in the following shape :—

" As some tall cedar, 'neath the summer skies
And winter snows of hoary Libanus,
Majestically lifts its hoary head ;

And year by year steals imperceptibly
Through the cleft air, its silent, heavenward march,
Unheard, unnoticed:

So Zion's temple rose ; no jarring note,
No crash of masonry, nor sound of axe,
Nor saw, nor plane, nor hammer's rattling din
Profaned the hallowed precincts ; awe profound
And reverent silence reign'd amidst the whole.
While *unobserved* the mighty structure grew
All noiselessly ; as though from earth it sprung
Spontaneous."

The prisoner at once pleading guilty;
we thus pass sentence — " Prisoner,
you stand in a position eminently
disgraceful to your literary character,
and still more to that of the great
University whose laurels you wear.
And here we would warn the awarders
of poetical honours in that seminary
seriously to consider the nature and
character of blank verse. A poem in
blank verse consists not only of a
number of lines set to one tiresome
monotony of cadence — the honey of
poetry cannot be made by bees who
attempt this second-rate manufacture,
simply because they have lost the sting
of rhyme. In the hands of Milton,
Wordsworth, Keats, Coleridge — in
some degree of Tennyson, and even
of Mr. Arnold, and Mr. Alexander
Smith, it is a sweet involution of
concentric rings of melody; not only
does it scan by the fingers taken *line-
wise*, but read from cadence to cadence,
from pause to pause, each clause, like
a cut worm, quivers with melody.
So true is this, that Shakspeare, a
mightier master of blank verse than
any that we have mentioned, does not

only manipulate his exquisite alliterations within one line, but even more; carries it on into that part of the next line which is read in the same breath therewith. Thus much for others. For you, prisoner, you have utterly destroyed that majestic palm, by turning it into a cedar; you have raised a mighty hubbub of words, ' silent, *unheard*, unnoticed, imperceptibly, reverent silence, unobserved, all noiselessly,' and much else, if so be you might hide your theft. But, because of your gown, and forasmuch as you are otherwise a good, and, it may be, even an able man, we dismiss you, on condition that you write no more verse — at least no more blank verse — seeing that that which you have already perpetrated is alike without music and without thought; being merely certain chapters of Kings and Chronicles, mangled and transposed; or rather an abridgment of Scripture history, so printed that every eleventh syllable begins with a capital letter."

On the whole, then, we are convinced that by thus referring the pleasure which he feels to permanent principles — such as those which, by way of sample, we have instanced — the student of poetry may turn fugitive delight into abiding profit. And if this be true of the less philosophical side of poetry, much more may it be predicated of that which the ancient critics considered of much greater importance — delineation of manners, and that "pleasing analysis whereby the poet — thrusting into the middest, even where it most concerneth him, and then recoursing to the things forepast, and divining of things yet to come—unwinds the intricate threads of events; not less distinctly,"[*] with reference to his end, than the " historiographer discoursing of affairs, orderly as they were done, and accounting as well the times as the actions."[†] But the rough sketch which we have chalked out at the commencement of this article, would be imperfectly coloured, indeed, if we said nothing of the bearing of true poetry upon the *moral* culture of *humanity*.

And here we are not aware of any *authority* adverse to our conclusion, save the weighty name of Plato. He,

as every one knows, drew a picture of an ideal state, from which he excluded Homer, and all poetry but hymns to the gods and panegyrics of the good. But a man like Plato must have seen much in heathen poetry to justify this severity. The golden songs of Homer represented that land which lies beyond the grave as a dark and cheerless portion even to the righteous; they painted gods who were excited with human laughter and melted with human tears—who quaffed the bubbling wine from the beaker, who were overcome by the unworthiest passions, and perpetrated the darkest crimes. The latter was an evil which at once arose from, and aggravated the depravity of the human heart. Men shaped out their notions of deity by looking upon it through the coloured medium of their own corrupt will, with the eye of the soul tinctured by the suffusion of their unhallowed lusts; and then, again, others derived a singular aptitude for wickedness from these conceptions, hardened into concrete representations, and might plead a divine example as a precedent for their sins. Hence, the lasting divorce between religion and morality, so that the moralist could inculcate the expulsion of obscenity from every other scene but the service of the gods — a divorce which has never been reconciled except in Him who " gave himself for us, that He might redeem us from all iniquity, who redeemed us from the curse of the law, that we might be under the law to him." Besides this, Plato considered the poetry of Greece a mere imitation of manners, and an imitation which was not beneficial to virtue. Thus the poet imitates, with pathos, an exhorbitant grief, such as a good man would think it sinful to exhibit himself. In this way, he unconsciously imbibed an influence which unnerved his soul in the hour when it was tried by the stern realities of life. Remembering, moreover, the old quarrel between poetry and philosophy, reason and imagination, slowly and reluctantly he passed the sentence of exile upon Homer and the tragedians; but it was a conditional sentence — *until* Poetry or her friends should make her defence.

---

[*] Εἰρωνεία.—Aristotle.
[†] E. Spencer's Letter to Sir W. Raleigh.

Surely that defence has been made. The spirit of poetry has been purified. He who objected to poetry as an imitative art, has, in another passage of his noblest work, where he speaks of painting (elsewhere placed by him in the same category), gloriously nullified his own objection. He who paints a beautiful picture cannot be coldly astricted to the demonstration of the objective existence of an equally beautiful prototype. His pencil does not copy that which is itself but a copy ; the eternal essential *idea* guides its work, which has a universal truth far above particular imitation. By this argument, in our own time, Dr. Milman vindicates the masterpieces of painting from peril of idolatry : men hang with the fondness of superstition upon the florid daub which is an individual likeness ; the painting is less and less likely to be idolised as it speaks an universal truth. Plato's vindication of painting is, *a fortiori*, the vindication of poetry, though he has not developed this conclusion ; nor can we do otherwise than wonder at the exaggeration of a great truth of our moral nature. True it is, certainly, that the strings of our passive emotions cannot be stirred without doing us harm, unless the active part of our nature is brought into play.* Compassion, the feeling that brings the choking to the throat, is the woman's voice in us that bids the man in us be up and doing. It is the music which excites the soldier to the war ; but not the sinew which gives him strength to strike, nor the will which makes him resolved to do or die. The chords of feeling cannot be played upon with impunity. If the will hears their alarm too often, it ceases to heed them altogether. But the danger of sympathy abused does not evacuate its legitimate office, its tendency to refine the character by liquefying the dross of selfishness. And can we, in the nineteenth century, doubt that the feud between Poetry and Philosophy is composed ? Indeed, the very childhood of the world—

"Wooed,
Even in its dawn of thought, Philosophy,
Though then unconscious of herself, *pardie*,
She bore no other name than Poesy."†

And now, in the maturity, or old age of the human race, poetry is the sweet smile of recollection — the look of youth that yet dwells beautifully on the wrinkled brow of Truth. It has been remarked of Homer, that all morality and all the laws of thought are to be found dispersedly in his writings. They are richly agglomerated in the " primitive synthesis" of his consciousness ; it required ages to analyse that consciousness into its separate elements — to develop the primary laws which presided over their creation. The poet's now is a harder task. He must, we believe, to gain a permanent hearing from this age, have analysed his consciousness ; and over the result of this analysis—whose apparent effect is to dissolve poetry, by removing the charm of wonder—he must be enabled to throw as fine a light as the blush of dawn which steeped the original elements. He must possess that mental science which is emphatically " *philosophia laudatarum omnium artium procreatrix et quasi parens*;" not a separate knowledge, nor a mere congeries of information, but a mastery of the inter-relations of knowledge — their points of contact, and position on the field of universal science. He must possess nearly that magnificent list of acquirements which Cicero has attributed to his ideal orator. For him, all sciences must have a delicate aroma, and wear unfamiliar looks of passionate beauty. It was not without a meaning beyond their developed knowledge that his contemporaries licensed the laurelled Petrarch to lecture upon all subjects whatever. How far Wordsworth or Tennyson may have attained this ideal, we will not take upon ourselves to pronounce. They have, at all events, answered this *item* of Plato's indictment.

Having thus taken the defensive, we cannot be contented with so low a position. It is the priestly office of poetry to engage the imagination and the affections on the side of virtue and of God, by pleasurable emotion. " It is the work of poets, says Hobbes, in delightful and measured lines, to avert men from vice, and incline them to virtuous and honourable actions." It is theirs, too, to touch and purify our hearts by sympathy ; to win us,

---

* " Butler's Analogy." Part i. c. 5.
† Coleridge. " Garden of Boccacio."

half unconsciously, to what is good, by showing us that it is also beautiful. In short, to use the words of Milton, "'These abilities, wheresoever they be found, are the inspired gift of God, rarely bestowed; and are of power, beside the office of a pulpit, to allay the perturbations of the mind, and set the affections in right tune; to celebrate, in glorious and lofty hymns, the throne and equipage of God's almightiness; to sing victorious agonies of martyrs and saints. Lastly, whatsoever in religion is holy and sublime, in virtue amiable or grave; whatsoever hath passion or admiration; in all the changes of fortune from without, or the wily subtleties and refluxes of man's thoughts from within; all these things, with a solid and treatable smoothness, to point out and describe: teaching over the whole book of sanctity and virtue with such delight, that, whereas the paths of honesty appear now rugged, they will then appear to all men both easy and pleasant. And what a benefit this would be to our youth may be guessed by the bane which they suck in daily from the writings of libidinous and ignorant poetasters, who, having scarce ever heard of that which is the main consistence of a true poem, do, for the most part, lay up vicious principles in sweet pills to be swallowed down." Under this head let it be noticed that the lovers of our modern poetry may thankfully trace one of its most distinctive and engaging features to the operation of Christianity. Modern poetry, as we have seen, clings to nature with a yearning tenderness, and colours her with the thoughtful hue of the mind contemplating. Not so the Greek or the Roman. Homer may paint the moonlight flooding the glens and sharp mountain peaks; Sophocles may sing of Colonos, where the nightingale wails in the thick greenery, unpierceable of sun or any storm; but they describe as coldly (to use Humboldt's language) as though they were speaking of a shield or a piece of embroidery. How was this? The Greek especially, at once so keenly observant and so deeply reflective — living so much in the open air — inhabiting a land which is indented by the sea, and thus presents the calm in its heavenliest sunniness of mood, the tempest in its wildest excitement — the mingling tints of earth and ocean, in soft-

est reconcilement, or most harmonious contrast—with its "old poetic mountains," and waves steeped at eventide of the long, long summer in that trembling haze of lustrous violet; how was it that the Greek failed to realise the finest teaching of nature? The growth of Christian literature answers the question. Our great poet has portrayed the tendency of the "lively Grecian's" mind, in a land like his, to personify the phenomena of nature. Those phenomena, then, were divorced from their proper associations, and blended with the factitious ones of an anthropomorphic religion. But the Gospel revelation, which showed that the things which are made are the work of one living and true God, gave men the habit of looking upon them as evidences of his power, wisdom, and goodness. The love and knowledge of God led to the love and knowledge of nature. Modern poetry and modern science are collateral results of Christianity, "after-growths" of pleasure and utility, "after the king's mowings" of souls brought to salvation. The first distinct evidences of that sweetly melancholy contemplation of nature which is so important an ingredient in modern poetry, might be articulately traced to the writings of certain of the Christian Fathers.

Again, those who are so sternly opposed to novel-reading should consider that poetry supplies more healthily the demand of the youthful mind, which it will otherwise assuredly gratify by novels. We, indeed, cannot agree with Edward Irving, when he declaims so picturesquely against Walter Scott: "The Magician of the North! a mighty one he is, possessed with a spirit of strong delusion. There is music in him to charm so sweetly that all who have not the safe keeping of the Spirit are carried captive with his strain. It is like the tradition told us by our mothers, of the travelling musician, who went from village to village, charming with his sweet pipe every one who was not protected by a branch of that tree whereon grows the crimson berry, like the drops of the Saviour's blood; and he would lead them dancing after him to the side of some beautiful green hill, which would straightway open at his approach, and enclose them all. A man of many inventions." Better were it for youth to be devouring three volumes a-day from the nearest circulating library, than listening to poor Irving, or his like. Still we are sensitively alive to the evils inseparable from much novel-reading by the young and inexperienced; to the expectations engendered of attaining ends in life without the use of the necessary means, as young heroes, with essenced hair and faultless waistcoats, marry heiresses of large fortune and incredible beauty; yet more, to the impression which they softly float in upon their current, that life, after certain unpleasing adventures, is unmixedly agreeable, that earth is a fit home for our affections, that marriage is practically heaven, and human love the satisfaction of the soul. But the only remedy is to fortify the mind generally: "*Potius ad fortiter vivendum quam ad caute abstinendum;*" to give it an internal principle which shall countervail the dangers to which it must needs be exposed. Now, the love and intelligent appreciation of good poetry can scarcely co-exist with a passion for the outrageous stimulant at least of *bad* novels. And if we be told that "Marmion," "The Princess," and many others, are merely novels in verse, we maintain that, even so, they are comparatively free from one, at least, of the evils of novels in prose: their very form makes all readers instinctively feel that they represent the ideal, and not the actual.

Of course, poetry has its own dangers. There is some whose characteristic is sickliness; which makes silly young ladies and moping affected young gentlemen. "Childe Harold" has, in the long run, done more harm than "Don Juan." Profligacy has sneaked, in disguise, into some of our poetry. We would recommend readers of the "Life-Drama," and of some other pretty poems of the day, to rub off the musical colouring of verse, and take a steady look into the face of the thought before them. Too many poets have been latitudinarian. This is the natural tendency, without due corrective, of the poetic instinct, which seeks to find love and beauty in every thing. The couplet which, in a pointed and popular shape, expresses the lati-

tudinarian sentiment, that acceptable virtue may exist without orthodox belief, has been borrowed by Pope from Cowley, speaking of Crashaw's secession to Rome:—

> "Even in error sure no danger is,
> When joined with so much piety as his;
> His *faith*, perhaps, in some nice tenets, might
> Be wrong—I'm sure his *life* was in the right."

The Papist Pope's plagiarised version,

> "For modes of faith let wrangling bigots fight,
> He can't be wrong whose life is in the right,"

has been so mischievously influential as to be esteemed worthy of distinct refutation by the acute Archbishop of Dublin. Or, once more. A peculiar difficulty seems to be felt at the present day, in admitting the eternity of future punishments. This, we venture to say, exists principally in legal minds attached to the Benthamite philosophy of jurisprudence. The habit of rejecting all punishment that is not plainly exemplary or reformative, prevents the mind from looking beyond these accidents to the characteristic of justice. Yet into how many minds have doubts of the Scripture representation of God's moral government been injected, like a dart of fire, by Burns, herein an unconscious Origenist:—

> "I'm wae to think upon that den,
> E'en for your sake." *

Above all, death has too often been objectionably treated by our poets. The prevalent idea that the souls of little children are metamorphosed into angels—one, with the denial of which we have known a pious simple believer greatly scandalised, is a part of the mythology of the heart, in a Christian shape, which poetry has enabled to pass current. But some of them are responsible for much worse than this beautiful fancy. How many have they led to believe practically, that death is but a sweet and dreamless sleep. Who can estimate the effects of the odious flippancy, for instance, with which it has been treated by Pope in his Epitaph on himself? Yet, after all drawbacks, we believe that there is a progress of poetry, as there is of society. And what is progress?—is it

---

* So Uncle Toby: " ' He is the father of lies, and is cursed already,' said Dr. Slop. ' I am sorry for it,' said my Uncle Toby." Such opinions have a more respectable pedigree than might have been imagined, as we could easily show.

the mere blind, undisciplined heaving of a lifeless tide of dissociated units, agitated by winds of chance? Not so; when we gaze at the gallant vessel on the horizon line, steering away to some distant harbour, we cannot see the pilot at the wheel, we cannot hear the word of command, but we know that there is a living hand that guides, and that the vessel obeys a living purpose. Such a purpose we trace in the progress of literature. In morality we find an unbeliever like Shaftesbury overruled to that theory of moral sentiment which, interrogated by Butler, becomes the witness to virtue, to duty, and to God. In poetry, after all temporary aberrations of taste, we find that ever living and ever moulding men's minds which is based upon a true view of our nature, and informed by the eternal principles of truth. Thus, the best manual of systematic morality in our language, Dr. Whewell's "Elements of Morality," is dedicated to Wordsworth, as due to one in whom the writer, "along with many others, found a spirit of pure and comprehensive morality, operating to raise his readers above the moral temper of those times." It has been falsely said that the immortality of man means that the species is imperishable, while the individuals are mortal; it may truly be predicated of bad poetry and bad poets, that the succession is continuous and unbroken, while the particular individuals have a name that, in one or two generations, perisheth out of the city.

And now, turning from the readers to the writers of poetry, seriously do we recommend to the consideration of our younger bards the memorable dictum of the heathen, that the good *poet* must be a good *man.* To Mr. Smith we would add, *ex abundanti*, that over and above purging away certain peccant humours, he must train his mind by severe discipline; that he must learn more truly and more deeply what human life is, before he can expect to dramatise it; that his comparisons, beautiful as they are, are too monotonous, and need fresh infusions from a larger knowledge. Let us whisper deferentially to Tennyson—let us say in bolder tones to Mr. Arnold, that Pliny esteemed it an unhopeful prospect for art, when sculptors, instead of charming by forms, made use of glittering sub-

stances and coloured rocks, to attract a gaping and ignorant wonder to those showy materials. Thoughts are to words as the form to the sculptor's materials. A glittering, affected language is the trick of the day; it may not last longer than the Elizabethian Euphuism — it will not please more generations than one.

A few concluding words. Poetry, we said, is the expression of the want of something better than this world can give. God has given us no want which has not its proper end, therefore poetry is a proof of man's immortality. This is not the fantastic argument of a dreamer; it is suggested by him who has given the name to that philosophy which multiplies the comforts and utilities of life, covers our land with a network of iron rails, and flashes thought along the wires. "If any man," says Bacon, "will look closely, poetry supplies proof that a mightier magnitude, a more perfect order, a fairer variety, is the aim of the human mind, than it may find in nature, since the fall." Poetry, then, is an historian and a prophet—the historian of a glory that is past — the prophet of a glory that shall be revealed. Our poetry is a voice of longing and of yearning, but in heaven, where the ideal and the actual coincide, the poetry is triumphant—"The Song of Moses" and "The Song of the Lamb." We may not have poetic power, we may not even have poetic taste, but we have the root of poetry in our souls.

We do not, then, esteem it a bad symptom of our age, that we have so many young poets—a fact which implies many readers. We are more than unwilling that the education of the poetical part of our nature should be eliminated. We will none of the theories which would give to God the reason only; the fairest products of the imagination are due to Him also. We have a symbol of this in the fragrant ointment and the alabaster box, more signally still in the Arimathean and Nicodemus. Linen of coarse texture may suffice for shroud and winding-sheet; nay, it shall be the finest and costliest the loom can weave. A moderate quantity of spices will be enough; nay. His body shall lie steeped in heaps of Arabian odours. A common sepulchre will serve for the resting-place of the corpse; nay, the clay shall not lie on Him who was the rose of Sharon and the lily of the valley; He shall not lie in the Potter's-field—His body shall have a garden of beauty, where trees shall wave over it all the summer long, and flowers shall make a pleasant smell. For Him, then, we claim the fine linen, and the spices of man's wonderful intellect, the ointment of thought in the alabaster box of poetic form. We would not only have the adoration of the shep-

herds; we love to see Bacon and Whewell, Buckland and Sedgewick, bringing to Him the gold of philosophy, and Butler the preserving myrrh of pure morality; and it is our earnest hope, that more and more of our poets may add to the grains of frankincense which have been already flung into the fire, which burns in the temple, by Keble and Heber, by Milton and Wordsworth.

SCOTTISH CAVALIERS AND JACOBITE CHIEFTAINS.[*]

THE passage of a people out of the barbaric but splendid era of chivalry, into that of peaceful economic development, is no doubt a subject well worthy of philosophic observation. But there are few men capable of harmonising both sides of such a picture. The economist is rarely philosopher enough to do justice to the hero, and the man of sentiment has as seldom the capacity to relieve the details of mere material progress from dryness and insipidity. Mr. Burton, our latest Scottish historian, aspires to present these two phases of his country's progress in artistic combination. We have the picturesque career of Dundee at one end of the composition, and the chimneys of Glasgow at the other. Mr. Burton is a scientific Whig, and has done the dull half of his work more agreeably than the lively one. He is a man of vigorous understanding, and of considerable, but not adequate, ability in writing. A laborious clumsiness mars many of his best reflections, and one cannot help wondering at the vanity and ambitious awkwardness of his language, while recognising, with agreeable surprise, the force and justice of the sentiments conveyed. But we must not quarrel with a man of ability, because his style is not equal to his matter, nor his treatment of the heroic equal to that of the economic half of his subject. In some moods of mind a philosophic man may regret that the arts of peace, in putting an end to the dangers and lawlessness of

the chivalrous times, have supplanted also their nobility of sentiment and their grace of genius. No inaugural odes of mechanics' institutes will ever equal the Jacobite songs of Scotland. No lectures on mental or moral philosophy will ever stir in the bosoms of the Scottish youth the sentiments of generosity, honour, and devotion which actuated thousands of men of all ranks in the days of Scotland's poverty and so-called ignorance. It seems, however, to be a law of social compensation, that as a people lose fervor, genius, and nationality, they gain the ability of producing and securing the enjoyment of wealth, and with wealth the advantages of every kind of mental and bodily cultivation. No one would wish, in his own person, to make a permanent change from the more prosaic to the more poetic period. Mr. Burton hardly feels at home in revisiting the ante-union epoch even on paper; and, truth to say, his post-union disquisitions are too cleverly discreet and too correctly dull to afford us any delight, however great the instruction we might draw from them if we needed anything to convince us of the advantages of peace, order, and a strong central government. But that cry of Sir Colin Campbell's, "We'll hae nane but Highland bonnets here," has stirred within us something of the spirit of the olden time, and we will leave the cold patriotism of the Dalrymples and even the calm wisdom of President Forbes at one side for the present, and

---

LITTLE LESSONS FOR LITTLE POETS.

THERE is a pleasant little superstition, not yet quite banished from the world, that to write and publish a book, especially a volume of poems, is an indication of some talent that distinguishes its fortunate possessor from the non-publishing portion of mankind. Authors, as a class, are regarded as persons superior in intellect and knowledge to their fellow-men who are innocent of printers' ink and know nothing of the mystery of proof-sheets. But as most advantages in this chequered life have their accompanying drawbacks, the same people who elevate writers of books into the kings of men, and the writers of poems into the aristocracy—the *crème de la crème*—of book-writers, believe that this favoured division of the human race is saddled with an incubus, plagued with a specific parasite, which vexes its peace, befouls its stately grace, and impairs its vitality; that as the whale has its louse, so the poet has his critic. In the former branch of this superstition we were at one time—as we suppose most other youths have been—devout believers; and the first day we beheld an author was a red-letter day in our calendar. Well, too, do we remember that at this credulous and enthusiastic period of life, if there was one man we envied and admired next to the writer of a volume of poems, it was the lucky individual—a master in the school which had the honour of our education—who was in the habit of receiving parcels of books for review, and had, so far as our knowledge of the transaction extended, the books he reviewed for his sole *honorarium* and reward; and richly did we think he was rewarded for what we imagined to be one of the most ennobling and delightful occupations. Wide as is the gulf which separates us from those days of long ago—difficult as it would be to realize again, in any one direction, 'the hopes, the fears of childhood's years' — no youthful experience seems so alien to our present judgment, no youthful delusion has been so completely turned inside out, as this of the glory of seeing one's name on a title-page, and the felicity of receiving gratis a constant supply of new books on condition of reviewing them, or even of reading them. In regard to the superior faculties of the literary class, the truth would seem to be that, beyond requiring the elementary accomplishments of reading and writing, that occupation demands and obtains no more ability, nor ability of a higher order, than most other of the employments in use among us—far less than many; that it is practically the refuge of persons who have not steadiness, energy, or ability for the more manly and active employments; and that it is so because, like needlework, it requires no special training. We are not by any means sure that the classification which assigns the highest rank among men to the great poets is the truest; we find in the great poets themselves—in Shakspeare, in Dante, in Homer— no trace of the feeling that they are greater than the men whose deeds they sing: but we are sure that the glory reflected from these great poets upon literature in general, and especially upon poetry, is a light that leads men's imaginations astray—that makes many a young man and woman utterly misunderstand the purposes of their existence in the world, and ridiculously magnify the relative importance of certain talents which they possess in common with, and in no higher degree than, the majority of mankind; and as the result, deluges our contemporary literature with productions which, calling themselves by the venerable name of poetry, indicate in their authors nothing which distinguishes them from nine-tenths of their fellow-countrymen of the same age, except a deficiency of modesty and good sense, and an utter insensibility to the characteristics of good poetry. There may be a question whether Shakspeare or Sir Philip Sidney was the higher kind of man; there is none whatever that Jones, after publishing a volume of doggrel verse, is a more undeniable ninny than when he was content

to blush unseen,
And waste his sweetness on the desert air.

A 'mute inglorious Milton' may be a loss to the human race ; but to Jones, ere he determine to unseal his lips, touched, as he thinks, with a coal from the altar, we recommend to ponder well the profound sentiment of Keats—

Heard melodies are sweet, but those unheard
Are sweeter.

But some reader of tender disposition and genial sympathies will say—Is this the mood of mind in which justice can be done to even the smallest poets ? Is not this mere savage fury, the expression of a natural indifference and a hardened dislike to poetry ? And are we not constantly told that it is the besetting sin of the critic to fancy himself the judge instead of the pupil of the poet—to set up his preconceived notions of what poetry ought to be, instead of humbly receiving the poet's higher inspiration as law and gospel in one, as a message from a better world, that pleads at no critical bar, is amenable to no critical rule, and justifies itself by its welcome to the hearts of men ?

So much has been said of late years on the impossibility of judging poetry aright except by sympathy, on the folly of the 'carnal mind,'—by which is meant the analytic intellect—pretending to decide the claims of 'spiritual things,' that the balance of truth has, in our opinion, been a little overweighted in that direction. True enough it is that poets have occasionally met hard measure at the hands of critics ; that conventional rules of partial application have been stretched into universal principles ; that the taste of an age or even a man has been erected into a standard of humanity ; and great individual injustice has therefrom resulted. But if both critics and poets would remember what is implied in the word *critic* or *judge*, all misapprehension as to the true position and powers of the critic would vanish, however imperfectly the function might continue to be discharged and the power exercised in particular cases. A judge is one who expounds the laws, and gives sentences in accordance with his exposition ; and the use of the title as applied to persons whose profession it is to estimate the pretensions of poetical writers, implies that there are laws to which both critic and poet are amenable. All that has been said of the superiority of the poet as poet, to his critic as critic, is true exactly in proportion as the poet class generally has a stronger hold of, and a deeper insight into, these laws than the critic class ; just as we may say that in a certain sense the practical chemist or manufacturer who employs the agencies and instruments of his art in obedience to the natural laws, has a stronger hold of, and a deeper insight into, these natural laws, than the philosopher in his closet, who studies them for speculative purposes merely. The parallel may not run on all-fours, but the analogy is sufficiently illustrative. And we should all think it a strange and absurd proceeding if the class of men who deal practically with natural materials, in obedience to natural laws, were to set up the claim of not being amenable to the judgment of men who have a speculative knowledge of those laws, simply because their knowledge is speculative science and not manual skill. And not less absurd if, because practical knowledge and manual skill have wrought marvels on the face of the earth, every new pretender to either was to be exempt from judgments founded on previous experience ; and though manifesting a total ignorance of the hitherto known laws of nature, was to be trusted on his mere claim to practical knowledge, as the discoverer of new powers, and his nostrums heralded as a panacea from Heaven to be used and not analysed. And yet this is something like the claim set up for poets or would-be poets ; and critics are asked to do what is impossible—to forget their common sense, their knowledge of literature and of its laws, and not to pronounce sentence of condemnation on an apparent nincompoop, lest he be a Tennyson in the chrysalis state, an undeveloped Goethe, or an immature Keats. If the critic deserves the name, his respect is for the laws of art, his tenderness for the ideal beauty, his homage for the true and the good, of which he is the priest, though it be of a different order, as well as the poet; and his especial business it is to assert the awful sovereignty of the laws of the true and the good over priest of both the poet and the critic order, to resist all attempts to degrade those laws to compliance with individual caprice, and, as the chief means of fulfilling his office, to raise himself above all partial and personal arbitrariness of judgment, to that temper of mind which we in England understand by the term judicial. Published criticism, if it is to be anything more than a means of gratifying friendly or malignant feeling towards individuals, anything better than a testimonial of Smith's personal regard for, or dislike to Jones, than a publisher's advertisement of his own works, must be regardless of individuals. There is no medium. The institution might be of great service to literature and art; even now, impaired as its utility is by the action of personal regards and literary partisanship, it is of service in maintaining a higher acknowledged standard of taste and morals, than would be maintained without it by the simple action of unaided public opinion; and so far as it does this service it is by being administered in a strictly judicial spirit. And as our national experience of the value of judicial integrity and strict impartiality has developed among us such a regard for these qualities, that it would surprise us to hear of a man being offended with a judge for giving a decision against him, so in time the same feeling might be expected to grow up about literary criticisms: and, personal regards once habitually banished from the literary judgment seat, we should find poets and painters no more offended with the individuals who pronounced unfavourable judgments on their works, than in their civic capacity they would be angry with the judge who found the law opposed to their claims, and gave judgment against them. If we valued as we ought the influence of literature and art upon the nation, if we remembered that bad books displace good ones, for a time at least; that faculties uselessly exercised on literary employment might do the State good service if properly suited with occupation; that the standard of excellence is lowered by the toleration and laudation bestowed upon bad books and stupid writers,—we should perhaps begin to see that a strict judicial temper of criticism was no unimportant element in the vigorous and sound mental health of the nation, and should look upon the critic who ignorantly or wilfully misplaced his praise and blame, as we do upon the judge who, from ignorance of the law or corrupt intention, perverts justice and undermines the bulwarks of social order and prosperity.

The batch of books which stand in long array upon our table, and which consists of about twenty volumes of verse, published within the last twelve months, is, with the striking exception of *Aurora Leigh*, as wretched a specimen of a year's productions as ever came before us for judgment. Of course it forms but a small portion of the article verse-books turned out of the London and provincial press within the year; but we have no reason for supposing it other than an average portion, fairly enough representing the quality of the whole annual produce. Nor are we so green as to be particularly disappointed at finding but the faintest indications of true poetic gold among these results of laborious word-grubbing. But it is strange that so little thought, knowledge, feeling, or mental product of any kind, should be discoverable; that the mere faculty of arranging words metrically should be able to pass, with a large number of persons of literary habits and tastes, as a sufficient substitute for all else that makes up the spirit, the body, and the form of poetry. We have no intention of reviewing these books, or of investigating the pretensions of their writers to the possession of the poetical faculties; but from a few of them we shall select the texts of some very elementary lessons which our experience of these very books proves to be needed, but which those persons who fancy they do not need any lesson, elementary or advanced, may leave alone, if they are so minded.

It may seem to be a lesson too elementary for any use, too barren a truism to be by any possibility overlooked, that a man must have something to say before he says it, and that before a man can write poems he must have poems in his mind. Truism it may indeed be; but if our writers would mark, learn, and inwardly digest it, the result would be the saving of more printed paper than our statistical arithmetic cares to calculate. Gratiano the Venetian is a type of one large class of writers in verse who speak an infinite deal of nothing; and Mr. Albert Smith's famous engineer Edwards, of another large class who have nothing to say and can't say it. In the former class, poetic matter is wanting, but a wonderful fluency of words that mean nothing to the purpose keeps up in the writer and in the inferior class of readers the delusion that poetry is being created; in the latter class, it is difficult to understand how either writer or reader can be deceived by the incoherent phrases and 'damnable iterations' that betray a mind struggling to deliver itself of its own flatulent emptiness. Almost anything is capable of poetic treatment. We at least are not going just now to lay down any eclectic theory which shall separate the world into its poetic and prosaic elements— which shall say to the poet, 'Thus far shalt thou go, and no farther;' beyond these limits all is common and unclean. An event in history, a phenomenon of nature, an individual life, a human character, a mood of mind, a single passing thought or feeling, are all adequate subjects for poems, and noble poems have been times beyond number made out of each of them. The primary condition of poems being written on these subjects is, that they should present themselves to a writer's mind with sufficient reality for him to individualize them—to see them separate from the class to which they belong—from the general terms which express the qualities they have in common with other objects of the same class. The more completely this realization of a poetical theme as something *sui*

generis is attained,—the more the features essential to the individual and not common to the class are predominant and vivid in the poet's mind, the more perfectly has he mastered the primary condition of the production of a poem. What sort of a poem he will produce will then depend upon the peculiar bias of his mind to this or that of the myriad aspects which every object presents to men, upon the stage of the language in which he writes, upon the degree in which he is master of its powers, upon the general knowledge and refinement of his age, and the degree in which he partakes of them. Coleridge has defined life to consist in individualization; and we know no larger or more exhaustive or more intelligible definition of poetry, in its comprehensive sense, as the product of the imaginative faculty, than to describe it as the transcript of life, as the delineation of objects by their individual characteristics, more or less complete according to the nature of the poet's design, but always distinguished by the presence of some one or more attributes not included in the general term which designates the class to which they logically belong. Of Milton's three essentials of poetry, 'simple, sensuous, and passionate,' we fix upon the middle term as expressing its fundamental quality, and should prefer, as more accurate and exhaustive, the word *concrete*. The concrete element in human thought, and in the literature which represents human thought, is the substance of poetry; and where that concrete element is wanting in the mind of a writer, and consequently in the language that expresses his mind, however much clever writing there may be, there is no poetry.

Whatever subject a poet deals with is real to his mind, present as an actual thing which is stirring his sympathies to song; and what he undertakes in writing a poem about it, is to make it present to his reader's mind, and by the phrases and the rhythm which are his instruments of expression, to make that reader share his emotion. Whether the subject be a tale of human joy and sorrow, a passing sentiment of pensive solitude, a thought of mightiest grandeur, a freak of fancy, a lovely flower, or the destiny of worlds, the poet's brain must be a mirror in which the object is actually present in its living characteristics, a theatre in which real forms mimic the scenic evolutions of life. And whatever ghosts are allowed upon that stage, the actors must in no case be reduced to the thin and bodiless abstraction undistinguishable in feature, shape, or limb, by which on the one hand the ordinary utilitarian thinking of men is carried on almost unconsciously, and which logical science on the other hand is ever striving to reduce to a still more impalpable and unreal condition. When Coleridge, struggling after that most difficult attainment, an exact definition of poetry, rests with all his emphasis upon this one quality of a poem, that it should 'communicate from each part the greatest immediate pleasure compatible with the largest sum of pleasure on the whole,' he expressed the direct result of the truth that, in whatever the poet deals with, he never loses hold for a moment longer than is necessary from the imperfection of language, of the real aspects of things, those aspects which arouse our emotional nature out of the lethargy of habit and familiarity, in discerning and appropriating which true life of mind, that mind which half creates and half perceives, may be said to consist. The mere act of writing a poem, if it is anything more than a copy of verses, means that some particular aspect of an object has revealed itself to the mind with a power and a glory which can only be expressed by singing; and as the poem developes itself in the mind, each phase of that development is a new revelation of qualities in the object, so exciting, so vividly present, so real to the sympathies and the senses, that ordinary prose language and ordinary prose arrangement are not adequate to express the singer's sense of the spectacle, and his whole being is raised into a state of excitement finding its vent, its satisfaction, and its natural expression, in 'thoughts that breathe and words that burn.' For any man to assume the form of poetry when he sees nothing and feels nothing, has no-

thing in his brain but the echo of other men's emotions, is a singular proof of the vast power of words and the associations they gather round them, of their power to call up in the mind a reference to the things they have stood for, sufficiently intelligible to cause a pleasurable excitement even where there is the most unquestionable evidence that the things themselves are not pictured to the imagination, and cannot therefore be transmitted to others by the person thus affected.

And thus we return to the truism with which we started, and the first lesson we would impress upon the minds of persons who are fond of writing verses, and meditate ever publishing a volume of 'poems,' is, that to write poems they must have poems in their minds; that the phrases and the rhymes they write down upon paper must be, if they are good for anything, the imperfect transcript of bright living pictures photographed direct from nature upon their brains. We are not pretending here to discuss the qualifications of the poet, as the singer, distinguished from the artist who writes prose fictions. Imaginative power is essential to both; the difference lies rather in the kind of sensibility awakened by the objects to which imagination is directed in the two cases, and consequent upon this sensibility in the degree of relative importance assigned to particular details. And we know no better test of the value of any poetic composition than just to turn it into prose. Lose, of course, it will, if the poetic form be the result of genuine inspiration; but it will yield as its residuum the sterling ore of which the

Cup of gold,
All rich and rough with stories of the Gods,

was framed, if a poet had the making of it. It is the nature of the kind to work in gold with more or less alloy; and the rich and jewelled form is only the fit adornment of what is itself the most precious of materials. Strip a genuine poem, however slight, of its metrical arrangement, of its merely ornamental similes—mercilessly throw it into the melting-pot, and reduce it, so far as it is possible, to pure thought as yet unexpressed in language—conceive it as it rose in vision before the poet's mind, ere his tongue had fitted it to articulate speech, and it will be found that there still remains a precious seed implicitly containing, and capable of again evolving, all the beauty that has been destroyed: or subject it to a process more capable of practical application, and translate it into a foreign tongue, all its grace of form necessarily vanishes ; but under the most disadvantageous circumstances, there remains the fresh aspect of some fact of life, some object of nature, which stirred the poet into song. We do not of course propose to institute this kind of test as the standard of the relative merits of particular poems ; but no poem that utterly breaks down under the test can be a true poem, can be anything but an imposture, a Brummagem counterfeit ; and it would certainly be a safe rule for a young poet to publish nothing that would not stand this test.

It is remarkable that of the great quantity of verse that the war has elicited, so little is tolerable. There is one noble exception in the small volume entitled *La Nation Boutiquière*, by Henry and Franklin Lushington, published about eighteen months ago. A volume of more genuine poetry, of the political and military order, we know not ; and the preface by the elder of the two accomplished brothers—who has since died in the prime of life, but late enough to have left a name that neither men of letters nor men whose souls glow with sympathy for political liberty and political justice will easily let die—is, to our thinking, the finest political essay that the English press has for many years sent out, both in style and thought. Besides this volume, a few of the war sonnets published by Mr. Alexander Smith and Mr. Sydney Dobell jointly, were specimens of high merit. But generally the newspaper correspondents gave a far more vivid and life-like picture of the battles—far more spirited representations of all 'the pride, pomp, circumstance of glorious war'—far

more appalling photographs of the misery and suffering of the camp and of the trenches, of the hospital and the field of death ; while the letters of the soldiers themselves, published in great numbers in the earlier portions of the campaign, tell us those details of their own feelings, of their military spirit, their religious hopes, and their domestic longings, which throw into the shade all attempts on the part of the poets to realize them by invention. Mr. Tennyson is unquestionably a poet of far higher order than Mr. Campbell, and his poem on the Balaklava charge is not unworthy of him ; but it would, we think, be rash to prophesy for it anything like the same popularity as has been attained by *Hohenlinden* and *The Battle of the Baltic*. Many of the volumes now before us contain poems on the great events of the war ; and there is this merit in the mere fact of selecting these subjects, that they may be presumed to have been written from that genuine interest in the events and the men who took part in them, from which scarce any Englishmen or Englishwomen were free. Among the authors of these poems, Mr. Gerald Massey has received from the contemporary press the most flattering notices. One eminent journal, an established authority in poetical criticism, tells its readers that his *Glimpses of the War* 'forms the most spirited accompaniment to the whole tale of the late war, that has been produced by any of our English minstrels.' This, perhaps, is not very high praise, if the language be strictly interpreted, excluding comparison with all the exceptions which we have noted above to the general flatness of the war poems. But a monthly magazine of some reputation improves on this, by saying that 'some of these are magnificent war-strains, *equalling anything ancient or modern*'— praise which, if justified, would certainly leave Mr. Massey little to desire—less to aim after. We derive this information from a long list of flattering criticisms appended to the volume by Mr. Massey, entitled *Craigcrook Castle*, and published last autumn. Let us test the poet and his critics by his poem on the Balaklava Charge, No. viii. of the *Glimpses of the War.* The poem is in the form of an address, delivered, it would appear, in the course of the charge, by the commanding officer — at least, by one who took part in it. It is a kind of accompaniment of talk or song to the action. We fancy those men said little to one another, and that the Earl of Cardigan said less, after the final order was once given to the Light Brigade. What passed in their hearts is probably supposed here by Mr. Massey to be uttered aloud, which, in the first place, is an awkward 'poetical' artifice, entailing in this particular instance the additional mistake of converting British cavalry soldiers into stage heroes soliloquizing in verse. A little expenditure of ingenuity would have enabled Mr. Massey to avoid this error; and it is the worse error in him because, whatever talent for poetry of a certain kind he may possess, he does not exhibit the faintest trace of dramatic talent, and can no more talk like a British dragoon than Sergeant-Major Smith of the Hussars could write his poems. Already in the choice of this form there is indicated a complete absence of any imaginative realization of the action he undertakes to record. We beg Mr. Massey to understand us. It is the specific charge of the British Light Cavalry at Balaklava that he is writing about, not an ideal charge of ideal cavalry, in no time and at no place, and belonging to no particular country. What the British cavalry soldier could and would by no possibility say in substance, Mr. Massey has no business to make him say, and he would not have made him talk to himself or his comrades what follows, if Balaklava had been to him a reality, or anything more than an Astley's Theatre pageant of men of straw. Lord Cardigan has talked enough since, but he did not start the Light Brigade with this lilt:

Sit proud in your saddles! grip tighter each blade!
We ride, ho, we ride a magnificent raid!
To-day win a glory that never shall fade.
Old England for ever! Hurrah!

We doubt whether any man in those two lines of horsemen thought they were riding 'a magnificent raid' —thought of glory or of country in the 'old England for ever' sense, —or of anything but of the stern necessity of obeying a mad and reckless order, of the death into which they were rushing, the loved ones whose faces they were never more to see, and the foe before them. These were most likely the thoughts which swelled their hearts as their lips closed with a tight set, and they looked straight before them over that mile and a half of country across which they had to ride in the teeth of the iron storm. But Mr. Massey was thinking of the jolly excitement of a rush of six hundred horsemen with plumes waving, sabres high in the air, trumpets blowing the charge, horses neighing, and the spectators cheering on the gallant race. Did Mr. Massey ever ride a steeple-chase, or did he ever see one ridden? Let him ask one of the riders what he thinks about when he comes to the fence and ditch that he is pretty sure will throw him; let him ask even the rowers in a boat-race what they think about when they see their rival bow-and-bow with them. If they tell him that they have any thoughts to expend upon glory, or the magnificence of their efforts, we will allow some slight chance that the British dragoon at Balaklava thought—not spoke, be it remembered—the sentiments put into his mouth by Mr. Massey. But nothing short of a written declaration, signed, sealed, and delivered in the presence of witnesses, by all the survivors of the Balaklava charge, shall make us believe that the sentiments which follow belong in any shape, prose or verse, thought or speech, to the British dragoon:—

Oh the lightning of life! O the thunder of steeds!
Great thoughts burn within us like fiery seeds,
Swift to flame out a red fruitage of deeds.
Old England for ever! Hurrah!

O the wild joy of Warriors going to die,
All Sword, and all Flame, with our brows lifted high!
Ride on, happy band, for thy glory swims nigh.
Old England for ever! Hurrah!

Chariots of fire in the dark of death
    stand;
Down thro' the battle-cloud reaches a
    Hand
To crown all who die for their own dear
    land.
    Old England for ever! Hurrah!

Whether the peculiar assignment of capital letters to some of the noun-substantives in these verses adds any peculiar force or beauty to them, we are not prepared to decide, not precisely knowing what the effect intended may be. But if this is the sort of war-poetry that ' equals anything ancient or modern,' all we can say is, that ancient and modern war-poetry must have been all written by persons who knew no more of war, of the spirit of battles, and the feelings of soldiers, than a tailor can learn at Astley's, which we take to be upon the whole not a reliable source of military history. We cite all this stuff, as it appears to us, not to disprove Mr. Massey's claim to the praise he has received from his critics, who no doubt have their sufficient reason for their opinions, but to illustrate a prevailing habit of writing poems on subjects which the writer makes no attempt to conceive truly. So long as a certain amount of sounding lines and unusual phrases can be put together, no matter whether the subject is presented or not, the object seems to be attained. We believe in this particular case Mr. Massey has far too much talent not to perceive at once that his poem, put into the mouth of a cavalry soldier charging at Balaklava, is a ludicrous absurdity; but it never once occurred to him that truth of representation was just the one fundamental quality of a poem, just the one function of imagination, without which all the ornaments of poetry are so much tawdry finery, and the office of imagination so much depravation of good sense and perversion of history. We are not criticising his poem except from one point of view—its utter falsity of representation, or we should object to such puerile misuse of language as ' great thoughts burning *like fiery seeds,*' a species of seed of which we have no instance, except in the case of grains of cayenne or capsicum seeds; and we should

object on critical ground to a gentleman making seeds of any kind '*flame out*' any fruitage — much more—red fruitage of deeds. But thus it is. One falseness leads to another. The neglect of the first great law of imagination naturally leads a man to neglect all its minor proprieties; and he who cares not to represent a great historic fact truly, to the best of his power, will be little likely to care whether his details of phrase represent anything in heaven or earth. And yet Mr. Massey has some of the gifts of the poet in no mean degree. If he would always rigorously ask himself whether he had anything to say before he said it,—if he would bind himself over to eschew tawdry finery of phrase, and would remember that truth is the first and highest object of poetry, and that metaphors and similes are worth less than nothing if not true, he would by strenuous labour and self-restraint reach a place among English poets which, on his present system, we tell him emphatically—and the more emphatically because the press generally has done nothing but foster all his bad tendencies—he has little chance of ever reaching. His range of thought, his power of imaginative sympathy, is at present very limited; he does not know enough of either human life or the face of nature to furnish the substance of any large amount of poetry; and his art is not advanced enough to make what knowledge he has of so much use to him as it should be. The lesson he has mainly to learn is, that the beauty in life and nature after which he seeks is to be found in life and nature, and not put there by his fancy; that the language in which he seeks to express the beauty that fascinates him is not subject to his caprices, but is ruled by laws as stern and unbending as nature herself,—laws not to be broken with impunity, but in obedience to which the greatest minds have found a perfect freedom. Mr. Massey must enlarge his experience vastly, and his range of thought must stretch almost beyond the visible and intellectual universe, before he will find any real occasion for innovating on the English language. At present he uses strange forms of phrase and commits solecisms in grammar because he does not know the capacities of that noble instrument, the English language. He is like a person who has been at a kind of High-Life-below-Stairs feast of the poet's valetry, and has stolen the scraps that have fallen from 'my Lord Duke' and 'my Lady Charlotté!' All this must be mended, and he may gain a rank worth having in our literature. Meanwhile, he can sometimes write with true feeling, and occasionally with great felicity of phrase and melody of rhythm. His 'Ode to Miss Nightingale' would have been more striking if he had been more determined to make every phrase mean something definite, and to use the simplest phrases that would express his meaning. But with its faults both of conception and of form, its jauntiness of tone, and its want of sustained individuality of treatment, it is a lyric of great merit and promise:—

You brave, you bonny Nightingale,
　You are no summer Bird ;
Your music sheathes an Army's wail
　That pierces like a Sword.
All night she sings, brave Nightingale,
　With her breast against the thorn ;
Her saintly patience doth not fail,
　She keepeth watch till morn.

Ah, sing, you bonniest Bird of God,
　The night is sad and long ;
To dying ears—to broken hearts—
　You sing an Angel's song !
She sings, she sings, brave Nightingale,
　And weary warrior souls
Are caught up into Slumber's heaven,
　And lapped in Love's warm folds.

O sing, O sing ! brave Nightingale,
　And at your magic note
Upon Life's sea victoriously
　The sinking soul will float.
O sing, O sing ! brave Nightingale,
　And lure them back again,
Whose path is lost and spirit crost,
　In dark wild woods of Pain.

She sings, she sings, brave Nightingale,
　She breathes a gracious balm ;
Her presence breaks the waves of war,
　She smiles them into calm.
She sings, she sings, brave Nightingale,
　Of auld Langsyne and Home ;
And life grows light, the world grows
　bright,
　And blood runs rich with bloom.

Day unto day her dainty hands
　Make Life's soiled temples clean,
And there's a wake of glory where
　Her spirit pure hath been.

At midnight, thro' that shadow-land,
　Her living face doth gleam ;
The dying kiss her shadow, and
　The Dead smile in their dream.
Brave Bird of Love, in Life's sweet May,
　She rose up from the feast,
To shine above our Banner,
　Like God's Angel in the East.
Brave Bird of Life, wave healing wings
　O'er that gray Land o' the Dead ;
God's heaven lie round you like a shield,
　Earth's blessings on your head.

If Mr. Massey wants a proof of the value of truth, or what we have previously termed individuality of representation in poetry, let him ask any of his friends which are the best four lines in this poem. We will guarantee that the four selected are these—

At midnight through that shadow-land
　Her living face doth gleam ;
The dying kiss her shadow, and
　The Dead smile in their dream.

And they owe their beauty solely to the striking trait conveyed in the words we have marked with italics, which is copied from the newspaper correspondence of the time, to the best of our recollection. The last line is obscure, though we suppose it means that there is a smile upon the face of the dead, as though they had fallen asleep in a happy dream. Before parting with Mr. Massey, we would protest against the notion that our remarks are intended as any complete estimate of his powers, much less as a complete criticism of his last volume of poems. We repeat that we are not reviewing books or deciding the claims of authors in this paper, but merely selecting texts from a few books of verse recently published, for some elementary remarks on poetry. It would be most unjust to the writers we happen to mention, to mistake a partial fault-finding criticism for a comprehensive estimate of their powers, or a balanced judgment of their productions.

Thus, in selecting for a text, from one of the volumes before us, a poem on the loss of the *Birkenhead*, we have no intention of offering it as a fair specimen of the writer's powers. We do not think he was intended by nature for a poet ; nor does he seem to have cultivated the art of writing poetry to such a point as sometimes men of imitative talent and a taste for poetry are able in our day, when good poetry of all ages and kinds is accessible, to reach. We select this particular poem for comment, because it furnishes the most striking illustration of the necessity of our truism, that when a man has nothing to say, he had better not say it. If the writer had asked himself before he wrote, or at least before he published, his poem, whether he had such a sense of that terrible catastrophe, ennobled by heroism, the sublimity of which only strikes us the more because it seemed the natural and effortless attribute of British soldiers under good officers,—such an impression of the scene, with all its overwhelming characteristics of terror and of grandeur, of pictorial splendour and of moral beauty, as to justify him in attempting to record it for the benefit of his countrymen and the glory of the actors in the tragedy, perhaps he would have been content to leave it with no loftier monument, no more lasting inscription, than the memorable words uttered in the House of Lords by the Duke of Wellington. It was indeed one of those events, numerous enough in history and in personal experience, which paralyse rather than excite the powers of imagination, by the consciousness how weak words are to express the unutterable terror and pathos of the scene, while yet they tempt the poet by the attraction of a realized ideal that far transcends his own stretch of invention. The true poet would either leave the actual scene entirely to the imagination of his readers, and exhaust his power of language in some few mighty lines, bringing out in massive monumental simplicity and force the moral significance and national interest of the soldiers' act; or, if he tried to paint the scene, would do it so that we who read his description should go through the horrors of that night with those who were there—should start with them at the shock which broke their last slumber on earth, —should awake to the sudden certainty that a horrible death stared us in the face,—should be nerved with them to that simple

submission to an orderly passiveness which was the most marvellous characteristic of the whole drama,— and should wait with them those long hours, each moment of which must have seemed drawn out to a secular duration, while they held death at bay, with no hope of finally escaping, but knowing their duty as men and soldiers, and unconscious—which is the sublimest trait of all—that they were all that time presenting a spectacle on which the angels of Heaven must have looked down with admiring sympathy. Now let us see how much of this the writer of the poem we are commenting on has realized with his imagination, how much he has felt of the awful but beautiful poem, that life under one of its commonest incidents — a shipwreck — was presenting on the world's stage, not without scenic accompaniments of mere physical grandeur, striking enough in themselves to have furnished the material of a great poem. He dashes *in medias res*, as if the whole scene were before him.

Thus he spake, in tone collected,
‘ Quickly, soldiers, to the poop !’
Thus their colonel,—thus directed,
Thither mount the scattered troop.
‘ Here fall in.’ In serried column,
Straightway, rank and file unite,
Hushed in silence, stern and solemn,
Shadowed o'er by middle night.
Thus, in wonted order planted,
Calmly they confront the foe,
Gravely, but with mien undaunted,
Looking on the sea below,
Where no rival ensign, streaming,
Floats o'er hostile ship unfurled.
Speckless, in the moonlight gleaming,
Watery folds are round them curled.
Moonlight its smooth mirror glazing,
Coldly gleams the quiet bay,
Like a serpent coldly gazing
On its fascinated prey.
And, as with a serpent, vainly
Might the spell-bound victim cope,
Well the doomed brigade, and plainly,
Know, that nought is left for hope.
Well they know that yawning ocean
Soon shall start from seeming sleep,
Suddenly with whirlpool motion
Whelming them in lowest deep;
Yet not less the serried column,
Steadfast stands, and unappalled,
Hushed in silence, stern and solemn,
As by magic charm enthralled.

So far good; we have been told simply in these thirty-two lines that the colonel told his men to fall in, that they fell in, and gazed on the sea 'speckless,' whatever that may mean, 'in the moonlight gleaming,' knowing well 'that nought is left for hope;' in plain English, that there was no hope left. No ingenuity can make more of the information given, than these few words tell with equal force and power of painting. The image of the ocean compared to 'a serpent coldly gazing on its fascinated prey,' is open to the double objection of grievously diminishing the terror of the situation, and grievously libelling the calm obedience of the soldiers. The true imagination—the faculty which would have made the scene present to the mind of the writer as if he had been one of the doomed company himself, would have saved him from this double mistake. But to proceed. He is started off by the phrase 'magic charm' in the last line, to ask

Else, how could men of mortal
Mould, in chill suspense, await
On Eternity's dark portal,
Glared at by triumphant Fate?

What they are 'awaiting,' the sentence does not inform us, and we therefore presume that it is modern English for *wait*. But that is a trifle. What is more important to notice is, that this solution of the 'magic charm' is final as regards the present writer. For he goes on to discuss at considerable length the comparative ease of heroism in meeting death and facing danger under opposite circumstances; then puts the contrast thus:—

But, in still expectance, bidden
Horror's grisly form to brave
In his inmost lair, unhidden
By the pale transparent wave!
But, while torpor slowly curdles
Life's stagnating stream, to stand,
Watching how Destruction girdles
Closelier their devoted band,
Watching here and there an eddy,
Whose thin flakes of foam reveal
That the prowling shark already
Snuffs from far his promised meal,
Watching thus, as sheep to slaughter
Mutely led, their turn abide,
Watching till the riven water
Gulph them in its volvent tide!

In which description note that the presence of sharks is the only fact expressed in intelligible sensuous images; that the last thing an actor

or a spectator of such a scene would think of would be such notions as 'Horror's grisly form,' or 'Destruction,' or any such cold abstractions and personifications; that all his senses would be absorbed by the terrible enemies that were let loose upon that devoted band, in forms, alas! too real to be abstracted, too grimly literal to be personified. Nor do we feel that the familiar image of 'sheep to slaughter mutely led,' adds much to the imaginative grandeur of a scene which resembles a common shambles in nothing but the fact of death, while the heroic self-restraint of the men is again by this simile distorted into a brute incapacity of resistance or complaint. Sure we are that sheep and their butchers would have been the last analogy that the real scene would have suggested. And we know no other test for the fitness of an image. But after this contrast of the position of the men who are meeting death in this shipwreck with that of men who face it heroically on the battle-field, we expect the motive spring of the former heroism to be touched. Not at all; we are simply informed of what we knew before:—

Oh! beneath that lingering anguish
Stoic's iron nerve might fail,—
Stanchest resolution languish;
Unrebuked, might terror wail.

There is the sort of 'makeshift' with which the want of any imaginative realization of a scene is compensated. The story seems to be proceeding, but nothing that adds a feature, or a colour, or a shade, is given: words! words! 'an infinite deal of nothing.' And now the whole story, except the final catastrophe, is told; and, supposing the reader to know nothing more of the troops that were on the *Birkenhead* when she struck than he has learnt from this poem,—to have realized the scene only so far as this writer's word-painting has enabled him to realize it,—to have had his sympathies excited by no other perception of the nobility of the men and the sublime circumstances of their last moments than he has gained from the verses we have cited, would he care more for the final catastrophe than if he read in a newspaper paragraph that 'the *Birkenhead*, steam-frigate, was unfortunately lost on the —th instant on the east coast of Africa. The conduct of the troops on board was excellent: they waited in perfect order and quiet, in obedience to their colonel, till the women and children were got out in the boats, with as many of the passengers as the boats would hold. Those who could swim then attempted to make for the shore; the rest were drowned on the breaking up of the vessel.'? Would he indeed care as much? For this paragraph, stating facts in the simplest outline, with no pretension to give either the pictorial or the moral grandeur of the scene, would leave his imagination free to fill up the picture, and his heart free to vent its natural emotions; while the lines we, have quoted shock the imagination and chill the sympathies. Here is the catastrophe; and we cannot certainly charge the poet with any inequalities of style.

But not less the troop, unshrinking,
    Stand, while yet endures the wreck,
Nor, when filling fast, and sinking,
    Low it leans with toppling deck,
When, with groan like crash of thunder,
    Overstrained by lengthened lunge,
Poop from prow is torn asunder,
    Breaking down with headlong
        plunge,—
Not e'en then, by cry or murmur,
    Nature's agony is marked,
Not more stout of heart, nor firmer,
    Were they when at first embarked,
When, by shouting crowds attended,
    Up the transport's side they sprung,
Than when now, their voyage ended,
    Down the gaping chasm flung.
Sound of grief or fear, none utter;
    Only, rising wild and shrill,
Comes a wailing from the cutter,
    Which their wives and children fill.
And that lonely shriek in quiet
    Soon is hushed of speechless woe,
When the waves, recalled from riot,
    Smoothly o'er the buried flow,
Bubbling, as they mantle o'er them,
    With their victims' dying breath,
Gasped, while low the vortex bore
        them
    In the stifling gripe of death.

If we venture to say that the prettiest thing we have found in Mrs. Phillipson's volume, entitled *Lonely Hours,* is her own portrait by Hayter, at the beginning, we merely intend to imply that the portrait is very pretty, and that we have only glanced at one or two of the poems, which strikingly exemplify our remark that a large class of verse-writers have nothing to say, and substitute words for sense. How can Mrs. Phillipson suppose that the public can be interested, for instance, in the following statement, which forms the only information she gives about the persons of the poem, entitled 'Scenes from Life'—

I see upon a grassy lawn
    Two youthful maiden forms;
Each in their spring's resplendent dawn
    Unshaken by life's storms!
I hear their converse low and sweet,
    And mark their sunny air;
That grassy bank is desolate,
    And they're no longer there!

Within that narrow fir-grove shade
    I hear their footsteps sound;
Their laughter by the breeze convey'd
    Towards the green fields round!
I see their floating dresses pass,
    At evening's solemn hour,
Now waves o'er one the churchyard
        grass,
    The worm was in the flower!

Yet side by side those sisters grew,
    Their haunts, their hearts the same;
With feelings to each other true,
    Despite their kindred's blame!
They gazed upon the sunset skies
    With the deep love of youth,
And fancied all beneath their eyes
    Was fraught with love and truth!

Alas! alas! those sunny themes
    Have long been with the dead,
And Hope and Joy's delusive dreams
    From both poor hearts have fled!
Love was the guide of those pure hours,
    The sunshine round their way;
But even from Earth's loveliest bowers
    False Love is apt to stray!

We say nothing about the slipshod language which talks of 'spring's resplendent dawn *unshaken by storms,*' of 'sunny themes that have long been with the dead,' though we were not aware that 'themes' were destined to coexist with us in Hades; but what we complain of is that the two youthful ladies in this picture have no individual features by which we can possibly, however quick our sympathies may be to gentle feelings, be interested. Miss A and Miss B are bodiless abstractions for us, as they must have been to Mrs. Phillipson while she was writing these verses. She may have had some real case with individual traits dimly in her eye

while writing, but she had no real
sense of the fact; and she consequently writes so weakly and in
such general terms as to entirely
fail in awakening any interest, any
feeling whatever but weariness, in
her readers.

Here, too, in another poem,
called 'The Nun', are clearly shown
the fatal effects on poetry of
writing without realizing the scenes,
the persons, and their speech under
actual circumstances. If Mrs.
Phillipson had but asked herself
what was the usual language of a
young gentleman when he despairs
of succeeding in his suit to a young
lady, and rather than subject her
to the persecution of her relatives,
buries his passion in his own
bosom; and if, in addition to this
knowledge of the expression the
thoughts of a lover would take on
such an occasion, she wished to
excite in her readers an interest in
the young gentleman, and not to
represent him as a simpleton who
could not express himself, could she
have put such language as this into
his mouth—

Oh! I felt it then, and I feel it now,
It was hard indeed to thy will to bow;
For I'd friends most anxious to urge my
claim,
I'd earthly honours and a noble name;
Broad lands, and all that would quickly
move
And obtain thy parents' speedy love.
Much as they priz'd thee, thy fate were
seal'd,
If once thy secret to them revealed!

The struggle was hard, but the will was
strong,
Though the love of self did the fight
prolong;
But 'twas vanquish'd; for, oh! I could
not bear
To cast o'er thy forehead a shade of care,
To dim the light of those beauteous
eyes,
Or fill thy spirit with ceaseless sighs.
'Twere much more natural—better far,
The strong should suffer, than thou,
sweet star!

I gave the promise—then turn'd away
To hide the anguish that in me lay.
My heart throbb'd loud, and I dared
not speak,
Though the will was stubborn, the flesh
was weak;
And I dreaded lest thou, my own,
should'st see
The *all* I had yielded for love of thee!

Hadst thou dreamt of my sorrow wild
and deep,
'Twould have haunted the dreams of thy
peaceful sleep!
'Twould have cast a shade o'er thy
morning hours,
And blighted the radiance of Spring's
sweet flowers;
Have sown with sadness the land of
light
Spread out by Fancy before thy sight;
Have dimm'd the rapture of Love's
young dream,
And reveal'd thee Sorrow's painful
gleam;
Have broken, in short, through the
blissful spell
Which circled thy footsteps wherever
they fell!

If this is the language of a lover,
it is of a lover who has learnt a sort
of Euphuistic jargon that is as inconsistent with true passion or feeling of any kind as it is with good
sense. Fancy the bathos of that
close of the second verse—

'Twere much more natural—better far,
The strong should suffer, than thou,
sweet star!

Then the last verse is one tissue
of weak, false, incoherent images.
The man intends to say simply that
if the woman for whom he made the
sacrifice had dreamt of the greatness
of that sacrifice, it would have sad-
dened her joy at her own release.
But, like the lady in the fairy tale,
who cannot open her mouth to speak
without a shower of pearls and
jewels of all kinds instead of words,
he cannot express his meaning for
the crowd of fine things that he has
to utter, not one of which, by the
bye, is anything better than a most
hackneyed poetical commonplace;
and finally, as if he felt that he was
getting tiresome, like a popular
orator when he has exhausted his
rhetorical resources and his audience,
he brings himself up with that wonderful bathos—

Have broken, *in short*, through the
blissful spell
Which circled thy footsteps wherever
they fell!

What a queer notion of the real
value of poetical imagery a lady
must have who winds up her passionate expansion of the one fundamental idea, the fruit and flower
upon the stem of her poetry, with
such a colloquial phrase as *in short*,

always expressing, as it does, that
the speaker is conscious of having
said too much upon a subject, and
yet does not exactly know how to
leave off with a climax. We cannot
be surprised that where such viola-
tions of the higher and essential
truths of poetry are not avoided,
the minor proprieties of grammar
and rhyme should be treated *de haut
en bas*, and that the verse should
frequently halt. How does Mrs.
Phillipson's ear, for instance, allow
her to insert a pure iambic verse in
the midst of these cantering rhythms?
or does she consider these two verses
of a similar rhythm—

For I'd friends most anxious to urge my
claim,
I'd earthly honours and a noble name.

If she left out the article *a*, the
verse would run smoothly enough,
and the grammar would not be
violated. We wonder what she
would think if any one wrote to her,
even in a familiar letter, so awkward
a phrase as 'moving and obtaining
thy parents' speedy love,' or such
an imperfect sentence as 'if once
thy secret to them revealed,' though,
indeed, the absolute construction is
not uncommon in very concise expressions, if Mrs. Phillipson's style
were what it certainly is not. Then
we do not talk in English, even in
colloquial English, of 'revealing
thee a thing,' but of *revealing to
thee ;* and in no English, colloquial
or poetic, can we understand how
the same event could do all the wonderful things attributed to it in the
last of the four verses we have
quoted, even if we allowed the possibility of any event performing the
incomprehensible feat of 'revealing
thee sorrow's painful gleam,' not in
the least knowing what sort of
gleam sorrow's is, nor how any gleam
can be painful, except to weak eyes.
In the verse next to the one last
quoted, we find a false rhyme and
an atrocious vulgarism together—

The idol was shattered, and never *again*
Could I build up another to worship *the
same,*

where *the same* stands for *like the
former.* False rhymes, indeed, seem
this lady's favourite caprice. In the
very next verse we have *seem* rhyming to *been,* and *mine* to *time.*
Surely Mrs. Phillipson would not

be the worse for very elementary
lessons in English composition.

There seems to be an opinion very
prevalent among the writers of verse-
volumes, that the sonnet is especially
exempted from any necessity of
being imaginative, either in substance or in language ; that its difficulties of construction are so great,
we suppose, as to render it sufficient
triumph for the sonneteer if he can
get his fourteen lines to run smooth,
and rhyme in due sequence, without
caring whether the thought they
express is one fit to be expressed in
verse, or even worth expressing at
all. The example of our great
writers of sonnets will scarcely bear
out this claim of that particular form
of poetry to immunity from the laws
of poetry ; though undoubtedly,
Shakspeare, Milton, and Wordsworth, who are pre-eminent among
English writers of sonnets, are among
the most philosophical thinkers, as
well as the greatest poets, our
country has produced, and have instinctively felt that the sonnet was
not a form that admitted of the free
play of fancy, or of any large use of
the ornaments of poetry. Their
sonnets, generally speaking, unfold
a single weighty thought, a single
impressive aspect of some living,
concrete fact or object, in a group
of co-ordinated images that make up
a whole at once 'simple, sensuous,
and passionate.' It would be impossible for any person to misunderstand the essentially imaginative
character of these works, who did
not begin by misunderstanding the
function of the imagination, and by
confounding it with the wholly subordinate and ministerial function of
fancy. Mr. Edmund Peel, however,
seems to be one of those persons ;
and to carry his notions of the
exemption of the sonnet from the
laws of poetry to such an extent that
he employs upon it neither his
imagination, nor his fancy, nor his
intellect, in any sense or degree.
Our readers will remember the
sonnet in which Wordsworth describes the various characteristics of
previous sonnet writers ; as also the
series in which he speaks of his
favourite poets, and his favourite
characters in their works, ending
with these charmingly finished
lines—

The gentle lady married to the Moor
And heavenly Una with her milk-white
lamb.

Now Mr. Peel addresses a sonnet
to Mr. Tennyson, enumerating various well - known poems by the
laureate, and asking why he buries
himself in silence.   The notion
might have led to a sonnet of felicitous criticism like those of Wordsworth's to which we have alluded,
and we should have had in weighty
and picturesque phrase the leading
characteristics of Mr. Tennyson's
principal poems ; what we actually
get is about as poetical and about
as critical as so many lines printed
off from the index to Mr. Tennyson's
poems.   Here it is :—

O for another, such another strain,
As bowed the gentle Dora to the ground !
As made one *Garden* evermore resound
With joy, one *Hall** of cruel wrong com-
    plain !
O thou that in the barge of woe and pain
Didst gird with prayer the dying hero
    round
To the calm region of Avilion bound,
Tennyson, wherefore do we call in vain ?
With great Ulysses doth thy spirit range
The world beyond the flood, rounding
    the deep ?
Mourn with Œnone over time and
    change ?
Dream in the Lotos-land ? or shunning
    sleep
(With ' Mariana in the moated grange'),
Watch for the hope that cometh not,
    and weep !

If this is poetry, what is prose ?
If this is worth printing and publishing, we may as well have all the
notes of compliment that have ever
passed between Mr. Peel and his
friends at once set to verse, and
issued in post octavo, with illustrative portraits.   Surely, if Mr.
Peel had attended to our truism,
and, having nothing to say, had not
said it, the public would have been
no losers.

We might go on to any length to
illustrate from the volumes before
us the intellectual deficiencies of
the writers, their utter ignorance of
the first principles of poetry and of
poetical composition.   For the most
part, however, they are harmless
noodles, entertaining none but virtuous sentiments, and plainly not
the victims of tempestuous passion

in any of its Protean forms of
seductive beauty or lurid glory.
Most of them would seem from
their writings to be wanting even
in the average share of ' animalism,'
healthy or morbid.   But we find
one gentleman, who writes *Student
of Christ Church*, after the name of
Edward Henry Pember, giving himself the airs of a Don Giovanni,
without the smallest provocation
from any extra liveliness of imagination or strength of feeling with
which his nature has been endowed.
He writes a poem, which he calls
Marriage, but the proper title of
which would be *Meritorious Adultery*, in which he tells us that—

I had a cottage, where I dwelt alone,
Whose lawn sloped down with daisies to
    the sea ;
And there I stood, while winds did
    roughly moan,
And waves did writhe and struggle up
    to me.

The cottage must have been situated
in a botanical region hitherto unexplored by science, for the lawn
up which waves ' do writhe and
struggle' would not, in an ordinary
experience, grow daisies.   However,
standing on this extra-mundane
daisied lawn, like King Canute with
the waves roaring round his feet,
the student of Christ Church, Oxford, beholds a ' fairy boat,' with
' wavering helm' and ' streaming
sail,' bearing as its freight ' a moody
man and wan,' with ' a lady pale.'
' The boat,' he tells us,

        was fair and delicately built,
A *child begotten on some sunnier shore ;*

and then, forgetting that congruity
is the law of images, except where
incongruity dramatically marks a
state of passionate agitation, adds
that the child's sails were silken,
her prow gilt, and her sides azure.
At one look from the lady as she
floats by on the crazy boat, which
is at once a boat and a child, our
adventurous gownsman rushes into
the water, ' accoutred as he was'
(he does not tell us whether he was
in cap and gown, or in shooting-coat
and rustic *déshabille*), and the neat
little allegory thus proceeds :—

Ere eve we anchored on a peaceful lake ;
    I sat in dreams below the lady's knee,

---

* Query, Sam 'all of Coal-Hole celebrity.

And said, 'I have left all things for thy
    sake—
Oh, tell the story of thy days to me.'
The dark cold man stood forward on the
    prow,
He neither heard nor cared : then
    answered she,
    *   *   *   *
' My life is lost to his beyond all cure ;
He must bide here, but oh! abide
    thou too!
The hated bonds that shackle me, tho'
    sure,
Are loose enough to let me turn to
    you.'

Perhaps the reader will conclude
'the bonds' were not the only
thing ' loose' in the case. But as
nothing is complete, since the rage
for Villikins and Dinah, without its
' moral;' hence Mr. Pember — in
the form of a query, addressed
either to the reader or the authorities of Christ Church—says :

Say, was it sin to stay and sweeten
    woe,
Say, were it virtue to have clenched
    that pain.
And left a soul, more bright than aught
    below,
To writhe and darken in the storm
    again ?

We should like to hear what Mr.
Pember's Dean would reply to this
naïve question. Pending that
answer *ex cathedrâ*, we venture to
refer this ingenuous young Oxo-
nian to the Ten Commandments, and
to suggest to him that genius may
gain some sort of toleration for
immorality, but that verses at once
more than ordinarily stupid and
uncommonly immoral, are not tolerated in the present day, even
though their authors have not the
official obligation to morality imposed by a college Fellowship. So
far as the mere poetry of this composition is in question, Mr. Pember
has made the not uncommon mistake of confounding the cold transformations effected by a fancy
stored with the commonplaces of
the simile manufactory, with the
genuine ' fusing power' of imagination which clothes ideas in facts,
and interpenetrates facts with ideas,
so that life always mirrors itself to
the true poet like the ' swan on
sweet St. Mary's lake,' which, as
the most imaginative of philosophic
poets tells us, ' floats double swan
and shadow.'

Our task is nearly finished ;
but, before we close, we wish
to show that the land is not
wholly barren from Dan to Beer-
sheba. The year has produced Mrs.
Browning's *Aurora Leigh*, without any question the greatest of her
works, and rich in beauties of high
order and great variety. Neither
our space nor our immediate
object permits us to criticise this
poem at present ; for Mrs. Browning is not ' a little poet,' nor would
it be fair to lecture her on her
faults of construction, and the occasional carelessness of her diction,
unless we could at the same time
do ample justice to the large
development of her genius, her
knowledge, and her taste, within
the last few years. Then Mr.
Coventry Patmore's Second Part of
The Angel in the House falls within
the year, and though we have previously expressed our opinion that
this poem laboured under radical
error of construction, it would be
ridiculous to class Mr. Patmore
among the poets whom we are
entitled to lecture on the elements
of their art ; his genius, his intellect,
and his taste, have already been
exhibited in forms that have won
the admiring sympathy of those
whose praise is fame, and that
those who can. appreciate poetry,
the essential charm of which is the
combination of the subtlest thought
with the finest sensibility, profound
reflection with the tenderest affection, will not let die. Mr. Patmore is among the few truly original
writers of poetry living. But among
the volumes now before us we find
indications of a genuine feeling for
poetry, and a power of producing
poems which, if they are not original,
are at least not unworthy copies of
good originals ; and to call them
copies is going too far ; they are
rather the results of the strong
impression made upon susceptible
minds by the originals, and are, we
should say, original studies moulded
more or less consciously upon the
style of particular favourite masters.
Mr. W. C. Bennett, for instance,
would perhaps never have written
the best poems in the volume entitled *Queen Eleanor's Vengeance,
and other Poems,* had not Mr.
Tennyson written before him. But

it is impossible to deny the genuine pictorial power of the mind from which this description, that might stand for a translation into words of Titian's *Bacchus and Ariadne*, in our National Gallery, proceeds :—

Lo! wild flush'd faces reel before mine
 eyes,
And furious revels, dances, and fierce
 glee,
Are round me, tossing arms and leaping
 forms,
Skin-clad and horny-hoofed, and hands
 that clash
Shrill cymbals, and the stormy joy of
 flutes
And horns, and blare of trumpets, and
 all hues
Of Iris' watery bow, on bounding
 nymphs,
Vine-crown'd and thyrsus-sceptred, and
 one form,
God of the roaring triumph, on a car
Golden and jewel-lustred, carved and
 bossed,
As by Hephæstus, shouting, rolls along,
Jocund and panther-drawn, and, through
 the sun,
Down through the glaring splendour,
 with wild bound,
Leaps, as he nears me, and a mighty
 cup,
Dripping with odorous nectar, to my
 lips
Is raised, and mad sweet mirth—frenzy
 divine
Is in my veins ; hot love burns through
 mine eyes,
And o'er the roar and rout, I roll along,
Throned by the God, and lifted by his
 love
Unto forgetfulness of mortal pains,
Up to the prayers, and praise, and awe
 of earth.

Perhaps a famous song of Shelley's may have been echoing in Mr. Bennett's brain when he wrote this 'Summer Invocation ;' but no one that was not a true poet could have reproduced the echo with such a sweet melody, and such delicate touches of his own.

O gentle, gentle, summer rain,
 Let not the silver lily pine,
The drooping lily pine in vain
 To feel that dewy touch of thine ;
To drink thy freshness once again,
O gentle, gentle, summer rain.

In heat, the landscape quivering lies ;
 The cattle pant beneath the tree ;
Through parching air and purple skies,
 The earth looks up in vain for thee :
For thee, for thee, it looks in vain,
O gentle, gentle, summer rain.

Come thou and brim the meadow streams,
 And soften all the hills with mist ;
O falling dew, from burning dreams,
 By thee, shall herb and flower be kiss'd :
And earth shall bless thee yet again,
O gentle, gentle, summer rain.

Altogether Mr. Bennett's volume appears to us full of promise ; though we warn him that he needs to look on life with his own eyes, and to avoid certain tricks of phrase on which he sets an undue value, even if they were original

Mr. Walter R. Cassels, too, has a vein of lyric poetry in him worth the working. We specify the *lyric*, because in the two dramatic fragments of his volume, 'Mabel,' and 'Llewellyn,' a total absence of dramatic faculty is observable. This, of 'The Raven,' is striking, both for its general pictorial power and for the imaginative idealism which constructs external scenery to clothe or frame an idea. It is landscape painting true to nature, and at the same time subordinated to, and interpenetrated by, a dominant idea.

There sat a raven 'mid the pines so dark,
 The pines so silent and so dark at
  morn
A ragged bird with feathers rough
 and torn,
Whetting his grimy beak upon the bark,
 And croaking hoarsely to the woods
  forlorn.

Blood red the sky and misty in the east—
 Low vapours creeping bleakly o'er
  the hills—
The rain will soon come plashing on
 the rills—
No sound in all the place of bird or beast,
 Save that hoarse croak that all the
  woodland fills.

A slimy pool all rank with rotting weeds,
 Close by the pines there at the highway side ;
No ripple on its green and stagnant
 tide,
Where only cold and still the horse-leech
 breeds—
 Ugh! might not here some bloody
  murder hide!

Pshaw! . . . . Cold the air slow stealing
 through the trees,
Scarce rustling the moist leaves beneath its tread—
A fearful breast thus holds its breath
 for dread !
There is no healthful music in this
 breeze,
 It sounds . . . . ha! ha! . . . . like
  sighs above the dead !

What fri̱ᵤᵤᵤ yon raven 'mid the pines
so dark,
The pines so silent and so dark around,
With ne'er accomplish'd circlings to
the ground
Ruffling his wings so ragged and so
stark?
Some half-dead victim haply hath he
found.

Ho! raven, now with thee I'll share the
spoil!
This way, methinks, the dying game
hath trod—
Ay! broken twigs, and blood upon
the sod—
These thorns are sharp! well! soon will
end the toil—
This bough aside, and then the prize.
: .... My God! ...

Emmeline Hinxman (we know
not whether to put Mrs. or Miss
before the name) writes with power
and grace. In a poem called 'The
Wraith,' with which her volume
begins, the pictures of nature are
very clear and true, and the story is
treated with a delicate slightness
which itself indicates power by its
reserve. There is no impotence
of self-restraint, no hysterics, no
spasms; all is quiet, defined, and
truthful. We have only space for
the opening picture—

Four maidens on a summer Saturday
Went up the hill against whose pleasant
green
The grey roofs of the village street re-
clined.
The air was sweet that met them, yet it
lacked
The wonted hilly freshness,—and the
girls
Sauntered and sat, and plucked with
idle hands
Late roses here, a single raspberry there,
Where straggling brushwood clothed a
ledge of rock;
And, loitering thus, marked not that
one dull hue
Had grown o'er all the heavens, until
they heard
The muttering thunder close them round,
and felt
Large drops fall ominous on hand and
brow.
How dreary were the uplands now,
that late

Seemed so familiar! and how far away
The village, hidden by the winding gorge,
When peal and bolt were in the home-
ward path!
But near at hand a covert lay, well
known:
Two rocks, together leaning, made a
cave,
Where oft, by storm surprised, the
sportsman sat,
Or herdsman harboured thro' a day of
rain.
Thither the maidens sped, and nestled
down
A fluttering covey, while the tempest
broke;
The light'ning from its rolling darkness
slid,
The thunders leapt from its continuous
roar;
A roar of struggling winds and clouds
above,—
Of rushing rains upon the further
peaks,—
Of waters maddened at their secret
source,—
And of what other powers, unknown to
man,
Nature in these her most inmost haunts
may work
When the hour of strength is on her.
But awhile
And the great tumult dwindled: weak
and few
The flashes fell, the tempest lifted up
His skirts from off the shoulders of the
hills,
And muttering hied him westward—
rain he left,
And tattered clouds, but bore his terrors
far.

There are besides some sweetly-
composed poems of sentiment in
this volume, but our space is exhausted. We only have to beg our
readers, if they are tempted to think
our earlier strictures unnecessarily
harsh, to judge whether our standard of excellence is over high or
over narrow by the praise we have
with sincere pleasure bestowed upon
the three last writers from whom
we have quoted, and to remember
that indifferent poetry is about the
most irritating diet possible, another
reason against encouraging its production.

Enoch Arden, &c. By Alfred Tennyson, D.C.L., Poet Laureate.
Dramatis Personæ. By Robert Browning.

WE couple these two books together, not because of their
likeness, for they are as dissimilar as books can be, nor on
account of the eminence of their authors, for in general two
great authors are too much for one essay, but because they
are the best possible illustration of something we have to say
upon poetical art—because they may give to it life and freshness. The accident of contemporaneous publication has here
brought together two books, very characteristic of modern
art, and we want to show how they are characteristic.

Neither English poetry nor English criticism have ever
recovered the *eruption* which they both made at the beginning
of this century into the fashionable world. The poems of Lord
Byron were received with an avidity that resembles our present
avidity for sensation novels, and were read by a class which at
present reads little but such novels. Old men who remember
those days may be heard to say, "We hear nothing of poetry
now-a-days; it seems quite down." And "down" it certainly
is, if for poetry it be a descent to be no longer the favourite
excitement of the more frivolous part of the "upper" world.
That stimulating poetry is now little read. A stray school-
boy may still be detected in a wild admiration for the
Giaour or the *Corsair* (and it is suitable to his age, and he

should not be reproached for it), but the *real* posterity—the quiet students of a past literature—never read them or think of them.   A line or two linger on the memory; a few telling strokes of occasional and felicitous energy are quoted, but this is all.   As wholes, these exaggerated stories were worthless; they taught nothing, and, therefore, they are forgotten.   If now-a-days a dismal poet were, like Byron, to lament the fact of his birth, and to hint that he was too good for the world, the *Saturday Review* would say that "they doubted if he *was* too good; that a sulky poet was a questionable addition to a tolerable world; that he need not have been born, as far as they were concerned."   Doubtless, there is much in Byron besides his dismal exaggeration, but it was that exaggeration which made "the sensation," which gave him a wild moment of dangerous fame.   As so often happens, the cause of his momentary fashion is the cause also of his lasting oblivion. Moore's former reputation was less excessive, yet it has not been more permanent.   The prettiness of a few songs preserves the memory of his name, but as a poet to *read* he is forgotten. There is nothing to read in him; no exquisite thought, no sublime feeling, no consummate description of true character. Almost the sole result of the poetry of that time is the harm which it has done.   It degraded for a time the whole character of the art.   It said by practice, by a most efficient and successful practice, that it was the aim, the *duty* of poets, to catch the attention of the passing, the fashionable, the busy world.   If a poem "fell dead," it was nothing; it was composed to please the "London" of the year, and if that London did not like it, why it had failed.   It fixed upon the minds of a whole generation, it engraved in popular memory and tradition, a vague conviction that poetry is but one of the many *amusements* for the light classes, for the lighter hours of all classes.   The mere notion, the bare idea, that poetry is a deep thing, a teaching thing, the most surely and wisely elevating of human things, is even now to the coarse public mind nearly unknown.

As was the fate of poetry, so inevitably was that of criticism. The science that expounds which poetry is good and which is bad is dependent for its popular reputation on the popular estimate of poetry itself.   The critics of that day had *a* day, which is more than can be said for some since; they professed to tell the fashionable world in what books it would find new pleasure, and therefore they were read by the fashionable world.   Byron counted the critic and poet equal.   The *Edinburgh Review* penetrated among the young, and into places of female resort where it does not go now.   As people ask, "Have you read *Henry Dunbar?* and what do you think of it?" so they then asked, "Have you read the *Giaour?* and what do you think of it?" Lord Jeffrey, a shrewd judge of the world, employed himself in telling it what to think; not so much what it ought to think, as what at bottom it did think, and so by dexterous sympathy with current society he gained contemporary fame and power. Such fame no critic must hope for now. His articles will not penetrate where the poems themselves do not penetrate. When poetry was noisy, criticism was loud; now poetry is a still small voice, and criticism must be smaller and stiller. As the function of such criticism was limited so was its subject. For the great and (as time now proves) the *permanent* part of the poetry of his time—for Shelley and for Wordsworth—Lord Jeffrey had but one word. He said* "It won't do." And it will not do to amuse a drawing-room.

The doctrine that poetry is a light amusement for idle hours, a metrical species of sensational novel, has not indeed been without gainsayers wildly popular. Thirty years ago, Mr. Carlyle most rudely contradicted it. But perhaps this is about all that he has done. He has denied, but he has not disproved. He has contradicted the floating paganism, but he has not founded the deep religion. All about and around us a *faith* in poetry struggles to be extricated, but it is not extricated. Some day, at the touch of the true word, the whole confusion will by magic cease; the broken and shapeless notions cohere and crystallise into a bright and true theory. But this cannot be yet.

But though no complete theory of the poetic art as yet be possible for us, though perhaps only our children's children will be able to speak on this subject with the assured confidence which belongs to accepted truth, yet something of some certainty may be stated in the easier elements, and something that will throw light on these two new books. But it will be necessary to assign reasons, and the assigning of reasons is a dry task. Years ago, when criticism only tried to show how poetry could be made a good amusement, it was not impossible that criticism itself should be amusing. But now it must at least be serious, for we believe that poetry is a serious and a deep thing.

There should be a word in the language of literary art to express what the word "picturesque" expresses for the fine arts. *Picturesque* means fit to be put into a picture; we want a word *literatesque*, "fit to be put into a book." An artist goes through a hundred different country scenes, rich

* The first words in Lord Jeffrey's celebrated review of the "Excursion" were, "This will never do."

with beauties, charms, and merits, but he does not paint any
of them. He leaves them alone ; he idles on till he finds the
hundred-and-first—a scene which many observers would not
think much of, but which *he* knows by virtue of his art will
look well on canvas, and this he paints and preserves. Susceptible observers, though not artists, feel this quality too ;
they say of a scene, " How picturesque ! " meaning by this a
quality distinct from that of beauty, or sublimity, or grandeur
—meaning to speak not only of the scene as it is in itself,
but also of its fitness for imitation by art ; meaning not only
that it is good, but that its goodness is such as ought to be
transferred to paper ; meaning not simply that it fascinates,
but also that its fascination is such as ought to be copied by
man. A fine and insensible instinct has put language to this
subtle use ; it expresses an idea without which fine art criticism
could not go on, and it is very natural that the language of
pictorial should be better supplied with words than that of
literary criticism, for the eye was used before the mind, and
language embodies primitive sensuous ideas, long ere it
expresses, or need express, abstract and literary ones.

The reason why a landscape is " picturesque " is often said to
be that such landscape represents an " idea." But this explanation, though in the minds of some who use it it is near
akin to the truth, fails to explain that truth to those who did
not know it before ; the word " idea," is so often used in
these subjects when people do not know anything else to say ;
it represents so often a kind of intellectual insolvency, when
philosophers are at their wit's end, that shrewd people will
never readily on any occasion give it credit for meaning
anything. A wise explainer must, therefore, look out for
other words to convey what he has to say. *Landscapes,* like
everything else in nature, divide themselves as we look at
them into a sort of rude classification. We go down a river, for
example, and we see a hundred landscapes on both sides of it,
resembling one another in much, yet differing in something ;
with trees here, and a farmhouse there, and shadows on one
side, and a deep pool far on ; a collection of circumstances
most familiar in themselves, but making a perpetual novelty
by the magic of their various combinations. We travel so
for miles and hours, and then we come to a scene which also
has these various circumstances and adjuncts, but which
combines them best, which makes the best whole of them,
which shows them in their best proportion at a single glance
before the eye. Then we say, " This is the place to paint
the river ; this is the picturesque point ! " Or, if not artists
or critics of art, we feel without analysis or examination that

somehow this bend or sweep of the river, shall, in future, *be the river to us :* that it is the image of it which we will retain in our mind's eye, by which we will remember it, which we will call up when we want to describe or think of it. Some fine countries, some beautiful rivers, have not this picturesque · quality : they give us elements of beauty, but they do not combine them together; we go on for a time delighted, but *after* a time somehow we get wearied ; we feel that we are taking in nothing and learning nothing ; we get no collected image before our mind; we see the accidents and circumstances of that sort of scenery, but the summary scene we do not see ; we have *disjecta membra,* but no form ; various and many and faulty approximations are displayed in succession ; but the absolute perfection in that country or river's scenery— its *type*—is withheld. We go away from such places in part delighted, but in part baffled ; we have been puzzled by pretty things ; we have beheld a hundred different inconsistent specimens of the same sort of beauty ; but the rememberable idea, the full development, the characteristic individuality of it, we have not seen.

We find the same sort of quality in all parts of painting. We see a portrait of a person we know, and we say, " It is like—yes, like, of course, but it is not *the man ;*" we feel it could not be anyone else, but still, somehow it fails to bring home to us the individual as we know him to be. *He* is not there. An accumulation of features like his are painted, but his essence is not painted ; an approximation more or less excellent is given, but the characteristic expression, the *typical* form, of the man is withheld.

Literature—the painting of words—has the same quality but wants the analogous word. The word *" literatesque,"* would mean, if we possessed it, that perfect combination in the *subject-matter* of literature, which suits the *art* of literature. We often meet people, and say of them, sometimes meaning well and sometimes ill, " How well so-and-so would do in a book ! " Such people are by no means the best people; but they are the most effective people—the most rememberable people. Frequently when we first know them, we like them because they explain to us so much of our experience ; we have known many people "like that," in one way or another, but we did not seem to understand them ; they were nothing to us, for their traits were indistinct ; we forgot them, for they *hitched* on to nothing, and we could not classify them ; but when we see the *type* of the genus, at once we seem to comprehend its character ; the inferior specimens are explained by the perfect embodiment ; the approximations

are definable when we know the ideal to which they draw
near. There are an infinite number of classes of human
beings, but in each of these classes there is a distinctive type
which, if we could expand it out in words, would define the
class. We cannot expand it in formal terms any more than
a landscape or a species of landscapes; but we have an art,
an art of words, which can draw it. Travellers and others often
bring home, in addition to their long journals—which though so
living to them, are so dead, so inanimate, so undescriptive to
all else—a pen-and-ink sketch, rudely done very likely, but
which, perhaps, even the more for the blots and strokes, gives
a distinct notion, an emphatic image, to all who see it. They
say at once, *now* we know the sort of thing. The sketch has
hit the mind. True literature does the same. It describes
sorts, varieties, and permutations, by delineating the type of
each sort, the ideal of each variety, the central, the marking
trait of each permutation.

On this account, the greatest artists of the world have ever
shown an enthusiasm for reality. To care for notions, and
abstractions; to philosophise; to reason out conclusions; to care
for schemes of thought, are signs in the artistic mind of
secondary excellence. A Schiller, an Euripides, a Ben Jonson,
cares for *ideas*—for the parings of the intellect, and the distillation of the mind; a Shakespeare, a Homer, a Goethe, finds his
mental occupation, the true home of his natural thoughts, in
the real world—" which is the world of all of us"—where the
face of nature, the moving masses of men and women, are ever
changing, ever multiplying, ever mixing one with the other.
The reason is plain—the business of the poet, of the artist,
is with *types ;* and those types are mirrored in reality. As a
painter must not only have a hand to execute, but an eye to
distinguish—as he must go here and then there through the
real world to catch the picturesque man, the picturesque scene,
which are to live on his canvass—so the poet must find in that
reality, the *literatesque* man, the *literatesque* scene which
nature intends for him, and which will live in his page. Even
in reality he will not find this type complete, or the characteristics perfect; but there, at least, he will find at least *something,* some hint, some intimation, some suggestion ; whereas,
in the stagnant home of his own thoughts he will find nothing
pure, nothing *as it is,* nothing which does not bear his own
mark, which is not somehow altered by a mixture with himself.

The first conversation of Goethe and Schiller illustrates
this conception of the poet's art. Goethe was at that time
prejudiced against Schiller, we must remember, partly from

what he considered the *outrages* of the *Robbers* partly because of the philosophy of Kant. Schiller's " Essay on *Grace and Dignity*," he tells us, "was yet less of a kind to reconcile me. The philosophy of Kant, which exalts the dignity of mind so highly, while appearing to restrict it, Schiller had joyfully embraced: it unfolded the extraordinary qualities which Nature had implanted in him; and in the lively feeling of freedom and self-direction, he showed himself unthankful to the Great Mother, who surely had not acted like a step-dame towards him. Instead of viewing her as self-subsisting, as producing. with a living force, and according to appointed laws, alike the highest and the lowest of her works, he took her up under the aspect of some empirical native qualities of the human mind. Certain harsh passages I could even directly apply to myself: they exhibited my confession of faith in a false light; and I felt that if written without particular attention to me, they were still worse; for in that case, the vast chasm which lay between us, gaped but so much the more distinctly." After a casual meeting at a Society for Natural History they walked home and Goethe proceeds.

"We reached his house; the talk induced me to go in. I then expounded to him, with as much vivacity as possible, the *Metamorphosis of Plants*,* drawing out on paper, with many characteristic strokes, a symbolic Plant for him, as I proceeded. He heard and saw all this, with much interest and distinct comprehension; but when I had done, he shook his head and said: ' This is no experiment, this is an idea.' I stopt with some degree of irritation; for the point which separated us was most luminously marked by this expression. The opinions in *Dignity and Grace*, again occurred to me; the old grudge was just awakening; but I smothered it, and merely said: 'I was happy to find that I had got ideas without knowing it, nay that I saw them before my eyes.'

" Schiller had much more prudence and dexterity of management than I; he was also thinking of his periodical the *Horen*, about this time, and of course rather wished to attract than repel me. Accordingly he answered me like an accomplished Kantite; and as my stiff-necked Realism gave occasion to many contradictions, much battling took place between us, and at last a truce, in which neither party would consent

---

* A curious physiologico-botanical theory by Goethe, which appears to be entirely unknown in this country: though several eminent continental botanists have noticed it with commendation. It is explained at considerable length, in this same *Morphologie*.

D

to yield the victory, but each held himself invincible. Positions like the following grieved me to the very soul: *How can there ever be an experiment, that shall correspond with an idea? The specific quality of an idea is, that no experiment can reach it or agree with it.* Yet if he held as an idea, the same thing which I looked upon as an experiment; there must certainly, I thought, be some community between us some ground whereon both of us might meet!'"

With Goethe's natural history, or with Kant's philosophy, we have here no concern, but we can combine the expressions of the two great poets into a nearly complete description of poetry. The "symbolic plant" is the *type* of which we speak, the ideal at which inferior specimens aim, the class-characteristic in which they all share, but which none shows forth fully: Goethe was right in searching for this in reality and nature; Schiller was right in saying that it was an "idea," a transcending notion to which approximations could be found in experience, but only approximations—which could not be found there itself. Goethe, as a poet, rightly felt the primary necessity of outward suggestion and experience; Schiller as a philosopher, rightly felt its imperfection.

But in these delicate matters, it is easy to misapprehend. There is, undoubtedly, a sort of poetry which is produced as it were out of the author's mind. The description of the poet's own moods and feelings is a common sort of poetry—perhaps the commonest sort. But the peculiarity of such cases is, that the poet does not describe himself *as* himself: autobiography is not his object; he takes himself as a specimen of human nature; he describes, not himself, but a distillation of himself: he takes such of his moods as are most characteristic, as most typify certain moods of certain men, or certain moods of all men; he chooses preponderant feelings of special sorts of men, or occasional feelings of men of all sorts; but with whatever other difference and diversity, the essence is that such self-describing poets describe what is *in* them, but not *peculiar* to them,—what is generic, not what is special and individual. Gray's *Elegy* describes a mood which Gray felt more than other men, but which most others, perhaps all others, feel too. It is more popular, perhaps, than any English poem, because that sort of feeling is the most diffused of high feelings, and because Gray added to a singular nicety of fancy an habitual proneness to a *contemplative*—a discerning but unbiassed—meditation on death and on life. Other poets cannot hope for such success: a subject, so popular, so grave, so wise, and yet so suitable to the writer's nature is hardly to be found. But the same ideal, the same unautobiographical character is to be found in the writings of meaner men.   Take sonnets of Hartley Coleridge, for example:—

I.

TO A FRIEND.

"When we were idlers with the loitering rills,
  The need of human love we little noted:
  Our love was nature; and the peace that floated
On the white mist, and dwelt upon the hills,
To sweet accord subdued our wayward wills:
  One soul was ours, one mind, one heart devoted,
  That, wisely doating, ask'd not why it doated,
And ours the unknown joy, which knowing kills.
But now I find, how dear thou wert to me;
  That man is more than half of nature's treasure,
Of that fair Beauty which no eye can see,
  Of that sweet music which no ear can measure;
And now the streams may sing for others' pleasure,
  The hills sleep on in their eternity."

II.

TO THE SAME.

"In the great city we are met again,
  Where many souls there are, that breathe and die,
  Scarce knowing more of nature's potency,
Than what they learn from heat, or cold, or rain,
The sad vicissitude of weary pain;—
  For busy man is lord of ear and eye,
  And what hath nature, but the vast, void sky,
And the thronged river toiling to the main?
Oh! say not so, for she shall have her part
  In every smile, in every tear that falls,
And she shall hide her in the secret heart,
  Where love persuades, and sterner duty calls:
But worse it were than death, or sorrow's smart,
  To live without a friend within these walls."

III.

TO THE SAME.

"We parted on the mountains, as two streams
  From one clear spring pursue their several ways;
  And thy fleet course hath been through many a maze
In foreign lands, where silvery Padus gleams
To that delicious sky, whose glowing beams
  Brightened the tresses that old Poets praise;
  Where Petrarch's patient love, and artful lays,
And Ariosto's song of many themes,
Moved the soft air.   But I, a lazy brook,
  As close pent up within my native dell,
Have crept along from nook to shady nook,
  Where flowrets blow, and whispering Naiads dwell.
Yet now we meet, that parted were so wide,
  O'er rough and smooth to travel side by side."

The contrast of instructive and enviable locomotion with refining but instructive meditation is not special and peculiar to these two, but general and universal. It was set down by Hartley Coleridge because he was the most meditative and refining of men.

What sort of literatesque types are fit to be described in the sort of literature called poetry, is a : atter on which much might be written. Mr. Arnold, some years since, put forth a theory that the art of poetry could only delineate *great actions*. But though, rightly interpreted and understood—using the word action so as to include high and sound activity in contemplation—this definition may suit the highest poetry, it certainly cannot be stretched to include many inferior sorts and even many good sorts. Nobody in their senses would describe Gray's *Elegy* as the delineation of a "great action;" some kinds of mental contemplation may be energetic enough to deserve this name, but Gray would have been frightened at the very word. He loved scholarlike calm and quiet inaction; his very greatness depended on his *not* acting, on his "wise passiveness," on his indulging the grave idleness which so well appreciates so much of human life. But the best answer—the *reductio ad absurdum*—of Mr. Arnold's doctrine, is the mutilation which it has caused him to make of his own writings. It has forbidden him, he tells us, to reprint *Empedocles*—a poem undoubtedly containing defects and even excesses, but containing also these lines:—

> "And yet what days were those, Parmenides!
> When we were young, when we could number friends
> In all the Italian cities like ourselves,
> When with elated hearts we join'd your train,
> Ye Sun-born virgins! on the road of Truth.
> Then we could still enjoy, then neither thought
> Nor outward things were clos'd and dead to us,
> But we receiv'd the shock of mighty thoughts
> On simple minds with a pure natural joy;
> And if the sacred load oppress'd our brain,
> We had the power to feel the pressure eas'd,
> The brow unbound, the thoughts flow free again,
> In the delightful commerce of the world.
> We had not lost our balance then, nor grown
> Thought's slaves, and dead to every natural joy.
> The smallest thing could give us pleasure then—
> The sports of the country people;
> A flute note from the woods;
> Sunset over the sea:
> Seed-time and harvest;
> The reapers in the corn;
> The vinedresser in his vineyard;
> The village-girl at her wheel.

Fullness of life and power of feeling, ye
Are for the happy, for the souls at ease,
Who dwell on a firm basis of content.
But he who has outliv'd his prosperous days,
But he, whose youth fell on a different world
From that on which his exil'd age is thrown;
Whose mind was fed on other food, was train'd
By other rules than are in vogue to-day;
Whose habit of thought is fix'd, who will not change,
But in a world he loves not must subsist,
In ceaseless opposition, be the guard
Of his own breast, fetter'd to what he guards,
That the world win no mastery over him;
Who has no friend, no fellow left, not one;
Who has no minute's breathing space allow'd
To nurse his dwindling faculty of joy;—
Joy and the outward world must die to him
As they are dead to me.

What freak of criticism can induce a man who has
written such poetry as this, to discard it, and say it is not
poetry? Mr. Arnold is privileged to speak of his own
poems, but no other critic could speak so and not be laughed
at.

We are disposed to believe that no very sharp definition
can be given—at least in the present state of the critical art—
of the boundary line between poetry and other sorts of imaginative delineation. Between the undoubted dominions of
the two kinds there is a debateable land; everybody is
agreed that the " Œdipus at Colonus" *is* poetry: everyone
is agreed that the wonderful appearance of Mrs. Veal is *not*
poetry. But the exact line which separates grave novels in
verse like *Aylmer's Field* or *Enoch Arden,* from grave novels
not in verse like *Silas Marner* or *Adam Bede,* we own we
cannot draw with any confidence. Nor, perhaps, is it very
important; whether a narrative is thrown into verse or not
certainly depends in part on the taste of the age, and in part
on its mechanical helps. Verse is the only mechanical help
to the memory in rude times, and there is little writing till
a cheap something is found to write upon, and a cheap
something to write with. Poetry—verse at least—is the literature of *all work* in early ages; it is only later ages which
write in what *they* think a natural and simple prose. There
are other casual influences in the matter too; but they are
not material now. We need only say here that poetry,
because it has a more marked rhythm than prose, must be
more intense in meaning and more concise in style than prose.
People expect a " marked rhythm" to imply something worth
marking; if it fails to do so they are disappointed. They are

displeased at the visible waste of a powerful instrument; they call it "doggrel," and rightly call it, for the metrical expression of full thought and eager feeling—the burst of metre—incident to high imagination, should not be wasted on petty matters which prose does as well,—which it does better—which it suits by its very limpness and weakness, whose small changes it follows more easily, and to whose lowest details it can fully and without effort degrade itself. Verse, too, should be *more concise*, for long continued rhythm tends to jade the mind, just as brief rhythm tends to attract the attention. Poetry should be memorable and emphatic, intense, and *soon over*.

The great divisions of poetry, and of all other literary art, arise from the different modes in which these *types*—these characteristic men, these characteristic feelings—may be variously described. There are three principal modes which we shall attempt to describe—the *pure*, which is sometimes, but not very wisely, called the classical; the *ornate*, which is also unwisely called romantic; and the *grotesque*, which might be called the mediæval. We will describe the nature of these a little. Criticism we know must be brief—not, like poetry, because its charm is too intense to be sustained—but on the contrary, because its interest is too weak to be prolonged; but elementary criticism, if an evil, is a necessary evil; a little while spent among the simple principles of art is the first condition, the absolute pre-requisite, for surely apprehending and wisely judging the complete embodiments and miscellaneous forms of actual literature.

The definition of *pure* literature is that it describes the type in its simplicity, we mean, with the exact amount of accessory circumstance which is necessary to bring it before the mind in finished perfection, and *no more* than that amount. The *type* needs some accessories from its nature—a picturesque landscape does not consist wholly of picturesque features. There is a setting of surroundings—as the Americans would say, of *fixings*—without which the reality is not itself. By a traditional mode of speech, as soon as we see a picture in which a complete effect is produced by detail so rare and so harmonised as to escape us, we say how "classical." The whole which is to be seen appears at once and through the detail, but the detail itself is not seen: we do not think of that which gives us the idea; we are absorbed in the idea itself. Just so in literature the pure art is that which works with the fewest strokes; the fewest, that is, for its purpose, for its aim is to call up and bring home to men an idea, a form, a character, and if that idea be twisted, that form be involved, that character perplexed, many strokes of literary art will be needful. Pure art does not mutilate its object: it represents it as fully as is possible with the slightest effort which is possible: it shrinks from no needful circumstances, as little as it inserts any which are needless. The precise peculiarity is not merely that no incidental circumstance is inserted which does not tell on the main design: no art is fit to be called *art* which permits a stroke to be put in without an object; but that only the minimum of such circumstance is inserted at all. The form is sometimes said to be bare, the accessories are sometimes said to be invisible, because the appendages are so choice that the shape only is perceived.

The English literature undoubtedly contains much impure literature; impure in its style if not in its meaning: but it also contains one great, one nearly perfect, model of the pure style in the literary expression of typical *sentiment;* and one not perfect, but gigantic and close approximation to perfection in the pure delineation of objective character. Wordsworth, perhaps, comes as near to choice purity of style in sentiment as is possible; Milton, with exceptions and conditions to be explained, approaches perfection by the strenuous purity with which he depicts character.

A wit once said, that "*pretty* women had more features than *beautiful* women," and though the expression may be criticised, the meaning is correct. Pretty women seem to have a great number of attractive points, each of which attracts your attention, and each one of which you remember afterwards; yet these points have not *grown together,* their features have not linked themselves into a single inseparable whole. But a beautiful woman is a whole as she is; you no more take her to pieces than a Greek statue; she is not an aggregate of divisible charms, she is a charm in herself. Such ever is the dividing test of pure art; if you catch yourself admiring its details, it is defective; you ought to think of it as a single whole which you must remember, which you must admire, which somehow subdues you while you admire it, which is a "possession" to you "for ever."

Of course no individual poem embodies this ideal perfectly; of course every human word and phrase has its imperfections, and if we choose an instance to illustrate that ideal, the instance has scarcely a fair chance. By contrasting it with the ideal we suggest its imperfections; by protruding it as an example, we turn on its defectiveness the microscope of criticism. Yet these two sonnets of Wordsworth may be fitly read in this place, not because they are quite without faults, or because they are the very best examples of their kind of style; but because they are *luminous* examples; the compactness of

the sonnet and the gravity of the sentiment, hedging in the
thoughts, restraining the fancy, and helping to maintain a
singleness of expression.

THE TROSACHS.

"There's not a nook within this solemn Pass,
But were an apt Confessional for one
Taught by his summer spent, his autumn gone,
That Life is but a tale of morning grass
Withered at eve.   From scenes of art which chase
That thought away, turn, and with watchful eyes
Feed it 'mid Nature's old felicities,
Rocks, rivers, and smooth lakes more clear than glass
Untouched, unbreathed upon.   Thrice happy guest,
If from a golden perch of aspen spray
(October's workmanship to rival May)
The pensive warbler of the ruddy breast
That moral teaches by a heaven-taught lay,
Lulling the year, with all its cares, to rest !"

COMPOSED UPON WESTMINSTER BRIDGE, SEPT. 3, 1802.

"Earth has not anything to show more fair:
Dull would he be of soul who could pass by
A sight so touching in its majesty:
This city now doth, like a garment, wear
The beauty of the morning; silent, bare,
Shops, towers, domes, theatres, and temples lie
Open unto the fields and to the sky;
All bright and open in the smokeless air.
Never did sun more beautifully steep
In his first splendour, valley, rock, or hill;
Ne'er saw I, never felt, a calm so deep !
The river glideth at his own sweet will:
Dear God !   The very houses seem asleep;
And all that mighty heart is lying still !

Instances of barer style than this may easily be found,
instances of colder style—few better instances of purer style.
Not a single expression (the invocation in the concluding
couplet of the second sonnet perhaps excepted) can be spared,
yet not a single expression rivets the attention.   If, indeed, we
take out the phrase—

"The city doth like a garment wear
The beauty of the morning."

and the description of the brilliant yellow of autumn—

"October's workmanship to rival May,"

they have independent value, but they are not noticed in the
sonnet when we read it through; they fall into place there,
and being in their place are not seen.   The great subjects of
the two sonnets, the religious aspect of beautiful but grave

nature—the religious aspect of a city about to awaken and be alive, are the only ideas left in our mind. To Wordsworth has been vouchsafed the last grace of the self-denying artist; you think neither of him nor his style, but you cannot help thinking of—you *must* recall—the exact phrase, the *very* sentiment he wished.

Milton's purity is more eager. In the most exciting parts of Wordsworth—and these sonnets are not very exciting—you always feel, you never forget, that what you have before you is the excitement of a recluse. There is nothing of the stir of life; nothing of the *brawl* of the world. But Milton though always a scholar by trade, though solitary in old age, was through life intent on great affairs, lived close to great scenes, watched a revolution, and if not an actor in it, was at least secretary to the actors. He was familiar—by daily experience and habitual sympathy—with the earnest debate of arduous questions, on which the life and death of the speakers certainly depended, on which the weal or woe of the country perhaps depended. He knew how profoundly the individual character of the speakers—their inner and real nature—modifies their opinion on such questions; he knew how surely that nature will appear in the expression of them. This great experience, fashioned by a fine imagination, gives to the debate of Satanic Council in Pandæmonium its reality and its life. It is a debate in the Long Parliament, and though the *theme* of *Paradise Lost* obliged Milton to side with the monarchical element in the universe, his old habits are often too much for him; and his real sympathy—the impetus and energy of his nature—side with the rebellious element. For the purposes of art this is much better—of a court a poet can make but little; of a heaven he can make very little, but of a courtly heaven, such as Milton conceived, he can make nothing at all. The idea of a court and the idea of a heaven are so radically different, that a distinct combination of them is always grotesque and often ludicrous. *Paradise Lost,* as a whole, is radically tainted by a vicious principle. It professes to justify the ways of God to man, to account for sin and death, and it tells you that the whole originated in a *political event;* in a court squabble as to a particular act of patronage and the due or undue promotion of an eldest son. Satan may have been wrong, but on Milton's theory he had an *arguable* case at least. There was something arbitrary in the promotion; there were little symptoms of a job; in *Paradise Lost* it is always clear that the devils are the weaker, but it is never clear that the angels are the better. Milton's sympathy and his imagination slip back to the Puritan rebels whom he loved, and desert the courtly angels whom he could not love although he praised. There is no wonder that Milton's hell is better than his heaven, for he hated officials and he loved rebels, for he employs his genius below, and accumulates his pedantry above. On the great debate in Pandæmonium all his genius is concentrated. The question is very practical; it is, "What are we devils to do, now we have lost heaven?" Satan who presides over and manipulates the assembly—Moloch

> "the fiercest spirit
> That fought in Heaven, now fiercer by despair,"

who wants to fight again; Belial, "the man of the world," who does not want to fight any more; Mammon, who is for commencing an industrial career; Beelzebub, the official statesman,

> "deep on his front engraven
> Deliberation sat and Public care,"

who, at Satan's instance, proposes the invasion of earth—are as distinct as so many statues. Even Belial, "the man of the world," the sort of man with whom Milton had least sympathy, is perfectly painted. An inferior artist would have made the actor who "counselled ignoble ease and peaceful sloth," a degraded and ugly creature; but Milton knew better. He knew that low notions require a better garb than high notions. Human nature is not a high thing, but at least it has a high idea of itself; it will not accept mean maxims, unless they are gilded and made beautiful. A prophet in goatskin may cry, "Repent, repent," but it takes "purple and fine linen" to be able to say "Continue in your sins." The world vanquishes with its speciousness and its show, and the orator who is to persuade men to worldliness must have a share in them. Milton well knew this; after the warlike speech of the fierce Moloch he introduces a brighter and a more graceful spirit.

> "He ended frowning, and his look denounced
> Desp'rate revenge, and battle dangerous
> To less than Gods. On th' other side up rose
> Belial, in act more graceful and humane:
> A fairer person lost not Heaven; he seem'd
> For dignity composed and high exploit:
> But all was false and hollow, though his tongue
> Dropt manna, and could make the worse appear
> The better reason, to perplex and dash
> Maturest counsels: for his thoughts were low;
> To vice industrious, but to nobler deeds
> Tim'rous and slothful: yet he pleased the ear,
> And with persuasive accent thus began:"

He does not begin like a man with a strong case, but like a man with a weak case; he knows that the pride of human nature is irritated by mean advice, and though he may probably persuade men to *take* it, he must carefully apologise for *giving* it. Here, as elsewhere, though the formal address is to devils, the real address is to men: to the human nature which we know, not to the fictitious demonic nature we do not know.

> "I should be much for open war, O Peers!
> As not behind in hate, if what was urged
> Main reason to persuade immediate war,
> Did not dissuade me most, and seem to cast
> Ominous conjecture on the whole success:
> When he who most excels in fact of arms,
> In what he counsels and in what excels
> Mistrustful, grounds his courage on despair,
> And utter dissolution, as the scope
> Of all his aim, after some dire revenge.
> First, what revenge? The tow'rs of Heav'n are fill'd
> With armed watch, that render all access
> Impregnable; oft on the bord'ring deep
> Encamp their legions, or with obscure wing
> Scout far and wide into the realm of night,
> Scorning surprise. Or could we break our way
> By force, and at our heels all hell should rise
> With blackest insurrection, to confound
> Heav'n's purest light, yet our Great Enemy,
> All incorruptible, would on his throne
> Sit unpolluted, and th' ethereal mould
> Incapable of stain would soon expel
> Her mischief, and purge off the baser fire
> Victorious. Thus repulsed, our final hope
> Is flat despair. We must exasperate
> Th' Almighty Victor to spend all his rage,
> And that must end us: that must be our cure,
> To be no more? Sad cure; for who would lose,
> Though full of pain, this intellectual being,
> Those thoughts that wander through eternity,
> To perish rather, swallow'd up and lost
> In the wide womb of uncreated night,
> Devoid of sense and motion? And who knows,
> Let this be good, whether our angry Foe
> Can give it, or will ever? How he can
> Is doubtful; that he never will is sure.
> Will he, so wise, let loose at once his ire
> Belike through impotence, or unaware,
> To give his enemies their wish, and end
> Them in his anger, whom his anger saves
> To punish endless? Wherefore cease we then?
> Say they who counsel war, we are decreed,
> Reserved, and destined, to eternal woe;
> Whatever doing, what can we suffer more,
> What can we suffer worse? Is this then worst,
> Thus sitting, thus consulting, thus in arms?
>   *   *   *   *   *   *

And so on.

Mr. Pitt knew this speech by heart, and Lord Macaulay has called it incomparable; and these judges of the oratorical art have well decided. A mean foreign policy cannot be better defended. Its sensibleness is effectually explained, and its tameness as much as possible disguised.

But we have not here to do with the excellence of Belial's policy, but with the excellence of his speech; and with that speech in a peculiar manner. This speech, taken with the few lines of description with which Milton introduces them, embody, in as short a space as possible, with as much perfection as possible, the delineation of the type of character common at all times, dangerous in many times; sure to come to the surface in moments of difficulty, and never more dangerous than then. As Milton describes, it is one among several *typical* characters which will ever have their place in great councils, which will ever be heard at important decisions, which are part of the characteristic and inalienable whole of this statesmanlike world. The debate in Pandæmonium is a debate among these typical characters at the greatest conceivable crisis, and with adjuncts of solemnity which no other situation could rival. It is the greatest *classical* triumph, the highest achievement of the *pure* style in English literature; it is the greatest description of the highest and most typical characters with the most choice circumstances and in the fewest words.

It is not unremarkable that we should find in Milton and in *Paradise Lost* the best specimen of pure style. He was schoolmaster in a pedantic age, and there is nothing so unclassical — nothing so impure in style — as pedantry. The out-of-door conversational life of Athens was as opposed to bookish scholasticism as a life can be. The most perfect books have been written not by those who thought much of books, but by those who thought little, by those who were under the restraint of a sensitive talking world, to which books had contributed something, and a various eager life the rest. Milton is generally unclassical in spirit where he is learned, and naturally, because the purest poets do not overlay their conceptions with book knowledge, and the classical poets, having in comparison no books, were under little temptation to impair the purity of their style by the accumulation of their research. Over and above this, there is in Milton, and a little in Wordsworth also, one defect which is in the highest degree faulty and unclassical, which mars the effect and impairs the perfection of the pure style. There is a want of *spontaneity*, and a sense of effort. It has been happily said that Plato's words must have *grown* into their places. No one would say so of Milton or even of Wordsworth.

About both of them there is a taint of duty ; a vicious sense
of the good man's task.   Things seem right where they are,
but they seem to be put where they are.   *Flexibility* is essential
to the consummate perfection of the pure style because the
sensation of the poet's efforts carries away our thoughts from his
achievements.   We are admiring his labours when we should
be enjoying his words.   But this is a defect in those two writers,
not a defect in pure art.   Of course it *is* more difficult to write
in few words than to write in many ; to take the best adjuncts,
and those only, for what you have to say, instead of using all
which comes to hand ; it *is* an additional labour if you write
verses in a morning, to spend the rest of the day in *choosing,*
or making those verses fewer.   But a perfect artist in the pure
style is as effortless and as natural as in any style, perhaps is
more so.   Take the well-known lines :—

> There was a little lawny islet
> By anemone and violet,
>   Like mosaic, paven :
> And its roof was flowers and leaves
> Which the summer's breath enweaves,
> Where nor sun, nor showers, nor breeze,
> Pierce the pines and tallest trees,
>   Each a gem engraven.
> Girt by many an azure wave
> With which the clouds and mountains pave
>   A lake's blue chasm.

Shelley had many merits and many defects.   This is not
the place for a complete or indeed for *any* estimate of him.
But one excellence is most evident.   His words are as flexible
as any words ; the rhythm of some modulating air seems to
move them into their place without a struggle by the poet
and almost without his knowledge.   This is the perfection of
pure art, to embody typical conceptions in the choicest, the
fewest accidents, to embody them so that each of these
accidents may produce its full effect, and so to embody them
without effort.

The extreme opposite to this pure art is what may be
called ornate art.   This species of art aims also at giving a
delineation of the typical idea in its perfection and its fulness,
but it aims at so doing in a manner most different.   It wishes
to surround the type with the greatest number of circumstances which it will *bear*.   It works not by choice and
selection, but by accumulation and aggregation.   The idea is
not, as in the pure style, presented with the least clothing
which it will endure, but with the richest and most involved
clothing that it will admit.

We are fortunate in not having to hunt out of past literature an illustrative specimen of the ornate style. Mr. Tennyson has just given one admirable in itself, and most characteristic of the defects and the merits of this style. The story of " Enoch Arden " as he has enhanced and presented it, is a rich and splendid composite of imagery and illustration. Yet how simple that story is in itself. A sailor who sells fish, breaks his leg, gets dismal, gives up selling fish, goes to sea, is wrecked on a desert island, stays there some years, on his return finds his wife married to a miller, speaks to a landlady on the subject, and dies. Told in the pure and simple, the unadorned and classical style, this story would not have taken three pages, but Mr. Tennyson has been able to make it the principal—the largest tale in his new volume. He has done so only by giving to every event and incident in the volume an accompanying commentary. He tells a great deal about the torrid zone which a rough sailor like Enoch Arden certainly would not have perceived; and he gives to the fishing village, to which all the characters belong, a softness and a fascination which such villages scarcely possess in reality.

The description of the tropical island on which the sailor is thrown, is an absolute model of adorned art :—

> " The mountain wooded to the peak, the lawns
> And winding glades high up like ways to Heaven,
> The slender coco's drooping crown of plumes,
> The lightning flash of insect and of bird,
> The lustre of the long convolvuluses
> That coil'd around the stately stems, and ran
> Ev'n to the limit of the land, the glows
> And glories of the broad belt of the world,
> All these he saw ; but what he fain had seen
> He could not see, the kindly human face,
> Nor ever hear a kindly voice, but heard
> The myriad shriek of wheeling ocean-fowl,
> The league-long roller thundering on the reef,
> The moving whisper of huge trees that branch'd
> And blossom'd in the zenith, or the sweep
> Of some precipitous rivulet to the wave,
> As down the shore he ranged, or all day long
> Sat often in the seaward-gazing gorge,
> A ship-wreck'd sailor, waiting for a sail:
> No sail from day to day, but every day
> The sunrise broken into scarlet shafts
> Among the palms and ferns and precipices ;
> The blaze upon the waters to the east;
> The blaze upon his island overhead ;
> The blaze upon the waters to the west;
> Then the great stars that globed themselves in Heaven,
> The hollower-bellowing ocean, and again
> The scarlet shafts of sunrise—but no sail."

No expressive circumstance can be added to this description, no enhancing detail suggested. A much less happy instance is the description of Enoch's life before he sailed:—

> "While Enoch was abroad on wrathful seas,
> Or often journeying landward; for in truth
> Enoch's white horse, and Enoch's ocean spoil
> In ocean-smelling osier, and his face,
> Rough-redden'd with a thousand winter gales,
> Not only to the market-cross were known,
> But in the leafy lanes behind the down,
> Far as the portal-warding lion-whelp,
> And peacock yew-tree of the lonely Hall,
> Whose Friday fare was Enoch's ministering."

So much has not often been made of selling fish.

The essence of ornate art is in this manner to accumulate round the typical object, every thing which can be said about it, every associated thought that can be connected with it without impairing the essence of the delineation.

The first defect which strikes a student of ornate art—the first which arrests the mere reader of it—is what is called a want of simplicity. Nothing is described as it is, everything has about it an atmosphere of *something else.* The combined and associated thoughts, though they set off and heighten particular ideas and aspects of the central and typical conception yet complicate it: a simple thing—" a daisy by the river's brim "—is never left by itself, something else is put with it; something not more connected with it than " lion-whelp" and the " peacock yew-tree" are with the " fresh fish for sale " that Enoch carries past them. Even in the highest cases ornate art leaves upon a cultured and delicate taste, the conviction that it is not the highest art, that it is somehow excessive and over-rich, that it is not chaste in itself or chastening to the mind that sees it—that it is in an unexplained manner unsatisfactory, " a thing in which we feel there is some hidden want! "

That want is a want of " definition." We must all know landscapes, river landscapes especially, which are in the highest sense beautiful, which when we first see them give us a delicate pleasure; which in some—and these the best cases—give even a gentle sense of surprise that such things should be so beautiful, and yet when we come to live in them, to spend even a few hours in them, we seem stifled and oppressed. On the other hand there are people to whom the sea-shore is a companion, an exhilaration; and not so much for the brawl of the shore as for the *limited* vastness, the finite infinite of the ocean as they see it. Such people often come home braced and nerved, and if they spoke out the truth, would have only to say " We have seen the horizon line; " if they were let alone indeed, they would gaze on it hour after hour, so great to them is the fascination, so full the sustaining calm, which they gain from that union of form and greatness. To a very inferior extent, but still, perhaps, to an extent which most people understand better, a common arch will have the same effect. A bridge completes a river landscape; if of the old and many-arched sort it regulates by a long series of defined forms the vague outline of wood and river which before had nothing to measure it; if of the new scientific sort it introduces still more strictly a geometrical element; it stiffens the scenery which was before too soft, too delicate, too vegetable. Just such is the effect of pure style in literary art. It calms by conciseness; while the ornate style leaves on the mind a mist of beauty, an excess of fascination, a complication of charm, the pure style leaves behind it the simple, defined, measured idea, as it is, and by itself. That which is chaste chastens; there is a poised energy—a state half thrill, and half tranquillity —which pure art gives; which no other can give; a pleasure justified as well as felt; an ennobled satisfaction at what ought to satisfy us, and must ennoble us.

Ornate art is to pure art what a painted statue is to an unpainted. It is impossible to deny that a touch of colour *does* bring out certain parts, does convey certain expressions, does heighten certain features, but it leaves on the work as a whole, a want, as we say, " of something;" a want of that inseparable chasteness which clings to simple sculpture, an imparing predominance of alluring details which impairs our satisfaction with our own satisfaction; which makes us doubt whether a higher being than ourselves will be satisfied even though we are so. In the very same manner, though the *rouge* of ornate literature excites our eye, it also impairs our confidence.

Mr. Arnold has justly observed that this self-justifying, self-*proving* purity of style, is commoner in ancient literature than in modern literature, and also that Shakespeare is not a great or an unmixed example of it. No one can say that he is. His works are full of undergrowth, are full of complexity, are not models of style; except by a miracle nothing in the Elizabethan could be a model of style; the restraining taste of that age was feebler and more mistaken than that of any other equally great age. Shakespeare's mind so teemed with creation that he required the most just, most forcible, most constant restraint from without. He most needed to be guided of poets, and he was the least and worst guided. As a whole no one can call his works finished models of the pure style, or of any style. But he has many passages of the most pure style, passages which could be easily cited if space served. And we must remember that the task which Shakespeare undertook was the most difficult which any poet has ever attempted, and that it is a task in which after a million efforts every other poet has failed. The Elizabethan drama —as Shakespeare has immortalised it—undertakes to delineate in five acts, under stage restrictions, and in mere dialogue, a whole list of *dramatis personæ*, a set of characters enough for a modern novel, and with the distinctness of a modern novel. Shakespeare is not content to give two or three great characters in solitude and in dignity, like the classical dramatists; he wishes to give a whole *party* of characters in the play of life, and according to the nature of each. He would "hold the mirror up to nature," not to catch a monarch in a tragic posture, but a whole group of characters engaged in many actions, intent on many purposes, thinking many thoughts. There is life enough, there is action enough, in single plays of Shakespeare to set up an ancient dramatist for a long career. And Shakespeare succeeded. His characters, taken *en masse*, and as a whole, are as well-known as any novelist's characters; cultivated men know all about them, as young ladies know all about Mr. Trollope's novels. But no other dramatist has succeeded in such an aim. No one else's characters are staple people in English literature, hereditary people whom everyone knows all about in every generation. The contemporary dramatists, Beaumont and Fletcher, Ben Jonson, Marlowe, &c., had many merits, some of them were great men. But a critic must say of them the worst thing he has to say; "they were men who failed in their characteristic aim;" they attempted to describe numerous sets of complicated characters, and they failed. No one of such characters, or hardly one, lives in common memory; the "Faustus" of Marlowe, a really great idea, is not remembered. They undertook to write what they could not write, five acts full of real characters, and in consequence, the fine individual things they conceived are forgotten by the mixed multitude, and known only to a few of the few. Of the Spanish theatre we cannot speak; but there are no such characters in any French tragedy: the whole aim of that tragedy forbad it. Goethe has added to literature a few great characters; he may be said almost to have added to literature the idea of "intellectual creation," —the idea of describing great characters through the intellect; but he has not added to the common stock what Shakespeare added, a new *multitude* of men and women; and these not in simple attitudes, but amid the most complex parts of

E

life, with all their various natures roused, mixed, and strained.
The severest art must have allowed many details, much overflowing circumstance to a poet who undertook to describe
what almost defies description.   Pure art would have *com-
manded* him to use details lavishly, for only by a multiplicity
of such could the required effect have been at all produced.
Shakespeare could accomplish it, for his mind was a *spring,*
an inexhaustible fountain of human nature, and it is no
wonder that being compelled by the task of his time to let
the fulness of his nature overflow, he sometimes let it overflow
too much, and covered with erroneous conceits and superfluous
images characters and conceptions which would have been far
more justly, far more effectually, delineated with conciseness
and simplicity.   But there is an infinity of pure art *in* Shakespeare, although there is a great deal else also.

It will be said, if ornate art be as you say, an inferior
species of art, why should it ever be used?   If pure art be the
best sort of art, why should it not always be used?

The reason is this: literary art, as we just now explained,
is concerned with literatesque characters in literatesque situations; and the *best* art is concerned with the *most* literatesque
characters in the *most* literatesque situations.   Such are the
subjects of pure art; it embodies with the fewest touches, and
under the most select and choice circumstances, the highest
conceptions; but it does not follow that only the best subjects
are to be treated by art, and then only in the very best way.
Human nature could not endure such a critical commandment
as that, and it would be an erroneous criticism which gave it.
Any literatesque character may be described in literature
under *any* circumstances which exhibit its literatesqueness.

The essence of pure art consists in its describing what is
as it is, and this is very well for what can bear it, but there
are many inferior things which will not bear it, and which
nevertheless ought to be described in books.   A certain
kind of literature deals with illusions, and this kind of literature has given a colouring to the name romantic.   A man
of rare genius, and even of poetical genius, has gone so far
as to make these illusions the true subject of poetry—almost
the sole subject.   "Without," says Father Newman, of one of
his characters, "being himself a poet, he was in the season of
poetry, in the sweet spring-time, when the year is most beautiful, because it is new.   Novelty was beauty to a heart so open
and cheerful as his; not only because it was novelty, and had
its proper charm as such, but because when we first see things,
we see them in a gay confusion, which is a principal element
of the poetical.   As time goes on, and we number and sort

and measure things,—as we gain views,—we advance towards philosophy and truth, but we recede from poetry.

" When we ourselves were young, we once on a time walked on a hot summer-day from Oxford to Newington—a dull road, as any one who has gone it knows ; yet it was new to us ; and we protest to you, reader, believe it or not, laugh or not, as you will, to us it seemed on that occasion quite touchingly beautiful ; and a soft melancholy came over us, of which the shadows fall even now, when we look back upon that dusty, weary journey. And why ? because every object which met us was unknown and full of mystery. A tree or two in the distance seemed the beginning of a great wood, or park, stretching endlessly ; a hill implied a vale beyond, with that vale's history ; the bye-lanes, with their green hedges, wound on and vanished, yet were not lost to the imagination. Such was our first journey ; but when we had gone it several times, the mind refused to act, the scene ceased to enchant, stern reality alone remained ; and we thought it one of the most tiresome, odious roads we ever had occasion to traverse."

That is to say, that the function of the poet is to introduce a " gay confusion," a rich medley which does not exist in the actual world—which perhaps could not exist in any world— but which would seem pretty if it did exist. Every one who reads *Enoch Arden* will perceive that this notion of all poetry is exactly applicable to this one poem. Whatever be made of Enoch's, " Ocean spoil in ocean swelling over," of the " portal-warding lion-whelp, and the peacock yew-tree," everyone knows that in himself Enoch could not have been charming. People who sell fish about the country (and this is what he did, though Mr. Tennyson won't speak out, and wraps it up) never are beautiful. As Enoch was and must be coarse, in itself the poem must depend for its charm on a " gay confusion "—on a splendid accumulation of impossible accessories.

Mr. Tennyson knows this better than many of us—he knows the country world ; he has proved it that no one living knows it better ; he has painted with pure art—with art which describes what is a race perhaps more refined, more delicate, more conscientious, than the sailor—the " Northern Farmer," and we all know what a splendid, what a living thing, he has made of it. He could, if he only would, have given us the ideal sailor in like manner—the ideal of the natural sailor we mean—the characteristic present man as he lives and is. But this he has not chosen. He has endeavoured to describe an exceptional sailor, at an exceptionally refined port, performing a graceful act, an act of relinquishment. And with this task before him, his profound taste taught him that ornate art was a necessary medium—was the sole effectual instrument—for his purpose. It was necessary for him if possible to abstract the mind from reality, to induce it *not* to conceive or think of sailors as they are while they are reading of his sailors, but to think of what a person who did not know might fancy sailors to be. A casual traveller on the seashore, with the sensitive mood and the romantic imagination Mr. Newman has described, might fancy, would fancy, a seafaring village to be like that. Accordingly, Mr. Tennyson has made it his aim to call off the stress of fancy from real life, to occupy it otherwise, to bury it with pretty accessories; to engage it on the " peacock yew-tree," and the "portal-warding lion-whelp." Nothing, too, can be more splendid than the description of the tropics as Mr. Tennyson delineates them, but a sailor would not have felt the tropics in that manner. The beauties of nature would not have so much occupied him. He would have known little of the scarlet shafts of sunrise and nothing of the long convolvuluses. As in Robinson Crusoe, his own petty contrivances and his small ailments would have been the principal subject to him. " For three years," he might have said, " my back was bad, and then I put two pegs into a piece of drift-wood and so made a chair, and after that it pleased God to send me a chill." In real life his piety would scarcely have gone beyond that.

It will indeed be said, that though the sailor had no words for, and even no explicit consciousness of the splendid details of the torrid zone, yet that he had, notwithstanding, a dim latent inexpressible conception of them: though he could not speak of them or describe them, yet they were much to him. And doubtless such is the case. Rude people are impressed by what is beautiful—deeply impressed—though they could not describe what they see, or what they feel. But what is absurd in Mr. Tennyson's description—absurd when we abstract it from the gorgeous additions and ornaments with which Mr. Tennyson distracts us—is, that his hero feels nothing else but these great splendours. We hear nothing of the physical ailments, the rough devices, the low superstitions, which really would have been the *first* things, the favourite and principal occupations of his mind. Just so when he gets home he *may* have had such fine sentiments, though it is odd, and he *may* have spoken of them to his landlady, though that is odder still,—but it is incredible that his whole mind should be made up of fine sentiment. Beside those sweet feelings, if he had them, there must have been many more obvious, more prosaic, and some perhaps more healthy. Mr. Tennyson has shown a profound judgment in distracting us as he does. He has given us a classic delineation of the " Northern

Farmer " with no ornament at all—as bare a thing as can be—
because he then wanted to describe a true type of real men :
he has given us a sailor crowded all over with ornament and
illustration, because he then wanted to describe an unreal type
of fancied men,—not sailors as they are, but sailors as they
might be wished.

Another prominent element in "Enoch Arden" is yet more
suitable to, yet more requires the aid of, ornate art. Mr.
Tennyson undertook to deal with *half belief.* The presentiments which Annie feels are exactly of that sort which everybody has felt, and which everyone has half believed—which
hardly anyone has more than half believed. Almost everyone,
it has been said, would be angry if anyone else reported that
he believed in ghosts; yet hardly anyone, when thinking by
himself, wholly disbelieves them. Just so such presentiments
as Mr. Tennyson depicts, impress the inner mind so much
that the outer mind—the rational understanding—hardly likes
to consider them nicely or to discuss them sceptically. For these
dubious themes an ornate or complex style is needful. Classical
art speaks out what it has to say plainly and simply. Pure
style cannot hesitate; it describes in concisest outline what
is, as it is. If a poet really believes in presentiments he can
speak out in pure style. One who could have been a poet—
one of the few in any age of whom one can say certainly that
they could have been, and have not been—has spoken thus :—

> " When Heaven sends sorrow,
>   Warnings go first,
>   Lest it should burst
>   With stunning might
>   On souls too bright
> To fear the morrow.
>
> Can science bear us
>   To the hid springs
>   Of human things ?
>   Why may not dream,
>   Or thought's day gleam,
>   Startle, yet cheer us ?
>
> Are such thoughts fetters,
>   While faith disowns
>   Dread of earth's tones,
>   Recks but Heaven's call,
>   And on the wall,
>   Reads but Heaven's letters ?"

But if a poet is not sure whether presentiments are true
or not true; if he wishes to leave his readers in doubt; if he
wishes an atmosphere of indistinct illusion and of moving
shadow, he must use the romantic style, the style of miscel-

laneous adjunct, the style "which shirks, not meets" your intellect, the style which as you are scrutinising disappears.

Nor is this all, or even the principal lesson, which "Enoch Arden" may suggest to us, of the use of ornate art. That art is the appropriate art for an *unpleasing type.* Many of the characters of real life, if brought distinctly, prominently, and plainly before the mind, as they really are, if shown in their inner nature, their actual essence, are doubtless very unpleasant. They would be horrid to meet and horrid to think of. We fear it must be owned that "Enoch Arden" is this kind of person. A dirty sailor who did *not* go home to his wife is not an agreeable being: a varnish must be put on him to make him shine. It is true that he acts rightly; that he is very good. But such is human nature that it finds a little tameness in mere morality. Mere virtue belongs to a charity school-girl, and has a taint of the catechism. All of us feel this, though most of us are too timid, too scrupulous, too anxious about the virtue of others, to speak out. We are ashamed of our nature in this respect, but it is not the less our nature. And if we look deeper into the matter there are many reasons why we should not be ashamed of it. The soul of man, and as we necessarily believe of beings greater than man, has many parts beside its moral part. It has an intellectual part, an artistic part, even a religious part, in which mere morals have no share. In Shakespeare or Goethe, even in Newton or Archimedes, there is much which will not be cut down to the shape of the commandments. They have thoughts, feelings, hopes—immortal thoughts and hopes—which have influenced the life of men, and the souls of men, ever since their age, but which the "whole duty of man," the ethical compendium, does not recognise. Nothing is more unpleasant than a virtuous person with a mean mind. A highly developed moral nature joined to an undeveloped intellectual nature, an undeveloped artistic nature, and a very limited religious nature, is of necessity repulsive. It represents a bit of human nature—a good bit, of course—but a bit only, in disproportionate, unnatural, and revolting prominence; and, therefore, unless an artist use delicate care, we are offended. The dismal act of a squalid man needed many condiments to make it pleasant, and therefore Mr. Tennyson was right to mix them subtly and to use them freely.

A mere act of self-denial can indeed scarcely be pleasant upon paper. An heroic struggle with an external adversary, even though it end in a defeat, may easily be made attractive. Human nature likes to see itself look grand, and it looks grand when it is making a brave struggle with foreign foes. But it does not look grand when it is divided against itself. An excellent person striving with temptation is a very admirable being in reality, but he is not a pleasant being in description. We hope he will win and overcome his temptation, but we feel that he would be a more interesting being, a higher being, if he had not felt that temptation so much. The poet must make the struggle great in order to make the self-denial virtuous, and if the struggle be too great, we are apt to feel some mixture of contempt. The internal metaphysics of a divided nature are but an inferior subject for art, and if they are to be made attractive, much else must be combined with them. If the excellence of Hamlet had depended on the ethical qualities of Hamlet, it would not have been the masterpiece of our literature. He acts virtuously of course, and kills the people he ought to kill, but Shakespeare knew that such goodness would not much interest the pit. He made him a handsome prince, and a puzzling meditative character; these secular qualities relieve his moral excellence, and so he becomes "nice." In proportion as an artist has to deal with types essentially imperfect, he must disguise their imperfections; he must accumulate around them as many first-rate accessories as may make his readers forget that they are themselves second-rate. The sudden *millionaires* of the present day hope to disguise their social defects by buying old places, and hiding among aristocratic furniture; just so a great artist who has to deal with characters artistically imperfect will use an ornate syle, will fit them into a scene where there is much else to look at.

For these reasons ornate art is within the limits as legitimate as pure art. It does what pure art could not do. The very excellence of pure art confines its employment. Precisely because it gives the best things by themselves and exactly as they are it fails when it is necessary to describe inferior things among other things, with a list of enhancements and a crowd of accompaniments that in reality do not belong to it. Illusion, half belief, unpleasant types, imperfect types, are as much the proper sphere of ornate art, as an inferior landscape is the proper sphere for the true efficacy of moonlight. A really great landscape needs sunlight and bears sunlight; but moonlight is an equaliser of beauties; it gives a romantic unreality to what will not stand the bare truth. And just so does romantic art.

There is, however, a third kind of art which differs from these on the point in which they most resemble one another. Ornate art and pure art have this in common, that they paint

the types of literature in as good perfection as they can.
Ornate art, indeed, uses undue disguises and unreal enhancements; it does not confine itself to the best types; on the
contrary it is its office to make the best of imperfect types
and lame approximations; but ornate art, as much as pure
art, catches its subject in the best light it can, takes the most
developed aspect of it which it can find, and throws upon
it the most congruous colours it can use. But grotesque art
does just the contrary. It takes the type, so to say, *in difficulties.* It gives a representation of it in its minimum development, amid the circumstances least favourable to it, just while
it is struggling with obstacles, just where it is encumbered with
incongruities. It deals, to use the language of science, not with
normal types but with abnormal specimens; to use the language
of old philosophy, not with what nature is striving to be, but
with what by some lapse she has happened to become.

This art works by contrast. It enables you to see, it makes
you see, the perfect type by painting the opposite deviation.
It shows you what ought to be by what ought not to be, when
complete it reminds you of the perfect image, by showing you
the distorted and imperfect image. Of this art we possess in
the present generation one prolific master. Mr. Browning is
an artist working by incongruity. Possibly hardly one of his
most considerable efforts can be found which is not great
because of its odd mixture. He puts together things which
no one else would have put together, and produce on our
minds a result which no one else would have produced, or
tried to produce. His admirers may not like all we may have
to say of him. But in our way we too are among his admirers.
No one ever read him without seeing not only his great
ability but his great *mind.* He not only possesse superficial
useable talents, but the strong something, the inner secret
something which uses them and controls them; he is great, not
in mere accomplishments, but in himself. He has applied a
hard strong intellect to real life; he has applied the same
intellect to the problems of his age. He has striven to know
what *is:* he has endeavoured not to be cheated by counterfeits,
to be infatuated with illusions. His heart is in what he says.
He has battered his brain against his creed till he believes
it. He has accomplishments too, the more effective because
they are mixed. He is at once a student of mysticism,
and a citizen of the world. He brings to the club sofa distinct
visions of old creeds, intense images of strange thoughts: he
takes to the bookish student tidings of wild Bohemia, and
little traces of the *demi-monde.* He puts down what is good
for the naughty and what is naughty for the good. Over

women his easier writings exercise that imperious power which belongs to the writings of a great man of the world upon such matters. He knows women, and therefore they wish to know him. If we blame many of Browning's efforts, it is in the interest of art, and not from a wish to hurt or degrade him.

If we wanted to illustrate the nature of grotesque art by an exaggerated instance we should have selected a poem which the chance of late publication brings us in this new volume. Mr. Browning has undertaken to describe what may be called *mind in difficulties*—mind set to make out the universe under the worst and hardest circumstances. He takes "Caliban," not perhaps exactly Shakespeare's Caliban, but an analogous and worse creature; a strong thinking power, but a nasty creature—a gross animal, uncontrolled and unelevated by any feeling of religion or duty. The delineation of him will show that Mr. Browning does not wish to take undue advantage of his readers by a choice of nice subjects.

> " ['Will sprawl, now that the heat of day is best,
> Flat on his belly in the pit's much mire,
> With elbows wide, fists clenched to prop his chin ;
> And, while he kicks both feet in the cool slush,
> And feels about his spine small eft-things course,
> Run in and out each arm, and make him laugh ;
> And while above his head a pompion-plant,
> Coating the cave-top as a brow its eye,
> Creeps down to touch and tickle hair and beard,
> And now a flower drops with a bee inside,
> And now a fruit to snap at, catch and crunch : "

This pleasant creature proceeds to give his idea of the origin of the Universe, and it is as follows. Caliban speaks in the third person, and is of opinion that the maker of the Universe took to making it on account of his personal discomfort :—

> " Setebos, Setebos, and Setebos !
> 'Thinketh, He dwelleth i' the cold o' the moon.

> " 'Thinketh He made it, with the sun to match,
> But not the stars ; the stars came otherwise ;
> Only made clouds, winds, meteors, such as that :
> Also this isle, what lives and grows thereon,
> And snaky sea which rounds and ends the same.

> " 'Thinketh, it came of being ill at ease :
> He hated that He cannot change His cold,
> Nor cure its ache. 'Hath spied an icy fish
> That longed to 'scape the rock-stream where she lived,
> And thaw herself within the lukewarm brine
> O' the lazy sea her stream thrusts far amid,

A crystal spike 'twixt two warm walls of wave ;
Only she ever sickened, found repulse
At the other kind of water, not her life,
(Green-dense and dim-delicious, bred o' the sun)
Flounced back from bliss she was not born to breathe,
And in her old bounds buried her despair,
Hating and loving warmth alike : so He.

" 'Thinketh, He made thereat the sun, this isle,
Trees and the fowls here, beast and creeping thing.
Yon otter, sleek-wet, black, lithe as a leech ;
Yon auk, one fire-eye, in a ball of foam,
That floats and feeds ; a certain badger brown
He hath watched hunt with that slant white-wedge eye
By moonlight ; and the pie with the long tongue
That pricks deep into oakwarts for a worm,
And says a plain word when she finds her prize,
But will not eat the ants ; the ants themselves
That build a wall of seeds and settled stalks
About their hole—He made all these and more,
Made all we see, and us, in spite : how else ? "

It may seem perhaps to most readers that these lines are
very difficult, and that they are unpleasant. And so they are.
We quote them to illustrate, not the *success* of grotesque art,
but the *nature* of grotesque art. It shows the end at which
this species of art aims, and if it fails it is from over-boldness
in the choice of a subject by the artist, or from the defects of
its execution. A thinking faculty more in difficulties—a great
type,—an inquisitive, searching intellect under more disagree-
able conditions, with worse helps, more likely to find falsehood,
less likely to find truth, can scarcely be imagined. Nor is the
mere description of the thought at all bad: on the contrary, if
we closely examine it, it is very clever. Hardly anyone could
have amassed so many ideas at once nasty and suitable. But
scarcely any readers—any casual readers—who are not of the
sect of Mr. Browning's admirers will be able to examine it
enough to appreciate it. From a defect, partly of subject, and
partly of style, many of Mr. Browning's works make a demand
upon the reader's zeal and sense of duty to which the nature
of most readers is unequal. They have on the turf the convenient expression " staying power": some horses can hold on
and others cannot. But hardly any reader not of especial and
peculiar nature can hold on through such composition. There
is not enough of " staying power" in human nature. One of
his greatest admirers once owned to us that he seldom or never
began a new poem without looking on in advance, and fore-
seeing with caution what length of intellectual adventure he
was about to commence. Whoever will work hard at such
poems will find much mind in them : they are a sort of quarry

of ideas, but who ever goes there will find these ideas in such a jagged, ugly, useless shape that he can hardly bear them.

We are not judging Mr. Browning simply from a hasty recent production. All poets are liable to misconceptions, and if such a piece as " Caliban upon Setebos " were an isolated error, a venial and particular exception we should have given it no prominence. We have put it forward because it just elucidates both our subject and the characteristics of Mr. Browning. But many other of his best known pieces do so almost equally; what several of his devotees think his best piece is quite enough illustrative for anything we want. It appears that on Holy Cross day at Rome the Jews were obliged to listen to a Christian sermon in the hope of their conversion, though this is, according to Mr. Browning, what they really said when they came away :—

> "Fee, faw, fum! bubble and squeak!
> Blessedest Thursday's the fat of the week.
> Rumble and tumble, sleek and rough,
> Stinking and savoury, smug and gruff,
> Take the church-road, for the bell's due chime
> Gives us the summons—'t is sermon-time.
>
> "Boh, here's Barnabas! Job, that's you?
> Up stumps Solomon—bustling too?
> Shame, man! greedy beyond your years
> To handsel the bishop's shaving-shears?
> Fair play 's a jewel! leave friends in the lurch?
> Stand on a line ere you start for the church.
>
> "Higgledy, piggledy, packed we lie,
> Rats in a hamper, swine in a stye,
> Wasps in a bottle, frogs in a sieve,
> Worms in a carcase, fleas in a sleeve.
> Hist! square shoulders, settle your thumbs
> And buzz for the bishop—here he comes."

And after similar nice remarks for a church, the edified congregation concludes :—

> "But now, while the scapegoats leave our flock,
> And the rest sit silent and count the clock,
> Since forced to muse the appointed time
> On these precious facts and truths sublime,—
> Let us fitly employ it, under our breath,
> In saying Ben Ezra's Song of Death.
>
> "For Rabbi Ben Ezra, the night he died,
> Called sons and son's sons to his side,
> And spoke, 'This world has been harsh and strange;
> Something is wrong: there needeth a change.
> But what, or where? at the last, or first?
> In one point only we sinned, at worst.

" 'The Lord will have mercy on Jacob yet,
And again in his border see Israel set.
When Judah beholds Jerusalem,
The stranger-seed shall be joined to them:
To Jacob's House shall the Gentiles cleave.
So the Prophet saith and his sons believe.

" ' Ay, the children of the chosen race
Shall carry and bring them to their place:
In the land of the Lord shall lead the same,
Bondsmen and handmaids.   Who shall blame,
When the slaves enslave, the oppressed ones o'er
The oppressor triumph for evermore?

" ' God spoke, and gave us the word to keep:
Bade never fold the hands nor sleep
'Mid a faithless world,—at watch and ward,
Till Christ at the end relieve our guard.
By His servant Moses the watch was set:
Though near upon cock-crow, we keep it yet.

" ' Thou! if Thou wast He, who at mid-watch came,
By the starlight, naming a dubious Name!
And if, too heavy with sleep—too rash
With fear—O Thou, if that martyr-gash
Fell on Thee coming to take Thine own,
And we gave the Cross, when we owed the Throne—

" ' Thou art the Judge.   We are bruised thus.
But, the judgment over, join sides with us!
Thine too is the cause! and not more Thine
Than ours, is the work of these dogs and swine,
Whose life laughs through and spits at their creed,
Who maintain Thee in word, and defy Thee in deed!

" ' We withstood Christ then? be mindful how
At least we withstand Barabbas now!
Was our outrage sore? But the worst we spared,
To have called these—Christians, had we dared!
Let defiance to them pay mistrust of Thee,
And Rome make amends for Calvary!

" ' By the torture, prolonged from age to age,
By the infamy, Israel's heritage,
By the Ghetto's plague, by the garb's disgrace,
By the badge of shame, by the felon's place,
By the branding-tool, the bloody whip,
And the summons to Christian fellowship,—

" ' We boast our proof that at least the Jew
Would wrest Christ's name from the Devil's crew.
Thy face took never so deep a shade
But we fought them in it, God our aid!
A trophy to bear, as we march, Thy band
South, East, and on to the Pleasant Land!' "

It is very natural that a poet whose wishes incline, or
whose genius conducts him to a grotesque art, should be

attracted towards mediæval subjects. There is no age whose legends are so full of grotesque subjects, and no age where real life was so fit to suggest them. Then, more than at any other time, good principles have been under great hardships. The vestiges of ancient civilisation, the germs of modern civilisation, the little remains of what had been, the small beginnings of what is, were buried under a cumbrous mass of barbarism and cruelty. Good elements hidden in horrid accompaniments are the special theme of grotesque art, and these mediæval life and legends afford more copiously than could have been furnished before Christianity gave its new elements of good, or since modern civilisation has removed some few at least of the old elements of destruction. A *buried* life like the spiritual mediæval was Mr. Browning's natural element, and he was right to be attracted by it. His mistake has been, that he has not made it pleasant; that he has forced his art to topics on which no one could charm, or on which he, at any rate, could not; that on these occasions and in these poems he has failed in fascinating men and women of sane taste.

We say " sane " because there is a most formidable and estimable *insane* taste. The will has great though indirect power over the taste, just as it has over the belief. There are some horrid beliefs from which human nature revolts, from which at first it shrinks, to which, at first, no effort can force it. But if we fix the mind upon them they have a power over us just because of their natural offensiveness. They are like the sight of human blood : experienced soldiers tell us that at first men are sickened by the smell and newness of blood almost to death and fainting, but that as soon as they harden their hearts and stiffen their minds, as soon as they *will* bear it, then comes an appetite for slaughter, a tendency to gloat on carnage, to love blood, at least for the moment, with a deep eager love. It is a principle that if we put down a healthy instinctive aversion, nature avenges herself by creating an unhealthy insane attraction. For this reason the most earnest truth-seeking men fall into the worst delusions ; they will not let their mind alone ; they force it towards some ugly thing, which a crotchet of argument, a conceit of intellect recommends, and nature punishes their disregard of her warning by subjection to the holy one, by belief in it. Just so the most industrious critics get the most admiration. They think it unjust to rest in their instinctive natural horror : they overcome it, and angry nature gives them over to ugly poems and marries them to detestable stanzas.

Mr. Browning possibly, and some of the worst of Mr.

Browning's admirers certainly, will say that these grotesque
objects exist in real life, and therefore they ought to be, at
least may be, described in art. But though pleasure is not
the end of poetry, pleasing is a condition of poetry. An
exceptional monstrosity of horrid ugliness cannot be made
pleasing, except it be made to suggest—to recall—the perfection, the beauty, from which it is a deviation. Perhaps in extreme cases no art is equal to this; but then such self-imposed
problems should not be worked by the artist; these out-of-the-
way and detestable subjects should be let alone by him. It is
rather characteristic of Mr. Browning to neglect this rule. He
is the most of a realist, and the least of an idealist of any poet
we know. He evidently sympathises with some part at least
of Bishop Blougram's apology. Anyhow this world exists.
"There *is* good wine—there *are* pretty women—there *are*
comfortable benefices—there *is* money, and it is pleasant to
spend it. Accept the creed of your age and you get these,
reject that creed and you lose them. And for what do you
lose them? For a fancy creed of your own, which no one
else will accept, which hardly anyone will call a 'creed,'
which most people will consider a sort of unbelief." Again,
Mr. Browning evidently loves what we may call the realism,
the grotesque realism, of orthodox christianity. Many parts
of it in which great divines have felt keen difficulties are
quite pleasant to him. He must *see* his religion, he must have
an "object-lesson" in believing. He must have a creed that
will *take*, which wins and holds the miscellaneous world,
which stout men will heed, which nice women will adore. The
spare moments of solitary religion—the "obdurate question-
ings," the high "instincts," the "first affections," the "shadowy
recollections,"

> " Which, do they what they may,
> Are yet the fountain-light of all our day—
> Are yet a master-light of all our seeing ; "

the great but vague faith—the unutterable tenets—seem to
him worthless, visionary; they are not enough immersed in
matter; they move about "in worlds not realised." We
wish he could be tried like the prophet once; he would
have found God in the earthquake and the storm; he
could have deciphered from them a bracing and a rough
religion: he would have known that crude men and ignorant
women felt them too, and he would accordingly have
trusted them; but he would have distrusted and disregarded the "still small voice;" he would have said it was
"fancy"—a thing you thought you heard to-day, but were

not sure you had heard to-morrow: he would call it a nice
illusion, an immaterial prettiness; he would ask triumphantly
" How are you to get the mass of men to heed this little
thing?" he would have persevered and insisted " *My wife* does
not hear it."

But although a suspicion of beauty, and a taste for ugly
reality, have led Mr. Browning to exaggerate the functions, and
to caricature the nature of grotesque art, we own or rather we
maintain that he has given many excellent specimens of that
art within its proper boundaries and limits.   Take an example,
his picture of what we may call the *bourgeois* nature in *diffi-*
culties; in the utmost difficulty, in contact with magic and
the supernatural.   He has made of it something homely, comic,
true; reminding us of what *bourgeois* nature really is.   By
showing us the type under abnormal conditions, he reminds us
of the type under its best and most satisfactory conditions :—

" Hamelin Town's in Brunswick,
By famous Hanover city;
    The river Weser, deep and wide,
    Washes its walls on the southern side;
    A pleasanter spot you never spied;
By, when begins my ditty,
    Almost five hundred years ago,
    To see the townsfolk suffer so
        From vermin, was a pity.

    " Rats!
They fought the dogs, and killed the cats,
    And bit the babies in the cradles,
    And ate the cheeses out of the vats,

    And licked the soup from the cook's own tables,
Split open the kegs of salted sprats,
Made nests inside men's Sunday hats,
And even spoiled the women's chats,
        By drowning their speaking
        With shrieking and squeaking
In fifty different sharps and flats.

At last the people in a body
    To the Town Hall came flocking :
' 'Tis clear,' cried they, ' our Mayor's a noddy;
    And as for Corporation—shocking
To think we buy gowns lined with ermine
For dolts that can't or won't determine
What's best to rid us of our vermin!
You hope, because you're old and obese,
To find in the furry civic robe ease?
Rouse up, Sirs! Give your brains a racking
To find the remedy we're lacking,
Or, sure as fate, we'll send you packing!'
At this the Mayor and Corporation
Quaked with a mighty consternation."

A person of musical abilities proposes to extricate the civic dignitaries from the difficulty, and they promise him a thousand guilders if he does.

"Into the street the Piper stept,
 Smiling first a little smile,
As if he knew what magic slept
 In his quiet pipe the while;
Then, like a musical adept,
To blow the pipe his lips he wrinkled,
And green and blue his sharp eye twinkled
Like a candle-flame when salt is sprinkled;
And ere three shrill notes the pipe uttered
You heard as if an army muttered;
And the muttering grew to a grumbling;
And the grumbling grew to a mighty rumbling:
And out of the houses the rats came tumbling.
Great rats, small rats, lean rats, brawny rats,
Brown rats, black rats, grey rats, tawny rats,
Grave old plodders, gay young friskers,
 Fathers, mothers, uncles, cousins,
Cocking tails and pricking whiskers,
 Families by tens and dozens,
Brothers, sisters, husbands, wives—
Followed the Piper for their lives.
From street to street he piped advancing,
And step for step he followed dancing,
Until they came to the river Weser
Wherein all plunged and perished!
—Save one who, stout as Julius Cæsar,
Swam across and lived to carry
(As he, the manuscript he cherished)
To Rat-land home his commentary:
Which was, 'At the first shrill notes of the pipe,
I heard a sound as of scraping tripe,
And putting apples, wondrous ripe,
Into a cider-press's gripe:
And a moving away of pickle-tub boards,
And a leaving ajar of conserve-cupboards,
And a drawing the corks of train-oil flasks,
And a breaking the hoops of butter-casks;
And it seemed as if a voice
(Sweeter far than by harp or by psaltery
Is breathed) called out, Oh rats, rejoice!
The world is grown to one vast drysaltery!
So, munch on, crunch on, take your nuncheon,
Breakfast, supper, dinner, luncheon!
And just as a bulky sugar-puncheon,
All ready staved, like a great sun shone
Glorious scarce an inch before me,
Just as methought it said, Come, bore me!
—I found the Weser rolling o'er me.'
You should have heard the Hamelin people
Ringing the bells till they rocked the steeple.
'Go,' cried the Mayor, 'and get long poles
Poke out the nests and block up the holes!

Consult with carpenters and builders,
And leave in our town not even a trace
Of the rats!'—when suddenly, up the face
Of the Piper perked in the market-place,
With a, 'First, if you please, my thousand guilders!'

" A thousand guilders! The Mayor looked blue;
So did the Corporation too.
For council dinners made rare havoc
With Claret, Moselle, Vin-de-Grave, Hock;
And half the money would replenish
Their cellar's biggest butt with Rhenish.
To pay this sum to a wandering fellow
With a gipsy coat of red and yellow!
'Beside,' quoth the Mayor with a knowing wink,
'Our business was done at the river's brink;
We saw with our eyes the vermin sink,
And what's dead can't come to life, I think.
So, friend, we're not the folks to shrink
From the duty of giving you something for drink,
And a matter of money to put in your poke;
But as for the guilders, what we spoke
Of them, as you very well know, was in joke.
Beside, our losses have made us thrifty.
A thousand guilders! Come, take fifty!

"The piper's face fell, and he cried,
'No trifling! I can't wait, beside!
I've promised to visit by dinner time
Bagdat, and accept the prime
Of the Head-Cook's pottage, all he's rich in,
For having left, in the Caliph's kitchen,
Of a nest of scorpions no survivor—
With him I proved no bargain-driver,
With you, don't think I'll bate a stiver!
And folks who put me in a passion
May find me pipe to another fashion.'

" 'How?' cried the Mayor, ' d'ye think I'll brook
Being worse treated than a Cook?
Insulted by a lazy ribald
With idle pipe and vesture piebald?
You threaten us, fellow? Do your worst,
Blow your pipe there till you burst!'

Once more he stept into the street;
    And to his lips again
Laid his long pipe of smooth straight cane;
    And ere he blew three notes (such sweet
Soft notes as yet musician's cunning
    Never gave the enraptured air)
There was a rustling, that seemed like a bustling
Of merry crowds justling at pitching and hustling,
Small feet were pattering, wooden shoes clattering,
Little hands clapping and little tongues chattering,
And, like fowls in a farm-yard when barley is scattering,
    Out came the children running.

F

All the little boys and girls,
With rosy cheeks and flaxen curls,
And sparkling eyes and teeth like pearls,
Tripping and skipping, ran merrily after
The wonderful music with shouting and laughter
*   *   *   *   *   *   *   *
And I must not omit to say
That in Transylvania there's a tribe
Of alien people that ascribe
The outlandish ways and dress
On which their neighbours lay such stress,
To their fathers and mothers having risen
Out of some subterraneous prison
Into which they were trepanned
Long time ago in a mighty band
Out of Hamelin town in Brunswick land,
But how or why, they don't understand.

Something more we had to say of Mr. Browning, but we must stop. It is singularly characteristic of this age that the poems which rise to the surface, should be examples of ornate art, and grotesque art, not of pure art. We live in the realm of the *half* educated. The number of readers grows daily, but the quality of readers does not improve rapidly. The middle class is scattered, headless; it is well-meaning but aimless; wishing to be wise, but ignorant how to be wise. The aristocracy of England never was a literary aristocracy, never even in the days of its full power—of its unquestioned predominance did it guide—did it even seriously try to guide—the taste of England. Without guidance young men, and tired men are thrown amongst a mass of books; they have to choose which they like; many of them would much like to improve their culture, to chasten their taste, if they knew how. But left to themselves they take, not pure art, but showy art; not that which permanently relieves the eye and makes it happy whenever it looks, and as long as it looks, but *glaring* art which catches and arrests the eye for a moment, but which in the end fatigues it. But before the wholesome remedy of nature—the fatigue arrives—the hasty reader has passed on to some new excitement, which in its turn stimulates for an instant, and then is passed by for ever. These conditions are not favourable to the due appreciation of pure art—of that art which must be known before it is admired—which must have fastened irrevocably on the brain before you appreciate it— which you must love ere it will seem worthy of your love. Women too, whose voice in literature counts as well as that of men—and in a light literature counts for more than that of men—women, such as we know them, such as they are likely to be, ever prefer a delicate unreality to a true or firm art. A dressy literature, an exaggerated literature seem to be fated to us. These are our curses, as other times had theirs.

> " And yet
> Think not the living times forget,
> Ages of heroes fought and fell,
> That Homer in the end might tell;
> O'er grovelling generations past
> Upstood the Gothic fane at last;
> And countless hearts in countless years
> Had wasted thoughts, and hopes, and fears
> Rude laughter and unmeaning tears;
> Ere England Shakespeare saw, or Rome
> The pure perfection of her dome.
> Others I doubt not, if not we,
> The issue of our toils shall see;
> And (they forgotten and unknown)
> Young children gather as their own
> The harvest that the dead had sown.

W. B.

MODERN VERSE WRITERS.

BETWEEN the first of January 1865 and the first of January 1866 there were published in the United Kingdom two hundred and seventy-five volumes of verse. If we but consider the mental and physical disease, the unrest, the baffled ambitions, the piteous wrestling with circumstances which these volumes typify, we shall say that in the social history of that year there are few more pathetic facts to be met with. Clever newspaper-writers, applying to such a statement their handy trade-gauge of utilitarianism, would probably dismiss it into the limbo of treated topics with a few happy remarks concerning the new deluge. But the fact remains: whether we regard it as a symptom of the unhealthy tendencies of modern life, or of a growing want of judgment on the part of amateur versifiers, or of the unconscionable negligence of critics. Probably at no period since the ingenuity of man lit upon the fatal 'accomplishment of verse' has there been any lack of those young gentlemen who love to rhyme in secresy. Had Lydia truthfully replied to the question of Horace, she would most likely have said that Sybaris, shunning the sunlit field of Mars, was only trying to write ridiculous sapphics about her pretty eyes, or fingers, or feet; while it is morally certain that numbers of Roman youths must have been in the habit of privately composing Æneids with their own foolish self for hero and with no adventures to speak of. In those days, so far as we can learn, Sybaris was content if his jolting dactyls won a kiss from the lady they celebrated; and the authors of spurious Æneids got through the measles of imitation without harm to themselves or trouble to their friends. Pretty nearly all Shakespeare's lovers are rhymers; but where do we find one of them trying to sell the feeble offspring of his love to a Moloch of a publisher? Valentine himself, when at the end of a sonnet he had anticipated in one line—

Sylvia, this night I will enfranchise thee—

a great political project of the present day, stuffed poetry and politics together into his cloak-pocket, and had nigh gone mad when the duke brought them to light. It has been reserved for the civilisation of a later age to create, during one year, in the minds of nearly three hundred men and women, the conviction of the possession of heavenborn genius.

One cannot avoid a suspicion that much of this hallucination and of its consequent misery has been produced by careless criticism. Versifiers depend upon reviews for what recognition, correction, and guidance they are likely to receive, simply because reviewers alone read their volumes. This is a duty entrusted by society to the conscience of critics. It may be said that the duty is a public one; that, to avoid the painful possibility of a struggling genius being crushed down by neglect, we ought to inform ourselves of the actual merit of each of these books. The principle is praiseworthy; but its application will become possible only when man's life ceases to be narrowed by the limits of birth and death. Not even in the exhaustive catalogues of human duty furnished by Lothario, or Jarno, or Wilhelm himself, do we find that it is demanded of us to read all contemporary literature—and all previous literature, for the matter of that, in order to form just comparisons. Mankind have other and as important duties to perform, the omission of which would be virtual suicide. We therefore ask the critic to tell us what is of value in such volumes

as come before him ; and how does
he do his work ? ' Why,' he says,
' I am paid by the length of the
review which I write. Most books
of verse are only worth four lines ;
many of them the newspaper, or
magazine, or review for which I
write would not mention at all. If
I were to spend my time gratuitously
in reading each volume carefully,
I should starve ; and there is no
divine law which commands me to
starve for the benefit of any verse-
writer, big or little.' The critic,
therefore—we speak now only of the
average critic as he is to be found in
modern journalism—cultivates the
art of saying nothing gracefully ;
and the book is shut with a few
faint sentences of approval. So far
well. The next best thing for a
man who cannot do good is to refrain from doing ill. Occasionally,
however, the critic loses sight of
the great merit of saying nothing.
Perhaps some not unnatural wish
to vary the monotony of such a
column of colourless criticism leads
him to depart from his theory of
negation, and he commits himself
to rash verdicts which may be productive of the saddest consequences.
Let us take an instance. Mr. John
Harris is a ' Cornish poet ' who has
written some decent verse, chiefly
descriptive of rustic life and natural
scenery. We choose the following
specimens of his lines solely because
they happen to be the first and last
verses of the ' Minor Poems ' in his
most recently published volume :

> In Windsor's royal chapel,
>   The nobles of the land,
> The flower of dear old England,
>   Assemble heart and hand ;
> And mitred bishops cluster
>   Around the royal pair,
> Far Denmark's bud of beauty
>   And Albion's noble heir.

> ' Good evening, Enoch Elk,' said I,
>   ' Good evening, sir,' said he :
> ' If men would only seek the Lord,
>   I know they'd happy be ;
> For He has sent His Spirit down
>   And whispered peace to me.'

Now let us look at what reviewers
have said of a man to whom the
writing and publishing of these
verses (amongst others greatly better, be it said), was a possible thing.
' The genius exhibited in the book
to which we are drawing the reader's
attention is of the highest order,'
says one. ' His lays abound with
some of the finest ideas we remember ever to have read,' says another.
' A man whose soul glows with the fire
of genuine inspiration,' says a third.
' John Harris has written his name
indelibly among the poets of the
age,' says a fourth. ' The " Mountain Prophet " contains some of the
finest lines in the language,' says
yet another. The *Athenæum* observes that his writing ' stirs the
blood like wine, and fills us with a
fuller strength ;' the *Literary Gazette* styles him, ' one of the truest
poets of our time.' Is it to be wondered at that Mr. Harris should in
his pages continually talk of himself as a ' poet,' and give the history
of his life as ' Peeps at a Poet,'.
without seeming to have the remotest glimmering of the grandeur
of the title he so easily assumes ?
Is it to be wondered at that men
who know their verses are incom-
parably superior to those we have
quoted should fling themselves into
print in the hope of obtaining an
equally flattering recognition ? Mr.
Harris we believe to be personally
a most worthy man ; and there is
something which stirs the heart
towards him in the circumstances
which prompted even such bald
lines as the following :

> The last eleven months thou'st been too
>   hard—
> Ten pence per day is all I've had of thee,
> And this has caused the silent tears to flow ;
> My wife and I have sat beside the hearth,
> And told our sorrowing tale, with none to
>   hear,
> But Him who listens to the raven's cry.
> My silent lyre has rusted in my cot,
> Or if 'twas strung, 'twas strung to notes of
>   woe, &c.

but there is cruelty as well as dishonesty in proclaiming him a true poet. If he is one of the few great ones whom the earth has from time to time received, he may well be bitter with the world for so far neglecting his books as to leave him in a position where he cannot procure 'the better education of his children,' which he seems to desire.

We have made it our business to read with some attention a tolerably large number of recent verse writers, especially that class which does not usually obtain for itself notice in current reviews. The task has not been wholly unprofitable. 'A vein of Poetry,' says Mr. Carlyle, 'exists in the hearts of all men. . . A man that has *so* much more of the poetic element developed in him as to have become noticeable, will be called Poet by his neighbours.' In these volumes the most unobservant reader cannot fail to be struck with occasional glimpses of better material among heaps of undeniable rubbish ; and the question naturally suggests itself whether, in the event of such a thing being possible, the boiling down of the three hundred volumes of any year would leave as residue one book of true poetry. Before proceeding, however, to adduce a few of the peculiarities of the most characteristic rhymers we have encountered, it will be necessary to show the reader on what principle we have endeavoured to distinguish between different kinds of verse. That principle may be thus briefly stated, — *Nothing is poetry which could as well have been expressed in prose,* or, more correctly, *That idea is not poetical the conception of which does not suffer by being expressed in prose.* The test, we admit, is a somewhat severe one. It strikes whiteness into manifold passages in Byron, for example, and obliterates whole pages of Wordsworth, while it leaves Shelley and Keats almost untouched. We nevertheless believe it to be practically sound. Let the most skilful and graceful prose-

writer of the century endeavour to embody in prose the conception of even such simple poems as Motherwell's 'Jeannie Morrison,' Heine's 'Die schöne Augen,' or Shelley's 'Lines to an Indian air.' He may adhere as he likes to the choice diction of the original, and paraphrase the lines without a word of commentary, yet the subtle aroma of the verses will assuredly be gone. The rule is not without exceptions ; but it will serve our present purpose. For in most volumes such as these we proceed to notice, not even paraphrase is necessary to show the absence of poetry : if the lines are but 'run on,' to use a printer's phrase, the dullest of prose is the result.

He who reads for the first time *Disappointed Aspirations, a Satire upon the Present State of Literature,* by Mr. F. A. White, will probably consider it an effort to make fun of the morbid fantasies of a disappointed poet ; but further study of this singular little book will do more than merely suggest the fact of Mr. White being the real plaintiff in a serious case. If we err in this conviction, it must be acknowledged that Mr. White pleads warmly, earnestly, and withal gracefully for the imaginary 'Leonard Leanheart' who is the hero of the volume, and the author of its largest poem. 'My life,' says this Leanheart, 'has, alas! been frittered away in the vain pursuit of an empty shadow. I have at length ceased from pursuing, but not from longing.' Doubts of his own inspiration struggle with bitter thoughts of his ill success being the consequence of neglect. He complains that a modern critic will at a glance dispose of the poem over which he has spent his life. He maintains that he has 'a sacred right to a hearing,' and advocates the formation of an office under Government, which shall receive, read, and give a definite opinion regarding all MSS. submitted to it. 'From a

Government that so liberally pensions successful genius, struggling genius has a claim for some assistance; if it protects a Copperfield's literary property *in esse*, it should protect mine *in posse*.' Against 'Copperfield,' whom we take to be Mr. Dickens, Mr. Leanheart is very bitter; perhaps because of the rejection of certain contributions offered to *All the Year Round*. 'Even he,' writes Mr. Leanheart—

Had he been trod on as he treads on me,
By those that then were as he now is, never
Had made a name that shall endure for
    ever,
But long had banished from life's busy scene,
Forgot with 'Boz' in *Ainsworth's Magazine*.

He owns his incapability of writing to please 'Copperfield.' 'In the attempt I lose all the magic fire of heaven, and sink into the frozen feebleness of imbecility. It would be to the full as fair to ask him to give us a new *Principia*, a book of essays, such as Bacon's, or a scheme of government equal to one of Sièyes'. It is as unfair as absurd. But Talent can do all this; while Genius can utter not one word either less or more than is in its sacred commission. Talent can perform to order whatever style of work is for the time being most in request—is, in a word, what Johnson erroneously defined Genius to be.' Crushed by poverty, tortured by doubt, and consumed by a burning sense of wrong, Leanheart, so far as we can gather, takes to drink, and insanely fancies that a writer in *Somebody's Luggage* wishes to make cruel sport of him. 'Nothing short of instinct could have supported me under the agony of so many wretched years that might have been most happy; and yet you jeer at me as a drunkard; you, who yourself by your heartless cruelty taught me and myriads like me so truly devilish, treacherous a remedy for our careless malady.' It is not of poverty but of neglect that Mr. Leanheart complains. He does not seek an extension of the Literary Fund for the benefit of such persons as Poet Close and the Orange Minstrel, Robert Young. He would probably give assent to the view which Mr. Carlyle, with so much good feeling and bad argument,[1] takes when he hints that some modest portion of starvation may be deemed beneficial in the great 'Organisation of Men of Letters,' which the future is to develop. But the same objection applies to his scheme for the recognition of struggling genius, and the scheme for the pecuniary relief of poor literary men. Who is to be the arbiter? Genius only can recognise genius. Must we, then, transfer our best writers to a sort of literary Lying-in Hospital, and make them sit up all night to watch the birth of infantine men of letters? Or shall we, as we do now, leave the decision in the hands of some Prime Minister who has just been called upon to settle the design for a new National Gallery or put a finishing touch to a Reform Bill scheme? Thereof come Messrs. Close and Young.

The four 'Laments,' to which is given the title of *Disappointed Aspirations*, are merely the thoughts contained in the dedication paraphrased in verse. The third 'Lament' is much the finest of the four, in which he prays God to spare his children 'the fell infection of my Siren song.' It is an ener-

---

[1] 'Byron, born rich and noble, made out even less than Burns, poor and plebeian.' Why? Because Byron had not the natural gifts of Burns. Byron in Burns's position would probably have drunk himself to death without writing a line. Burns in Byron's position would have enriched the world with further song instead of breaking his heart on the bleak pasturage of Ellisland. Goethe, with all his severe adhesion to self-culture, says that he never would have risen above the writing of Wertherism, had he been compelled by need of money to pander to the popular taste he had himself created.

getic, sometimes incoherent, protest against the inhumanity of neglect, and contains 'a chorus of victims of the arch-fiend Cruelty, awaiting their murderers here in the nethermost hell below.' Homer, Socrates, Tasso, Camoens, Kepler, Shakespeare, Bacon, Rousseau, Chatterton, and Marat appear and recite their wrongs or the crimes to which they have been driven. The fourth 'Lament,' ostensibly written by Mr. White, tells the story of Leonard's life, and also how, having been jilted by his sweetheart and despised by cold-hearted editors and publishers, he commits suicide. Leonard thus anticipates his end :

Curst be the law that blocks the avenues
Of Fame's dear temple with a hireling crowd,
That come not in themselves, nor suffer
    others!
Cowed by the hubbub, stifled in the press,
Meek, inert genius, with a sigh, gives way
To bustling talent, skill'd in puffing fraud,
And in some dark retreat, lone as the grave,
All broken-hearted pines away and dies.

There is no incontinent screeching against destiny in 'Patrick Scott, Esq.' He relates these *Legends of a State Prison* with a grave, majestic air, a grand unconsciousness of bathos, which overpower and awe the querulous judgment. Reading them, we fancy ourselves listening to the grandiloquent speech of a provincial recorder, whom it would be frank blasphemy to interrupt. The legends relate to various historical celebrities who have at one time or another been inmates, against their will, of the Tower of London ; and are written in the irregular octosyllabic measure which *Marmion* made popular. Several situations in the stories are dramatically conceived ; but we have looked in vain through the entire volume for the tiniest bit of poetical description or feeling. Here is a picture of Sir Walter Raleigh being led out to execution, which may indicate Mr. Scott's manner :

No more he stands ornately drest,
But in plain mourning-suit, and meek
And loving, one whose better mood
Had thriven on sacramental food.
A haggard beauty stamps his face,
But on it there exists no trace
Of trouble ; nought to mark the sense
Of the wrong done him, for he calls
That world a larger prison, whence
Some hourly are ta'en out to die,
As he from his own narrower walls
This day, while others longer lie,
Making but little difference.

A marked characteristic of most verse writers is their fun. A man who has produced an almost perfect imitation of Mr. Tennyson's *In Memoriam,* and who writes apparently in the deepest sadness, will suddenly break out into a hectic laugh and cut antics like a penny showman. It seems to be a want of self-control which prevents these gentle imitators preserving their secret ; or perhaps it is an inordinate desire to show their wit as well as their wisdom. Men whose writing is calm, thoughtful, and even readable so long as they confine themselves to what is sad or tender, betray a hopeless imbecility and a grossly bad taste whenever they try to be funny. And it is not wild mirth which they chiefly affect ; godless satire and Bacchanalian fervour are equally distant from these mild pages. We have, instead, a playful chattiness, an air of knowing shrewdness, with here and there a pun, and here and there a little modest bit of cynicism ; in short, we have Mr. Sala or Mr. Yates done into rhyme. Mr. J. G. Maxwell, M.A., adopts another plan, however, and boldly arranges his poems into three divisions, calling the volume *Sighs, Smiles, and Sketches.* Mr. Maxwell's 'Sighs' are good in tone ; several of his 'Sketches' are well written ; but his 'Smiles' are somewhat sad efforts. They form an unpleasant anticlimax to much that is full of fine feeling in the previous portions of the book. At one time he would be merry, and writes a letter to Mr.

E. Capern, 'the poet-postman of Bideford,' congratulating him on having 'tallow on his ribs ;' at another he would be droll, and puts down the love-breathings of a young woman who has caught a severe cold. Amidst such material, 'A lay of love on Dartmoor' is wholly out of place. There is in this quaint little effort a blowing of fresh wind which reminds us of Allan Ramsay :

'Midst Dartmoor's rugged Torrs, one summer's day,
  Among bright heather bells and furzo brakes yellow,
Where golden plover breed and fox cubs play,
  A strapping damsel met a lusty fellow ;
With drooping head and half-averted glance,
  Twiddling her thumbs the bashful maiden stood ;
The bolder swain first grinned, then looked askance,
  And thus poured forth his passion's rising flood.

The damsel has lost her way on the moor, and the swain, about to show her the path, wishes to take her hand, which she refuses to give him :

JAN.

Cum, Girzie, dan't be zo onkind,
  I only want vor pit e straight ;
Zartin the way ee'l never vind
  Naw, dan't e walk at zich a rate.

Thee warn't zo crass ta Okinton,
  To Giglet market t'ither day ;
Thee never aimed to squall or rin,
  When Tummas kissed e there, no vay !

GIRZIE.

Why, what a lyart, Jan, thee be !
  A niver didn't no zich thing ;
A warn't be kissed by zich as he,
  A han't a zeed mun zince the spring.

Cum, dan't e go vor crame my arm,
  Zo zure as life a'll scat the vace ;
What was't I yeared 'bout Varnie Varm,
  Why don't e go vor thacce place ?

Jan indignantly denies that he has anything to do with Fernie Farm or the people who reside there, and says he cares not if it were burnt. He denies all knowledge of a certain 'Nan ;' and a reconciliation, followed by a betrothal, are the natural consequences. These closing stanzas

show that Mr. Maxwell can write deoently when he forbears to be funny :

The thin grey mist along the hill side crept,
  And slowly spread its curtain o'er their way;
The speckled trout in every deep pool leapt,
  Sprinkling its darkening face with silvery spray.
The sun's last rays were glancing on the scene—
  Yes-torr and Hazle glittered in their light,
Old Cawsand's rugged side warmed in their sheen,
  And glowed with purple deep and gold bedight.
The sparkling Taw was rushing on its course,
  Gurgling hoarse music to its granite bed;
The green rush waving marked each streamlet's source,
  And o'er its breast its downy snow-flakes shed.
The water ouzel skimmed along the stream,
  The raven sought his mate on Haytorr's height ;
The heron left the shallows with a scream,
  And noisy rooks winged home their straggling flight;
The shadows lengthened on the fern-clad hill,
  As Jan and Girzie left their love tryst there,
But somehow in the lanes they lingered still,
  For Girzie never got to Morton fair.

The mirth of verse writers is, generally speaking, not exhilarating ; but their copying of the mirth of other writers is simply intolerable. This is a deep into which, it must be confessed, few fall ; even an imitator knows how much better it is for him to go into the house of mourning. For, indeed, a certain amount of poetical sympathy is at the root of all this imitation—a certain amount of native tenderness which instinctively clings to the more sentimental of our poets. Milton is seldom copied ; Shakespeare almost never. Our minor poets may adopt or borrow from the dramatic terseness, the keen analysis, and occult thought of Robert Browning ; but our verse writers prefer the melody, the felicitous phrasing, and sensitiveness of Tennyson. What shall we say, how-

3 B

ever, of the gentleman who falls down and worships the *Ingoldsby Legends?* These legends are clever enough, as every one knows, and sufficiently pleasant reading; but imitations of them—witness the *Bentley Ballads*—have hitherto been deplorable. Mr. E. C. Nugent, in his apology for *Anderleigh Hall*, ingenuously asks, ' Is Ingoldsby inimitable ?' and proceeds to tell a long story in that hysterical rhyme which has awakened his imitative faculties. The amount of labour bestowed on this little book is considerable. The cadence of the lines is almost perfect; and in the 112 pages there is scarcely to be found a false rhyme. The same quantity of work, otherwise expended, would surely have produced something better than *Anderleigh Hall*, which is merely a novelette, with conventional characters and a worn-out plot, rendered further unreadable by being put into verse. The author appears to have aimed at smartness rather than humour, and has attained his object; but the result is neither interesting nor cheerful.

A very different volume is *Philoctetes: a Metrical Drama, after the Antique.* The author of *Philoctetes* is unknown to us, but we should not be surprised to see him ere long remove himself from the ranks of mere verse writers. He seems to be a skilled and practised writer, who has not yet learned to trust his own choice of subject. The finely modulated blank verse and pure English of these pages are linked, in the first place, to a subject which Sophocles has suggested to a host of poets, and, in the second place, to shades of thought which bear the impress of Shelley and Tennyson. He has taken for the subject of his poem little else than the interview between Ulysses and Philoctetes in the island of Lemnos, having cunningly interwoven some subsidiary interest with

the story of Ægle, a girl who has attended the hero in his sufferings. The complaints of Philoctetes against the tyranny of Zeus are well written; but the finest passages in the book are undoubtedly to be found in a conversation between the wounded man and this Lemnian maiden. He says :

Thou comest to me like music, and my pain
Ebbs out before thee. Thou dost lay thy
    hand
In comfort on the throbbing and it dies.
Thou bringest about me thy light beautiful
    hair,
And thy sweet serviceable hands and warm
Bendings beside me helpful, the live glance
Sweetening the tact of aidance.

She deprecates the warmth of his gratitude in some lines of charming simplicity :

O hero, had I wisdom in my brain,
As ample as the pity which dissolves
My very nature, seeing thee so great,
Greatly afflicted, silent in the joy
Of time, a life secluded, an orphan soul—
Since it is given thee to endure these dregs
Of bitterness—I then might comfort thee.
But a mere maid most simple I can bring
Nothing to help thee save a few warm tears.
For thou art wise and I am no such thing ;
And heroes speak thy name, but I am set
To graze my kids unnoticed in a small
Corner of this small island. So shall I
Meet at God's hand hereafter silent days,
And no man after I am dead shall say
She lived in any honour, no not one.
But the sea fed the labour of her sires
Ignoble, and the earth is on her breast,
Ay, and so sleep she.

In his reply, Philoctetes speaks of the disappointment attending upon those nobler destinies which she had unknowingly envied, and of man's perpetual unrest :

But those old common duties and desires,
Monotonies of home and kindred love,
He lays them by disdaining: in his hall
The bride may chaunt alone her cradle song
Fortunate islands beckon him away ;
And nobly fronted in the yellow dawn
Their cliffs are gleaming: night goes down
    behind :
And one by one the stars break from the
    grey.
Ye surely now find haven. Can ye hear
The boughs at music and the infinite voice
Of the sweet inland waters? swallows cry
And flit between the aloes : the lark goes

Away in heaven : the almond orchards heave,
The harbour margin is one marble stair,
Copsed in with myrtle : and the maidens
　　sing,
'The heroes come, they come !' and hold
　　their arms
Seaward.—Ah, fools and blind, Charybdis
　　churns
In all her caverns yonder and your keels
Are driving on her.

In *Philoctetes*, Ulysses figures as a paltry trickster, a sort of Grecian Barnum ; or rather a conceited old wiseacre, who blunders at every effort he makes, like the Mephistopheles of German burlesques of *Faust*. At the close, Ægle accompanies Philoctetes when he leaves to smite the Trojans with the arrows of Hercules ; and the action of this section of a drama ends. The choruses, occurring at intervals throughout the book, are very musical, and are creditable imitations of the antique ; but our chief hope for the author of *Philoctetes* lies in his blank verse. He must avoid, however, the too frequent use of an allowance which is delicately and moderately used by Mr. Tennyson, but which has become a positive nuisance in Mr. Swinburne —the breaking of the monotonous fall of the ten syllables by irregular accents. Sparingly used, this interruption of the regular cadence is not unpleasant ; carried to excess, it becomes an offensive vice.

In Mr. Alfred B. Richards, we find another type of verse-writer, almost as rare as the preceding. Gifted with a clear intelligence, with sound and generous sympathies, possessed of much reading, and boasting a singular acquaintance with poetic forms and symbols, in the combination of which he exhibits a wonderful manipulative power, Mr. Richards produces something which, if not poetry, is marvellously like it. Mr. Richards' imagination does not deal with ideas acquired by personal experience, but with expressions of ideas which he has learned in books.

This whipping-up of metaphor and sentiment is varied and beautiful ; but an occasional repetition suggests the true original, as, for instance, when he speaks of one—

Whose eyes, like blue forget-me-nots in
　　rain,
Deepening, o'erwaved by mist of shadowy
　　hair, &c.

And elsewhere varies the simile by adopting the botanical name of the forget-me-not :

Her eyes, myosotis fresh deepened with dew,
In a cloud-mist of gold waves her banner
　　of hair.

We have 'red Days of Fear,' 'storm-vext seas,' ' dusk Oblivions, girt by awful Shapes,' ' midnight Oceans in the starless gloom,' in every second page—in short, a very torrent of phrasing ; but we fear to say how little impression is produced by Mr. Richards's gracefully written rhetoric. Occasionally, indeed, we come across some really fine lines, such as these :

Hark ! how the hollow thunder
　　Smites dumb the shuddering bay ;
Out leaps the tawny levin,
　　As serpents strike their prey ;
Till the loud surges answer,
　　Like wolves from out the dark,
And foaming worry ribless,
　　The seaman's shattered bark.

or these :

Weep for Ophelia, cold as rain-beat stone,
　　With purple eyelids in death's shadow
　　　set ;
Like Sorrow's effigy by wind o'erthrown
　　On bruisèd snow-drop and pale violet.

The subjects treated by Mr. Richards, in his *Religio Animæ*, &c., are numerous, and such as would naturally occur to any educated gentleman who looks abroad on passing events, and strives to clear his vision from the fogs and mists of English ' Philistinism.' We find, however, in these philosophical and social speculations of Mr. Richards nothing which might not have been a great deal better set down in prose, whether he speaks of a possible immortality or the treatment of paupers. The blind infatuation which, at this present time, is prompting one or two of the most promising of our young writers to use a vehicle which directly militates against the force and practical value of their thought, has also tempted Mr. Richards to embody in pointless rhyme many sound and sensible suggestions, which might have been of definite use elsewhere. The tone of a few foot-notes scattered throughout this volume shows us very clearly that Mr. Richards would do more good to the world by writing in a penny newspaper, than by striving to earn the thankless renown of a minor poet.

We now come to by far the largest class of verse writers: those, namely, who have no characteristics whatever. Their name is legion; and their work is the most puzzling which can be set before a reviewer. There is not a point or angle which he can touch: he attempts to seize some thought or expression of opinion, and the lines run through his fingers like sand. There is nothing bad enough to be blamed, nothing good enough to be praised, in these colourless pages, where the very blankness of desolation dwells. Thin indignation, imbecile mirth, vapid rhapsodies, and moral twaddle, are the plums which are sparsely stuck into a pudding of hopeless mediocrity. All this one recognises at a first glance. But who is to tell of the trembling anxiety, the wild dreams, the good intentions, with which these poor volumes have been given to the world? We can conceive of no sadder destiny than that of him who has the desire, but not the power, to be a great poet, and who sets his life to the accomplishment of an impossible end. While other men are toiling all around him at work which gives

its daily tangible product, he alone, hoping against hope, struggles year after year to reach forward his hand and anticipate the clutching of the golden crown which he dimly sees before him in the treacherous future. It is well, indeed, with him if death, instead of disappointment, draw a thin veil of blindness over his eyes; if he is permitted to finish the struggle without the conviction of his own feebleness being thrust upon him.

We do not now speak of those versifiers whose vanity has prompted them to publish, for their own gratification, the inane trifling of leisure moments; but of men in whom nervous disorganisation, or heart-disease, or a certain mental weakness, has awakened a consuming passion to be recognised as of divinely poetic origin. They are more numerous than most people not acquainted with certain phases of modern life would imagine. There is no occasion to burden these pages with quotations from their writings. Whether the offender is a mere complacent jingler of rhymes, pleased with the tinkling of meaningless words, like a monkey with its cap and bells, or a poor enthusiast, whose feverish ambition and helpless poverty of brain are likely to procure for him only a swift extinction from the earth, to pillory him or his productions were surely unnecessary cruelty. The only use of criticism in such a case is, that it may possibly have a deterrent influence upon others likely to become the victims of a similar infatuation. The critical sword need not be drawn against these poor people in punishment of their misdeeds: the soft hand of Oblivion steals quietly down and erases the sad, blurred lines, as the rain washes out the figures that children have drawn on the sand.

WHAT is Poetry in the common meaning of the word, poetry as apart from ordinary prose, poetry as we understand it in all its manifold shapes, from a psalm of David to an idyll by Tennyson, from Homer's Iliad to Browning's "Dramatis Personæ," from an ode of Horace to "Edwin of Deira?" What is it that distinguishes even third-rate verse from the most poetic prose? Why do we naturally think of Swinburne and Buchanan, let us say, as artists differing in kind from Carlyle and Ruskin? Both the latter have written passages, pages, whole volumes, brimming over with poetic fancy; and yet we never think of classing them among poets proper. Writers of prose-poems they may sometimes be called, but poets in the vulgar sense, never.

Of many possible answers to such questions, the most obvious may also be accepted as the most true. Verse after all is verse, and prose prose, though each might sometimes be mistaken for the other. Everything in nature has its own distinctive form, its own outward and visible sign of an existence, otherwise ideal and incomplete. The vague thoughts that brood within us are born into the world through form only, through this or that outward vehicle of artistic, scientific, or mechanical energy. In the world of our daily experience form and essence are found wedded together as inseparably as living soul with living body. In art, as in social life, the style is part of the man, because it is the shape in which his thoughts evolve themselves, the mould into which they have been run. A man's foot, his arm, his facial outlines, all bear witness in their several ways to corresponding features of his inward temperament; a witness to which ancient sculpture was marvellously alive, and which the popular instinct has never entirely overlooked.

In all good verse one feels how largely the form determines the effect produced, how different are the thoughts expressed therein from the same thoughts expressed in mere prose. The poet thinks in musical phrases, the prose-writer in the terms of ordinary speech. The one paints, the other describes. The one sings, the other recites. Poetry is to prose what the Taj-Mahal at Agra is to a London warehouse or a Lancashire mill; what "Israel in Egypt" or Beethoven's Fifth Symphony is to an oration by Mr. Mason Jones; what graceful dancing is to graceful walking; what the Belvedere Apollo is to a portrait-bust of the Queen. Music, in one shape or another, is the natural language of artistic emotion, the language of the painter, the sculptor, the architect, the musician, the poet. A keen sense of melody, whether simple or harmonised, underlies all the arts, suggesting to sculpture its noblest outlines, to architecture its fairest proportions, to painting its softest harmonies of shade and colour, to music its most exquisite blending of sweet sounds, to poetry its most graceful turns of phrase and rhythm. All true art in short is uttered music, and music is but another name for poetry.

But is there no poetry in well-written prose, no music in the tones and turns of ordinary speech? Is not all nature alive with melody, from the thunder of waves upon the shore or the soughing of the wind in a pine-forest, to the quiring of birds in spring and the buzzing of innumerous bees among the heather? Yes, indeed; but the melodies of nature form, as it were, the raw material for the melodies of art, and the melodies of written or spoken prose are at best but rude outshapings of the subtler melody that breathes in all genuine verse. Art, like the bee, gathers honey from all sweet things of nature ; and poetry may be called the quintessence, the concentrated spirit of the roses blowing in the domains of literature. Song, in short, in its twofold aspect of musical verse and rhythmical music, is the fruitful flower and ripe fruit of the tree whose leaves represent the less rhythmical utterances, the *numeri lege soluti* of work-a-day prose. The poet and the prose-writer are fellow-travellers in the same broad realm of nature. Each looks around him with open eyes and ears attentive, swift to discover the things that best suit his genius, hungry to take up within himself all kinds of seminal facts, images, windfalls, waifs, suggestions, which, after due transmission through the power-looms of his mind, shall come forth again in full coherent shapeliness, for the profit and delight of his fellow-men. Each fulfils his proper mission : the one appealing to the mind mainly through the processes of ordinary logic ; the other mastering the soul through the "simple, sweet, and sensuous" utterances of a creative fancy.

The prose-writer may also be an artist ; but art is an accident, not the essence of his work. The poet, on the other hand, is nothing if he be not all artist ; and as art is eminently rhythmical, poetry, the natural outcome of melodious thoughts, cannot help speaking in phrases more or less rhythmically tuneful. Prose too has rhythmical cadences, a not inaudible music of its own, rising and falling gratefully on the ear like the words of the "clear-toned Pylian speaker." But the freer it is from set musical turns, from regular recurrences of marked rhythm, the less often we strike on passages that look like prose but read very like broken verse, by so much the nearer does the form of it correspond to its inward character, and come up to our instinctive conception of what prose should be.

In all good prose-writing you may catch undoubted undertones of rhythmical harmony. Milton, Clarendon, Jeremy Taylor, Dryden, Addison, Fielding, Goldsmith, Burke, and Hume, will at once strike the English reader as splendid examples of a fact discernible in all literatures, from the days of Cicero and Livy to those of Emerson, Michelet, Carlyle, and Victor Hugo. Well-fitting words and

phrases, fair-flowing sentences, finely modulated periods, paragraphs that sway the mind with a rare succession of long-drawn, noble, satisfying harmonies, such things, all or some of them, are sure to enhance the mental pleasure we derive from reading or hearing a speech of Mr. Bright's, a chapter from a novel by Mr. Charles Reade or George Eliot, a page from the histories of Mr. Froude or Dean Milman, or a calmly reasoned, carefully worded essay by Mr. J. S. Mill. But the undertones here must still be undertones. Prose ceases to be prose, becomes a mere slipshod caricature of verse, when those suggestions of underlying music blend themselves into forms more definite than the roaring of the sea, or the distance-softened voices of a neighbouring city. The speaker should never let his audience fancy they are listening to a singer out of place.

Some of our greatest prose-writers have, indeed, been poets, poets often of the first rank. But their works, even while they illustrate the points of family likeness, show yet more clearly the gulfs of essential difference between verse and prose. Writers like Milton, Campbell, Southey, Moore, were too good artists to ignore that difference ; had far too much sense to borrow from poetry her peculiar graces in order to lend prose an air of wishing to be poetry if it could. For each kind of work they reserved the befitting treatment, and their excellence in the field of prose, if largely owing to that gift of expression which prose-writers enjoy in common with poets, was further heightened by a wise forbearance from all attempts to make their homelier utterances ape the music and the imagery of heaven-reaching song. Beer is good, and wine is good, and both contain a certain amount of alcohol and water, but to mix them together in one draught would commonly be deemed the surest method of spoiling each.

Tunefulness and rhythm, rhythmical form and tuneful essence, these are the main distinguishing marks of all good poetry. The same thing may be said of music proper ? True, for is not music inarticulate poetry, even as poetry may be called articulate music ? In discussing the latter there is no need to draw further distinctions between sisters so nearly alike. Enough for present purposes, to dwell on the supremely musical origin of verse. The analysis may not be exhaustive : what analysis of things human ever is ? But it claims at any rate to lay hold of one indispensable clue to the right appreciation of poetry as apart from prose. In talking of poetry or verse as articulate music, we mean always music in its widest sense. The thoughts that breathe must be musical thoughts ; the words that burn must keep fair time and tune with the fancies that inspire them. In other words, verse is or should be the due rhythmical embodiment of the thoughts and feelings conceived by a truly musical soul.

The closer the correspondence between the original thoughts and their outward clothing, between the musical essence and the rhythmical form, the more agreeably on the whole will our minds be swayed, soothed, uplifted by the results produced. When the execution matches the conception, like the marriage of "perfect music into perfect words," then, of course, the pleasure derivable from the whole reaches its utmost height. It is a perfect pleasure, varying in quality with the quality of the thought conceived. The one will be deeper and more abiding in proportion as the other is fairer, worthier, or more sublime. Like to the pre-eminence of Raphael among painters, of Handel or Mozart among musicians, is the pre-eminence of a Homer or a Shakespeare among poets. In those great masters of their several arts one sees the marvellous union of vast imaginative power with superlative skill in expressing it through worthy forms.

Marvellous union ; but for that very reason how much too rare ! How sadly common it is to see great conceptions altogether marred by weakness of expression, and strength of expression lavishly squandered on poor conceptions ! It is the old story of Socrates and Xantippe ; of the fairy who came unasked to the christening ; of ill-mated unions everywhere in all times. A Haydon fails to embody conceptions to the height of which an Etty or a Reynolds, for all his mastery of expression, could never rise. Cromwell's

speeches fell as much below his best thoughts as those of Cicero towered above his best. Nature seems to take a cruel delight in spoiling her fairest handiwork, yoking together things unequal or inconsistent, jangling her sweetest harmonies into discords, jumbling up good with evil, strength and frailty, wisdom and foolishness, in a strange unreasonable way. Once in a thousand years she produces a Socrates or a Shakespeare, as if to remind us common men of the possibilities latent in her wildest moods. At all other times we are bidden, perhaps in mercy, to gaze on excellences more or less blurred by defects from the faded glories of him who "took all nature for his province" to the grovelling genius of poor Edgar Poe. Even a Shakespeare, if we look more closely at him, sinks on the whole below our sense of his highest powers. He is always greater than his noblest utterances. There are flaws in that outward image of him, his printed plays, which he himself in his brighter moments must have regretted as keenly as the most loyal of his critics could regret for him now. And there are other flaws which it seems idle to regret, because he does but share them in common with all who wield the two-edged weapon of human speech. It was something more than mere cynicism which prompted Goldsmith's saying about language being given us to conceal our thoughts ; for all too certain it is that speech does partially hide or misrepresent too many of the thoughts we strive in the purest faith to utter. It serves at the best of times but as a veil that floats between us and the outer world ; and veils, however transparent, have a trick of altering, not always indeed for the worse, the character of the faces behind them.

More plastic than the sculptor's marble, words are also far more uncertain. The despair of sculptor or painter in trying to reach up to the height of his own ideals, cannot be greater than the despair of the poet, to whom language furnishes at once the shifting material, and the roughly fashioned tools of his art. Within limits easy to define, one can imagine the sculptor gazing on his work, and calling it very good. His marble poem may live unchanged, unmarred for ever, teaching nearly the same lesson to men of all ages, and almost every clime. To the intelligent Englishman of to-day, the Belvedere Apollo speaks as eloquently as it did to the average Roman of eighteen centuries ago. But with means apparently larger and more manageable, the poet has commonly far fewer chances of fulfilling his aim. His words, however beautiful to the men of one age, may lose half their lustre or their meaning in the next. How many Frenchmen were ever in perfect sympathy with our world-remembered Shakespeare? To how many Englishmen, nay, to how many modern Greeks, does old Homer reveal the fulness of his poetic worth? Byron is only now rising from undeserved eclipse. Moore's sun is gone or going down. Pope lingers in pale twilight, like the shade of Achilles in realms Plutonian. Is Spenser, is Chaucer read, loved, thoroughly digested by readers even of high and varied culture? Even with regard to Shakespeare himself, how vast the number of those admirers who bestow their admiration wholly or mainly upon trust; while of the remainder how very few are likely to grasp the full range of their idol's powers, to follow his every turn of thought and feeling, to weigh in perfectly equal balance his excellences and his defects!

Time and fashion, manifest destiny and seeming chance, the force of habit, of mental associations, the growth of popular misconceptions, changes slow or sudden in national manners and modes of thought; all those regular and irregular processes, which account for the alternate corruption and renewal of a nation's language, add continually fresh folds to the veil originally flung between the poet's innermost ideas and his formal utterances. Look, for example, at the clouds of commentative dust raised by a swarm of rival interpreters round hundreds of doubtful passages in the Bible or in Shakespeare's plays. How are you to extract the pure gold of natural meaning from out that dross of perplexed, and perplexing words? In vain does a

Jowett point out the only rational mode of interpreting the one; and a Payne Collier furnish an almost unfailing means for repairing manifest flaws in the other.* Commentators would keep on wrangling, and enforcing their pet conclusions on a puzzled world, even if Isaiah or Shakespeare were to rise from the grave, and bring out an authentic edition, duly annotated, of his own works.

But again, if the lapse of time bears hard upon the poet, not seldom has the poet borne hard upon himself. His attempts to alter, to improve, to remodel his handiwork, too often lead to the marring of its better without mending its worse parts. Byron's poems are among the very few which have gained by after revision, more than they have lost. Gray and Campbell pruned away excrescences which some at least of their critics would willingly have spared. Tennyson himself, in one or two well-known instances, notable in the stanzas altered from "The Princess" for his volume of Selections, has replaced a beautiful line, or poem, by one less beautiful. It is dangerous for a poet in after years, or in cooler moments to meddle with the fruits, however faulty, of an inspiration always surest when least conscious of its own workings. Great things are done offhand, unconsciously, in great moments. Sober criticism may have its uses, may sometimes serve as a beacon to the doing of yet greater things, by the light it throws on this or that shortcoming in the past. But it can never fill the place of true poetic insight. The iron must be heated over again if you would alter its shape or mend its character. Inspiration must be left to judge of inspiration. If you cannot put old heads on young shoulders, neither can you expect the poet's fancy to burn always at white heat. Apollo's bow is not always bent, nor would it be half so powerful if it were. Genius also has its ebbs and flows, its creative and its critical moods; and only on pain of utter failure may it seek to reproduce the one directly through the other. Critical insight and creat-

---

* It seems strange to me how any intelligent, thoughtful, unbiassed reader can doubt the self-evident rightness of all the more important emendations contained in the Collier folio. Whoever put them there, they speak for themselves—even in the case of the "table of green frieze."

ive power are not indeed always, and altogether foes ; for a broad bottom of spiritual sympathy underlies them both, giving to each its proper starting-point, and bearing each as it were to a common goal. But so rare is their perfect union in the same minds, still more at the same moment, that for practical purposes, the contrast popularly drawn between the poet's fancy and the critic's judgment may be accepted as a general truth. The sun and the stars shine together in the same universe ; but to the dwellers on this earth, the stars grow visible only when the sun has passed below the horizon.

When the glow of a poet's inspiration dies off, the light of critical reflection gleams bright but cold upon the gathering darkness. At such a time may the poet think calmly over what he has done, measure the distance between the issue and the aim, and store up rare instructions for his future work. But let him beware of tampering overzealously with his former utterances, lest he succeed in maiming what he only meant to prune. After due pondering, let him wait quietly for the returning sunrise. Even so, he cannot secure himself against the difference between one day's brightness and another's. The old inspiration may never quite return, just as a dream once broken can never be quite renewed. The thought that yesterday, that an hour ago, filled him with its informing energy, may by this time have faded into the pale dim ghost of its younger self. His fancy flickers as his judgment burns clearer ; youth wanes and manhood melts into age ; Homer nods and Shakespeare droops his wing ; the poet of "Paradise Lost' betrays an old man's fondness for his "Paradise Regained ;" and the Second Part of Goethe's "Faust" lacks half the dramatic force and fulness of the First. Age hath, indeed, its own autumnal glories ; but the poet's prime claims nearest kinship with the teeming freshness of a full-blown spring ; and, like the spring, its hours of fairest sunshine are sometimes interspersed with hours of chilling gloom.

Let us grant, then, the too frequent inequality between the poetic thought and its translation into words—an inequality varying with every in-

stance ; for if the thought be sometimes greater than the words, the words are not seldom greater than the thought. But the admission makes nothing against our rule. In dealing with the fruits of human genius we have always to allow for the proofs of human imperfection. We must strike a fair balance between theoretic likelihoods and patent facts, between our standards of ideal excellence and our experience of actual results. Within due limits the critic, like the astronomer, will always count on the presence of disturbing forces. Enough for him if the discrepancies between aim and issue be not too marked, if the poet's language prove, on the whole, a fair translation of the poet's thought, if the rhythmical form correspond as nearly as may be with the musical essence.

The closer the correspondence, the more successful will the poem itself be, viewed as a work of art. But closeness of correspondence means something very different from uniformity of treatment. Poetry, like painting, can be tested only by general rules. Two or three great artists will handle the same subject in as many different ways, and yet the work of each, taken separately, shall seem the fittest from its own point of view. And so of a genuine poet we may say that whatever garb he chooses for the clothing of his thought seems to be the only natural, therefore the fittest garb. His utterances fall naturally as it were into a certain harmony of duly rhythmical cadences, with effect as satisfying as that which follows every movement of a really graceful child. In respect of this wild propriety, this artless-seeming unison of form with spirit, very few poets can be compared with Shelley. Wander with him where you will, you feel yourself listening to one of nature's sweetest voices, bodying forth

"In profuse strains of unpremeditated art,"

the quick-springing emotions of a marvellously tuneful soul. Whether he is dramatising the crimes and sorrows of the Cenci family, or exulting with Prometheus in the overthrow of long-triumphant wrong, or chaunting with the Greeks the new birth of freedom and Hellas, or soaring heavenward with the lark in a long burst of lyric ecstasy, or trilling some tender lay in honour of evening and his best beloved, you feel that the poet's fancies cannot help taking the form in which his happy artlessness or his unrivalled art has clothed them. In his case form and essence are supremely one. His poetry may sometimes be too ethereal or too diffuse, some of his graver utterances may lack the coherent force, the lifelike breadth and clearness of more human if not always greater bards ; but the magic warble of his many-cadenced verse, and the masterly graces of a diction never forced, never too ornate, severely simple at need as that of Dante, and always tuneful as if Italian, not English, were the instrument he had to play upon, claim for Shelley the poet a close spiritual kinship with the prince of born melodists, Mozart. There is no need, of course, to push the comparison too far, else were it easy to show how widely in many things the poet of " Prometheus Unbound " and the " Revolt of Islam " differs from the composer of " Don Juan," and the " Twelfth Mass." But in the one great gift of musical expression the two are wonderfully and essentially alike.

SCEPTICISM AND MODERN POETRY.

THERE are doubts and doubts. Not so many, perhaps, as is generally supposed, of those "honest" ones in which there lives—according to Tennyson—"more faith than half the creeds." It has, in fact, become the fashion in certain quarters to over-compassionate the doubter, to accredit him with a greater depth, and even with a more thorough conscientiousness, than the man convinced. But with every desire to find the reasonableness of such a view, we have entirely failed to discover why the holding of a creed should imply a smaller share either of intelligence or honesty than the holding of a doubt. Credulity has its negative side as well as its positive one, and there is as much room to slip on the one side as on the other. Clough—himself the most conscientious of poetical sceptics—admits, that if on the one hand "hopes are dupes," on the other, "fears may be liars;" and, in short, there is no good reason, other things being equal, for supposing that the man who rejects evidence may not be quite as great a fool as the man who accepts it. Creeds, no doubt, are easily adopted. We in a sense fall heirs to them. They lie about us from our very infancy, and as soon as we are able to think, they are recommended to us by those whom we very naturally respect. In this way, it is not to be denied that we are apt to creep into them with only too little inquiry. But on the other hand, are the great majority of doubts not only equally weak at the root and held with infinitely more self-complacency, not to say conceit? Search faith for its foundations, and in too many cases we daresay they will be found loose and flimsy enough: but subject doubt to a like scrutiny—strip it of all the mystical generalities it seeks to clothe itself in, and the pensive poetical sadness it so frequently affects—and in all but the rare exceptions, you will find that it is neither more nor less than our old friend Sir Oracle in a new disguise. The philosophy that questions everything with a regretfully necessitous air, and a sorrowful shake of the head, passes with too many for originality, and even profundity, until the trick is found out. That there are honest doubts, however, and honest doubters, we do not mean to question — godly doubters even — doubters of the order of "that white soul," as a living poet so beautifully says of Socrates—

"Which sat beneath the laurels day by
        day,
And, fired with burning faith in God and
        Right,
        Doubted men's doubts away "—

doubters whose doubts ultimately tend to broaden and deepen the foundations of faith rather than undermine them. Doubt of this description is but faith's handmaid, and to whom faith is perpetually indebted, whether it has the candour to acknowledge the debt or not. In a certain sense it is the test of truth itself, and no faith is worth the name that cannot pass through its fires unscathed.

Perhaps there has been nothing more suicidal to the real interests of religion than the shallow theology which without distinction, and without a hearing, bundles all scepticism into that too convenient limbo of certain minds to which are relegated the works of the devil. The easiness of the process might itself cast a doubt on its efficiency.

For on the supposition even that the classification is correct, and that scepticism without discrimination might be put down in the diabolical category, those who know the devil best—or at least the spiritual difficulty his name is made to represent —know well, that he is not to be balked in this way by a mere wave of the hand.

In fact there is no question as to whether we shall be troubled with doubt or not : we must. In a mixed world of good and evil, a state of things is not even conceivable that would afford "no hinge or loop to hang a doubt on." The world where it is not, must be one either altogether sacred to truth, or wholly abandoned to lies. Doubt and faith live under the same imperfect conditions, and the point at which one dies, the other also and consequently dies. And if the necessity of the case could only teach the impossible purist who wishes to ignore the existence of doubt altogether, to look it more steadily and honestly and thoughtfully in the face, where he has found only the devil before, he might possibly discover the presence of God as well, in the periodical recurrence of the doubter in the history of all living faith. The damage that "honest" doubt can do to the real supports of faith must ever be trivial ; while its use in knocking away the conventional props of it is inestimable. The common and easy acceptance by the many of that rather vulgar personage—the regulation Mephistopheles of poetry and the drama—has probably done a good deal in modern times to instruct that prevailing incapacity to disassociate the questioning spirit from the diabolical. But in order to see that such a conclusion is the shallowest of generalities, the weakest of confusions, it is only necessary to fall back on the history of Christianity itself. The most

important of truths were doubts once. Those soul certainties which men can plant their feet upon, and feel with Milton that—

> "If this fail
> The pillared firmament is rottenness,
> And earth's base built on stubble"—

were nearly all dangerous heresies at one period of their history. The strength of the Christian religion in our day is as much indebted to her heretics as to her saints ; or rather, should we say the maturer verdict of time in many cases has pronounced these two titles to be one ?

But, however gladly men may acknowledge the existence of these honest doubts, which, closely looked into, are but the transitional phases of faith, they must also admit that these are few compared to the unnumbered host of doubts which have little or no root in conscience, and which appear rather to proceed from a self-satisfied indifference to any faith at all. This kind of doubt has none of the troubles that afflict the genuine and honest article. Its deepest pains seem to be readily assuaged in a kind of sentimental and *quasi*-philosophical regret.

It is mostly this half-hearted and half-affected variety of doubt that has taken a poetical form in modern times, and the fact to us affords a perfectly sufficient reason why a great deal of the poetry produced under such conditions has never risen above mediocrity. There are perhaps few things in themselves more irrecoverably prosaic than doubt. Few, on the other hand, more evocative of the poetic faculty, or more susceptible of poetical treatment, than faith.

Doubt disintegrates, disperses, repels. Faith attracts and knits together. It acts as a kind of centre of gravitation in the planetary system of things ideal, controlling the most erratic of orbits : standing to the intellect in much the same overmastering relation that Cressida's love stood to all her other feelings, when she declares—

> " My love
> Is as the very centre of the earth
> Drawing all things to it."

Faith is the tonic of the poetical scale, the key-note to which the most wildly discursive imagination must return in the end before the ear can rest satisfied. Hence we have absolutely no poetry in which doubt is anything like the central or dominant interest; while we have, as in the Hebrew poetry, as gorgeous palaces as imagination ever sanctified, whose material is supplied and whose genius is inspired from faith alone. When doubt is made use of at all in poetry, as in that highest quotable example, the Book of Job, it is introduced more as a foil to faith — the intense shadow of an intenser light—a wrestler brought into the arena only to be overthrown by his mightier opponent. Doubt can command no prolonged sympathy, and consequently can find no permanent footing in any of the higher places of poetry. Faith, on the contrary, seems to clothe itself with poetry without effort; attracts all poetry to it as a seemingly natural consequence ; interwinds and interweaves its life with it, until—to use the strong Shakespearian phrase—the two have "grown together," and their parting would be "a tortured body." They are the dermis and the epidermis of the ideal anatomy, and their severance means mutilation. Poetry can find no more than a partial and passing attraction in anything that is doubtful ; she is at best but a stranger and a pilgrim in the debatable land. Her final election and abiding home is faith. She clings to faith as a child to a mother, and will not be shaken off, as plainly

as if she had declared, once for all, *thy God shall be my God, and thy people my people.*

The poetical scepticism of the present day has of course retired from the gloomy atheism of the beginning of the century. The old controversies, deistical and theistical, have nearly died out in literature. The world at length seems to have lost patience with the philosophy that does not at least postulate a god of some kind or another to begin with ; at all events, any such philosophy has been left high and dry by the poetical tide of the present generation. And, to tell the truth, there was no choice. One or other must perish : they could not live together. The dewless desert of blank and barren denial was no place for the gentle muse. Imagination cannot breathe its atmosphere and live. And yet, though not present themselves, these old controversies have left us an inheritance. The times have changed, and we have changed with them. The gloomy, not to say stagey atheism that had a certain fascination for the youth of thirty or forty years ago, has given place in our day to a refined and vaguely idealistic pantheism, which, without any of the old obtrusion of unbelief (it has even a kind of niggardly recognition of a personal God about it), still exercises a limiting influence on poetry —a weaker solution of the strong waters of atheism, not so objectionable as the old form, on account of what it admits of evil, as of what it excludes of good. Without attempting any hard-church definition of its influence — and indeed we question much if many of its poetical exponents themselves could give a perfectly lucid account of what they believe and what they do not believe—we are yet of opinion that it puts a limitation on genius, and especially on poetical genius, in nearly the same proportion that it falls short of a definite faith.

Leaving all moral considerations out of sight as not within our province, it seems to be necessary, for æsthetical reasons alone, that the poet, of all other artists, should possess a belief that shall at least be clear to himself. Above all other men it behoves him, in the words of one of the greatest of his brotherhood, to be—

"One in whom persuasion and belief
Has ripened into faith, and faith become
A passionate intuition."

There is a certain degree of heat at which language fuses, and becomes the possible vehicle of poetical feeling, and the point of liquefaction is never registered below conviction, but above it. We do not say conviction is all that is necessary. Oxygen itself would quickly consume life, yet a man must consume oxygen to live. Conviction alone will not produce poetry, but it is an essential component of the atmosphere in which alone poetry can be sustained. At the degree in the mental thermometer which chronicles conviction, the possibility of poetry begins. Anything below that lacks one of the first conditions of its existence.

The poetry that has been produced without due regard to this essential quality, has seldom outlived its own generation; and, in fact, any attempt to get the materials of poetry out of half belief, argues a defective poetical perception at the outset. It is possible indeed, leaping to the opposite extreme, to get something like poetry out of the gigantic and passionate denial of Satan himself, as Milton has abundantly proved; or even, to a certain degree, out of the pagan abhorrence to the God of Christianity, as illustrated by a living poet. For, waiving altogether any question as to the moral fitness of rehabilitating even under an im-

personal or dramatic mask that which, in the hearing of the majority of his audience, can only be regarded as flat blasphemy, there can be no doubt that Mr Swinburne has reached his highest poetical possibility in what we may classify as his ethnical poems. Without troubling ourselves about whether the inspiration comes from above or below, there is a force about his audacious profanity that we do not so readily find in his other efforts. Good or bad, Mr Swinburne's capacity for blasphemy is unquestionably *une qualité*, as the French would say, with their subtle substratum of meaning.

In the hands of a poet like Milton, the Titanic war against heaven is capable of a certain amount of diabolical picturesqueness; but the merely human unbelief, the distracting doubt, and the shuffling ingenuity that nibbles at this creed and that without arriving at any definite conviction of its own, is the most unpoetical thing in the world.

No amount of artistic skill can make its effusions pleasing. Seeking sympathy and finding none, they seem to be all conceived in the melancholy minor, without any of the natural plaintiveness of that key, and with a double share of its hopeless dejection. There appears to be a place in the realms of the imagination for either God or devil; but upon the Laodicean lukewarmness, upon the apathetic neutrality that is neither cold nor hot, poetry turns her back.

To trace the effects of scepticism, and the stern limitation put upon poetical genius by the want of that faith which ripens into Wordsworth's "passionate intuition," would open up too wide a field, extending as it does through all the infinite phases and degrees of doubt, from the first shadowy suggestion down to the ultimate utter denial. But that each step downward is hurtful in its degree, whatever disguise it assumes, could be easily proved. Even the affectation of atheism, as in much of Byron's poetry, is an artistic expedient fraught with infinite danger to the user of it. Although one feels that the atheism of Byron is not real, but in most cases a mere stage property, one gets thoroughly sick of it before all his scowling heroes : the Laras, the Corsairs, the Giaours are painted in on the same gloomy and threadbare background—a varied fugue on the one everlasting theme—a change of costume, but the same old unhallowed anatomy visibly sticking through. Nothing short of the genius of Byron could have achieved even a partial success with such a clogging nightmare on its back.

It is perhaps not to be so much regretted that atheism should prove such a complete extinguisher to anything like second-rate poetical power, as that it should have sometimes dragged down to the second place gifts that should have ranked with the highest. It overshadows the resplendent genius of Shelley like a black thunder-cloud above a rainbow, and gives everything he has left behind him a phantasmagoric and evanescent character. Reading his works is like walking through the dreamlike palace of Kubla Khan. On every side, and in such profusion as has never been approached by man, lie the potentialities of poetry, but yet in a great measure only the potentialities. He has left no palace behind him worthy of his genius or his materials. If ever mortal had the materials, and the power of the enchanter to call them forth, it was he. No one ever possessed in a greater degree the faculty of bringing himself *en rapport* with the hallucination of the moment.

Images of the most ethereal ten-

uity, that would have presented themselves to other men's minds in some vague and nebulous way, stood forth to the order of that imperial imagination with the distinctness and precision of objective realities. And yet with all this power he is still but the enchanter. Wherever you go it is fairy-world still, and affords no solid ground for mortal foot ; and though you cannot resist its haunting beauty, you are equally haunted by a sense of its almost ghastly unreality. The kindred points of heaven and home are even more nearly akin than they are commonly supposed. Shelley's inability to conceive a heaven with a God in it to whom he could pay reverence, seemed to drain away all humanness and homeliness out of him, until his poetry became quite as unearthly as his adverse critics judged it unheavenly. Starving one side of his moral nature, the other side was supersaturated, and rendered morbid by an overflow of the imaginative secretions that should have fed both. This insubstantial characteristic of his work was unfortunately one upon which Shelley rather prided himself. Writing to a friend, he says he "does not deal in flesh and blood." "You might as well," says he, "go to a gin-shop for a leg of mutton, as expect anything earthly from me." That want of fixity, too, which the absence of central faith invariably induces, that want of a peaceable mental anchorage—the green pastures and the still waters of the Hebrew poet, with whom, however, he has so much in common—acts as a continual drag on his powers. There is a provoking absence of that massive and leonine repose which usually consorts with the greatest gifts, and which one naturally looks for as a concomitant of his. But we look for it in vain. He was always in an ecstasy, in the somewhat lost but literal meaning of the word—always *out of himself.* If his genius had a fault, it was too impressionable. The merest mouthful of the Delphian vapour put him into fits. He was ever on the tripod, and is only a modern incarnation of that priestess of Apollo, mentioned by Plutarch, who raved herself to death in the temple. His Pegasus in this way was good for a short run, but had little waiting power. Consequently, the defect does not interfere with the perfection of his shorter lyrics, which are simply unique and unapproached; but its limiting influence is painfully apparent in all his works (though less marked in the Cenci) that require any long sustained effort. The deficiency was one well understood and keenly felt by Shelley himself. In a letter to Godwin, he says,—"I cannot but be conscious, in much of what I write, of an absence of that tranquillity which is the attribute and accompaniment of power."

Sad indeed that this defect, this want of reference to the fundamental key-note of power, should have marred the music of such an otherwise heavenly instrument.

That the atheism—or at least the pantheism—of Shelley, was a mental unsoundness of a constitutional and hereditary kind, does not, we think, admit of a doubt. In these days of irresponsible faultiness, studded over with dipso- and klepto-maniacs, when so many are anxious to prove that we are "villains by necessity," as Shakespeare would have put it, —"fools by heavenly compulsion ; knaves, thieves, and treachers by spherical predominance,"—we have often wondered that some charitable *doctrinaire* with a scientific turn of mind has never started his atheomaniac. If the world could be convinced—and there is no lack of plausible argument to prove it—that

the different degrees of unbelief are frequently no more than the varied phases of mental disorder, and that absolute atheism itself, in the vast majority of cases, is only an irresponsible mania, proceeding from sheer intellectual defect, — if we could only have it settled that our sceptics, and more especially our cultured and scientific sceptics, are what they are by "a divine thrusting on," they might possibly be taught to hold their views with a little more humbleness of mind than they have hitherto done. In Shelley's case, atheism was a thing that ran in the blood. His father seems to have had a fame for eccentricity in the direction of profanity, and was said to have been a disciple of the Chesterfield and Rochefoucauldean school ; while Shelley himself declares—in an unpublished letter quoted by Mr Rosetti—that his grandfather, old Sir Bysshe, "was a complete atheist, and *founded all his hopes on annihilation.*"

To a somewhat similar cause— the want of any deep-rooted conviction in the author's mind—may be attributed, we think, a great deal of that watery and Werthery instability that characterises too many of Goethe's heroes, although in his case in a more modified degree. Goethe's unbelief did not kick at heaven as Shelley's did in the Prometheus. His scepticism was of a milder and more passive type, or perhaps it might be more accurately described as a kind of moral *juste milieu,* with a singular inaccessibility to attraction on one side or the other. His moral sense was insulated, so to speak—encased by a coating of intellect which was an absolute non-conductor. There is no better representative than he of the spirit described by Tennyson as

"Holding no form of creed,
But contemplating all."

With less of this power to maintain an attitude of moral neutrality, Goethe's own character, as well as that of many of those he created, would have been much more humanly and poetically complete. His shortcoming in the direction of personal faith cannot be kept down, and is continually cropping out in his heroes. In many of the leading men he has drawn there is hardly any strong moral aspiration, and in some no discoverable preference or predilection whatever. The only exception to this we can think of is in the character of "Goetz von Berlichingen," and that was a production almost of the author's boyhood, or at least at an age before men have begun to question or doubt. There was evidently a lurking suspicion in Goethe's maturer mind that anything like well-defined religious views in a man argued weakness, and weakness was the one vice Goethe abhorred, even to a weakness. But that he was equally well convinced, on the other hand, that no feminine character could possibly be complete without such views, may be as safely inferred. His women are singularly rich by the very excess of those qualities of faith and trust so conspicuously awanting in his men.

This absence of any kind of moral partiality in the author found its counterpart in the moral tenuity and aimless vacillation of Werther, Egmont, Wilhelm Meister, and Faust. Beside the intense purpose of Shakespeare's heroes, such men as these are little better than shadows. Even in the presence of Shakespeare's secondary characters —of his villains even—we are never altogether out of an atmosphere of faith. Among the very worst there is an implied recognition of God, a power without and beyond them, in an accusing if not approving conscience.

Without any of that modern moral attitudinising that pirouettes on a pivot of its own self-consciousness (and which the world could so well do without), no man's work carries upon it more clearly and unmistakably the marks of an over-ruling conviction and a dominant purpose. So evident is this quality in Shakespeare's works that one might almost imagine that—like every fresh effort of Haydn's genius —they were commenced with prayer and carried out under the power of old Herbert's motto—

"Think the king sees thee still, for his　King does."

Perhaps the most striking illustration in more modern times of the manner in which the poetical faculty may be overridden and paralysed by the action of doubt, is to be found in the life and writings of Arthur Hugh Clough. The more his life is studied, the more it appears to rise above the common conventionality of doubt, and to represent the highest possible phase of conscientious scepticism — one, indeed, of those sacrificial souls which the Creator seems to throw from Him at intervals into the ocean of religious opinion to keep the waters in a healthy fermentation, and save them from stagnating by tradition, or freezing by convention into mere lifeless forms. His case presents many unique and interesting points. Differing from Shelley, inasmuch as the very elements left out in Shelley's half - human composition were amongst Clough's most conspicuous endowments,—the social side of genius—its simple homeliness, and the keenness of its human sympathies—was in him beautifully complete. Differing, again, from the scepticism of Goethe—for Clough's moral predilections were strong, and anything like indifference was with him impossible — his scepticism seemed rather to rise out of an almost morbid over-keenness and over-sensitiveness to the requirements of conscience. With a strong and perpetual craving for some solid ground of belief, he would yet have no part of his faith at second hand. Following Clough's career from his school-days at Rugby onwards, it is a melancholy and even a humiliating thing to find how much even of the unseen and spiritual force of a great man's mind is overruled by the irresponsible circumstance of its earthly surroundings. With all its unquestionable excellences, there was a fatal flaw in the Rugby training under the Arnold *régime*. In many cases—and these cases necessarily the most important—it had a tendency to over-stimulate the moral sense. It sent boys out into the world with a dangerously premature moral equipment; an education that yielded a good deal of dogmatic brain-force, but at the sacrifice of intellectual accuracy and the finer moral discriminations. An old head upon young shoulders is a doubtful blessing in any case; but when it takes the special form of an adult faith grafted on a spiritual anatomy whose bones are set not yet, there is no doubt in the matter. With the great majority of strong natures, it is simply the best conceivable arrangement for ultimate moral shipwreck. Not the most carefully administered education, accompanied by the utmost solicitude of parents, can ever take that highest part of every man's education out of the hands of his Maker. Father or mother or teacher may in some measure mould the outward frame, but God alone can breathe into its nostrils the breath of life, and make such an education a living thing. Clough (who by the inherent tendency of his nature would have been a seeker after God, had he had no higher advantages than a heathen)

has always seemed to us to have been the victim of a premature moral development. He came from Rugby with the Arnold mint-marks fresh and strong upon him, with his mind fully made up, and an amiable determination to do battle, if need be, for all the theories of his worthy master. But man proposes, God disposes. A moral influence was lying in wait for him that he had never taken into account, and which proved to be the turning-point of his life. When he went into residence at Oxford in 1836, the Tractarian movement was at its height. Newman was stretching out, through pulpit and platform, through verse and prose, those subtle prehensile tentacles of his, that touched so softly, and yet have closed so firmly, upon modern thought. It was an atmosphere Clough had never breathed before, and it proved too much for his tender years. Speaking of it afterwards, he says that for a long time he was " like a straw drawn up the draught of a chimney."

The fierce struggle he passed through can never be altogether known, and is only shadowed here and there in his poems, and a few chance exclamations in his correspondence; but of the severity of it there can be no doubt. His mind was not altogether unhorsed—he had too firm a seat for that—but he may be said to have lost his stirrups, and never again to have recovered them until the harrowing interregnum that dates between doubt and well-assured belief had done its work upon him, and worn him down to the brink of the grave. Torture like his turns the confident cant of your easy-minded believer into something that almost approaches blasphemy.

All that he suffered in that pitiless purgatory will never be revealed —that valley of the shadow of death, so thickly strewn with the bones of the spiritually dead, by what inscrutable decree of Providence we know not ; but that all was borne without a murmur, and with a rare humility and integrity, his life is a sufficient guarantee. With all his doubts and difficulties, we should be inclined to question the catholicity of the Church that refused to extend to him the invitation of Laban, " *Come in, thou blessed of the Lord : why standest thou without ?* "

But for the fate that brought him so directly under the wheels of the Tractarian movement, he might have been living yet ; and few, who have paid his works any attention, will doubt but that he would have been one of the greatest of living men. That this unfortunate interruption and harassing mental conflict fatally interfered with his æsthetic development as a successful poet, is very abundantly proved by nearly all the poetry he has written. He carried his doubts about him by force of habit, and not least doubted his own powers, and the quality of his own productions. His doubts to him indeed

> " Were traitors,
> And made him lose the good he might
>   have won,
> By fearing to attempt."

He kept his most important poem, the " Amours de Voyage," in MS. beside him for nine years, and only published it at last in a kind of modestly furtive way in an American periodical — the ' Atlantic Monthly.' His doubt seemed to find him out and to hunt him to cover whenever and wherever he ventured out. He could not escape it. There was nothing left for him, but, in his own melancholy words, " to pace the sad confusion through." Baffled and tempest-tost by conflict-

ing opinions, he exclaims, in one of his poems :—

> " O may we for assurance' sake
> Some arbitrary judgment take,
> And wilfully pronounce it true."

We almost wish he could have done so, even at some little intellectual sacrifice. But that was just the thing he could not do. He was too keenly suspicious of his intellectual life. With him there was no deeper form of dishonesty than that which shrinks from its own conviction. There never was a character more spotlessly free from anything even approaching compromise in this respect. His intellectual honesty was without a flaw. Everything went down before his convictions —his living at Oxford (it should not be forgot that in his position pecuniary sacrifice meant poverty), and with it, in many men's eyes, his social status as well. And last, what to him was of far more value than these, the confidence of his dearest friends, and at the head of the list Arnold himself. Happiness, health, all went ; and in their place, to use a phrase of his own, came "spiritual vertigo and megrims unutterable," and loneliness and misery. Everything his conscience required of him was paid down to the last farthing. All was given away, till only his great unrooted honesty remained to him. Religion would indeed be a rhapsody of words if in such a case a man could not spend his life and yet in the highest sense possess it. *Whosoever shall lose his life shall preserve it.* It is a beautiful belief, and it never was beat out into the metal of actual hard fact with a sublimer self-denial than in the life of Clough.

Culture and Modern Poetry.

———

IT must have frequently occurred to the readers of modern poetry, that the ancient and time-worn dictum, assuring us that a poet is born, not made, must in our day have lost, if not some of its force, then certainly some of its fitness. To this conclusion we must come if the word *poet* has not changed its signification. The original genius ("his soul is with the saints we trust") who first propounded the *poeta nascitur* dogma, had his eye no doubt upon certain of the stiffnecked and rebellious, who clung to the condemned creed, that, given a fair average quantity and quality of mental fibre, a poet might after all, and with some little trouble, be made. Dr. Johnson held that a given amount of ability may be turned in any direction, "even as a man," he argued, "may walk this way or that." "And so he can," answered in our day Archbishop Whately, "because walking is the action for which his legs are fitted; but though he may use his eyes for looking at this object or that, he cannot hear with his eyes, or see with his ears. And the eyes and ears are not more different than, for instance, the poetical faculty and the mathematical."

Notwithstanding the completeness of this answer, there is room for grave suspicion that the Doctor's theory has still, not only its believers, but its school and its disciples. If we are to judge by the living facts around us, and seek a conclusion through the philosophy that teaches by examples, that conclusion must inevitably be—either, that we have still amongst us crowds of heretics who abide by the belief in the manu-factured article, or that the poetic faculty is a very much more common production than it used to be. Nor is the alternative very puzzling. Any one who takes the trouble of looking into the titles of the several claimants of the laurel as they rise, must get himself more and more con-vinced that the poet made is rampant, and that the real possessor of what Mrs. Browning called "the sorrowful great gift,"—the poet born of the old dogma—is as rare as he has ever been, and in fact, there are not a few who do not hesitate to declare he is as dead as the Dodo.

Many of those in the present day who approach nearest to the old standard of the poet born have, in addition, so much about them of the poet made, that the proverb no longer fits, and, we may add, have so much about them of what is so elaborately made, that one is tempted to believe some of them might have been greater men at less pains.

Macaulay declared that "as civilization advances, poetry almost necessarily declines." Without denying that the assertion at first sight has an appearance of plausibility, we are inclined, on closer examination, to set it down as one of those half-truths which the brilliant essayist's partiality for a telling antithesis frequently led him into : just one of those picturesque announcements, which Mr. Spedding—speaking of Macaulay's extravagant strictures on Lord Bacon—characterizes as proceeding from " the love of rhetorical effect in a mind rhetorically disposed." If indeed we are to suppose civilization in Macaulay's phrase to be in this case synonymous with education, as it is loosely understood, then the statement does contain a certain amount of truth. But if we mean by education what it should be rather than what it is—a drawing out of a man's emotional nature, as well as his merely mental qualities, then the statement not only contains in it nothing that is true, but something that is pretty nearly pernicious. If even we could be brought to admit the possibility of poetical decline from such a cause, we would not the less strenuously deny the *necessity* of any such decline. Certainly nothing will contribute more surely to the decline of poetry than the civilization which forgets to educate those very faculties and parts of a man's nature by the exercise of which alone poetry can either be produced or appreciated. And if, in addition to the neglect of these faculties, we give an exaggerated importance to the education of the faculties which naturally counteract them, we at length reach tangible grounds and get something more than a glimpse of the civilization in which poetry necessarily declines. Under like conditions, would it be a matter of surprise that Logic, Metaphysics, Science, or any of the mathematical or mechanical arts should also decline? Physiologists have long ago agreed that the inordinate exercise of one set of muscles invariably results in the impoverishment of the corresponding set, and it is quite as possible in the mind as in the body, by excessive exercise, to strengthen one set of faculties to the permanent weakness and injury of the others. Nor can it be denied that the prevailing partiality for scientific and mechanical pursuits, by keeping imagination out in the cold, has had the effect of making our more recent advances rather a one-legged progress.

By exclusive attention to the education of the emotional side of a man's nature, you will no doubt succeed in creating such a milksop as shall hardly supply fibre enough for the hero of a penny novel; but, on the other hand, by an equally exclusive cultivation of the rationalistic side, you will develop something quite as weak, and as dangerous, and a good deal more intolerable. To look strongly at anything with one eye, it is natural to close the other, and so with reason's eye riveted, one need not be surprised to find the eye of imagination shut.

In the civilization whose progress is thoroughly sound, the education of the head and of the heart should go abreast, and the assumed advancement in which poetry declines is more than likely to be the civilization of an age that sacrifices its emotions to its reason. If this be true, we must be prepared to see a good many other things decline. First after poetry, perhaps religion, and after that the possibility of political cohesion.

If we read history carefully enough, we shall find in most cases, that this lopsided civilization, under some very high-sounding aliases, "Perfectibility of Human Nature," "Age of Reason," and so forth, has a trick of moving in a circle, and playing itself out. By-and-by the neglected half of human nature has its revenge. The fatal flaw in this emotionless culture is that it contains no sort of human amalgam strong enough to bind society together. The individual forces composing it are what Lord Palmerston would have called "a fortuitous concourse of atoms," and possess no element of political adherence. The forgotten thing that under the name of Emotion was allowed to fall asleep as quiet as a lamb—the busy worshippers of Reason taking no note of the fact—awakens one day with a changed name and a changed nature. It is now a lion. Spurned Emotion has grown to Rage, an easy transition. Renewed by his sleep, the lion rises up and scowls around him, rushes into society with his tail in the air, inaugurates a Reign of Terror, and reasserts the sovereignty of the brute. When the mad fit has gone, and the long arrears to the heart have been paid for in blood, cash down, society sits down again clothed and in its right mind. The Sisyphus of civilization finds himself again at the foot of the hill, glad to accept a philosophy that, if less high-sounding and pretentious, is at least a good deal more human.

That in the progress of the civilization worth the name, the arts should, and actually do extend their influence and empire, hardly requires to be argued. It is rather a matter of historical demonstration than a matter of opinion, and the immensely wider field and increased appreciation of the particular art of poetry might be amply illustrated by simple reference to fact. We do not mean to assert, however, that the publication of any number of editions of the best poets, with an almost universally reading public, necessarily involves the more frequent recurrence in society of the poet born. The times and seasons of genius are as inscrutable as the thing itself. It is one of those things (for there are a few of them yet left) that has not as yet been altogether circumvented by the rationalist. The natural law—as he would probably call it—that evolves its higher immortals, that drops down here and there, over three or four centuries, its Raphaels, Shakspeares, and Beethovens, is one of those that has not been quite accounted for by that science of Averages which promises to make everything so easy by-and-by. We can see no good reason, however, for concluding that in such an improved condition of society as this advanced civilization brings about, the poetical gift amounting to genius should occur less frequently, although it may be easy to conceive that it may be born under the unlucky star of having its lot cast in a mechanical civilization unfavourable to its development. It must be admitted also that the same artificial education that stimulates mediocrity so wonderfully, seems sometimes, not only to obscure, but even to interfere with and impede the more original gift. And yet these unfavourable influences once overcome, civilization stands no longer in the way, but rather pays tribute. We need not look for the removal of these obstacles, nor is civilization altogether to blame for them. It must legislate in the interests of the majority, not the minority—the rule, not the exception—and even if it were advisable, it would yet remain impossible to make educational provision, to fit at all points such exceptional cases as genius presents. The ideal *milieu* that would do justice to every variety and degree of natural gift, and injustice to none, is as far off as ever, and will probably remain what it ever has been, a world-without-end desideratum. But what if these very obstacles of genius, the earthly incompatibilities, the uncongeniality of atmosphere, which always have been, and from the nature of things must continue to be, its never-ending complaints—what if these are only the providential and appointed spurs in the side of genius, intended to take the place of the more ordinary educational stimulants that serve the purpose of mediocrity? It might be fairly argued from the lives of great men, that there is a given amount of genius at which education becomes almost impossible, and which, in fact, defies education in the ordinary sense of the word. There seems to be a degree reached in the brain barometer, at which faculty undergoes a chemical change and slips through the fingers of the educational manipulator in an imponderable ether. Let the earth rejoice that this abnormal gift usually brings with it the gift to educate itself. Sir Humphry Davy, in a letter to his mother, making reference to the way in which his schoolmaster had neglected him when he was a child, declares he was fortunate in such neglect, and adds, " I perhaps owe to this circumstance the little talents I have and their peculiar application." Sir Walter Scott, who cut but a poor figure at school, says that " the best part of every man's education is that which he gives himself." William Blake goes a good deal further, and boldly says—

> Thank God, I never was sent to school
> To be flogged into following the style of a fool.

Leslie, again, declares that it was Fuseli's " wise neglect " of young Landseer that helped to make him what he afterwards became. Turner's father put him to school to learn drawing, and in a short time his teacher, a most competent man, brought the pupil back, fairly beaten, and told his father it was no use, the case was hopeless. Many such anecdotes from the lives of great artists might be added to these, but perhaps poetry's more nearly related sister art of music supplies us with the most striking illustrations. On that auspicious morning, which must ever be held in grateful remembrance by all lovers of music, when the Duke of Saxe-Weissenfels caught a little boy surreptitiously amusing himself on his chapel-organ, ordered him up before him, and settled his career from that day forward, by then and there finding him guilty of genius, no one was more astonished at the verdict than the said boy's own father, who could throw very little light on how young Händel came by his accomplishment, and none at all on how he came by his

32—2

genius—a thing he had never even been suspected of. Again, Schubert's instructor complained that he was always making the mortifying discovery that he could tell his pupil nothing but what he knew beforehand. When young Nicolo Paganini—a mere boy—was sent to Parma to study under Alessandro Rolla, the great musician, on hearing him play, told him to go home, he could teach him nothing. Moschelles told the parents of young Mendelssohn the same thing, and when that excellent couple had at length prevailed on him to give their son lessons, he knew and openly confessed the thing was a mere form. In the recently-published Life of Moschelles we find an entry in his diary dated November 22nd, 1824 (Mendelssohn being then fourteen), to the following effect : " This afternoon I gave Felix Mendelssohn his first lesson without losing sight for a single moment of the fact, that I was sitting next a master, not a pupil." Mozart, again, was the despair of his instructors. And what indeed could any one be expected to teach a boy who could write tunes at four years old, and was a master himself, and the astonishment of masters, at an age, in ordinary cases, before education can be said to have properly begun ? Then again, Beethoven, how he laughed at the idea of even Haydn having taught him anything. He was a standing puzzle to the professors, and to the end of his life used to enjoy their helpless perplexities, and would chuckle over the difficulties they could not explain by reference to any authoritative thorough-bass book. Cases like these set all ordinary method at defiance.

The difficulty of bringing musical genius under any systematic educational training is even aggravated in the poet's case. If the gift indeed be small enough, education is everything, and in such a case it will teach the poet to be a more elegant *rimeur* of the *vers de société* stamp, and the musician an endless producer of what are called *morceaux de salon,* but one naturally does not look for anything corresponding to the " Samson Agonistes " or the Sonata " Pathétique " from such quarters. The artificial soil that hurries into fruit the smaller faculty may not always be the most suited for the development of the deeper rooted gift. On the contrary, we suspect that the civilization that levels up the lower endowment, sometimes involves a corresponding liability to level down the higher. Again, in a condition of society so almost universally informed, if not cultivated, the recognition of anything short of towering genius is hardly to be expected. Who could bring himself to believe, for example, that if three-fourths of the poets eulogized in Johnson's " Lives," or gathered together in Chalmers' Collection, were walking in the flesh amongst us now, it would make any appreciable difference? Not that any one begrudges them the niche they have earned, only were it to be earned again, and upon the same work, who can reasonably doubt but that an immense preponderance of them would pass on to their graves unnoticed?

Critical discernment, and discrimination between gift and gift, seems to increase in difficulty with the progress of civilization. In an age when education was the privilege and luxury of the few, the greater gift made its mark readily, but when the advantages of culture become more generally distributed, it is not so readily recognised and the man of talent—more especially the man of mimetic talent—is by the great majority not to be distinguished from the man of genius. In much of the criticism issuing from even authoritative quarters, one not unfrequently sees the work of the merely dexterous performer passing off for the outcome of inspiration. In the interests of art it would pay well if every critic were gagged who did not know the difference. Not to hint for one moment that a perfect knowledge and use of the instruments of his art can be dispensed with, even by genius itself, we still hold that it is mainly to this educated rattle of the tools without the gift, that we are indebted for the abundance of modern poetry so called. Perhaps it is one of the inevitable hostages we must pay to universal civilization, but it is surely worth an effort to keep the two products apart. The difference of value is discriminated by all in the more ordinary affairs of life. An illustration may be taken from an art which every one practises more or less, the art of speech. A man may talk the purest rubbish in the purest English, perfect in style, faultless in grammar. What is called his "delivery" may be perfect, while the thing itself delivered is utterly worthless; dear at the breath it cost to deliver it, dearer still at the effort to listen. Now this of course is mere platitude. Nobody disputes it, because there is almost nobody but what has to endure it now and then. But it does not strike us all so forcibly that there is an analogous case to this in all the other and higher arts. The analogy in music, for instance, is not so commonly perceived. Change the medium of expression from words to sound, and some will even deny that such analogy exists. Amongst so-called musicians themselves, nevertheless, nothing is more common than for a man to convince himself that he is giving the world music, when he is only giving them grammatical noise under cover of musical speech. In his sphere he is neither more nor less than an idealess chatterer of correctly worded nonsense.

Many who can clearly discern this in the case of speech, seem to fall short of the perception that in music—which is only after all a subtler form of speech—it is equally necessary to have something to say worth saying, before the thing said can have any value. The analogy holds good with all the arts—for all are but different modes of conveying thought and feeling. It is not alone sufficient that a musician should know thorough-bass and counterpoint, or a painter the laws of perspective and chiaroscuro,—or in short that any artist, whatever that art may be, should have a perfect knowledge of his subject, and a perfect mastery of its minutest appliances. Unless there goes along with these the ability to use them in the conveyance of original thought, his execution may be admirable, he may be the most skilful of artificers, if you will, but an artist never. Lord Bacon says of studies, "They teach not their own use: but that is a wisdom without them and above them." This is the part of every artist's education no man can give him, and is not to be confounded with technical dexterity. This last contribution to his efficiency and the one that lifts him out of mediocrity cannot be attached by any amount of educational fitting and screwing. It is the gift specially contributed by his Maker—that impalpable gift beyond the reach of criticism or definition, and in the artist's case his greatness will mainly depend on his clear perception of what that gift consists, and the devout loyalty with which he is prepared to live for it.

The commonness of the extrinsical, and what may be called the ingrafted talent, as compared to that which is intrinsical and indigenous, is sufficient to account for the greater bulk and abundance of its products. In poetry we have a hundred volumes coming from this ingrafted talent, for one that issues from natural gift : work that may be considered the result of a cultivated taste and a fair education, and in many cases accompanied with great technical adroitness. Now it would be ungrateful not to acknowledge that many of these volumes are most interesting, and untrue to say they are perfectly devoid of natural gift. The work they represent may be, and sometimes is, more conscientiously creditable in a certain sense than the work of genius itself, and cultivation is as great a duty in their case as in the other. The commandment is as binding on the one talent as the ten, and if we had no higher motive than personal satisfaction, better cultivate ever so little a patch than none. Better that a man should grow mignonette on a window-sill than no flowers at all. But yet in the interests of art and art-criticism, it is essential that the two kinds of work—for the difference is one of quality as well as degree— should be broadly distinguished and clearly discriminated. The ingrafted faculty for poetry, sustaining itself mainly from memory and the radiation of greater minds, and building out of its funded educational acquirements, however highly cultivated and however artistically it may clothe itself with words, will never take the place or work the miracles of that simpler and deeper endowment that derives its nurture more directly from its own heart, and bases its power upon the exercise of its own intrinsic capabilities. The products of the two are as widely different as their sources, and let no poet deceive himself, the difference is readily recognized, and keenly appreciated by the most unsophisticated apprehensions, and pronounced upon with unerring instinct, by thousands who know nothing of the wherefore of the difference, and who could not for the life of them give a reason for their preference. Such preference, however, let it be remembered, is not the less deeply rooted because it is arrived at by no conscious process. Nor, on the other hand, are the dislikes in such cases to be pooh-poohed simply because the explanation of it is not always at hand—.

> Je ne vous aime pas, Hylas ;
> Je n'en saurais dire la cause,
> Je sais seulement une chose ;
> C'est que je ne vous aime pas—

and there is no help for it.   No amount of agonised excogitation, no
amount of the most masterly manipulation of the implements of the art,
will ever succeed in giving us the tiger-like spring of the original conception—the leap in the air as of an unsheathed sword—that characterizes the genuine inspiration.   Those conceptions of the poet that strike
the deepest and live the longest do not come to him by any long-sustained
and elaborate process; but finely sensitive to Nature's ordinary influences
at her slightest touch,

> Across his sea of mind,
> The thought comes streaming like a blazing ship
> Upon a mighty wind.

The true gift does not go out of its accustomed way for its effects; does
not dive to the bottom of its own consciousness to bring up with infinite
labour its brightest pearls.   If the thought be there, the faintest breeze
will give it wing.   Boasting no mysterious power or process, it rather
takes delight in clothing things familiar and palpable with "golden
exhalations of the dawn."   An over-critical fondness for the manner of
the poet's speech may interfere with the vigour of it.   The gift will not
stand a too artificial treatment.   A native plant taken from the hillside
to the garden, notwithstanding the greatest care—as those who have
tried it can tell—is apt to become enfeebled.   Culture in this way
becomes sometimes a very questionable benefit to the poet.   To the man
of talent, and especially to the critic, it is of the last importance, but it
is quite possible for the poet to wear his culture in such a way as to
impede and enfeeble him that wears it.   The educated and literary
poet—except when endowed with the very highest power—can never
sufficiently forget and shake himself free of the critical element, and
seldom attains that perfect, because unconscious, *ars celare artem*, which
characterizes the more robust and less elaborated gift.   It may occur to
many that the poetry of Mr. Browning may serve as an illustration
here.   But his case is not so much to the point as many others.   His is
rather a unique example.   In him it is difficult to draw the line between
information and inspiration; one cannot well conceive of them apart.   Take
away his culture, or even reduce it to mediocrity, and you withdraw his
essential element, and, in fact, put his genius in a receiver and pump the
air away.   Without elaborate and excessive culture the lever of Mr.
Browning's genius would have found no fulcrum, and we question much
if in a less cultured age he would have had temptation enough to have
become a poet at all.

   There are many and much more fitting illustrations than his case
affords.   The very highest genius is not altogether untouched by it.
Who would not even gladly accept a less completely informed Milton,
instead of the one we have, bristling all over with a quickset of mytho-
logical briers, which ninety-nine out of a hundred of his admirers prefer
leaping over to walking through, and which they do leap over?   Cowley
again, "the poet of the brain," as M. Taine so justly calls him, affords a

less important, but yet a more striking case; in fact, he is one of the best examples we have of the purely literary poet. If we could take from his poetry those ingenious absurdities, and affected prettinesses, with which a lettered overniceness so plentifully strewed it; or if we could only have kept his poetry as sweetly simple as his prose, how much more readable it would have been. The genius of Burns itself—and Nature never sent anything out of her heart with a clearer directness than *that*—is not altogether untainted in this respect. If ever there was a poet born on purpose to illustrate the difference between the poetry of genius and the poetry of talent, between the poetry of impulse and the poetry of effort, between the poetry of inspiration and the poetry of gestation; in short, between the intrinsical and the extrinsical gift—surely that poet was Burns. One can hardly open his works at random without finding some proof of what we say. His worship of the true fire, and his almost godlike revelry in the use of it, may be inversely estimated by his corresponding contempt of the borrowed light. His perception of the infinite value of the one, and the pretentious hollowness of the other, were equally clear and strong; and in making allusion to their respective claims, he was not in the habit of mincing matters.

> What's a' your jargon o' your schools,
> Your Latin names for horns and stools;
> If honest Nature made you fools,
>   What sairs your grammers?
> Ye'd better ta'en up spades and shools
>   Or knappin-hammers.
>
> A set o' dull conceited hashes
> Confuse their brains in college classes!
> They gang in stirks, and come out asses,
>   Plain truth to speak.
> And soon they think to climb Parnassus
>   By dint o' Greek.
>
> Gie me ae spark o' Nature's fire!
> That's a' the learning I desire.
> Then though I trudge through dub and mire,
>   At pleugh or cart,
> My muse, though hamely in attire,
>   May touch the heart.

And yet—not to detract one moment from the infinite credit he had in the little culture he so manfully strove to give himself—who can read his letters without perceiving that even that little made him not a little pedantic sometimes? And in his poems, too, we have now and then a phrase such as "the tenebrific scene," and a few others of that description, not many, but yet just enough to make every lover of true poetry inwardly thank God that the poet's culture went no further in that direction, and that he escaped the vice of "fine writing" by a happy ignorance of it. Again, in Goethe it may be questioned whether the philosopher and man of science did not sometimes super-saturate the poet. Even in Shakspeare himself we are perhaps more indebted to his "little Latin and less Greek" than we commonly suppose. Better for us it may be, after all, that like his own Holofernes, and Nathaniel in *Love's Labour's Lost*, he did not manage to steal from the great feast of languages any more than the scraps. Had he been more perfectly equipped, we might have had more of his learning and less of his genius : the one we could have had as well from any one else ; the other, from no one else.

Now if the poet born runs this risk, and even suffers by it, to some degree, notwithstanding the continually counteracting influence of his genius, we need not perhaps be so surprised to find that the smaller talent of the poet made is sometimes overpowered by it, or that in a highly-educated age the artificial modifications of the poetic faculty should be so common.

By far the most admissible ground lying between the poet born and the poet made is unquestionably occupied by the purely critical and reflective writer of verse. Most admissible because he cultivates that little isthmus which may be said to stretch between the two, but which properly belongs to neither. What he produces is not so much poetry as a kind of sublimated prose ; just such thoughts as may occur to any educated person, carefully chiselled into rhythmical form. The words of such writers are not winged, but are rather arrows skilfully feathered. Their productions have none of the marks of an overmastering inspiration. They possess their genius, but are never possessed by it : poets *minus* the passion, and consequently have none of the creative fire and lofty utterance that passion alone can give. We suspect that the most successful cultivators of this isthmus know better than to lay any claim to being the real inheritors of Apollo's laurel bough ; and yet this half-way house between Poetry and Prose is often frequented by the highest genius. Coleridge, with a humility that should not be without its lesson—we had almost said its rebuke—for a good many versifiers of the present day, designated some of his poems "rhymed prose." But that intermediate retreat had far more frequent visitors than he. Wordsworth may be said to have rented permanent apartments there, for-keeping out of sight in the meantime his unsurpassed and unsurpassable inspirations, he certainly wrote more rhymed prose than any other possessor of the real gift that ever lived. In fact, it is mainly to the influence of Wordsworth's rhymed prose that we owe the existence of this half-way school ; and although it has a numerous and influential following, and numbers among its productions nearly all that such writers as Clough have produced, we are by no means clear that that influence has been an unmixed good. There is reason to suspect that a good deal of a kind of verse the world might have done very well without has been contributed by that modern modification of the faculty—so wonderfully prolific since Wordsworth's day—which fails to recognize with sufficient discrimination the line between rhymed prose and poetry. In an eloquent passage in the *Excursion* the author deplores the loss of those poets who, as he says, " go to the grave unthought of "—

<blockquote>
men endowed with highest gifts,
The vision and the faculty divine,
Yet wanting the accomplishment of verse.
</blockquote>

Our misfortune is just the opposite of all this. In too many cases we have the " verse " without the vision.

In attempting to trace the historical fluctuations and modifications of poetry one cannot but remark the continual tendency of the art to fall into artificial and conventional forms; a proneness to drift into positive schools with accepted models, and fixed and final laws, and which an extreme culture is apt to regard with something like superstition. It would seem that in the history of art, as well as in politics or theology, there exists a periodical necessity for revolution. Around it, as around these, gathers a tangle of tradition that now and then must be kicked off in the interests of further progress. Art has been as stubborn a conservator of this sort of *impedimenta* as theology; and just as the Church, as some suppose, has suffered the letter to overgrow the spirit, and now totters beneath a burden of exanimate dogma, which it ought to have allowed to fall in its proper time, like dead leaves that had already served their purpose—in like manner art has frequently been found in an almost breathless condition from the sheer weight of its traditionary harness. In its history we can trace where this hardening process begins, and follow its gradually increasing pressure until the chain begins to gall, and the soul of art begins to sicken under its ever-accumulating burden. Then enters the reformer—some Cromwell of art—who, by the inherent unfetterability of genius, snaps the chain in two and orders the bauble away.

Never was there a greater innovator, or one who shocked the art proprieties with greater effect than Shakspeare himself; and, dating from his time, it is interesting to watch this ebb and flow, or rather this alternate heating and cooling process in the history of the poetic faculty, the oscillation between the claims of the natural poet and the literary and partially made one. Poetry in the Elizabethan era was poured out molten and alive, so much so, that some of its creations—built out of airy nothing—are yet to us more real than the realities of that time. It was not to be expected that the poetical thermometer could have remained long at that height, so we find that it gradually cooled down and hardened, until Dryden and the Restoration group brought back in some measure its wonted fire and vigour; yet only to fall back again and freeze more completely than ever into the cold monotony and prim formality of the poets of Queen Anne. Again the blood began to warm in the veins of Gray, and Cowper, and Campbell, till at last it reached its modern climax in the glowing passion—not altogether free from fever—of Lord Byron.

The tide turned again, and retreated according to its law, till it reached the cultured serenity of Windermere, the placid and almost oriental quietism of Wordsworth. And through his influence we arrive at our own time, with all its advantages and disadvantages, waiting for the next deliverer, as some would almost imply, who do not hide their impatience and restlessness under the artificialities of modern culture. Nor, notwithstanding all the unquestionably high poetry our time has yielded, is their impatience altogether without reason. Unreasonable it might appear, if applied to particular cases, but any one paying attention to the general tenor and teaching of much of the poetical criticism now obtaining, must have observed how frequently it is hinted—and more than hinted—that if we are to pass for judges at all, we must give our hearty approval in many instances to poetry that has little else to recommend it than a certain technical finish, and musical completeness, and that even for the sake of these artistic advantages, we must be prepared to overlook other qualities that are clearly and unquestionably objectionable. Such critics may carry a few readers with them ; but it is too far on in our day to expect of the majority of men that they dance to the piping of an educated satyr, even if his exquisite music should compel them to admit that he has found the reed of Pan himself. We make no reference to the metrical attitudinizing of the school which mistakes a cultured eccentricity for genius, and which seems to think it a duty to train Pegasus, as if he were a circus hack, to do nothing but tricks. Such extravagances may be safely left to cure themselves. But leaving these out of sight, men have a right to express their disappointment, when they believe they have amongst them possessors of the real gift, who have allowed the subject to decline in their hands until it has become little better than a lay figure, upon which they are contented to display the mere millinery of poetical thought : inheritors of a real inspiration, misled by the affectation of the hour, allowing themselves to be tempted into the tricks of the literary *costumier*, who clothes his muse with "samite" and puts a " cithern" in her hand, and instructs her in all the mannered mimicry of an obsolete English. There is no doubt a sweet and dainty delight in much of this poetry. In many instances it is a real gift exercised only in a wrong direction. There is a quaint prettiness about it that reminds one of an old enamel, an antique Watteau-like artificial simplicity, that has its peculiar charm. It is clearly a step in advance of the Damons and Delias, the Chloes and Phillises, the imitation shepherds and shepherdesses, and all the book-rural mockeries of nature and human nature, that so daintily disfigured what is commonly called the classical period of English literature. It is the same in kind, however ; the same misdirection of the same faculty, developed under slightly modified conditions. Better bred if you choose, and more elaborately cultured, but nearly identical. Time has changed the actors and the *mise en scène*, but the thing produced is just a revival of the old farce. Such poetry will always have its admirers of a kind, just as there are

still readers living who can convince themselves they find nature and
reality in the Pastorals of Pope, or the amatory ditties of Shenstone
and others of his time.　We do not at all quarrel with the fact; only
let no critic attempt to foist upon us such things, as if they belonged
to the order of that poetry which holds the mirror up to nature, when
they do not even hold it up to art in any dignified sense so much as to
artifice.

The "classic period of English literature," how easy to expand the
title—and the fatal sarcasm that time will clothe it in—to a whole chapter
on the influence of supposed culture on the poetic faculty.　Showing, as
it might be made to show, the easiness of writing the most polished verse
and the difficulty of writing even the roughest of true poetry.　How easy
to illustrate from much of the verse called classic that inveterate tendency
of art to run into mere drapery, to the almost burial and oblivion of the
thing draped.　And in our time the danger is imminent.　In our anxiety
"to paint the outward wall so costly gay," the soul of the thing itself
seems to be escaping us.　With all deference to one or two great poetical
names amongst us, we cannot help thinking that seldom has a time stood
more in need than the present of the advent of a soul great enough to be
simple, and bringing with it the sacred fire that burns convention to a
cinder.

It is not to be disguised that many readers of present-day poetry
would gladly hail a reversion in favour of

> The few strong instincts, and the few plain rules,

that Wordsworth spoke of.　They complain, and not altogether without
reason, that too much of what is offered for their delectation wants the
freshness and fragrance of Nature, nor are they content, just yet, to accept,
in the place of Nature's growths, the most carefully cultivated of exotics.
Perfect of its kind as much of our later poetry may be, its perfection is
too studied and finically correct to give general or abiding satisfaction,
and carries too plainly upon it the marks of the supersubtle manipulation
of the modern *littérateur*.　These trim gardens of thought are pleasant
enough in their way, but in every healthy estimation they will never be
preferred—nay, nor compared—to those unbroken acres of wilderness
and wild flowers where the indigenous forces of Nature are at work, and
God only is the gardener.

The almost universal cultivation of music, and the rapidly increasing
appreciation of the highest kinds of it, are certainly features upon which
the age may be fairly congratulated, and it is not to be supposed that
such a wonderful development of the art could possibly fail to make its
mark upon contemporary poetry.　When the poetry of the Victorian
era has receded far enough in time to admit of a final and unbiassed
summing-up, we make no question but that one of its most conspicuous
excellencies will be found to be its musicalness.　The exquisite melody
alone of Mr. Tennyson is more than sufficient to consecrate a muse far less

profound than his. Beyond doubt the most perfect passages in poetry
have always been the most musical, but to say that on that account they
can dispense with meaning, or even consider it a thing of minor importance, would be ridiculous. On the contrary, one has only to take
to pieces any of those exquisite passages which, by reason of their perfection, have become permanently embedded and interwoven with the
very texture of our language, "those jewels five-words long," as Mr.
Tennyson calls them—

> That on the stretched forefinger of all time
> Sparkle for ever—

in order to come to a very different conclusion. Take any such passage
and examine it minutely, and you will find that its perfection consists
of a subtle interfusion of sound and sense, and a perfect equipoise of
meaning and melody, that sacrifices not so much as a hair on either side.

One cannot but regard the culture of sound for poetical purposes—
and, as far as that goes, for prose as well—as of the highest consequence.
To a certain extent we are all victims, consciously or unconsciously, of
the Mesopotamian fallacy, whether we care to admit it or not. That
mere noise, mere colour, mere form, mere motion, altogether apart from
any intellectual association or moral insignificance, do of themselves
affect us, is not to be denied, and therefore need not be laughed at. And
that euphonious sound gives wings to thought as nothing else does,
whether we can explain it or not, is a simple fact that transcends the
region of argument. It has the power even of endowing very commonplace thought with a kind of fictitious immortality. In all languages
some of the weakest and most childish of proverbs have held their place
for ages by reason only of the musical mould in which they have been
cast. Many of them owe their continued existence to a mere trick of
sound, some catching rhyme, or euphonious alliteration, some silvery
see-saw of sibilants, or, perhaps most of all, to a dexterously balanced
distribution and modulation of vowel sounds. In the world of art the
end justifies everything, and any limitation as to means is not for a
moment to be considered. We do not trouble ourselves to inquire too
minutely whether or not Turner produced those wonderful effects of
surging sea by a twirl of his thumb-nail. For us it is sufficient that the
effect is there. The water is alive, and Genius is justified of her children.
No exercise of faculty can be too mean or too minute as long as it is
controlled by the inspiration, and is not permitted to sink into the region
of mere mechanism.

The art of good writing, either in prose or poetry, was defined by
Shenstone as consisting of "spontaneous thought and laboured expression," and the definition has a certain scope that gives it a fitness for
all the other arts. Elaboration can hardly be overdone as long as the
thought which sustains and directs it is the *vrai feu*, and not the *ignis
fatuus* of a mistaken ambition. The capacity, in fact, for minute refinement in detail, and infinite loving labour, is an instinct of all truly

artistic genius.   But it should not be forgotten that art in these matters
of detail, except in the most competent hands, is apt to degenerate into
artifice, until the means and expedients called in for the purpose of
enforcing thought are found only to hamper and enfeeble it.   To attempt
the finish of Rembrandt one must have his insight as well.   In such a
case music degenerates into mere " *Musikmacherei*," and poetry becomes
the mechanical trick of the rhyming " *Wortmacher*," the work not of the
artist, but rather of the weak artificer, whose pottering demon tempts
him on to

> Add and alter many times
> Till all is ripe and rotten.

Given the strong poetical thought, and we question much whether or
not it is possible to give it an embodiment that shall be too musical; but
when critics can show such fondness for the vehicle of poetical thought
rather than the thing itself, as shall lead them to avow that if language
be only musical enough it does not matter if it mean nothing, it is surely
time to enter a protest, if poetry has not to sink into an empty jingle,
and become to us the trick *of one that hath a pleasant voice, and can
play well on an instrument.*

The abuse of the music-worshippers in poetry is capable of illustration from an exactly diverse quarter.   Wagner and his school are
endeavouring to enforce a theory, which, as it seems to us, is rooted in
an error on the exactly opposite side.   By an attempt to get out of music
an amount of dramatic meaning, which from the very nature of music,
and the character of its art implements, it cannot be made to render up,
they are making the same mistake—on the other side—with those who
attempt to load poetry with more music than the nature of articulate
language will artistically admit of.   To claim anything like originality
for Wagner's theory is almost puerile.   It is as old as the phenomenon
of sound, or the sense of hearing; a thesis universally received, only
pushed to an unreasonable and untenable extreme.   No one ever doubted
that music and poetry possessed much in common, and must of necessity
play into each other's hands.   Nevertheless, the products of each art
must stand or fall alone.   Beethoven's music to *Egmont*, or Mendelssohn's to *A Midsummer Night's Dream*, or Schumann's to *Manfred*,
have distinctive merits of their own, altogether independent of the names
Goethe, or Shakspeare, or Byron.

No doubt the association and conjunction of exquisite words with
exquisite music is an encounter worthy of the gods themselves, and in
every case to be desired.   And unfortunately it is not to be denied that
only too many of our *libretti*, even to this day, go to prove the justice of
Beaumarchais' sarcasm in the *Barber of Seville*, " Ce qui ne vaut pas la
peine d'être dit, on le chante."   But had these *libretti* been perfect,
would the music have been other than it is ?   No; genius by itself must
justify itself, or nothing.   No possible poverty of sound-accompaniment
could ever successfully veil the grandeur of Shakspeare's genius, just as

no conceivable triviality of word-accompaniment could alter by a cubit the stature of Beethoven's soul. Bad music just remains bad music, and the bray of the beast is not to be concealed, clothe it as you will in the bravest lion's skin of words. On the other hand, the exploded divinities of poetry—your Beatties, Klopstocks, Blackmores, *et hoc*, would in all likelihood continue to hug the ground if their words were yoked to the song of the morning stars.

The two arts are not only to be much better judged apart, but they can be drawn so near as to destroy and neutralise the special perfection that distinctively belongs to each. They must not move on the same line, but rather glide forward on imperceptible parallels, that, by the nature of the case, can never touch. To take an illustration from music itself; it is not the similarity but the difference between a note and its minor third that makes their harmony so sweetly plaintive and pathetic. You have only to draw them closer together by a very few vibrations in order to set your teeth on edge. And so

> If music and sweet poetry agree
> As they must needs, the sister and the brother,

let the very fact of their family connection forbid the banns of a closer alliance. Except by a violation of their nature they can never become one flesh, or one art, in the Wagnerian sense. Where such an alliance has been attempted, the offspring has been some beautifully brainless poetry on the one side, and on the other, music, of which a great part, at least, is unintelligible even amongst musical people. Whether the nonsense or the noise of to-day will ever become, in either case, the wisdom or the music of the future, is a question we are quite contented to let the future settle for itself. But unless these good people—so seemingly essential to every age—who display such an indecent haste in the matter of the millennium, are much nearer their final triumph than we have any sober means of computing, we suspect that our grandchildren will probably find with us, that a good deal more than sufficient unto the day are the impossible theories thereof.

J. B. S,

Ethics and Aesthetics of Modern Poetry.

In the history of every art there are continually recurring periods at which artistic progress, and sometimes almost artistic life, seems to be threatened by those obstructive theories and conventional rules to which art every now and then is authoritatively asked to submit. Just as religion, in its purest and most spiritual aspects, seems to lose ground in nearly the same proportion as dogmatic theology gains it, true art becomes weakened by the overgrowth and imposition of its authoritative and arbitrary methods.

Poetry, for example, was never more seriously hampered and handicapped than by the superstitious observance of the old dramatic unities of time and place. Although to all but a very small number that doctrine looks ridiculous enough from our modern point of view, and is not likely seriously to trouble us again, it was only one out of many difficulties of a similar nature which periodically arise to vex such questions. Fallacious theories in matters of art, as well as morals, will probably continue to come up for discussion, with average regularity, as long as art is cultivated.

The theory of the dramatic unities itself was only the logical consequence of Aristotle's narrow definition of poetry, as nothing more and nothing higher than imitation. It was but an extension and application of the iron law of literal imitation to the particulars of time and place. As the world progresses, or thinks it progresses, each cultus brings along with it its besetting snares, and even old theories, supposed to be long ago historically dead and buried, seem to come back to life with such confident rejuvenescence, and clothed so cunningly in the fashionable costume of the hour, that many of them are daily passed off, among the inexperienced, as actual novelties. Just as we have had the atomic theory and fortuitous Cosmos of Democritus and Epicurus—we say nothing of the soundness or unsoundness of the theory—rehabilitated in nineteenth-century English, as the newest thing in science; just as we have in theology the pantheism known to India for thousands of years, formulated in the mythology of Greece, and revived by Spinoza in the seventeenth century, again served up in the mystical prose-poetry of its fashionable preachers and teachers; so, in literature and art, more than half of the disputations arising out of such subjects are neither more nor less than revivals of old discussions with new names.

One of the most fashionable fallacies that have recently cropped up, and engaged the attention of artists and art critics, has been discussed under the attractive and, to some extent, misleading title of "Art for Art's Sake," misleading in the first place, because the whole argument turns upon the definition of the word "art," and the exact ground, ethical and æsthetical, which that word legitimately covers. The extreme supporters of the art for art's sake theory seek, indeed, to draw an impassable line between the ethical and æsthetical, and declare that, however they may have been mixed up by morally disposed but stupid people, art and morals have really nothing to do with each other. The doctrine is based upon one of those half-truths which, viewed exclusively from one side, appears to be exceedingly plausible, but which, upon closer acquaintance and viewed as a whole, is altogether unsound, and as full of danger to art as to morals.

Its reference to morals we do not care to touch, but would rather leave that question to the care of those professional gladiators of the consecrated ring who, so to speak, have taken out a licence to treat that side of the subject, and with whose trade monopoly we have no desire to interfere. Its reference to art, however, and especially to poetry, is another matter, and one in which a large portion of the world, licensed and unlicensed, may fairly be supposed to take an interest. It is somewhat ominous that, in its relation to poetry, the doctrine has been already set up by some of its supporters, in extreme cases, not as an argument in the interests of art, so much as a shelter and attempted justification of artistic uncleanness. In so doing, the supporters of such a view may be said, in some sort, to have supplied an answer to their own arguments; for if it be beyond the province of art, and inconsistent with her legitimate object and aim, that she should ever become the exponent of morality, it must surely be admitted that it is equally foreign to her nature to become the exponent of immorality. These are but the two segments of the same argument, and, knocking out the key, the two must fall together. That morals and art, however, broadly speaking, are each in possession of distinct kingdoms of their own, is a general statement of the case, that no one, we dare say, will care to dispute; but that the two powers have given and taken from each other, or, in other words, that art has been largely indebted to morals, and that religion has largely availed itself of the assistance of art, is equally indisputable. The artistic instinct may be one, and the moral and religious quite another; but that third instinct, which, in the whole history of the human race, savage and civilised, has invariably joined the two in one, suggests a *tertium quid* which cannot be left out of the argument, and which proves the existence of an instinct as strong as either. That mysterious longing for the manifestation of some higher power than we possess, which underlies the history of art and religion in every phase, and at every stage and step of its development, is always looking about it for some tangible and visible incarnation. Art, indeed, may be very well defined as the result of that instinct which propels a man towards the outward embodiment and expression of the highest thought of which his nature is capable; and no human being, savage or civilised, has ever been able to shake himself altogether clear of the desire. The barbarian who carved his first idol was impelled by this joint instinct, and it would be clearly useless to attempt to separate the art motive from the religious motive in the force that impelled him. Mean and rudimentary as his work must necessarily have been, he was moved to the performance of it by the same instinct which suggested the statue of Zeus to Pheidias, or an *Ecce Homo* to Guido or Correggio. Poor and elementary as his conception of the Deity must also have been, he was, unconsciously and according to his lights, working at the root of that tree of which Christianity itself is the crown and flower. The great work of Pheidias affords an exact illustration of the action of this joint instinct amongst a people ethnologically unique, and in a state of civilisation, as regards art, certainly unsurpassed. Strabo relates that the declared intention of the artist in that great work was to illustrate and give a visible embodiment to the mighty lines in the *Iliad*, in which Homer represents Olympus trembling at the nod of Zeus. The statue was not only considered the masterpiece of Greek art, but an actual representation of the deity, "the Father of gods and men;" and the epigram of Philip of Thessalonica, in the Greek anthology, which declares that before the production of so marvellous a work could become possible, God must have either come down to earth on purpose to show Himself to the artist, or Pheidias himself must have been taken up into heaven, seems clearly to indicate the belief that the inspiration sprung from the two combined and indivisible sources—religious and artistic. It would not be difficult to prove the existence and operation of this double instinct in the history of every nation, and in all the departments of work, aspiring to the name of art, whether in poetry, painting, sculpture, or architecture. The winged Assyrian bull, with its soulless and yet half-human face, and its cruel iron talons, the fossil remnant of a long-forgotten faith—"the dead disbowelled mystery," which has given Mr. Rossetti a theme for one of the most perfect poems of the century; the sphinxes of Egypt, those passionless creatures that seem to be lifted above the cares of a fleeting world, and to live in an atmosphere of everlasting repose—

> Staring right on with calm eternal eyes;

Greek sculpture; Italian painting at its highest period; the architecture of the middle ages, all these are but the varied answer to the one ever-present instinct. It may be objected that many of these earlier works were the unworthy attempts of half-civilised peoples to realise their own gross conceptions of the Deity, and not to be called religious in the sense in which we use the word. But it is enough for our argument that on their moral side many of them were deifications, and that on their artistic side they were all, more or less, an answer to that unquenched and unquenchable cry in the breast of every intelligent human being, which impels him in the search to find what Mr. Tennyson calls "that

type of perfect in his mind." And even in a religious point of view,
when we consider the periods which produced them, it may be after all
fairly open to question, whether some of those primitive and barbarous
attempts to embody and express religious feeling and religious faith were
not quite as noble, quite as religious, and quite as intelligent as the stolid
fetichism of a later and more pretentious cultus.

It is this longing to embody his highest aspiration in which the
morality of the artist consists ; and the history, poetry, or artwork of a
people only becomes of importance in proportion as it is informed and
penetrated by this instinct. It is its profound moral significance which
gives the secret charm to Hebrew history and Hebrew poetry, bestowing
upon it that unique flavour which sets it above all others in human
interest. It is the strange blind groping after the perfect type, after God
and the Godlike in all its art-worship, which gives that deathless and
unaccountable fascination to "the glory that was Greece," and which in
its highest period makes the sublimities of Æschylus read like passages
from Isaiah. In such cases art is no more independent of morals than
morality is of art.

With those, however, who argue for the impassable line between
ethics and æsthetics, on the ground that it is not desirable that art
should be a mere teacher of morality, we perfectly agree, only that does
not preclude the possibility of art becoming an admirable exponent of
morality without any obvious didactic intention. A man may come
under moral influence without any design upon him to that end, and in
fact one of the most direct means of getting him, morally speaking, to
kick over the traces, is to buttonhole him over a sermon. It is not safe
even to commend him for his moral excellence. "Dub not my likings
virtues," says George Eliot—

> lest they get
> A drug-like taste, and breed a nausea ;
> Honey's not sweet commended as cathartic.

It dashes the native power and natural lustre of a good deed to
have the light of the moral lantern turned too fully upon it. It should
rather be kept dry, and in the dark, like grain seed, in order to preserve
its power of germination in perfect efficiency. An obvious exhibition of
morality is apt to defeat its own end. In Richardson's *Pamela*, for
example (that in many respects admirable work of art), it is difficult to
say whether the occasional indecency of the book, or the obtrusive
morality with which it is interlarded, is the more mischievous or reprehensible element of the two. It is doubtful enough whether any modest
young woman could write to her friend a glowing description of how she
was *not* seduced by the squire, but in the moral tag to such a story, the
step for most of us has been taken between the doubtful and the disgusting. Again, in Hogarth's pictures of the same era, in such a series,
for example, as the "Harlot's Progress," no possible parade of moral purpose can ever hide the gross realism and the glut of uncleanness which

characterise them as a whole.   Preaching of such a kind was much better calculated to gratify a prurient curiosity than send any pitiful Magdalene back to the shelter of God.   Saviour-less sin is an ugly thing at best, and there is neither reason nor morality in the exhibition of it. Putting the question of art aside, its moral method is unsound, and, except among the more extreme supporters of the Calvinistic heresy, happily all but obsolete.   Such teaching—if there was any religion in it at all—was too exclusively based upon the purblind devil-worship of those with whom the good old orthodox damnation seemed the only safe road—moralists who mainly regarded religion as a deterrent, and upon whom " the pity of it, Iago," would have been uselessly thrown away. The simple word of the Master on the same subject, " Neither do I condemn thee, go and sin no more," reduces morality like this to ashes.

It has always been a somewhat dangerous expedient to use art for a directly moral purpose, or indeed to use it as an exponent of anything but itself.   Even in the two arts which lie most closely akin—music and poetry—it is not to be attempted except at some slight sacrifice, and violence done to one or the other.   The marriage of music to immortal verse was after all the dream of a poet—the ideal union of that " orb of song, the divine Milton "— a marriage made in heaven, rather than any alliance capable of being successfully consummated and ratified on earth. There are words in our poetical anthology which refuse to set themselves to music (except indeed to the native rhythm which belongs to all beautiful speech) by reason of their very loftiness and grandeur—passages so profound and impressive that, like the names of God, are hardly to be uttered in other attitude than that of worship, and not to be felt in their fulness except by ourselves alone.   In the latter half of the sixteenth century—that great spring-tide of English poetry—" Marlowe's mighty line " only became possible through the poet's determination to discard what he called—

> The jigging veins of rhyming mother wits,
> And such conceits as clownage keeps in pay—

all the beggarly elements, that is to say, of the elder drama, the vulgar accessories, and jingling couplets with which his predecessors had so long tickled the ears of the groundlings.   The deliberate adoption also of the new method by Shakspeare (who evidently profited by Marlowe's example) proved beyond a doubt, that even the modified music of rhyme could be safely dispensed with, and was no longer necessary to the very loftiest poetical expression.   Music, on the other hand, has also her sacred groves, and her rapturous moments into which words may not and cannot enter ; those sublime soliloquies, for example, of Beethoven, that master-magician, upon whose great sound-wave words perish and melt like snow that falls upon the sea.   The soul of the hearer, under such a mighty spell as his, mounts into a region where the methods of language are superseded.   He confers not with flesh and blood.   A messenger has reached him with authentic tidings of invisible things, before whom the

world and its wordy doctrine stands dumb. With him who saw the
heavens open and the angels ascending and descending, things of sense and
time are consumed and swallowed up in the eternal chasm, as through
the open gates he hears the far-off echo of a song which sings to him—

> of what the world will be
> When the years have died away.

No, the marriage between music and words is not consummated, and,
the genius of Wagner notwithstanding, never will be consummated on
earth.   There is a kind of music to which words would only be a drag
and an intrusion, while on the other hand there are words so sweet, so
profound, and so full of a strange fascination for us, that their best
possible accompaniment, and their most powerful exponents, will be
found in solitude and silence.   Herr Wagner may give us a new creature,
the joint issue of music and the drama, but neither his theory nor his
practice—wonderful as the latter unquestionably is—will ever advance
music to a greater height, or poetry to a greater height, than each of
these can achieve by itself alone.

If there be a danger then in asking the kindred arts of music and
poetry to become the exponents of each other, the danger is greatly
magnified when we come to ask the divine spirit of Poesy—

> The singing maid with pictures in her eyes—

to become the exponent of the proprieties, and a sort of moral maid of all
work.   It would be an unpardonable stupidity to insist that she should
attune her heavenly voice to the screech of Minerva's owl, and to bind
the ægis about her tender flesh and put her in a pulpit would be to
strike her dumb.   And yet without agreeing with Dryden and the elder
authorities, that " the chief design of poetry is to instruct," it is not to be
denied that the best art *does* instruct, and that in the highest sense of the
word.   It is only when the didactic design is put in the front, and
obtruded on us, that it becomes obnoxious, and indeed intolerable.   To a
certain extent this holds good, as we have said, even in moral teaching
itself.   Men must be taught as if you taught them not, whether the
medium of instruction be a picture, a poem, or a sermon.   The artist in
either case who imagines that, being an artist, he can disregard the
opinions of the rest of the world as to the morality or immorality in the
choice of his subject, or thinks that he can succeed by addressing men as
if they occupied a distinct moral platform from that upon which he himself stands, is grievously deceiving himself.   Any such assumption, on
the part of either artist or moralist, is based upon a professional fallacy ;
and indeed, in the case of the preacher, this tacit assumption is the real
reason why the average sermon in every educated community becomes
daily more ridiculous and intolerable, and more and more provocative of
that refractory frame of mind which reaches a climax in Goethe's ejacu-
lation, "five minutes more of this, and I confess everything."   The
question for both moralist and artist is not how to separate themselves

from their fellow-men, but how to lose sight of any such distinction, how to combine and transfuse themselves into the great soul and common mind of the world. It will not do for the artist to address men as his inferiors, but as equals. Even if they should be his inferiors, and deny his art, and laugh him to scorn, it will not serve him, like Byron in his day, to lose his temper at a public which refuses to appreciate his work. Far better is it to work on in silence, in the well-grounded assurance that the secret sanhedrim, which always judges righteously in the end, and which is always alive somewhere in the world, will one day do him justice. Rather than be tempted by such hostility to seek a separation from the world, he should descend lower yet to meet them, compelling his soul into the highways and byeways, and walking if need be with the publican and sinner, if by any means he can get his feet upon the common rock, and lay his hand at least on the common heart of humanity. By this means only can the artist draw all men to him, and by the light of his tardily acknowledged fitness compel the world at last to read the central purpose of his life, and to judge his work as a whole. In art as well as morals, the basis of all true power is in humility and self-oblivion, and nothing more completely defeats artistic effect than professional self-assertion. There is a stern independence in all healthy human nature which will not suffer itself to be patted on the back, instructed as a younger, or humoured as an invalid. Where a sense of equality or fellow-feeling is lost, artistic and moral effect goes along with it. All idea of difference between artist and audience must be cancelled, all thought of superior personality put out of the way, before art can have its perfect elemental freedom. No human breath must stain the glass, through which art at its best can be apprehended. The medium through which we perceive and appreciate what is beautiful in art should be as nearly as possible the medium through which we apprehend the beautiful in nature. It should be atmospheric and invisible. The moment at which the attention is diverted from the thought to the utterer of the thought, from the thought to the vehicle of the thought, a false step has been taken. The presence of an obvious apparatus is fatal to artistic effect. In literature, for example, as soon as the writer reveals the trick of his school, or in any way shows the self-consciousness of the literary craftsman, his style is ruined. At that point a poison enters his pen, which affects injuriously everything he utters. Whatever is attempted, the true secret of the highest method of art expression is the result of professional self-forgetfulness. It is the perfect self-negation, the almost ghostly withdrawal of Shakspeare's personality, which loads his words with that oracular significance the word of no other man possesses. It is, again, the exquisite simplicity of Homer, in which the literary performer is altogether lost sight of, set aside, sunk, and superseded in the thing performed, the unconscious "garrulous God-innocence,"—as Mrs. Browning called it—of the simple story-teller, which gives him his ever fresh fascination. This secret power of self-surrender and self-disappearance is even strangely characteristic of the highest spiritual fact within man's cognizance. Although there has never been awanting an intense and even a morbid curiosity on the subject, what a complete withdrawal of everything like earthly personal basis, what an infinite height and depth of distance, what an impenetrable veil stands between us and the human Personality that laid in the earth the living seeds of that miracle of miracles—Christianity.

Most readers must have noticed the peculiar charm bestowed on all that Shakspeare has ever written, by the conspicuous absence of any apparent didactic purpose. In his profoundest moments he never buttonholes you. He never attempts to point the moral or improve the occasion, except where the dramatic fitness of the situation, or the character of the speaker, demands it; in such cases, for example, as Jaques and Polonius, who, of course, would be entirely out of keeping with their character if they did not preach and moralise. It was the want of this deliberate moral finger-post in Shakspeare's work which made him the stumbling-block he was to the critics of the eighteenth century. Dr. Johnson was disgusted with his reckless indifference to the poetical and moral proprieties, in making the innocent Cordelia die on the breast of Lear, and quite approved of Nahum Tate's " revival with alterations," in which that wretched creature—who wrote a poem on syphilis and rhymed the Psalms of David with the help of Dr. Brady —kept Cordelia alive, married her to Edgar, and so settled the point of poetical justice and outraged morality. Poor Nahum, from a cursory perusal of the Psalms he rhymed, had probably convinced himself that it was highly improper that the wicked should be allowed to spread himself like a green bay-tree, while the righteous went to the wall, and thought that he might as well readjust the little matter the gods had somehow overlooked, and so proceeded to do so to the satisfaction of the moralists of his time. A little further insight into the philosophy of the two great poets he, for the time being, was born to mutilate, might have taught him the working of that higher law, under which to represent virtue as a policy, and offer it any other inducement or reward than that which it offers itself, is to turn the truth of God into a lie.

Shakspeare's morality was of a kind which Johnson and his school could hardly understand, because it belonged to an order, not more honest perhaps, but infinitely higher and wider than their own. If Shakspeare's story and his art-method do not of themselves impress their moral, there are no instructions left. Through death and disaster the sun shines and birds sing, and his eyes are motionless and silent as the eyes in a mask of marble. With a moral design as clear as air, he never tells you what that design is. Like his own Æneas, in *Troilus and Cressida*—

the secrets of nature
Have not more gift of taciturnity.

He that hath ears to hear let him hear, as for the others, he does not care even to speak to them.   Just as we see in nature and life itself, he uses facts sometimes in a way which seems to contradict the accepted moralities.   His noblest creature starts back from the very thought of dissolution with an undisguised shudder, while his most godless worldling goes to his death in a pleasant dream, in which he " babbles o' green fields."   That he looked upon the art of the mere preacher with a wise contempt is capable of abundant proof.   In Jaques he makes the preacher's gift the cynical conceit of a played-out *roué*; while in Polonius he gathers up the preacher's wisdom in words that have never been surpassed, in order to fit them to the mouth of a meddling and contemptible busybody.   Notwithstanding this well-marked peculiarity in Shakspeare, there are no writings which more deeply impress the reader with a profound moral intention.   It would savour of special pleading to attempt to prove such a fact by mere reference to isolated passages, although there are enough of these to found such a school of moral philosophy as one would look for in vain from the work of any other man.   The stronger proof lies in the broad moral tendency of his work as a whole, and the moral build of his matchless men and women, for whom he asks, not our admiration alone, but our respect.   He knew, none better, that life was a mingled yarn, good and ill together, and that " cakes and ale " in some shape or other had their roots in human nature.   By reason of his measureless receptivity he took the good and evil up under that massive frontal arch of his, and held them there without disturbance or displacement until the hour came for using the material in his art, when, without any conscious theory about either art or morals, he instinctively used the darker tints of humanity in such a way as brought its higher and fairer aspects into full relief.   In *King Lear*, for example, Goneril and Regan form but the dark background upon which the artist limns the white soul of Cordelia.   In *Othello*, again, he paints the unsullied fame and the too trusting simplicity of the open-hearted soldier on the still blacker canvas of Iago's villany. Everywhere the good and bad are used as contrasts, and in a sense exponents of each other—Lady Macbeth over against the blameless Duncan, the thoughts of whose innocent blood at length unseat her reason; Henry V., Shakspeare's ideal man of the world, is contrasted with Sir John and his good-for-nothing tatterdemalion crew ; while in his most spiritual sphere we have Prospero and Miranda set against the hardly human group of Caliban, Stephano, and Trinculo.   In all these we have the good and ill, the noble and ignoble, together, but we are never left one moment in doubt as to which side engages the artist's moral sympathies ; while there are single characters in which the moral qualities more distinctly predominate, such as Prospero, Cordelia, Hermione, or the Fool in *King Lear*, so utterly spotless, and even holy, both in conception and execution, that they might have been drawn, as was said of some of Fra Angelico's pictures of saints and angels, when the artist was on his knees.   There is clearly one law controlling all that is truly beautiful either in the physical, moral, or artistic world.   If beauty do not naturally belong to the artistic work, if it is not interfused and made one with it in the original casting, it cannot afterwards be superadded. If Aphrodite herself have not the beauty of the living flower, the bloom cannot be laid on.   Any such attempt in the case of physical beauty is a hindrance rather than a help, and in the region of æsthetics, whether moral or poetical, an artistic blunder.

M. Taine, who seems, by the way, to be as blind to Shakspeare's moral method as Dr. Johnson was (only with infinitely less excuse), has insisted upon a theory, which, if accepted by the poet, enables him to shift the entire moral responsibility of any perilous stuff he may have written, clean off his own conscience on to that of his age, and the social circumstances by which he is surrounded; although, curiously enough, the critic forgets to apply his favourite test to Shakspeare's own case, and exhausts his ingenuity to prove our great dramatist's immorality, ignoring the fact that Shakspeare was not only cleanly above his age, but that in one of his undoubtedly autobiographical sonnets he bitterly complains of the ill-fortune that threw him on a public whose manners were far below his moral standard, and in which he pitifully asks forgiveness for any shortcomings arising out of associations with which his public life necessarily brought him into contact.   Surely such a confession as this might have helped the critic to discriminate between the licence characteristic of an era and that personal and premeditated uncleanness which so frequently disfigures Dryden and the Restoration group. Moreover, M. Taine's theory of environment affects only one side of the truth, and is therefore valueless as a test.   To speak of an age as a separate entity controlling the units who constitute that entity, is to a certain extent a fallacy.   It is just such a theory as the criticism of Olivia's Clown in the *Twelfth Night* would dispose of as " the cheveril glove to a good wit; how quickly the wrong side may be turned outward !"   For, if there be any truth in the theory at all, the inverse proposition is quite as true—viz. that the leading minds of any age give tone to, and in a sense control, the social aggregate of which they themselves are the most influential units.   To insist on either proposition as representing the whole truth would be to dogmatise on a half truth. What we call the spirit of the age is not to be caught in a trap which can be turned so easily inside out, nor can it be so readily formulated or manufactured into a critical tape-line by which every case may be exactly measured, least of all the case of genius.   It might indeed be said with far more show of truth, that the law of environment controls all mental phenomena below the standard of genius, but at that point ceases to have any influence, and in the case of great genius even provokes a contrary current.   Ordinary mental power is fenced round by that chain of outward circumstance which genius breaks ; there are set bounds for the rule, but none for the exception.   The theory altogether is one of those complete little pocket oracles, which it has been too much the fashion of late to apply indiscriminately to literary and art questions, and which are held to settle everything out of hand. The doctrine, like a good many short-cuts to hard-and-fast conviction, has not that final importance which in some quarters has been rashly credited it. The dogma in art or religion (and in many other places where its presence is less suspected) which proposes to supersede the necessity for any further hard thinking, naturally recommends itself to the majority. Anything that invites a man to fold his brains up and put them away in a napkin is eagerly closed with in these days of mental strain and pressure. But fortunately, or unfortunately, things are not necessarily true because they save trouble and provide an armchair for intellectual inaction. M. Taine has supplied one of these patent processes eagerly accepted by the crowd, and which has been applied in a manner and with a completeness its original propounder did not perhaps think of. In a time like ours, when, for the education of men, all periods, and the literatures of all ages, are equally laid under contribution, the theory of environment ceases to have any tangible meaning, and genius in such circumstances is moulded by its own predilections. Such a theory may have a limited application in a literary clique, but in the great broad world its effect becomes quickly invisible. It falls into the vast ocean of modern life and merely makes

a circle in the water,
Which never ceaseth to enlarge itself
Till by broad spreading it disperse to nought.

If there were any really controlling principle in it, one would expect to find a striking resemblance between the poets of the same period, and this is never observable except in poetry of the poorest and most conventional description. Between the poets of our own nineteenth century, discarding the mere imitators, we find no such family likeness ; on the contrary, we are rather astonished at the extraordinary variety of character and quality of gift we so often see in the same family. There is nothing in common between the scowling cynicism of Byron and the placid serenity of Wordsworth ; nothing between the matter-of-fact realism of Crabbe and the idealistic tenuity of Coleridge ; nothing between the open-hearted manliness of Scott and the sugar-water imitation sentiment of Tom Moore ; nothing in common between the somewhat solid pudding of Southey's muse and the phantasmal spirituality of Shelley. Such contrary currents as these in the same period are surely enough to stagger the most devout believer in the iron law of environment. This diversity of gift and moral purpose is by no means confined to the poets of the present age. The greatest single figure in authenticated English history, as scholar, statesman, and poet, a greater *personage* than Shakspeare, and beyond question our greatest poet next to him, presents us with the most remarkable example. Milton is almost the lonely figure in an age whose morality is happily unparalleled

28—2

in the history of his country. What sympathy, moral or artistic, what likeness either in the conception or execution of his work, was there between him and the dissolute rhymesters and dramatists of his time? Looking back upon his life and its moral environment, we seem to see a colossal statue of Apollo, his eyes lifted up to the empyrean as he watches the arrow-flight of his immortal song; while round about his feet, all but unconscious of the godlike presence, hand in hand with their painted and patched bacchantes, dance the wine-stained satyrs of that never-to-be forgotten court.

Turning aside, however, from the moral action and counteraction of an age and its greatest artists, it is somewhat extraordinary to find that it has been left to the nineteenth century to propound the dogma that art to be worthy of the name must be cut off from all moral significance, and that the artist, especially the poet, before he begins his work, must carefully lay aside his moral consciousness, as if that were some kind of detached movement of his being he could take up or lay down at will. The doctrine was tolerable as long as it went no further than that youthful enthusiasm of beauty for beauty's sake, which young Hallam, for example, at the age of twenty, insisted upon when reviewing Mr. Tennyson's first volume in 1831. But when it is argued to the exclusion and expulsion of all moral sense, it is a very different thing; and that Mr. Tennyson gives his countenance to any such doctrine is sufficiently disproved by all his highest and best work. In such poems as the *Palace of Art*, *The Two Voices*, *The Vision of Sin*, and *In Memoriam*, in which a profound moral sense bulks most largely, his imagination finds its greatest scope, and in the particular sphere to which these poems belong, the artist reaches a higher point than has ever yet been chronicled in the same direction in the entire history of English poetry. *The Palace of Art*, indeed, is a poetical and philosophical treatise bearing upon the very subject under discussion; and in which the question is plainly put and plainly answered—whether or not it be possible that a human soul can lay aside its ethical instinct, and live happily and exclusively for the gratification of its æsthetic sense, whether or not a man can successfully detach and lay aside his moral nature, and find the aims and objects of existence served and satisfied in the worship of beauty for beauty's sake? It is no new question, and many a soul besides the one in Mr. Tennyson's poem has undergone a similar test, and returned from the battle with a hard-won experience and in a more or less vanquished condition. Nor is it new as a theme for poetical treatment. It is the central idea in Goethe's *Faust*, in which the trampled moral nature of the hero has its revenge upon him, and reasserts itself so completely that the devil at last is duped of his dupe, and has to take his departure without him. The theme, indeed, is common to many great works representing that struggle with self and sin through which in some shape or other every soul must pass. The work, however, in which we find the most striking prototype of Mr. Tennyson's poem is the Book of

Ecclesiastes. The "Preacher" in that moral monologue, and the "Soul" in the laureate's poem—both of them dramatic personations—proceed on the same lines. "I made me great works," says the hero of the Hebrew drama, "I builded me houses ; I made gardens and orchards ; I gathered me silver and gold, and the peculiar treasure of kings : " while the "Soul" in the *Palace of Art*, in varied phrase to the same effect, begins—

> I built my soul a lordly pleasure house,
> Wherein at ease for aye to dwell.

The Hebrew philosopher says to his heart, "Go to now, I will prove thee with mirth, therefore enjoy pleasure ; " while the modern poet, in what sounds almost like a paraphrase of the same words, says—

> O Soul, make merry and carouse,
> Dear Soul, for all is well ;

and so the two set out upon that quest which has ever had but one end— vanity and vexation of spirit.

It is interesting to note the points of difference, as well as resemblance, in the dramatic treatment of the same idea, by writers so widely asunder in point of time as well as environment. Each story represents its hero at the commencement as one who has already attained great worldly eminence. Both are men of position and power, of unbounded means, and great culture ; men who, even exposed to the danger of such an experiment, may be stained, but not retained by evil as a habit, caught but not held by the senses, as the sequel in each case proves. The eye takes in at a glance the structural beauty of the modern poem, its clear definition, and its gorgeous imagery, while the ear is held by the fascination of its deep resounding harmony ; and though the subject is of necessity profound and mysterious, as all spiritual conflicts must be, there is no tinge of that obscurity, and repetition, which has made the work of the Hebrew author such a puzzle to the annotators. But the wider difference between the two will be found to lie in the moral standard accepted by the respective authors. The hero of Ecclesiastes seems to undergo a series of indulgences, with moral pauses between, in which the ever-recurring burden of *Vanitas vanitatum* is introduced, not as a *miserere*, as we are accustomed to find it under similar conditions in the Psalms, but rather with a kind of moral flourish of trumpets. This alternation of good and evil, preacher and sinner, by turns, no doubt suggested the attempt on the part of some of its early commentators to divide the poem into strophe and antistrophe, but it certainly lowers its moral tone. The hero retires from each successive trial a wiser rather than a better man, and comes back to the burden of his song, not so much with contrition as vexation of spirit, discontent rather than sorrow. The discovery of failure and the conviction of sin do not much disturb the placid scepticism of the Hebrew, and instead of repentance, or even regret, we have only dejection, disappointment, and satiety, with now and then a half-pitiful, half-sardonic grin at the utter insignificance of man's life.

Even when he reaches the sad conviction that the same event happens alike to fool and wise, and that death is the hopeless and final end of all, in which a man has no pre-eminence over a brute, he goes on making his admirable proverbs as if nothing had happened.   One cannot help suspecting that he knew all through that the experiment he was making was an ungodly one, and that he was attempting to juggle his conscience into the belief that wisdom gained by a knowledge of evil was a per-mitted path for princes.   Such experiences were probably looked upon by him in the light of contributions to what Goethe called the "pyramid of his existence."   One is hardly surprised to learn that the question of the canonicity of the book has afforded such endless matter for discussion, or that by tradition it was placed amongst those works that were not to be read by anyone under thirty.

As late as the Christian era, heretics, so-called, have attempted to reject it on account of its dangerous teaching.   Its many and peculiar excellences, however, are beyond question.   It is one of those books which will continue to stand upon the broader canonicity of its own merits.   Its keen insight into the ways and working of the world of man, and the incisive language in which its verdicts are embodied—although its direct relation to Christianity may be difficult to see—will always make it a favourite with men of the world.

Turning to the modern poem, what difference do we find there on the discovery of failure and sin !   The moment the truth flashed in upon the Soul in the *Palace of Art* that her life had been an acted lie—

> she fell,
> Like Herod when the shout was in his ears
> Struck through with pangs of Hell !

No time with her for moral reflection on the vanities or insignificances of life ; the new significance of it has struck her dumb ; and when at last speech comes, there is no breath left for a proverb—she cried aloud—

> I am on fire within :
> What is it that will take away my sin
> And save me lest I die ?

To compare language like this to the proverbial philosophy of the moral experimenter of Ecclesiastes, would be to compare the moral method of the jailor of Philippi with that of the Duc de la Rochefoucault.

Mr. Tennyson, then, utters no uncertain sound upon the subject of beauty for beauty's sake, when that theory involves the exclusion from art of all action or correspondence with the moral instinct, and sets its worshipper on some fancied intellectual height which cuts him off from the moral sympathy of his fellow-men.   His verdict is contained in a short prologue to the poem, which, like many prefaces, was perhaps an epilogue in the order of the poet's mind, and from which we quote four lines, containing, for us, the essence of the argument, and what the author of Ecclesiastes would call the conclusion of the whole matter.   The verdict is this—

> That Beauty, Good, and Knowledge are three sisters,
> That dote upon each other, friends to man,
> Living together under the same roof,
> And never can be sundered without tears.

Where the non-moral argument in poetical art is stretched, as it has been, so as to cover the immoral and justify positive uncleanness, we do not follow it.   A modern singer of no small power, and possessing a lyrical gift perhaps unsurpassed amongst living poets, has lent his eloquent advocacy to this extreme view, and has solemnly assured us that the " Lesbian music, which spends itself on the record of fleshly fever and amorous malady, has a value beyond price and beyond thought."   But the Nemesis that overtakes uncleanness in literature is inexorable. Nothing more quickly reduces the power of the artist, or takes him out of that atmosphere of repose in which alone the highest work is possible.   Life gets soured in the repeated and hopeless defence of the indefensible.   Thought becomes thin and querulous.   The finer balance is lost, and power is frittered away on distracting and profitless animosities, until at last the victim becomes incapable of artistic work that does not carry upon it the plain marks either of dotage or delirium.

Man's highest and purest culture reaches him through the gates of his imagination, and it is of consequence that only those things which are lovely and of good report should enter in.   The art which does not elevate, ennoble, and refine the thing it touches, but tends rather to degrade it, has no right of entrance there ; and when it forces a way in the disguise of poetry, it is at best a traitor to the household.   There is little chance, however, that the Lesbian school of poetry, which makes it a boast that it does not write for mothers or children, will ever gain a solid footing on English ground.   Most men are disinclined at the out-set to accept a poetical theory based upon productions that must be read by stealth.   The reverence for mothers and children, too, has still a pretty firm hold of the earth, and does not seem likely to be uprooted and replaced by anything else just yet.   An instinct rooted in human nature, and hallowed by its most sacred associations, and which—if their highest works may be called in as evidence—the greatest artists of the greatest art age delighted to honour, is not likely to be seriously affected by the Lesbian school of poetry or any other ; and in all probability mothers and little children will still continue to form no inconsiderable part of that "poetry of earth which never dies."   There is happily, too, a strong prejudice abroad, both amongst fathers and mothers, that when all is said and done, the poetical laurel does some-how look

> greener on the brows
> Of him that utters nothing base.

J. B. S.

A DIALOGUE ON POETIC MORALITY.

God sent a poet to reform His earth.
A. MARY F. ROBINSON.

"AND meanwhile, what have you written?" asked Baldwin, tickling the flies with his whip from off the horse's head, as they slowly ascended, in the autumn afternoon, the hill of Montetramito, which, with its ilex and myrtle-grown black rocks, and its crumbling mounds, where the bright green spruce pine clings to the washed-away scarlet sand, separates the green and fertile plain of Lucca from the marshes of the Pisan sea-shore. The two friends had met only an hour or so before at the foot of the Apennine pass, and would part in not much more again. "And what have you written?" repeated Baldwin.

"Nothing," answered the younger man, drearily, leaning back languidly in the rickety little carriage. "Nothing, or rather too much; I don't know which. Is trash too much or too little? Anyhow, there's none of it remaining. I thrust all my manuscripts into my stove at Dresden, and the chimney took fire in consequence. That's the tragic history of all my poetical labours of the last two years." And Cyril, lying back in the carriage with his arms folded beneath his head, smiled half sadly, half whimsically in the face of his friend.

But Baldwin did not laugh.

"Cyril," he answered, "do you remember on a birthday of yours—you were a tiny boy, brought up, like a girl, with curls and beautiful hands—one of your sisters dared you to throw your presents into the garden well, and you did it, before a number of admiring little girls: you felt quite a hero or a little saint, didn't you? And then my little hero was suddenly collared by a big boy fresh from school, who was his friend Baldwin, and who pulled his ears soundly and told him to respect people's presents a little more. Do you remember that? Well; I now see that, with all your growing up, and writing, and philosophizing and talking about duty and self-sacrifice, you are just the self-same womanish and uncontrolled *poseur*, the same romantic braggadoccio that you were at seven. I have no patience with you!" And Baldwin whisked the whip angrily at the flies.

"Mere conceit: effeminate heroics again!" he went on. "Oh no, we must do the very best! Be Shakespeare at least! Anything short of that would be derogatory to our kingly nature! No idea of selecting the good (because in whatever you do there must be talent), and trying to develop it; no idea of doing the best with what gifts you have! For you are not going to tell me that two years of your work was mere rubbish—contained nothing of value. But, in point of fact, you don't care sufficiently for your art to be satisfied to be the most you can; 'tis mere vanity with you."

Cyril became very red, but did not interrupt.

"I am sorry you think so ill of me," he said sadly, "and I daresay I have given you good cause. I daresay I am all the things you say— vain, and womanish, and insolently dissatisfied with myself, and idiotically heroic. But not in this case, I assure you. I will explain why I thought it right to do that. You see I know myself very well now. I know my dangers; I am not like you—I am easily swayed. Had those poems remained in existence, had I taken them to England, I am sure I should not have resisted the temptation of showing them to my old encouragers, of publishing them probably; and then, after the success of my other book, and all their grand prophecies, the critics would have had to praise up this one too; and I should have been drifted back again into being a poet. Now, as I wrote you several times— only of course you thought it all humbug and affectation—such a poet as I could be I am determined I will not be. It was an act of self-defence—defence of whatever of good there may be in me."

Baldwin groaned. "Defence of fiddlesticks! Defence of your vanity!"

"I don't think so," replied Cyril, "and I don't think you understand me at all in this instance. There was no vanity in this matter. You know that since, sometime I have been asking myself what moral right a man has to consume his life writing verses, when there is so much evil to remove, and every drop of thought or feeling we have is needed to make the great river which is to wash out this Augean stable of a world. I tried to put the doubt behind me, and to believe in Art for Art's own sake, and such bosh. But the doubt pricked me. And when suddenly my uncle left me all he had, I felt I must decide. As long as I was a mere penniless creature I might write poetry, because there seemed nothing else for me to do. But now it is different. This money and the power it gives are mine only as long as I live; after my death they may go to some blackguard: so, while I have them, I must give all my energies to doing with them all the good that I possibly can."

"In that case better give them over to people who know best what to do with them—societies or hospitals, or that sort of thing—and write your verses as before. For I don't think your thoughts will add much to the value of your money, Cyril. You've not a bit of practical head. Of course you may, if you choose, look on idly while other people are using your money. But I don't think it is specially worth doing."

Cyril sighed, hesitated, and then burst out rapidly—

"But it is the only thing I *can* do—do you understand? I can't write poetry any more. Perhaps that may be the only thing for which I was ever fit, but I am fit for it no longer. I cannot do what I have got to despise and detest. For I do despise and detest the sort of poetry which I should write—mere ornamental uselessness, so much tapestry work or inlaid upholstery. You believe in Art for Art's own sake—Goethianism—that sort of thing, I know. It is all very well for you, who have an active practical life with your Maremma drainings and mine diggings, a life in which art, beauty, so forth, have only their due share, as repose and refreshment. It was all very well in former days also, when the people for whom artists worked had a deal of struggle and misery, and required some pure pleasure to make life endurable; but now-a-days, and with the people for whom I should write, things are different. What is wanted nowadays is not art, but life. By whom, do you think, would all the beautiful useful things I could write, all the fiddle-faddle about trees and streams and statues and love and aspiration (fine aspiration, which never takes a practical shape!) be read? By wretched overworked creatures, into whose life they might bring a moment of sweetness, like a spray of apple blossom or a bunch of sweet-peas into some black garret? Nothing of the kind. They would be read by a lot of intellectual Sybarites, shutting themselves out, with their abominable artistic religion, from all crude real life; they would be merely so much more hothouse scents or exotic music (*con sordino*), to make them snooze their lives away. Of course it is something to be a poet like those of former days; something to be Tasso, and be read by that poor devil of a fever-stricken watchmaker whom we met down in the plain of Lucca; but to be a poet for the cultured world of to-day—oh, I would rather be a French cook, and invent indigestible dishes for epicures without any appetite remaining to them."

So saying, Cyril jumped out of the gig, and ran up the steep last ascent of the hill. He had persuaded himself of his moral rightness, and felt quite happy.

Suddenly the road made a sharp bend between the overhanging rocks, grown in all their fissures with dark ilex tufts and yellow broom and pale pink cyclamen; it turned, and widened into a flat grass-grown place, surrounded by cypresses on the top and ridge of the hill. Cyril ran to the edge and gave a cry of pleasure. Below was stretched a wide strip of Maremma swamp-land, marked green and brown—green where the grass was under water, brown where it was burnt into cinders by the sun; with here and there a patch of shining pond or canal; and at the extremity of this, distinguishable from the greyish amber sky only by its superior and intense luminousness, the sea—not blue nor green, but grey, silvery, steel-like, as a mirror in the full sunshine. Baldwin stopped the gig beneath the cypresses.

"Look there," he said, pointing with his whip to a dark greenish band, scarcely visible, which separated the land from the sea; "those are the pine woods of Viareggio. It was into their sand and weeds that the sea washed Shelley's body. Do you think we should be any the better off if he had taken to practical work which he could not do, and declared that poetry was a sort of French cookery?"

Baldwin tied the reins to the stem of a cypress, and threw himself down on the warm sere grass on the brow of the hill, overlooking the tangle of olive and vine and fig-tree of the slopes below.

"In Shelley's time," answered Cyril, leaning his head and shoulders against one of the cypresses, and looking up into its dark branches, compact in the centre, but delicate like feather and sparkling like jet where their extremities stood out against the pale blue sky—"in Shelley's time things were rather different from what they are now. There was a religion of progress to preach and be stoned for; there was a cause of liberty to fight for—there were Bourbons and Lord Eldons, and there was Greece and Spain and Italy. There was Italy still when Mrs. Browning wrote: had she looked out of Casa Guidi windows now, on to the humdrum, shoulder-shrugging, penny-haggling, professorial, municipal-councillorish Italy of to-day she could scarcely have felt in the vein. The heroic has been done—"

"There is Servia and Montenegro, and there are Nihilists and Democrats," answered Baldwin.

"I know—but we can't sing about barbarous ruffians, nor about half-besotten, half-knavish regicides; we can't be Democrats nowadays—at least I can't. Would you have a man sing parliamentary debates, or High Church squabbles, or disestablishment, or woman's rights, or anti-communism? sing the superb conquests of man over nature, &c., like your Italian friends, your steam-engine and mammoth poet Zanella? The wonders of science!—six or seven thousand dogs and cats being flayed, roasted, baked, disembowelled, artificially ulcerated, galvanized on ripped-up nerves, at Government expense, in all the laboratories of Christendom, in order to discover the soul-secreting apparatus, and how to cure old maids of liver complaint! Thank you. My Muse aspires not thereunto. What then? Progress? But it is assured. Why, man, we can't even sing of despair, like the good people of the year '20, since we all know that (bating a few myriads of sufferers and a few centuries of agony) all is going to come quite right, to be quite comfortable in this best of all possible worlds. What then remains, again? Look around you. There remains the poetry of beauty—oh yes, of pure beauty, to match the newest artistic chintzes; the poetry of artistic nirvana, of the blissful sleep of all manliness and energy, to the faint sound (heard through dreams) of paradisiac mysticism sung to golden lutes, or of imaginary amorous hysterics, or of symphonies in alliteration. And this when there is so much error, so much doubt, so much suffering, when all our forces are required to push away a corner of the load of evil still weighing on the world : this sort of thing I cannot take to." And Cyril fiercely plucked out a tuft of lilac-flowered thyme, and threw it into the precipice below, as if it had been the poetry of which he was speaking.

" Do you know, Baldwin," went on Cyril, " you have destroyed suc. cessively all my gods ; you have shown me that my Holy Grails, in whose service one after another I felt happy and peaceful to live, like another Parzival, are not the sacred life-giving cup brought down by angels, but mere ordinary vessels of brittle earth or stinking pewter, mere more or less useful, but by no means holy things ; ordinary pots and pans, barber's basins like Mambrino's helmet, or blue china teapots (worst degradation of all) like the Cimabue Browns'. I believed in the religion of Nature, and you showed me that Nature was sometimes good and sometimes bad ; that she produced the very foulness, physical and moral, which she herself chastised men for ; you showed me whole races destined inevitably to moral perversion, and then punished for it. So I gave up Nature. Then I took up the fashionable religion of Science, and you showed me that it was the religion of a sort of Moloch, since it accustomed us to acquiesce in all the evil which is part and parcel of Nature, since it made us passive investigators into wrong when we ought to be judges. After the positive, I threw myself into the mystic—into the religion of all manner of mysterious connections and redemptions ; you showed me that the connections did not exist, and that all attempted sanctification of things through mysticism was an abomination, since it could not alter evil, and taught us to think it might be good. O my poor Holy Grails ! Then I took up the religion of love ; and you pro- ceeded to expound to me that if love was restricted to a few worthy individuals, it meant neglect of the world at large ; and that if it meant love of the world at large, it meant love of a great many utterly unworthy and beastly people. You deprived me of humanitarianism, of positivism, of mysticism ; and then you did not even let me rest peaceably in pessimism, telling me that to say that all was for the worst was as unjust as to say that all was for the best. With a few of your curt sentences you showed me that all these religions of mine were mere idolatries, and that to rest in them for the sake of peace was to be utterly base. You left me nothing but a vague religion of duty, of good ; but you gave me no means of seeing where my duty lay, of distinguishing good from evil. You are a very useful rooter up of error, Baldwin ; but you leave one's soul as dry and barren and useless as sea shingle. You have taken away all the falsehoods from my life, but you have not replaced them by truths."

Baldwin listened quietly.

" Would you like to have the falsehoods back, Cyril ?" he asked. " Would you now like to be the holy knight, adoring and defending the pewter basin or blue china teapot of humanitarianism, or positivism, or mysticism, or æstheticism ? And what becomes of the only religion which I told you was the true one—the religion of good, of right ? Do you think it worthless now ?"

"I think it is the religion of the Unknown God. Where shall I find Him ?"

" In yourself, if you will look, Cyril."

Cyril was silent for a moment. " What is right ?" he said. " In the abstract—(oh, and it is so easy to find out in the abstract, compared to the concrete !)—in the abstract, right is to improve things in the world, to make it better for man and beast ; never to steal justice, and always to give mercy ; to do all we can which can increase happiness, and refrain from doing all which can diminish it. That is the only definition I can see. But how vague !—and who is to tell me what I am to do ? And when I see a faint glimmer of certainty, when I perceive what seems to me the right which I must do, who again interferes ? My friend Baldwin, who after preaching to me that the only true religion is the religion of diminishing evil and increasing good for the sake of so doing, coolly writes to me, in half a dozen letters, that the sole duty of the artist is to produce good art, and that good art is art which has no aim beyond its own perfection. Why, it is a return to my old æsthetic fetish worship, when I thought abstract ideas of beauty would set the world right, as Amphion's harp set the stones building themselves. . . . . Am I justified in saying that you merely upset my beliefs, without helping me to build up any ; yes, even when I am striving after that religion of right doing which you nominally call yours——— ?"

" You always rush to extremes, Cyril. If you would listen to, or read, my words without letting your mind whirl off while so doing——"

" I listen to you far too much, Baldwin," interrupted Cyril, who would not break the thread of his own ideas ; " and first I want to read you a sonnet."

Baldwin burst out laughing. " A sonnet ! one of those burnt at Dresden—or written in commemoration of your decision to write no more ?"

" It is not by me at all, so there's an end to your amusement. I want you to hear it because it embodies, and very nobly, what I have felt. I have never even seen the author, and know nothing about her except that she is a woman."

" A woman !" and Baldwin's tone was disagreeably expressive.

" I know ; you don't believe in women poets or women artists."

" Not much so far, excepting Sappho and Mrs. Browning, certainly. But, come, let's hear the sonnet. I do abominate women's verses, I confess; but there are such multitudes of poetesses that Nature may sometimes blunder in their production, and make one of them of the stuff intended for a poet."

"Well then, listen," and Cyril drew a notebook from his pocket, and read as follows :—

> " God sent a poet to reform His earth,
> But when he came and found it cold and poor,
> Harsh and unlovely, where each prosperous boor
> Held poets light for all their heavenly birth,
> He thought—Myself can make one better worth
> The living in than this—full of old love,
> Music and light and love, where saints adore,
> And angels, all within mine own soul's girth.
> But when at last he came to die, his soul
> Saw Earth (flying past to Heaven) with new love,
> And all the unused passion in him cried :
> ' O God, your Heaven I know and weary of,
> Give me this world to work in and make whole.'
> God spoke : ' Therein, fool, thou hast lived and died.' "

Cyril paused for a moment. "Do you understand, Baldwin, how that expresses my state of feeling ?" he then asked.

"I do," answered the other, "and I understand that both you and the author of the sonnet seem not to have understood in what manner God intended that poets should improve the earth. And here I return to my former remark, that when I said that the only true religion was the religion not of nature, nor of mankind, nor of science, nor of art, but the religion of good, and that the creation of perfect beauty is the highest aim of the artist, I was not contradicting myself, but merely stating two parts—a general and a particular—of the same proposition. I don't know what your definition of right living may be ; mine, the more I think over the subject, has come to be this:—the destruction of the greatest possible amount of evil and the creation of the greatest possible amount of good in the world. And this is possible only by the greatest amount of the best and most complete activity, and the greatest amount of the best activity is possible only when everything is seen in its right light, in order that everything may be used in its right place. I have alway preached to you that life must be activity ; but activity defeats itself if misapplied ; it becomes a mere Danaides' work of filling bottomless casks—pour and pour and pour in as much as you will, the cask will always be empty. Now, in this world there are two things to be done, and two distinct sets of people to do them : the one work is the destruction of evil, the other the creation of good. Mind, I say the *creation* of good, for I consider that to do good—that is to say, to act rightly—is not necessarily the same as to *create* good. Every one who does his allotted work is doing good; but the man who tends the sick, or defends the oppressed, or discovers new truths, is not creating good, but destroying evil—destroying evil in one of a hundred shapes, as sickness, or injustice, or falsehood. But he merely removes, he does not give ; he leaves men as poor or as rich as they would have been had not disease, or injustice, or error stolen away some of their life. The man who creates good is the one who not merely removes pain, but adds pleasure to our lives. Through him we are absolutely the richer. And this creator of good, as distinguished from destroyer of evil, is, above all other men, the artist. The scientific thinker may add pleasure to our lives, but in reality this truth of his is valuable, not for the pleasure it gives, but for the pain it removes. Science is warfare; we may consider it as a kind of sport, but in reality it is a hunting down of the most dangerous kind of wild animal—falsehood. A great many other things may give pleasure to our lives—all our healthy activities, upper or lower, must; but the lower ones are already fully exercised, and, if anything, require restraint; so that French cooks and erotic poets ought rather to be exterminated as productive of evil than encouraged as creative of good. And moral satisfaction and love give us the best pleasures of all; but these are pleasures which are not due to any special class created on purpose for their production. Oh, I don't say that any artist can give you the pleasure you have in knowing yourself to be acting rightly, or in sympathizing and receiving sympathy; but the artist is the instrument, the machine constructed to produce the only pleasures which can come near these. Every one of us can destroy evil and create pleasure, in a sort of incidental, amateurish way, within our own immediate circle; but as the men of thought and of action are the professional destroyers of evil, so the artists are the professional creators of good—they work not for those immediately around them, but for the world at large. So your artist is your typical professional creator of pleasure; he is fitted out, as other men are not, to do this work; he is made of infinitely finer stuff than other men, not as a whole man, but as an artist: he has much more delicate hearing, much keener sight, much defter fingers, much farther-reaching voice than other men; he is specially prepared to receive and transmit impressions which would be as wasted on other creatures, as the image in the camera on unprepared, ordinary paper. Now, what I maintain is simply this, that if, according to my definition, the object of destroying as much evil and creating as much good can be attained only by the greatest activity rightly applied, it is evident that a man endowed to be an artist—that is to say, a creator of good for the whole world—is simply failing in his duty by becoming a practical worker; that is to say, an amateur destroyer of evil. What shall we say of this artist? We shall say that in order to indulge in the moral luxury, the moral amusement, of removing an imperceptible amount of pain, he has defrauded the world of the immense and long-lasting pleasure placed in his charge to give; we shall say that, in order to feel himself a little virtuous, this man has simply acted like a cheat and a thief."

Baldwin had spoken rapidly and earnestly, with a sort of uniform or only gradually rising warmth, very different from the hesitating, fluctuating sort of passion of his companion. There was a short silence; Cyril was still seated under the tall, straight cypress, whose fallen fruit, like carved balls of wood, strewed the sere grass, and whose compact hairy trunk gave out a resinous scent, more precious and strange than that of the fir: he felt that he was momentarily crushed, but had a vague sense that there lurked somewhere reasons, and very potent ones, which prevented his friend being completely victorious; and Baldwin was patiently waiting for him to muster his ideas into order before continuing the discussion. A slight breeze from the over-clouded sea sent a shiver across the olives into the ravine below, turning their feathery tops into a silver ripple, as of a breaking wave; the last belated cicalas, invisible in the thick plumy branches of the cypresses, sawed slowly and languidly in the languid late afternoon; and from the farms hidden in the olive yards of the slope came faint sound of calling voices and barking dogs—just sound enough to make the stillness more complete. "All that is very true," said Cyril at last, "and yet—I don't know how to express it—I feel that there is still remaining to me all my reason for doubt and dissatisfaction. You say that artistic work is morally justifiable to the artist, since he is giving pleasure to others. From this point of view you are perfectly right. But what I feel is, that the pleasure which the artist thus gives is not morally valuable to those who enjoy it. Do you follow? I mean that the artist may be nobly and generously employed, and yet, by some fatal contradiction, the men and women who receive his gifts are merely selfishly gratified. He might not perhaps be better employed than in giving pleasure, but they might surely be better employed than in merely receiving it; and thus the selfishness of the enjoyment of the gift seems to diminish the moral value of giving it. When an artist gives to other men an hour of mere enjoyment, I don't know whether he ought to be quite proud or not."

Baldwin merely laughed. "It is droll to see what sort of hyper-moral scruples some people indulge in nowadays. So, your sense of the necessity of doing good is so keen that you actually feel wretched at the notion of your neighbours being simply happy, and no more, for an hour. You are not sure whether, by thus taking them away for a moment from the struggle with evil, letting them breathe and rest in the middle of the battle, you may not be making them sin and be sinning yourself! Why, my dear Cyril, if you condemn humanity to uninterrupted struggle with evil, you create evil instead of destroying it; if mankind could be persuaded to give up all of what you would call useless and selfish pleasure, it would very soon become so utterly worn out and disheartened as to be quite powerless to resist evil. If this is the system on which poets would reform the world, it is very fortunate that they don't think of it till they are flying to heaven."

"I can't make it out. You seem to be in the right, Baldwin, and yet I still seem to be justified in sticking to my ideas," said Cyril. "Do you see," he went on, "you have always preached to me that the highest aim of the artist is the perfection of his own work; you have always told me that art cannot be as much as it should if any extra-artistic purpose be given to it. And while listening to you I have felt persuaded that all this was perfectly true. But then, an hour later, I have met the same idea—the eternal phrase of art for art's own sake—in the mouths and the books of men I completely despised; men who seemed to lose sight of all the earnestness and duty of life, who had even what seemed to me very base ideas about art itself, and at all events debased it by associating it with effeminate, selfish, sensual mysticism. So that the idea of art for art's own sake, has come to have a disgusting meaning to me."

Baldwin had risen from the grass, and untied the horse from the trunk of the cypress.

"There is a storm gathering," he said, pointing to the grey masses of cloud, half-dissolved, which were gathering everywhere; "if we can get to one of the villages on the coast without being half-drowned while crossing the swamps, we shall be lucky. Get in, and we can discuss art for art's own sake, and anything else you please, on the way."

In a minute the gig was rattling down the hill, among the great blasted grey olives, and the vines with reddening foliage, and the farm-houses with their fig and orange trees, their great tawny pumpkins lying in heaps on the threshing-floor, and their autumn tapestry of strung-together maize hanging massy **and** golden from the eaves to the ground.

Baldwin resumed the subject where they had left it: "My own experience is, that the men who go in for art for art's own sake, do so mainly from a morbid shrinking from all the practical and moral objects which other folk are apt to set up as the aim of art; in reality they do not want art, nor the legitimate pleasures of art: they want the sterile pleasure of perceiving mere ingenuity and dexterity of handling; they hanker vaguely after imaginary sensuous stimulation, spiced with all manner of mystical rubbish, after some ineffable half-nauseous pleasure in strange mixtures of beauty and nastiness; they enjoy above all things dabbling and dipping alternately in virtue and vice, as in the steam and iced water of a Turkish bath. . . . . In short, these creatures want art not for its own sake, but for the sake of excitement which the respectabilities of society do not permit their obtaining, except in imaginative form. As to art, real art, they treat it much worse than the most determined utilitarian: the utilitarians turn art into a drudge; these æsthetic folk make her into a pander and a prostitute. My reason for restricting art to artistic aims, is simply my principle that if things are to be fully useful, they must be restricted to their real use, according to the idea of Goethe's Duke of Ferrara :—

' Nicht alles dienet uns auf gleicher Weise :
Wer viel gebrauchen will, gebrauche jedes
Nach seiner Art : so ist er wohl bedient.'

I want art in general not to meddle with the work of any of our other energies, for the same reason that I want each art in particular not to meddle with the work of any other art. Sculpture cannot do the same as painting, nor painting the same as music, nor music the same as poetry; and by attempting anything beyond its legitimate sphere, each sacrifices what it, and no other, can do. So also art in general has a definite function in our lives; and if it attempts to perform the work of philosophy, or practical benevolence, or science, or moralizing, or anything not itself, it will merely fail in that, and neglect what it could do."

" Oh yes," continued Baldwin after a minute, as they passed into the twilight of a wood of old olives, grey, silvery, mysterious, rising tier above tier on either side of the road, a faint flicker of yellow light between their feathery branches,—" oh yes, I don't doubt that were I a writer, and were I to expound my life-and-art philosophy to the world, the world would tax me with great narrowness! Things are always too narrow for people when they are kept in their place—kept within duty and reason. Of course there is an infinite grandeur in chaos—in a general wandering among the Unknown, in an universal straining and hankering after the Impossible; it is grand to see the arts writhing and shivering to atoms, like caged vipers, in their impotence to do what they want. Only it would be simpler to let those do it who can; and my system is the only one which can work. Despair is fine, and nirvana is fine; but successful and useful activity is a good deal finer. Wherefore I shall always say—' Each in his place and to his work'; and you, therefore, my dear Cyril, to yours, which is poetry."

" I think your philosophy is quite right, Baldwin, only—only somehow I can't get it to suit my moral condition," answered Cyril. " I do feel quite persuaded that sculptors must not try to be painters, nor musicians try to be poets, nor any of them try to be anything beyond what they are. It is all quite rational and right and moral, but still I am not satisfied about poetry. You see a poet is not quite in the same case as any other sort of artist. The musician, inasmuch as musician, knows only of notes, has power only over sounds; and the painter similarly as to form and colours; if either be something more, it is inasmuch as he is a mere man, not an artist. But a poet, inasmuch as he is a poet, knows, sees, feels a great many things which have a practical and moral meaning: just because he is a poet, he knows that there is something beyond poetry; he knows that there are in the world such things as justice and injustice, good and evil, purity and foulness: he knows all this, which the mere musician, the mere painter, does not—and knowing it, perceiving, feeling, understanding it, with more intensity than other men, is he to sweep it all out of his sight? is he to say to justice and injustice, good and evil, purity and foulness, ' I know you, but my work lies not with you?' Is he to do this? Oh, Baldwin, if he be a man and an honest one, he surely cannot: he cannot set aside these ideas and devote himself to his art for its own sake."

Baldwin listened attentively to the passionate words of his companion, and twitching at a sprig of olive as a branch swept across their heads in their rapid movement through the wood, he answered quietly :

" He will not set aside the ideas of justice and injustice, of good and evil, of purity and impurity, Cyril. He will make use of them even as the musician uses his sounds, or the painter uses his colours. Such ideas are at least one-half of the poet's material, of the stuff out of which he creates—the half which belongs exclusively to him, which he does not share with any other artist ; the half which gives poetry a character in many respects different from that of painting or music. I have always laughed at the Ruskinian idea of morality or immorality in architecture, or painting, or music, and said that their morality and immorality were beauty and ugliness. I have done so because moral ideas don't enter into the arts of line, or colour, or sound, but only into the subjects to which their visible and audible works are (usually arbitrarily) attached. But with poetry the case is different ; and if the poet has got a keener perception (or ought to have) of right and wrong than other men, it is because a sense of moral right and wrong is required in his art, as a sense of colour is required in painting. I have said ' art for art's own sake,' but I should have been more precise in saying ' art for beauty's sake.' Now, in poetry, one half of beauty and ugliness is purely ethical, and if the poet who deals with this half, the half which comprises human emotion and action, has no sense of right and wrong, he will fail as signally as some very dexterous draughtsman who should have no sense of physical beauty and ugliness, and spend his time making wonderful drawings of all manner of diseased growths. Of course you may be a poet who does *not* deal with the human element, who writes only about trees and rivers, and in this case your notions of right and wrong are as unnecessary to you as an artist as they would be to a landscape painter. You use them in your life, but not in your art. But as soon as a poet deals with human beings and their feelings and doings, he must have a correct sense of what in such feelings and doings is right and what is wrong. And if he have not this sense, he will not be in the same case as the painter or musician who is deficient in the sense of pictorial or musical right and wrong. The wise folk who have examined into our visual and acoustic nerves seem to think, what to me seems extremely probable, that the impression of æsthetic repulsion which we get from badly combined lines or colours or sounds, is a sort of admonition that such combinations are more or less destructive to our nerves of sight or of hearing ; so, similarly, the quite abstract aversion which we feel to an immoral effect in literature, seems to me to be the admonition (while we are still Platonically viewing the matter, and have not yet come personally into contact with it) that our moral sense—what I may call our nerves of right and wrong—is being disintegrated by this purely intellectual contact with evil. And, moreover, our nerves of right and wrong are somehow much less well protected than our visual or acoustic nerves : they seem to be more on the surface of our nature, and they are much more easily injured : it takes a good deal of bad painting and bad music to deprave a man's eye or ear, and more than we can well conceive to make him blind or deaf; but it takes less than we think of base literature to injure a man's moral perception, to make him see and hear moral things completely wrong. You see, the good, simple, physical senses look after themselves—are in a way isolated; but the moral sense is a very complex matter, and interfered with in every possible manner by the reason, the imagination, the bodily senses—so that injuring it through any of these is extremely easy. And the people whom bad painting or bad music had made half-blind or half-deaf would be less dangerous to themselves and to others than those who had been made half-immoral by poetry."

"But at that rate," said Cyril, "we should never be permitted to write except about moral action ; if the morally right is the same for the poet as the pictorially right for the painter. Baldwin, I think, I fear that all these are mere extemporized arguments for the purpose of making me satisfied with poetry, which I never shall be again, I feel persuaded."

"Not at all," answered Baldwin. "I mean that the moral right or wrong of poetry is not exactly what you mean. If we were bound never to write except about good people, there would be an end to half the literature of the world."

"That is exactly what I saw, and what showed me the hollowness of your theory, Baldwin."

"Because you mistook my theory. There could be no human action or interest if literature were to avoid all representation of evil : no more tragedy at any rate, and no more novels. But you must remember that the impression given by a play or a poem is not the same as that given by a picture or statue. The picture or statue is all we see ; if it be ugly, the impression is ugly. But in a work of literature we see not only the actors and their actions, but the manner in which they are regarded by the author ; and in this manner of regarding them lies the morality or immorality. You may have as many villains as you please, and the impression may still be moral; and you may have as many saints as you please, and the impression may still be immoral."

The road had suddenly emerged out of the olive woods covering the lowest hill ranges, and in a few minutes they were driving through a perfect desert. The road, a narrow white ribbon, stretched across a great flat tract of country : field after field of Indian corn, stripped of its leaves and looking like regiments of spindles, and of yellowish green grass, half under water ; on either side a ditch full of water-lilies, widening into sedge-fringed canals, in which the hay of coarse long grass was stacked in boats for sheer want of dry soil, or expanding into shallow patches of water scarcely covering the grass and reflecting, against the green of the meadow below, the boldly peaked marble mountains of Carrara, bare, intensely ribbed, veined, and the blue sky and rainy black clouds. Green, brown fields, tufts of reed, hill and sky reflected in the inundated grass—nothing more, not a house, or shed, or tree for miles around—in front only the stormy horizon where it touched the sea.

" This is beautiful," cried Cyril ; " I should like to come and live here. It is much lovelier and more peaceful than all the woods and valleys in creation."

Baldwin laughed. " It might be a good beginning for final nirvana," he said; " these are the sea-swamps, the *padule,* where the serene Republic of Lucca sent its political offenders. You were locked up in a tower, the door bricked up, with food enough to last till your keeper came back once a fortnight ; the malaria did the rest."

" It is like some of our modern literature," answered Cyril, with a shudder; " Maremma poetry—we have that sort of thing, too."

" By the way," went on Baldwin ; " I don't think we quite came to the end of our discussion about what a poet ought to do with his moral instincts, if he has any."

" I know," answered Cyril, " and I have meanwhile returned to my previous conclusion that, now that all great singable strifes are at an end, poetry cannot satisfy the moral cravings of a man."

" You think so ? " asked Baldwin, looking rather contemptuously at his companion. " You think so ? Well, therein lies your mistake. I think, on the contrary, that poetry requires more moral sense and energy than most men can or will give to it. Do you know what a poet has to deal with, at least a poet who does not confine himself to mere description of inanimate things ? He has to deal with the passions and actions of mankind—that is to say, with a hundred problems of right and wrong. Of course, men who have deliberately made up their mind on any question of right or wrong, are not shaken by anything in a book; nay, they probably scarcely remark it. But if you remember that in the inner life of every man there must be moments of doubt and hesitation, there must be problems vaguely knocking about, you will understand that for every man there is the danger that in such a moment of doubt his eyes may fall upon a sentence in a book—a sentence to other men trivial—which will settle that doubt for ever, rightly or wrongly. There are few of us so strong that the moment does not come when we would ask, as a good Catholic does of a confessor, what is right and what is wrong, and take the answer which is one of the two that have been struggling within himself, as definitive ; and to us, who do not go to confession, a book, any book casually taken up, may be this terribly powerful spiritual director. People used to exaggerate the influence of books, because they imagined that they could alter already settled opinions; nowadays I deliberately think that they underrate this influence, because they forget how it may settle fluctuating opinion. The power of literature is in this way very great."

"It has been, formerly—yes, I grant it," answered Cyril; "but it is no longer what it was; in our cut-and-dry days it is necessarily smaller."

"On the contrary, much greater now than perhaps almost at any other time. These are not cut-and-dry days, Cyril, but the very reverse; you must not let yourself be deceived by a certain superficial regularity, by railway journeys and newspapers, and a general civilization of hand-books and classes. In reality there is more room for indirect moral perversion or enervation in our days than there has been for a good while; for the upsetting of ideas, the infiltration of effete or foreign modes of thought and feeling, is much greater in this quiet nineteenth century than it was, for instance, in the Renaissance or the eighteenth century. With all their scepticism, the people of those days had a great fund of tradition about everything; they were floating about a good deal, I admit, but they were fully persuaded of the existence of certain very solid moral rocks, to which they might always tie their boat when it grew over-rough; rocks of religion or deistic mysticism, or of social *convenances*, which we have now discovered to be by no means granite, but some sort of sea deposit, of hardened sand, whose formation we understand and no longer rely upon. The most arrant sceptics of the past had always one great safety, that they were in a groove; they saw, understood, sympathized with only their own civilization. What they thought right they had never seen questioned—they never imagined any one could regard as wrong; hence the most liberal thinkers of former days always strike us, with their blindness to all but their own civilization, as such Philistines. Things have changed since then; they began to change already, as soon as men began to look at other civilizations; and the suggestive first-fruit of this early ethnographic eclecticism may be seen in Diderot's very beastly books: he found that South Sea Islanders had not, on the subject of incest, the same views as Christian folk; whereupon it struck him that those views might be due to prejudice. It was not the development of the natural sciences, but rather of the historic and ethnographic, which upset people's ideas; it was the discovery of how our institutions, moral and social (hitherto regarded as come straight from heaven), had formed themselves, and how they were subject to variation. Speaking of poets, look at a pure man, I believe a very pure man, Shelley, if you want to understand the necessity of poets having a greater solidity of moral judgment than the mere Jones and Browns who stick to their shop, and are not troubled with theories. Add to the influence of scientific doubt, of the doubt created by books on the origin of ideas and institutions (showing of what moonshine they are often made), the utterly confusing effect of our modern literary eclecticism, our comprehension and sympathy with so many and hostile states of civilization, our jumbling together of antique and mediæval, of barbarous and over-ripe and effete civilizations, our intellectual and moral absorption of incompatible past stages of thought and feeling, with the follies and vices inherent in each ;—sum up all this, and you will see that, with our science and our culture, our self-swamping with other folk's ideas, we are infinitely less morally steady than the good sceptics of the days of Voltaire, who always believed in the supremacy of their own century, their own country, their own institutions, their own conventionalities ; who were in danger only from their own follies and uncertainties, while we are in danger from the follies and uncertainties of every past century from which we have inherited. And you will see, if you look, that that sceptical eighteenth century, which was very much more credulous and conservative than ours, was very little divided and upset in its ideas ; certain things were universally admitted, and certain others universally rejected ; in that day there was always the master of the ceremonies—Propriety. He knew exactly what could be permitted : in the dining-room, drunkards yelling filthy jests ; in the drawing-room, polite gentlemen stalking or tripping through their minuets. It is different nowadays.

Cyril nodded. "I understand what you mean," he said, " but I don't see the application yet."

" Well," answered Baldwin, " I will show you one instance of the application. Have you ever thought over the question of—how shall I call it ?—the ethics of the indecent ?"

Cyril stared. " No, it never struck me that there were any. I don't write indecent things, it doesn't amuse me, I feel not the smallest desire to do so ; if anything, I feel rather sick at such things ; that is all."

" That is all for you, but not all for other people. You don't feel attracted to write on some subjects ; well, other people not only feel attracted, but imagine that it is their duty even if they are not."

" They are pigs ; I have nothing to do with them." And Cyril looked as if he had settled the matter.

" But they are not pigs ; at least, not all of them ; or they are not entirely pigs, by any means," insisted Baldwin. " You are not going to tell me that a man like Walt Whitman is a mere pig. Still, there are things of his which to you are simply piggish. Either Whitman is a beast or you are a prude."

" That depends upon difference of nature," said Cyril quickly, vaguely desirous of putting an end to a discussion which brought forward an anomaly.

" That is merely repeating what I said,".replied Baldwin. " But in reality I think it is *not* a difference of nature. I think it depends on a difference of reasoned opinion—in short, upon a sophistication of ideas on the part of Whitman. I think it depends, in him and the really pure men who uphold his abominations, upon a simple logical misconception ; a confusion of the fact that certain phenomena have been inevitable, with the supposition that those same certain phenomena are therefore desirable—a confusion between what has been, and could not help being, and what may be and ought to be. It is the attempt to solve a moral problem by an historical test."

" I don't understand in the least, Baldwin."

" Why, thus : our modern familiarity with the intellectual work of all times and races has made people perceive that in past days indecency was always part and parcel of literature, and that to try to weed it out is to completely alter the character of at least a good half of the literature of the past. Hence, some of us moderns, shaken as we are in all our conventional ideas, have argued that this so-called indecency is a legitimate portion of all literature, and that the sooner it is re-introduced into that of the present the better, if our literature is to be really vital and honest. Now, these people do not perceive that the literature of the past contained indecencies, merely because, being infinitely less self-conscious, less responsible than now, the literature of the past contained fragments of every portion of the civilization which produced it. For besides what I might call absolute indecency, in the sense of pruriency, the literature of the past is full of filth pure and simple, like some Eastern town ; a sure proof this, that if certain subjects which we taboo were not tabooed then, it was not from any conscious notion of their legitimacy, but from a general habit of making literature, like the street of some Oriental or mediæval town, the scene of every sort of human action, important or trifling, noble or vile ; regarding it as the place for which the finest works were painted or carved, and into which all the slops were emptied. Hence, in our wanderings through the literature of the past, our feet are for ever stumbling into pools of filth, while our eyes are seeking for the splendid traceries, the gorgeous colours above ; our stomachs are turned by stenches even while we are peeping in at some wonderful rose garden or fruit orchard. I think you might almost count on your fingers the books, up to the year 1650, in which you are sure of encountering no beastliness— choice gardens or bowers of the soul, or sacred chapels, kept carefully tidy and pure—viz., Milton, Spenser, the *Vita Nuova*, Petrarch, Tasso—things you see mainly sacred or spiritualistic—sort of churches where only devotion of some sort goes on ; but if we go out to where there is real life, life complete and thoughtless—Shakspeare, Rabelais, Molière, Ariosto, Cervantes, Aristophanes, Horace—the evil odours meet us again at every step. Well, nowadays this has all been misunderstood. People have imagined that an inevitable nuisance of the past ought also to be a deliberately chosen nuisance of the present : a line of argument which appears to me to be similar to that of a man, who, because the people of Lisbon used, in the days of my grandfather, to practise a very primitive system of sewerage, should recommend that the inhabitants of modern London should habitually empty their slops on to the heads of passers-by. I am crude ? Well, it is by calling nasty things by beautiful names that we are able to endure their existence. I think that people who should attempt such literary revivals ought to be fined, as the more practical revivers of old traditions certainly would be.'

Cyril paused a moment. " I think that these sort of offenders, like Whitman, are not evil-doers, but merely snobs : they offend not good morals, but good taste."

" That's just such an artistic and well-bred distinction as I should expect from you," answered Baldwin, rather contemptuously. " I wonder what that word ' good taste ' signifies to your mind ? Everything and nothing. They are offenders against good taste, you say. Well, let us see how. If I hang a bright green curtain close to a bright blue wall-paper, you will say it is bad taste; if I set Gray's " Elegy " to one of Strauss's waltzes, that is bad taste also; and if I display all my grand furniture and plate (supposing I had it) to my poor neighbour, whose chintz chair is all torn, and who breakfasts out of a cup without a handle, that also is bad taste. Each for a good reason, and a different one; in each case I am inflicting an injury, too slight and inadvertent to be sin, against something : the green curtain and blue paper combination pains your eye; the Gray's " Elegy" and Strauss's waltz combination annoys your common sense ; the contrast between my riches and your poverty inflicts a wound on your feelings : you see that all sins against taste are merely a hurting of something in somebody. So that, if writing in-decent poems is an offence against good taste, it means that it also inflicts some such injury. That injury is simply, as the world has vaguely felt all along, an injury to your neighbour's morals."

" But," put in Cyril, " such a man as Whitman has no immoral intention, nor is he immoral in the sense that Ariosto and Byron are sometimes immoral. The man is not a libertine, but a realist. He wishes people to live clean lives ; all he says is, that everything which is legitimate, innocent, necessary in life is also legitimate and innocent in literature. And although I should rather select other subjects to write about, and would rather he did so likewise, I cannot deny that there is logic in saying that there can be no harm in speaking of that which there is no harm in doing."

" Yes," said Baldwin, " that is just the argument of such men. And the answer is simply that there are things which are intended to be done and *not* to be spoken about. What you call logic is no logic at all, but a mere appeal to ignorance. It so happens that the case is exactly reversed—that there are a great many things which there is not the smallest immorality in speaking about, and which it would be the most glaring immorality to do. No one shrinks from talking about murder or treachery ; nay, even in the very domain of sexual relations there need not be the smallest immorality, nothing at all perverting, in a play which, like the whole Orestes trilogy, or *Othello*, or *Faust*, turns upon adultery or seduction; no one also has the slightest instinct of immorality in talking about the most fearful wholesale massacres. Yet the world at large, ever since it has had any ideas of good and evil, has had an instinct of immorality in talking of that without which not one of us would exist, that which society sanctions and the church blesses. And this exactly because this is as natural as murder—of which we speak freely—is the contrary. For exactly because certain instincts are so essential and indispensable, Nature has made them so powerful and excitable; there is no fear of their being too dormant, but there is fear of their being too active, and the consequences of their excess are so hideously dangerous to Nature itself, so destructive of all the higher powers, of all the institutions of humanity; the over-activity of the impulses to which we owe our birth is so ruinous of all that for which we are born, social, domestic, and intellectual good, nay, to physical existence itself, that Nature even has found it necessary to restrain them by a counter-instinct—purity, chastity—such as has not been given us to counteract the other physical instincts, as that of eating, which can at most injure an individual glutton, but not affect the general social order. Hence, the slightest artificial stimulus is a danger to mankind, and the giving thereof a crime; for the experience of all times tells us, what modern psychology is beginning to explain—viz., the strange connection between the imagination and the senses, the hitherto mysterious power of awakening physical desires, of almost reproducing sensation, possessed by the mind, even as the mention of dainty food is said to make the mouth water, and the description of a surgical operation to make the nerves wince. So that the old intuition, now called conventionalism, which connects indecency with immorality, is entirely justified. Crime may be spoken of just because it is crime, and our nature recoils therefrom; indeed, I think that nowadays, when our distructive instinct (except in small boys and professors of physiology) is becoming effete, there has ceased to be any very demoralizing influence in talking even of horrors. But the immorality of indecency is quite unlike the immorality of—how shall I distinguish?—of ordinary immorality. In the case of the latter the mischief lies in the sophistication of the reason or the perversion of the sympathies; as, for instance, in Machiavel's 'Prince,' or any of a hundred French novels. In the former case, that of indecency, the immorality lies in the risk of inducing a mood which may lead to excess— that is, to evil. And, as a rule, I think this inducing of a mood is the commonest source of moral danger, whether the mood be a sensual or a destructive one."

" I don't see how you make that out; although I now understand what at first seemed to me mere inexplicable instincts—founded on nothing."

" Some things are inexplicable perhaps, but be sure instincts are not founded on nothing. Misconceptions are mere false conceptions; but a good half of what people call social convention is based upon a perfectly correct conception, only mankind has forgotten what that conception was. Well, I should place the various sorts of demoralization of which literature is capable in this order: No. 1, and least dangerous, sophistication of judgment; No. 2, and more dangerous, perversion of sympathy; No. 3, and most dangerous, inducement of questionable frame of mind. And I place them thus because it seems to me that this is the order of facility, and consequently universality; I mean that fewest people can be found who depend sufficiently on their deliberate ideas, and most effort is required to sophisticate them; whereas least effort is required, and most effect produced, in the matter of inducing a mood; the perversion of sympathy is half-way. Of course, if we could imagine (as once or twice has actually been the case) that the moral ideas of a whole people were sophisticated, that would be the worst, because the least remediable; but, in the first place, people act but little from ideas, or few persons do, and it is difficult to alter people's ideas; and, in the second place, the sophistication of conscience of single individuals is kept in check by the steadfastness of the mass of mankind, and consequently, as in such men as Diderot, reduced to mere talk, without corresponding action. But a mood is easily induced without the reason even perceiving it, and the more necessary the mood is to nature, the more easily it will be aroused—the more unnatural an evil, the less danger of it; the more an evil is the mere excess of the necessary, the more danger there is of it."

"It is curious how you marshal ideas into their right places," said Cyril. "There remains one thing to be said about the ethics of impropriety. The people who go in for writing upon subjects which thirty years ago would have distinctly been forbidden, do not all of them write as Whitman does: they are not all what I should call openly beastly. They do their best, on the contrary, to spiritualize the merely animal."

"That is just the most mischievous thing they could possibly do," interrupted Baldwin. "I know the sort of poets you mean. They are the folk who say that things are pure or impure, holy or foul, according as we view them. They are not the brutal, straightforward, naturalistic school; they are the mystico-sensual. Of the two, they are infinitely the worse. For the straightforward naturalistic pigs generally turn your stomach before they have had a chance of doing you any harm; but these persuade themselves and you that, while you are just gloating over sensual images, you are improving your soul. They call brute desire passion, and love lust, and prostitution marriage, and the body the soul. Oh! I know them; they are the worst pests we have in literature."

"But I don't think they are intentionally immoral, Baldwin."

"Do you think any writer ever was intentionally immoral, Cyril?"

"Well, I mean that these men really intend doing good. They think that if only some subjects be treated seriously, without any sniggering or grimacing, there ceases to be any harm in them. They say that they wish to rescue from out of the mire where prudery has thrown it, that which is clean in itself; they wish to show that the whole of Nature is holy; they wish to purify by sanctifying."

Baldwin listened with a smile of contempt. "Of course such words seem very fine," he said ; " but a thing is either holy or is not holy : all the incense of poetry and all the hocus-pocus words of mysticism cannot alter its nature by a tittle. And woe betide us if we once think that any such ceremony of sanctification can take place ; woe betide us if we disguise the foul as the innocent, or the merely indifferent as the holy ! There is in Nature a great deal which is foul : in that which men are pleased to call unnatural, because Nature herself chastises it after having produced it : there is in Nature an infinite amount of abominable necessity and abominable possibility, which we have reason and conscience to separate from that which within Nature itself is innocent or holy. Mind, I say innocent *or* holy ; for innocence and holiness are very different things. All our appetites, within due limits, are innocent, but they are not therefore holy ; and that is just what mystico-sensual poetry fails to perceive, and in giving innocence the rank of holiness it makes it sinful. Do you know what is the really holy ? It is that of which the world possesses too little, and can never possess too much : it is justice, charity, heroism, self-command, truthfulness, lovingness, beauty, genius ;—these things are holy. Place them, if you will, on a poetic altar, that all men may see them, and know them, and love them, and seek after them lifelong without ever wearying. But do not enshrine in poetic splendours the merely innocent ; that which bestows no merit on its possessor, that which we share with every scoundrel and every animal, that which is so universal that it must for ever be kept in check, and which, unless thus checked by that in ourselves which is truly holy, will degrade us lower than beasts. For in so doing—in thus attempting to glorify that in which there is nothing glorious—you make men think that self-indulgence is sanctity, you let them consume their lives in mere acquiescence with their lusts and laziness, while all around is raging the great battle between good and evil. Worst of all, in giving them this worship of a mystic Ashtaroth or Belial, you hide from them the knowledge of the true God, of the really and exclusively holy, of good, truth, beauty, to know and receive which into our soul we must struggle lifelong with the world and with ourselves—yes, struggle for the sake of the really holy with that mere innocence which is for ever threatening to become guilt."

Baldwin paused ; then resumed after a moment : " I believe that mankind as it exists, with whatever noble qualities it possesses, has been gradually evolved out of a very inferior sort of mankind or brutekind, and will, I hope, be evolved into a very superior sort of mankind. And I believe, as science teaches us, that this has been so far effected, and will be further effected henceforward, by an increased activity of those nobler portions of us which have been developed as it were by their own activity ; I believe, in short, that we can improve only by becoming more and more different from the original brutes that we were. I have said this to explain to you my feelings towards a young poet of

my acquaintance, who is very sincerely smitten with the desire to improve
mankind; and has deliberately determined to devote a very fine talent
to the glorification of what he calls pure passion, pure in the sense that
it can be studied in its greatest purity from the brute creation."

Cyril made a grimace of disgust.

"No, indeed," continued Baldwin, "that poet is not one of the
æsthetic-sensual lot you seem to think. He is pure, conscientious,
philanthropic; but he is eminently unreasoning. He is painfully
impressed by the want of seriousness and holiness with which mankind
regards marriage, and his ambition is to set mankind right on this
subject, even as another young poet-philanthropist tried to improve
family relations in his ' Laon and Cythna.' Now, if you were required
to use your poetical talents in order to raise the general view of
marriage, in order to show the sanctity of the love of a man and a
woman, how would you proceed?"

"I have often thought about that," answered Cyril; "but it has been
done over and over again, and I think with most deliberate solemnity
and beauty by Schiller and Goethe in the ' Song of the Bell' and in
' Hermann and Dorothea.' Well, I think that poetry can do good work
in this line only if the poet see where the real holiness of such love lies;
in the love not of the male and the female, but of the man and the
woman. For there is nowhere, I think, greater room for moral beauty
and dignity than in the choosing by a man of the one creature from whom
only death can separate him; of the one friend, not of a phase of his
life, but of his whole life; of the one soul which will grow and mature
always by the side of his, and having blossomed and borne fruit of
good, will gently fade and droop together with his. But this is not the
most holy part of the choice, for he is choosing also the mother of his
children, the woman who is to give half their nature, half their training,
to what children must mean to every honest man—the one chance he
possesses of living as he would have wished to have lived, of being what
he should wish to have been; his one chance of redeeming his errors, of
fulfilling his hopes, of realizing in a measure his own ideals. And to
me such a choice, and love in the sense of such a choice, become not
merely coldly deliberate, but passionately instinctive, are holy with the
holiness that, as you say, is the only real one; holy in all it implies of
recognized beauty and goodness, of trust and hope, of all the excellence
of which it is at least the supposed forerunner; and its holiness is that
upon which all other holiness, all the truthfulness and justice and
beauty and goodness of mankind, depends. This is how I view the
sanctity of the love between man and woman; how all the greatest
poets, from Homer to Schiller, and from Schiller to Mrs. Browning,
have viewed it; and it is the only possible view that I can conceive."

Baldwin nodded. "That is how I also see the question. But my
young poet is not satisfied with this: he wishes to make men believe in
the holiness of that which is no more holy, and far oftener tends to be

unholy, than eating or drinking; and in order to make mankind adore, he lavishes all his artistic powers on the construction of an æsthetical temple wherein to enshrine, on the preparation of poetic incense with which to surround, this species of holiness, carefully separated from any extraneous holiness, such as family affection, intellectual appreciation, moral sympathy; left in its complete unmixed simplicity of brute appetite and physical longing and physical rapture; and the temple which he constructs out of all that is beautiful in the world is a harlot's chamber; and the incense which he cunningly distils out of all the sights and sounds of Nature are filthy narcotics, which leave the moral eyes dim, and the moral nerves tremulous, and the moral muscle unstrung. In his desire to moralize he demoralizes; in his desire to sanctify one item of life, he casts aside, he overlooks, forgets, all that which in life is already possessed of holiness. Thus my young poet, in wishing to improve mankind, to raise it, undoes for the time being that weary work of the hundreds of centuries which have slowly changed lust into love, the male and female into a man and a woman, the life of the body into the life of the soul; poetry, one of the highest human products, has, as it were, undone the work of evolution; poetry, which is essentially a thing of the self-conscient intellect, has taken us back to the time when creatures with two legs and no tail could not speak, but only whine and yell and sob,—a mode of converse, by the way, more than sufficient for the intercourse of what he is pleased to call the typical Bride and Bridegroom."

They had got out of the strange expanse of brown and green swamp, and after traversing a strip of meagre redeemed land, with stunted trees and yellowish vines, had reached the long narrow line of pine woods which met the beach. They passed slowly through the midst of the woods, brushing the rain-drops off the short bright green pines, their wheels creaking over the slippery fallen needles embedded in the sand; while the setting sun fell in hazy yellow beams through the brushwood, making the crisp tree-tufts sparkle like green spun-glass, and their scaly trunks flush rosy; and the stormy sea roared on the sands close by.

" I think your young poet ought to be birched," remarked Cyril; " and if anything could add to my aversion, not for poetry, but for the poetic profession, this would, which you have just told me. You see how right I was in saying that I would have more moral satisfaction in being a French cook than in being a poet."

" By no means," answered Baldwin. " In the first place, my young poet ought not to be birched; he ought to be made to reflect, to ask himself seriously and simply, in plain prose, what ideal of life he has been setting before his readers. He ought to be shown that a poet, inasmuch as he is the artist whose material is human feeling and action, is not as free an artist as the mere painter or sculptor or composer; he ought to be made to understand that nowadays, when the old rules of conduct, religious and social, are for ever being questioned, every man

who writes of human conduct is required, is bound, to have sound ideas
on the subject : that because nowadays, for better or for worse, poetry
is no longer the irresponsible, uncontrolled, helter-skelter performance
of former times, but a very self-conscious, wide-awake, deliberate matter,
it can do both much more harm and much more good than it could do
before."

They were slowly driving along the beach, among the stunted pine
shoots and the rough grass and yellow bindweed half buried in the sand,
and the heaps of sea-blackened branches, and bits of wood and uncouth
floating rubbish which the waves had deposited, with a sort of ironical
regularity, in a neat band upon the shore ; down here on the coast the
storm had already broken, and the last thin rain was still falling, dimp-
ling the grey sand. The sun was just going to emerge from amidst the
thick blue-black storm-clouds, to descend into a clear space, like
molten amber, above the black, white-crested roaring sea ; it descended
slowly, an immense pale luminous globe, gilding the borders of the
piled-up clouds above it, gilding the sheen of the waves and the wet
sand of the shore ; and as it descended, the clouds gathered above it
into a vast canopy, a tawny orange diadem or reef of peaked vapours
encircling the liquid topaz in which the sun moved ; tawnier became
this garland, larger the free sky, redder the black storm masses above ;
till at last the reddening rays of the sun enlarged and divided into
immense beams of rosy light, cutting away the dark and leaving un-
covered a rent of purest blue. At last the yellow globe touched the
black line of the horizon, gilding the waters ; then sank behind it and
disappeared. The wreath of vapours glowed golden, the pall of heaped-
up storm-clouds flushed purple, and bright yellow veinings, like fila-
ments of gold, streaked the pale amber where the sun had disappeared.
The amber grew orange, the tawny purple, the purple a lurid red, as of
masses of flame-lit smoke ; all around, the sky blackened, until at last
there remained only one pile of livid purple clouds hanging over a
streak of yellow sky, and gradually dying away into black, with but
here and there a death-like rosy patch, mirrored deadlier red in the
wet sand of the beach. The two friends remained silent, like men
listening to the last bars, rolling out in broad succession of massy,
gradually resolving chords, of some great requiem mass—silent even for
a while after all was over. Then Cyril asked, pointing to a row of
houses glimmering white along the dark lines of coast, below the great
marble crags of Carrara, rising dim in the twilight—

" Is that the place where my friends will pick me up ?"

" Yes," answered Baldwin, "that's the place. You will be picked up
there, if you choose."

" I must, you know." And Cyril looked astonished, as if for the first
time it struck him that there might be no *must* in the matter. " I
must—at least I suppose I ought to—go back to England with them."

" You know that best," replied Baldwin, shortly. " But before we
get there I want to finish what we were saying about the moral value

of poetry, if you don't mind. I gave you the instance of Whitman and the mystico-sensual school merely because it is one of the most evident; but it is only one of many I could give you of the truth of what I said, that if a poet, inasmuch as he is a poet, has—what the painter, or sculptor, or musician, inasmuch as they are such, have not—a keener sense of moral right and wrong than other men, it is because his art requires it. Consider what it is deliberately to treat of human character and emotion and action; consider what a strange chaos, an often inextricable confusion of clean and foul, of healthy and pestilent, you get among, in penetrating into the life of the human soul; consider that the poet must pick his way through all this, amidst very loathsome dangers which he often cannot foresee; and not alone, but carrying in his moral arms the soul of his reader—of each of his thousands of readers—a soul which, if he see not clearly his way, if he miss his footing, or tread in the soft, sinking soil (soft with filthy bogs), may be bespattered and soiled, perhaps for ever—may be sucked into the swamp pool or poisoned by the swamp air; and that he must thus carry, not one soul, but thousands of souls, unknown to him—souls in many cases weak, sometimes already predisposed to some loathsome moral malady, and which, by a certain amount of contact with what to the poet himself might be innocuous, may be condemned to life-long disease. I do not think that the poet's object is to moralize mankind; but I think that the materials with which he must work are such that, while practising his art, he may unconsciously do more mischief than all the professed moralists in Christendom can consciously do good. The poet is the artist, remember, who deliberately chooses as material for his art the feelings and actions of man; he is the artist who plays his melodies, not on catgut strings or metal stops, but upon human passions; and whose playing touches not a mere mechanism of fibres and membranes like the ear, but the human soul, which in its turn feels and acts; he is the artist who, if he blunders, does not merely fatigue a nerve or paralyze for a moment a physical sense, but injures the whole texture of our sympathies and deafens our conscience. And I ask you, does such an artist, playing on such an instrument, not require moral feeling far stronger and keener than that of any other man, who, if he mistake evil for good, injures only himself and the few around him? You have been doubting, Cyril, whether poetry is sufficient work for a man who feels the difference between good and evil; you might more worthily doubt whether any man knows good from evil with instinct sure enough to suffice him as a poet. You thought poetry morally below you: are you certain that you are morally up to its level?"

Cyril looked vaguely about him: at the black sea breaking on the twilit sands, at the dark outline of pinewood against the pale sky, at the distant village lights—vaguely, and as if he saw nothing of it all. The damp sea-breeze blew in their faces, the waves moaned sullenly, the pines creaked in the wind; the moon, hidden behind clouds, slowly silvered into light their looser, outer folds, then emerged, spreading a broad white sheen on the sands and the water.

"Are you still too good for poetry?" asked Baldwin; "or—has poetry become too good for you?"

"I don't know," answered Cyril, in the tone of a man before whose mental eyes things are taking a new shape. "I don't know—perhaps."

VERNON LEE.

ÆSTHETIC POETRY:

DANTE GABRIEL ROSSETTI.

IN December last, the President of the Royal Academy delivered an interesting lecture to the students of the Academy, in which he addressed himself to the question, What is the proper end and aim of Art, and in what relation does Art stand to Morals and Religion? In answering these questions, Sir Frederick Leighton set himself vigorously to combat the didactic theory of Art—that which maintains that the first duty of all artistic production is to inculcate a moral lesson or a Christian truth, and that the worth and dignity of a work of art is to be measured by the degree in which it performs this duty. Yet, while entirely repudiating this view, he strongly maintained that the moral force or weakness of the artist's character would reveal itself in his work—that the *ethos* of the artist tinges every work of his hand, and moulds it silently, but with the certainty of fate.

With regard to the didactic theory of Art, he showed very clearly that it did not hold in the case of Spanish painting, especially in that of its greatest master, Velasquez; neither did it square with all the facts regarding either the Italian or the Flemish school of painters. But in arguing the whole question, Sir Frederick Leighton narrows the issue to the direct inculcation of some moral truth, and by so narrowing it has no difficulty in overthrowing the didactic theory. For the purpose of inculcating moral precepts, teaching definite truths to the understanding, the simplest spoken homily, if sincere in spirit and lofty in tone, is more effective, as he tells us, than all the creations of all the most pious painters and sculptors, from Giotto to Michael Angelo. This is true. But it is one thing to disprove the didactic theory—quite another to invalidate the moral significance of art. There are many avenues by which the soul can be reached, stirred, and elevated besides the understanding. Do not indirect and quite inarticulate influences often melt into us more powerfully, do us more good, than the clearest, most forcible appeals to the intellect? Who has not felt if, after listening to the best spoken discourse, he has wandered forth alone into the fields, that there was something in the silent face of Nature which sank more into him, more soothed and reconciled his whole inner being, than any words of man? The same is the effect of the finest music, though no one could express in language what it conveys.

Sir Frederick's own view is that the function of Art is to speak to the emotional sense—to awaken the emotions throughout their whole range up to the highest in the scale. If so, he would, no doubt, allow that the highest emotions are those which are born in the highest regions of man's nature, which connect themselves with the greatest ideas of the intellect, the deepest ethical truths, and the noblest spiritual faiths. Art, if it is high art, cannot stop with the exhibition of colour, or form, or sound, however exquisite. These sensible media it employs, not for their own sakes, not to produce merely pleasant sensations, or to convey clear-cut conceptions, but the artist so touches these that through them he may set vibrating fine spiritual echoes, and prolong them endlessly 'through the sounding corridors of the soul.' And in proportion to the mass, the variety, the complexity, and the elevation of these emotional echoes which he awakens, is the dignity and excellence of his work. This is a very different thing from saying that Art must directly inculcate ethical truth. The mind which is in the didactic attitude, which sets instruction of any kind before it as its purpose, is by that very act cut off from the true sources of inspiration. By all means let art be free to range over the whole expanse of Nature and of human life, and to express, as far as it can, *all* the emotions which these awaken in men. We must not limit its province to the ethical or the religious region—much less must it impose on itself a didactic aim, or confine itself to this. Indeed, the idea of imposing on it any aim beyond that of expressing the delight it has in the objects it loves, and the thrilling emotions which spring from the contemplation of these, is alien to the very nature of poetic or artistic inspiration. It is the characteristic of genius that it is unconscious alike of its methods and its aims. It cannot tell how it produces its results, or why. It is something more than a merely natural power, this which we call inspiration. It proceeds by a path we cannot trace, works in a way inexplicable by the understanding. This is so; therefore let genius work as it lists, untrammelled by didactic purpose. And yet, if we can suppose two men of equal genius, of equal artistic power, one of whom dwells by instinct and habitually on the higher moral and spiritual levels, while the other is conversant only with things earthly and mundane—can any one doubt whose hand of the two would mould the finest creations? Genius, whether pictorial or poetic, achieves the noblest results, when it is led, not of set purpose, but by unconscious sympathy, to live in the highest regions of being, and to express the emotions which are native there. And the art of such a one will be, in the truest sense, moral and religious, though it never dreamt of inculcating anything. It will be so in the best way, that is, by instinct and unawares. So, then, we conclude, that while it is true that art is the vehicle to express *all* emotions, it is at the same time true, as has been said, that 'it has always found itself at its best when its instinct has led it to express the higher religious and moral emotions.' As a friend lately well expressed it, 'Our sense of beauty is so allied and akin to our moral sense that whenever *mere* beauty is aimed at in a work of art, we feel a deficiency. The beauty is ten times as lovely if there is a soul of moral purity seen through it by the eye that seeks the inward beyond the outward.' It comes, then, to this, that if we would reach the highest beauty, we must forget beauty and ascend beyond it. One instance more of a well-known law of ethics, that it is not always true " that to get a thing you must aim at it. There are some things which can only be gained by renouncing them." And the highest beauty is one of these. Or to adapt words from Cardinal Newman: 'The highest beauty and moral goodness are inseparably connected, but they who cultivate the goodness for the beauty's sake are artistic, not moral, and will never reach the beauty, because they can never really love the goodness.' For the apprehension of the highest beauty, there is needed not merely a fine sensibility and a cultivated taste. The sense of it does not come merely from the intellect, or from the æsthetic faculties, as they are called—something more is needed, even a heart, pure and right.

Mr. Ruskin has told us that if the sense of beauty begins with pleasure at the sight of an object, it does not stop there, but includes joy in and love of the object, then a perception of kindness in a superior intelligence—finally thankfulness and reverence towards that intelligence. To borrow words of the lately-departed Dr. John Brown, 'All beauty of thought, passion, affection, form, sound, colour, and touch, whatever stirs our mortal and immortal frame, not only comes from, but is centred in God, in His unspeakable perfections. This we believe to be not only morally, but, in its widest sense, philosophically true, as the white light rays itself out into the prismatic colours, making our world what it is—as if all that we behold were the spectrum of the unseen Eternal.'

This, the moral theory of beauty, Mr. Ruskin has unfolded throughout his works, and especially in the second volume of his 'Modern Painters;' and he deserves our gratitude for the strong witness he has borne to the doctrine, that all sublimity and all beauty is an adumbration of the unseen character of the Eternal One.

I am well aware that there are other theories of Beauty than this, which measure it by quite other standards. There are those who hold that Beauty should be sought for its only sake, quite apart from any moral meaning it may be alleged to have. They proclaim loudly what is called the moral indifference of Art, and that to try to connect it with moral ideas or spiritual reality is to narrow and sectarianize it. They deprecate entirely in their idea of Beauty any transcendental reference, and say that it has certain occult qualities of its own, which may be known and appreciated only by a refined nature and a cultivated taste. Such persons, one soon perceives, mean primarily by Beauty, sensuous beauty, grace of form and outline, richness or delicacy of colour. Painting, as the highest of those arts which deal with sensuous beauty, they take especially under their wing, and not painting only but all the arts which minister to the adornment of outward life. But such a pursuit of Beauty, genuine though it may be at first, because it has no root in the deeper, more universal side of human nature, swiftly degenerates into a mere fashion. What is new, rare, or antique, or out of the way, gets valued because it is so, not from any spiritual meaning or intrinsic worth it possesses. A surprise, a new sensation comes to be the one thing desired. Hence comes affectation, and artificial, as opposed to natural and healthy, sentiment. Mannerism, modishness, exclusiveness, the spirit of coterie, are the accompaniments of this mental habit, which craves for beauty, divorced from truth of life, without any really human and ethical root.

What this spirit is producing in the region of Art it is not for me to say —many of my readers know this for themselves. Do not its results meet us at this moment in all our galleries ? It more concerns me here to note how a kindred spirit reveals itself in our poetry and criticism. In these, too, there has been for some time apparent a tendency—perhaps born of the artistic tendency, certainly closely allied to it—to make much of sensuous beauty, apart from any inward meaning it conveys. We have a poetry in which beauty of form and outline, gracefulness of attitude, richness of colouring are attempted to be portrayed in the most elaborate, sometimes affected, diction, and with the most high-wrought and luscious melody of words. In the pursuit of this sensuous beauty men have gone back, as they supposed, to the Greeks, whom they fancied to be the great masters of it. But they have forgot that in the best and greatest of the Greeks—in Homer, Pindar, Æschylus, and Sophocles— colour and grace of attitude are rigorously subordinated to the exhibition of great human qualities, or of moral truths. Indeed this worship of sensuous beauty, for its own sake, is not the growth of a vigorous age, strong in manhood, but is the mark of a late and decadent civilization. To appeal to the imagination chiefly through the eye, divorced from high thought, tends very surely to degrade the imagination and to lower the soul. The boundary line between the sensuous and the sensual may not in theory be easily defined, but in practice it is easily crossed, and there are not a few instances in modern literature in which it has been crossed very decidedly. If when the eye discerns beauty, the beauty does not become the index of something higher than itself, if to the soul it is not a step by which it springs upward, very speedily it becomes a snare to lure it downward. The senses of sight and smell, gorgeous colour, and richness of perfume, these minister most readily to sensuous delight, and these are the sensations which sensuous poets most affect. The ear is a more spiritual sense, and so we find the spiritual poet making sound, not sight, ally itself to the finest beauty.

> . . . ' She shall lean her ear
> In many a secret place,
> Where rivulets dance their wayward round,
> And beauty born of murmuring sound
> Shall pass into her face.'

But the poet who is chief favourite with all the modern beauty-worshippers is Keats. In his earliest poem, ' Endymion,' there is little else but a revelling in sensuous delights; but, before his brief life closed, he had begun, as Mr. Arnold has lately well shown, to feel his way upward, to apprehend a severer, more spiritual beauty. Had he lived he would probably have risen from sensuous impressions to the moral meanings of things. As it is, the works he has left exemplify the first part of his famous line ' Beauty is Truth.' The second part, ' Truth is Beauty,' he had not yet attained to show. Keats has had many followers among recent poets, but they have mostly seized on his lower phase and exaggerated it, and have not risen to the height towards which he himself was latterly tending. If Keats is their prime favourite, there are others of our poets whom this school have, in an exclusive sort of way, appropriated as their own possession. Shelley, Coleridge, and Blake are high in the admiration of the abler men of the school, while their second-rate followers affect to despise Wordsworth as a tiresome proser, Byron and Scott as shocking Philistines; even Shakspeare they would taboo, if they dared. Such are the vagaries of some, but it would not be fair to credit the stronger heads of any school with the absurdities of its weaker brethren.

One of the latest and greatest of the school of Keats, if we may venture so to tabulate him, has but recently passed from amongst us. This sudden and lamented loss has probably made many look into the poetry of Dante Rossetti, who before had been strangers to it. There exists, I believe, a circle of intimate friends, who have long known his powers, and admired the fruits of them, and the views of these admirers are to be met with, at times, in contemporary literature. It may perhaps be worth while for one of the uninitiated to give the impressions this poetry has made on him, coming to it recently with a fresh eye and an unprejudiced mind.

Mr. Rossetti's poetry is contained in two volumes, one published in 1870, the other in 1881. To begin with the first volume, you cannot open it without being struck by the marked individuality of manner, and also by the signs of poetic power which meet you on the surface. When you have entered a little farther into the precinct, you become aware that you have passed into an atmosphere which is strange, and certainly not bracing—the fragrances that cross your path are those of musk and incense rather than of heather or mountain thyme. It takes an effort to get into the mood which shall appreciate this poetry—you require to get acclimatized to the atmosphere that surrounds you. And, as you proceed, you meet with things which make you doubt whether you would much desire the acclimatization. At the same time you are aware of the presence of genuine poetic power, even though you may be far from admiring some of its manifestations.

It would have been much more grateful to me, if of a man of genius, both a painter and a poet, so lately departed, one who by his works and character attracted to himself many admiring friends, I could have spoken only that to which I could expect them to respond. But as Dante Rossetti's poetry has probably already influenced the tone of our poetic literature, and may still further influence it, I feel bound to say what seems to me the truth regarding it, while I at the same time endeavour to do so with consideration for the feelings of others. It must be remembered, all that is here said now is the impression made on the writer by the study of these two volumes, which contain all he knows of their author.

I shall first notice what seem to be the weaknesses and faults of this poetry, then pass to the more pleasing duty of trying to show some of the beauties it contains.

As to the manner or style, the first thing that strikes one is that many of these poems take, as has been said, a great deal of reading. And even when you have given this, and gone over them many times, there are not a few, for which one would not like to be made responsible to furnish the explanation. I know not whether these particular poems will ever be thought worthy of the attention of those societies which meet nowadays for the purpose of illustrating poets who are obscure, but are believed to be oracular. There are various kinds of obscurity in poets, and various causes for it. In the case of Rossetti it would seem to come from too much after-thought and over-elaboration. If the poems had been struck off under the first access of emotion, and been fully pervaded by it, one cannot think that we should ever have had many of the subtleties and out-of-the-way thoughts and over-driven metaphors, which darken the meaning of many of the poems. But if after the emotion has cooled down, ingenuity, no longer supported by the inspiring heat, went to work upon the subject, then would appear just such far-fetched thoughts, passing into conceits, such linked subtleties long drawn out, as we here too often meet with. Hence it is that few of the poems arrest you and carry you along with a spontaneous interest. They require rather a set purpose to study them, an effort to get at their meaning. The art, in short, is stronger than the inspiration. No doubt when you have pierced the cloud of redundant imagery and the encrustation of elaborate diction, you do find that the poet has ' rescued some inward and delicate moods ' from the border-land of ' inarticulate meditation.' Yet even for these evanescent moods, which can only be hinted at, not expressed, the pure style, which is simple, transparent, unloaded with ornament, is, we believe, the fittest vehicle.

We regret to see so much of whatever poetic feeling is amongst us, overlaid nowadays with this artificial diction, this cloying ornamentation. Whenever a stronger, manlier inspiration shall come and breathe on poetic hearts, it will, we believe, scatter before it the unhealthy sentiment which now prevails, the overwrought imagery, dainty sweet, which is its accompaniment.

As to the substance of the first volume, the tone of sentiment which certainly predominates is the erotic. So we call it, for it has little in common with the pure and noble devotion which the best of our older poets have immortalized. This amatory or erotic sentiment is unpleasant in the poem called ' Eden Bower, or Lilith ;' it is revolting in the ballad of ' Troy Town.' But the taint of fleshliness which runs through too many of the other poems reaches its climax in some of the twenty-eight sonnets, entitled, ' The House of Life.' These sonnets not only express, but brood over thoughts and imaginations which should not be expressed, or even dwelt on in secret thought. Not all the subtle association or elaboration of words, nor dainty imagery in which they are dressed, can hide or remove the intrinsic earthliness that lies at the heart of them. One cannot imagine why—one cannot but regret that—they should even have been composed by a man of so much genius. What would become of our English homes if an atmosphere like this were allowed to pervade them ? It was in no such atmosphere that the noble manhood and pure womanhood of the England of past time were reared. From such an atmosphere minds used to the noble love that Scott depicted, imaginations fed by the portraits of Desdemona, Portia, Cordelia, instinctively turn away. Rossetti is said to have formed himself mainly on Shakspeare. If so, it is the young and voluptuous Shakspeare of Lucrece and Venus and Adonis which these sonnets recall, not the Shakspeare of the great tragedies, or of Cymbeline and The Tempest.

It has been said that these sonnets contain an allegory. If so, the allegory is well concealed—the unpleasant images are plain and patent. Again, we know the nonsense that is talked about poetry of this kind being the natural recoil from asceticism and Puritanism. We are aware of the talk of certain cliques about the soul being not more than the body. But poetry like these first twenty-eight sonnets, instead of making the body sacred, degrades both body and soul alike. It has taken eighteen centuries of Christianity to make practical among men the true idea of purity. And are we now, under the guidance of a morbid and unmanly art and poetry, to return to that from which the best Pagan poets, Virgil, Æschylus, Sophocles, would have recoiled ? The laws of modesty have been well ascertained, and are as truly natural, as deeply rooted in the best part of human nature, as is the law of truthfulness. It is an evil sign that there exists in so many quarters a disposition to rebel against these laws. Unless the moral plague can be stayed, and the higher literature kept clear of it, it is a sure prelude of moral decadence in a nation.   Having said so much against a tendency, which we deeply regret to have found in a poet in many ways so gifted, we gladly turn to the more pleasing aspects of his genius.

The poems fall into three forms :—1st, Ballads, archaic in form, quaint in thought and expression, all more or less touched with glamourie and trenching on the supernatural.   2nd, Sonnets, some such as I have spoken of, others expressing natural feeling and sentiment in fitting language.   3rd, Songs and lyrics, of very diverse quality, some of very condensed passion, others fantastic and subtilized till they have become remote from reality.

The first poem of the first volume, the ballad of 'The Blessed Damozel,' said to have been written when the author was only nine-teen, contains at the outset an example of the author's strength and his weakness—the power of bodying forth strange and out-of-the-way situa-tions, and the tendency to do this in a guise and diction so quaint that it verges towards the affected.   The whole attitude and scenery of this poem are eminently pictorial, and the subject must, we should think, have engaged the author's pencil as well as his pen.

There is one other ballad in this volume—that of 'Sister Helen'—which, after 'The Blessed Damozel,' stands quite alone in its power and pathos.   The story is that of a girl who has been forsaken, and then, in order to revenge herself on her false lover, calls in the aid of an old superstitious rite, and melts the waxen image of him for three days before a slow fire.   She does this knowing that the result of it must be the loss of his soul and of her own.   The tale is told, in a strikingly suggestive way, in a dialogue between Sister Helen and her little brother, who sees the charm working on the body and soul of the lost man, and reports what he sees to his sister.   She replies in few, terse words, in which weird phantasy, rooted revenge, and terrible pathos meet :—

> 'Ah! what white thing at the door has crossed
> .Sister Helen?
> Ah! what is this that sighs in the frost?
> A soul that's lost as mine is lost,
> Little Brother!'

In another mood is the touching poem, named 'The Portrait,' on the picture of a lady who is loved and gone :—

> 'This is her picture as she was;
> It seems a thing to wonder on,
> As though mine image in the glass
> Should tarry when myself am gone.
> I gaze until she seems to stir,—
> Until mine eyes almost aver
> That now, even now, the sweet lips part
> To breathe the words of the sweet heart—
> And yet the earth is over her.

*   *   *   *

'Yes, this, of all love's perfect prize,
    Remains; save what in mournful guise
    Takes counsel with my soul alone,—
    Save what is secret and unknown;
    Below the earth, above the skies.'

'A Last Confession' is a narrative in blank verse, very powerfully told. It is the story of a Lombard refugee in hiding from the Austrians, who reared a little orphan-girl—her parents had died in the famine, or fled elsewhere—up to womanhood; he grew to love her and she him. But in time she became estranged—loved some one else—and he stabbed her, and years after he confesses the whole story to a priest. The poem is more direct, full of strength, and less artificial than most of these poems. One could wish that the author had oftener wrought after this fashion. The subject is no doubt a painful one, as are most of the subjects in the first volume. For it seems to be characteristic of the school to which Rosetti belongs that calm joy seems gone from their world. Either the brief rapture of the most high-strung passionate emotion, or the long languor, exhaustion, despair, which come as the sequel. But the painfulness of the 'Last Confession' is relieved by touches of rare beauty, as—

'Life all past
    Is like the sky when the sun sets in it,
    Clearest when farthest off.'

Or this description of the heroine—

'As the branch sustains
    The flower of the year's pride, her high neck bore
    Her face, made wonderful by night and day.
                Her great eyes,
    That sometimes turned half dizzily beneath
    The passionate lids, as faint, when she would speak,
    Had also in them hidden springs of mirth,
    Which, under the dark lashes evermore
    Shook to her laugh, as when a bird flies low
    Between the water and the willow-leaves,
    And the shade quivers till he wins the light.'

These seem to be the best poems in the first volume, with the exception of one called " Jenny," on which I do not care to dwell now, and some of the sonnets and songs to be noticed presently.

The volume published last year contains three new ballads, two of them long and very elaborate, and all more powerful than the ballads in the earlier volume, except perhaps 'Sister Helen.' 'Rose Mary,' the first, is the most studied and elaborately wrought of all the author's ballads. The story is laid in the mediæval time, and turns upon the magic power which resides in a Beryl stone. Rose Mary's lover, Sir James Heronhaye, is about to ride to a shrift at Holycleugh, and her mother has heard that an ambush lies in wait for him by the way. But there are two roads, either of which he can take. And as the Beryl stone has the power to show to a pure maiden whatever she would wish to see, her mother calls Rose Mary to look into the magic stone, and see by which of the two ways it would be safe for Sir James to go. But Rose Mary is not now what her mother takes her to be. By her sin the good angel has been driven out of the Beryl stone, and evil spirits have taken possession of it. She reads the stone amiss. By her advice the knight takes the wrong road, is waylaid by his mortal foe, the Warden of Holycleugh, and foully slain. The mother discovers her daughter's secret, tells her that her lover has perished on the road by which she bade him ride. The knight's body is borne back to the castle, but under his mail the mother finds love-tokens, which prove that he had plighted his troth to the Warden's sister of Holycleugh, and that when he went to the shrift he was going to meet her. Rose Mary, when she knew the truth, lay long in a swoon, but when she awoke, she ascends to a secret chapel, where the Beryl stone lay on the altar. With her father's sword she cleaves the stone in twain, and so drives out the evil spirits which had come into it and deceived her, and brings back the good angel who had been driven forth by her sin. As she dies, the angel receives her, assures her of forgiveness, and of a place in Blessed Mary's Rose-bower. The ballad is an excellent example of the elaborately wrought and highly orna-mented kind. It has many merits; but one it has not—simplicity and directness, which we take to be the chief characteristics of the real old ballad. Each feeling Rose Mary has, each situation, is over-described; and the pathos of the whole is smothered beneath a cloud of imagery. For instance, at the beginning of the third part, when Rose Mary wakes from her swoon, her sensations are described in nine stanzas, in which heaven and earth, and air and sea, and the nether world, are ransacked to supply illustrative images. This kind of thing, however well done, palls at last, and by the multitude of details destroys the total impres-sion. The Beryl songs interlaid in the ballad do not help forward the action at all, and seem forced and artificial. Indeed, it would be im-proved by their omission. The same may be said of most of the refrains with which the other ballads are interlaid.

If we would see how a ballad of elaborate workmanship looks by the side of one in the simple direct style, we may compare ' Rose Mary ' with Scott's ' Eve of St. John.' Both deal with tales of lawless love, both draw largely on the supernatural element: which of the two is the most effective—which leaves the deepest total impression? I, for my part, cannot doubt. For real impressiveness the pure style rather than the elaborately ornamental is surely the most suitable and effective. It is refreshing to pass from ballads whose scene is laid in an unreal and fantastic world, to two which deal with actual historic events. The first of these is entitled ' The White Ship,' in which the Butcher of Rouen, the only survivor, relates the shipwreck and the loss of the son of Henry I. of England. The narrative is told with as much force and directness as could be desired, without circumlocution, and without those strained similes and images which disfigure ' Rose Mary ' and others. But best of all Rossetti's ballads, and probably his greatest poem, is ' The King's Tragedy,' founded on the murder of James I. of Scotland at midnight in the Charter-house of Perth. Here we see how much the poet's genius is enhanced, when he chooses a subject not from fantasy or dreamland, but from historic events, 'supplementing,' as has been said, ' his mortal weakness by the strength of an immortal subject.' James I. was the greatest king, except Robert Bruce, who ever reigned over Scotland. A poet, a musician, a warrior, a statesman, he was the most accomplished sovereign, perhaps the most accomplished man, in Europe in his day. On his return to Scotland from his English captivity, he had set himself to reduce his distracted kingdom to law and order, and to curb the proud and turbulent barons who had for long lorded the land uncontrolled. He and his queen, Lady Jane Beaufort, whom he had wooed during his captivity at Windsor—his first sight of whom he had described so gracefully in his poem of ' The King's Quhair'—they two had journeyed to Perth to pass their Christmastide in the monastery of the Black Friars there. During their stay, some nobles in the wild north, who had suffered by the king's vigorous rule, conspired together to take his life as he lived securely in the Charter-house. The tale is told by Catharine Douglas, the noble lady who thrust her arm into the empty staple in the attempt to bar out the king's murderers, and received from that the name of ' Kate Barlass.'

She tells how on their journey towards Perth, when they reached ' the Scottish Sea,' that is the Forth, and were about to cross it, at the Queen's Ferry, an ancient beldame appeared, and warned the king not to cross the water, for if he did, he would meet his doom. The king heard her, and replied, that if it had come—

> ' The day when I must die,
> That day by water or fire or air,
> My feet shall fall in the destined snare,
> Wherever my road may lie.'

He crossed the Forth, and rode on with his queen by his side to Perth. Nearly two months were passed in the Charter house, when on a stormy night in February, while the wind is loud without, the king and queen within revert to the day they first met at Windsor, and to the scene described in the ' King's Quhair.'

As they are in the midst of their loving talk,

> ' Beneath the window arose
> A wild voice suddenly :
>
> ' And the King reared straight, but the Queen fell back,
> As for bitter dule to dree,
> And all of us knew the woman's voice,
> Who spoke by the Scottish Sea.
>
> ' " O King," she cried, " in an evil hour
> They drove me from thy gate :
> And yet my voice must rise to thine ears
> ·But, alas ! it comes too late !

> ' " Last night at midwatch, by Aberdour,
>   When the moon was dead in the skies,
> O King, in a dead light of thine own
>   I saw thy shape arise.
>
> ' " And in full season, as erst I said,
>   The doom had gained its growth ;
> And the shroud had risen above thy neck,
>   And covered thine eyes and mouth.
>
> ' " And no moon woke, but the pale dawn broke,
>   And still thy soul stood there ;
> And I thought its silence cried to my soul
>   As the first rays crowned its hair.
>
> ' " Since then I journeyed fast and fain,
>   In very despite of Fate,
> Lest Hope might still be found in God's will,
>   But they drove me from thy gate.
>
> ' " For every man on God's ground, O King,
>   His death grows up from his birth,
> In a shadow-plant perpetually ;
> And thine towers high, a black yew tree,
>   O'er the Charter-house of Perth." ' '

The voice had hardly ceased when the king and the queen and their attendants heard ' the tread of the coming doom,' and the clang of the arms of Graham and his three hundred men.   Then follows the well-known scene, Catharine Douglas rushing to the door and thrusting her arm through the staples, to supply the place of the bars which had been removed—

> " Like iron felt my arm, as through
>   The staple I made it pass—
> Alack ! it was flesh and bone—no more !
> 'Twas Catharine Douglas sprang to the door,
>   But I fell back Kate Barlass."

The king, raising a plank, and plunging down into a vault—the room thronged with armed men—who, not finding him they sought, depart to search elsewhere, then return, guided by one who knew the chamber well to the hiding-place, in which, after the naked unarmed king had fought manfully, he is overpowered and slain.

All this is told directly and simply, but at somewhat too great length, and in too circumstantial detail.   The whole ballad would have been more effective, if more condensed.   But with whatever defects, it stands a noble rendering of a famous historic scene—a poem more likely to survive, I believe, than any other of the long ones in these two volumes.

Mr. Rossetti was evidently devoted to the Sonnet as the form in which he could best express his favourite thoughts and sentiments. This was natural in one who had begun his poetic career by translating many sonnets from the early Italian poets, and of whom we are told that his earliest and latest model, in all condensed utterance, whether of sonnet or song, was Shakspeare.   For the obscurity of meaning which meets us in most of Rossetti's sonnets, the example of Shakspeare might perhaps be pleaded.   But it should be remembered that those sonnets of Shakspeare, which take the heart and dwell on the memory, are not obscure, but transparent, and that we know not how much of the difficulty of those which we find obscure, may be due to our ignorance of the subject he was writing of, and to the euphuistic contagion of his time, which even Shakspeare did not escape.   We regret to see that Mr. Rossetti's second volume should have reproduced from the first volume most of the unpleasant sonnets we have already complained of.   Some of the most offensive indeed have been omitted, but some in the same vein have been added.   The more these are veiled in obscurity the better.   But there are other sonnets that breathe a different sentiment, whose meaning we would gladly have been able to read plainly.   Yet in most of these the sense is so buried beneath a load of artificial diction and laboured metaphor, that we believe few but special admirers will take the trouble to unearth their meaning.   Wordsworth had thoughts to convey at least as deep as any Rossetti was a master of; yet we doubt if even Wordsworth's obscurest sonnet is not transparent compared with even the average of Rossetti's.   We all know the maxim of Horace—

' Si vis me flere, dolendum est
Primum ipsi tibi ;'

and Shelley's saying of poets, that—

' They learn in suffering what they teach in song.'

Here is a way into which Rossetti beats out that truth in his sonnet called ' The Song Throe' :—

' By thine own tears thy song must tears beget,
O singer ! magic mirror hast thou none
Except thy manifest heart ; and save thine own
Anguish and ardour, else no amulet.
Cisterned in Pride, verse is the feathery jet
Of soulless air-flung fountains ; nay, more dry
Than the Dead Sea for throats that thirst and sigh,
That song o'er which no singer's lids grew wet.

' The Song-God—He the Sun-God—is no slave
Of thine : thy Hunter he, who for thy soul
Fledges his shaft : to no august control
Of thy skill'd hand his quivered store he gave :
But if thy lips' loud cry leaps to his smart,
The inspired recoil shall pierce thy brother's heart.'

This is the kind of thing we complain of—this elaborate un-simplicity.

As one reads them one is reminded of a passage from Milton's Second Book on ' Church Government' (quoted by the late Dr. John Brown, when speaking of Bailey's 'Festus') :—'The wily subtleties and influxes of man's thoughts from within' (which is the haunt and main region of Rossetti) 'may be painted out, and described with a solid and treatable smoothness.' Would that all our inward and analyzing poets nowadays would paint out and describe after this manner!

Here are a few samples of his work, where it leaves the shade, and comes out into open day. In a sonnet entitled 'The Hill Summit,' having told how he has loitered on the hillside all day, and only reached the top at sunset, he concludes thus—

> ' And now that I have climbed and won this height,
>   I must tread downward through the sloping shade,
> And travel the bewildered tracks till night.
>   Yet for this hour I still may here be stayed,
>   And see the gold air and the silver fade,
> And the last bird fly into the last light.'

There is a sonnet on 'Lost Days,' which has a serious, practically earnest spirit, the more impressive that this tone is not very frequent in these poems. Equally impressive are six fine lines which conclude a sonnet on 'Inclusiveness.'

One also called 'The Monochordon' has been often alluded to. It hints with great power what is so undefinable, the inarticulate yet absorbing emotions so multitudinous, yet so opposite, which are awakened by the finest music. This is the conclusion—

> ' Oh, what is this that knows the road I came,
>   The flame turned cloud, the cloud returned to flame,
>   The shifted lifted steeps, and all the way ?
> That draws round me at last this wind-warm space
> And in regenerate rapture turns my face
>   Upon the devious coverts of dismay ?'

What 'regenerate rapture' may exactly mean, I must leave others to find out for themselves, but the sonnet as a whole is finely suggestive.

Amid so many morbid fancies and such super-subtilized phrases as these sonnets contain, we welcome all the more gladly a few which are purely objective and clothed in plain vigorous English. Such is the sonnet on 'The Last Three from Trafalgar,' and one on 'Winter,' and one on 'Spring;' the latter two, reproducing so faithfully the English landscape, without being imitations, recall the best manner of Keats. Here is the last of these :—

> ' Soft littered in the new year's lambing-fold,
>   And in the hollowed haystack at its side,
>   The shepherd lies o' nights now, wakeful-eyed,
> At the ewe's travailing call through the dark cold.
> The young rooks cheep 'mid the thick caw o' the old ;
>   And near unpeopled stream-sides, on the ground,
>   By her spring cry the moorhen's nest is found,
> Where the drained flood-lands flaunt their marigold.

' Chill are the gusts to which the pastures cower,
　　And chill the current where the young reeds stand
　　As green and close as the young wheat on land :
　Yet here the cuckoo and the cuckoo flower
　Plight to the heart Spring's perfect imminent hour,
　　Whose breath shall soothe you like your loved one's hand.'

Perhaps the divisions between the different months may be here somewhat obliterated ; yet as we read sonnets like this with their refreshing out-of-door feeling we are inclined to say, ' O si sic omnia !'

One word on the lyrics and songs, for each volume contains a different set of these. Of the eleven short pieces in the first volume the last four are all more or less simple and intelligible in style, and condense into a few felicitous lines some fleeting mood, or some one thought which, coming for a moment, would have been lost, had it not been fixed in words. Such are the songs or poems named, ' The Wood-spurge,' which compresses much sadness into little space, ' Honeysuckle,' ' A Young Fir-wood.' The lines named ' Sea Limits,' express well the feeling that there is one life pervading all things in some mysterious way.

' Consider the sea's listless chime :
　　Time's self it is, made audible,—
　　The murmur of the earth's own shell.
　Secret continuance sublime
　　Is the sea's end.　Our sight may pass
　　No furlong further.　Since time was
　This sound hath told the lapse of time.

　　　*　　　　*　　　　*　　　　*

' Listen alone beside the sea,
　　Listen alone among the woods ;
　　Those voices of twin solitudes
　Shall have one sound alike to thee :
　　Hark, where the murmurs of thronged men,
　　Surge and sink back and surge again—
　Still the one voice of wave and tree.

' Gather a shell from the strewn beach,
　　And listen at its lips : they sigh
　　The same desire and mystery,
　The echo of the whole sea's speech.
　　And all mankind is thus at heart,
　　Not anything but what thou art :
　And earth, sea, man, are all in each.'

In the second volume the lyrics have all more or less an undertone of sadness for some loved and lost one, which breaks out here and there into a passionate cry. They dwell mainly on the mystery of our life here and of our destiny. This is expressed in the last of the series, ' Cloud Confines,' which the author himself, we are told, regarded as his finest lyric work. It repeats the old truth of the inexorable Silence which encompasses us, behind, before, and above.

'Our past is clean forgot,
  Our present is and is not,
  Our future's a sealed seed-plot,
    And what betwixt them are we?

'We who say as we go,
  Strange to think by the way,
  Whatever there is to know,
    That shall we know some day.'

There is also a very touching lament named, 'Alas! so long!' This and other of these lyrics close with a faintly breathed hope, so little removed from uncertainty that it does not relieve the oppressive sadness—the hope that there may be a meeting hereafter—

'Is there a home where heavy earth
  Melts to bright air that breathes no pain,
  Where water leaves no thirst again,
    And springing fire is Love's new birth?'

Rossetti does not rank with the poets of denial and decided unbelief; there is in his poetry a desire, that almost becomes a hope, for better things. But it is a hope so faint that it seems almost next door to despair, and is nearly as sad as despair. Of this kind of poetry, which is unillumined by the sense of the Divine Presence in the world, and by the hope of immortality, we have surely had enough in this generation. To young poets we should say, Till you have learned something better to tell us on man's life and destiny, had you not better be silent? The world is weary of these moanings of despair, and can well dispense with any more of them. It is really not worth your while to trouble it with your pipings till you have something to tell it; some authentic message to bring of man and of God, and of man's relation to God.

On the whole, we must again repeat our regret that poetic genius, real within a certain range, such as Mr. Rossetti possessed, should, if judged by any high standard, seem to a large extent to have spent itself in vain. The worth of his poetry is vitiated by two grave errors. The first of these is the unwholesome sentiment and the esoteric vein of thought into which he allowed himself to diverge. The second is the exotic manner and too elaborated style, which, for whatever reason, he adopted.

If future poets wish to win the ear of their countrymen, and to merit the honour accorded to the highest poetry, they would be wise to cultivate manlier thought and nobler sentiment, expressed in purer and fresher diction, and to make their appeal, not to the perfumed tastes of over-educated coteries, but to the broader and healthier sympathies of universal man.

J. C. SHAIRP.

Poetry and Culture.

———

Two facts are forced upon the attention of all who care to study the tendencies and characteristics of their own days. The first and perhaps the more striking of the two is the extraordinary interest, activity, and laborious zeal that pervades all classes with respect to education. Brief reference to the number, variety, and excellence of the educational works which are now annually, almost daily, pouring from the press, would be alone sufficient to give some notion of the marvellous development which has been attained in this direction during the past thirty years. The second fact to which I allude is the no less unmistakeable preponderance which positive or scientific branches of knowledge are gradually but rapidly gaining as elements in education over acquirements purely literary. All the signs point the same way : we are becoming more material, more utilitarian—more sordid and earthly in our lives and in our aspirations. The voices of Mr. Matthew Arnold and many others are lifted up in this modern wilderness to protest against the vandalism that would still further narrow the limits of literature in education, the arms of many who have themselves received the priceless boon of a liberal educa- tion, are raised to endeavour to stem the approaching tide of science, which threatens to swallow up schools, universities, and examining boards alike, at least by engrossing their energies. As with Catholics the truth of what they believe is not a matter of opinion but of knowledge and of faith, the certainty of which is above all merely human know- ledge, so those whose minds and powers have been trained by literature do not merely *think*, but they *know*, that no amount of science and mathematics can possibly supply the deficiency of an education that is in great part at least literary. Just as that indescribeable air of refinement, the nameless charm of a perfect manner, is never attained under any conditions by those who, neither bred or born gentlemen, have never mixed in good society when young, so it has been abundantly proved that that peculiar character of mind, thought, and feeling which we instinctively associate with the idea of a well-educated man, is not to be attained by the most devoted, exclusive attention to the 'ologies.

In the face, however, of these two facts of the day, the universal thirst for knowledge, and the encroaching, nay, almost hostile, attitude to letters assumed by science, perhaps the partisans of the old classical and literary training cannot employ themselves more usefully than by endeavouring to investigate still further the relations between literature and culture. Even if there be nothing absolutely new to say on the subject, we may perchance be doing good service by an attempt to put some old trite truths in a new form, or even by mere repetition.

"It seems to me," writes Mr. M. Arnold,[1] "that those who are for giving to natural knowledge, as they call it, the chief place in the education of the majority of mankind, leave one important thing out of their account—the constitution of human nature." Now it has long been admitted that this human nature of which Mr. M. Arnold writes, may, for educational purposes, be considered as made up of two parts. There is the *intellectual* and the *emotional* side of human nature; the judgment and the understanding, and the feeling and imagination. If it can be shown that the study of geometry and logic and physiology braces the intellectual muscles and strengthens all the reasoning and judicial powers a man possesses, it is no less susceptible of strict demonstration that attention to poetry and all the language akin to poetry, such as fiction without verse, to humane letters as they are justly called, in a word, that attention to literature is the chief means provided by Providence for developing and giving power to the nerves and fibres of the feelings and the imagination. The argument is in each case strictly empirical. Appeal is made to no *à priori* method, but simply to experience and fact. We see that since science and letters have been it is so; and we may each of us, if we choose, compare the different effects produced upon our own minds by a page of Euclid and a page of Keats.

But here the difficulty begins, because as if the burden of proof lay with us rather than our adversaries, they ask us:

[1] *Nineteenth Century,* August, 1882, "Art, Literature, and Science."

Why is it that letters produce one effect on the mind of a boy or a man, and science another? or putting precisely the same question in another way, they require to know *how* it is that poetry and eloquence come to have the power which science has not, of calling out the emotions? and again, *how* do they exercise this power? A fool, we know very well, may ask a question which a wise man can't answer. And Mr. M. Arnold, who in matters of culture at least is proverbially a wise man, would appear to think that not impossibly we may have here an instance of the saying's truth. "This," he says, "is perhaps a case for applying the Preacher's words: 'Though a man labour to seek it out, yet he shall not find it; yea, further, though a wise man think to know it, yet he shall not be able to find it.' Why should it be one thing, in its effect upon the emotions, to say, 'patience is a virtue,' and quite another thing, in its effect upon the emotions, to say with Homer: τλητὸν γὰρ Μοῖραι θυμὸν θέσαν ἀνθρώποισιν—'for an enduring heart have the Fates appointed to the children of men'?"

Whether it be possible or not to analyze the workings of a man's mind so as perfectly to solve the problem we may well leave to the metaphysicians; or perchance the mental physiologists of the day may later on succeed in throwing some light on an obscure subject by careful examination of our cerebral convolutions. I venture to hope that at least some difficulties may be cleared away and the ground prepared for future research by diligent investigation of the essential and eternal relations between literature and the emotional side of our nature. By literature I mean in the first place poetry, and secondly all language akin to poetry, such as is to be found in books of fiction and art, as opposed to such as treat of fact, historical or scientific.

What is poetry? Never perhaps has a question been more often asked, more variously and less satisfactorily answered. And no wonder. The very idea of poetry is of its very nature so subtle and refined, so various in form, so changeable in colour, that any attempt to define its essential constituents except by their effects may well seem hopeless. Proteus-like, it ever eludes our mental grasp, like the chameleon its hues seem hardly the same one hour and the next.

One valuable result, however, of the criticism of the day has been to establish on a firm and solid basis a truth with regard to poetry—not indeed new, but lost sight of in that age of prose, the eighteenth century—the truth that whatever else poetry may be, its first and most essential characteristic is that it appeals not to the reason but to the imagination. "Poetry," says Mr. Mark Pattison in his valuable review of Milton's poems[2] in Mr. Ward's edition of *The English Poets*, "poetry must be a vehicle of emotion. Poetry is an address to the feelings and imagination, not to the judgment and the understanding. The world and its cosmical processes, or nature and natural scenery, are in themselves only objects of science. They become matter for the poet only after they have been impregnated with the joys and distresses, the hopes and fears of man." Hence, "the doctrine that human action and passion are the only material of poetic fiction was the first theorem of Greek æsthetic."

To illustrate the same truth from the views of Mr. M. Arnold. Why is it that he and others of his school of criticism boldly refuse the title of poetry to the writings, didactic and descriptive, of men whose names stand so high as those of Dryden and Pope, whilst they unhesitatingly award the meed of true poetic merit to Keats and even Gray? Why, but because, as has been most truly said, the verses of Pope are conceived and elaborated in the *wits* of their author and not in his *soul*. "The difference," writes Arnold, "between genuine poetry and the poetry of Dryden, Pope, and all their school, is briefly this: their poetry is conceived and composed in their wits, genuine poetry is conceived and composed in the soul. The difference between the two kinds of poetry is immense. They differ profoundly in their modes of language, they differ profoundly in their modes of evolution. The poetic language of our eighteenth century in general is the language of men composing *without their eye on the object*, as Wordsworth excellently said of Dryden; language merely recalling the object as the common language of prose does, and then dressing it out with a certain smartness and brilliancy for the fancy and understanding. This is called 'splendid diction.' The evolution of the poetry of our eighteenth century is likewise intellectual; it proceeds by ratiocination, antithesis, ingenious turns, and conceits. This poetry is often eloquent, and always, in the hands of such masters as Dryden and Pope, clever; but it does not take us much below the surface of things, it does not give us the emotion of seeing things in their truth and

[2] *The English Poets*, vol. ii. Edited by T. H. Ward.

beauty. The language of genuine poetry, on the other hand, is the language of one composing with his eye on the object; its evolution is that of a thing which has been plunged in the poet's soul until it comes forth naturally and necessarily." [3]

Elsewhere the same critic tells us that "we are to regard Dryden as the puissant and glorious founder, Pope as the splendid high-priest, of our age of prose and reason, of our excellent and indispensable eighteenth century."

Mr. Mark Pattison, too, writing of the same classics, says they wanted "inspiration, lofty sentiment, the heroic soul, chivalrous devotion, the inner eye of faith—above all—love and sympathy. They could not mean greatly. But such meaning as they had they laboured to express in the neatest, most terse, and pointed form which our language is capable of. If not poets they were literary artists."

I have thought it worth my while to make here these somewhat lengthy extracts from the writings of two distinguished literary critics, because they appear to me to suggest a really good answer to the question we started with: What is Poetry? If the view of Mr. Arnold and his school is the true one, this at least is clear, that poetry is above all things a genuine appeal to the emotions. The very essence, the very innermost being of all true poetry is its power of calling out the emotions. Alliteration rhyme, even rhythm itself, is an accident of poetry, not the substance of poetry in its true and widest sense. The one thing poetry cannot be without, the one quality which makes poetry what it is, is that inherent power it has of playing upon the feelings, the imagination, the emotions.

Here, too, is found its specific difference to prose. The whole, or at least the characteristic, scope of the latter lies precisely in this, that leaving the feelings to look after themselves, it addresses itself alone to the judgment, reason, and intellect of its audience. Now if this be the case, it further follows—a deduction indeed most pertinent to our subject—that poetry, whether in verse or not, is opposed to prose in exactly the same way that fiction is opposed to fact. And how is this? Not surely in that fact is truth and fiction falsehood, for this would be tantamount to saying that fact is beauty and fiction all that is loathsome and ugly. How then? In this way, that fact is what may be called objective or historic truth, and fiction is ideal or philosophic truth. Both are true,

---

[3] *The English Poets*, Gray, vol. iii. p. 314.

only the truth of fiction is of a higher and more sublime order than the truth of fact. Poetry, I say then, and prose are similarly opposed. The latter possesses as its own the truth and beauty which are inseparable from all honest and genuine appeals to right reason ; but poetry, using the term always in its wide sense, claims a higher truth and a more perfect beauty of its own, for it is its own peculiar boast to address itself alone to that higher and more elevated portion of man's nature, his whole moral being, his feelings, his sympathies, his affections, his passions, his love of all that is high and good and pure and true. Hence again flows a second very important corollary, and that is, that poetry is ideally at least *the* language of fiction, as prose is of fact.

Here, however, I would guard myself from a double mis-apprehension. And first when I say that poetic language is the language of fiction, I by no means imply that fiction is necessarily true poetry, that the two are identical. Far from it ; fiction may be as worthless as what pretends to be historical truth or fact. Fiction may be merely not fact, without any of the positive good qualities that it ought to possess, that is to say, without appealing in the least to the imagination, the emotions of its readers, or what is far worse, appealing indeed to our passions but in a spurious, degenerate way. Fiction is not necessarily poetry or akin to poetry, any more, surely, than much of the so-called history or " Special Correspondent " news of the day is fact or akin to fact. But in spite of this it still remains true that fiction ought to be poetry, or at least akin to it, and poetic language recognized as such, whether by the rhythm or the words and phrases employed, is fiction's most becoming attire, its full dress. It never appears to such advantage, and displays all its charms so effectively, as when thus arrayed. Thus the connection between poetry and fiction is apparent—they are not identical or even inseparable, at least as far as spurious fiction is concerned, but they naturally go hand in hand. We see, then, that all fiction is not poetry, but only the best. And this leads us to consider the further and no less interesting question, whether poetry itself is necessarily *exclusive* of fact or historic truth. At first sight it might appear as if what has been said would imply this too ; but a little thought will show the case to stand very differently. Genuine poetry no more excludes historic truth for its foundation than a genuine house prefers stone to the exclusion of bricks. Poetry, as such, neither includes or excludes fact; but holds itself perfectly indifferent to its presence or absence. To poetry, as such, historic truth is neither a disfigurement nor an ornament.

Hence we have Shakspere's historic plays as well as *Othello* and the *Midsummer Night's Dream;* hence we have *Kenilworth* and the *Heart of Midlothian,* as well as the *Abbot* and the *Bride of Lammermoor;* hence we constantly have true fiction founded on fact. But though Richard may be personally more interesting to us, because the poet has taken much from More's *Life* and Holinshed's *Chronicles,* and in fact built the entire plot upon these foundations, yet the question whether Richard's nephews were by his order murdered in the Tower or not, whether Richard is answerable for the death of Clarence or not is beside the point,—it in no way affects the value of the play as a dramatic poem. Merely as a poem *Richard the Third* would be quite as noble a monument of Shakspere's genius if Edward had never had any children and Bosworth had never been. Thus, again, to criticise Shakspere unfavourably, because he makes the gentle dew to drop from heaven, is simple ignorance of the difference between scientific and poetic truth and beauty—a very fair specimen of *ignoratio elenchi.* The question whether dew really drops from heaven or not, is not worth considering here for a moment, all that we have to look to is whether the idea is poetically true or false. To take one more example from the only English poet who ever rivalled Shakspere, and from the most exquisite, the most sublime of Milton's masterpieces, *Lycidas.* On the lines:

> Batt'ning our flocks with the fresh dews of night,
> Oft till the star that rose at ev'ning, bright,
> Toward heav'ns descent had sloped his westering wheel,

Keightley remarks: "The evening star appears, not rises, and it is never anywhere but *on* heaven's descent."

Quite so. But is this any reason why Milton should not make Hesperus to rise and set? Surely none. The scientific description of astronomical phenomena is not poetry, and as long as it is not poetically an unsound idea to represent the evening star as rising, we need trouble ourselves about nothing else. Naturalistic or scientific solecism counts for nothing in Milton or Shakspere.

And now to retrace our steps. We started with the assumption that the moral or emotional side of human nature was at least as deserving of culture and education or training as the reasoning faculties are. I have endeavoured to point out how it is of the very essence of literature or poetry, taken in its widest and truest sense, to address itself primarily and above all things to the imagination, to call out the emotions. Hence the doctrine that human action or passion is the only subject of poetry; for human action or passion alone of themselves can evoke these emotions, and if other subjects appear to do so, the extent and feeling they excite is really caused only by their reference to man. Moreover, I have tried to establish the relations between fiction and poetry, historic fact and prose.

It remains for us now to put two and two together, and ask ourselves, Is not Mr. Matthew Arnold right when he finds that "those who are for giving to natural knowledge, as they call it, the chief place in the education of the majority of mankind, leave one important thing out of their account—the constitution of human nature?" If one half of our nature, and the better half, is, as far as mere books are concerned, to be trained and educated by works of the imagination, and, if the entire scope of the literature of fiction is what we have seen it to be, this would certainly appear to be the case. And then, what is to become of a man who resolutely refuses to sully himself even with a smattering of letters? His understanding and judgment may indeed be developed, but the development will be abnormal, he will be an intellectual monstrosity, there will be no balance of power, and the entire man will be a one-sided being. Of course there always remains the hope and the chance that exceptionably favourable external circumstances may, in great measure, remedy the deficiencies of education. But neither are natural or even supernatural virtues, nor again are domestic sympathies and ties either capable or designed by Providence to supply altogether the place of education and the mental culture to be gained by application and study. Books and living books or masters may be said to be an integral and indispensable factor in the training of a man's mind.

Culture, therefore, requires something more than even virtue, natural or supernatural, to make it what it is—and that something is literature. "The aim of culture," writes Mr. Mallock in a very fine passage, "the aim of culture is indeed to make the soul a musical instrument, which may yield music either to itself or to others, at any appeal from without; and the more elaborate a man's culture is, the richer and more composite can this music be. The minds of some men are like a simple pastoral reed. Only single melodies, and these unaccompanied, can be played upon them, glad or sad ; whilst the minds of others, who look at things from countless points of view, and realize, as Shakspere did, their comparative nature, their minds become, as Shakspere's was, like a great orchestra . . . or sometimes when he is a mere *passive* observer of things, letting impressions from without move him as they will. I would compare the man of culture to an Æolian harp, which the winds at will play through,—a beautiful face, a rainbow, a ruined temple, a death-bed, or a line of poetry wandering in like a breath of air amidst the chords of his soul, touching note after note into soft music, and at last gently dying away into silence."

Here, then, is the man of culture, presented to us, as well perhaps as any words can paint him. Whether it be desirable or not to be so cultivated we need not inquire, but only ask ourselves now, how is such a man likely to be formed ? *Poeta nascitur non fit*, you answer. True no doubt, but even of a poet not all the truth ; for as old Ben Jonson wrote :

> For though the poet's matter nature be
> His art doth give the fashion ; and that he
> Who casts to write a living line, must sweat
> (Such as thine are) and strike the second heat
> Upon the muse's anvil, turn the same
> And himself with it, that he thinks to frame ;
> Or for the laurel he may gain to scorn ;
> For a good poet's *made as well as born.*

And, if this is true of the poet, how much more true will it be of the man of culture !

Mr. Darwin, we are told, felt the need in his existence neither of poetry nor of religion—science and the domestic affections were enough for him. "But then," as Mr. Arnold naively adds, "Darwins are very rare." And perhaps as the great naturalist could do without religion, in this world at least, as well as without poetry, which is not so indispensable after all, because we need not all be men of culture, this rarity is rather a merciful dispensation of Providence. The sentiment, however, naturally suggests one word, and only one, because the subject is a long one, as to the part played by religion in education, considered from a purely human point of view. Here, then, as we have been treating of poetry and culture, it will be sufficient to say that though the educational functions of religion and literature are to some extent analogous, both dealing with man's higher and moral nature, they are not identical, nor can religion, much less the domestic affections, pretend utterly to supersede letters. A man may well be a saint without a tincture of purely natural mental cultivation.

I conclude, then, with one more striking extract from Mr. Mallock's *New Republic*, and I adopt his words in preference to my own, and all others, because they seem to me to express and sum up the views I have been trying to advocate as well as words can.

"Here we come to our friends the books again. Not, however, to such books as histories, but to books of art, to poetry, and books akin to poetry. The former do but enlarge our common experience. The latter are an experience in themselves, and an experience that interprets all former experience. The mind, to borrow an illustration, is a sensitized plate, always ready to receive the images made by experience on it. Poetry is the developing solution, which first makes these images visible. Or, to put it in another way, if some books are the telescopes with which we look at distant facts, poetry—I use the word in its widest sense—is a magic mirror which shows us the facts about us reflected in it as no telescope or microscope could show them to us. Let a person of experience look into this, and experience then becomes culture. For in that magic mirror we see our life surrounded with issues viewless to the common eye. We see it compassed about with chariots of fire and with horses of fire. Then we know the real aspect of our joys and sorrows. We see the lineaments, we look into the eyes of thoughts (compare Wordsworth's "writing with the eye on the object"), and desires and associations, which had been before unseen and scarcely suspected presences—dim swarms clustering around our every action. Then how all kinds of objects and of feelings begin to cling together in our minds! A single sense or a single memory is touched, and a thrill runs through countless others. The smell of autumn woods, the colour of dying ferns, may turn by a subtle transubstantiation into pleasures and faces that will never come again—a red sunset and a windy seashore into a last farewell and the regret of a life-time."

C. COWLEY CLARKE.

MACMILLAN'S MAGAZINE.

DECEMBER, 1885.

POETRY AND POLITICS.

THE separation of literary criticism from politics appears to have been a gain both to politics and to literature. If Mr. Swinburne, for example, speaks unkindly about kings and priests in one volume, that offence is not remembered against him, even by the most Conservative critic, when he gives us a book like 'Atalanta,' or 'Erechtheus.' If Victor Hugo applauds the Commune, the Conservative M. Paul de Saint Victor freely forgives him. In the earlier part of the century, on the other hand, poems which had no tinge of politics were furiously assailed, for party reasons, by Tory critics, if the author was a Whig, or had friends in the ranks of Whiggery.[1] Perhaps the Whiggish critics were not less one-sided, but their exploits (except a few of Jeffrey's) are forgotten. Either there were no Conservative poets to be attacked, or the Whig attack was so weak, and so unlike the fine fury of the Tory reviewers, that it has lapsed into oblivion. Assuredly no Tory Keats died of an article, no Tory Shelley revenged him in a Conservative 'Adonais,' and, if Lord Byron struck back at his Scotch reviewers, Lord Byron was no Tory.

In the happy Truce of the Muses, which now enables us to judge a poet on his literary merits, Mr. Courthope has raised a war-cry which will not, I hope, be widely echoed. He has called his reprinted essays 'The Liberal Movement in English Literature,'[2] and has thus brought back the howls of partisans into a region where they had been long silent. One cannot but regret this intrusion of the factions which have "no language but a Cry" into the tranquil regions of verse. Mr. Courthope knows that the title of his essays will be objected to, and he tries to defend it. Cardinal Newman, he says, employs the term "Liberalism" to denote a movement in the region of thought. Would it not be as true to say that Cardinal Newman uses "Liberalism" as "short" for most things that he dislikes? In any case the word "Liberal" is one of those question-begging, popular, political terms which had been expelled from the criticism of poetry. It seems an error to bring back the word with its passionate associations. Mr. Courthope will, perhaps, think that the reviewer who thus objects is himself a Liberal. It is not so; and though I would fain escape from even the thought of party bickerings, I probably agree with Mr. Courthope in not wishing to disestablish anything or anybody, not even the House of Lords. None the less it is distract-

[1] Compare Maginn's brutal and silly attack on Shelley's 'Adonais,' recently reprinted in Maginn's 'Miscellanies.' Sampson Low and Company.

[2] John Murray, London, 1885.

ing, when we are occupied for once with thoughts about poetry, to meet sentences like this : " Life, in the Radical view, is simply change ; and a Radical is ready to promote every caprice or whim of the numerical majority of the moment in the belief that the change which it effects in the constitution of society will bring him nearer to some ideal state existing in his own imagination." Or again : " How many leagues away do they " (certain remarks of Mr. Burke's) " carry us from the Liberal Radical- ism now crying out for the aboli- tion of the hereditary branch of the Legislature ? " and so on. One ex- pects, in every page, to encounter the deceased wife's sister, or " a cow and three acres." It is not in the mood provoked by our enthusiasm for the hereditary branch of the Legislature, it is not when the heart stands up in defence of the game laws, that we are fit to reason about poetry. Con- sequently, as it appears to me, Mr. Courthope, in his excitement against Radicalism, does not always reason correctly, nor, perhaps, feel correctly, about poetry.

As far as I understand the main thesis of Mr. Courthope's book, it is something like this. From a very early date, from the date certainly of Chaucer, there have been flowing two main streams in English literature. One stream is the Poetry of Romance, the other is the Poetry of Manners. The former had its source (I am in- clined to go a great way further back for its source) " in the institutions of chivalry, and in mediæval theology." The other poetical river, again, the poetry of manners, " has been fed by the life, actions, and manners of the nation." One might add to this that the " life and actions " of our people have often, between the days of the Black Prince and of General Gordon, been in the highest degree " romantic." This mixture, however, would confuse Mr. Courthope's system. Drayton's 'Agincourt,' Lord Tennyson's 'Revenge' may be regarded at will, perhaps, as

belonging to the poetry of romance, or the poetry of national action. Mr. Courthope does not touch on this fact, but the reader will do well to keep it in mind, for reasons which will appear later.

The fortunes of the two streams of poetry have been different. The romantic stream was lost in the sands of Donne, Crashaw, Cowley, and the rest, but welled up again in the begin- ning of our own century, in Scott, Coleridge, and others. The poetry of manners, on the other hand, had its great time when men, revolting from the conceits of degenerate romanticism, took, with Pope, Dryden, Thomson, and Johnson, to " correctness," to working under the " ethical impulse." Now the " correctness " and the choice of moral topics which prevailed in the eighteenth century were " Conserva- tive,"and the new burst of romantic poe- try was " Liberal," and was connected with the general revolutionary and Liberal movement in politics, specu- lation, and religion. Finally, Mr. Courthope thinks that " the Liberal movement in our literature, as well as in our politics, is beginning to lan- guish." Perhaps Mr. Chamberlain and his friends are not aware that they are languishing. In the interests of our languishing poetry, at all events, Mr. Courthope briefly pre- scribes more " healthy objectivity " (the words are mine, and are slang, but they put the idea briefly), and a " revival of the simple iambic move- ments of English in metres historically established in our literature."

In this sketch of Mr. Courthope's thesis, his main ideas show forth as, if not new, yet, perfectly true. There is, there has been, a poetry of romance of which the corruption is found in the wanton conceits of Donne and Cra- shaw. There is, there has been, a poetry of manners and morals, of which the corruption is didactic prosi- ness. In the secular action and re- action, each of these tendencies has, at various times, been weak or strong. At the beginning of this century, too, a party tinge was certainly given, chiefly by Conservative critics, to the reborn romantic poetry. Keats cared as little as any man for what Marcus Aurelius calls "the drivelling of politicians," but even Keats, as a friend of "kind Hunt's," was a sort of Liberal. But admitting this party colouring, one must add that it was of very slight moment indeed, and very casually distributed. Therefore, one must still regret, for reasons which will instantly appear, Mr. Courthope's introduction of party names and party prejudices into his interesting essays.

It is probably the author's preoccupation with politics which causes frequent contradictions, as they seem, and a general sense of confusion which often make it very hard to follow his argument, and to see what he is really driving at. For example, Scott, the Conservative Scott, whom Mr. Courthope so justly admires, has to appear as a Liberal, almost a revolutionary, in verse. Mr. Courthope quotes Coleridge's account of the origin of Lyrical Ballads as "the first note of the 'new departure,' which I have called the 'Liberal Movement in English Literature.'" Well, but the Tory Scott was an eager follower of Coleridge's; he played (if we are to be political) Mr. Jesse Collings to Coleridge's Mr. Chamberlain. This, by itself, proves how very little the Liberal movement in literature was a party movement, how little it had to do with Liberalism in politics.

Again, when Mr. Courthope is censuring, and most justly censuring, Mr. Carlyle's grudging and Pharisaical article on Scott, he speaks of Carlyle as a "Radical," and finds that "our Radical Diogenes" blamed Scott "because he was a Conservative, and amused the people." Now Carlyle, of all men, was no Radical; and Scott, as a Conservative, is a queer figure in a Liberal movement. Another odd fact is that the leaders of the Liberal movement "steeped themselves" in the atmosphere of feudal romance. Whatever else feudal romance may

have been, it was eminently anti-Radical, and, to poetic Radicals, should have been eminently uncongenial. Odder still (if the Liberal movement in literature was a party movement to any important extent) is Mr. Courthope's discovery that Macaulay was a Conservative critic. Yet a Conservative critic Macaulay must have been, because he was in the camp opposed to that of Coleridge and Keats. Macaulay was a very strong party man, and, had he been aware that his critical tastes were Tory, he would perhaps have changed his tastes. Yet again, Mr. Courthope finds that optimism is the note of Liberalism, while "the Conservative takes a far less sanguine view of the prospects of the art of poetry," and of things in general. But Byron and Shelley, in Mr. Courthope's argument, were Liberal poets. Yet Mr. Courthope says, speaking of Shelley, "like Byron, he shows himself a complete pessimist." For my own part (and Mr. Courthope elsewhere expresses the same opinion), Shelley seems to me an optimist, in his queer political dreams of a future where Prometheus and Asia shall twine beams and buds in a cave, unvexed by priests and kings—a future in which all men shall be peaceful, brotherly, affectionate sentimentalists. But Mr. Courthope must decide whether Byron and Shelley are to be Conservatives and pessimists, or Liberals and optimists. At present their position as Liberal pessimists seems, on his own showing, difficult and precarious. Macaulay, too, the Liberal Macaulay, is a pessimist, according to Mr. Courthope. All this confusion, as I venture to think it, appears to arise, then, from Mr. Courthope's political preoccupations. He shows us a Radical Carlyle, a Conservative Macaulay; a Scott who is, perhaps, a kind of Whig; a Byron, who, being pessimistic, should be Conservative, but is Liberal; a Shelley, who is Liberal, though, being pessimistic, he ought to be Conservative. It is all very perplexing, and, like most mischief, all comes out of party politics. It is less easy to demonstrate, what I cannot help suspecting, that Mr. Courthope's great admiration of the typical poetry of the eighteenth century comes from his persuasion that that poetry, like Providence, "is Tory." This may seem an audacious guess. I am led to make it partly by observing that Mr. Courthope's own poems, especially the charming lyrics in 'The Paradise of Birds,' have a freedom and a varied music, extremely Liberal, extremely unlike Johnson and Thomson, and not all dissimilar to what we admire in the Red Republican verse of Mr. Swinburne. Now, if Mr. Courthope writes verse like that (and I wish he would write more), surely his inmost self must, on the whole, tend rather to the poetry he calls Liberal, than to that which (being a politician) he admires as Conservative, but does not imitate. All this, however, is an attempt to plumb "the abysmal depths of personality." We are on firmer ground when we try to show that Mr. Courthope expresses too high an opinion of the typical poetry of the eighteenth century. Now this really brings us face to face with the great question, Was Pope a poet? and that, again, leads us to the brink of a discussion as to What is poetry? On these matters no one will ever persuade his neighbours by argument. We all follow our tastes, incapable of conversion. I must admit that I am, on this point, a Romanticist of the most "dishevelled" character; that Pope's verse does not affect me as what I call poetry affects me; that I only style Pope, in Mr. Swinburne's words, "a poet with a difference." This is one of the remarks which inspire Mr. Courthope to do battle for Pope, and for Thomson and Johnson, and the rest. Mr. Matthew Arnold, too, vexes Mr. Courthope by calling Pope and Dryden "classics of our prose." Why are they not poets? he asks; and "Who is a poet if not Pope?" Who? Why from Homer onwards there are many poets: there

are "many mansions," but if Pope dwells in one of them I think it is by courtesy, and because there are a few diamonds of poetry in the fine gold of his verse. But it is time to say why one would (in spite of the very highest of all living authorities) incline to qualify the title of "poet" as given to Pope. It is for a reason which Mr. Courthope finds it hard to understand. He says that Mr. Matthew Arnold and Mr. Swinburne deny Pope the laurel without assigning reasons. They merely cry, in a despotic fashion, *stet pro ratione voluntas.* They do not offer argument, or, if they argue, their arguments will not "hold water." But Mr. Courthope himself justifies the lack of argument by his own reply to certain reasonings of Wordsworth's. "Your reasoning, no doubt," says Mr. Courthope to the Bard of Rydal, "is very fine and ingenious, but the matter is one not for argument, but for perception."

Precisely: and so Mr. Arnold and Mr. Swinburne might answer Mr. Courthope's complaints of their lack of argument,—"The matter is one not for argument, but for perception." One feels, or perceives, in reading Pope, the lack of what one cannot well argue about, the lack of the indefinable glory of poetry, the bloom on it, as happiness is, according to Aristotle, the bloom on a life of goodness. Mr. Swinburne, avoiding "argument," writes, "the test of the highest poetry is that it eludes all tests. Poetry in which there is no element at once perceptible and indefinable by any reader or hearer of any poetic instinct may have every other good quality ... but if all its properties can easily or can ever be gauged and named by its admirers, it is not poetry, above all it is not lyric poetry, of the first water." In fact, to employ the terms of Mr. Courthope's own reply to Wordsworth, "the matter is one not for argument, but for perception." Now this "perceptible and indefinable" element in poetry, is rarely present in Pope's verse, if it is ever present at all. We can "gauge and name" the properties of Pope's verse, and little or nothing is left unnamed and ungauged. For this reason Pope always appears to me, if a poet at all, a poet "with a difference." The test, of course, is subjective, even mystical, if you will. Mr. Courthope might answer that Pope is full of passages in which he detects an indefinable quality that can never be gauged or named. In that case I should be silenced, but Mr. Courthope does not say anything of the sort. Far from that, he says (and here he does astonish me) that "the most sublime passages of Homer, Milton, and Virgil, can readily be analysed into their elements." Why, if it were so, they would indeed be on the level of Pope. But surely it is not so. We can parse Homer, Milton, and Virgil; we can make a *précis* of what they state; but who can analyse their incommunicable charm? If any man thinks he can analyse it, to that man, I am inclined to cry, the charm must be definable indeed, but also imperceptible. Take Homer's words, so simply uttered, when Helen has said that her brothers shun the war, for her shame's sake—

Ὣς φάτο· τοὺς δ' ἤδη κατέχεν φυσίζοος αἰα,
Ἐν Λακεδαίμονι αὖθι, φίλῃ ἐν πατρίδι γαίῃ.[1]

Who can analyse the subtle melancholy of the lines, the incommunicable charm and sweetness, full of all thoughts of death, and life, and the dearness of our native land?

In Virgil and Milton it is even easier to find examples of this priceless quality, lines like

"Fluminaque antiquos subterlabentia muros,"[2]

or

"Te, Lari maxime, teque
Fluctibus et fremitu assurgens, Benace, marino!"[3]

---

[1] "So spake she, but them already the mother earth possessed, there in Lacedæmon, their own dear native land."

[2] "And rivers gliding under ancient walls."

[3] "Thee, mightiest Laris, and thee Benacus, rising with waves and surge as of the sea."

Mr. Courthope himself quotes lines of Milton's that sufficiently illustrate my meaning—

"And ladies of the Hesperides that seemed
Fairer than feigned of old or fabled since
Of faery damsels met in forest wide
By Knight of Logris or of Lyones,
Lancelot, or Pelleas, or Pellenore."

There is something in the very procession and rhythmical fitness of the words, there is a certain bloom and charm, which defies analysis. This bloom is of the essence of poetry, and it is *not* characteristic of the typical verse of Mr. Courthope's Conservative eighteenth century. He enters into argument with Mr. Swinburne, who quotes, as an example of the indefinable quality—

"Will no one tell me what she sings?
Perhaps the plaintive numbers flow
For old, unhappy, far-off things,
And battles long ago."

Mr. Swinburne says that "if not another word was left of the poem in which those two last lines occur, those two lines would suffice to show the hand of a poet differing, not in degree, but in kind, from the tribe of Byron or of Southey"—the Conservative singer of Wat Tyler. As to Byron I do not speak; but certainly the two lines, like two lines of Sappho's, if they alone survived, would give assurance of a poet of the true gift, of the unimpeachable inspiration. Such a line as

Ἦρος ἄγγελος ἱμεροφωνος ἀήδων,[4]

or

ὡς δὲ παῖς πεδὰ μάτερα πεπτερύγωμαι,[5]

is not a more infallible proof of the existence of a true poet.

Mr. Courthope does not see this in the case of Wordsworth. He says the beauty of the fragment depends on the context. I quote his remark, which proves how vain it is to argue about poetry, how truly it is "a

---

[4] "The dear glad angel of spring, the Nightingale."—BEN JONSON.

[5] "Even as a child to its mother I flutter to thee." Both these passages are fragments of Sappho.

matter of perception." Mr. Courthope says, "The high quality of the
verses depends upon their associations
with the image of the solitary Highland reaper singing unconsciously her
'melancholy strain' in the midst of
the autumn sheaves; detached from
this image the lines would scarcely
have been more affecting than our
old friend, 'Barbara, celarent, &c.'"
By an odd coincidence, and personal
experience, I can disprove (in my own
case) this dictum of Mr. Courthope's.
When I was a freshman, with a great
aversion to Wordsworth, and an almost
exhaustive ignorance of his poetry, I
chanced to ask a friend to suggest a
piece of verse for Latin elegiacs. He
answered, "Why don't you try

> ' Will no one tell me what she sings?
> Perhaps the plaintive numbers flow
> For old, unhappy, far-off things,
> And battles long ago.'"

I did *not* attempt to convert the lines
into blundering elegiacs. I did not
even ask for the context, but the
beauty and enchantment of the sounds
remained with me, singing to me, as
it were, in lonely places beside the
streams and below the hills. This is,
perhaps, evidence that, for some hearers, the high quality of Wordsworth's
touch, "when Nature took the pen
from him," does *not* depend on the
context, though from the context
even that verse gains new charms.
For what is all Celtic poetry but a
memory

> "Of old, unhappy, far-off things,
> And battles long ago"?

In the long run, perhaps, as Mr.
Courthope says, Mr. Swinburne "only
proves by his argument that the
poetry of Byron is of a different
kind from the poetry of Wordsworth
and Shelley, and that he himself
infinitely prefers the poetry of the
two latter." Unluckily argument
can prove no more than that the
poetry which we "infinitely prefer"
is of a different kind from the poetry
of Pope and Johnson, and even from
most of Thomson's. One cannot *de-*

monstrate that it is not only of a
different kind but of an infinitely
higher kind. That is matter for perception. But this one may say, and
it may even appear of the nature of
an argument, that the poetry of "a different kind," which I agree with so
much more competent a judge as Mr.
Swinburne in preferring, is not peculiar to any one people, or time, or
movement. It is *quod semper, quod
ubique, quod ab omnibus.* I find this
flower on the long wild, frozen plains
and steppes, the *tundras,* of the Finnish
epic, the 'Kalevala':—"The cold has
spoken to me, and the rain has told
me her runes; the winds of heaven,
the waves of the sea, have spoken and
sung to me, the wild birds have
taught me, the music of many waters
has been my master." So says the
Runoia, and he speaks truly, but wind
and rain, and fen and forest, cloud
and sky and sea, never taught their
lesson to the typical versifiers of the
Conservative eighteenth century. I
find their voices, and their enchantment, and their passion in Homer and
Virgil, in Theocritus, and Sophocles,
and Aristophanes, in the *volkslieder*
of modern Greece, as in the ballads of
the Scottish border, in Shakespeare
and Marlowe, in Ronsard and Joachim
du Bellay, in Cowper and Gray, as in
Shelley and Scott and Coleridge, in
Edgar Poe, in Heine, and in the Edda.
Where I do not find this natural
magic, and "element at once perceptible and indefinable," is in the
'Rape of the Lock,' 'The Essay on Man,'
'Eloisa to Abelard,' 'The Campaign,'—
is in the typical verse of the classical
and Conservative eighteenth century.
Now, if I am right in what, after all,
is a matter of perception, if all great
poetry of all time has this one mark,
this one element, and is of this one
kind, while only the typical poetry of
a certain three generations lacks the
element, and is of another kind, can
I be wrong in preferring *quod semper,
quod ubique, quod ab omnibus?*
The late Rector of Lincoln College
(a Liberal, to be sure, alas!) has defined

that which we consciously miss in Pope and Johnson as " the element of inspired feeling." Perhaps we cannot define it, and perhaps it is going too far to say, with the Rector, that " it is by courtesy that the versifiers of the century from Dryden to Churchill are styled poets." Let us call them " poets with a difference," for even Mr. Courthope will probably admit (what he says Mr. Swinburne has " proved " about Byron) that they are poets " of a different kind." Then let us prefer which kind we please, and be at rest. We, who prefer the kind that Homer began, and that Lord Tennyson continues, might add, as a reason for our choice, that our side is strong in the knowledge and rendering of Nature. Wordsworth, in a letter to Scott,[1] remarked that Dryden's was " not a poetical genius," although he possessed (what Chapelain, according to Théophile Gautier, *especially* lacked), " a certain ardour and impetuosity of mind, with an excellent ear." But, said Wordsworth, " there is not a single image from nature in the whole body of his works," and, " in his translation from Virgil, wherever Virgil can be fairly said to have had his *eye* upon his object, Dryden always spoils the passage." So, it is generally confessed, does Pope spoil Homer, Homer who always has his eye on the object. I doubt if Chapman, when he says—

" And with the tops he bottoms all the deeps, And all the bottoms in the tops he steeps,"

gives the spirit of a storm of Homer's worse than Pope does, when he remarks—

" The waves behind roll on the waves before."

Or where does Homer say that the stars—

" O'er the dark trees a yellower verdure shed, And tip with silver every mountain head ?"

Πάντα δὲ εἴδεται ἄστρα,[2]

says Homer, and it is enough. The " yellower verdure," and the silver,

[1] Lockhart's ' Memoirs of the Life of Sir Walter Scott,' ii. 89.

[2] " And all the stars show plain."

and the rest of this precious stuff come from Pope, that minute observer of external nature. Mr. Courthope numbers Dryden, with Shakespeare, Chaucer, and Scott, among poets with " the power of reproducing the idea of external nature." It may be my unconscious Liberalism, but I prefer the view of that eminent Radical, William Wordsworth. Mr. Courthope elsewhere asserts that the writers of the best poetry of the eighteenth century (meaning Pope, I presume, and the rest), " faced nature boldly, and wrote about it in metre directly as they felt it." Probably, by " nature," Mr. Courthope means " human nature," for I cannot believe that Pope, boldly facing Nature on a starlit night, really saw a " yellower verdure " produced by " that obscure light which droppeth from the stars."

Before leaving the question of the value of typical eighteenth century poetry, one would recall Mr. Courthope's distinctions between the poetry of manners and national action, and the poetry of romance. I said that there was much romance in our national actions. Now, outside the sacred grove of Conservative and classical poetry, that romance of national action has been felt, has been fittingly sung. From the Fight of Brunanburh, to Drayton's ' Agincourt,' from Agincourt to Lord Tennyson's ' Revenge,' and Sir Francis Doyle's ' Red Thread of Honour,' we have certain worthy and romantic lyrics of national action. The Cavalier poets gave us many songs of England under arms, even Macaulay's ' Armada ' stirs us like ' Chevy Chase,' or ' Kinmont Willie.' The Conservative and classical age of our poetry was an age of great actions. What, then, did the Conservative poets add to the lyrics of the romance of national action ? Where is *their* ' Battle of the Baltic,' or their ' Mariners of England ' ? Why, till we come to Cowper (an early member of " the Liberal movement,") to Cowper and the ' Loss of the Royal George,' I declare I know not where to find a poet who has discovered in national action any romance or any inspiration at all! What do we get, in place of the romance of national adventure, in place of 'Lucknow' and 'The Charge of the Light Brigade,' from the classical period? Why, we get, at most, and at best,

" Though fens and floods possessed the middle
  space
  *That unprovoked they would have feared to
  pass,*
  Nor fens nor floods can stop Britannia's
  hands,
  When her proud foe ranged on their border
  stands." [1]

I recommend the historical and topographical accuracy of the second line, and the musical correctness of the fourth. Not thus did Scott sing how—

" The stubborn spearsmen still made good
  Their dark impenetrable wood,"

and I doubt if Achilles found any such numbers, when Patroclus entered his tent, ἄειδε δ'ἄρα κλέα ἀνδρῶν.[2] The Conservative age, somehow, was less patriotic than the poets of "the Liberal movement."

Space fails me, and I cannot join battle with Mr. Courthope as to the effect of science on poetry, and as to the poetry of savage times and peoples, though I am longing to criticise the verses of Dieyries and Narrinyeries, and the *karakias* of the Maoris, and the great Maori epic, so wonderfully Homeric, and the songs of the Ojibbeways and Malagasies. When Macaulay said, "as civilisation advances, poetry almost necessarily declines," I doubt if much Dieyri or Narrinyeri verse was present to his consciousness. But this belongs to a separate discussion.

I have tried to show that, by introducing political terms into poetical criticism, and by having his eye on politics when discoursing of poetry, Mr. Courthope has not made obscure matters clearer, and has, perhaps, been betrayed into a strained affection for the Conservative and classical school. His definition of what gives a poet his rank, "his capacity for producing lasting pleasure by the metrical expression of thought, of whatever kind it may be," certainly admits Pope and some of his followers. But, as a mere matter of perception, I must continue to think them "poets with a difference," different from Homer, Sappho, Theocritus, Virgil, Shelley, Keats, Coleridge, and Heine. This is the conclusion of a romanticist, who maintains that the best things in Racine, the best things in Aristophanes, the best things in the Book of Job, are romantic. But I willingly acknowledge that the classical movement, the Conservative movement, the movement which Waller began and Pope completed, was inevitable, necessary, salutary.

I am not ungrateful to Pope and Waller; but they hold of Apollo in his quality of leech, rather than of minstrel, and they "rather seem his healing son," Asclepius, than they resemble the God of the Silver Bow. As to the future of our poetry, whether poets should return to "the simple iambic movements" or not, who can predict? It all depends on the poets, probably unborn, who are to succeed Mr. Matthew Arnold and Lord Tennyson. But I hope that, if our innumerable lyric measures are to be deserted, it may be after my time. I see nothing opposed to a moderate Conservatism in anapæsts, but I fear Mr. Courthope suspects the lyric Muse herself of a dangerous Radicalism.

ANDREW LANG.

---

[1] Of course there are better things than this in the 'Campaign' of the inspired Mr. Addison.

[2] " And he was singing of the glorious deeds of men."

POETRY AND POLITICS: FORM AND SUBJECT.

WE may congratulate ourselves on having at last approached a period when it will be possible for those who differ fundamentally on questions of taste to express their differences without calling each other "malignants," or "asses," or even "criticasters." I think myself happy that my book on *The Liberal Movement in English Literature*, should have been reviewed in a spirit of courteous antagonism by one so well qualified as Mr. Andrew Lang to speak on behalf of romantic theory and practice. If he has at times employed the arts of light banter and ridicule, in which he has few equals, to obscure the real nature of my position, he has in no way exceeded the rights of a controversialist; while by his counter-statement of his own position he throws a new and suggestive light on the whole question. As the counsel who opens the case has the right of reply, I may be allowed, under these circumstances, to clear up for the jury, as far as I can, the few points on which Mr. Lang has (no doubt unintentionally) misrepresented me, and then to examine the nature of the real issue between us.

Mr. Lang accuses me of having, by the title of my book, "raised a war-cry," and "brought back the howls of partizans into a region where they had been long silent." Supposing that I am justly chargeable with this abominable conduct, am I the sole, or indeed the first, offender? Is it really the case that poets and critics have long been living in the pastoral, the stormless Eden which Mr. Lang describes? I seem to remember, not so many years back, that the warmth with which one eminent poet expressed his opinions about the morals of another, led the two to carry their differences into the law-courts. I should have said that Mr. Swinburne's late attack on Byron was not altogether unaccompanied by ululation. And when Mr. Arnold pronounces *ex cathedrâ* that Dryden and Pope are "not classics of our poetry," it appears to me that the verdict, however decorously delivered, is based, not simply on the "literary merits" of these writers, but on the prejudices of a "partizan."

What is meant, however, of course, is that I allow my political feelings to warp my literary judgments. It is suggested that I am reviving the malpractices of that malignant Tory Maginn

* *Macmillan's Magazine* for December.

who, in the early part of the present century, attacked Byron and Shelley. With very great deference I deny that I am doing anything of the kind. Maginn condemned the romantic poets on account of their political and religious *opinions*; whenever I have examined the nature of any poet's opinions, it has always been with reference to some influence which, in my judgment, these have exerted on the principles of his *art*. I appeal with confidence to those who have read my book, to decide whether it can be justly characterized as " the howl of a partizan."

" Well, but," says Mr. Lang in effect, " waiving that point, your political preoccupations have led your judgment all wrong. Your excitement causes you to see everything in a red light, and when you ought to be thinking in a serene literary atmosphere about Byron and Shelley and Wordsworth, you constantly use political phrases which show you to be full of apprehensions about the Establishment, the Game Laws, and the three acres and the cow."

Admirable fooling, but not, I think, sound argument. Mr. Lang is seeking to win the sympathies of the English reader who, when he sees the word "Liberal" used, thinks immediately of Mr. Gladstone sitting opposite to Sir Michael Hicks Beach. It is surely, however, the height of insularity to tie down the term "Liberalism" to a Parliamentary meaning. It came to us from the Continent, and, question-begging though it may be, it was undoubtedly first used to signify the movement of emancipation from feudal custom and religious dogma associated in our minds with the French Revolution. Cardinal Newman employs it in the sphere of religious thought, and—though Mr. Lang asserts that he " uses it as short for most things that he dislikes "—as a matter of fact defines very precisely the sense he attaches to it in his *History of My Religious Opinions*. Even, however, if Mr. Lang objects to Cardinal Newman as an authority, he can scarcely object to Heine, in whose writings the word is constantly found with the same broad sense which I have given to it.* In its application to literature I have used the word " Liberal" as almost equivalent to " romantic," and I have preferred the former term chiefly on account of the moral, social, and political explanation which it seems to offer of the latter.

---

* Compare Heine's comments on our insular party names : " The English do not, however, let themselves be led astray by these party names. When they speak of Whigs, they do not form, in so doing, a definite idea, as we do in speaking of Liberals, when we at once bring before us certain men who are from their souls sincere as to certain privileges of freedom—but they think of an external union of people, of whom each one, judged by his private manner of thought, would form a party by himself, and who, as I have already said, fight against the Tories through the impulse of extraneous causes, accidental interests, and the associations of enmity or friendship."— *Reisebilder.*

If Mr. Lang had borne in mind the definition which I gave in my preface, I venture to think he would not have found so much difficulty in understanding my meaning.

"Mr. Courthope," he says, "shows a Radical Carlyle, a Conservative Macaulay; a Scott who is, perhaps, a kind of Whig; a Byron who, being pessimistic, should be Conservative, but is Liberal; a Shelley who is Liberal, though, being pessimistic, he ought to be Conservative. It is all very perplexing, and, like most mischief, all comes out of party politics."

Carlyle was not a Radical like Mr. Chamberlain, of course; but for all that he was a Radical, as I understand the word, socially and artistically. He was content, with Professor Teufelsdröck, that "old sick Society should be burned, in the hopes that a phœnix might arise out of its ashes." Such "content" I hold to be Radicalism pure and simple. Macaulay is politically a Whig or Moderate Liberal; but that does not prevent him from being a Conservative in taste as opposed to Carlyle. His whole method of common-sense criticism is merely a development of modes of thought handed down to him from the eighteenth century: his English is the natural social idiom of his time formed on the best prose models since Addison. Without any great strain on the understanding, this may surely be called literary Conservatism. Carlyle's criticism is all introspective; his style belongs to nobody but himself; in relation to preceding writers it is complete topsy-turveydom. This, again, looking to my definition, is of the nature of artistic Radicalism. As to Scott, he is in literature a Moderate Liberal. Though his imagination is romantic, all his judgments of men and things are, as I have argued in my essays, founded on the sane ways of thinking of the eighteenth century. Mr. Lang, indeed, says, in his mischievous vein, that "Scott played (if we are to be political) Mr. Jesse Collings to Coleridge's Mr. Chamberlain." I confess I think this criticism is quite at fault. Though the metrical movement of the *Lay of the Last Minstrel* was strongly influenced by *Christabel*, I should have supposed it to be impossible to study Scott without perceiving that the body of his diction was a development, under altered circumstances, of the mixed social and literary idiom inherited, through a long succession of poets, from Dryden. As to optimism and pessimism, I never said that Conservatives were pessimists. True Conservatism I hold to be founded on Christian doctrine; and a belief in the corruption of the human will undoubtedly involves an element of pessimism, but this is mitigated by the principles of religious Faith and Hope. Optimism, on the other hand, is, as I have said, the characteristic note of the French Revolution; nor do I find anything extraordinary in the fact that one who embraced revolutionary principles, as Shelley did, in their plenitude, should have fallen from the heights of rapture into the abysses of despondency.

I have said all that I wish to say in defence of my title from Mr. Lang's strictures. I come now to the far more important question between us: what it is that constitutes the nature of poetry. Pope, we are told, is no poet. Mr. Arnold's *fiat* has gone forth, and he is to be banished from our English Parnassus. Well, some of us Englishmen who still love Liberty, naturally ask, "Why, what evil hath he done?" and Mr. Lang undertakes to supply the arguments which justify Mr. Arnold's sentence. As his reasoning is very suggestive, I give what he says at full length :—

We can "gauge and name" the properties of Pope's verse, and little or nothing is left unnamed and ungauged. For this reason Pope always appears to me, if a poet at all, a poet "with a difference." The test, of course, is subjective, even mystical, if you will. Mr. Courthope might answer that Pope is full of passages in which he detects an indefinable quality that can never be gauged or named. In that case I should be silenced, but Mr. Courthope does not say anything of the sort. Far from that, he says (and here he does astonish me) that "the most sublime passages of Homer, Milton, and Virgil can readily be analysed into their elements." Why, if it were so, they would, indeed, be on the level of Pope. But surely it is not so. We can parse Homer, Virgil, and Milton; we can make a *précis* of what they state ; but who can analyse their incommunicable charm? If any man thinks he can analyse it, to that man I am inclined to say, the charm must be definable, indeed, but imperceptible. Take Homer's words, so simply uttered, when Helen has said that her brothers shun the war for her shame's sake—

Ὡς φάτο· τοὺς δ'ἤδη κατέχεν φυσίζοος αἶα.
Ἐν Λακεδαίμονι αὖθι, φίλη ἐν πατρίδι γαίῃ.

Who can analyse the subtle melancholy of the lines, the incommunicable charm and sweetness, full of all thoughts of death, and life, and the dearness of our native land?

In Virgil and Milton it is even easier to find examples of this priceless quality, lines like—

" Fluminaque antiquos subterlabentia muros " ;

or—

" Te, Lari maxime teque
Fluctibus et fremitu assurgens, Benace, marino."

Mr. Courthope himself quotes lines of Milton's that sufficiently illustrate my meaning :—

"And ladies of the Hesperides, that seemed
Fairer than feigned of old or fabled since
Of faery damsels met in forest wide
By Knight of Logres, or of Lyones,
Launcelot, or Pelleas, or Pellenore."

There is something in the very procession or rhythmical fitness of the words, there is a certain bloom and charm which defies analysis. *This bloom is of the essence of poetry, and it is not characteristic of Mr. Courthope's Conservative eighteenth century.*

Hence Pope may be justly and legitimately exiled from Parnassus. Q.E.D. Now on this reasoning I have two main observations to make. In the first place, I do not think it would be possible to find a passage that illustrates more forcibly than the above that tendency in the Romanticism of the period, on which I have dwelt in my book, to insist that poetry inheres in the form without reference to the subject, to identify poetry, in fact, as closely as possible with *music*. I had hoped, indeed, that Mr. Lang would have perceived, from what I said about Coleridge, that I was by no means insensible to the subtle charm of metrical music pure and simple. But let that be. To say, however, that this is of the essence of *all* poetry is to say what is demonstrably false. According to Mr. Lang, poetry should lie entirely in the expression independently of the conception, whereas, in truth, it lies in conception and expression taken together, but the highest part is in the conception. Does Mr. Lang hold that there is no poetry in the irony of *Œdipus Tyrannus*? Surely he does not. But if he does not, then nothing is more certain than that, in such an atmosphere of terror, any approach to that charm and softness and bloom of expression which is found in the passages he cites would be entirely out of place. I said that the *most* sublime passages in Homer, and Virgil, and Milton, could readily be analysed into their elements; and so they can, as far as their subject-matter goes, as one sees from Longinus's analysis of the passage in the *Iliad* describing the combats of the gods, and from many other examples in the section of his *Treatise on the Sublime* dealing with *Elevation of Thought*. In the same way, when Satan, in *Paradise Lost*, weeps before his address to the fallen angels, we readily apprehend the *idea* that gives poetical sublimity to the passage, though I fully allow that we cannot analyze or fathom the beauty of the *form* in which the idea is expressed. The particular passages which Mr. Lang cites are by no means the most sublime in Homer or Milton. I do not for a moment deny the existence of an indefinable charm in them : I only say that it is a mistake to suppose that this is an essential element in *all* poetry.

Let me illustrate my point a little further. Mr. Swinburne quoted Wordsworth's beautiful stanza from *The Highland Reaper*,—

> Will no one tell me what she sings?
> Perhaps the plaintive numbers flow
> For old, unhappy, far-off things,
> And battles long ago,

and said, " If not another word was left of the poem in which those two last lines occur, those two lines would suffice to show the hand of a poet differing not in degree, but in kind, from the tribe of Byron or of Southey." Upon this I remarked : —

Supposing that the two lines—

> For old, unhappy, far-off things,
> And battles long ago,

had been all of the poem which was in existence, their pathos and beauty and harmony would have been entirely lost. The high quality of the verses depends on their association with the image of the solitary Highland reaper singing unconsciously her melancholy strain in the midst of the autumn sheaves : detached from this image the lines would scarcely have been more affecting than our old friends, " Barbara celarent, &c."

In order to show that I am completely wrong in this view, Mr. Lang cites his own experience when the *whole stanza* was first repeated to him as an undergraduate at Oxford. He says :

1 did not even ask for the context, but the beauty and enchantment of the sounds remained with me, singing to me, as it were, in lonely places beside the stre⁞ ⁞ and below the hills.

I can readily understand this : a man of imagination hearing the stanza for the first time would probably be able to supply something like the context ; but the question is, would Mr. Lang have been thus affected if he had only heard the two last lines ? For obviously in that case he would have known nothing about the *song,* and nothing about the *mystery* and *plaintiveness* connected with the song. Mr. Swinburne formed his judgment of the two last lines with his mind full of the harmonious associations of the poem as a whole. But if Mr. Lang had only had the two isolated lines to judge from, he would not have got the "beauty and enchantment of the sounds" which set the song going in his imagination. And even though he did not care to look up the context, I suppose he would not deny that the stanza becomes infinitely more poetical when taken with its context than when read in its isolation. You get, then, this result—that until the last two lines of the stanza are supplemented by the two that precede them, the mind is unable to form any complete or harmonious image, while the beauty and music of the stanza is wonderfully increased when it is taken as part of the poem as a whole. All this seems to me to show that the larger, the finer element in poetry is something quite independent of " that bloom and charm which defies analysis," " the procession and rhythmical fitness of the words."

The first main point of difference between Mr. Lang and myself is, then, that he holds (or so I understand him) subject in poetry to count for no more than theme in music, and to be only valuable in so far as it gives opportunity for the production of those effects of metrical harmony which he particularly admires. I maintain, on the contrary, that the essence of poetry lies quite as much in the design or conception or idea of the poet as in the form in which he clothes it ; and that, in fact, the rank of a poet is determined by the quality of the thought and feeling for which he has been able to find a completely harmonious expression.

And I am saying only what Dante said with regard to subject and form :—

> O divina virtù, se mi ti presti
> Tanto che l' ombra del beato regno
> Segnata nel mio capo io manifesti,
> . Venir vedra' mi al tuo diletto legno,
> E coronarmi allor di quelle foglie
> Che la materia e tu mi farai degno.*

The second point of difference is in respect of poetical expression. Mr. Lang, applying his principles, would exclude from the circle of genuine poets all those whose choice of subject virtually prohibits them from producing his required metrical effects. I claim to take a more liberal view of the art of poetry than my Liberal critic. I say that the range of subjects open to the poet is ample and various ; that the poetical capacity of any idea means simply its power to awaken imaginative associations of any sort in the mind ; and that the true test of a poet's art is the reader's sense that something has been said better in metre than it could have been said in prose. Within a certain range of associations it is almost impossible to decide beforehand that there is any subject for which a metrical form cannot be found to satisfy this test. *Solvitur ambulando*. It is, of course, the case that it would be impossible to argue a proposition of Euclid in metre. Frere, however, has written what I should certainly call a good poem on *The Loves of the Triangles* ; and, generally speaking, there is a large class of poetry represented by such names as Horace, Ariosto, Pope, and Goldsmith, most of whose work entirely excludes romance in Mr. Lang's sense of the word, while it at the same time exhibits a certain *curiosa felicitas* in the diction, equivalent to the "bloom and charm which defies analysis" in the romantic style. Here I quite grant we must fall back on ultimate perceptions. I have no hope whatever of persuading Mr. Lang—because he insists on the necessity of the romantic element ; but I would ask the general reader, whose mind is still open on the subject, to consider whether any of the following passages, selected from the metrical writer over whose body Mr. Lang and I are fighting, could possibly have been expressed so well in prose as they are in verse. I do not choose my examples from the fanciful *Rape of the Lock*, or the passionate *Eloisa to Abelard*, for here, Mr. Lang might say, the romantic element came in: I take them one and all from Pope's *ethical* poems, from which this element is necessarily excluded. The first is the opening of the *Essay on Man* :—

> Awake, my St. John! leave all meaner things
> To low ambition and the pride of kings.
> Let us (since life can little more supply
> Than just to look about us and to die)

* *Paradiso*, Canto i. 22.

Expatiate free o'er all this scene of man ;
A mighty maze ! but not without a plan;
A wild where weeds and flowers promiscuous shoot,
Or garden tempting with forbidden fruit.
Together let us beat this ample field,
Try what the open, what the covert yield ;
The latent tracts, the giddy heights explore
Of all who blindly creep or sightless soar ;
Eye nature's walks, shoot folly as it flies,
And catch the manners living as they rise ;
Laugh where we must, be candid where we can,
But vindicate the ways of God to man.

This is not sublime or profound ; the range of imagination is limited ; but, within that range, how perfect it all is ! The animation of the somewhat homely metaphors so exactly appropriate to the subject, the terseness and pregnancy of the words chosen, the musical movement of the whole paragraph—is there not in all this an indefinable something which indicates the presence of a poet of genius ? The next passage is in a higher vein : the concluding lines of the *Epistle to the Earl of Oxford* after his disgrace :—

In vain to deserts thy retreat is made ;
The Muse attends thee to the silent shade.
'Tis hers the brave man's latest steps to trace,
Re-judge his acts, and dignify disgrace.
When Interest calls off all her sneaking train,
And all the obliged desert, and all the vain,
She waits, or to the scaffold or the cell,
When the last lingering friend has bid farewell.
E'en now she shades thy evening walk with bays,
(No hireling she, no prostitute to praise !)
E'en now, observant of the parting ray,
Eyes the calm sunset of thy various day ;
Through Fortune's cloud one truly great can see,
Nor fears to tell that Mortimer is he.

If this is not noble poetry I do not know what is. In another vein, take the well-known description of the Duke of Buckingham's death-bed :—

In the worst inn's worst room, with mat half-hung,
The floors of plaster, and the walls of dung,
On once a flock-bed, but repaired with straw,
With tape-tied curtains never meant to draw,
The George and Garter dangling from that bed,
Where tawdry yellow strove with dirty red,
Great Villiers lies—alas ! how changed from him,
That life of pleasure and that soul of whim !
Gallant and gay, in Clievden's proud alcove,
The bower of wanton Shrewsbury and love ;
Or just as gay at council, in a ring
Of mimic statesmen and their merry king.
No wit to flatter, left of all his store,
No fool to laugh at, which he valued more ;
There, victor of his health, of fortune, friends,
And fame, this lord of useless thousands ends !

This is the man who is henceforth only to be reckoned a "classic of our prose!" I will only add one more extract, because it may be said that, though Pope could be animated brilliant, lofty, picturesque, he could not be pathetic.

> O friend, may each domestic bliss be thine!
> Be no unpleasing melancholy mine.
> Me let the tender office long engage
> To rock the cradle of reposing age;
> With lenient arts extend a mother's breath,
> Make languor smile, and smooth the bed of death;
> Explore each want, explain the asking eye,
> And keep awhile one parent from the sky.

Mr. Lang is ready to allow Pope to be a "poet with a difference." This is only a way of saying, politely but dogmatically, that he is not a poet at all. It appears to me that he might say with equal reason that Gerard Douw was a painter with a difference. I appeal to the tribunal of *common* sense to decide whether the man who, from the simple metrical instrument at his disposal, could evoke all this varied harmony of feeling, may not be reckoned in his own order (a far lower order, of course, than Homer's, Virgil's, and Milton's) a poet in the most absolute sense of the word.

And now I have a few words to say in conclusion. Mr. Lang divines that in the "somewhat strained affection that I bear to the poetry of the eighteenth century," I am reasoning against my natural literary instincts, and am prompted by my "excitement against Radicalism." In one sense I can assure him that this is not the case. I can remember, as long as I can remember most things, the avidity with which I read both the poetry and the prose of the master writers of the eighteenth century, and my admiration for their style dates from a period long before I was capable of knowing my real reasons for admiring. If I have now endeavoured to put these reasons into a systematic form, my first motive has been a desire to vindicate the fame of those for whom I feel strong gratitude and affection, and whom some of the most distinguished critics of our time have combined to deprive of laurels which, by common consent, they have worn for generations. It appeared to me that those who judged our great classical writers in this narrow and grudging spirit were falling into precisely the same error as the critics of the beginning of the century who excommunicated Wordsworth, and Shelley and Keats. The one set condemned the new romantic poets because their work did not conform to the requirements of conventional classical rules; the other are for disparaging the poetry of Dryden and Pope because it lacks the element of romance. All this proscription and exclusion is an abomination. It has its origin in party pride, which I agree with Mr. Lang in regarding as the root of almost all evil.

But I am not ashamed to confess that, in another sense, my literary reasoning is associated with my "excitement against Radicalism." Radicalism, as I understand it, would rob me of most of what makes life dear to me. I value life because I am a member of a free *Society*, a society whose conceptions of duty and charity are derived from a religion, laws, and institutions springing out of a far distant past into which the mind, when moved by the electricity of association, can travel back in a moment along the continuous line of history. One of the chief cements of such a society is the power of using justly in metre the historic language which has grown with the nation's growth, and which is the finest instrument for the expression of its collective thought. Whatever nobility there is in the life of the nation should find utterance in its verse. The element of romance forms part of the nobleness of our history, and I am in the fullest agreement with Mr. Lang when he says that much of our national action and manners has been romantic. I gladly add my own respectful tribute of admiration to what he says in praise of Drayton's *Agincourt*, Lord Tennyson's *Revenge*, and Sir Francis Doyle's *Private of the Buffs*, poems which are all full of incentive to manly action. I delight in verse that genuinely arouses ideas

> Of old unhappy far-off things
> And battles long ago.

But I cannot forget that the end of all noble poetry, as of noble playing, is, in Shakespeare's words, "to hold as 'twere the mirror up to nature, to show virtue her own feature, scorn her own image, and the very age and body of the time his form and pressure." Nor do I think that Mr. Lang will deny that there is a tendency in the present day, as there has been for the last two generations, to take romance as an opiate or an anæsthetic, which has the power to make the mind insensible to the actual ills of life. Some rare and delicate intelligences have even presented this as the *duty* of art. "De nos jours," says George Sand, contrasting her own time and practice with Dante's, "plus faible, et plus sensible, l'artiste, qui n'est que le reflet et l'écho d'une génération assez semblable à lui, éprouve le besoin impérieux de détourner la vue et de distraire l'imagination, en se reportant vers un idéal de calme, d'innocence, et de rêverie. C'est son infirmité qui le fait agir ainsi, mais il n'en doit point rougir, car c'est aussi son devoir." But it is to be remembered that these are the words of a woman, and of a woman writing in the midst of a nation which has severed its connection with its past history. I appeal to Mr. Lang, as he has indirectly appealed to me, whether, with the strong sense of patriotism which breathes in his own writing, he considers that *bergerie* of any kind is the first duty of an English artist in the present day. For my own part, while I cannot help thinking it a great mistake to apply the word *criticism* to poetry, and while I am quite unable to accept his views as to the nature of classic poetry, I think that Mr. Arnold is substantially right when he says that "poetry is at bottom a true criticism of life"; or, as I should prefer to say, it has its roots in conceptions of human interest and action, derived from a noble national history. With an abominable spirit of political lying abroad, and seeking to undermine all that is historic in our institutions, it certainly does appear to me that what we want to cultivate is rather the almost lost art of speaking out in verse with strength, dignity, and lucidity, than the *rêverie* which weakens in the mind all conceptions of manly action, national or individual. I lately read some lines in an evening paper which struck me.* Speaking of those who declare that England is no longer a name to conjure with, the poet (if I may be allowed to call one who writes in so direct a fashion a poet) said :—

> Nay, if indeed that name no more
> Must, like a trumpet, stir the blood,
> Of all our fathers did and bore
> For England on the field or flood,
> If nought endures, if all must pass,
> Then speed the hour when we shall be
> Unmoved and mute beneath the grass,
> Deaf to the mountains and the sea !

These fine lines were signed "A. L." Their author seems to have a truer appreciation of the nature of poetry than the accomplished depreciator of Pope. The poet understands what it is to belong to a great nation with a continuous history. The critic would strike out of the history of our national poetry a whole century of verse because it lacks "the bloom and charm" of romance. In an age when every kind of social hypocrisy is rampant, when affectation in art and literature has become a cult, when a virulent faction is striving to obliterate all landmarks that are notably and historically English, he puts his ban on that truly English style which is represented by *Absolom and Achitophel*, the *Lines on the Death of Oldham*, *The Epistle to Arbuthnot*, and *The Castaway.*

* *St. James's Gazette,* December 9th, 1885.

WILLIAM JOHN COURTHOPE.

POETRY AND POLITICS.[1]

WITH almost all that Mr. Lang has said on this subject[2] I entirely agree. It appears to me to be manifest that political party names ought not to be allowed to beset the mind when it is engaged to the enjoyment and estimation of poetry. And he would be a hard-hearted man who would not sympathise with Mr. Lang's distress at this confusion of boundaries. He feels the pang of a romantic traveller confronted by a London advertisement in a mountain glen. Like some hart in a secret covert, he starts sadly as he hears, or thinks he hears, the political horn wound suddenly in the grove of the Muses, and the hunter preparing to

" lay his hounds in near
The Caledonian deer."

It appears to me also plain that although such argument and analysis as are undertaken by Mr. Courthope in his ingenious, but rather confusing book, may incidentally, perhaps accidentally, throw light on poetical qualities, yet they may more easily lead to fallacies and strained judgments. Above all do I most emphatically agree that in such lines as those quoted by Mr. Lang from Homer and Virgil, and Milton and Wordsworth (to which hundreds more might, happily for the world, be added), there dwells a peculiar enchantment at once indefinable and

[1] Since I wrote this paper I have read Mr. Courthope's reply to Mr. Lang in the ' National Review.' With part of it I can agree ; with part I cannot. But as it belongs to a special controversy, I think that probably any value my remarks may possess will be better retained by leaving them as they are than by modifying them to follow the course of Mr. Courthope's argument. I need hardly say that this is from no want of respect toward what he has written, but, on the contrary, because I would avoid the least semblance of a pretension to play the arbiter between him and Mr. Lang.
[2] ' Macmillan's Magazine,' December, 1885.

indispensable to the highest poetry ; and that the appreciation of this quality is matter " not of argument, but of perception."

Being thus so entirely at one with Mr. Lang as to his main positions and his mental attitude toward poetry, I am disappointed to find, further on in his paper, what seems to make an exception to this agreement. The attitude with which I sympathise is that of distrust and aversion toward the arbitrary labels which many attempt to affix to the works of poets, and toward the exaggerated desire to classify and assign them to definite " schools." But Mr. Lang himself seems to lend some countenance to the mistaken hankering after such labels in his use of the cant terms " classical" and "romantic," as applied to poetry. The terms, I conceive, were first used in French or German literature, and it might be of a certain interest to trace their origin in those countries ; but I cannot but think that they are likely to do at least as much ill service as good in general discussion of the poetry of any race or country, and especially of our own. When Mr. Lang says that he is " a romanticist," and that "the best things in Aristophanes, and Racine, and the Book of Job, are romantic," what does he mean ? Does he mean anything more than that the best things are what he likes best ? What will he say of the two lines concerning Helen's brothers which he quotes from the third book of the ' Iliad,' or of the other lines from Virgil ? Are these " romantic ? " If the epithet " classical " has any meaning applicable to poetic qualities, it would surely be the appropriate one in these cases. It should, I imagine, imply restrained force, chastened grace, pregnant simplicity of phrase, as opposed to more fantastic and startling methods of appealing to the imagination; and such force, grace, and simplicity are eminently present in these passages. Is Mr. Lang, then, as a "romanticist" to recant or qualify his admiration of them? And why is this misused epithet of "classical" to be bestowed on the English poets of the eighteenth century? What makes poetry classic unless it be the possession of high poetic genius? Even by the admission of its admirers, the genius of the eighteenth century poets was prosaic compared with that of those preceding and succeeding them. It cannot be held that there is more to be found in this period of either the spirit or the form (if, indeed, these can be rightly viewed apart in poetry) of the great poets of antiquity. What influence from antiquity is to be found here seems rather to be that of the silver age of Latin poetry. Shall we not do more wisely to discard, or at least use with great wariness, all such cant terms as these of "classical" and "romantic," as belonging, or tending to belong, to a cloud of parasitic pedantries, invented for the benefit of lecturers and critics, but merely obscuring and obstructing our enjoyment of poetry? Undoubtedly a poet is influenced by his age and its action, and also by his predecessors and contemporaries in his own art, as well as by the more permanent elements of human life, and by the phenomena of the visible universe. But who shall foretell from his multiform "environment" what part of it is to find expression in his poetry? That depends on his own free genius.

No definitions of the nature of poetry can ever be entirely satisfactory, but it is generally interesting to hear what a poet has to say of his art. Well worthy of attention is Mr. Swinburne's remark, quoted by Mr. Courthope, that the two primary and essential qualities of poetry are imagination and harmony. There is no discrepancy, and no less significance, in the words of an older poet, a fold of

whose lyric mantle has fallen on Mr. Swinburne. Pindar is somewhere speaking of the qualities by which poetry lives. It will live, he says, "whensoever by favour of the Graces the tongue hath drawn it forth out of the depth of the heart."[1] The favour of the Graces—that is, the power of imagination to conceive, and of harmonious words to express—this is indispensable; but so also is a certain state of the heart, of the feelings. It is not meant, of course, that a poet has deeper or stronger feelings than men who have not the gift of expressing them in poetry, still less that his feelings need exceptionally affect his moral action. Very likely they are too transient or too imaginative, or have little reference to practical life. A man of any other kind is as likely to "make his life a poem." But strong and pervading feeling, however transient, however merely imaginative, there surely must be to produce real poetry. Whatsoever things are lovely, or majestic, or piteous, or terrible (if there be beauty in their pity and terror) —all these can draw poetry from a poet, and that whether the images come to him in woods and mountains, or in oral tradition, or in books, from his own time, or from times remote. No classification as "classical" or "romantic" can debar him from his common rights on all these pastures of the mind. Only these things must have possessed his imagination, and through his imagination his feeling, before they will call forth his best poetry. It is indeed this need of penetrated and penetrative feeling, and presentation of beauty and grandeur, combined with the intellectual formative effort, that makes the production of poetry of sustained excellence so hard and rare, and makes us feel that almost all poems would have been better if they had been shorter. Now in this newly-revived question of the claims of Pope and kindred writers to be counted poets, is it not primarily the continuous absence of deep imaginative

[1] 'Nemean,' iv. 7, 8.

feeling which prevents some of us from so counting them in any but a very imperfect sense? Neglect of inanimate nature—possibly even glaringly false description of it, as in Pope's Homer—need not argue the absence of poetry, any more than mere accurate and picturesque description need argue its presence. Descriptions of picturesque phenomena are used with much greater reserve by the great poets of antiquity than by most English writers since Thomson and Cowper; yet they are by no means used with less effect, for they are always strictly relevant to the human interest. But the most fatal want in Pope and his fellows is a want of passion. By passion is not necessarily meant, of course, any tumult of the mind; more often a kind of fervent stillness; but at any rate a condition in which the intellectual perception is, so to speak, steeped throughout in emotional contemplation of a possessing idea, with which it is for the time identified, yet without losing its intellectual formative energy. Only by " possession " of this kind, coinciding with the requisite faculty of words, is the perfect poetic expression of the idea elicited. Though it often includes, it yet differs from, that " ardour and impetuosity of mind " allowed by Wordsworth to Dryden. Ardour of this kind is necessary to the orator also, but then the orator is always thinking first, or at least equally, of his audience, and the effect of his words on them : the poet is entirely occupied with the object of his imagination. In this lies the reason why didactic poems are in continual danger of degenerating into mere rhetorical verse—a danger which even the genius of Lucretius could not altogether surmount, and which repeatedly compelled Virgil to choose in the ' Georgics ' between instruction and poetry. He seldom fails to choose the latter alternative. It is not of students of agriculture that he is thinking when he loses himself in imagination among the cool glens of Hæmus, beneath the umbrage of the giant boughs. But in Pope and Addison and Dryden, and the eighteenth-century poets generally, the rhetorical quality is predominant, and it is only in this rhetorical quality that I can see plausible justification of Mr. Courthope's attributing to that century a closer connexion between poetry and public life than is found during other periods. In the sonnets alone of the recluse Wordsworth there would seem to be more memorable witness to things of national concern.

It is by no means intended here that a man may not be both a rhetorician and a poet. Macaulay, for instance, was both ; and though his vein of poetic metal is a small thing among the vast mines of his rhetoric, it runs pure and unconfused when it appears in his ' Lays.' Rhetoric must be included in the genius of a dramatic, and even of an epic, poet. Yet there are few momentous speeches in Homer or in Shakespeare which do not contain a poetic element far beyond the rhetoric with which it blends. Through the stern brief utterances of Achilles avenging, pierce such haunting strains as the lines—

ἔσσεται ἢ ἠὼς ἢ δείλη ἢ μέσον ἦμαρ
ὁππότε τις καὶ ἐμεῖο Ἄρει ἐκ θυμὸν ἕληται,
ἢ ὅγε δουρὶ βαλὼν ἢ ἀπὸ νευρῆφιν ὀϊστῷ.[1]

It is only through the presence of imaginative passion that the metrical form of expression justifies its use, at once as a necessity, and as an inexhaustible charm. Metre not only provides, as has not seldom been remarked, a balance and law which harmonises the passionate flow of imaginative emotion ; but it also deepens and intensifies that emotion by bringing it into accord, so to speak, with the inner music which is at the heart of things, and through which alone their existence can have its fullest meaning, and be the object of vivid conception. Thus the art of poetry, instead of removing us from nature, brings us closer. This

[1] " There cometh morn or eve or some noonday when my life too some man shall take in battle, whether with spear he smite or arrow from the string."

2

is an effect of metre far beyond the conciseness and power of impressing the memory in which Pope seems to have seen its chief merits.

The things which fertilise one poet's imagination may be very different from those which fertilise another's; the seed may be wafted from mediæval romance, or from Hellenic mythology, from the idea of the fall of man, or of the founding of a state, from clouds or from flowers, from mountains or from the sea. It may even be found, under limitations to which I will return, in some of the political interests shudderingly repudiated by Mr. Lang. But whatever it may be, it is something which the poet must transfer, so to speak, from his imagination to ours, by means of his art and his feeling combined, or rather interfused. Some degree of sympathy, of course, is needed : the subject which interests him may seem so remote from humanity in general, or perhaps so trivial, that such transference is hardly possible ; but this is only a question of degree. Now Pope not only generally chooses things to write about which are unlikely to inspire poetic feeling ; but even when his subjects are moving (as the grief of Eloisa), they seem to contend in vain with the antithetical point-making of the expression. The fact of his writing in metre, and giving his readers pleasure by his epigrammatic skill in wielding it, is surely beside the mark in considering whether he is to be called a poet. The mere terseness and compendious convenience of metre can give pleasure when they fix a witty epigram on the mind, but this is not a poetic pleasure. Pope's deficiency may be well seen by comparing him with Gray, of whom Mr. Courthope speaks as " carrying on the ethical impulse communicated to poetry by Pope." Many lines of Gray share largely the mannerism of Pope's age, and yet by their interpenetrative glow of imaginative feeling are stamped as indisputable poetry. And not only in Gray, but also in Crabbe, there is at times imaginative passion ; it is

lack of beauty, rather than lack of passion, that gives Crabbe but a low place among poets. For in high poetry this penetrative feeling must have its cause, however indirectly, in the contemplation of beauty of some kind ; this is part of what Pindar means when he speaks of the favour of the Graces as indispensable. Verse of which the pervasive feeling and imagination are mainly excited by mean or hideous things may attain great power as satire, but not as pure poetry. It is as a satirist rather than as a poet that Byron seems to me to be entitled to rank high, in spite of the directness and facility, the rhetorical force which his prodigious ability gave him on subjects of many kinds. The ' Vision of Judgment ' and ' Don Juan ' seem to me his most successful works. I do not forget that this postulate of beauty might seem to deprive most of Dante's ' Hell ' of its place in pure poetry. Some parts must be so excepted, I think, and also such parts of the ' Purgatory ' and ' Paradise ' as treat of matters where there is not enough feeling transmitted to the reader to prevent his thinking that they might as well have been in prose. Such are most of the theological and philosophical disquisitions. But even in the ' Inferno,' besides the broken lights of pathetic beauty, such as the meetings with Francesca, or with Brunetto Latini, the horrors are redeemed to poetry by the sense both of the noble and melancholy presence of the guide Virgil, and of the righteous judgments of God which overshadow the whole. Nor can there be a nobler poetical idea than that of the progress and purgation of the human spirit, symbolised through the entire poem by Dante's upward journey through hell and purgatory to the spheres of heaven.

The argument has somewhat led us away from the title of this paper and of Mr. Lang's, but a few further remarks more directly relevant to it may yet find room. On the principles suggested above, it is plain what kind of power political theories or interests may have in affecting poetry. If they attract a poet's imagination by something in them which he happens to feel vividly noble or imposing, they may contribute an element to his poetry. But it is also plain that this is not likely to happen in the case of contemporary party politics, because these are commonly involved in a cloud of prosaic and even mean associations, which render an imaginative presentment practically impossible. Of course a poet may be a politician, like any one else, when not concerned with his art, and the broad fundamental principles on which his politics are based may be capable of poetical expression. But it can only be when remoteness has caused the prosaic details to disappear that the imagination will be sufficiently impressed by some moral or picturesque beauty discoverable beneath these to find material for poetry. And English politics of the eighteenth century would be among the least likely to afford such material. In the preceding age there was obviously far more idealism in the political world. And a knowledge of Milton's ardent political aspirations, and of his part in public affairs, repeatedly add great interest to his poetry. But from his poetry itself politics are excluded, unless it be in a few of his sonnets. Even these, though they are inspired by contemporary men and things, deal only with the generalities and moralities of politics. Scott also, though of course in a far less degree, was involved in the party politics of his time. But it is one of the especial glories of his sane and kindly genius that this fact could never be discovered from his works of imagination. When he presents historical characters and parties in which analogies to modern politics might be found, no tinge of partisanship ever disturbs the serene and frank impartiality with which he depicts all the lights and shades of the "mighty opposites," who have, under whatever flag, animated the stage of human life by battling for the fulfilment of some political or religious

ideal, or, it may be, for little but the satisfaction of a barbaric love of strife. It is only natural, perhaps, that, among political ideas, those of a "Liberal" or progressive kind should have been more often and more directly expressed in poetry, for the vague future lends itself more readily to the moulding of imagination than the familiar order of things seen in the light of common day. Even if the idealisation be of the past, this is hardly more corroborative of a practical and political Conservatism of existing institutions. But happily the instinct of poets has pretty nearly banished party politics and definite political specifics of all kinds from poetry—at any rate from the best. The one great exception is an exception that may really be said to go far to prove the rule. Dante not only argued systematically for his cherished political theory in prose, but also eagerly welcomed all occasions for vindicating it in his great poem. The doctrine of the divinely appointed ordinance of the Holy Roman Empire may be said to be incorporated in the fabric of the 'Divina Commedia.' Going beyond generalities in praise of freedom or tradition, progress or order, Dante urges his specific remedy for the political ills and difficulties of the world—its repose under the wing of the imperial "bird of God." But then this was a remedy at which no practical politician had at that time any intention of aiming. Doubtless the idea of the Roman Empire had still some traditional authority over the minds of men. But the then emperor was too fully occupied with affairs on a much smaller scale to listen to Dante's cry to him on behalf of "widowed" Rome. As to the Ghibellines, they only profaned *il sacrosanto segno* by usurping it.

" Faccian gli Ghibellin, faccian lor arte
 Sott' altro segno ; chè mal segue quello
 Sempre chi la giustizia e lui diparte." [1]

---

[1] " Let the Ghibellines practice their arts. under some other banner than this ; for ever is he an ill follower thereof who dissevers it from justice."

If the universal empire of Rome had been before Dante's view as a militant or a triumphant reality, instead of as a visionary ideal of the reign of justice and peace, it would probably soon have lost its power of inspiration.

When we speak of the failure of politics to inspire poetry, it need hardly be said that such politics do not include the sentiment of patriotism, of resistance to oppressors or invaders, or to national enemies generally. This is happily a sentiment which has known no distinction of parties in our country, and has found expression alike in the Conservative Wordsworth, the Liberal Tennyson, and the Radical Burns; and I am glad to see that Mr. Lang reminds his readers that in the falsely-named " classical period " of the eighteenth century English patriotism found no poetic expression comparable to that achieved in the age when it has been alleged that the Revolution had corrupted our literature with cosmopolitan indifference. To the eighteenth century in England belong great and solid achievements, but not the imaginative aspirations of the Reformation, or of the Revolution, or of the age of the Crusades and the foundation of the great monastic orders of Dominic and Francis. Out of all the nineteen centuries since the Christian era, only in the three periods containing those three great movements can Europe claim to have felt the full influence of those " golden stars " beneath which poets are said to be born.

But such wide fields of disquisition are not to be entered now. In conclusion I would merely say a word to deprecate any imputation of dogmatism in these matters. In the first place, I am well aware that if several people write about a subject of this kind they are very likely to misunderstand each other, and also to use the same words in senses that differ with the user. They may be repeating when they mean to controvert, and possibly controverting when they mean to repeat. Further, with regard to the view here

supported—the view that the estimate of poetry is ultimately a matter of perception rather than argument, that the highest poetic qualities are apprehensible but indefinable — those who think thus are by virtue of their faith especially bound (however hard it seem) to be most careful to hold frankly to the principle, and not merely to "respect the right of private judgment," but to try to believe that when a judgment differs from theirs it may be based on some real perception of qualities not apparent to themselves, perhaps overlaid with defects which their idiosyncrasy makes exceptionally disfiguring in their eyes, perhaps appealing to associations which to them are insignificant. Personally, for instance, I would most willingly sacrifice the whole of ' Childe Harold,' if need were, to preserve Coleridge's ' Kubla Khan,' or Wordsworth's ' Solitary Reaper,' or one of Macaulay's ' Lays.' Yet it is undeniable that a great body of opinion would be opposed, that a great number of persons who derive genuine pleasure from poetry think as highly of Byron as a poet as I think of him as a satirist. Others, again, may hold Wordsworth's ' Reaper ' a simple and graceful piece without any especial rare and penetrative charm. Others (including a greater number of respectable judges) will allow little to Macaulay's poetry except "a certain ardour and impetuosity." Dr. Mommsen classes the ' Æneid ' with the ' Henriade'; and we know Voltaire's opinions on Dante and Shakespeare. All this only shows how subtle is the appeal of poetry, and on what complex associations it depends in each individual case. Probably, therefore, not very much is to be gained by discussion of whether this or that is true poetry, still less by too elaborate attempts at artificial classification of poets. Let us by all means know all we can of what there was in the concerns of a poet's age,—political, religious, social, literary, artistic — which was likely to influence his mind and his work, so that we may hereby apprehend more fully the significance of what he wrote. There will be natural and legitimate occasions when such knowledge will contribute an element in our appreciation of him. But let his poetry be judged as poetry, on the ground of its own merits, its own appeal to the perception of the reader, and without reference to theories as to its supposed connexion with something else, to find which the mind must leave its due enjoyment, and travel forth on a barren quest among academic formulæ and illusive classifications and definitions of the indefinable.

Ernest Myers.

THE POETIC IMAGINATION.

"Forms more real than living man,
Nurslings of immortality."

SHELLEY.

PHYSIOLOGISTS would, I suppose, tell us that imagination is a reflex action of the brain, a definition more concise than helpful. It is to the psychologists that we shall more naturally look for assistance on this subject. According to the most recent English work on the subject, Mr. Sully's 'Outlines of Psychology,' imagination is the picturing of objects and events in what are called images. If, he says, the images are exact copies of past impressions, the process is called reproductive imagination, or memory. If, on the other hand, the images are modifications or transformations of past impressions, the process is marked off as productive or constructive imagination. This latter process, Mr. Sully points out, answers roughly to the popular term imagination. But, as he says, this kind of imagination not only transforms or idealises past impressions, it also works them up into new imaginative products. Further, he might have added, imagination is interpretative; it interprets the facts of the world of sense, or, in Wordsworth's phrase, it explains "the moral property and scope of things." If, then, we take into account these three functions of the imagination, shall we not pronounce that there is after all more similarity than dissimilarity between the memory and the imagination? Shall we not say that memory is concerned with what is old, imagination with what is new; that memory is reproductive, imagination productive; that memory is imitative, imagination original? Allowing then for the obvious metaphor in the use of the word seeing, may we

not accept James Hinton's definition of imagination as "the power of seeing the unseen"?

It should here be noticed that formerly the word fancy was used to denote what we now term imagination. Thus Milton speaks of Shakespeare as "fancy's child." It was Coleridge who first distinguished between fancy and imagination, and, though the distinction is not considered of any account by modern psychologists, it is, I believe, a real one. Coleridge defined fancy as "a mode of memory emancipated from the order of time and space; and blended with and modified by that empirical phenomenon of the will, which we express by the word choice;" and he pointed out that "equally with the ordinary memory it must receive all its materials ready-made from the law of association." The term imagination he reserved for the creative faculty, but unfortunately the full and complete account of its powers which he intended one day to write, remained one of the many projects which he never put into execution. In the few but pregnant hints, however, which he has left us on the subject, he especially insists on the unity of the imagination, coining for it the epithet esemplastic (εἰς ἓν πλάττειν, i.e. to shape into one) and saying that it sees il più in uno. The same idea is carefully worked out by Mr. Ruskin in his account of the imagination in 'Modern Painters,' where he points out with great appositeness of illustration the difference between mere composition, or patchwork, and true imaginative production. Indeed, one of the strongest arguments in favour of what may be called the transcendental theory of the imagination is the immeasurable distance that separates the patchwork of an inferior artist from the seamless garment woven by a master's hand. So immeasurable is it that it is impossible to accept the explanation that the secret of true imaginative work consists merely in modifying and piecing together past impressions so rapidly and so deftly that we cannot detect the join.

" All imaginative activity," truly says Mr. Sully, "involves an element of feeling." Love, pity, horror, joy, indignation, all serve to kindle the imagination. But the emotions which beat in closest unison with it are the æsthetic emotions, that group of nameless and mysterious feelings which are generated by the presence of beauty. Seeing, then, that the true characteristic of the imagination is its creative and life-giving power, and that it has an intimate relation with the æsthetic emotions, it is not surprising that it should be especially the art-faculty, the faculty which comes into play in the production of all works of art. The sculptor must be able to model, the painter to draw and to colour, the architect to build, the musician must be a master of melody and harmony, the poet of language and rhythm ; but all alike must have imagination.

Take, for instance, one of those Dutch pictures, for which Mr. Ruskin has such contempt and George Eliot such sympathy. The exclusive worshipper of high art condemns it at once as wholly devoid of imagination. But let us try the picture by a simple test. Let us set ten painters down to paint a study from the life of an old woman scraping carrots. What will be the result ? For certain, no two of their pictures will be exactly alike. Each painter will have added something new, something which to the eye of the ordinary observer did not appear in the actual scene ; and this addition, this idealisation, as we should call it, will have come from the painter's imagination.

We speak of imagination as the idealising faculty ; but it is a mistake to suppose that to idealise necessarily means to make beautiful. Idealisation consists rather in throwing into relief the characteristic parts of an object, and discarding unimportant details ; in short, in presenting an idea of the object to the mind which, by virtue of this rearrangement makes a deeper and more lasting impression ; and for this reason, that artistic truth has been substituted for scientific truth, life for death.

Not only is imagination necessary for the production of a work of art, but it is also necessary for the understanding of it. The conception which is born of imagination can only be apprehended by imagination. Hegel indeed makes a distinction between the active or productive imagination of the artist, and the passive or receptive imagination of the beholder of a work of art, and calls them by different names ; but in reality the difference between them is one of degree and not one of kind. The impression which is made upon the beholder of a work of art, though doubtless far less intense, is no doubt similar in kind to that which the artist himself had when he conceived it.

It must be admitted that the law that imagination is necessary to the production of a work of art does not apply so strictly to poetry as to the other fine arts, and for this reason, that poetry stands on a somewhat different footing from other arts. It is, so to speak, less strictly an art. In the first place, not only, as is the case with other time arts, such as music, is the impression which it makes upon the imagination spread over a period of time instead of being almost instantaneous, as it is in a space art like painting, but it is not always even continuous. When Edgar Poe declared that a poem which could not be read through at a single sitting was an anomaly, thus excluding the ' Iliad ' and other epics from the category of poetry, he was only following out to its logical conclusion, his theory that poetry, like music, is a pure art. But the common-sense of many generations, which is a higher court than any theory, has ruled him to be wrong. The explanation is that poetry is not a pure art.

Secondly, there is this vital distinction between poetry and the other fine arts. They are addressed immediately to the senses, and through the senses to the emotions and the imagination; but poetry, though it is in some measure addressed to the ear and so far partakes of the nature of music, is chiefly and primarily addressed to the intellect—for language implies intellect to understand it—and through the intellect to the emotions and the imagination.

There follow from these special characteristics of poetry two notable results. First, the impression made upon the imagination by a poem being often spread over a considerable space of time, which may not even be continuous, we can dispense with imaginative treatment in some parts of a poem, and we do not necessarily condemn a whole poem because it contains some unimaginative passages. Secondly, poetry not being addressed primarily to the senses, there is a marked difference between the function of the imagination in poetry and its function in a sensuous art like painting. In both arts alike it is the function of the imagination to represent both the visible and the invisible world, both the sensuous object and the inward spiritual meaning of that object; but in painting the sensuous object is directly presented, while the spiritual idea can only be suggested; in poetry, on the other hand, it is the object itself which can only be suggested, it is the spiritual idea which receives direct presentment.

It is most important that poets and painters should bear in mind this distinction. To paint pictures vague in outline and blurred in colour under the impression that they thus become spiritual, is as foolish as to write poems full of detailed and matter-of-fact descriptions of material objects in order to make them sensuous. It is quite true that painting should be spiritual, it is equally true that poetry should be sensuous; but this must be effected by the method proper to each art, not by confusing their two methods.

It will be remembered that in those noble chapters of 'Modern Painters' in which Mr. Ruskin treats of the imagination he classifies its powers under three heads, Associative, Penetrative, and Contemplative. By Associative imagination he means the power of constructing images, or, as Coleridge calls it, the shaping power of the imagination. Contemplative imagination is, as I shall try to show presently, merely a form of this, which I prefer to call by the more ordinary term Constructive. On the other hand, a faculty of the imagination which Mr. Ruskin has omitted in this classification is the idealising faculty. I would therefore propose to substitute for Mr. Ruskin's terminology the terms Constructive, Idealising, and Penetrative, as expressing the various powers of the imagination.

Let us consider now what is the part played by the imagination in the genesis of a poem. First, it is to the imagination that the first conception of every true poem is due. Some external object, either animate or inanimate, either a face or a landscape, sends a rush of emotion to the poet's soul and kindles his imagination. What Turgénieff says of himself is probably true of most great poets and novelists, that they never start from the idea but always from the object. The imagination being thus called into life exercises its powers by an instantaneous and involuntary process. It transports the poet from the world of sense to the spiritual world beyond; it reveals to him as in a vision the inward meaning of the sensuous fact which has aroused his emotions, while in one and the same moment the vision is embodied in the form of a poem, the general idea of which, along with the rhythmical movement, flashes upon the poet instantaneously. Then follows the "accomplishment of verse," the filling up the details of the poet's design, in order to communicate his vision to those denser intelligences which lack the "divine faculty." With the true poet, to borrow the words used by Monro of Catullus, "there is no putting together of pieces of mosaic; with him the completed thought follows at once upon the emotion, and the consummate form and expression rush to embody this thought for ever."

Of course it is only short poems that require, as it were, but a single draught of inspiration from the imagination for their production. In longer poems the poet must be constantly calling upon his imagination for fresh efforts. But he must call upon it as a master, and he must never lose sight of the original impulse which gave birth to his work, of the guiding idea which ought to be the central point of his poem. The reason why so many poets who excel in short poems fail when they try a longer flight is that they have not sufficient power of mental concentration to keep their imagination steadily fixed on one point. They follow it instead of guiding it, and it sometimes leads them into grievous quagmires. The imagination is partly an active and partly a passive faculty. Visions often come to us without any effort of our own; it is only the supreme artist, the really great man, who can control his visions.

The intensity and the quality of the imagination in a poem will vary according to the nature of the poet's genius and the special mood engendered in him by the motive of the poem; the character of the imagination will determine that of the poem. Thus, if the imagination be directed chiefly towards the human passions and the infinite variations of them which make up individual human character, the result will be a drama, or at least a dramatic poem. If on the other hand it is rather on the actions than on the passions of men, rather on human nature in its broad outlines than on the characteristics which mark off one human being from another, that the imagination loves to dwell, we shall have a narrative, possibly an epic, poem. If the imagination is strongly emotional the result will be a lyric; if it suggest a train of thought rather than of images it will produce an elegy.

Even from the two kinds of poetry which are rightly accounted the lowest, inasmuch as their aims are only in a small measure artistic, namely satire and didactic poetry, imagination is by no means absent. There is imagination in the descriptions of persons, and in the pictures of social life which satire, not wholly unmindful of her early Italian home, sets up as a mark for her arrows; there is imagination in the images and metaphors, and in the concentrated and pregnant language by which a didactic poem like 'The Essay on Man' seeks to render its reasoning more pointed and impressive.

The images evoked by the Constructive imagination are of two kinds. They are either complex images representing some new combination of actually existing objects, or they are simple images of wholly new objects, of objects which have no existence in the world of sense. The former class of images only require a somewhat low degree of imagination for their production, and ordinary persons, who are neither novelists nor poets, have frequent experiences of them. They supply what are called the scenes or situations of fiction, in which some new and ideal combination either of man or nature, or of both together, is presented, and which form the framework for all narrative and dramatic poetry, as well as for all novels.

The most obvious instance of the second class of images are what are called imaginary creatures, such as

Milton's Satan, Ariosto's Hippogriff, Dante's Nimrod, Shakespeare's Ariel. But what are we to say of those far higher creations, the human beings who live only in the world of fiction? Are they due to the Constructive power of the imagination, or to its Idealising power, or to its Penetrative power?

It may at once be granted that all fictitious characters which are drawn from existing persons must be ascribed to the Idealising imagination. But I believe that the majority of characters in fiction, and certainly all the greatest characters, are purely ideal representations and not portraits. Although some living person may have first suggested them, they are evolved by the imagination without any further reference to that person. A great many characters for instance in Alphonse Daudet's novels are said to be portraits; but they have been claimed as such by reason, not of any essential property of likeness, but of certain details of position and circumstances. Whether Numa Roumestan stands for Gambetta, or the Duc de Mora for the Duc de Morny or not, there can be no doubt that both Numa and Mora are absolutely new creations.

If then the characters of fiction are creations and not representations, they must, as far as regards the first conception of them, be ascribed to the constructive power of the imagination. But their evolution is surely due to its penetrative power. To evolve a great character of fiction requires a deep knowledge of the human heart, and so much of that knowledge as proceeds from intuition and not from actual experience can only come from the imagination as a penetrative faculty. It is Penetrative imagination that inspires the dramatist with those touches that reveal a whole world of passion at a flash; such touches as those cited by Mr. Ruskin, the "He has no children" of Macduff; the "My gracious silence hail!" of Coriolanus; the "Quel giorno piu non vi leggemeno avanti" of Francesca, or that wonder-

ful passage in 'Lear,' wonderful in its simplicity—

> "Pray, do not mock me :
> I am a very foolish fond old man,
> Fourscore and upward ; and, to deal plainly,
> I fear I am not in my perfect mind."

This intensity and energy of concentration are unfailing signs of Penetrative imagination, the imagination which pierces right to the heart of things, seizes hold of their most characteristic and life-giving quality, and reveals it in language as simple as it is pregnant.

What a picture of perfect beauty we have in these lines from 'Christabel'—

> "Her gentle limbs she did undress
> And lay down in her loveliness."

What intense imagination in the following from Keats—

> "Or like stout Cortez, when with eagle eyes
> He stared at the Pacific—and all his men
> Looked at each other with a wild surmise—
> Silent, upon a peak in Darien."

Or in this from Wordsworth's 'Yew-trees'

> "Nor uninformed with Phantasy, and looks
> That threaten the profane."

Or as an instance of a somewhat more elaborate, but still intensely imaginative, description we have Shelley's—

> "And in its depth there is a mighty rock,
> Which has, from unimaginable years,
> Sustained itself with terror and with toil
> Over a gulf, and with the agony
> With which it clings seems slowly coming down ;
> Even as a wretched soul, hour after hour,
> Clings to the ways of life ; yet clinging leans,
> And, leaning, makes more dark the dread abyss
> In which it fears to fall. Beneath this crag,
> Huge as despair, &c."

Or Milton's description of Satan, the sublimest portrait ever painted in words—

> "He, above the rest
> In shape and gesture proudly eminent,
> Stood like a tower ; his form had yet not lost

All her original brightness ; nor appeared
Less than archangel ruined, and the excess
Of glory obscured : as when the sun, new
    risen,
Looks through the horizontal misty air
Shorn of his beams.

        Darkened so, yet shone
Above them all the archangel ; but his face
Deep scars of thunder had intrenched ; and
    care
Sat on his faded cheek ; but under brows
Of dauntless courage, and considerable pride,
Waiting revenge."

There are some lyrics which exhibit in the highest degree this penetrative faculty of the imagination, concentrating themselves on some object of nature, and revealing in one luminous flash of song the secret of its spiritual life. Such are Wordsworth's 'Daffodils', 'To the Cuckoo', and 'To a Skylark'; Herrick's 'To Blossoms' ; Goethe's 'Auf allen Gipfeln'. But on the whole this intensity of imagination is to be found more often in sonnets than in those poems to which the name of lyric is generally restricted. The very form of the sonnet, its forced concentration, its division into two parts, its sober but stately rhythm, makes it an admirable instrument for the purpose of calling up before the mind the twin image of a sensuous object and a spiritual idea. Wordsworth's sonnets especially are characterised by this high imaginative power, and of his sonnets there is no finer example than the well-known one 'Upon Westminster Bridge.'

" Earth has not anything to show more fair :
Dull would he be of soul who could pass by
A sight so touching in its majesty :
This city now doth like a garment wear
The beauty of the morning; silent, bare,
Ships, towers, domes, theatres, and temples
    lie
Open unto the fields and to the sky,
All bright and glittering in the smokeless
    air.
Never did sun more beautifully steep
In his gilt splendour valley, rock, or hill ;
Ne'er saw I, never felt, a calm so deep !
The river glideth at his own sweet will :
Dear God ! the very houses seem asleep ;
And all that mighty heart is lying still ! "

In the great majority of lyrical poems which deal with some external object, and not with the poet's own passion, the poet plays round his subject rather than penetrates it, contemplates it rather than interprets it. Thus, sometimes his imagination, instead of remaining concentrated on the object which has inspired the poem, flies off to fresh images, and so becomes creative instead of penetrative. This is what Mr. Ruskin means when he speaks of the imagination in its contemplative mood. We have a good instance of it in those beautiful lines from Keats's 'The Eve of St. Agnes,' where the soul of the sleeping maiden is said to be—

" Clasped like a missal, where swart Paynims
    pray ;
Blinded alike from sunshine and from rain,
As though a rose should shut, and be a bud
    again."

Here the poet, after describing the soul as

" Blissfully havened both from joy and pain,"

—a touch of really penetrative imagination—is, as it were, distracted by fresh images ; first, that of a missal clasped tight for safety in a land of pagans, and then that of a rose-bud. Sometimes the imagination gives place for a time to fancy, and then, instead of images which have an essential likeness to the object which is being described, we get images which have only some external and accidental likeness. There is no better example of the difference between fancy and imagination than that instanced by Mr. Ruskin, Wordsworth's poem, 'To the Daisy'—the one beginning, " With little here to do or see." Here the flower is compared successively to a " nun demure," a " sprightly maiden," a " queen in crown of rubies drest," a " starveling in a scanty vest," a " little cyclops," a " silver shield with boss of gold," and a " star " ; and the poet himself notes the ephemeral character of these images, which start up one after the other at the bidding of fancy—

" That thought comes next—and instantly
    The freak is over."

At last his mind ceases from wandering, cleaves to the flower itself with intensity of gaze, and illumines it with true penetrative imagination.

" Sweet flower ! for by that name at last
  When all my reveries are past
  I call thee. and to that cleave fast,
    Sweet silent creature !
  That breath'st with me in sun and air,
  Do thou, as thou art wont, repair
  My heart with gladness, and a share
    Of thy meek nature !"

Defective imagination in lyrical poems is also due to the poet's vision being dimmed by the shadow of his own personal joys and sorrows. Instead of projecting himself by the force of sympathy into the external world, whether of man or nature, he makes it sympathise with him. Consequently, though he gives us a faithful representation of his own feelings, the image that he presents of the external world is blurred and misty. It is the great weakness of Byron, as an imaginative poet, that his personal aspirations and regrets are continually passing across the field of his vision, and, as it were, distorting his imagination. Thus, even in the splendid description of the Lake of Geneva in the third canto of ' Childe Harold,' passages of a really high order of imagination are interrupted by egoistic and commonplace outbursts, which go far to spoil that illusion which it is the business of all poetry to create. The same kind of defective imagination is shown in Byron's often-noticed incapacity to create real human beings, his attempts at creation being for the most part merely copies of himself.

Shelley, who with a love even greater than that of Byron for the elemental forces of nature had an ear for her more hidden harmonies which was wholly wanting to the other poet, shows a finer quality of imagination in his treatment of nature. But intensely penetrative though his imagination sometimes is, it is on the whole less remarkable for intensity than for sensibility and productiveness. No poet's emotions were more easily aroused, and no poet's imagination was in such intimate sympathy with his emotions. In the presence of nature to see with him was to feel, and to feel was to imagine. But his poetry for the most part rather charms us by the marvellous delicacy and variety of its images than seizes hold of us by the force of its imaginative truth. It is not often that he attains to that luminous and concentrated depth of imagination which distinguishes 'The Cenci', and 'Adonais'. His poem 'To a Skylark' is probably far better known than Wordsworth's poem on the same subject ;[1] in splendour of colour and movement it far surpasses its modest grey-toned companion ; but I question whether out of all its wealth of beautiful and subtle images there is one that shows such high imaginative power, such intense penetration, as the line which forms the climax of Wordsworth's poem—

" True to the kindred points of Heaven and
  Home."

It is, of course, not enough for a poet to have a powerful imagination ; he must be able to embody his visions. " Poetry is not imagination, but imagination shaped." [2] The instruments at his command are two, language and rhythm, and it is his business to use these in such a way as to assist as much as possible the imagination of his readers in realising his conceptions. In the first place then, his vocabulary should be as large as possible ; the better the instrument, the easier it is to play on. But he must also know how to play on it : he must know how to vary his method with his theme : he must remember that when he is portraying great passion his language cannot be too simple—the death of Desdemona, the closing lines of 'The

---

[1] I mean the one beginning—
" Ethereal minstrel ! pilgrim of the sky ! "
[2] F. W. Robertson, in his lecture on the ' Influence of Poetry on the Working Classes,' which, with his lecture on Wordsworth, I warmly commend to all those who are not already acquainted with them.

Cenci,' Heine's and Catullus' lyrics, are models in their bare simplicity of language. He must also remember that when he wishes to call up before the mind of his readers some sensuous object, he must do this not by an accurate and detailed description of that object, but by using some word or expression which, by the force of association, immediately suggests an imaginative impression of that object. It has been truly said that the poet is a namer ; that all language was in its origin poetry, and that prose is fossilised poetry. By which it is meant that, in the early stages of human society, things were named after their chief characteristic—were called by some symbolical name which not only served to mark them off from other things, but interpreted their properties and meaning. Thus, man is the thinker, the moon is the measurer, the sun is the begetter, the serpent is the creeper.[1] But in the process of time the meaning of these names has been forgotten ; they no longer appeal to the imagination, they are fossil names. It is therefore the business of the poet to invent new names— names which do appeal to the imagination, which do reveal to us some new quality in the object named. The difference between false poets and true poets is that the false poet goes for his names to the poetical dictionary, the true poet finds them in his own breast. The names of the one, though they were living in the hands of their makers, are cold and dead ; the names of the other breathe with a vital energy. It is only the real poet, the real maker of names, who can touch our imagination.

The second instrument which the poet has at his disposal is rhythm. Its effects are far more subtle than those of language, and consequently far more difficult to analyse. But the intimate connection between rhythm and emotion has been pointed out by several writers, notably by Mr. Herbert

[1] Professor Max Müller, 'Lectures on the Science of Language,' i. p. 434.

Spencer. Not only does strong emotion find a natural expression in the rhythmical movement or language, but conversely the effect of rhythm is to excite emotion. It may therefore be reasonably inferred that the function of rhythm in poetry is to predispose the mind of the reader to emotional impulses, and thus make it more sensible to the influence of imagination. Rhyme, of course, is merely a method of measuring rhythm, but it also serves to keep the reader's mind concentrated, to produce that feeling of expectancy which is so effective in stimulating the imagination. The same purpose is served by the various forms of repetition used in poetry, from alliteration or the repetition of consonantal and vowel sounds, to the refrain or the repetition of a whole sentence.

The art of using all these rhythmical effects so as to heighten the imaginative impression of a poem, to vary them " in correspondence with some transition in the nature of the imagery or passion,"as Coleridge says, is one of the poet's most incommunicable secrets, and I for one shall not try to surprise it. I will only point to that supreme example of rhythmical effort in our language, Coleridge's ' Christabel.' How weird is the rhythm of these two lines !—

" Is the night chilly and dark ?
The night is chilly, but not dark."

And how the effect of weirdness is sustained by the repetition at intervals of " The night is chill " ! and how the rhythm dances in the following !—

" The one red leaf, the last of its clan,
That dances as often as dance it can."

Such are the methods which the poet uses to bewitch our imagination, to draw us with him into that region of truth and beauty and love that lies beyond the senses' ken. But we must meet him half-way. Our imagination must not be utterly dead, or his most potent efforts will fail to elicit a response. People are gifted with imagination in a very various degree, but every one can cultivate his imagination, can make it more sensible to the calls of beauty and sympathy. People whose lives are shut in by sordid and commonplace surroundings have very little imagination. But the spark is there, it only wants fanning. By seeing great pictures, by reading good literature, whether it be poems or novels, above all by intercourse with nature, the imagination may certainly be stimulated. What is the aim of art for the people, and parks for the people, but that they may become more sensible to the influences of the spiritual world, that their lives may be made brighter by contact with the ideal? But it is in the power of all of us, the educated and the uneducated alike, either to quicken or to deaden our imagination. Sympathy with our fellow-men, high aspirations, purity, unworldliness, these are the helps to the imagination. Selfishness, unbelief, sensuality, worldliness, these are the hindrances; these are the chains which bind us to the earth, these are the clouds which hide from us the light of heaven.

ARTHUR TILLEY.

THE MUSICAL AND THE PICTURESQUE ELEMENTS IN POETRY.

THE view of art that is expressed by the phrase " imitation of nature " has left traces in nearly all criticism—in criticism of literature, as much as in criticism of art in the more restricted sense. One example of the influence of this definition is the stress that is often laid on " the imagination " as the principal faculty at work in poetry. For when in poetical criticism imagination rather than passion is regarded as the essential thing. the reason seems to be that the imagination, being visual, keeps itself in contact with external nature, while passion, or feeling, remains merely internal. Imitation of nature is thought to give a certain superiority to the kinds of art in which it has a greater place, as making them somehow less purely personal, more disinterested. Some such view as this seems to be implied in parts of the article on " Poetic Imagination," by Mr. Arthur Tilley, in the January number of this Magazine.

It is not sufficient for those who disagree with this view to point to the indefinable personal quality present in all poetical work, and indeed in all art, whether specifically personal or impersonal in its attitude towards nature and man. Those who have a preference for the objective, imitative, element in art, would admit the presence of this personal quality just as much as any one else. And they could defend their position in this way. Taking this quality—which, they might point out, is exactly the element that eludes analysis—as " a constant," as something always present in anything that can be called poetry, they might insist that an impartially objective view of the world is that which characterises the highest poetry ; and that poets are to

be placed higher or lower according to the degree in which they succeed in being objective and impartial. This objective character, they might say, is best described as a character of " the poetic imagination."

To this it may be replied that insight into the reality of things is not precisely imagination any more than it is passion ; that this insight is rather a part of the meaning conveyed by poetry than an element of its form, and has just as much relation to one formal quality as to another. In fact, we have got away from what ought to be a distinction between formal elements to a distinction of content from form. But the first question for criticism is, in which of the formal elements that can be detected by analysis does the indefinable, unanalysable quality of poetry most of all express itself.

Imagination, as a name for one of the formal elements in poetry, is too wide. It always suggests more than the power of constructing and picturing shapes of external things ; and it has sometimes been used to describe the formative power generally, the power of giving shape to the feelings within, as well as to the images of the world without. On the other hand, passion refers properly to the material or basis of poetry, and not to its form at all.

There is, however, another current distinction of poetical criticism—that of " musical " and " picturesque " qualities—by which the difficulties of clearly distinguishing passion and imagination are avoided. Both these terms refer entirely to form ; and they divide between them all the formal qualities of poetical work. For the term " picturesque," though strictly it ought only to be applied to those characters of the imagery of a poem that recall the effects of a picture, has come to be applied in practice to the whole of the qualities that depend on visual imagination. The explanation of this extension of meaning is that, just as the imaginative characters of ancient poetry are most related to the effects of sculpture, so the imaginative characters of modern poetry are most related to the effects of painting. With the extension that has been given to it, the term "picturesque" describes half the formal qualities of a poem. The other term of the anti-thesis, which is again a purely formal one, and therefore to be preferred to "passionate," describes the other half of all the formal qualities of poetry; for musical quality and the element of passion are names for the same thing (considered artistically). Rhythmical movement is the expression of emotional movement; and in poetry the material of passion, or feeling, assumes metrical, that is, "musical" form. Thus the antithesis of "musical" and "picturesque" is at once clear and perfectly general.

Are the two elements distinguished by these terms of equal value? Or is one of them the essential poetic quality, and the other a subordinate element to be taken into account by criticism in an estimate of the total artistic value of poetical work, but not directly affecting its value merely as poetry?

Closer consideration of the two terms will make it clear that the essential element in poetry is that which is described by the first of them when properly interpreted. The true interpretation of both may be arrived at by developing the consequences of Lessing's theory of the limits of poetry and painting.

Lessing proved in the 'Laocoon' that the method of the poet must be different from that of the painter (or of the sculptor); that the poet cannot imitate the painter in his treatment of subjects they have in common, and that the painter cannot imitate the poet. He shows by examples what difference of treatment actually exists, and deduces it from the necessary conditions of the arts of expression in words and in colours. There is this difference of treatment, because in poetry images are represented in their relations in time, while in painting objects are represented in their relations in space. In detailed descriptions of beautiful objects the poet cannot equal the painter; but he is not confined, like the painter, to a single moment of time. The poet describes the effects of things, not merely the things themselves; and thus he can convey ideas of beautiful objects by methods of his own which the painter cannot employ. But to produce a "poetic picture," that is, a picture not of an object but of an action or event, which consists of successive phases related in time, not of coexistent parts related in space, is the true aim of the poet.

Now Lessing's conception of a poetic picture—a picture in words of a series of images related in time—is not a perfectly simple conception. We may discover in it by analysis those suggestions of distinct pictures which, as Lessing admits, are made incidentally by the poet without attempting anything beyond the limits of his own art. The words of the poet call up images of what existed at those particular moments which the painter might select if he were working on the same subject. Is it, then, the mere relation of these images in time, or is it some remaining thing, that makes the picture poetic? That it is some remaining thing, and that this is the "musical element," will become clear from an example. We will select one from Milton—

> "Down a while
> He sat and round about him saw unseen.
> *At last, as from a cloud, his fulgent head
> And shape star-bright appeared or brighter,* clad
> With what permissive glory since his fall
> Was left him or false glitter."

This passage is a perfect example of a "poetic picture" in Lessing's sense;

and there is no difficulty here in detecting the presence of the two elements. The poetic effect does not proceed merely from the vivid objective representation of the phases of an action or event as they follow one another in time. A particular image out of the series—that which is contained in the italicised lines—rises before the imagination. The movement in which the mind is really absorbed is not the external movement, but the musical movement of the verse ; and on the stream of this musical movement there is the single image appearing. But since Milton is especially a musical poet, we will also take an example from a picturesque and objective poet ; let us take Homer's description of the march of the Grecian army :—

" ἠΰτε πῦρ ἀΐδηλον ἐπιφλέγει ἄσπετον ὕλην
οὔρεος ἐν κορυφῇς, ἕκαθεν δέ τε φαίνεται αὐγή,
ὣς τῶν ἐρχομένων ἀπὸ χαλκοῦ θεσπεσίοιο
αἴγλη παμφανόωσα δι' αἰθέρος οὐρανὸν ἶκεν." [1]

Do we not here perceive as separate images, first, the blaze of the forest, and then the gleam that is compared with it, of the armour? We are at the same time conscious of the march of the army ; but this movement is, as it were, identified with the rhythmical movement of the verse. Here, as before, a particular image rather than the whole objective movement is realised in imagination. To this realisation of definite pictures is added the rhythmical movement, in other words, the musical element, of the verse. This alone is the element in poetry that has time for its condition ; and time, not space, is, as we have seen, the fundamental condition of poetic representations. Of the two formal elements of poetic effects, therefore— musical movement and separate suggestions of picturesque imagery— it is clear that the first, since that

alone depends on the fundamental condition of poetic representations, must be regarded as the essential element.

Thus, by considering the nature of the formal conditions of poetic expression, we find that the effects which recall those of painting (and sculpture) are subordinate to the musical element. But in order to meet a possible objection, it is necessary to point out that the effects of music itself and of poetry are not, as is implied in some criticisms, identical. Sometimes the remark is made about verse that possesses musical quality in a very high degree that it "almost succeeds in producing the effect of music." Such criticisms convey the idea that the effort after intensity of musical effect in verse is an attempt to pass beyond the limits of verbal expression, and therefore that it does not properly belong to poetry. But the musical effect of verse is of its own kind, and is produced by methods peculiar to the poet. The resemblance that there is between musical verse and music is due to resemblance in the general conditions of their production ; music, like poetry, has time for its formal condition, and in music as in poetry the effect depends immediately on sequences of sound ; but there need not be any imitation either on the part of the poet or of the musician. This becomes evident from the observation that many people who are very susceptible to music care little for metrical effects in poetry ; while on the other hand those who care most for lyric poetry have often no peculiar susceptibility to music.

For those who can accept provisionally the conclusion that the musical element is the essential element in poetry, an examination of the characteristics of the poets in whose work musical quality becomes most manifest, as a quality distinct from all others, will not be without interest. In the first place it may be asked, is there any mode of dealing with life and with external nature that is

---

[1] " Like as destroying fire kindles some vast forest on a mountain's peak, and the blaze is seen from afar ; so, as they marched, the dazzling gleam of their awful armour reached through the sky even unto the heavens."—Il. ii. 455-8.

characteristic of those poets who display this quality pre-eminently? Admitting that all material is of equal value to the artist, we may still find that some particular mode of treatment of that which is the material of all art is spontaneously adopted by poets who manifest the essential poetic quality both in its highest degree and in such a manner that it is perceived to be distinct from all others.

Artistic qualities generally become most distinct, most separable in thought from other qualities, in lyric poetry. If, then, there should be any discoverable relation between mode of treatment of material and mode of manifestation of poetic quality, this will be found most easily by studying the work of poets whose genius is of the lyric order. It is even possible that such a relation may exist in lyric poetry only. We may see reason for concluding that a certain mode of treatment of life is characteristic of the greatest lyric poets, but this conclusion may have no further application.

The general condition of the manifestation of lyrical power may be found without much difficulty. This condition is expressed in the remark so frequently made that lyric poetry is "subjective." As it is used in criticism the term is sometimes rather vague; but it really describes very well the change that all actual experience undergoes in becoming material for lyric poetry. The lyric poet resolves all human emotion and all external nature into their elements, and creates new worlds out of these elements. Now this process has a certain resemblance to the resolution of things into their elements by philosophical analysis. The method of the poet of course does not end in analysis; but that resolution of emotion into a few typical poetic motives, and of nature into ideas of elementary forces and forms, which is the first condition of the creation of the new poetic world of the lyrist, resembles the analytical process of the philosopher taken by itself in that it is subjective. The term has therefore not been misapplied in this case in being transferred from philosophy to literary criticism.

The subjective character of lyric poetry is so obvious that it has been noticed as a fact even by those who have not seen the reason that determines it. The reason why the lyric poet must be "subjective" is this : in order to produce a distinct impression by the form of his work, he must have the material perfectly under his control. Now the material cannot be under the control of the poet unless he selects from that which he finds in life, accentuating some features of experience, and suppressing others. To make this selection possible analysis is necessary ; and then, the more complete the transformation of human emotion with all its circumstances into a new "subjective" world, the more complete is also the detachment of form from matter, the more intense is the impression given by the form alone.

This transformation may be brought about in two different ways. One of these consists in contemplating from the point of view of a peculiar personality the few typical emotions and ideas to which analysis reduces all the rest. A new world is created in which some effect of strangeness is given to everything. After the treatment of earlier artists has been studied, an effort is made to express what has been left by them incompletely expressed—all those remoter effects of things which they have only suggested. Baudelaire, who has carried this method to its limits, has also given the theory of it. He called it the research for "the artificial," and regarded it as the typical method of modern art. The other method is to give to the mood that is selected as the motive of a poem a special imaginative character by associating with it some typical episode of life, colouring this brilliantly, and isolating it from a background that is vaguely thought of as made up of common-place experience. This mode of treatment of life is to a certain extent that of all poets ; but some lyrists—Heine, for example—have carried it to greater perfection as a poetic method than the rest. Lyrics such as Heine's have for their distinctive character an intensity of emotional expression which has led some critics to praise them as not being "artificial." But they are really quite as artificial, in a sense, as those with which they are contrasted. For nothing in them is taken directly from life. The episode that is selected has a certain typical character by which it is removed from real experience ; in being emphasised by intensity of expression and by contrast it is of course equally removed from the world of abstractions. Thus it is true here, as everywhere else, that "art is art because it is not nature."

But among the lyric poets themselves there are some in whose verse the musical quality becomes more distinct than it does in the verse of those who may be characterised by their use of one of the two methods described. The musical quality in the verse of the poets referred to above is of course unmistakable, but it is not the quality which we select to characterise them. In the one case intensity in the expression of a mood is most characteristic, in the other strangeness in the colouring. But there are some poets who are pre-eminently "musical," whom the musical quality of their verse would be selected to characterise. Is there any peculiarity in their mode of treating the material of all poetry, by which this still greater detachment of form from matter can be explained?

In order to determine this, the best way of proceeding seems to be to compare the poets of lyrical genius of some one literature, and to try to discover what those poets have in common who, in musical quality of verse, are distinguished above the rest. For this purpose we may be allowed to choose English literature.

The first great English poet who is above all things musical is Milton. The distinction of musical from picturesque qualities has indeed been used as a means of defending Milton's claim to be placed in the first order of poets against those critics who have complained that he does not suggest many subjects for pictures. And we must place Milton among poets whose genius is of the lyrical kind, though most of his work is not technically lyrical—especially if we accept as universal among the greater poets the distinction of lyric from dramatic genius. Spenser's verse is, of course, extremely musical ; but we do not think of the music of his verse as that which is most characteristic of him. His distinction consists rather in what Coleridge described as the dream-like character of his imagery. After Milton, the next great poet who is eminently musical is Shelley. It will be said that Coleridge and Keats are, equally with Shelley, poets whose verse has the finest qualities of rhythm. But in Keats, what Mr. Arnold has called his "natural magic," and in Coleridge certain other imaginative qualities, are what we think of as characteristic ; for these qualities are scarcely distinguishable from the medium of expression ; the music of the verse is not felt as something that produces an effect of its own apart from the effect of other artistic qualities. Now in some of Shelley's lyrics no formal quality seems to exist except the music; a clear intellectual meaning is always present, but often there is scarcely any suggestion of distinct imagery. The power that he shows in these lyrics of giving music of verse an existence apart from all other formal qualities is what makes Shelley more of a musical poet than Coleridge or Keats ; and no other poet of the same period can be compared with these in this quality of verse. From the period of Shelley to the present time the poet who is distinguished above the rest by the musical quality of his verse is Mr. Swinburne. And he has, in common with Milton and Shelley, the power, which Shelley perhaps manifests most of all, of detaching musical quality from all other formal qualities. If the same poets have also something in common in their selection of material, then it is probable that this will be found to have some relation to their attaining the last limit of detachment of the essentially poetic quality from all others.

A ground of comparison is found in the power these poets have of expressing what may be called impersonal passion. Like all other poets of lyrical genius, they often express personal emotions; but they also give peculiarly distinct expression to emotions that have an impersonal character—emotions that are associated with a certain class of abstract ideas. What, then, is the nature of these abstract ideas?

They are ideas that may be found by analysis in all poetry. By some poets they are distinctly realised, but oftener they make their influence felt unconsciously; and when they are distinctly realised they may or may not be the objects of emotion. They represent the different ways in which the contrast is conceived between the movement of external things on the one hand, and the desires and aspirations of man on the other. The opposition of man and things outside is implicit in Greek tragedy, for example, as the idea of fate. And both in ancient and modern lyric poetry the conception of the dark background of necessity gives by contrast an intenser colouring to the expression of particular moods. There can be no finer example of this than the fifth ode of Catullus, where the peculiar intensity of effect is given by the reflection that is interposed :—

> " Soles occidere et redire possunt ;
> Nobis, cum semel occidit brevis lux,
> Nox est perpetua una dormienda." [1]

---

[1] " Suns may set and rise again ; we, when once our brief light has set, must sleep for ever in perpetual night."

But this contrast may not be employed merely to give emphasis to personal moods ; it may become independently the object of an emotion. Now the three English poets whom we have seen grounds for comparing, all express an aspiration towards a certain ideal of freedom. This aspiration is, on the emotional side, sympathy with the human race, or with the individual soul in its struggle against necessity, against external things whose "strength detains and deforms," and against the oppression of custom and arbitrary force ; on the intellectual side it is belief in the ultimate triumph of the individual soul over the circumstances that oppose its development, or of man over destiny. But with fundamental identity, both of ideas and of sentiments, there is difference in the form they assume. The exact difference can only be made clear by a comparison of particular poems.

In his essay on Mr. Matthew Arnold's poems, Mr. Swinburne has said that the ' Thyrsis ' of Mr. Arnold makes a third with ' Lycidas ' and ' Adonais,' and that these are the three greatest elegiac poems, not only in the English language, but in the whole of literature. Some readers may be inclined to add Mr. Swinburne's own ' Ave atque Vale' to the scanty list. If we compare his elegy with the elegies of Milton and Shelley, the difference in the form assumed by the idea the three poets have in common becomes distinct. For Milton the constraint that is exercised by things, their indifference to man, is embodied in "the blind fury with the abhorred shears ;" with Shelley the mutability of all the forms in which life manifests itself is the intellectual motive of this as of many other poems ; while Mr. Swinburne brings the permanent background of silence and unconsciousness into contrast with the individual spirit. and represents it as absorbing all things into itself. Though in all three poems the idea of future fame as a compensation for the temporary vic-

F F

tory of blind forces is suggested, there is nevertheless a difference in the form in which confidence in the final victory of the soul over destiny expresses itself ; but this is seen more clearly in other poems than in these, which are partly personal in motive. The triumph of the human soul is conceived by Milton as a supremacy of the individual will over circumstance. This conception is above all that of 'Samson Agonistes.' Shelley expresses the belief in the permanence of certain ideas, such as that of "intellectual beauty," under all changes of superficial appearance. And with Mr. Swinburne, just as the opposition of man and destiny is represented in its most general form—

" Fate is a sea without shore, and the soul is
    a rock that abides ;
  But her ears are vexed with the roar and
    her face with the foam of the tides : "

—so the triumph of man over destiny is represented in its most general form as the conquest of external things by "the spirit of man."

It is through this power they have of representing an ideal as triumphant that poetic form becomes more separate in the work of these than of other poets. The general relation between manifestation of lyrical power and mode of treatment of the material presented by life was found at first to be that the more completely experience has been resolved into its elements and transformed into a new subjective world, the more distinct must formal poetic qualities become. It was said that this transformation may be brought about either by the interpreting power of a peculiar personality, or by a heightening of the colours of some typical episode of human experience. But, as we have seen, there is a further stage of this transformation. By a kind of insight that belongs to the highest class of poetic minds of the lyrical order, certain tendencies for ideals to be realised are selected from among all actual tendencies of things, and then become

the objects of emotion which embodies itself in poetic form. Now to associate emotion in this way with abstract ideas is a means of making the "criticism of life" that is contained in poetry still more remote from life itself. The power of expressing impersonal passion is, therefore, on its intellectual side merely the most complete development of the way of looking at life that was found to be characteristic of the lyrist.

The connection that actually exists between the highest qualities of rhythmical expression and a certain way of viewing the world, is thus seen to have grounds in the nature of things. But when the detachment of poetic form as a thing existing by itself is said to be the effect that is characteristic of a particular group of poets, it must not be understood that these poets are limited to effects of one kind. They are able to deal with subjects and to produce effects that are outside the sphere of other lyric poets ; but this does not prevent them from having equal powers with the rest within that sphere. Hence there are differences in the effect of their work as a whole, depending on differences in the combination of other artistic qualities with the essentially poetic quality, besides the differences already discussed. This will be seen if we carry the parallel a little further.

There is, for example, a difference between Milton's treatment of external nature under its imaginative aspect and that of the two later poets. In reading Milton, the peculiar imaginative effect experienced is that which is produced by the contemplation of enormous spaces. The later poets, on the other hand, give a characteristic quality to their imaginative representations of nature by endowing the elementary forces and forms of the world with a kind of life. Objects are not described as portions of a mechanism, but are identified with a spirit that gives them motion. Two equally perfect examples of this are the description of dawn at the opening of the fourth act of 'Prometheus Unbound' and the description in one of the choruses of 'Erechtheus' (in the passage beginning "But what light is it now leaps forth on the land " . . .), of the sudden re-appearance of the sun after having been obscured. There is nothing in Milton corresponding to this mode of conceiving nature. The spheres, with him, are guided by spirits that act on them from outside ; they are themselves lifeless.

In some respects, however, Mr. Swinburne resembles Milton and is unlike Shelley. This is the case as regards specially picturesque effects. Shelley suggests a greater number of distinct pictures corresponding to particular moments; with Milton and with Mr. Swinburne the picturesque effect is not so easily distinguished at first from the musical effect, but there is a stronger suggestion of a background that remains permanent while individual objects disappear. As has been already said, Shelley does not always attempt picturesque effects ; the imagery in some of his lyrics is of the faintest possible kind ; it is something that is vaguely suggested by the idea that gives shape to the poem and the emotion that animates it, rather than something that exists for its own sake. But when he does attempt picturesque effects he becomes one of the most picturesque of the poets who can be compared with him as regards music of verse. It is the peculiar character of the effects he produces that prevents this from being always recognised. Many of Shelley's descriptions are exact representations of the more indistinct impressions that are got from natural things ; as it has been put by some critics, he describes temporary forms of things rather than permanent objects. His pictures have the effect of a combination of form and colour that has only existed once and will never exist again ; of a phase in a series of transformations in the clouds, for example. That is, in describing those changes that are the

material of "poetic pictures," he does not select for most vivid representation the moments that convey the strongest suggestion of permanence, but rather those that convey an idea of fluctuation. When this is considered, the want of suggestions of permanent backgrounds, of solid objects, cannot be regarded as a defect ; for the presence of these would be inconsistent with the production of a picture of the kind described. It is possible, however, that a relation might be discovered between Shelley's power of producing pictures of this kind and a certain want of artistic completeness that is noticed in some of his work. Whatever may be the cause of it, much of Shelley's work appears to have been less elaborated than that of Milton or of Mr. Swinburne. There is less "form" in the more restricted sense—that is, less purely literary quality. In Milton there are always present certain qualities of style that could not be imagined by a critic to be the result of anything but the most complete artistic consciousness. A similar quality of style is perceived in Mr. Swinburne's work. As an example of the extent to which he manifests this quality, it is sufficient to refer again to 'Ave atque Vale.'

The difference between the picturesque qualities of Shelley's work and of Mr. Swinburne's may be illustrated by comparing their mode of treatment of such a conception as that of a procession of divine forms. There is in one of the best known lyrical passages of 'Hellas' a description of "the Powers of earth and air" disappearing from the eyes of their worshippers—

> " Swift as the radiant shapes of sleep
> From one whose dreams are Paradise."

If we compare this with the passage in 'The Last Oracle' beginning

> " Old and younger gods are buried and begotten," . . .

the difference that has been pointed out becomes quite clear. Shelley's imagery is in itself more consistent :

although the images that are suggested are vague and fluctuating, yet they call up a picture that can be realised as a whole by the imagination. The passage in Mr. Swinburne's poem does not suggest imagery that can be realised so distinctly merely as imagery; but the forms that "go out discrowned and disanointed" give the impression of being more concrete than those described by Shelley: a more vivid sense is also conveyed of something that remains while all forms perish one after the other; the "divers births of godheads" are contrasted with "the soul that gave them shape and speech." An idea similar to this is indeed suggested in the chorus of 'Hellas,' but it is not brought out so distinctly. Shelley makes the idea of the changing phases of the perpetual flux of forms most vivid; Mr. Swinburne, on the other hand, makes most vivid the idea of that which is contrasted with all temporary forms of things. Thus it has been remarked that he often employs conceptions like those of the avatars in Hindu mythologies. In the poems of 'Dolores' and 'Faustine,' for example, there are conceptions of this kind. The ideal figures in these poems are not ghosts like Heine's "gods in exile," but embodiments of a spirit that is conceived as having remained always the same while changing its superficial attributes in passing from one age to another.

Returning from this attempt to characterise some of the resemblances and differences in the work of those poets who have more in common than any other of the greater English poets, we come upon the question whether the general idea that has been partially developed can be applied to dramatic as well as to lyric poetry. In its application to dramatic poetry (supposing this to be possible), it could not, of course, receive the development of which it is capable when applied to the work of poets whose genius is of the lyrical order. The dramatic is more dependent than the lyric genius on the unanalysed material that life presents to it directly; and the conditions of the drama prevent that almost complete detachment of the essentially poetic element which we perceive in some lyrics. On the other hand, this element is intrinsically the same in the drama and in the lyric, though it differs in its mode of manifestation. While it seems in the lyric to assume an existence apart, in the drama it emerges at particular moments in the progress of the action. From the poetic point of view all other parts of the drama exist for the sake of these. And this poetic effect, being produced, like the effect of lyric verse, by the rhythmical expression of emotion, is best described as "musical." No difficulty is presented by dramatic poetry, therefore, as to the central part of the view that has been taken. And if, as has been said, the particular conclusions arrived at in considering lyric poetry are not applicable to the drama, it must at the same time be remembered that the conditions of success in dramatic and in lyric poetry cannot be (as is sometimes thought) altogether unlike. For a lyric element is perceptible in most dramatic poets; and the greatest among those poets who are usually thought of as lyrists have written dramas that rank next to those of the greatest dramatists.

THOMAS WHITTAKER.

THE PROVINCE AND STUDY OF POETRY.[1]

THE Chair which I have the honour of filling presents difficulties, so many and so great, that the first words of any one who has been chosen to the post must, almost inevitably, be words of a somewhat earnest entreaty for the goodwill, the kind excuses, the patience, of his hearers. So far as I know, this is the only professorship in any civilized country—in any European country at least, which has for its exclusive subject nothing less than the whole field of Poetry, from old Homer in the isle of Chios, to our own venerable Epic Poet in the Isle of Wight. Within this period, how many thousand poets, nay, hundreds of thousands, have lived and worked and passed away, unknown or known, but each adding his voice to "the still sad music of humanity,"—that great song which is always going up—now harsh and thin, perhaps, now sweet and resonant, —from this prosaic and material world! The conditions of human life may, as we often hear it said of our own age, and as it has been said, I imagine, of every age in turn, be unpropitious to Poetry ; but the Poets are still adding, eagerly and daily, to their vast Treasury-hive, like the bees in Virgil :

—Genus immortale manet, multosque per annos
stat Fortuna domus, et avi numerantur avorum.[2]

When the brief occupant of this Chair looks at the vast array and family of his Ancestors, how should not a certain terror seize him—how should he venture to judge and value them ;—how even number them ?

We all vaguely know how vast this field of Poetry is ; how long it has been cultivated ; how varied and magnificent the harvests,—if I may thus carry on the metaphor,—which it has borne for the pleasure and advantage of mankind. But it is probable that to no man, even if he devoted to the subject the labours of a life, could it now be possible to explore, much less to be familiar with and know it, in its completeness. Some eighteen hundred years ago, indeed, a short critical review of the poetry of the then civilized European races was attempted by the Latin writer Quintilian. He had before him only the literatures of Greece and the first and best portion of that of Rome. Yet even of these he has attempted no more than a sketch. And this sketch, though of the highest value from the writer's own acuteness of judgment and from the traditional criticisms of previous days which he has obviously followed and preserved for us, yet covers little more than the chief poets. To do more was not, indeed, Quintilian's object ; had he tried to make his view complete, his one chapter, even in that terse ancient style which, unhappily, the modern world cannot endure, would have swelled to volumes. Since his time, besides the latter portion of the Roman Poetry which barbarian ravage has left us, has been added all the poetry of the Romance languages, all that of the Teutonic races, all that of the Celtic. Basque and Finlander, Arabia and China,—I know not whether we should not add, Assyria and Egypt,

[1] An Introductory Lecture, by Francis T. Palgrave, Professor of Poetry in the University of Oxford.
[2] "The race maintains its immortality, and through the length of years the happy destiny of the family stands firm, and can count up the ancestors of ancestors."

nay, Oceana in all her vastness,—like the Queen who came before the throne of Solomon,—offer their gifts. And, as if this vast world of verse were insufficient, we in Oxford may lawfully pride ourselves on the possession of two men, each of true world-wide eminence,—(a phrase how often abused !) —who call us to view, as an essential and inevitable portion of the History of Poetry, the hymns and epics of that great Indian civilization, which, if I understand them rightly, hand down to us, if not the actual words, yet at least the modes of thought by which, in the remotest ages, "the supreme Caucasian mind" was characterized.

Even in this brief and imperfect outline, how vast, how magnificent a subject opens before us !—Poets best do justice to Poetry ; and those of my hearers who have the good fortune to be familiar with the 'Paradise Regained,' may recall some splendid passages in the third and fourth books, where Milton presents a picture closely analogous, in breadth and variety, to the sketch which I have just given. I refer of course to that panorama of the kingdoms of this world and their glory which the Tempter sets before the eyes of Our Saviour from the "specular mount," as the poet terms it, of Temptation. There he takes us in vision from Asia

As far as Indus east, Euphrates west,

with its early capitals, Nineveh, Babylon, Persepolis, Ecbatana, Seleucia, and a long roll of other memorable names, to the

Great and glorious Rome, queen of the earth ;—

with all the nations of the world bringing her, as tribute, all the fruits of civilization, from India to Britain, from Ceylon to Germany ; thence carrying us, lastly, with the finest poetical instinct, from these mythic or material images of splendour, to behold—

Where on the Ægean shore a city stands,
Built nobly, pure the air, and light the soil,
Athens, the eye of Greece— ;

while there he enumerates first, as though Poetry were the finest flower and fruit of the Hellenic intellect, those Masters of song, from whose charm eighteen hundred years and more have taken nothing of its first force and freshness.

Hardly less varied, and greatly more extended, than Milton's visionary landscape, is the field of Poetry before us. This is the subject matter with which it is my arduous but honourable duty to attempt to deal. In attempting this, in the poet's words, "we must learn to live in reconcilement with our stinted powers." In any but the most fractional degree it is obviously impossible that I can fulfil my office. It is even more impossible that I can do it with comfort to myself and with advantage to you, unless I am favoured with the patience, the goodwill, the sympathy of my hearers.

The Statute establishing this Chair lays down no special rules for the Praelector's guidance. Only a phrase occurs which was quoted by Lowth in his able and scholarly lectures, near a century and a half ago (1741-1751); —That the study of Poetry was of value in the University, as tending to the improvement of the chief sciences there pursued, sacred and secular. But I read in this, not so much a suggestion for the matter of the lectures, as a recognition of Poetry as a high and holy Art, as a motive power over men,—in opposition to the sentiment which regards it as the creation and the recreation of an idle day,—as a mere source of transient or sensuous pleasure. From that loftier aspect Poetry, it seems to me, should be regarded and approached ; and not least in Oxford; here, at the meeting-point between the spirit of Youth and the spirit of Study. Perhaps you smile at this. And these powerful spirits, doubtless, are not always upon friendly terms ;—there are rumours, indeed, of an ancient feud between them ; *res olim dissociabiles*, as Tacitus said once of Order and

Liberty.[1] Yet when, by happy fortune, Study and Youth do meet in amity, great is the gain to both; youth strengthens itself with power through study; study is inspired with freedom by youth. In words which at the present time may speak with a peculiar force to the memories of many among us, *Imperium* and *Libertas* are united.

Had my own younger days, in truth, been more faithful to this doctrine, I might have felt more confidence in regard to the task towards which I am now addressing myself. Even however from those days onward it has always seemed to me,—as it must have seemed to others,—that English literature calls loudly for full and free recognition as one of the studies of an English University. If ever so recognized, I claim for Literature,—Art though it be,—the whole rights and methods of scientific pursuit. And for those who thus may pursue it, I claim also, in the highest measure, all that Science, in the latest and widest sense of the word, offers in the way of intellectual advance, of moral invigoration and pleasure, as the reward of her votaries. In this direction, at any rate, my wish, within my limited sphere, is to work; encouraged by recent signs which seem to indicate that the current of University thought is now, in some degree, running propitiously. To offer details on the scheme for this systematic study, (should it ever become such,) as an integral portion of the Humanity School, would be out of place and presumptuous. But I hope I may be allowed briefly to express a very strong conviction upon two points, which impressed me greatly when, in former years, it was my work to teach this subject under the direction of my fellow-collegian, equally eminent and admirable, the present Bishop of London. First; the thorough study of English literature, as such—literature, I mean, as an Art; indeed, the finest

¹ 'Agricola': c. iii.

of the Fine Arts,—is hopeless, unless based on equally thorough study of the literatures of Greece and Rome. But secondly; when so based, adequate study will not be found exacting, either of time or of labour. To know Shakespeare and Milton is the pleasant and crowning consummation of knowing Homer and Æschylus, Catullus and Virgil. And upon no other terms can we obtain it.

Poetry, it need hardly be said, as by general consent it is the finest flower of literature, would enter largely into such systematic, positive, scientific study. Whether any idea of this nature was before the mind of the liberal founder of the Professorship, I am ignorant. But 1708,—the date of the first Lectures, — is the time when Dryden and Locke, the fathers respectively of analytical criticism and analytic psychology in England, were just dead; when Pope was beginning that brilliant career which a distinguished member of New College is doing so much to elucidate; when men like Swift, Addison, Arbuthnot, Bolingbroke, with other lights of a literature essentially modern in its character, were in the ascendant. It is hence possible that some anticipatory impulse may have then existed towards such a study of poetry as I have just described. But, whether this were so or not, a scheme of this broad character is manifestly beyond the limits of the Professorship, even if English literature were already admitted to a humble entrance within that Palace of Art, the sacred precinct of the Schools. It is more probable that simply to aid in the creation of Good Taste, or Gusto as it might then have been called, was the dominant purpose of the University; such models of criticism as were given in Pope's celebrated Essay (written in 1709), and by the writers whom Pope enumerates, being in the Founder's mind. And to do what I can in this direction will be my object as your Professor.

At this point, I ask leave to offer

a little personal explanation, requesting your pardon for an egotism which I shall do my best afterwards to avoid. My wish was, at first, when beginning my work, to dispense with general statements as to Poetry, the theory of it as a Fine Art, the nature of its influence upon the world, the laws of criticism and good taste, and the like. These somewhat abstract considerations it is difficult to make clear, more difficult to make accurate,—most difficult of all, maybe, to make interesting. Yet on the whole it seems most useful in itself, and most respectful to you, my hearers,—some of whom, at least, I could with more fitness and advantage learn from than lecture,—if, as the saying is, I should "begin from the beginning," in the old-fashioned way. And there may be the more reason for this course, because I do not find that it has been definitely attempted by any holder of the Chair during the last half-century ; not, indeed, since it was adorned by the exquisite taste and lofty feeling of Keble. Following him then, *haud passibus aequis*, I shall try to set forth at once a few broad general principles upon the subject as a whole, with the hope hereafter to illustrate and vivify them by lectures of a more detailed character. Every one has seen the plain outline maps which are found in Guides and Handbooks, and serve to show the traveller his way through those elaborate and confusing charts, by whose aid he does not so much learn his road, as the crowd of wonders he is to find while pursuing it. In offering such an outline, a lecturer runs the risks, alas ! like Dogberry, of bestowing all his tediousness upon your worships. But to the best of my power I shall avoid technical and abstract terms. Nor shall I trouble you now with any essay at a definition-in-form of Poetry. Many men of genius,—some of my predecessors included,—have made the attempt. But they have rather given us beautiful phrases describing certain aspects of Poetry, than a complete definition. This Proteus is a spirit too many-sided and vast, too simple and too subtle at once, to be thus caught and bound and exhibited. Such a definition may, indeed, rise in our souls when we are saturated with the best poetry,—at home with the Master-singers. But I think that we shall then be somewhat shy of trying to put it into words. In the beautiful phrase of Sir Joshua Reynolds upon his own Art, it will be an Idea which "subsists only in the mind. The sight never beheld it, nor has the hand expressed it ; it is an idea residing in the breast of the artist, which he is always labouring to impart, and which he dies at last without imparting." [1]

Taking my duty then to be, to aid, so far as I may, towards Good Taste in Poetry, these two words, it should be noticed, cover a very wide field of study. For Good Taste, when we look closely, means in truth nothing less than that familiarity which enables us to win from Poetry the greatest amount of pleasure : — the deepest draught of that relief, comfort, exhilaration, enlargement, elevation of mind which she has, in all ages, freely given to all who truly love her.

Good Taste in Poetry exists on the same ground as in the other Fine Arts. Three diverse elements, it would seem, combine always to form it. We must have (1) Natural bias and sympathy with the art in question ; (2) Familiarity with its masterpieces, Acquaintance with works of lesser degree ; (3) Knowledge of the conditions of the art as Art, of its own historical course, and of the parallel history of the country which produces it.

Some natural bias, first, towards the subject, some inborn and incommunicable sympathy must be presumed ; some portion, in short, of the gift which the Artist himself has in larger degree. For it is only a question of degree which separates him from those to whom his Art gives pleasure ; there

[1] Discourse ix. ; Oct. 17, 1780.

is something in us all of Homer, something of Shakespeare, when their works speak to us as soul with soul; when we triumph with Achilles in the trenches, or grieve with Lear over Cordelia. It is through this one touch of sympathy that the vitality,—what, by a phrase of somewhat pathetic irony, we call the immortality—of the masterpieces of art, those of Poetry in particular, is maintained. To judge any art truly, we also, in our measure, must be born artists. This natural basis must be set as the primary requisite for good judgment; as Plato once said of Virtue, this cannot be taught. Yet the difficulty thus seemingly presented to us at the outset is not really formidable. For in some natural bias towards the Beautiful in her many forms, most men, I fully believe, have their inborn share; Wordsworth's famous phrase,

—many are the Poets,

may thus, perhaps, be best interpreted.

That this favourable predisposition exists in you, I shall therefore assume, through the fact of your presence to-day; if anywhere, this instinct should be found in its freshness here; it is one of the best treasures of the spirit of Youth.

But, like all God's gifts to His creatures, our native sense of the Beautiful in Art is at once a help towards life, and a responsibility. Without this innate sympathy, judgment is a barren thing; but sympathy itself is all but barren, unless it be strenuously cultivated into judgment. This is but a commonplace; yet much current criticism, if it deserve the name, supported by natural indolence, practically sets aside the doctrine that we must work towards a faithful judgment of Art hardly less than the Artist; that Art's final result and overplus of pleasure is, itself, the fruit and the reward of pleasant labour.

From that of which we are heirs, I pass to that which we can acquire; from the natural groundwork of Taste, to what we must ourselves add;

Familiarity with masterpieces, Acquaintance with lesser work. Even limited thus, it is only a province or two in the United Kingdom of Poetry which the most energetic can hope in some degree to conquer. But it is one of the privileges of this art, that each great province, in essential features, is typical of the rest. Poetry is the mirror of mankind; of man's grand elementary passions and thoughts above all. He, then, who masters one natural group will have, thus far, laid sufficient foundation for right judgment.

Thirdly; to gain true Taste in Art, —which, let me again remind you, means simply the greatest power of enjoying and profiting,—we require knowledge of the formal rules of each art, of its own historical career, and relation to its own age. Every art, as words familiar in Oxford tell us, aims at some good end; this in Poetry, may be provisionally, at least, defined as pure, high, and lasting pleasure. As the medium through which the painter works is colour, that of the poet is language. Words are his colours; the dictionary is his palette; but he has upon it a thousand-fold more tints than the painter. Under what special conditions and rules must he use words for the creation of his poem? These are the technical laws of his art; to this belong questions of metre, rhyme, diction, style, species of poetry, as Epic or Lyric; choice and treatment of subject, and the like;—in short, all the points in which Poetry differs from the other Fine Arts.

These are the conditions under which the Poet must work; here are the tools of his trade, the word-material over which he is to show his plastic power. Why, then, it may be asked, should these be studied by us,—spectators only of his picture, readers of his poem? Why not "take the goods the Gods provide us," ask no more, and enjoy?[1]—Simply because we should thus

[1] This question arose of old with regard to Music. Τί δεῖ μανθάνειν. . . ., ἀλλ᾽ οὐχ ἑτέρων

inevitably and uniformly fail to obtain the fullest and most lasting enjoyment. We cannot do justice to the poet's work unless we know the strict limits and laws under which he produces it. These technical conditions were with him at every moment as he penned each line. These conditions also we, in some measure, must know, if we are truly to sympathize with poet and poem.

The aspect of Poetry which I have just touched on is the most peculiar to it, the most intimate. Farthest from it lies the historical career and development of poetry, and its relation, in each country, to that country's own contemporary life. Perhaps upon the necessity of studying these two closely-united subjects I need not now enlarge. It seems clear at once that, if isolated, no work of art can either be intelligently judged or duly enjoyed; to gain that vantage-ground we must know what led up to it, what followed. Nor is knowledge of the surrounding history, if I may be allowed the phrase, less essential. Poetry reflects life; it runs as a river through its own age, and all the currents of thought and of action fall into it. We must know what it imitates, if we are to judge and to enjoy the truth of the imitation.

In this somewhat lengthy preface my effort has been to lay down and define distinctly an outline of the different elements which Poetry presents for study. We must have, Sympathy, Familiarity, Knowledge of the Art and of its history. Or, looked at in another way, these two latter main roads towards Good Taste might be spoken of as Poetry viewed in its results, and Poetry viewed in its processes;—the poem given to the world, and the poet as an artist in his studio. I divide them for convenience of treatment; but it will be seen that they form only different faces of the same thing. By study of the specific rules of Poetry as a Fine Art, and of its historical course, we put ourselves in the proper light to examine and appreciate the Master-singers. By familiarity with Master-works, we find the technical rules of their art best exemplified and put vividly before us, and can also catch some glimpse at the working of the poet's special powers, — Invention, Fancy, Imagination; powers which we are constantly tempted to define, but which (it seems to me), like the essential spirit of Poetry itself, almost always elude definition.

These two main elements of study, which I hope constantly to have before me, it will be best, I think, to elucidate in a little detail. Poetry as an Art it is my wish to consider in the next lecture, comparing it with the other Fine Arts. It seems to suit a first discourse better, to dwell upon Poetry in its main effects on the mind, on Poetry as a motive force in the world, as an expression of our best and most intimate thoughts and feelings; Poetry, in short, as an integral part of the general history of mankind.

What, then, has been the main power of Poetry over mankind, and whence is that power derived? There have been spaces, more or less blank, when her descant has been hardly audible above the din of war, or stifled in the heavy air of vulgar and material civilization. But Poetry, whenever existing as a living force, to put it in a word, has simply been the voice through which the passions and imaginations of the race, as well as of the individual, have uttered themselves. And Poetry, at the same

---

ἀκούοντας ὀρθῶς τε χαίρειν καὶ δύνασθαι κρίνειν; ᾿Ωσπερ οἱ Λάκωνες· ἐκεῖνοι γὰρ οὐ μανθάνοντες ὅμως δύνανται κρίνειν ὀρθῶς, ὡς φασί, τὰ χρηστὰ καὶ τὰ μὴ χρηστὰ τῶν μελῶν: "Why need we study, and not rather learning of others gain power rightly to enjoy and judge? So do the Lacedæmonians; for they without study yet can judge rightly, as they say, what is good and not good in melody." (Arist. 'Polit.,' viii., 5.)—But no one, I will venture to say, who has learned no more, even, than one instrument, will agree with the Spartan critics.

time, has only given back what she has herself received. As the river shapes the valley, and the valley gives the river its bias, so the poet is at once moulded by the general current of thought and feeling prevalent in each age,—and then himself aids in moulding them. Poetry stands as a mediator between man's heart and mind, and the world in which he moves and exists. In the systematic lectures given here by Keble, the author of the 'Christian Year,' true to his own modest depth and delicacy of nature, treated his Art mainly in its effect upon individual men. The Poet's impulse he describes as a desire to give relief to an over-full heart; whilst the reader, in his turn, finds this relief from the poem. It is Poetry as a *vis Medicatrix*, in which Keble is most interested. What I desire now to dwell upon, is another aspect of the same power;—poetry as a *vis Imperatrix;* Poets as they have given aid and guidance to the men about them, enabling them to live again in the Past, or to anticipate the future; Poets, in a word, as leaders of thought, through the channels of emotion, and beauty, and pleasure.

In some words which many here will remember,[1] Mr. Arnold, with his usual happy eloquence, has dwelt upon what he names the "interpretative power" of Poetry. This interpretation is given in several ways. It may be, as he says in the passage alluded to, by those magical touches of pure imagination which awaken in us a new and intimate sense of "the real nature of things;" it may be by making us feel the inner beauty of what we have hitherto regarded as the barren commonplaces of life,—a function, amongst others, admirably fulfilled by Wordsworth. But nowhere, I think, does Poetry act as Interpreter more grandly, than when she shines forth as the practical guiding power over a whole nation, leading them to

[1] 'Essays in Criticism'; Article upon Maurice de Guérin.

higher, holier, and nobler things. The reproach has been often cast upon the Fine Arts, and justified often by the tone of those who love them unwisely, —that they serve only for the adornment and the amusement of life; that, because they are imperatively bound to move us through Pleasure, Pleasure is their final cause of existence. Above that reproach Poetry is lifted most when performing this imperial function. Perhaps I may here seem to magnify, if not my office, at any rate the Art which that office professes. Doubtless the history and development of nations have been greatly moulded by events over which Poetry has, unhappily, exercised no influence. We may not say with Shelley, in his fine frenzy, " Poets are the unacknowledged legislators of the world." Yet it is surely probable that if Greece could be imagined without Homer, Rome without Virgil, Italy without Dante, England without Shakespeare, not only would each nation have lost one of its highest sources of personal, and as it were, private, wealth, and we with it, but the absolute current of its history could not have followed its actual course; nay, that it would have missed, in each case, something of its best and most fertile direction.

By this I do not mean that a direct political influence over national history can be often traced to poetry. Indeed, we generally and not untruly think of it as standing in a kind of opposition to the prose of material advance, to the strife of party tongues, to the din of warfare. But beneath these and all other analogous forms of activity lies the broad basis of our common human nature; and no one, I think, even of those who would draw the line most trenchantly between the real and the ideal, between facts and visions, between Adam Smith, let us say, and Keats,—can deny that the sentiments of that common human nature are powerfully worked upon by Poetry, when given to us by the greater Masters and Makers. Nor would even a direct practical aim be alien from the genius of this Fine Art. The greatest of poets, on the contrary, so far as evidence enables us to judge, have been precisely those who were most completely and emphatically men of their day: "children," as the highest-hearted among German Master-singers has said, "of their age," though with the mission to "strengthen and purify it."

In what mode has the national influence which I here am ascribing to Poetry been felt ? It has been felt in what I would call the interpretation of each country to itself; in making the nations alive, in the first instance, to their own unity; afterwards, to their place in the whole comity of mankind. I may call it briefly, the Power of Poetry in the world. Let me give one or two examples,

So to interpose a little ease,

in a rather too abstract discussion.

Virgil I will take first, for two reasons. He has been familiarized to us, in all the fullness of his many-sided and exquisite genius, more than to the students of fifty years since; partly by two admirable editions which England owes, one to a great Cambridge scholar, the other to our own lost and lamented Conington; partly by that treatise on his age, life, and works, equally learned and sympathetic,—two things not often united,—by which my old College friend, William Sellar, has done honour both to Edinburgh and to Oxford. My other reason is that Virgil, by the character of his genius, gentle, gracious, supreme in Art, rather than energetic or creatively original, would not seem at first sight one of those poets who, in Lord Tennyson's phrase, are destined to "shake the world,"—or, rather, to give it strength and calmness after it has been shaken by civil war and revolution. Yet this great and beneficent work was really accomplished by the author of the 'Georgics' and the 'Æneid.' That poem, it has been eloquently said by Hallam,

"reflects the glory of Rome as from a mirror."[1] "It remains," says the historian of the early Empire, "the most complete picture of the national mind at its highest elevation, the most precious document of national history, if the history of an age is revealed in its ideas, no less than in its events and incidents."[2] But much more, with high probability, may be claimed for the 'Æneid.' Miserably imperfect as is our evidence for the inner life whether of the Romans or of the provincials whom they ruled and assimilated, enough remains to prove the depth and width of the impression which Virgil's work stamped upon the Empire, and thus upon all then existing Western civilization. I do not here allude to the effect, not always fortunate, which Virgil's style exercised over the later Latin Epics. But everywhere in Latin literature we find proof how deeply this poem touched thinking men. Nor was this influence confined to literature. We know that the 'Æneid' was a text-book in the popular schools; we see Virgil's verse yet scrawled on the roofless walls of Pompeii, and within the gloom of the Catacombs.

Those faults of idea and sentiment, the unsatisfying element which modern comparative criticism finds in the 'Æneid,' happily or unhappily for the reader, were then unfelt; what the ruling race seems, from the very date of its publication, to have recognized, was, that here was enshrined the representative idea of the City and the Empire; the poem in which Roman power and civilization were personified. The mirror reflecting the glory of Rome, past and present, was to the Romans also the glass in which they beheld her future and immortal glory :—

Imperium sine fine dedi.[3]

---

[1] 'Introduction to the Literature of Europe'; ii. v.

[2] Merivale's 'History of the Romans under the Empire'; ch. xii.

[3] "I have granted them Empire without end."

In its " long-resounding march " the ' Æneid' appealed to them through all the great sentiments and thoughts which had enabled Rome to conquer and to rule the world – to the mystical " Fortuna Urbis " ; to their love for their own beautiful land ; to the traditions of their origin and history ; to their proud confidence in themselves ; their strange but deeply-rooted sense of religion ; to their love of law and fixed government ;—above all, and in Virgil's time including all, the ' Æneid' appealed to " the imperial idea of Rome in its secular, religious, and personal significance. This idea," Professor Sellar adds, Virgil "has ennobled with the associations of a divine origin and of a divine sanction ; of a remote antiquity and an unbroken continuity of great deeds and great men ; of the pomp and pride of war, and the majesty of government : and he has softened and humanized the impression thus produced by the thought of peace, law, and order given to the world. . . . We are reminded only of the power, glory, majesty, and civilising influence with which the idea of Rome is encompassed." [1] Looked at thus, the ' Æneid' lifts itself above all Latin poetry, as the great Temple of Jupiter once raised its golden roof over all the temples and palaces of the City. It is the Capitol of Roman literature. When we add that this " glorified representation " of the State was borne in to men's hearts and memories by a poetical style so supreme and exquisite in charm that after nineteen centuries it retains all its unique fascination,—need we hesitate to believe that Virgil the Magician was an imperial power in the Roman world ? That his genius, penetrating the soul, was a bond of national unity to the Romans throughout the wide regions of the Empire ? That it taught them a lofty aim and ideal of public life during the years of Imperial prosperity ? That

[1] ' Virgil' ; by W. Y. Sellar, Professor of Humanity in the University of Edinburgh : 1883.

when the evil days of decay and invasion began, it nerved many a heart to endure, and many an arm to strike ? Oxford has scholars and historians to whose judgment I bow with due respect. If they should remind me how scanty, as I noticed before, is the *positive* evidence for the political impulse which I here assign to Virgil, and to Poetry through him, my reply would be, It is so. But I rest this argument upon deeper grounds than material proof ; upon the certainty that what has widely and deeply and long moved the minds and hearts of men, must have strongly influenced their lives and actions ;—I rely upon the common laws of human nature.

You will remember that I am now speaking of Poetry in her loftiest function ; of Poets as a vital energy in the course of the world. Is it not a singular fate which, in this character, unites in the closest bonds Virgilius Maro with Dante Alighieri ?—the Poet whose work was to impress the unity and meaning of the actual Roman Empire upon the minds of men,—and the Poet, who by his advocacy of an ideal Roman Empire, was to impress first upon Italy that impulse towards national unity which has accomplished itself in our own days ? For these two great men we may claim a living and moving force, a spiritual power and presence, through near two thousand years ; while it is to the earlier that the later looks up for guidance, not only in poetry, but in thought. Both were men of singular natural sensitiveness, delicacy of feeling, tenderness of nature ; yet both, drawn by the sure instinct of the Poet, discerned the national necessity of their day, and left home-life and love-songs, to become the inspired political leaders of Italy. It is Virgil whom Dante takes for his master ; in his immense task, that of seeing first and telling afterwards the long Pilgrimage through Hell by Purgatory to Heaven, " Virgil bids him lay aside the last vestige of fear. Virgil is to *crown him king and priest over himself,* for a higher venture than heathen poetry had dared;"[1] Virgil to him is "that lord of the loftiest song, who soars above the rest like the eagle."[2]

> Tu duca, tu signor, e tu maestro.[3]

But Dante's spirit is bolder than Virgil's, more confident, with more wisdom in regard to this world, more insight for the next; political impulse with him, is, also, only a portion of his task. Dante's style, again, though far below Virgil's in continuous grace and unfailing dignity, deserves the epithet *supreme* in another way. Even Shakespeare's is not so direct, so flexible, so incisively penetrating as Dante's. No words cut deeper than his. Nor was less power in his Art essential for the delivery of his message to his countrymen.

I have tried to sketch the power of the 'Æneid' over men. In what consisted the similar power of the 'Divina Commedia'? In defining this, I shall avail myself of the Essay by Dean Church,—the finest, the most complete single piece of criticism which our day, though not wanting critics of high quality, has produced. Italian life in Dante's time was a history, not of a country, but of cities; of their rivalries and their wars. Nay, it was a history of civil war within each city; castle against castle, family against family. Yet, beneath this wretched scene of jarring disintegration, reminding us often of what Milton termed the battles of kites and crows in old England,—beneath all this lay a deep memory of the historic Roman empire with its iron unity, a vague sense that Italy should rightly form one country at peace within herself. Some sought this union through the spiritual headship of the Papacy; some, through the German Emperors. Dante be-

longs strictly to neither side; he is Guelf and Ghibeline at once; his party, as he says, was one made by himself.[4] The Imperial power which he desired and advocated was an ideal empire, alien far from the material supremacy of Hohenstaufen and Hapsburg. "Dante's political views," says Dean Church, "were a dream : . . . a dream, in divided Italy, of a real and national government, based on justice and law. It was the dream of a real State." If the dream were blended with impossibilities, yet, "in this case, as in many others, he had already caught the spirit and ideas of a far distant future." We see Dante, like Virgil, conscious of greater issues than he could grasp,

> Tendentemque manus ripæ ulterioris amore.[5]

And his words, as we know, have run through Italy from his day till ours; at times as a hidden fire, at times as a beacon and a warning to his countrymen. We cannot strictly *prove* the influence of Virgil on the fortunes of the Empire. But no one can question the power which Dante has exercised towards that unification which is now working itself out,—to the satisfaction of most Italians, and (it is to be hoped), on the whole, to the gain of all.

By what poetical energies,—to revert to our immediate subject,—has the 'Commedia' exercised this power over Italy,—this power, it may be truly said, over Europe? Dante's appeal to his countrymen is through all the interests of their life. In his poem we find their history as heirs of Rome, united always with that of his own age. Virgil's Rhipeus, Cato, Trajan, in his liberal view, have their

---

[1] Dean Church ; 'Essay on Dante' : 1854.

[2] Quel signor dell' altissimo canto,
Che sovra gli altri, com' aquila, vola.

('Inferno': C. iv. 95, 96.)—Line 80 shows that Virgil, not Homer, is here intended.

[3] "Thou art my leader, lord, and master."

[4] A te fia bello
Averti fatta parte per te stesso.
"To thee it shall be honourable to have made thee a party for thyself" : 'Paradiso'; C. xvii. 69.—I quote from Mr. A. J. Butler's edition (1885): one of the most useful and scholarly pieces of work lately executed in England.

[5] "And stretching forth his hands for love of the further shore."

place among the saints of Paradise; we see all the leading Italians, his contemporaries, the true heroes and the false, the scenery and cities of his "fair country," the fresh rising art, Cimabue and Giotto. And above and beyond the framework and personages of his drama the poet's magic mirror repeats, interprets, and intensifies all the politics of his age, all its morality, all its theology. Nor are the contents of the poem more rich and impressive than its art. Wild and wandering as the scenes of his pilgrimage may be, one strong purpose traverses and animates the whole. As in the fourteenth century, so in the nineteenth, Dante breathes conviction into the heart by the sheer force of Poetry; by the austere yet subduing loveliness of his style; by the words which, in his own beautiful phrase, "carry their beauty with them."[1]

Thus far we have thought of Poetry in her loftiest function, as a motive force in the world's progress. This aspect of the Muse has been much put aside, especially in modern days, in favour of her more markedly narrative, personal, or subjective creations; or of criticism upon Poetry as an art. I have hence attempted to illustrate my proposition by the examples of Virgil and of Dante. But those whose assent I may have had the good fortune to gain will recognize that the same high place has been filled by others; that every race and country, in its turn, has, it is probable, found interpreters of itself to itself among its poets. Many such, doubtless, are now dimly known or forgotten, hidden away in the birthnight of the race,—as the early age of a rising nation is that in which this national power of song has most often been felt. What the tale of Arthur was in ancient Wales, what the original Gadhelic hero-legends, of which a phantom likeness is left to us under the name of Ossian, what their in-

fluence over the sensitive Celtic nature may have been, we shall never know. But we can yet trace the modifying and impelling action of David and Isaiah over the Hebrew mind, of Homer over the Hellenic. In the same class, though not of equal moment, we may, I think, rank the great romances—those of Charlemagne, of Arthur, of Perceval, during the middle age of Europe. Their influence runs parallel with, but counter to, the influence of the early Renaissance. Nor, in later days, have these great forces ceased operating. Goethe, Schiller, Shakespeare, Scott, Burns,—not to enter the debateable ground of our own century; do we not feel that these names represent

Full-welling fountain-heads of change,

of movement, of life? Do we not feel that these countrymen of ours, with others whom we may silently add, have distinctly co-operated, more or less, in proportion to their poetic gift, in framing what one of them calls, "our island-story;" that they have largely made the minds of Englishmen, not only during their own age, but in ours also?

If, however, this national motive power of Poetry be her highest function, it is also her rarest. Two greatly more popular provinces remain, which I hope to outline in fewer words. By far the largest number of poets have devoted themselves,—and perhaps from the earliest times,—on the one hand, to represent the world about them in the widest sense of that wide phrase, Man above all;— on the other hand, to putting their own personal thoughts and feelings into the music of verse. This is the range claimed for his Art by Wordsworth in that memorable Essay which on some points, indeed, is justly open to the criticisms it has received, in Wordsworth's own time from Coleridge, more recently from my own courteous and accomplished friendly

---

[1] 'Convito'; I: c. 8;—a quotation which I owe to Dean Church.

antagonist, Mr. Courthope. But one eloquent passage, describing the sphere of Poetry, may, I think, be advantageously quoted.

"Aristotle has said that Poetry is the most philosophic of all writing; it is so; its object is truth, . . . not standing upon external testimony, but carried alive into the heart by passion; Truth which is its own testimony. . . . Poetry is the image of man and nature. . . . The Poet writes under one restriction only, namely, the necessity of giving immediate pleasure to a human Being. . . . Poetry is the breath and finer spirit of all knowledge. . . . Emphatically may it be said of the Poet, as Shakespeare hath said of man, *that he looks before and after* . . . he binds together by passion and knowledge the vast empire of human society. . . . Poetry is the first and last of all knowledge—it is as immortal as the heart of man."

These are not rhetorical phrases; they express the reasoned convictions of one whose deep insight into the common heart of man and the soul of nature needs no praise of mine. Poetry, speaking of it in its higher forms, is the most vivid expression of the most vivid thoughts and feelings of man. And, as by the gift that was in them the Poets have spontaneously and inevitably known and felt more keenly, more warmly, I may say it with truth, more truly, than their fellows; so the pictures which they have left us, in exact proportion to their proper power in their Art, are more lively, more informed with soul, nearer the heart than any others. Poets, when they have rightly used their gifts, when they have written with their eye on their object, as Wordsworth said, not on themselves,— uniting disinterestedness with conviction,—Poets are the true Representative Men of their century; in Milton's majestic phrase, treating

Of fate and chance and change in human life, High actions and high passions best describing.

We are considering now, let me once more for clearness' sake remind you, Poetry in its results, rather than its processes; the finished work of Art, more than the laws which govern

the Artist. When Poetry as an Art is before us, will be the time to try to seize the limitations which oppose a direct treatment of History, Morals, Religion, or Science, in verse. But if these conditions place History or Morals in didactic form,—like the direct imitation of Nature in painting, —beyond the limits of Poetry, she gives us in compensation something more vital, more penetrative. Keeping in view still poems of impersonal, objective character:—beside their wider, national, functions, where is the temper of each race, the common life of city and country, painted more fully and brilliantly than in Homer or Dante? And with these great names we may join that long series of traditionary ballads which every nation owns, and which are to the Epic what the star-dust of the sky is to the great stars themselves. Even the most picturesque or brilliant of historians does not paint so tersely and truly, with such living tints, as we find in the historical pictures of the poets. At the best, historians only speak what the others sing. So again with novelists. If their narration has far more wealth in detail and fulness than the poet can compass, they cannot compete with him in vivid flashes of description or character, in the strokes which need no repetition. In this peculiar class of poetry, modern literature, our own, I think, in particular, has been fertile. I know what our debt is to the great romance-writers of the century. Yet in 'Auld Robin Gray,' in the 'Death of Sir John Moore,' in Wordsworth's 'Brothers,' in Lord Tennyson's 'Rizpah,'— to name a few only for example's sake,—will you not agree that we have tales in their essence, novels in three pages instead of three volumes, which even a Thackeray could not equal, or a Scott surpass?

If, again, we take a lower or narrower level of life as the poet's standing-ground, the manners and morals, frailties and fashions of the day, the tone of society, the current criticism on literature or art,—nowhere are these preserved for our pleasure with such brilliant clearness, such accurate lightness of touch, as by Aristophanes, Horace, Chaucer, or Pope. Drama stands in a peculiar region, midway between prose and verse. But when it is either poetry pure, as at Athens, or mixed, as in the England of Elizabeth and James, whilst the Dramatist is faithful to the higher traditions of his art, it yet fulfils its old Aristotelian office of purifying the passions, whilst it brings the past or present before us in an enchanted world of its own, and adds a charm to Poetry herself. Each century as it passes writes itself in light upon the mirror of the poet's mind, and is fixed for ever by the secret of his art in words livelier than the painter's tints, more durable than the marble of the sculptor.

What Epic poetry does for mankind, what we receive from Narrative, from Satire, from the Drama, I have now briefly sketched. All are, of course, given to us through the soul of the poet; rays of light refracted as it were and variously tinted by passage through his thoughts and feelings. But all these classes are alike, broadly speaking, in being representations of what is in itself external to the Poet: they are all, to use one of the few abstract metaphysical terms which it is difficult to avoid, forms of objective Poetry. This species, for the last hundred years or so, has been less fertile, and, perhaps, less popular, than during the former centuries of civilization. To take another phrase, we might call it synthetical Poetry; whilst what we are apt to prefer is largely of the analytical kind; personal, subjective, —in a restricted sense of the word, Lyrical. Time does not allow me here to enter into this point with any attempt at completeness. All I will venture now to say is, that the first or objective order of poems seems to

me the most healthy in its nature, the least distorted by caprice or fantasticality, above all, the more free from Egotism;—that suicidal, hidden canker-worm of Art and of life. It has certainly exercised the widest, the most massive, influence on the world; the creative, as contrasted with the penetrative, Imagination has in this field displayed its energies most widely. In support of this criticism, which I submit with diffidence, I may quote a striking passage from Goethe. It occurs among those conversations,[1] fortunately recorded by Eckermann, in which the *mitis sapientia* of the poet's old age often shines out with a peculiarly simple and attractive light. "The poet deserves not the name while he only speaks out his few subjective feelings; but as soon as he can appropriate to himself and express the world, he is a poet. Then he is inexhaustible, and can be always new; while a subjective nature has soon talked out his little internal material, and is at last ruined by mannerism. People always talk of the study of the ancients; but what does that mean, except that it says, turn your attention to the real world, and try to express it, for that is what the ancients did when they were alive." "Goethe" (Eckermann continues) "arose and walked to and fro, while I remained seated at the table, as he likes to see me. He stood a moment at the stove, and then, like one who has reflected, came to me, and with his finger on his lips, said, 'I will now tell you something which you will often find confirmed in your experience. All eras in a state of decline and dissolution are subjective; on the other hand, all progressive eras have an objective tendency.

[1] January 29, 1826. I quote from Mr. J. Oxenford's excellent translation; 1850.— In this book, Eckermann's naif honesty has not concealed Goethe's weak points as a critic; yet I doubt if any of the poet's writings, (the letters to Schiller included,) give so favourable, so human, a view of his nature.

Our present time is retrograde, for it is subjective; we see this not merely in poetry, but also in painting, and much besides. Every healthy effort, on the contrary, is directed from the inward to the outward world, as you will see in all great eras, which have been really in a state of progression, and all of an objective nature.'"

Goethe's criticism here is the more interesting and weighty because, as he seems to have correctly felt, his judgment was in contradiction to his own practice as a poet. And those who do not accept his view may point with triumph to some amongst his own many personal subjective lyrics. In the Lyrical region indeed, wherein I include the 'Faust,' and in this alone, so far as my knowledge extends,—may I confess it?—does the writer of first-rate genius strictly appear recognizable. With Goethe's name, I may, therefore, fitly preface the brief remarks with which I propose to-day to tax your patience upon the last great province of Poetry remaining for notice.

As a practical descriptive definition, we might characterize the Lyric as eminently the voice of passion and of impulse, uttering in verse, generally fervent and rapid, some single thought, feeling, or situation. The poet's art will hence be especially shown by the choice of a metrical structure appropriate to the subject, and of a subject marked by unity in its motive. Or, rather, to speak more truly, motive and metre and prevailing colour will have presented themselves together to his mind as it were in a predestined unity. Within these general limits, the lyric falls under the two main heads of Objective and Subjective, Impersonal and Personal, upon which Goethe comments. Of these the first is, doubtless, highest or largest in purpose; it is to this that we naturally give the great name of Ode, under which the most splendid and world-moving lyrics by common consent would be grouped. But here, also,

perhaps, are found the most ambitious failures of the lyric. A vast fervour of intensity, a rare command of his art, are demanded of the poet; the furnace must be seven times heated, which is to fuse and poetize this "large utterance" into unity. Hence that noble form of song often runs in the calmer current of narrative lyric, as the 'St. Agnes' of Keats, or the 'Ruth' of Wordsworth; or, as in Gray's exquisite lines, glides down into the Elegiac.

The personal or subjective lyric, I need hardly remark, is by far the most frequent form; it is also that which perhaps yields the most immediate pleasure and relief to the mind; it is especially the treasure-house for the Memory. Within this kind also our two main divisions reappear. The Lyric, whilst expressing individual feeling, may also represent universal feeling. The Poet's personality may be felt to be that of human kind. The objective quality may be latent in the subjective. I venture to ask your attention to this point; the distinction is one which cuts very deep, and the value of lyrical poetry as a living power is greatly affected by it. I will name a few examples; taking first the more absolutely and purely personal style,—the strictly subjective lyric.

The poem which expresses a single mind, which does not appeal to the common human heart, will often spring from an exceptional or fantastic temperament. Such are many of those fanciful lyrics of the seventeenth century which we owe to writers such as Donne, Crashaw, or Lovelace: nor is the race extinct in our own time. Such poems are seldom read, but never read without interest. Rarely, however, do they touch our feelings; for the ingenious is a foe to the pathetic. It is otherwise with those poems in which some morbid element, some too sensitive note, penetrates the strain with sadness. During this century, Italy has seen two singers of this character, strangely contrasted with the natural gaiety of the land : her own son Leopardi, and our exile Shelley. Upon the beauty of Shelley's lyrics, this is not the time to dwell ; my point here is, that their remoteness from ordinary feeling, their severance from humanity, set as they are to that weird melody of their own by the poet's mastery over his art, is no small cause of the fascination which they hold over us :

Coming one knows not how, nor whence,
Nor whither going.

Were Shelley's lyrics not thus exceptionally personal, thus aloof from experience,—a music of despair, such as Lucretius might have heard in fancy as he looked up at the " æther studded with shining stars,"—I think we could hardly enjoy them. In Mr. Arnold's beautiful phrase, he seems to

Wave us away, and keep his solitude,

at the moment when the witchery of his Eolian music most attracts us.

Shelley, however, is every way alone in his magic. Wordsworth in his solitary ' Highland Reaper ' expresses the quality which we look for most, and find most frequently, in first-rate lyrics ;—the voice of humanity, the cry of the heart ;—our own experience given back to us in song ; the commonplace of life transmuted into novelty and beauty ;

Some natural sorrow, loss, or pain,
That has been, and may be again.

Shakespeare has been our first grand-master in this style ; some half dozen songs of his, in Sappho's phrase, " sweeter than the harp, more golden than gold," unite universality of feeling with lovely uniqueness of style beyond anything in the language : Milton's too rare lyrics, many by Wordsworth, songs such as the ' Break, break,' or ' Ask me no more,' of our great living Lyrist, often coming near Shakespeare's in quality. But the field of the lyric is a world of beauty in itself, too large and too varied in its flowers that I should attempt to sketch it. One only specimen, how-

ever, I will venture to give, as an example of the personal lyric in its simplest form of perfection. It is some unknown lover's song of absence.

When I think on the happy days
  I spent wi' you, my dearie,
And now what lands between us lie,
  How can I be but eerie !

How slow ye move, ye heavy hours,
  As ye were wae and weary !
It was na sae ye glinted by
  When I was wi' my dearie.

These " slender accents of sweet verse,"—this little Romance of a life in eight lines, as I have elsewhere called it, has to me that beauty which almost calls forth tears ; and it is no wonder that Burns himself, despite two attempts, has failed to better it.

This lecture began with a historical outline of the realm of Poetry in its length and breadth. I have then tried, in similar outline, to set forth Poetry in its main results as a motive power in the world at large, and over the hearts of men ; a power expressing itself by those varied methods of appeal, which bear the name of styles or classes. For the next occasion when I have the privilege of addressing you, remains, I hope, Poetry as an art,— the conditions under which she has to exercise this power ; and, as my moral from the whole, the claim of Poetry to be treated as a subject for study not less scholarly and scientific than the other great studies of Oxford.

This is an ambitious attempt ; it asks your kind forbearance ; for a judgment tempered with mercy. Perhaps, indeed, any attempt to show what Poetry really is, is impossible. Let me quote a few beautiful lines applicable to this point, by that dear and high-hearted friend whose premature death has opened, sadly, my way to a Chair which, I may indeed occupy, but cannot fill as Shairp filled it. Some here may remember the lines ; though but scant justice, I think, was done during his lifetime to his own gift in poetry,—marked as it is everywhere by the tenderness, the gallantry, the patriotism, the lofty aspiration and deep, fervent Faith which were the notes of Shairp's character. After all our attempts (he is saying) to interpret the soul of those we love, an element remains, and this the central, the most important, which is beyond our finding out:

We gaze on their loved faces, hear their speech,
  The heart's most earnest utterance,—yet we feel
Something beyond, nor they nor we can reach,
  Something they never can on earth reveal.

This is the secret of the poet; this is that which, as one of them said, we *cannot show, but feel only.* For me, at least, whilst I hold this Chair, it will be enough if I can give some true insight into the character and course of Poetry, some aid towards understanding and judging; if by choice of specimens I can assist towards full initiation into the beauty of the great master-works; above all, and without which all is of no avail, if I can lead some to true study of the Poets, with love, with reverence, and with enthusiasm.

POETRY COMPARED WITH THE OTHER FINE ARTS.*

It is with the results of the art of Poetry that we have been thus far concerned : with the work produced, rather than the rules by which the workman, consciously or not, was guided : with the effect of his poem upon the world, more than with the peculiar personal gifts necessary for the poet : with the song, in a word, rather than the singer.

What was last in actual fact has thus been first in criticism. But my task is now to turn from effect to cause : to ask what are the special means by which the poet reaches his results : to look from the Substance to the Form of his art. This inquiry is less external in its nature, more intricate, and, if I may use the word, more intimate ;—hence more difficult. Yet, *tentanda via est*, the brief Introduction to poetry which I wish to offer would be but half completed without it. But so much that is technical and theoretical will force its way into an inquiry of this nature, that I ask pardon beforehand should a subject, curious and interesting in itself, prove obscure or dull through my insufficient handling. My wish, at least, is to put the case as plainly as possible, avoiding in particular those rhetorical decorations into which the fine arts are too apt to tempt us, to the damage of judgment and the loss of pleasure. For rhetoric is always near to partisanship, and dazzles in place of lighting.

Such a subject as this cannot be approached, as a great master of poetical analysis has said,

Without some hazard to the finer sense,†

lest the bloom and the odour of poetry should be hurt by the hard touch of definition, lest one should wander into egotism or fancifulness, and, in the fine phrase of Dante, "transmute thought into dreaming."‡ Yet, at a time when art, as, all the world over, it dies out in creative power, ever more and more is in the mouths of men, it may be of interest —I would hope, even of use—to com-

---

* A second Introductory Lecture, by F. T. Palgrave, Professor of Poetry in the University of Oxford.

† Wordsworth ; *Prelude*, xiv.

‡ *Purgatorio*, c. xviii. 145.

pare the differences and find the common principles between the Fine Arts, with especial reference to that which is my peculiar care—*mea cura, Poesis*. And a further inducement is, that I am not aware of any modern attempt at this comparison, except in an essay by Mr. J. A. Symonds,* to which I am indebted for a few suggestions.

For our starting-point let us take two broad principles, which are not likely to be contested. First, that the essential aim of all true art is to clothe human thought and feeling, experience and aspiration, in such permanent forms of beauty as may touch and elevate the beholder's soul with responsive emotion and pleasure ; secondly, that the excellence of each art lies in its individuality, in its truth to its own conditions, in its strict obedience to its natural limits, its perfect freedom within them.

Architecture is the bridge between the practically useful and the visibly beautiful,† between the prose and the poetry of human activity. Building becomes art so soon as the builder's mind endeavours to move our minds by something beyond utility. We may note in Architecture three ascending stages of art. Mere mass in a building is the first and easiest form of expressiveness. Beauty felt in . the proportions of the mass, even without decoration, follows, until Architecture reaches its highest and noblest point as a fine art, when massiveness, moulded into general beauty of form, is united with the grace and life of appropriate ornament. Here the same laws govern Poetry and Architecture. True proportion in a building answers to the general scheme or plot of a poem (as exemplified especially in narrative or dramatic works), and, further, to the sense of unity which all good art conveys ; whilst the ornamental details in each should always be felt by eye and mind to bud and flower out, as if by necessity, from the main object of the design. They should be like the trees in a native forest described by an old poet, "born of their own impulse, not planted."‡ Let me dwell on this for a moment.

Architecture, at the first glance, presents to the eye utility transforming itself into beauty. Hence every beautiful element thus interfused should not only be appropriate to the purpose of the building, but should express and emphasize it. The obvious difficulty of this union between use and ornament adds, also, the further pleasure which arises always when we are conscious of obstacles vanquished by patient skill or imaginative invention. In the

---

* *Italian Byways*, 1883.

† The sense of *moral* beauty which is roused when we see works of eminent usefulness, unless it be translated by art into word or form, belongs to another sphere of thought.

‡ Ingenio arbusta ubi nata sunt. non obsita.—Naevius, *Lycurgus*.

finest buildings we find nothing merely decorative; the one-sided demand, "Art for Art's sake," here, at least, can have no place. The mysterious creatures which guarded the palace-gates of Nineveh—the severe power of the Doric column in the Parthenon —the lovely capitals and wreaths which we see in the earlier structures of Venice—the figure-peopled front of Rheims or Wells— nay, every pinnacle and parapet in the days of living architecture, all, as a rule, serve to accentuate straightforwardly the functions of the building. And rightly so: for the eye is soon satisfied with seeing; any decoration beyond that which is really needed, any ornament which does not justify its existence, vexes us with satiety, rouses a sense of the intrusive, and weakens the very effect on the spectator's soul at which the designer aimed.

Here we meet with another law, one of the few—the very few, I am disposed to say—really common to all the Fine Arts, but in ncne more stringent than in architecture, what may be termed the law of Climax. It is generally agreed that every true work of art must form a whole, must lead us to a definite and perceptible end, should in a word, have unity. In Architecture, this law is often neglected. We find buildings, public and private (as, it must be confessed, we find poems), so lavishly clothed with decoration that eye and mind are oppressed only by a general sense of perplexing profusion. *All* ornament is little more satisfactory, little more effective, whether in poem, picture, or building, than *no* ornament. Here the law of climax has its place. Decoration should always be so managed as to carry us up to moments of intenser interest. These may be more or fewer, in proportion to the scale of the work. But such moments, in turn, must lead, with always increasing delight and wonder, to the last climax of significance and beauty. The end, in the old phrase, should crown the work.

But each Fine Art works with closely limited materials, sparing us, we should remember always, whether as artists or as beholders and judges, "narrower margin than we deem."* These conditions, if I may use words not too lofty or serious for the matter, are, in fact, part of the ever surrounding chains and mountain-walls of Necessity, in the battle between which and man's Free Will, all human life is involved; and, with it, all fine art, which is always and everywhere a mirror held up to life. Architecture, as the one fine art directly subserving utility, has special limits of its own. The employer, doubtless, invites art when, in the phrase of Tacitus, " he wishes not only for a shelter from rain and wind, but also for an object which should please his eye." " Non tantum eo vult tecto tegi quod imbrem ac ventum arceat, sed etiam quod visum et oculos delectet." The builder becomes artist when into

* M. Arnold; *Sonnet* V.

the language of arch and wall, roof and spire, he " translates emotion ; vague, perhaps, but deep, mute but unmistakable. When we say that a building is sublime or graceful, we mean that sublimity or grace is inherent in it."* But it is the practical purpose of the building, imposed from without upon its designer, which, in general, must govern also the spiritual or poetical impression it conveys. The architect is not, like poet or painter in modern days, free to choose his subject. Palace and cottage, town-house, or country-house, castle and church, railway station and inn, each embodies one great phase of human existence, with all its array of thought and feeling and activity ; for the prose of life is always inextricably intertwined with its poetry. This it is the artist's business to put into visible form. And this practical aim, while determining his materials, determines also, in a great degree, the character of the emotion which the architect is able to excite. Mass, solidity, permanence ; these are the first ideas which his materials carry with them. If he can render these ideas only with visible appropriateness and in satisfying propor- tion, the plainest work will be a work of art. Hence the master- pieces of architecture will generally be found expressive, not so much of beauty pure and simple, as of elevation of soul and sublimity, upon which last quality I can here only pause to remark that the Sublime, although often contrasted with the Beautiful, seems to me rather to be one form or mode of beauty. But the limit thus straitly fixed by the physical conditions, as ever is the case, adds to the vital force of the art, " turning its necessity to glorious gain." The permanent sublimity of a noble building appeals to one of the deepest cravings of the heart—

> The universal instinct for repose,
> The longing for confirmed tranquillity,
> Inward and outward :†

to " that peace which is at the centre of all agitation." This is the feeling expressed by those famous lines in Congreve's *Mourning Bride*, describing the interior of some Gothic cathedral, which Johnson said that he placed above any single passage of Shakes- peare ;—finding in them, doubtless, a tone in harmony with the pensive loftiness of his own mind.

The sense of aspiration and sublimity thus called forth is vague and general, compared with the more definite thought or emotion which we may owe to pictures or to poetry ; the moral impressed upon us more remote. It is a sort of counterpart to the delightful sense of unrealised desire, of the longing that cannot be put into words, which is, perhaps, the peculiar privilege of music. The

---

* J. A. Symonds ; *Italian Byways*.
† *Excursion* ; Book iii.

German critic, Schlegel, *aut quis fuit alter*, who spoke of a Gothic Cathedral as "frozen music," may have had in his mind this sublime vagueness. But, if architecture thus falls short of her sister fine arts, in clearness and variety of pleasurable effect, she finds a charm which they are all but without, in the permanence due to her purpose and her materials. The charm I speak of, in its best recognized form, lies in that union of the work of time with the work of beauty, which everyone of ordinary taste and education knows as Picturesqueness. This is probably the most common source of the pleasure which architecture gives; it is this which, in the popular mind, most connects it with art. But architecture brings often a further charm, also specially inherent in this fine art; which, to those who can feel it, is deeper far than picturesqueness; what I should call the magic of antiquity, the actual and tangible presence of the past. Statue or picture may also be ancient; yet their age is apt to impress us rather as a source of regret for the inevitable wrongs wrought by Time, than as a direct source of pleasurable interest. Between us and the poet the distance is wider still. Sophocles or Dante or Milton are not face to face with the modern reader in their works. It is through words, the full meaning of which no student can fully hope to penetrate, that they reach us—through words which, even if our own language, are but the symbols of the poet's thought, not the thought itself. But the building which entrances us by its grace or grandeur is not only the authentic creation of an artist long since passed from earth; it must be also the living handiwork of a whole crowd of others, those who set up and carved it—artists too, in their degree, all in some strange but real way surviving in their own creation.

This thought, if we consider it rightly, is deeply pathetic. As, when looking on some mountain-top or valley such as the poet describes,—

> Crag jutting forth to crag, and rocks that seem
> Ever as if just rising from a sleep,[*]

most men, in their imaginative moments, feel with Wordsworth somewhat of the presence of—

> The Visions of the hills,
> And Souls of lonely places;

similarly the spectator, if he has rendered himself worthy of the spectacle by a reasonable amount of knowledge, in dome or spire, arch or buttress, stable and motionless as the mountain, sees the souls of men, their thoughts and emotions and fancies, as it were making silent appeal to his sympathy from their prisons of stone, praying to be understood, and felt with as men by man, and gently handled, and spared from needless injury. And such a spectator

---

[*] Keats; *Hyperion*, Book ii.

hears not only thus the sweet, melancholy music of the long-vanished days. What to the uneducated or the prejudiced eye is a bare skeleton, to him is a living organism of the past. He will be aware how the style of the building before him was evolved from those that preceded it by laws, imperative almost as the laws of Nature, under the combined pressure of the material wants, the moral tone, the imagination and art of its own age: how that style, in turn, gave way to another which more accurately embodied and petrified the needs and wishes of a later period. He will hence learn patience with each, and be able to take an open-minded enjoyment in its beauty, even whilst maintaining the rights of a just judgment to give every style its due place in art. One cathedral shall thus bring before us that long evolution of human intelligence and invention which passes successively through Renaissance, Gothic, Romanesque, Roman, Greek; arrested only before Assyria and Egypt, like Geology when classifying the steps in organic life, by the failure of our evidence.

Thus, from any single work of art avenues, as someone has said, go forth to the Infinite. The building which to the uneducated eye is but a voiceless if impressive mass, to the informed taste will be a short history of art, a chronicle of human progress. And it would be idle to say that the pleasure which we may hence receive will be twenty-fold deeper, higher, and more permanent than that of the uninstructed passer-by: it will be something out of all comparison with it.

Architecture thus " connects itself indissolubly with the life, the character, the moral being of a nation and an epoch." The very fact that it subserves utility, compels it, as it were, to follow and to represent more closely than the other fine arts the spirit of its age: history here carves itself before us in broader lines, and covers more of human life in every rank and condition than even painting or poetry.

I wish that space allowed me to vivify these perhaps too general reflections by the example of some one famous building; by such an imaginary walk, for instance, as Addison led the men of his time through the Abbey of Westminster, or, in our own time, some of those present may have enjoyed with our accomplished and lamented Stanley. But my subject recalls me : I must linger no more on this favourite art, lest, as Virgil feared, I should fatigue my hearers,—

Singula dum capti circumvectamur amore.

Sculpture and painting, formative arts which represent to us human life, landscape, and all other appearances of Nature, bring us nearer Poetry. Their sphere is much wider, their appeal more direct and special, than that of Architecture. In place of the

general sense of grace or sublimity, they present, not indeed imitations of Nature, as is sometimes said, but her forms as seen
through the glass of the artist's own soul; individualized by its
varying tints and degrees of translucency, combined in new shapes
and new meanings by fancy and imagination. But upon these
points we need not dwell: Oxford has heard much eloquent teaching upon them. I pass on to my own immediate subject, the
special character of the formative arts in comparison with poetry.

Every Fine Art, let me repeat, may be said to conquer its specific
character by the artist's incessant battle with its physical conditions; he becomes master of his craft by turning his own limitations
into victory. Sculpture connects itself here with architecture, using
stone or metal, and expressing thoughts in solid, tangible form; it
also is the natural exponent of repose, of dignity, of permanent
beauty. The subjects in a high degree suited for sculpture—those
in which the special limits are best tenable—are hence comparatively few. They must be, first, expressible by pure form,
without the interpretative aid of colour, and with little aid from
background or accessories. Hence, more than any other art, they
require the spectator to bring knowledge of the subject treated
with him. Sculpture rarely explains itself, as painting often does,
and poetry should always. Landscape is wholly denied to her.
Living forms, pre-eminently human forms, are almost her whole
province.

This, truly, is but a small field compared with the world of
thought and feeling, of tale and landscape, free to poetry. Yet
from this limitation springs the peculiar power of Sculpture.
What she offers are the great elementary passions common to
mankind through all the ages; the actions which are most widely
known; the features which, through their intrinsic beauty or the
lives of their wearers, have a world-wide significance. The proper
appeal of Sculpture is to those thoughts and feelings which are
highest or deepest in us; to those which seem by nature to have
most of immortality in them. These the artist must render
through colourless human form. This brings before us another
general law of fine art—that the most important feature in every
work must be the most perfectly realised and rendered. We have
here another form of the law of climax. Hence ingenuities of carving
which attempt an absolute illusion of the sight, the veils that look
as if we could lift them, the fruit we might pluck, are but caricatures of the true art. The sculptor, that he may render human
form and human thought and feeling through it, with the highest
perfection, is compelled to render abstractly or conventionally every
minor, less important feature in his work. It is to Nature that
he returns, through deviations from Nature.

This law of abstraction in sculpture, I note in passing, seems to find its counterpart in what Keble and other authorities have spoken of as the law of reserve in poetry. All fine verse suggests whilst it reveals : the poet leaves much generalized or incomplete that he may give us the sense of completeness : his reticences enable him to speak more forcibly.

Sculpture being thus narrowly restricted, at once in her methods and her subjects, has to rely more than any other art on that common basis of them all—absolute beauty. Even when creating forms of grandeur and sublimity, she can hardly, like painting or poetry, place us in presence of the simply fearful or the unalloyedly grotesque : no form distinctly not beautiful being, I think, ever admitted in sculpture of high class, at least without great peril. And if, going beyond the familiar word "beauty," we ask which of the elements composing it (so far as they are definable) do really move and charm us most, our answer, it seems to me, must be these two—intensity and tenderness. All the highest work, if I do not dogmatize too much in saying it, in all the fine arts, has this note of perfection. It is a truth which I greatly wish to impress upon you : it is, at least, the underlying thought in all I have to offer.

Now sculpture, as the most concentrated of the fine arts, presents this mode of the beautiful in the highest degree. From her natural conditions she can, as it were, give but one stroke. But it is decisive. And this intensity and tenderness of beauty is not, as with painting, to be sought mainly in the human features ; it must be felt living through the whole figure, infused in every limb, inherent in every fold of drapery. To name these conditions is enough to make us feel, in some small degree, the amazing difficulty of the art ; enough to explain why true success in it is so rare. But hence, also, the strange, deep, mysterious pleasure which first-rate sculpture gives. Hence, again, in combination with its material, the permanence of its appeal to civilized man. Sculpture shares with architecture this prerogative of duration. It is through a frail and impalpable film that we know Titian or Raphael. It is only through serious toil that the symbols through which the poetry of Hellas or Rome is preserved become living words and thoughts to the modern reader. But the gods of the Acropolis and of Olympia are before us, as they were before Sophocles or Theocritus.

I might go on till all but I were weary upon this magical art, so cold to the careless spectator, so informed, I might almost say so white-hot, with inward passion to the soul of the true student. But we must return to the relations between sculpture and poetry. Close analogies are not here to be looked for. But where poetry gives the sense of sublimity in human character, of that rare pathos which is roused, not by pathetic words, but by the simple setting forth of a pathetic situation, where details are suppressed in favour of human interest; where, in fine, beauty is mainly presented through tenderness and intensity—there we may recognize the statuesque elements in poetry. Homer was long since known as the Master of Phidias. In their style, Aeschylus and Sophocles have the sculptural quality; Pindar (to me) far less constantly. Petrarch occasionally, Dante and Milton oftener, show it. Modern verse, however, is not rich in this quality. Even Keats, of all our poets since Milton, the most richly endowed with plastic genius, failed, and with his exquisite modesty confessed his failure, in *Hyperion*. In point of Form, the impersonal, or national ode, is nearest to a work of sculpture. Dryden (in a coarse, Renaissance style), Manzoni, Schiller, Wordsworth, here may supply examples. But in this region also, as in sculpture itself, success is of the rarest.

The material and technical differences between painting and sculpture reveal the nearer approach made by Painting towards poetry. The sculptor gives his thoughts to us in actual form. Colour is the only natural element which he requires the spectator to supply. The painter requires us, by a farther effort of imagination, to take a flat surface for solidity and distance, showing us his impression of Nature in that magical mirror of the mind, without which he himself could not have received the impression which he transfers to us. Painting here approaches Poetry, the fine art which has most of the symbolical, least of the sensuous, in its material. The painter also, although his canvas can only exhibit forms co-existent in space, not progressive in time, like those which pass before us in poetry, can indicate combined movement more than the sculptor; can imply the immediate before and after of the one moment which he has chosen. He can exhibit more of a connected story, more subtle and complicated feeling than sculpture, and can connect his work into a whole through landscape, through multitude of detail, through colour. Painting, hence, has a wider range of character than sculpture, and depends less upon absolute beauty. In all these points pictures come near to poems. Colour in particular, which, I think, answers in some respects to metre, allows the painter to give his work at the first glance a general tone of feeling, putting us in the right mood to understand and enjoy the scene which he offers for our study. Hence a likeness, true though shadowy, may be traced between the main currents of painting and poetry. Words such as epic, dramatic, idyllic, and even lyrical (as, for example, in the case of Correggio) are applicable to individual pictures, and to certain schools of art.

The natural limit which confines painting to presenting one moment, one aspect only, in completeness, gives this art, even more than sculpture, a great advantage, of which every poet must be conscious. The painter exhibits at one glance to the mind the beauty of face or figure or landscape which the poet can only exhibit in succession by separate touches. And, however skilfully he may select and arrange his words, he cannot help knowing that no reader will ever be able to recombine them in the whole which was before his own inner vision. But I must not allow myself to be tempted here into discussing that very curious subject, the limits of Descriptive Poetry.

Painting is nearest among the arts to poetry in the range, variety, and definiteness of its subjects; it is also the art, if we include light-and-shade designing, which lends to poetry the dubious aid of illustration. Why, then, is it natural to take Music for our final comparison? In her appeal to us music calls forth emotion even more general and indefinite than architecture, with less representation of nature, less power to supply or to arouse thought. The forms through which music speaks to the ear not only present none of those natural appearances which sculpture and painting and poetry imitate or suggest, but have scarce any real prototypes in the very sounds of Nature. The orchestra is as little indebted to the nightingale as the cathedral aisle to the forest avenue. The most limited of the fine arts, by her technical conditions, the most conventional in material and method, what right has Music to a place next to Poetry—of all arts the freest, the most varied in range of subject, the most intellectual—in short, the highest? I may reply in a single word, which I hope will not be considered too rhetorical: Music speaks. Further answer is scarcely needed: *causa finita est.*

As, however, I have tried in case of the other fine arts, let us attempt to compare with poetry this evanescent and impalpable spirit of music, which here I shall, so far as possible, think of as separated from the words of a song or the action of an opera— absolute music, according to the modern phrase. We have granted that it is nearest to poetry in its essence and in its effect on the hearer. But the reason often given for this, that music acts more immediately and closely upon the nerves than the arts which we have examined—and has, hence, a more absolutely spiritual influence over us—cannot, I think, be sustained. Hearing is known now to be a nervous function in no essential respect different from that of Sight, through which architecture, sculpture, painting, move our souls. The wave of sound has not, hitherto at least, been shown to penetrate the consciousness by any finer or closer channel than the wave of light. The true reason why music has this magical and

41 *

enthralling power, why it seems to steep us in the essence of poetry, lies more deep; it must be sought in a region where words, I fear, cannot enter without peril to the speaker. Analyse and define how we may, no one has ever caught and imprisoned in words the volatile vital element which makes poetry poetry. Could we define it, it would be that magical thing which we call poetry no longer; the spell would be broken by the word;—the fairy gift would fly. The poet himself cannot seize this essence. "I feel it only"—*sentio tantum*—is his last utterance. He is, at most, dimly conscious of a spirit moving in him, he knows not how. And we, the readers, may define and describe the outward, formal circumstances of poetry; may reckon and weigh the part which imagination and fancy, pathos and sublimity, heart and head, contribute to a poem; but this inner soul, this inspiration, remains always indefinable. Intensity with Tenderness is only the phrase in which I have tried to find an imperfect expression of it.

Now it is, I think, precisely this mysterious element, this soul of soul, which music offers to the sensitive nature. The spirit of poetry which we hear in music is even less embodied than that " half-graspable Delight " in the air above him, which Keats describes his Endymion as conscious of when he first meets his unknown goddess in the enchanted forest. Its invisibility is part of the magic and the entrancement; invisibility to the senses answering to the vagueness with which music appeals to the soul. It is the triumph of a poem to offer us definite images, distinct pictures; of music to dispense with them, and pass beyond to the inmost animating spirit which renders picture and imagery poetical. If any attempt at definition be not too hazardous, might we not, hence, define music simply as poetry without words?

But hence, also, this Fine Art differs essentially from the rest; they move us actively, they call forth our latent thoughts and feelings, they interpret our higher nature to ourselves. Music (speaking always now of music absolute), in place of leading, follows the moods of the mind, clothes them with poetry, soothes or exalts them accordantly with the temper of the moment. The melody which brings tears to one hearer shall give another consolation, beyond the reach of philosophy or poetry. A slight change in expression, even in time, will turn into a song of despair the symphony of triumph. This adaptive, living quality, this *immediateness* of music, if I may use the word, seems to arise from the material conditions of the art which here, as ever, secretly confine and govern it. Seemingly the most natural, music is, in fact, the most artificial of the arts, the most conventional. Our scale, our melody, our harmony, are meaningless if not discordant to the majority of human ears. Even among the races which employ them, they have proved arbitrary and fluctuating. Mathematics show that the very intervals of the scale are irreconcilable with natural law. The European ear is gradually learning new rules of harmony. Hence, perhaps, music is the most modern of the arts, not, of course, in its practice, but in the forms which now speak to us musically. Despite a few fragments, surviving rather as curiosities than as works of art, we can hardly realise what was the music which Dante heard in Paradise more than the music which accompanied the verse of Homer or Sophocles. Yet in this paradoxical art the peculiarities of music bring it nearer to the soul of poetry; they make it more fit to follow, to invest, to deepen our emotion; dissevering it from the associations of the past, they render it more immediately and purely pleasurable, make it a more pervading atmosphere of intensity steeped in tenderness; the interpreter of that sadness which lies always at the heart of joy. An old poet has sung this aspect of melody in two lines which have in them no little of the art they describe :

> The mellow touch of music most doth wound
> The soul, when it doth rather sigh than sound.*

But I must linger no more in these Elysian fields; *Quid multa* —to take the words of the most musically gifted among my predecessors—*Quid multa? Communis est hominum sententia, Musicam omnium plane artium proxime ad Poesin accedere.*† " Why say more? It is the common sentiment of mankind, that of all the arts music clearly comes nearest to poetry."

Much of interest has perforce been passed over in this comparison of the arts. But if, step by step, I have made the meaning clear, the special province of each art, the special powers of each to please and to move us, will also have defined the area left for poetry, whilst showing us, at the same time, what poetry cannot do. We have seen that the spell of every art over our souls is always limited by its material conditions, and by the technical rules which they necessitate. Through its conformity to these conditions, fine art gives pleasure; it rules, because it obeys. What, then, are the materials, the limits, and the laws of Poetry as an art ?

The brief statements of two great poets will be our best starting-point here. Milton defines poetry as " simple, sensuous, and passionate." Coleridge defines it as consisting of " the best words in the best places." Enlarge this, with what he would have been the first to add, into " The best words in the best places, for sense and sound and metre," and the definition of what we are seeking will be complete. With such words poetry " does the work in

---

* Herrick, *Hesperides.*
† J. Keble, *Prael.* III

turn of architecture, sculpture, painting, music." But whilst the material of these arts is tangible or audible, the very material of poetry is, if I may be allowed the phrase, immaterial. Words are signs only of things, not images; light and airy beings, as Plato unkindly describes the Poet himself; breath mysteriously blended with thought. The mind only—head and heart, but heart through head—is addressed by poetry. The single strictly sensuous element which she has in common with her sisters is found in so far as something remotely like music is felt or heard in rhythm and rhyme,—and through these the poet's material mainly takes its form.

When painting was before us I compared rhythm and rhyme to colour, because the metre chosen for a poem tints it at once and throughout with a peculiar tone. But the comparison has a deeper significance. Colour, it is generally agreed, is the element which divides painting from sculpture; it is the outer limit of the art. And I cordially agree with those who similarly hold metre, rhymed or unrhymed, as that material form which parts prose from poetry, which bounds it, which is of its essence. This view obviously excludes at once the extension of the name Poetry to prose writing. The "unheard melodies" which the sight of his Grecian Urn suggested to Keats might as well be termed actual music. Prose may be poetical, but remains always prose. I regret sincerely to find myself here opposed to many modern authorities, for it is doubtful whether the phrase, Prose-poetry, occurs till late in the eighteenth century. Shelley* speaks of Plato and Bacon as poets, and draws no line between them and Homer or Dante. This seems to me to turn metaphor into fact. But against Shelley in his youth may be set the mature judgment of Goethe and of Schiller, in one of the too-rare passages of helpful criticism which give value to their *Correspondence*.† And Schiller, in another letter, has a phrase which goes deeply, if somewhat obscurely, into the nature of metre. " Purity " (by which he means *strictness*) " of metre," he says, " serves as a sensuous representation of the inner necessity of the thought."‡ As I understand the passage, fixed metrical form answers to that inward impulse, that inspired movement or madness, as Plato calls it, which constrains the poet, in proportion to the force of his genius, to think, feel, and express himself as he does. Here, again, from another side, we find ourselves confronting that insoluble problem, what, namely, forms the innermost essence of poetry. This presence of necessity, though, perhaps, little noticed, is felt in all really fine art.

* *Defence of Poetry.*
† See Goethe's letter of November 25th, 1797.
‡ Schiller, August 9th, 1799.

It is implied in Wordsworth's profound criticism on Goethe, " that his poetry was not sufficiently *inevitable*." Rhythm and rhyme— our substitute for the ancient verse-systems framed upon quantity—rhythm and rhyme, by the inevitable bonds which they impose upon the poet, impress us with that silent sense of difficulty vanquished, of perfect freedom within the strictest bounds, which is one great source of poetical effectiveness and pleasure. Nor is this law confined to the poet. The artist's triumph always is when he can thus identify liberty with necessity, when his work strikes us at once as inevitable and spontaneous.

To conclude. My first lecture attempted to sketch the vast palace of art at which poets have been toiling almost from before the dawn of history ; " that great poem," as Shelley called it in his brilliant essay, " which all poets, like the co-operating thoughts of one great mind, have built up since the beginning of the world." To-day we have had less of the work than of the workman ; the formal conditions which the poet and his fellow-artists must obey ; the natural system of Art, if I may take the phrase from Science. Form as contrasted with substance, body with spirit, idea with realisation, style with matter—these and other phrases express, but express imperfectly, the two great elements which are found together in all the arts. The more intimate their union, the more equal their proportions, will the work be finer, more pleasurable, more durable. Probably, indeed, in all masterpieces the two elements have been given together ; soul and body have been born to the poet's mind at once ; Pallas has leapt forth, armed and perfect, from the head of her divine parent. An old remark which I have seen quoted, I know not whence, ingeniously expresses this balance between style and matter, as it should make itself felt in the finest works of art : *Simul, denique, eluceant opus et artifex.* As the last result, the work and the workman should shine forth on us together.

But this union of form and substance is often unequal and incomplete. Few, comparatively, are the poets who have steered true the narrow course midway between these opposing attractions, —led astray by the impulse to teach, or the impulse to display skill. Hence the endless battles which artists and students are always waging over this problem. Yet the dispute would hardly exist if beauty—beauty in its highest sense—were accepted, as it was by the Greeks, as the first and last word in art ; if poets and critics had taken to heart the single line in which Horace, with his exquisite skill in the use of words, has summed up the aim and method of poetry—

Animis natum inventumque Poema iuvandis—

where *iuvare* carries with it at once the image of aid and of

delight to the soul. Greek criticism and taste, and Roman following Greek, held the balance true between style and matter. But
the restless and fever-weakened modern world, which in its heart
prefers doubt and debate to truth, the novel to the beautiful, will
not have it so. Hence the quarrels and instabilities of criticism—
the one-sided judgments of literary coteries,—until the outer world
scornfully pushes aside the question with the proverb that we
cannot dispute about taste,—called forth by the eternal disputes
about it. Is the painter to aim at art for art's sake, or for his
subject's sake? Is the poet to satisfy himself with beauty devoid
of substance, or with matter imperfectly informed with charm of
imagery or language? All judgment on poetry is constantly
moving between these opposite yet eternally united poles. We can
trace the fluctuation in our own minds, as well as in our schools of
art and of criticism, as we are attracted in turn by the pole of
style or the pole of matter. But the final judgment, the central
estimate, poised and unwavering, and bringing with it the highest
and most endurable pleasure, will always be that which is evenly
balanced between them.

F. T. PALGRAVE.

POETRY AND PESSIMISM.

In the mind of a student of humanity, if he be also a reader of books, intellectual problems are apt to crystallise around individual personalities. A single poet, a single novelist, comes to stand to him for a whole complex of thought, a web of vague ideas and tendencies which are elsewhere, as we say, in the air, but which first become palpable when compelled by an artist's hand into the rigidity of the written word. This is especially the case with poets, for poetry, by its very nature, strikes to the heart of things and sets them before us in their naked essence, stripping away the vesture of irrelevant detail that, in the novel no less than in life, often veils and obscures them. It is by its poignancy, its directness of presentment, that poetry claims to be, as a medium of ideas, what Aristotle called it, most akin to philosophy.

The analysis, for example, of modern pessimism can scarcely be dissociated from the study of that gifted writer whose work it permeates and informs, Amy Levy. Two little volumes of her poems, in a dainty green-and-white binding, lie on my table, and have fascinated me for hours together. Vividly personal as they are, the pent-up sufferings of hundreds of souls throb through them, launching one on wide seas of melancholy speculation. Of Amy Levy's short and sad life I have no knowledge. She was, it would seem, by birth a Jewess, but one for whom the faith of her fathers had become an impossible thing. Gifted with brilliant intellectual powers, she spent a short time as a student at Cambridge, and then entered upon the perilous ways of literary life. It was not long before success appeared to be within her reach, but she was not destined to reap the fruition of it. A haunting shadow had fallen upon her path; she came to find the burden of life intolerable; and while still a girl was contented to yield up her share therein. Throughout all her work, prose and poetry alike, hand in hand with a sincere devotion to art, there runs a note of invincible sadness.

Such is the dominant impression that one gets from reading these volumes. Looked at purely as literature, they have a remarkable charm. They possess all the subtle workmanship, the delicacy of finish, the innumerable scholarly touches, which are so characteristic of the minor verse of our day. If they are somewhat full of echoes, there also they do not stand alone. But far beyond their merely artistic value, is their interest as the record of a soul. They are, indeed, a human document at least as rich with suggestion as the much discussed diary of Marie Bashkirtseff. And a document, one would think, far more legible ; for Marie, even in her most secret moments, was always and inevitably a *poseuse*, whereas Amy Levy is throughout absolutely genuine and sincere. How could it be otherwise ? Utterly disenchanted with the world, why should she try to keep up a brave show before it ? Her verse mirrors her thought, and its *leit-motif*, recurring with constant sad iteration, is· the consciousness of pain.

I suppose that the philosophical attitudes which we call optimism· and pessimism are generally less the result of mental conviction than· of individual temperament. They are moods, not systems. Life in· itself is iridescent with pleasure and pain : to one the richer hues, the lurking purples and leaping crimsons alone are visible ; another is spiritually colour-blind, and can see only the browns and drabs, the dusky shadows and more sombre depths of existence. Person-ality is a selective force, choosing from the vast mass of what is, by some subtle magnetism, just those elements which are most akin to its own nature. For all who attract pleasure, life is a triumph ; for the rest, a pilgrimage. This, no doubt, has been a universal law, no less true when the world seemed vanity to the author of *Ecclesiastes*, than it is now. Yet it will hardly be denied that, for whatever cause, pessimism is in an especial degree characteristic of our own· time and our own stage of development.

Our splendid literature is invested with melancholy. Tennyson· and Browning, indeed, are optimists, but their optimism is grave, not buoyant ; they walk by faith, not by sight. Browning twists· an assurance for the future out of the failures of the present, while Tennyson, in no less doubtful a strain, bids us "stretch lame· hands of faith " to a dimly felt Providence, and " faintly trust the· larger hope." So, too, with the rest. George Meredith saves him-self from pessimism by a strong will and an austere philosophy. Matthew Arnold and A. H. Clough are openly and profoundly despondent ; for them the light of the past is quenched, the future is beset with clouds ; they are for ever " wandering between two worlds, one dead, the other powerless to be born." Even in the Neo-Romantic poets, who least express the spirit of their age, the same tone may be discerned. Rossetti, though a lover, walked in Willow-wood all the days of his life. Morris, in youth, sought a refuge from the century's stress in the groves of an earthly Paradise, a dream-world of Greek and northern and mediæval legend. But his attempt was not all a success : the blitheness of Hellas was beyond recapture ; the violin-note of modern feeling rang incon-gruously through Arcadia, and in the end—

" he could not keep,
For that a shadow lour'd on the fields,
Here with the shepherds and the silly sheep."

He translated his ideals from the past to the future, and the "idle singer of an empty day" became the busy herald of a visionary hope. And if this sadness haunts the great poets of the age, still more is it noticeable in the lesser singers. Look at the pages of Mr. Miles's *Poets and Poetry of the Century.* There is a literature surcharged with tears, whose sure touch is on the pathetic, whose lyre sounds in groves that are shaded by cypresses and poplars, among roses that weep their petals.

When one turns from letters, the reflex of life, to life itself, the outlook is equally drear. We moderns find the world a very serious matter. Fifty years of individualism, of free thought, and unrestricted competition, have bitten their mark deep into our civilisation. The suffering which inevitably accompanies the struggle for existence is not less, but greater, for organisms upon a high level of self-consciousness. Flesh is ever but a transparent veil to spirit, and of this suffering we bear the plain sign upon our brows. It needs no wide knowledge of art to realise that the faces which Gainsborough painted differ notably in character and expression from those which fill the walls of a modern picture-gallery. The new type is as beautiful perhaps, more deeply intellectual, but certainly far more sad. It is scarcely fantastic to suggest that Leonardo's ironically named *La Gioconda*, an alien to our great-grandmothers, is curiously at home among the women of our own generation. By the same spirit our philosophy is coloured. Mr. Alexander, in his thoughtful book on *Moral Order and Moral Progress*, has singled out, as a central point in current ethical conceptions, the growing sense of the significance of pain. Pleasure was the loadstar of the earlier Hedonist; his modern successor, less exigent, would barter hopes of positive felicity to be quite sure of escaping suffering. This tendency to dwell on pain manifests itself among many who are by no means Hedonists. In it are rooted both strong and weak elements in our social organisation, the self-sacrifice of genuine philanthropy, as well as the excesses of sentimental humanitarianism.

It is difficult to analyse the causes which have made pain and pessimism so aggressive nowadays. Perhaps they are not really new dwellers among us, but only now for the first time becoming articulate, after long silent years in the heart of humanity. Partly they may be the outcome of fundamental changes in the religious consciousness. I do not mean the spread of unorthodoxy, but the disappearance of what George Eliot called "other-worldliness," that facile optimism which held this world as a vale of tears, to be compensated for by an eternity of pleasures in the next. More and more the conception that "I myself am heaven and hell," with all that it implies, is coming to be a fixed and abiding mode of belief. In part, also, a reason may be found in the intensity of our intellectual life, in the constant feverish speculation, the besetting desire to know. We are " sicklied o'er with the pale cast of thought." Only the superficial, the unreflecting, can dare to echo in all soberness the famous words of Mr. Pole ; " No one has said the world's a jolly world so often as I have. It's jolly ! " Given a temperament exceptionally sensitive to pain, and set in a modern environment, the result will be yet farther conditioned by individual characteristics. In the sympathetic, for whom the sufferings of others are no less real, no less vivid than their own, it will generally be devotion, in some one of its many forms, to the cause of humanity. In the self-centred, who have no safety-valve, it can hardly be other than a life of brooding misery. And such a life, faithfully presented, one would think, but at any rate with poignancy, is revealed to us in these poems of Amy Levy's. On opening them one's eye falls upon some such passage as this, lines in which the stored-up bitterness of the heart seems forcing itself into expression :

EPITAPH

ON A COMMONPLACE PERSON WHO DIED IN BED.

" This is the end of him, here he lies :
The dust in his throat, the worm in his eyes,
The mould in his mouth, the turf on his breast ;
This is the end of him, this is best.
He will never lie on his couch awake,
Wide-eyed, tearless, till dim daybreak ;
Never again will he smile and smile,
When his heart is breaking all the while ;
He will never stretch out his hands in vain,
Groping and groping—never again ;
Never ask for bread, get a stone instead,
Never pretend that the stone is bread ;
Never sway and sway 'twixt the false and true,
Weighing and noting the long hours through ;
Never ache and ache with the choked-up sighs :
This is the end of him—here he lies."

One turns instinctively to the portrait facing the title-page to see what manner of woman she was who could write thus, but the secret is hardly revealed. There is a face of no special beauty, the brow and eyes burdened with a weight of thought, the lips set as if in some reticence of sorrow. Baffled rather than satisfied, one goes back to the poems, anxious if possible to win the mystery from themselves. They are not many. A few lyrics and fragmentary snatches of verse, and a Browningesque monologue, *A Minor Poet*, clearly in some measure autobiographical. Brief as these records are, it is yet possible to decipher in them some image of the personality by which they were dictated. Amy Levy was in her way a passionate idealist. She entered upon life full of hope and strength and self-confidence, conscious of unbounded capacities for happiness and intensely eager to realise them. In the person of the Minor Poet she cries :

> " I want all, all ;
> I've appetite for all : I want the best,
> Love, beauty, sunlight, nameless joy of life."

Moreover, she was modern to the core, keen in relish of the pleasures of æsthetic and philosophical speculation ; sensitive, as only moderns can be, to the thousand charms and phases of Nature, in her infinite variety ; blessed with rich potentialities for friendship and love ; thirsting, like Tennyson's Ulysses, to " drink life to the lees." But it is part of the irony of things that those who have most power to enjoy are often those whom joy visits most rarely. Little by little, disillusion crept upon her ; overlooked by love, cheated in friendship by death and misprision, she discovered in girlhood that the universe was hollow, and life, for her at least, " a circle of pain," more terrible than death itself, although, or perhaps because, death bore no promise of a hereafter. As her capacity for joy had been deep, so her actual sufferings were intense ; they find some expression in these volumes, with their pitiful mottoes from Omar Khayyam, filled with poems of which each is a wail, only more penetrating for the artistic charm which makes of it a carven shrine for grief. The keynote of them all is struck in a half-serious, half-ironic imitation of Swinburne, by the lines :

> " I am I—just a Pulse of Pain—I am I, that is all I know.
> For Life, and the sickness of Life, and Death, and desire to die :
> They have passed away like the smoke, here is nothing but Pain and I."

And this dominant sense of a besetting personal pain is never far away, coming at last to bear the aspect of a fate, disastrous to all hope and all effort, a watcher at the threshold, of whose presence she is ever conscious, with bitterness, or with resignation, or with a half surprise, all alike unavailing. Desolation and solitude add a pang :

> " The people take the thing of course,
> They marvel not to see
> This strange unnatural divorce
> Betwixt delight and me."

Only most rarely, in the swing of a waltz, in some spiritual day of April or Midsummer, in the presence of an elect soul, does a moment of gladness come to her ; never is it more than a moment, and in most of her moods, even the intimations of beauty, moral and physical, are powerless. They speak to a deaf ear, and the heart regardeth them not :

> " Is it so much of the gods that I pray ?
>   Sure craved man never so slight a boon !
> To be glad and glad in my heart one day—
>   One perfect day of the perfect June.
>   *   *   *
> " I would hold my life as a thing of worth;
>   Pour praise to the gods for a precious thing.
> Lo ! June in her fairness is on the earth,
>   And never a joy does the niggard bring."

More cruel than all else is the contrast between what is and what
might have been, between the aspiring idealism of the past and the
sorry levels of the present. This is the burden of a striking little
poem called *The Old House :*

> " In through the porch and up the silent stair ;
>   Little is changed, I know so well the ways ;
> Here the dead came to meet me, it was there
>   The dream was dreamed in unforgotten days.
>
> " But who is this that hurries on before,
>   A flitting shade the brooding shades among ?
> She turned—I saw her face—O God, it wore
>   The face I used to wear when I was young.
>
> " I thought my spirit and my heart were turned
>   To deadness ; dead the pangs that agonise.
> The old grief springs to choke me—I am shamed
>   Before that little ghost with eager eyes.
>
> " O turn away, let her not see, not know !
>   How should she bear it, how should understand ?
> O hasten down the stairway, haste and go,
>   And leave her dreaming in the silent land."

Among thoughts such as these it is only natural that the image
of death, in its varied aspects, should be a familiar visitant, presenting itself now as a strong deliverer, now as a terrible veiled shape,
inscrutable, and therefore to be feared. As a matter of theory,
Amy Levy in her strenuous rejection of the religious standpoint can
only look upon death as the goal of existence and ultimate barrier
between human souls. And so, when one whom she had loved
passes away, the blank sense of loss is unrelieved by any hope.
Every link is shattered :

> " There is no more to be done,
>   Nothing beneath the sun.
> All the long ages through
>   Nothing—by me for you.
>
> " *All's done with* utterly,
>   *All's done with*. Death to me
> Was ever death indeed :
>   To me no kindly creed
>
> " Consolatory was given
>   You were of earth, not heaven."

This for her friends. But for herself death seems all the more a gracious thing in its finality. Annihilation might yield a rest unknown to sentience; the whirl of life might vanish for ever in a "poppied sleep." The thought of death makes strange disturbance in her heart, becoming at last an imperious summons not to be disregarded. It obtrudes itself, in unexpected places, at inappropriate moments, striking across every vein of reflection with ironic self-assertiveness, waiting at the close of every avenue of conversation.

> " It is so long gone by, and yet
>   How clearly now I see it all !
> The glimmer of your cigarette,
>   The little chamber, narrow and tall,
>
> " Perseus, your picture in its frame
>   (How near they seem and yet how far !)
> The blaze of kindled logs : the flame
>   Of tulips in a mighty jar.
>
> " Florence and Spring-time : surely each
>   Glad thing unto the spirit saith,
> Why did you lead me in your speech
>   To these dark mysteries of death ? "

And so the days pass by, and life becomes more intolerable, and the thought of the end more alluring, until the second volume of poems—of which, the publishers tell us, the proofs were corrected by the author about a week before her death—closes upon the ominous words :

> " On me the cloud descends."

The first effect of such a record as this upon the mind is purely an emotional one. " Sunt lacrimæ rerum et mentem mortalia tangunt." The pity, the infinite pity of it, resists all attempts to draw a moral. But before long the inevitable problem asserts itself. What help is there ? By what philosophy, what direction of will is a soul smitten with this *welt-schmerz*, this modern disease of pessimism, to shake off the paralysis, and get back into touch with the normal and saner aspect of things ? Many answers have been given and merit consideration; but it must frankly be admitted that they are none of them very cogent. Theories that challenge refutation when set forth in an essay or from the pulpit have a terrible way of shrivelling up and ceasing to convince when brought face to face with the concrete facts of an individual human life. Ideals are so often ineffectual from the mere lack of dynamic force. To the present difficulty both the moral philosopher and the plain man, influenced more or less consciously by centuries of Christian tradition, would probably offer the same very obvious reply. Pessimism, they would say, is rooted in self-absorption. Constant inward gazing upon the bare self can only beget a sense of emptiness and vanity. Fruition, and happiness therewith, can alone be attained

by contact with the other than self, by entering into some form of
sympathetic union with the universal life wherein each person is only
a unit. And this is perfectly true, as an ethical maxim. But it
does not meet the case of those who have not the gift of sympathy.
"He that loseth his soul, the same shall find it." But there are
those whose temperament does not permit them for one instant to
lose their souls. Take Miss Levy. What are the ways by which
the individual mingles with the universal? Love, Friendship,
Religion, the passion of Art, the passion of Humanity. For her, it
would seem, all these avenues were irretrievably closed. Friendship
and love she had grasped at, but they had proved bitter and elusive—
apples of Sodom in the mouth. Religion she held an unmeaning
thing. "Both for me and you, you know," she cries, "there's no
Above and no Below." Hers indeed was the saddest of all spiritual
states upon the earth, that of an awakened Israelite, cheated of the
hope of Israel. So, too, with Art: once she might have striven to
find a vocation in some mode of creative effort; but little by little
her early ambitions had been nipped by a chilling sense of impotence,
until all faculty of absorbing herself in them was gone. There
remains the service of Humanity, in which, no doubt, under its
various forms, many have found the consolation for which they had
sounded the depths of their own personality in vain. Yet one reads
a confession in *A Minor Poet*, which shows how little this could ever
have appealed to her :

> "Then, again,
> 'The common good,' and still 'the common good,'
> And what a small thing was our joy or grief
> When weighed with that of thousands. Gentle Tom,
> But you might wag your philosophic tongue
> From morn till eve, and still the thing's the same,
> I am myself, as each man is himself—
> Feels his own pain, joys his own joy and loves
> With his own love, no other's. Friend, the world
> Is but one man : one man is but the world.
> And I am I, and you are Tom, that bleeds
> When needles prick your flesh (mark, yours not mine).
> I must confess it ; I can feel the pulse
> A-beating at my heart, yet never knew
> The throb of cosmic pulses. I lament
> The death of youth's ideal in my heart ;
> And, to be honest, never yet rejoiced
> In the world's progress—scarce indeed discerned."

Ah no! it is idle to preach philanthropy to those who have not
the genius for sympathy. At bottom it is a matter of temperament.
"We are as the Fates make us." In spite of all gospels, the self-
centred will be self-centred still to the end of time, and must spin
their threads of interest from within, or not at all. And on this
rock of the essential difference between centripetal and centrifugal

natures, the Christian answer to the pessimistic problem necessarily founders.

The neo-paganism of the nineteenth century has also attempted its answers to this same problem. In the end these reduce themselves more or less directly to the idea of harmony with Nature. All alike preach self-surrender, acceptance of the inevitable, and a strenuous cultivation of the consciousness that only by his attempt to transcend Nature, and to live his life on another plane than hers, does man vex and fret himself away. One side of this philosophy addresses itself to the emotional correspondences between Nature and man. Nature is the universal Mother, the infinite comforter, consoling her lovers with subtle spells of forest and cloud and meadow, yielding to whoso will take it the cup of Lethe, the soporific that lulls doubt and destroys sorrow. It is in Wordsworth that this teaching first became articulate, and in virtue of it he has been enabled to dominate a whole century of poetry. It is the burden of his most inspired moods, of *Lucy*, of the lines on *Tintern Abbey*, of the *Ode on Immortality*. Matthew Arnold, with his accurate critical instinct in such matters, has touched this central point in Wordsworth's attitude to life and has in some measure learnt the lesson of it.

> " He found us when the age had bound
>   Our souls in its benumbing round ;
>   He spoke and loosed our heart in tears.
>   He laid us as we lay at birth
>   On the cool flowery lap of earth.
>   Smiles broke from us and we had ease ;
>   The hills were round us, and the breeze
>   Went o'er the sunlit fields again ;
>   Our foreheads felt the wind and rain,
>   Our youth returned, for there was shed
>   On spirits that had long been dead,
>   Spirits dried up and closely furl'd,
>   The freshness of the early world."

Transfigured and stamped with the impress of a wayward genius, the same ruling ideal appears in the Nature-poetry of George Meredith. For him the man who has attained is Melampus, the eyes open and ears unsealed for every secret of bird and beast and flower, in whom insight has been born of love.

> " Through love exceeding a simple love of the things
>   That glide in grasses and rubble of woody wreck."

Only in the " Woods of Westermain " may the riddle of life be read. Those who can walk there undismayed find all the joys of life and lose its hungers. Beauty and the meaning of beauty, passion and the seeds of passion, are made manifest to them ; they become interpreters and know themselves " kin of the rose " and of all delicious things. But not for every one is such transfiguration possible : it is reserved for those of a right heart and a right temper, those who

are by nature "servile to all the skyey influences," who can give an
absolute confidence, an absolute self-surrender. At a single hint of
mistrust, the spell of the woods is broken, terrible shapes possess
them.

> "Thousand eyeballs under hoods
> Have you by the hair!"

And this is why, for all its magic, the Nature-philosophy is no
panacea against pessimism. Like the ethical gospel, it is only true
for certain temperaments that have already a faculty of detachment
from self, and can greet the physician in his own spirit. And such
are not the stuff of which pessimists are made. Those on whom the
burden of the world presses most heavily are yet most strongly
drawn to it; they are linked to it for ever with adamantine fetters.
So it was with Amy Levy. The peace of Nature was to her merely
an Arcadia, a languid bower of bliss, impotent to satisfy her restless
perturbed spirit. "Fain would I bide," she moans, among the
lavender and lilies of a summer garden—

> "Fain would I bide, but ever in the distance
> A ceaseless voice is sounding clear and low:
> The city calls me with her old persistence,
> The city calls me—I arise and go.
>
> "Of gentler souls this fragrant peace is guerdon;
> For me, the roar and hurry of the town,
> Wherein more lightly seems to press the burden
> Of individual life that weighs me down."

But there is another aspect of the neo-pagan creed, Stoic rather
than Epicurean, in which the harmony to be set up between Nature
and man finds a basis not in the emotions, but in the intellect. Of
this, too, Meredith in certain moods is the best representative. He
conceives of life as a constant struggle between natural law rigid
and invincible and the idealism which strives to overleap law. So
long as the unequal battle lasts, the issue for the idealist must be
disastrous, tragic alternately and comic. Only when man wins
himself "more brain," and by coming to understand the laws of
Nature comes also willingly to submit to them, can he look for any
semblance of happiness. But rarely will he bring himself to this.
Love, for example, will yearn for immortality, forgetful that change
is the one fixed principle in things, although the annual process of
the seasons might so easily have taught the lesson:

> "'I play for Seasons, not Eternities!'
> Says Nature, laughing on her way. 'So must
> All those whose stake is nothing more than dust.'
> And lo, she wins, and of her harmonies
> She is full sure! Upon her dying rose
> She drops a look of fondness, and goes by,
> Scarce any retrospection in her eye;
> For she the laws of growth most deeply knows,

Whose hands bear here a seed-bag, there an urn.
Pledged she herself to aught, 'twould mark her end!
This lesson of our only visible friend
Can we not teach our foolish hearts to learn?"

And then, like all philosophers sooner or later, Meredith points
us to the flaw in his own doctrine. The idealist cannot accept law;
he would not be an idealist if he could. Emotion, after all, is the
strongest thing in man. Theories cannot quell it, nor syllogisms
subdue. From the ruins of them it arises craving and unassuaged.

"Yes! yes!—but oh, our human rose is fair.
Surpassingly! Lose calmly Love's great bliss,
When the renewed for ever of a kiss
Sounds through the listless hurricane of hair."

Christianity, then, and paganism alike attempt to provide the
pessimist with an antidote against his secret sickness, nor can either
claim to have effected a cure. One last alternative remains, that
"which Cato gave and Addison approved." Is the remedy for life
to be found in the will not to live, the high goal of man's hopes
and possibilities to be reached in his annihilation? Such, no doubt,
is the official teaching of pessimism. And some such dream haunts
line after line of Miss Levy's verse. But to defer the difficulty is
not to solve it. Long ago a great dramatist taught us that in the
supreme creation which has tasked the wits of three centuries. To
Hamlet, most modern of Elizabethans, the pessimist problem
presented itself. He, too, looked lovingly upon the white poppy of
death. "'Tis a consummation devoutly to be wished." And yet
the thought of what might be beyond stayed his hand. Let us not
be too hasty to ring down the curtain, for how if the gods do not
applaud? Better to wait and strive and, if it may be, pray; for
what is, is, and not even Zeus, as Agathon tells us, can make it as
though it were not. It were idle to suppose that the razor's edge
or a drop of dark liquid in a phial could erase the past, or cut the
thread of continuity with the future. And the pity of it is that in
her strong moments Amy Levy knew this well. How should the
argument against suicide be better put than in the farewell words of
Tom Leigh over the deathbed of the Minor Poet:

"Nay, I had deemed him more philosopher;
For did he think by this one paltry deed
To cut the throat of circumstance, and snep
The chain which binds all being."

E. K. CHAMBERS.

POETRY AND MUSIC.

No one can study the present state of music in England without being struck by an apparent paradox. We have, in the record of our literature, some of the finest and noblest of lyric poets : we have a school of living composers which can hold its own against all contemporaries ; and yet song is our weak place. When we look to our highest achievements in this form we are too frequently conscious of disappointment ; of effort that just misses the true success ; of eloquence that somehow is not wholly convincing. Now and again one of our greater artists offers us a lyric masterpiece, but such gifts are as yet too rare to form a tradition. And for the rest, our poetry goes its own way, claiming entire independence for its best work, and only tossing to music its weaker stanzas, while our music either joins unequal alliance with verse that was never meant for it, or, if it be of lesser mould, parts with its courage and sinks to the companionship of some mechanical librettist.

At a time when English music is beginning once more to attract the ears of Europe, this incongruity is a matter of serious importance. We cannot present ourselves to the countrymen of Goethe and Beethoven, of Schumann and Heine, with an art which is manifestly one-sided and imperfect. Indeed there are already signs that our position is growing untenable. The old drawing-room ballad is as dead as Thomas Haynes Bayly. The festival cantata is becoming a byword. And, as a climax, a popular man of letttes enters into the fray and tells us that "like most poets

he himself detests the sister art and knows nothing about it ; " and that the natural explanation of the breach between the two "is not flattering to musical people." So, while the attack is preparing upon every side, it may be of service to inquire into the history of the quarrel, and to see whether some admissible terms of peace can be suggested.

This is not the place for any discussion as to the relative artistic value of vocal and instrumental music, even if such a discussion were profitable or possible. But it is essential to notice at the outset that vocal music is by its very nature a composite art made up of two disparate factors, and that its success is attained not only by the perfection of its constituent elements, but in an even higher degree by their proper balance and interrelation. Again, the two arts that have been so conjoined are widely different in condition and character. Poetry, as compared with music, is definite and precise in meaning : it appeals to the reason first, to the emotions afterwards ; and the proof, if proof were needed, may be found in that disastrous heresy preached by Edgar Poe and sedulously maintained by his French followers. Once let the poet lose his grip upon rational significance, once let him find his ideal in vague indeterminate emotion, or, worse still, in mere collocation of sound, and he has started upon a downward path at the end of which he will find M. Stéphane Mallarmé lamenting because "La Pénultième est morte." On the other hand music, however suggestive, is essentially inarticulate, and it finds its true artistic function in a supremacy of pure form which the highest verse can never hope to rival. Not all the melody of Tennyson or Heine or Alfred de Musset, not all the native wood-notes of Shakespeare or the stately measures of Milton, can charm us with such consummate mastery of tone and rhythm as we find in the tunes of Schubert and Brahms and Beethoven. As a natural consequence, when the two arts are brought together they must each be content to counterbalance gain with loss. The one will retain its sweetness and significance, but will sacrifice a little of its precision; the other will give full rein to its emotional force, but will thereby lose something of its formal perfection. In a word, the laws of both will be modified by an equitable compromise, and will so grant its own territory and its own legislation to the border-kingdom of song.

Of this kingdom, during the earliest times into which it is pertinent to inquire, the poet seems to have held the government. In the few examples of Greek song which have been preserved to us the music appears to follow the verse with entire subordination; it hardly does more than emphasise and intensify the rise and fall of the reciting voice. No doubt our instances are not of the best period; no doubt there are many passages in Plato and Aristotle which still await an explanation; but all the evidence that we possess points to the belief that music had not as yet risen to the full dignity of comradeship, and that poetry had still the predominating influence. Indeed the very imperfection of the record is itself an important piece of testimony. If we compare our knowledge of the Greek poets with our knowledge of the Greek musicians we shall feel but little uncertainty as to their respective places in the history of art.

After Greece came one of Bacon's *eremi et vastitates*, barely occupied by a few anecdotes and some half score of theoretical tracts and commentaries. Under the rule of the medieval Church the story is resumed with an entire change of condition. The practice of music followed from the time of Dunstable to that of Palestrina was altogether different from that which we attribute to the Greeks: it disregarded dramatic expression; it left the growth of lyric melody to the profane and unauthorised efforts of troubadours and *trouvères;* it concentrated its whole attention upon the elaboration and development of vocal counterpoint. Possibly this movement originated in a feeling of reverence. The ecclesiastical composers had to deal, in the first instance, with the sublimest and most sacred of all texts, and they may have thought that it was in some sense irreligious to deck the words with any noticeable display of human emotion. In any case the tradition soon began to degenerate. Sobriety passed into indifference, indifference into total apathy; until at last the voice was treated merely as an instrument and the meaning of its speech was almost obliterated. If the tune of a popular song offered some opening for contrapuntal ingenuity, the song was borrowed, words and all, to serve as the *canto fermo* for a Mass: and thus one member of the choir would be rousing the cathedral echoes with a tavern-catch while his fellows were engaged upon their devotions. No doubt the practice became too great a scandal for even apathy to endure, and church-music, threatened by a Papal prohibition, was only saved by the reforms of Palestrina; but the very existence of such a system is conclusive testimony. The words of the Mass service must have lost their significance altogether before the public opinion of a religious age could have tolerated such desecration. And in Palestrina, though the gravity and dignity of the service were restored, there is very little attempt to adapt the melodies to the various requirements of the text. It is still a disputed question how far his work may be regarded as expressive, and how far it may be summed up as a magnificent edifice of pure beauty in sound; but at least any decision on the matter must take account of the famous Lamentations, in which the words *Incipit Lamentatio Jeremiæ Prophetæ*, and the names of the Hebrew initial letters, *Aleph, Beth, Gimel* and so on, are treated in precisely the same manner as the most impassioned utterances of the chapters which follow. A composer who can bring tears to our eyes with the word *Vau* is certainly not bound by any precise limitations on the score of meaning.

Meantime the same plan was adopted in the madrigal. At first there seems to have been some equality of collaboration, but before long the poet began to find that his most delicate fancies were being crushed out of all recognition by contrapuntal uniformity, and so gave up the partnership in disgust and left the task of libretto-making to the humbler and less exacting members of the craft. So, as the music of the madrigals improved, the verse steadily declined, until the climax of absurdity was reached in the following example preserved, for the admiration of posterity, in Percy's RELIQUES OF ANCIENT BRITISH POETRY:

Thule, the period of Cosmographie,
Doth vaunt of Hecla, whose sulphureous fire
Doth melt the frozen clime and thaw the skie,
Trinacrian Ætna's flames ascend not hier:

These things seeme wondrous, yet more wondrous I,
Whose heart with feare doth freeze, with love doth fry.

The Andalusian merchant that returnes
Laden with cutchinele and china dishes,
Reports in Spaine how strangely Fogo burnes
Amidst an ocean full of flying fishes:
These things seeme wondrous, yet more wondrous I,
Whose heart with feare doth freeze, with love doth fry.

Imagine a party of sane human beings standing up to sing about "Thule the period of Cosmographie." Assuredly it is sometimes true that *ce qui est trop sot pour être dit on le chante.*

In 1600 came the Florentine revolution, the ostensible aim of which was to restore the Greek ideal of dramatic expression. On such a quest it was necessary that poet and musician should again join hands, and thus the movement, apart from its technical interest in the history of the modern scale, is specially important as the peace-maker of a much needed reconciliation. Monteverde in Italy, Lulli in France, began once more to give adequate recognition to the poetic claims; and England, though she wrote little music for the theatre, offered her own contribution in that superb array of lyric song which lasts from Ford and Dowland to Henry Lawes and Purcell. Yet during this period the balance was not always maintained. There were still some illiterate composers, with no mind for poetry and no ear for verse, barbarians in the art, who overran the country in mere wantonness of ravage; and when opera itself degenerated the breach was once more established, and the quarrel broke out with renewed vigour. Addison tried libretto-writing and failed; Goldoni tried it and gave it up in despair; music began to devote more attention to instrumental forms; poetry left off singing and took to criticising life; once more the border-kingdom fell in danger of a double secession and saw its government passing into the hands of the undistinguished multitude.

From this it was partly rescued by the accession of Handel. But Handel, though, when he took the trouble, he was strong enough to maintain an equal administration, yet even in oratorio had his occasional moments of laxity, and throughout his long reign did very little for the lyric. Sometimes he transferred to one text music that had been originally composed for another, and so refuted in his own case any doctrine of a pre-established harmony. Sometimes he constructed a whole song,—first part, second part, and the inevitable *da capo,*—out of a single quatrain, repeating the words till their very sound was wearisome and their meaning lost in a tangle of reiterated clauses. In short, for all his power of vivid and picturesque expression, a power unsurpassed, perhaps, by any of his contemporaries, he was yet content to rule by conventional method, and only conceded as an occasional act of grace what, in the ideal commonwealth, poetry ought to claim as an inalienable right.

So there grew up in England a hopelessly inartistic fashion of regarding the tune as paramount and the words as of no importance. Our public listened complacently to foreign languages which it did not even pretend that it understood, or followed them in translations which it would have found itself wholly incompetent to parse. And the fashion has not yet entirely passed away. We still accept inarticulate singers and unknown tongues without any thought that the value of the song is thereby impaired to us. We still accept translations which it would be flattery to describe as doggerel, not because they are the best that we can get, but because we do not realise that there is anything amiss with them. Take Haydn's CREATION for example. During the better part of a century England has been tolerating a libretto of which the following may be given as a specimen:

The Heavens are telling the glory of God,
The wonder of His work displays the firmament.
To day that is coming speaks it the day,
The night that is gone to following night.
In all the lands resounds the word,
Never unperceived, ever understood.

This is bad enough in oratorio and opera, when the attention is divided among several points of interest; it is a thousand times worse when it appears, as it soon began to appear, in the closer concentration of lyric song. No wonder if our poets came away dissatisfied; no wonder if they concluded that anything was good enough for musical treatment. And when our dark age came and music itself was looked upon as a foreign import, both elements alike began to decay and to infect each other with a fatal taint of corruption.

On the Continent a better state of things was inaugurated by Gluck and carried on by the great masters of Germany and Austria. In some of Haydn's canzonets the balance is adequately maintained: then came Mozart's VEILCHEN, then Beethoven, then the Romantic school which gave due equality to the poet and brought song to the highest consummation that it has yet attained. But meanwhile the tide ebbed away from England, and its flood is but now returning. During the most active and strenuous period in all musical history our own art was virtually in abeyance; we held aloof from the struggle, we looked upon the leaders of advance with an unintelligent suspicion, and we paid the penalty not only by loss of repute, but by the heavier loss of power and opportunity. And now that our musicians are once more resuming the place which they held before the death of Purcell, it is only to find that the poets have forgotten the old terms of agreement, and have begun to set up new customs of their own. There is probably no lyric verse in the world so difficult to set to music as that of our English contemporaries; it has been written without thought of the composer, without regard to his special claims and requirements; it is too individual, too self-centred, to ask or admit the aid of the collaborator. In a word, though much must be allowed for particular conditions of character and temperament, one proximate reason of our failure in song is the present divergence between English music and English poetry; and of this one ultimate reason may be found in our fathers' maintenance of a bad musical tradition.

Now it is clearly best, as a matter of ideal, that the two elements in song should both be of the same age and of the same country. For in the first place art depends in some degree upon national characteristics, and is itself the purer for the purity of its lineage; and in the second place there have been successive stages in musical as in poetic expression, and it undoubtedly makes for unity that the two should pass through these stages together. Schubert, no doubt, occurs as an exception, but Schubert's whole position in music is exceptional. Schumann, Franz and Brahms are at their highest as song-writers when they are setting the poets of their own people; so are Grieg and Dvoràk, so are Gounod and Jensen and Hans Sommer. It is therefore only a partial solution of the problem if we bid our composers seek alliance from France and Germany, or even from our own lyric masters of the Stuart period. In the former case the music, to be congruous, will take a foreign tinge: in the latter it will be touched with archaism; and both alike will give us a sense of unreality that is fatal to art as a living force. With the Bible, with Shakespeare, the case is different; they have both grown up afresh in each successive generation and are as much a part of our own life as of our forefathers'. But the Bible lies beyond the limits of the present question; with much of Shakespeare we have been already forestalled, and our music has learned a different language from that known to Herrick and Suckling. It is to our own contemporaries, to Tennyson and Rossetti and Mr. Swinburne, that we should look for aid, and it is here, by the irony of circumstance, that aid is most unattainable.

In illustrating this point it is important not to confuse the issue by reference to our great choral compositions. Choral writing has its own special laws and characteristics, its own special qualities of mass and volume, and no inference can be drawn from it to the purely personal feeling of the lyric. It is no answer, therefore, to quote the magnificent work which Dr. Parry has done with Pope and Milton, or even such examples of noble achievement as THE LOTOS-EATERS, or THE REVENGE, or the ODE TO ETON. It is of lyric song that we are speaking; it is in lyric song that our art is, on the whole, most deficient. Every one remembers the sense of expectation which heralded the Tennyson volume a few years ago, and the bitter disappointment which ran through England on its appearance. Here were a score of poems written by Tennyson set by some of the greatest of our composers, and there was hardly a true song among them. Μία ἐκ πολλῶν οὐκ ἀπόμουσος; the rest were either preoccupied with some technical problem, or clearly overweighted by an unequal partnership. It would be hardly possible to find a more striking instance of our national disability.

On the causes, so far as they spring from the melodic side, we have already touched. They arise partly from a tradition of indifference, partly from its natural complement, a divergence of musical energy into directions other than lyric. But poetry itself has laid obstacles in the way of return. Allowed too little by a past generation, it is now claiming too much, and challenging the composer with difficulties which even the highest genius is not always adequate to surmount. In the first place the best English verse has come to exhibit a peculiar kind of flexibility to which no exact parallel can be found in the art of other nations. It relies mainly upon great variety of stress and accent, upon an extremely free treatment of the laws of scansion, upon a balance of rhythm in which there is as little as possible of exact recurrence. An extreme instance may be seen in those exquisite lines of Keats which were selected by a writer in THE QUARTERLY REVIEW as examples of bad prosody; and though the stupidity of the criticism has passed into a proverb, there still remains the fact which it illustrates. But music, though within certain limits it is more flexible than any verse, yet prefers, and indeed almost requires, that its lyric stanza should be marked by some definite recurrences of beat, particularly at the end of the clause where our verse is least inclined to grant them. A poet. for example, will rhyme the word *sky* with the word *silently*, and deliberately choose the rhyme because of its variety of stress. The musician can hardly follow him without breaking the entire design of the melody. Of course in declamatory song this difficulty does not appear,

and even in lyric song it is not always insuperable, but none the less it exists, and it is particularly noticeable in our own country. Again the frequent *enjambement* of the lines, which gives to English verse a special characteristic of beauty, itself affords a new problem to the composer. Shelley's poem " When passion's trance is overpast " would require very deft handling before it could be fitted to the exigencies of the musical stanza.

So far, however, the solution is merely a matter of skill. But a more serious question remains. It must be remembered that song is a combination of two arts, in which each must exercise its own function and must respect the office of the other. In the ideal lyric, such as those of Heine and Schumann, the poet draws an outline which the musician colours ; and where they are in perfect sympathy there will be perfect unity of result. But if the one goes on to complete the picture, if he prescribes every *nuance* and every detail, there is no collaboration possible, for nothing is left to the other but complete subservence. There will never be an adequate setting of the " Bugle Song " in THE PRINCESS, not because the verse is too musical, for such a plea is a contradiction in terms, but because the poem is too full. What is the composer to do with such a consummate line as,

Blow, bugle, answer, echoes, dying, dying, dying— ?

Shall he follow the suggestion of the words ? He is but echoing the echoes. Shall he disregard it ? He has missed the poet's meaning. The whole field has been occupied already, and if he claim a share of the tillage he must take station as a serf.

It is not pretended that this is true of all our best lyric poetry. If it. were we should not have the few masterpieces of song that have been given us, to name two examples, by Dr. Parry and Dr. Stanford. But it is true in a large number of cases, and wherever it is true, song in any real sense of the term is almost impossible. When CROSSING THE BAR was published, more than one of our composers took the poem in hand, and produced a set of *tours de force* of which some were brilliant and some were creditable, and not one was wholly satisfactory. The four stanzas have already attained finality and there is nothing left to add. The same holds good, though in varying degree, with our other great poets of the present age. Browning may almost be put out of consideration, he is no more a singer than his own Pacchiarotto : Rossetti often presents insuperable difficulties of phrase ; and though Mr. William Morris and Mr. Swinburne come nearer to the musician's ideal, since they love those broad lines of emotion which it is the function of his art to follow and illustrate, yet the former occasionally forgets that he is writing in the nineteenth century, while the latter, like Keats and Shelley, will only respond to certain musical moods. It is a far cry from even the most adaptable of our lyrics to WIDMUNG or FRUHLINGSNACHT or DU BIST WIE EINE BLUME.

This bare statement of cause and effect should not be pressed to the extremity of a hostile criticism. Song, in spite of M. de Banville, no more covers the whole of poetry than the whole of music ; it is but a province of march-land, ceded from the territory of two separate empires, and governed by the representatives of a joint administration. On either hand lie wide expanses that spread from the near frontiers of romance and elegy and dance-measure to the remoter regions of drama and epic, of sonata and symphony. In them the artist has free choice to take up his habitation : one may devote himself to the service of pure tone, another to the methods and ideals of pure literature ; and, if a man does the best work for which his genius fits him, it is idle that we should complain because he has wrought it on this or that side of a particular border-line. There is no more reason for demanding that every lyric should be a song than for demanding that every play should be an opera ; indeed the poet will often speak with a fuller meaning if he be bound by no restrictions but those of his own art. At the same time song is a possession that we would not willingly forego ; and song is neither music nor poetry, but both together. The two elements are combined as gold and silver were fused in the electrum, each, it may be, losing some feature of its own beauty, each bearing its part in a result that is worth the sacrifice. And the whole contention of the present paper is that in our English song we should require true gold and true silver, and that we should not rest satisfied with the substitution of a baser metal.

Yet recently our choice has lain, for the most part, between base metal and imperfect fusion. In many forms of expression we have learned to rival Germany, in song we are still far behind her ; and the reason is to be found less in the weakness of our music than in the alienation of our poetry. If we have no Heine we can have no Schumann ; the future of our song is a matter in which both arts are equally concerned. It only remains that each should more fully recognise the requirements of the other, and should so join in a common cause, of which there already stands over sea a living example and illustration.

1898.

POETRY, POETS, AND POETICAL POWERS.

"POET" is a word which naturally reminds us of the names of Kalidas and Bhababhuti, Shakespeare and Milton, Goethe and Schiller, names dearer to us than anything we have ever known. Each one of these names instils in us a feeling of unalloyed love and affection for the great masters of poetry. We forget the thousands of miles that lie between our birthplace and theirs. We forget the centuries that stand in the way of our direct and palpable touch with them. No traces are to be found of the ages when these dear children of God came to us with their divine messages—for God's message comes to the world only through two sources, the pen of the poet and the mouth of the prophet—all have been submerged in the span of that great enemy of man called Time which divides us from them; but their names are a living memory; they stand before us delivering their heavenly message. Why is all this? That is a question which comes naturally to the mind of every lover of art, poetry, and literature. None of us have seen these great masters, the most perfect specimens of human genius. We should all give anything to see them. But how many of us should care to see that Kalidas who was striking with his axe on the root of that branch upon which he was sitting, or that Shakespeare whose early genius was discerned in his skill as a deer-stealer? It is not that Kalidas, neither is it that Shakespeare, of whom we are enamoured. The Kalidas who stealthily saw the first bloom of love in the heart of the lovely, simple-hearted girl Sakuntala; who made Sakuntala establish a relationship with a roe by adopting it as her child; who witnessed her take the dust off the eyes of her future lord with her lips; who in the thick of the forest saw and felt for the love pangs of young Sakuntala's heart, and gave her his sympathy—it is that Kalidas whom we long to see. It is that Shakespeare, to see whom we should give all our possessions of this mundane world, who bore witness to the sufferings of disappointment of young Hamlet—a prince indeed, and a prince of men; who witnessed the cruel assassination of guileless and loving Desdemona by Othello; who amply congratulated himself on having been able to mete out a condign punishment to the unfaithful, treacherous Lady Macbeth;

who made Miranda confess that her ambition was humble because she had loved Ferdinand, the third person "she ever saw, and the first one she sighed for."

Speaking plainly, it is his poetry that makes the name of the poet a dear one to us. If I am asked the question, What is poetry ? I should say, "Tell me what is not poetry, and I will tell you what it is." It is easier to tell what poetry is when we know what it is not.

I will now attempt to make out what is not poetry. Byron has told us,

> " Freedom's battle once begun,
> Bequeathed by bleeding sire to son,
> Though baffled oft, is ever won,"

and it is truly said that genuine poetical powers are discernible in these three lines. The question will be asked, What is that in these three lines which is poetry ? They have rhyme ; it is clear that the poet thinks slavery to be an undesirable bondage—a curse ; the poet's love of freedom is also plain. Which one of the three things that we see in the lines is poetry ? If a verse, simply for the sake of its rhyme and melody, comes to be recognised as poetry, I am afraid our great masters, Shakespeare and Milton, would have to rest contented with the appellation of mere versifiers or poetasters, and would have to retire from the contest to make room for some divine Muse like our present Poet-Laureate or the poet of Asia and of the World. We often call these advertisements, in perhaps unblemished rhyme, poetry, and more often their writers poets. Even sublime thoughts only are not poetry. If they were so, certainly Bacon and Spenser, Voltaire and Rousseau, Carlyle and Emerson should be among the great poets of the world, or the following lines of J. Q. Adams should make him a great poet :

> " This hand, to tyrants ever sworn the foe,
> For freedom only deals the deadly blow ;
> Then sheathes in calm repose the vengeful blade,
> For gentle peace in Freedom's hallowed shade."

Adams's appreciation of freedom does not fall far short of Byron's, but that is a very poor reason why the former's four lines must be deemed as highly poetic as the three of the latter. It is difficult to establish a man's poetic powers even when in his verses there is a remarkable combination of perfect rhyme, melodious versification, high thoughts, and regular figures. Many of my readers will disagree with me, and call it a fine piece of poetry where they find the presence of all these characteristics. I do not venture to say that the presence of these features is not material to the making up of poetry, but that we always lose sight of the chief essence of poetry, preferring the less essential ones, and this chief essence is what we call "emotions or passions." I shall be asked why is it that I prefer to call Byron's lines real poetry, and not those of Adams? What is present in Byron's three lines which is absent in the lines of Adams? There is rhyme in both. But there is one feature—a grand transcendental feature—in Byron's which we fail to find in Adams's. And that is Byron's emotion, his love of freedom. This love of freedom is not his opinion; it is not a scientifically proven truth to him; it is not a discovery: it is his passion. The strength of this passion is a clear evidence of his high poetic powers. Without this passion his lines are dry and insipid, anything but poetry. Every one of us has noticed on various occasions that the awakening of passionate eloquence of a true orator simultaneously awakens the emotions and passions in the minds of his audience. John Stuart Mill, that great connoisseur of human character, observed this very clearly. The great scholars and critics of ancient Sanskrit literature have also said that this passion is the real test of poetry. "*Bákyam Rasátmakam Kábyam*" (Passionate words are poetry). Poetry is a combination of thought with emotion. Poetry has, indeed, nothing to do beyond what I call emotion or passion. It is no business of poetry to lead us to a new system of thought; let science and philosophy do that; poetry undertakes to kindle in us new sentiments and new emotions as well as the dormant passions.

When we keep these characteristics of poetry clearly before us, to single out true and genuine poetry becomes easier. A study of what does not awaken in us a feeling of emotion is no more poetry than Euclid's definition of a point or of an acute angle. The elegiac verse that fails to inspire in us a sense of affection and a feeling of deep sorrow is a poetry not worth the name. The lyric that cannot make us offer our deepest sympathy to the individual emotions of the poet is nothing short of versification. We have not unfrequently heard many a man of culture talk glibly about an author of some prose work being the happy possessor of poetic gifts, simply because, as it happens, it is impossible to make any improvement upon the beauty of his narrative. I have a serious quarrel with them. I fail to see why poetic powers must be necessary for arranging a story in prose or perfecting a narrative! Intelligence and imagination are all that is needful. Novels of this description are not poetry because they are mere narrative compositions, and as such are no part of what I call the emotions or passions of poetry. John Stuart Mill has told us that the period of our life, childhood, when the eagerness to hear stories and fables is most keen, is the period when our faculty to appreciate poetry is least developed. *Æsop's Fables, Tales from the Arabian Nights, Fairy Tales, Robinson Crusoe,* and *Adventures of Don Quixote* are the poetry of our childhood. Then we appreciate them more than Milton's "Lycidas"

or Tennyson's " In Memoriam," Shelley's " Skylark " or Gray's
" Elegy."

There is a popular belief that it is in childhood that we can study
poetry with the greatest profit, because, as is said, it is then that we
receive impressions quickest; and a study cannot fail to leave a
deep and lasting impression upon us even though we may not appreciate it—as a matter of fact we do not. This is a wholly contra-
dictory and erroneous belief. It seems difficult to understand how
a study that has not been enjoyed because not appreciated can leave
an impression upon any person. Impression without appreciation is
a contradiction. It is erroneous also because in childhood the first
bud of those feelings and emotions upon which alone poetry plays
is yet unborn, much less taken shape. There are others who believe
that a true poet must be gifted with the power of studying human
nature, manners and customs, closely and accurately. This appears
to be hardly anything like the qualification or a gift which the true
poet must possess. Professor Edward was an admittedly great
philosopher even though he could not tell his own horse from those
of his friends. In like manner, it is perfectly reasonable that one
completely ignorant of human nature, manners and customs, can be
a poet too. Indeed, when I recall the fact that most poets have
been utterly indifferent to human nature, human manners, and
human desires, if not complete ascetics in regard to them, I might
say without fear of contradiction that the exactly opposite view is
nearer the truth. A knowledge of human nature is a qualification
needful for the novelist, whose real art it is to paint truly human
character, act and deed, whose real skill is in being able to describe
graphically the feelings of others. Very different is the function of
the poet. The novelist gives us a true picture of others besides
himself, whereas the poet presents us with a picture of the waves
and emotions of his own heart. For lack of incidents, which in his
hands take the shape of a plot, the novelist is resourceless. But
the poet cares no more for those indispensable materials of the
novelist than he does for opinions opposed to the dictates of his
imagination. He takes a handful of sawdust and makes a present
of it to us a lump of gold. A formidably dark and gloomy night,
an uninhabited desert or a thick forest, a solitary dilapidated castle
or a superb palace, in them an exquisitely beautiful woman with all
the charms and virtues that is in the power of the Almighty to
bestow upon a dear child of His, these are some of the materials
without which the novelist is ill at ease, without which his imagination cannot play, without which the sentimental feelings of the
novel reader cannot be awakened. But the mere sight of the new
cloud was the cause of an overflow of sentiments and passionate
emotions of Kalidas such as the world has never seen before or
since. As a ploughman when tilling the land, the mere destruction

of an ant-hill drove Burns mad with rambling thoughts, and these are what richly adorn some of the pages of true poetry. The mere sight of a lark caused Shelley to give us what all the novelists put together could not give. Descriptive verse is truly poetry when surcharged with emotions. The mere fact of a description being put in verse has perhaps the poorest claim to be poetry.

There are, again, some who believe that drama is poetry and the dramatist is a poet. It is difficult to believe that this is so. There must be an equipoise of narration and emotion in a drama. Mill said that the presence of a consummate narrative skill with an abundance of heart's feelings and passions in his dramas is what has made Shakespeare a most perfect poet, what has made us value his works so highly, is what has made them so dear to us. Take any of Shakespeare's great tragedies, and you see how the narrative becomes thicker and thicker as you read scene after scene and act after act, until it comes to that when every event sends a thrill in your heart, when its awakening influence is felt to be so powerful that our emotions cannot remain any longer dormant; and our awakened passions now make us weep with sorrow and sympathy, and now rage with passionate fury.

The question—Why should not an orator be regarded as a poet in the light of the test of the true poet and manifestations of poetry laid down here?—is not an unnatural one, looking to the fact that he too expresses the emotions, waves, and thoughts of his own mind, and what is more, kindles the passions and awakens the emotional thoughts of his hundreds and thousands of audience. What may then be the distinction between poetry and oratory? Nobody has ever uttered a truer word about poetry than John Stuart Mill, when he said that " oratory is heard, but poetry is overheard." The meaning suggested in this sentence is clear. When the orator speaks, he begins with a consciousness of the presence of others before him, with a consciousness that he is speaking to them; but the poet, when beginning to write, is oblivious of the existence of any one in this world other than himself, he forgets that this world is peopled by anybody else. The orator takes pains to awaken and kindle the feelings in others by his eloquence, while the poet is anxious how best to express the thoughts of his own heart, to do which he starts with the idea that they do not concern anybody save himself. The first thought in the mind of the made poet, or one who falsifies the adage " A poet is born, not made," with his pen in his hand, is—how to write, what word to use that would be pleasing to the ear of man, delicious to his taste, enjoyable and delightful? and hence goes in quest of choice and suitable words, with the result that he partly succeeds in making his rhyme a soft and a tender one, but nothing more. The true poet is above all these troubles and exertions. He has no patience for it. All he attempts to do is to compose in that style and to use those words which in his opinion would delineate the truest picture of his own heart, by style and diction to make a mirror in which to see the clearest shadow of his own thoughts. Not unfrequently poverty of language prevents his passions from finding their fullest expression. But the thought which is distinct, which is clear, gives us a clue to the sublimity of a whole series of them that are not properly expressed. This is one of the many reasons why the composition of the true poet is more life-giving and exquisite, because he is able to express some of his thoughts clearly, and with regard to the rest is incapable of doing more than throwing a hint for us to find out what the whole is, just as a few strokes of the brush of the great artist give us an idea of how lovely and natural the picture would look when finished.

I have in the foregoing pages attempted to ascertain what poetry is. Now we shall try to find out who the poet is. This does not appear to be a task at all difficult. The test of poetry is to all intents and purposes the test of the poet. If emotional words are poetry, undeniably then the composer, or one who is capable of composing those emotional words, is the poet. That is to say, one whose composition is pregnant with ardent and intense feelings of the heart, and a study of whose composition awakens in the reader all his stagnant and motionless passions, is the poet. It is difficult to disagree with Mill when he says that a poet, the study of whose poetry leaves us in doubt whether or not he is a true poet, is in all probability not one.

It is a common belief that God has endowed certain persons with certain powers by which they are able to compose really good poetry. Nobody seems to have ever inquired into what these powers are or how they work. These powers are commonly called " poetic powers." It is said, " A poet is born, and no power on earth can deprive him of his gifts : one who is not a poet is not born so, and no amount of exertion can make him one." This is a very serious question. Those who do not admit the possibility of acquiring a second nature by habituating oneself to something, may ask that, placed under similar circumstances and training, why should it not be possible for every one of us to be a Shakespeare or a Kalidas ? In a later part of this paper I shall make an attempt to decide the question. At present I shall draw the attention of the reader to two things. We have known persons eager for a poetic fame. Their one and only subject of conversation is poetry, poetic powers, merits and demerits of a poet, and so on ; their delight is to compose poems, and, if favoured by fortune's smiles, they do not hesitate at all to publish their poems in book form. It is indeed a pity that none save themselves are found to appreciate their writings, and the real genius of their own powers is discerned by themselves only. Again, we have known persons who write poems occasionally, very occa-

sionally, and sometimes it is a most annoying task to make them
write one, and these have never been known to have given anything
but the most blissful delight to their readers. The excellence of
their thoughts and the beauty of their rhyme could not have failed
to impress upon them. This certainly tends to support the theory
that a " poet is born." On the other hand, we have known persons
who at one period of their life showed no poetic powers so called, but
have done so at a later one, and that of a perfect type. Kalidas is a
glorious illustration of this latter theory. It is certainly past the
imagination of man that the hand that wrote *Ritusamhara, Vikra-
morvasi,* or *Malavikagni,* was capable of composing *Sakuntala,
Meghduta,* or *Kumdra.* They are as unlikely the compositions of the
same hand as *Malatimadhava* or *Viracharita* as compared to *Uttara-
rama-charita* are those of Bhababhuti's. Both Milton and Cowper
stand arm in arm with Kalidas and Bhababhuti. Of Milton it is
said by one of his critics that he " was not a genius, ' a boy poet '
of the type of Chatterton and Shelley." Another critic of Milton
tells us that " he had not even produced school exercises of unusual
merit." There is an astounding and an unbelievable difference in
style, in thought, in true poetic genius, between what they wrote
when they were a few years over their teens and what they composed
twenty years later. As will appear, this supports the latter view.
I am aware some of the readers of this paper will hold the former
opinion and others the latter. My own opinion is that both the
theories have a great deal of truth in them, and both are reasonable,
inasmuch as there truly is to be found a gift which we call " poetic
gift," and that circumstances, and training too, have much to do
with the development or curtailment of that gift.

I have tried to prove before that without emotions of the heart
it is not poetry, and that without them poetic powers are absent in
the writer of verse. Some may ask whether the mother of · a dead
child, when she wails and weeps over her loss—when there is no
paucity of emotions or lack of feelings of the heart in her, when
her troubles not only excite the deepest sympathy with her of all
those who hear about it, but make them feel the loss as keenly as
the mother herself—whether that mother is a poet and her wailings
and her troubles that foment our passions are poetry? I am disposed to say they are not poetry, neither is she a poet, since the
cause of her sorrow is utterly devoid of any imagination, and is
only a palpable event and a loss, though the most serious one that
human being can suffer from. It is a loss which is equally grievous
to every one of us. Her sorrows and troubles are exactly what we
should feel when placed in a similar situation. But the poet's
imagination, tempered by his individual passions and thoughts, is
otherwise. It is his imagination that creates the beauty of his
poetry. The conclusion, therefore, that merely passions or emotions

of the heart are not poetic powers cannot be helped. Imagination is undoubtedly one of the chief features of poetic gifts; and not only imagination, but in the inmost depth of the poet's heart we find another feature so powerfully predominant that it cannot be ignored. It is the association of ideas. As various dreamy sights pass away before the eyes of a delirious patient, so it is by the miraculously divine power of the association of ideas that the poet in an instant sees before his mind's eye various events and feels multifarious emotion and a medley of thoughts. In the true genuine poet are visible the three most powerful characteristics—emotions, imagination, and association of ideas. To put it in order, at the idea of a certain thing inspiration dawns upon the poet, his imagination then clothes his inspiration with fashion of his own choice. The poet then forgets himself, he loses his self-consciousness, and is nothing but a lump of inspiration and imagination. If it is the deed of a hero that arrests his attention or commands his admiration, he becomes the hero himself, unconscious of his own individuality, unconscious of all things around him. Sometimes he marches on with his hero, at others he takes the tragic leave of her whom he considers to be nearer than the dearest thing could be, whom he holds dearer than even his own life. Thus his imagination sometimes becomes so overpowering, so vivid, that he can almost follow each footstep of his hero. With the brush of inspiration and the colour of imagination he paints a most faithful picture of the passions of his heart and the association of his ideas. His new ideas are associated by old ones. He does not think of them. They come to him of themselves with magic precision and faithfulness. This faculty or power is the association of ideas which enriches the poet's composition with similes that add force and strength to his own emotions.

Thus, when inspiration, imagination, and association of ideas come to him, the poet takes himself away from the ordinary vocations, bustles, and anxieties of life, and he holds his pen. Now he tries to choose his words—choose only those words which he thinks would be exactly expressive of what he means and would accurately represent the passions of his heart. His ability to do it calls forth our admiration of his choice of words. When he has done this he invites his faculty of harmony to help him to spinning these his chosen words into rhyme. Finally, if the poet is a man of refined tastes he is able to sort out emotional feelings from inspired thoughts, and puts them in their proper place to prevent a hopeless *abracadabra* marring the beauty and excellence of true poetry. All these faculties are certainly the natural possessions of a born poet, and the presence and co-existence of all of them in a person is what we call "poetic powers." One, the trend of whose mental constitution is not towards these, can no more be a poet than Shelley could be a physicist. They are better known as prosaic men—men whose emotions are domineered over by their reason and imaginations subordinated by facts.

There are two classes of poets even among those who are admitted on all hands to be poets, in most of whom we find all the faculties I have mentioned present, and whose works are acknowledged as true poetry. One is natural or born poet, the other is made poet. All the difference that there is between them is that inspiration comes first to the born poet and imagination and association of ideas next, only to thicken his inspiration; whereas the made poet inspires himself with the help of imagination and association. I shall attempt to show what I mean by a genealogical tree. If we take the cause to be origin of true poetry, the tree may be drawn as follows:

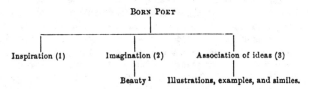

When we take the effect to be cause of true poetry, the tree is slightly altered in manner, but in matter it remains the same:

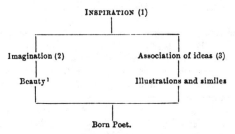

As regards his diction and rhyme, too, I shall attempt to draw another tree to make myself clearly understood.

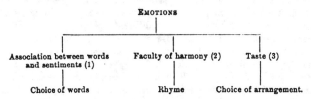

It is thus that we have chaste and animating diction and faultless rhyme in the born poet:

Creation of beauty and brilliancy of description.

In the made poet the order would be very much different from the born :

1. Imagination.
2. Association of ideas.
3. Inspiration.

Regarding diction and rhyme, the made poet can very well say to the born that his method is not dissimilar to his, and in that he stands on a par with him. To put it more explicitly and in fewer words, it might be that the born poet loses his individuality in inspiration, while the made poet has got to invoke inspiration. One might say it is quite possible for the made poet to lose like the born poet his individuality in the inspiration after invocation. Verily so. But inspiration is the domineering mistress of the natural or born poet—she fascinates the poet simultaneously with the awakening of his emotions, and who, as an unwilling guest of the made poet, cannot have that influence over him which she always has over her dearer lord. In the case of the former, his cup of passion is always warm and full to overflowing ; in that of the latter, he has got to warm it full to the brim. The verse of the one is thoughtful emotions, that of the other is emotional thoughts ; or rather, as Mill has said, that one sees and describes in poetry, the other sees in prose and describes in poetry. One has a natural irrepressible fountain of emotion ; the other has, with the aid of a pressure below, to show that his is a fountain too. The one makes use of the figures, similes, or thoughts that come across his emotions at the moment, else he loses sight of them ; he has no time, neither patience nor inclination, to go in quest of any of them ; the other is always, at every step, on the look-out for them, and invites them. His anxiety is to see his figures regular, his illustrations consistent, his feelings accepted as true.

Persons who are commonly called poets are certainly divided into two classes I have described. Of modern English poets, I take Burns, Byron, Shelley, Keats, and Swinburne to be natural or born poets, and Wordsworth, Southey, and Tennyson to be made poets. By way of illustration, I have classified the modern poets in a way which, I am afraid, might be taken serious objection to by many of my readers, who, I daresay, have a different opinion of them from what I have. So long as there is emotion, so long as there is passion, there is feeling of heart in the natural poet, there is that simplicity of his diction, that brilliancy of his description and regularity of his figures. It is on this account that he is seldom successful in describing a subject covering a very long period. As a rule, he is a much more brilliant success when he writes short pieces on solitary subjects ; here his composition is excellent, his performance glorious and life-giving. The made poet may be able to write poems at request, or, to put it in a more expressive but undignified phrase, may be able to compose poems to order, and there is a possibility, even probability, of their being very good; but the born poet is a huge failure when trying to make poems to order. He has to wait for inspiration to dawn upon him.

I might notice here that men with not more than two or three of the six qualities I have mentioned (inspiration, imagination, association of ideas, association between words and sentiments, faculty of harmony, and taste) have been reckoned among the poets. Men utterly devoid of the first three qualites, but richly possessing the last three, are commonly and widely known to be poets. I should be slow to call them by so supreme an appellation.

There is another question, an attempt to decide which might be made before I conclude: Whether circumstances and training help in the amelioration or in the deterioration of poetic powers? I cannot think of a more appropriate answer to the question than that when the poet's powers have only to do with his emotions they must suffer, either for better or for worse, according as the warmth or chilliness of the passions of his heart. In every-day life we see domestic troubles and anxieties, physical malady, painful sorrows, and various other causes have an irresistible effect upon the feelings or emotions of a man. If the poet passes through all these stages of severe mental agitation, it is no wonder, nay, it is only natural, that his poetic abilities should suffer because of the decrepitude which these ailments cannot fail to bring upon the emotional side of his nature. There is, again, an improvement in his poetical abilities when his mental constitution becomes healthier, and there is a marked deterioration in his powers with the weakening of the same constitution. Materialism, or the materialistic ideas of the age, are the deadliest enemy to poetry, poets, and their gifts. Materialism arrogantly and audaciously puts down emotions and sentimentalism as a sign of weakness utterly unworthy of man. To love deeply, to be devotedly fond and affectionate of a person is, say the materialists, the sign of a fevered and delirious brain, and not that of the man of reason. To shed tears for the sorrows of others becomes, they say, a woman, not a man. To feel sympathy for the suffering humanity ill suits a man of the world—a man of action, who, according to Goethe, "is conscienceless," as Mr. John Morley beautifully puts it in his recent Romanes lecture. This mischievous theory of materialism is not only injurious but damaging to the art and literature of poetry, and therefore to the finer nature of map. It is a deplorable fact that even those who are gifted by nature with poetic abilities, with a heart full of love, sympathy, and passionate emotions, are disgracefully trying their very best to suppress these feelings, to be carried away by them under the magic influence of materialism. Auguste Comte exhausted his unparalleled argumentative faculty and his vocabulary to put a check to the growth of this dangerous theory of materialism. It is undeniable that that theory which belittles the qualities of the heart and magnifies those of the brain is a dangerous one. Where on earth do we find a sweet repose from the turmoils, anguish, sorrow, and pains of life? Is it the head or the heart? Who can deny that it is the heart—that heart is the place of that blissful repose? Make man heartless, he is no other than a brute. John S. Mill, after serious thought, came to the conclusion that this material world is nothing but a "permanent possibility of sensation." But is that any reason why man —the young man—should bid adieu to the noble goddess of his affectionate fondness, the goddess of the feelings of his heart, as the "permanent possibility of sensation"? With Campbell he will in an unmistakable voice say:

> "I ask not proud philosophy
> To teach me what thou art."

There are two ways by which poetical powers could be improved. One is to study abundantly, over and over again, the writings of natural and born poets. This has a doubly beneficial effect upon us. First, the various feelings of our heart are awakened, dormant passions become fresher, and new emotions are infused. Secondly, that most important faculty of the choice of words is developed, with a large vocabulary at our command, simultaneously with the growth of the faculty of harmony (rhyme), and refinement of taste becomes distinctly visible. The other way is the association of women. To many, I am sure, this is a novel suggestion. Especially at this stage of our civilisation, and looking to the lamentable state of our relationship with intelligent women, it is difficult to put as innocent a construction upon it as I mean. Some may ridicule the bare possibility, for the close connection of the pure heart of woman with that of the pure man is what this generation of mankind cannot yet realise. Commonly speaking, intelligent feminine company means something unspeakable, something unholy; but let my meaning be clearly understood. What it is to love a pure woman as a friend and to have that love reciprocated is past the description of human intellect—nay, past all conception of human imagination. Perhaps, of all persons, Shelley was the one, and only one, destined to realise it when addressing to Emili Viviani:

> "Would we two had been twins of the same mother.
> *   *   *   *   *
> We—are we not formed, as notes of music are,
> For one another, though dissimilar?"

This is a feeling transcendental indeed. Auguste Comte realised that feeling, and that is why he devoted his whole intellect, energy, and life towards placing the woman on the highest pedestal—a pedestal even higher than the one which his God must occupy. The ancient Hindus deified the woman. Their Goddess of Fortune, Goddess of Learning, in fact, all their most powerful deities, were women. This is symbolical of a significant idea. Comte, following the Hindus, tried to deify the woman. A distinguished professor of Cambridge on one occasion spoke about the woman as "the princess." "She is the sleeping princess; the prince will have to come and wake her up." This is an exquisite idea. That the mere look in the most innocent sense of the woman inspires us with poetic thoughts cannot be denied, and this the ancient sages of the Hindus and of the Greeks saw vividly. This is exactly the re-echo of my sentiments about women. Those who are incapable of looking at the face of the woman with pure eyes are frivolous. One can only pity and commiserate them. To advise them would be a sheer waste of energy. My remarks are only meant for those who are capable of looking upon the woman as their goddess in life and those who are capable of seeing the holy sanctified halo round her face.

JUDIUS.

THE PHILOSOPHY OF POETRY

I

POETRY is not an art, but the excellency and the halo of all the arts—as also of life itself; and the great artist, like the great man, is generally a poet.

If a person, with certain powers of feeling and imagination, is fortunate enough to have some artistic talent as well, it is of no essential importance which art, or which particular form of any of them, is adopted in exploiting those powers, the possession and adequate representation of which constitute the poet and the artist. Thus he may write or paint or model or compose music or make designs, and, moreover, he may do so in whatever shape, form, or manner he chooses, and his work, provided it is the outcome of sensibility and imagination in an eminent degree, will be poetry. This I believe to be the true philosophy of poetry in its relation to art.

And this unsophisticated theory, if it is clearly accepted and borne in mind, will be found, I think, to provide us with an unfailing guide through the immense labyrinth of æsthetics; and it will, also, help to account for the inconsistencies and contradictions, and the general ambiguity of terms and principles, which make the usual views on this subject so unsatisfactory, and which, it seems to me, are caused mainly by the circumstance that this theory is not recognised—at least frankly and thoroughly, since, as a matter of fact, it is indirectly and unconsciously relied on very much in most æsthetic criticism. It was, indeed, simply because I so often observed it latently influencing such criticisms and opinions, and in some measure explaining their otherwise hopelessly confused nature, that I came to see in it a coherent answer to the fundamental and perplexing question, What is the meaning and place of poetry in all art and in life?

II

For, whenever a work of great imaginative power was under consideration—no matter where, when, or how it had come into being—I noticed that it was deemed 'poetic' and the author ' a poet.' Whether it happened to be some famous example of Greek sculpture, or of Gothic architecture or of Italian painting or of German music or of English literature, made no difference in this respect, since no particular form, or art, or craft, or class, or school, or fashion, or country, or tongue, or race, or faith, or age was apparently granted an exclusive possession of poetic genius, but it was acknowledged to be a universal endowment of the highest humanity all the world over, and to be capable of manifesting itself in a thousand different ways and times and places, and not alone in all of the fine arts and in every variety of them, but also in many other directions, not so evident or lasting.

Thus, while the writings of a Shakespeare or of a Shelley may be said to speak for themselves, can we not say that Michel Angelo, in those four great, silent, solitary years, painted the poem of humanity on the vault of the Sistine Chapel? And is there no feeling and imagination[1] on the frescoed walls of cloisters or in the illuminated pages of missals, where monks and holy men have 'muttered in green and purple and gold' their hopes and struggles and loves and losses? And, in our own times, what of Turner or Millet, or the works, with both brush and pen, of Blake and Rossetti? Again, does not the poetry of suffering and catastrophe speak to us in the Laocoön—although no sound escapes his lips? And have you never wandered round a carved poem—in some rough, old, gray-stone Breton Calvary? And are not Wagner's dramas or Beethoven's symphonies real poems—the musical expressions of human feelings and conceptions? And who objects to Handel being buried in the Poet's Corner in Westminster Abbey? And has not 'the poetry of architecture' been pointed out?

Is there not poetry, also, in some prose, just as there is in some verse—in much, say, of Newman and Carlyle, as of Wordsworth and Browning? Did not Matthew Arnold actually go to a prose work, the *Centaur* of Maurice de Guérin, in order to illustrate the characteristic merit of poetic thought? For, can there not be poetry even in a single word? And what about Plato, or those songs of praise and prayer, the Psalms? Where is there greater poetry than in parts of the Old and New Testaments? Where is the feeling more intense and the imaginative power higher? And do you care whether Lucretius wrote in prose or in verse? Does not St. Beuve call Montaigne 'a true poet'? And has not Jeremy Taylor been described as 'one of our noblest poets'? While of Ruskin's works it has been said that they are 'so full of analytical acumen and creative genius that they might be called the poems of criticism.' 'Our best history is still poetry' said Emerson,

---

[1] On another occasion I hope to describe the psychology of these qualities, which form the constituent elements of poetry.

and Professor Max Müller has gone so far as to call Froude a poet.
And has not Mr. Balfour declared that 'metaphysicians are poets'?

Vedic hymn, or Caledonian lay, or Hebrew chant; mediæval
romance, ancient ballad, or northern saga; the *Divine Comedy* of
Dante or the *Human Comedy* of Balzac; Herodotus or Malory;
Homer or St. Paul; Behmen or Rembrandt; Raphael or Mozart;
Strasburg Cathedral or the Dying Gaul; Egyptian pyramid or
Celtic monolith; Job or Brand, Prometheus or Hamlet; *Don
Quixote* or *Faust*; Siegfried or the Sower, Fingal or Zarathustra,
The Song of Myself or *The Story of my Heart*, *The City of God* or
The City of Dreadful Night, *The Dream of Gerontius* or *A Dream of
John Ball*, *The Imitation of Christ* or *The Apology of Socrates*,—
what does it matter? Temple, picture, play, novel, statue, oratorio,
essay, ode—is not poetry possible in all of these, nay, in all things—
not excepting even verse or rhyme? [2]

III

Is there not the poetry of science, or the speculative fervour and
intuition of man as seen in his researches through nature, and in
his brilliant inferences and theoretical conceptions? Has not
science given a more solemn significance, in the bosom of infinite
space and time, to the endless vitality and variety of creation?
Have not its truths, by their wider compass and by their disclosure
of marvellous adaptations and correspondences, greatly enhanced the
mystery and cohesive splendour of the universe? Is not the poetry
of astronomy, from the days of the Chaldean shepherds to our own—
the galaxy of the heavens, the stellar depths and solar system, the
countless worlds and clusters and forces, the origin of light and
heat—proverbial? And was it not Coleridge's opinion that if Sir
Humphry Davy 'had not been the first chemist he would have been
the first poet of his age'? And have we not Tyndall's eloquent
discourse on the scientific use of the imagination, in which he calls
that faculty 'the divining rod of the man of science—the mightiest
instrument of the physical discoverer,' and gives, as an example of
its poetic power 'Newton's passage from a falling apple to a falling
moon'?

Do we not speak, too, of the poetry of character, conduct, actions,
manners, speech, looks, motion, gesture? Was not the first poetic
artist probably a dancing savage—some sensitive and imaginative
creature who, by his primitive cries and gesticulations, sought to
impart to others his own frenzied feelings and conceptions? And
was not Fanny Elssler's dancing called 'poetry'? Among the
numerous means of expression is there not the language of nature
and man, as it were, combined—in face and feature, voice and

[2] Goethe, however, defined 'good' society as that which furnished no material
for poetry.

movement? For are not these the outward, partial appearances of corresponding powers and passions and affections within, which influence and actuate all that we do? So that it is no exaggeration to say that a poem—an exhibition of heart and soul, most graceful and strong and clear—may be seen in a smile or a touch, in an accent or a tint, or in a turn of the head, in a hand by the bedside, or in a knock at the door? Even in such small actions, it is as with the good dancer who does not use only his feet or his head or neck or arms or thighs—but the whole man, the spirit, more than all the body put together, is the moving and determining force.

And was it not said of Thoreau that his actual life was a poem? And has not Goethe entitled his own autobiography 'poetry'? And did not Milton say that the poet himself ought always to be a true poem, since poetry, rightly understood, is the offspring and part of the life and being of great individuality? And has any poetry, which has received artistic treatment, excelled that of certain lives which have been faithfully and bravely passed?—just as no painting or sculpture has ever equalled the living figure and countenance, nor word or sound conveyed the full meaning of thought and emotion? What of St. Francis of Assisi or Joan of Arc, General Gordon or Sir Thomas More, Telemachus or Lincoln, Marcus Aurelius or Christopher Columbus? Martyr, hero, prophet, mystic, Buddha, saint, or sage—what does it matter?

And, finally, can it not appear in political and social life, as in the immortal annals of Greece and Rome, or in the teaching and tradition of the great religions and civilisations of the world? What about the Crusades, and the pilgrimages and perilous expeditions, and every noble, emancipating movement of the spirit of man? And are not the saws and proverbs handed down to us often the accumulated poetry of generations? Life, art, science, religion, history, philosophy, knowledge, experience—is not poetry 'the breath and finer spirit of them all'? I stood for a long time on the Acropolis, wondering which was the greatest poet—Phidias, Ictinus, or Pericles. Does not religion appeal almost exclusively to the emotions and imaginative susceptibility of man? What are piety and worship, from the days when David danced before the Ark to these less demonstrative times, when, even still, a ballet is performed on certain occasions before the high altar in the Cathedral of Seville? And did not Napoleon declare that 'the world was governed by imagination'? And has not Horace ascribed the civilisation of mankind to poetry?

So great and universal, in fact, is the presence of poetry, that sometimes it seems to me as though all our beliefs and principles and ideals and morals, which we suppose to be based on logic or authority or education, are really born of and nurtured by the poetic faculties of man, to comfort our suffering hearts and souls,

What else are God, the soul, immortality, conscience, wisdom, beauty, virtue, holiness? 'The Church herself,' says Cardinal Newman, 'is the most sacred and august of poets.' Lacking certitude, the human spirit endeavours to console itself with poetry; and is it not only by thus keeping life at an emotional and imaginative pitch, by means of love, affection, loyalty, faith, honour, grace, trust, hope, duty, that we are reconciled to and manage to survive the ordeal of mortal existence?

IV

And yet, since men are for the most part, as regards their highest qualities, dumb creatures, how much of the poetry of the human race has remained silent! I believe there are many inarticulate poets. The meanest of mortals can share the poet's inspiration, though he may not have his gift of expression. Is not nearly every man, as has been said, a Shakespeare in his dreams? In the speechless depths of the heart and soul, do we not feel and see more than we can say or do? Whisperings of the mysterious meaning and gravity of all things haunt most of us. Emotions and visions occur, where words and images and shapes and colours and sounds or any visible token fail. There can be a rich poetic disposition, incapable of any kind of expression, just as there are many with remarkable artistic faculties and apparently little or no poetry. But the silent need not be less poetic than the articulate. 'To be is just as great as to perceive or tell.' A man is a poet according to his powers of feeling and imagination and not according to his learning or expository skill. He is an artist as well, if he possess in addition some talent or means of expression, whereby he can exercise and manifest these powers in εἴδωλα or sensuous images and effects.

But is it not absurd and idolatrous to confine poetry to any one of these numerous and different means?[3] For the particular form employed in no way affects the question of the presence and the quality of poetry. The mode of transmission is not the original creative force, as ether is not itself light, or air sound. A Hottentot can have a sense of poetry as strong as Wordsworth's. Natural qualities, like feeling and imagination, can be the same, however much tastes, arts, subjects, and customs—all the peculiar conditions of place and time—differ. With some learning and industry a man can write good verses or paint or compose well, but it is something much more earnest and personal and 'inevitable'—much more of the heart

[3] Yet such is commonly the case. Many opinions to this effect of even distinguished writers and critics—could be quoted. Quite recently, for instance, I read in Mr. Mackail's *Life of William Morris* that one day he said, when poetry was being discussed: 'That talk of inspiration is sheer nonsense, I may tell you that flat. There is no such thing; it is a mere matter of craftsmanship.'

that feels and loves and of the soul that sees and imagines than of the head and hand that execute—which make him a poet. Poetry has the same relation to all forms of art that the earth has to the plants that grow on it, and we might as well talk of the art of earth as of the art of poetry. In order to make the soil fruitful the art of cultivation according to our tastes and capacities may be employed, and in the same way the various arts embody the innate creations of the imagination.

There can, then, be poems in prose, and hexameters without the faintest suggestion of poetry. Metre, rhyme, and stanza distinguish verse, not poetry, from prose. A poet is no more a mere literary artist of a certain description than he is, as he was once considered, a wit or a man about town. Speech is but one of the instruments of poetry. Literature in all its forms is an art, but poetry is not, neither is truth, or beauty, or gracefulness, or heroism. Poetry was not an art in the East, in the early land of its birth, nor was it included among the fine arts when *l'Académie des Beaux-Arts* was established in France; and we know, on Cowper's authority, that it was not an art in Eden. Rhyme and metre were no marks of Indian or Hebrew poetry. 'The accomplishment of verse' has as much to say to poetry as alliteration or any other verbal or syllabic trick. It is but an arbitrary style of writing, a literary dress of a particular cut and measure, a dialect. All forms of linguistic inversion and metre are only modes of artistic exposition. They are often mere affectations, and were once far more elaborate, as in the conceits of the Restoration writers. Some people are good at acrostics and some at sonnets. Poetry has essentially no more connection with verse-writing than it has with pig-sticking.

And likewise with regard to the different arts—letters, music, painting, sculpture, architecture—they are but the sensuous vehicles of thought and emotion : but all of them are capable of poetry, and therein lies their real excellence. The poetry of any artistic creation is the poetic qualities, the imaginative genius displayed by means of it. It is never the art itself or the form. Art is the protean vesture that clothes in divers fashions the eternal, unchanging spirit of poetry whose unveiled purity is the poet's secret vision. All the succeeding stages and kinds of art in the world are manifestations under many guises and forms of one and the same presence—the abiding life and majesty of poetry. Arts are many, and they date from various mechanical discoveries. They are simply technical memoranda. Art means skill. Besides the five ordinary fine arts there are many others. The æsthetics of the dining table has been ably treated as a fine art, and murder also, and there is the black art. But poetry is one, and it has always been, although it has many voices and shapes and appearances. It is not itself a dress or vehicle, but it is a source and substance, issuing through innumerable talents and channels.

It is the root and succulence of a tree that has many shoots and ramifications—and some very lofty boughs. To be a poet it is not the art of verse that a man should study, but the poetry of life—its pathos and significance, which he should feel and see. For life, in its true light, is all poetry, and in relation to it, and not to any rule of art or conventional form or taste, must every poem be finally judged. As it is the source and origin, so is it the perpetual standard and test of all poetic effort, and solely according to its strength is there poetry in a man or in his acts or works, whatever may be the life he leads or the form his creations may happen to take. Fortunately the field of poetry is wide. All that is, has its poetic potency and expression. Any part of life, however sordid, savage, and commonplace, if it is once touched by the strong hand of imaginative genius—becomes for evermore poetry—steeped after its kind in all the unfathomable beauty of deep, sincere feeling and sympathetic interpretation. The truth is that life—if we are only conscious of its human and spiritual conditions, which are always present—cannot escape being poetry. The world is full of meaning. Radiations from the heart and penetrations of the soul draw us in every direction; and it would, indeed, have been a narrow and pedantic arrangement, if only the artist or student, forsooth, could know and represent the poetry of life.

V

But poets vary, of course, greatly in artistic capacities, from the illiterate peasant up to the highest expressive talent. Rich though the soul often is or may be, the utterance may yet be very feeble; and I believe that many people differ, not so much in their feelings and insight as in their powers of expression, and that the delight of genuine appreciation consists largely in welcoming the appearance of our own dormant thoughts and emotions. The poet announces what others feel and see, and therefore hail as true. He is not merely dumbfounded by the mystery of life, but, finding speech, he is relieved, and recovers from the shock, and we, who, although inarticulate, have perhaps gone through the same experiences, and are as sensitive and imaginative, gladly recognise echoes and memories, and shadows, of the loves and the hopes, and the dreams of our own elusive lives. Or, with his greater powers of feeling and discernment, he interprets what we have only dimly felt or darkly seen, and so actually enlarges the sphere of our vital consciousness. And the creative joy and artistic skill of the poet lie in rescuing from such Nemesis, or oblivion and indifference, and embodying in lasting form, some idea or light, however partial and shadowy, with regard to the dark and thoughtless space we live in; and it is by so doing that he 'enriches the blood of the world'—feeling and revealing the eternal significance and freshness of life—adding and fixing for others new thoughts and sympathies and relations, which would otherwise have been but fleeting visions and momentary impressions, hopelessly lost in the wreckage and futility of what is past and forgotten. The whole world cries to heaven for interpretation. The poetry of life has hardly found expression at all. There have been but few voices and lights to break the silence and dispel the gloom. Patiently the world lies before us, like a great block of unhewn marble, containing within itself, as Michel Angelo said, all the images and secrets that the greatest poet could ever dream of or desire to know.

But, even in the case of the greatest artist and poet, feeling and imagination far outstrip expression. No word or image has limned the heart and soul of man. Voice is itself but an echo, colour a reflection, form a shadow. Art matches poetry about as well as dogma does religious exaltation, or language the reverie of thought. At best it is never more than a miserable representation of the original—a clumsy image of its spiritual counterpart. The symbol can only suggest ' the light that never was on sea or land.' There is no real equation between what is within and its external makeshift. The countenance, voice and action, how weak and deceptive they can be ! Body and soul are generally a hideous misfit. The most eloquent often see more than they can name or depict. The spirit that built and still illuminates the cathedrals and shrines of the middle ages is greater than the buildings themselves. However beautiful, they are only the halting, sepulchral effigies of a vanished dream of the divine presence.

For the spirit of poetry exists apart from any incarnation of it. What, for instance, is more poetic often than mere affinity, recollection, association, reticence ? The soul can conceive without the use of language. Thought preceded speech. Poetry—feeling and insight—was in the world long before printing or writing or even speaking were heard or thought of, or any instrument of art invented, and it would survive, even if knowledge of all the arts were completely lost.

And the attempt to arrive at adequate expression has been a long and stuttering course. The rudiments and science of the language of art, the elaboration of signs and the perfecting of instruments, whether in writing, perspective, or notation, were with great difficulty reached, and sounds, pictures, words, and shapes so made capable of fixing and communicating their contents. But the tools with which we endeavour to hack out our meaning are still very blunt and unsatisfactory. Was Swedenborg so eccentric, when he held that our finest thoughts could only be expressed ' by variegations of heavenly light ? ' Does not every poet know well how inferior his means of communication are to his inspiration ? They are as wild and futile as Romeo's passionate contradictions or Tristan's musical

transports in their efforts to describe love.   Like the prophet of old,
can we do more than speak of 'the appearance of the likeness,'
'the voice of the cry'?   The greater the poet and artist is,
the nearer will be his approach to true expression of the internal
life and import—and so on, until every secret shall be detected
and named, and the game of thought and interpretation at an
end ; but, in the meantime, so poor a thing is expression of any
kind, that on great occasions do we not instinctively make no
attempt whatever to give utterance to our thoughts and feelings ?
We foresee and shudder at the awful disparity, and so refrain.   ' Be
silent, and know that I am God' sums up many a situation.

VI

Thus have we briefly seen how the whole life and history and
circumstances of the human race, from the beginning of the creation
to the end, are suffused with the divine breath and sustenance of
poetic power.

For God, in truth, is the supreme and only original poet—the
Maker or Creator ; and His poem—the everlasting Book of Life.   He
is, too, the great imaginative artist ; and the visible universe—His
work of art.   In splendid style has He shaped the earth into man
and beast and every living thing ; and man, also, can shape some
lovely images and ideas.   But the creation of the world was not a
masonic act but a spiritual breathing ; and man creates and is a poet
in so far as he sees and partakes of this divine life and presence.
Just as God is Pure Being itself, the poetry of anything is its share
of such perennial essence.   From the central fire of Life radiate waves
of love and light, permeating the hearts and souls of men, and
bodied forth in the glorious births of imaginative expression.   The
poetic artist is like a refracting prism, decomposing the sun's purity
into an infinite number of shades of varying force and amplitude,
and his works may be compared to the order and nature of the
different broken tints of the solar spectrum—red, orange, yellow,
green, blue, indigo, violet.   On the sensitive retina of one life
oscillates into luminous images of colour and light and form and
design ; on the delicate tympanum of another it vibrates into
rhythmic chords of sound ; in the cerebral consciousness of another
it thrills into glowing words of speech.   O to see and to hear !
Voice and vision !   Light and sound !—undulating through the
world in a myriad radial arteries, and exciting to elastic response the
throbbing heart and flashing imagination of man !

Thus does a great wave of the divine spirit, which is the eternal
life and current of the universe, pass over a dark, unmeaning, arid
world, and they drown themselves in it—who haply can.   The heavens
are opened, and extraordinary inspiration and gifts are showered on the

chosen ones. 'The spirit of God shall come over you.' The poet sees that the whole universe is a manifestation of spiritual being and significance; and this insight constitutes distinct poetic creation. To be inspired is to hear, however faintly, the reverberation 'down the ringing grooves of change,' of the divine Word—ὁ Λόγος—which created the world and which still sustains it and is its ineffable oracle. The first and the last and the only word of all creation is: Let there be light. This is how the poet is really ὁ ποιητής, or maker—as God is. Poetry is the human counterpart of the divine creativeness of the world. It is an unconscious secret force, composing 'the life of things,' which the imaginative genius of man discloses and renders conscious. It is a partial revelation of the creative spirit of the universe, and is itself the creative principle of all spiritual life and understanding. There can be no real religion without a poetic sense—not that the spiritual consciousness of the poet is the same as the dogmatic, spiritualistic faith of the believer. The latter refers to another world—of spirits or in the future—apart from this. But poetry is thoroughly terrestrial and natural to man; it is a present insight into the spiritual in this actual world around us; and, without it, all gifts intellectual, moral, or physical are incomplete, and no man, in any path of life, can be great. The soul should have a sense of poetry as the will has a sense of duty or the mind a sense of logic; but the faculty of expression may be as weak and uncommon as right conduct or true reasoning are. But to the great man the transcendent poetry of life is revealed, and his words and acts abide. Beneath all its shapes and guises, his sympathetic insight discerns and evokes the unchanging spirit of the manifold universe. The mystic unity of life finds an echo in the lonely grandeur of his soul. He sees the universal significance and relationship of what is otherwise dead and meaningless and discordant; and life becomes one harmonious vision.

MARTIN MORRIS.

Art. VIII.—THE CONDITIONS OF GREAT POETRY.

NO two domains of thought could, at first sight, seem farther apart than those of poetical criticism and of sociological science. They are, however, in reality very closely connected, though the nature and importance of the connexion has only become apparent through the gradual comprehension of certain facts and principles which has taken place during comparatively recent years. Few conceptions have done more to transform the aspect which existence generally presents to the human mind than the principle now known to us under the familiar name Evolution. It has not only exhibited to us in a wholly new light the sequence of all phenomena, physical, mental, and social; but in the case of each class of phenomena it has cast a light equally new on the fact of their co-existence, revealing it to us as an inter-dependence. It has shown us that, as nothing can be understood apart from the things preceding it, so nothing can be understood apart from the things surrounding it. It has shown us this relativity in the sphere of commerce and industry, in the sphere of political government, in the sphere of class relationships. It has shown us the same thing with regard to thought and literature. There is no order of phenomena which is not conditioned by its environment, which does not depend on circumstances outside itself; and of this great rule poetry is a signal example. The greatness or the littleness of the poetry of any given period depends to some extent on the faculties of the poets themselves; but to some extent also, and far more than was once thought, it depends on the social conditions into which the poets have been born : and poetry being thus connected with social history, the criticism of it, within certain limits, is a portion of the science of sociology.

In pre-scientific days this truth was perceived but dimly. The greatness of the greatest poetry was once attributed without qualification to the peculiar congenital faculties comprised in the personality of the poets; and if the poetry of certain epochs and peoples has been on the whole greater than the poetry of others, the fact was explained solely by reference to the further fact, itself unexplained and inexplicable, that among certain races there appeared at certain epochs an unusual number of unusually gifted individuals. Modern scientific thinkers, among them Mr. Herbert Spencer, have been led, in their protests against the insufficiency of this theory, into an error which is even greater than that which they are anxious to displace. In emphasising the fact that the greatness of great poetry is not due entirely to the greatness of the poet himself, they have tended to lose sight of the greatness of the poet altogether, and have treated his personal gifts as though they were practically a negligible quantity. The nature of the temptation which has led them to do this is intelligible. Their desire has been to reduce history to a series of calculable phenomena, to redeem it from the dominion of chance or from the arbitrary interpositions of a Deity; and they have no doubt been able to exhibit these phenomena under their wider aspects as arising and succeeding one another in obedience to certain general laws. But the phenomena of exceptional genius have entirely eluded their explanations. They can tell us why one race is intellectually more feeble than another; they can tell us why one age is intellectually less active than another; but they cannot tell us why, among men of the same race, individuals or groups of individuals appear from time to time, incalculably more gifted than the great mass of those whose racial antecedents and whose social circumstances are the same. The appearance of great genius, and of poetic genius especially, remains still an inscrutable mystery; nor is there any reason for supposing that the causes, which make one member of a family a genius and leave the rest dunces, belong to the same order of causes as those which make the average intelligence of the European greater than that of the Hottentot, or which made the intellectual atmosphere of the time of Queen Elizabeth more stimulating than that of the time of William the Conqueror. In so far therefore as exceptionally great genius is a factor in the production of exceptionally great poetry, the causes of great poetry are inaccessible to the science of the sociologist; and in the interest of his science he is consequently tempted to minimise them. He is tempted to argue that the greatness of such works as the 'Divine Comedy' or 'Hamlet' was due in reality not to the author but to the age. The truth of the matter is that both these causes were essential to the result, and that to dwell on the character of the age and practically ignore that of the author—as is done by Mr. Herbert Spencer—is as nonsensical as to dwell on the author and practically ignore the age. The man with the greatest congenital gift for poetry may be unable to produce any poetry that is really great if he lives in an age that is unsuited to its production; but the age most suited to its production will be no less barren unless, by a happy coincidence, it chance to possess the man whose exceptional poetic powers will respond to the stimulus which it applies to them.

Having, however, recognised that the personal, the incalculable element in poetry retains its importance despite all the attacks of the sociologists, we may profitably direct our attention to the truth on which the sociologists insist. Premising, then, that no great poetry can be written except by men with congenital faculties of an exceedingly rare kind, we must admit that such men might be very great poets in one age but would be very inferior poets, or hardly poets at all, in another; and we shall then see that the broad facts of history provide us with a partial, though not a complete, explanation of the curiously intermittent and irregular manner in which great poets and poetry have always made their appearance.

We have been led to direct attention to this aspect of the question by the condition of English poetry at the close of the nineteenth century, as compared with its condition during the larger part of that period. During the earlier portion of the century this country possessed poets in whose works the nation found an echo, and often a revelation, of all that was highest and deepest in its thoughts, its aspirations, and its feelings. Byron, Shelley, Keats, and Wordsworth, in their respective manners and degrees, dealing with life as seen through the medium of emotion, grasped it and interpreted it in such a masterly way that all contemporary emotion gradually ran itself into the moulds with which these poets supplied it; and when Wordsworth died, having long outlived his coadjutors, successors had already arisen to his position and theirs, in the persons of Tennyson and Robert Browning, and—at least during his earlier years—in the person of Mr. Swinburne. We have mentioned thus far poets of the first order only; but contemporary with these, and sharing not a little of their influence and inspiration, were Scott and Coleridge during the earlier decades of the century, and in later years D. G. Rossetti, William Morris, and Matthew Arnold. But now, since the deaths of these three last-named writers, together with those of Tennyson and Browning, and the gradual exhaustion of Mr. Swinburne's earlier and most distinctive inspiration, poetry of the first order has become practically extinct among us. To this observation we must make one partial exception, which we shall mention presently; but in a general sense it is true. We have still poets, no doubt, who are distinguished by many excellences. But true poetry, and even poetry perfect of its kind, need not be great poetry; and the voice of great poetry is, for the time, silent. We hear the notes of experts who are performing on minor instruments, but the sound of the great organ which flooded the aisles has ceased.

What, then, we ask, is the reason of this cessation? The

old-fashioned answer would have been that great poetry has ceased simply because the Deity or the incalculable operations of Nature had produced no new individuals with genius sufficient to write it. Whatever element ,of truth there may be in this answer, we shall invite the reader to consider whether, in the present case, there is not another, the scope of which has already, in general terms, been indicated. We shall invite the reader to consider whether poetry, at the close of the nineteenth century, may not owe its lack of greatness less to the deficiencies of its poets than to various changes which have come over the world generally—changes in the ideals and the political outlook of nations, and in the spiritual and intellectual atmosphere of the world at large. This is an enquiry which suggests to us many questions, highly interesting in themselves, apart from their present application. It involves, firstly, a consideration of what the general conditions are which history shows us to have been favourable to the production of great poetry in the past; and, secondly, it involves a consideration of what great poetry is. We will begin with the general conditions.

Under what conditions, then, did the great poets produce their masterpieces? Let us take Æschylus and Sophocles; let us take Horace and Virgil; let us take Dante; let us take Shakespeare and Milton; let us take Goethe and Schiller, and lastly the great English poets who have flourished during the' nineteenth century. We shall find that all these writers produced their works during periods in which their respective countries were in a state of heightened national vitality; or in which mankind generally were dominated by some strong religious convictions; or in which old convictions were being discarded, and new ones were with eagerness being foreshadowed, sought out, and formed; or in which some or all these conditions to some degree co-existed. Thus the period of the production of the great Greek tragedies was the period during which Athens, as a State, rose to its brief pre-eminence; when the guardian Goddess of the Acropolis, shining 'through the most pellucid air,' was more than a work of art, more even than an object of worship; when she was a visible and triumphant symbol to the City of the Violet Crown of a national life exulting over all rivals, in a solemn yet buoyant consciousness of freedom, strength, and beauty. And what the exquisite microcosm of Athens was to Æschylus and Sophocles the august macrocosm of Rome was to Horace and Virgil. Its effects upon the poetry of Horace are not, perhaps, immediately obvious; but in the 'Æneid' they are such that he who runs may read them. Rome would never have possessed an 'Æneid' if it had not possessed a Virgil; but no Virgil could have written an 'Æneid' if he had not been a citizen of Rome. When we come to Dante the case is somewhat different. The conditions of Florence, and of his own life as affected by them, had no doubt a certain effect on his genius; but the most important relation of his personal gifts to his environment was not his relation to any secular State. It was his relation to the spiritual empire of mediæval Catholicism. In the 'Divine Comedy' we have a revelation of his own gifts and character. We see them in his mastery of language, in the rigid clearness of his imagination, in his unflinching judgments of individuals, in his passion for Beatrice, and in his sympathy for the lovers who kissed each other and who 'that day read no more.' But through all these, beyond all these, and greater than all these, we see an image of Christianity as it was in the Age of Faith—the depths, the heights, the terrors, the probations, and the blessedness which it created or revealed as possibilities for the human soul. In the case of Shakespeare, as has often been observed before, we see the poet set in an age of great national expansion, partly political, partly religious and intellectual; new continents offering themselves to the enterprise of action, new regions of speculation offering themselves to the enterprise of the mind, and new splendours and amenities introducing themselves into social life. Milton presents us with a phenomenon of the same kind. His genius too was conditioned by special and unusual circumstances. What the Renaissance of art and thought and the blossoming of a monarchical civilisation were to Shakespeare, the anti-monarchical revolt of the Puritans was for Milton; and for Milton the religion of the Puritans was what Catholicism was for Dante. The genius of Schiller and Goethe, that of Goethe more especially, was conditioned by circumstances which were less national than cosmopolitan. It developed itself and worked in an atmosphere of political calm; but its mental environment was that stress and ferment of thought by which all Europe was at the time agitated—the seeking for new philosophies, new spiritual ideals, and new conceptions of the manner in which the individual man might realise most fully the highest possibilities of his existence.

Of the environment of the great poets with whom we are more specially concerned—namely, those who have flourished in England during the nineteenth century—we will speak presently; but let us dwell a little longer on that of those with whom we have just been dealing. These poets are so eminent and representative that they afford us materials from which to generalise with regard to the present question. They suffice to justify us in saying that great poetry is never produced except in periods in which the minds of men are excited by strong feelings, dominated by strong beliefs, or animated by strong hopes, which the poet, at starting, has had no share in producing. He may react on them by means of his poetry. He may stimulate them, he may clarify them, he may add to their vitality, he may exalt them; but he finds them ready to hand, as the materials with which his art must work. These feelings, beliefs, and hopes are, as we have seen already, national, religious, or philosophic, or all three in combination. To describe them thus, however, is not sufficient for our purpose. It is necessary that we should analyse them further.

Let us begin with those which are national—which spring into exceptional vitality in connexion with some expansion or development of national life and power. The principal point which is here to be observed is this. Every national expansion or development of the kind in question may be generally and broadly divided into two stages: the first being the stage of struggle through which victory and success are reached; the second being the stage during which the resources that victory has won are being consciously appreciated, and applied to further uses; and it is the latter stage alone which is favourable to great poetry. All the evidence of history tends to support this conclusion. Great poetry has no doubt been produced in nations which have not been going through this latter stage of success; but it has never been produced in nations during the stress and struggle that have preceded it. To illustrate this fact it will be enough to turn again to the age of Shakespeare. In the sphere of politics, of national religion, and of social civilisation alike, England was then, as it were, entering into a new inheritance. It was no longer fighting for its treasures. It was sorting them, admiring them, employing them in many ways, and dreaming of other ways in which they might be employed some day. The same thing may be said of the great poetic epochs of Athens and Rome, and of France under Louis XIV. But it is not necessary here to go into further details. Stated briefly, the truth amounts to this: that the national conditions most favourable to the production of great poetry are conditions of national vigour, confident of success and looking forward to further triumphs. Under these conditions the minds of men generally are in a state which is midway between the calm of speculation and reflection and the preoccupation of practical endeavour. It unites the intellectual vision of the one with the ardent passion of the other. It is this state of mind to which the poet appeals, and which in the great poet reaches its most complete development.

We do not say that these national conditions are indispensable to the production of great poetry; but if they are absent, then it is all the more necessary that the conditions of religion or thought should be favourable. If we consider religious conditions, we shall find the one which most strongly affects the production of poetry to be a religious belief at once generally diffused and accepted with unquestioning and intense conviction. This of itself may be sufficient to admit of the production of great poetry, apart from any special heightening or development of national life; but, whenever such a development of national life takes place, religious belief is directly or indirectly an element of it. The precise nature of the belief—as we see in the case of Dante—will necessarily affect the character of the poetry that is produced under its influence; but the essential point is that the belief, whatever it may be, shall not be a belief confined to the poet himself, or to a band of struggling propagandists, but shall be accepted by the whole public whom he addresses, with a faith equal to his own. It must not be a flame which he has to kindle and tend, and which only shines precariously from the spot which he himself occupies. It must be a flame which burns for him and for all alike, illuminating life for all of them in the same way, and producing the same effects of spiritual light and shade. Dante, however devout a Catholic himself, could never have written his 'Inferno' had his lot been cast in a generation which, before it could listen seriously to any account of Hell, required to be persuaded that such a place as Hell existed; nor could Milton ever have written his 'Paradise Lost' in an age when no Christian of attainments similar to his own any longer believed that there was any literal truth in the Hebrew account of the genesis of the human race. Unless the poet's religion is, without any effort of his own, shared by his audience, and unless he can take it for granted in them, it will, if it moves him to public utterance at all, move him to use his genius, not as a poet, but as a missionary.

Finally, let us consider the philosophic or intellectual conditions favourable to great poetry — conditions which may co-exist with the others, or else may take the place of them. That some great and general outburst of intellectual and philosophical activity may have on poetry an effect very similar to that of some great national development, or of strong religious belief, is attested by the case of Goethe. In certain instances such a movement may assume a national character; but the case of Goethe shows us that this is by no means essential. What influenced his genius was a quickening of thought throughout Europe, which had nothing to do with the fortunes of the State of Weimar. And just as it was independent of the life of any special nation, so was it independent of the dogmas of any special religion. It was not only independent of them; it represented a revolt against them; or at all events it involved a repudiation of them in their literal sense. Now if strong religious belief is favourable to great poetry, we might naturally expect that the disintegration of it, at the hands of philosophy, would be the reverse; and we might easily adduce examples to show that such is the case. The fact is, however, that philosophy, when it frees itself from dogmatic religion, and endeavours to reach truth by independent means of its own, is capable of doing this in two widely different ways. It may do so in a spirit which, so far as definite belief is concerned, is mainly negative and destructive; and it may do so in a spirit which, in the very act of negation, conceives itself to be re-expressing what it denies, and re-expressing it more completely. In the former case we have an extinction of belief; in the latter we have a transformation; and whilst an intellectual movement which tends to the extinction of belief is unfavourable to poetry, an intellectual movement which tends to the transformation of it may be no less favourable than the settled belief itself. For such a movement, so long as it remains in this stage, is practically an equivalent of the very thing which it seems to be destroying. It is itself a religion which, whilst it is losing the stimulus of definite conviction, gains what for the time is equally operative on the mind, namely, the stimulus of indefinite hope. Such was the movement in the midst of which the genius of Goethe expanded itself. It was a movement inspired by an exceptionally vivid belief in exuberant possibilities of life which till then had been hampered by man's unsuccessful attempts at expressing them, and which seemed to be then at last thronging vaguely into sight, ready, at the spell of genius, to assume some intelligible form. The words of religious dogma might be only 'sound and smoke'; but behind them was the 'heaven's glow' which they had obscured, and which would shine on us when they were swept aside. Who, asks Faust, can say he believes in the Deity? And yet who, having felt, can say, 'In Him I do not believe'? An intellectual movement which, whilst repudiating one set of beliefs, is not vivified by the conviction that it is replacing them by others

M 2

equally inspiring, may be favourable, or not unfavourable, to many efforts of human genius—to progress in the arts of life, to the advance of positive knowledge; or, as we see by the example of Rome, when its ancient faith was leaving it, to the elaboration of a great system of jurisprudence. But to great poetry such a negative movement is unfavourable: we may say, indeed, that it renders it impossible. But when an intellectual movement, however destructive on one side, is simultaneously constructive on another, the case, so far as regards great poetry, is reversed.

The explanation of this fact is simple, and is to be found in a general principle which applies equally to the connexion with great poetry of a quickening of the national life and of intense religious conviction. This principle is that at the root of all great poetry there is some form or other of strenuous and impassioned optimism, some heightened sense of the value and importance of existence. And this is as true of the poetry which expresses sadness, or even deliberate pessimism, as it is of the poetry which expresses the delights of love, hope, and endeavour, the beauty of good, or the majesty of great conduct. For all pessimism that is really impressive in poetry is neither more nor less than the shadow of some vivid optimism; and the gloom of the shadow is in proportion to the brightness of the light that casts it, just as the bitterness of a lover's loss is in proportion to the intensity of his passion. It is easy to see that a development of the national life such as that which took place in this country during the age of Shakespeare, and an intellectual movement such as that which conditioned the career of Goethe, were essentially optimistic, in the sense that they intensified men's consciousness of the value and richness of existence, and made them regard it with heightened and deepened feelings; and a moment's reflection will make it equally clear that the Catholicism of the Age of Faith, in spite of the terrors of its Inferno, and what many regard as the tyranny which it exercised over the human spirit, was an optimism, in the sense in which we are now using the word, of the most absolute and overwhelming kind. It was founded on a belief in the unerring justice of God, and it impressed on men, with a vividness which has never since been equalled, the inconceivable preciousness of every human soul. To these observations there is one more to be added, or rather to be repeated, for it is an observation we have made already. The hopes, the feelings, the beliefs, which are favourable to great poetry, which the great poet focalises, and which we have classed together under the name of optimism, must not be the precarious possession of some small clique or party. They must be generally diffused throughout the poet's own country or throughout the world ; and they must have a vigorous existence independent of the poet himself. His province must be not to initiate them, but to absorb, to reproduce and to interpret them.

And now let us turn at last to the poets of our own country who have flourished between the beginning of the nineteenth century and its close, and see how they have been affected by one or other, or all, of those conditions which we have just been examining. We will take Byron and Shelley, with whom we may associate Keats, as representing poetry during the earlier portion of that period ; treating Wordsworth, whose full development belonged to a later time, subsequently. We will then pass on to Tennyson, Browning, and Mr. Swinburne.

Byron and Shelley, it is hardly necessary to say, were surrounded by the same general intellectual atmosphere as that which surrounded Goethe, though they assimilated its various elements in a very different manner. Goethe assimilated them as a philosopher, Byron as a practical man, and Shelley as a prophetic dreamer ; but all three assimilated them as idealists. They all three gave expression to the hope of some larger and freer life, and they all found these hopes alive in the air around them—hopes partly generated by the political and the military convulsions of the time, partly by the growth of the democratic and the scientific spirit. But the idealism of Byron, and even that of Shelley, contained far more of the national and political elements than Goethe's ; and these elements likewise were supplied by contemporary circumstances. Political ideas and ideals of the most incongruous and indeed conflicting character were then germinating in this country, and being more or less fused together in the crucible of the national imagination. On the one hand there was the democratic idea, which had been expressed by such writers as Godwin. On the other there was the remains of a sort of Strawberry-Hill mediævalism, with which the upper class invested itself, applauded and assisted by the public. Byron absorbed and reflected both sets of ideas, which, however otherwise opposed, possessed alike the charm of innovation, and appealed alike to some living faith in the future. Byron was, indeed, equally sincere in his passionate response to both. Shelley was touched almost exclusively by the former. But the two poets alike concentrated and reproduced ideas, hopes, feelings, passions, and aspirations which were not peculiar to themselves, but belonged to their generation, and were due to far-reaching and widely-extended causes. The same observation applies also to Keats. The same comprehensive spirit of sanguine and adventurous unrest, which spoke through Byron and Shelley as a spirit of romance and freedom, spoke through Keats as the spirit of a paganism born again, which to the life of sensuous beauty should give back the spiritual charm of which Christian spiritualism had defrauded it. The general optimism of the period was, in the case of each poet, coloured by his own genius and character. Whatever the conditions of the age in which each lived, he would probably have written poetry of some sort or other; but in each case the poet's volume of meaning, and the confident passion which inspired it, and which stimulated and sustained his utterance, were derived from that quickening of new hopes, sentiments, and philosophies which pervaded Europe at the dawn of the nineteenth century.

Let us now take the case of Wordsworth. If Byron, Shelley, and Keats were the exponents of a revolutionary optimism, that optimism was succeeded, and for a time accompanied, by a corresponding optimism of reaction, and Wordsworth was the exponent of this. During his earlier years, indeed, he too had been touched by the revolutionary fervour. His bringing poetry back to the realities of the simplest life was in itself a response to, and an expression of, the general revolutionary movement; and a response to it yet deeper was the quasi-pantheistic mysticism which led him to invest, like Shelley, the beauties of external nature with the spiritual and emotional meanings of a self-revealing religion. But for Wordsworth, unlike Shelley, this self-revealing religion was practically but another aspect of orthodox and dogmatic Christianity. And yet Wordsworth, no less than Shelley, was inspired and stimulated by a spirit which was diffused amongst a multitude of his contemporaries, and which therefore possessed a vitality altogether independent of himself. In spite of the non-orthodox transcendentalism which had spread itself through Europe, orthodox Christianity, especially in this country, retained a vigorous hold on many of the most powerful intellects, and the pulses of the old faith quickened under the attacks of the new philosophies. Wordsworth's poetry was an attempt to take the new philosophies captive, and apply them to the service of the old religion; and it was the religious faith and feeling still alive amongst multitudes, who were at once touched by the spirit of progress and distrustful of it, which sustained and stimulated him in constructing a retreat for the soul, in which faith and reason might together find rest amongst the most profound realities.

The genius of Tennyson developed itself amongst a different set of influences, and in a world which has been fast vitalised by faiths of a new kind. As a great poet, and in his greatest poems, he represents the optimism of the earlier Victorian period. His very patriotism was a refinement of the patriotism of Mr. Podsnap. Everything seemed to him to be for the best in this best of all possible countries; and the same opinion was rife in the air around him. As we look back at it now, we can see that this opinion was exaggerated; and many of the hopes associated with it have by this time been falsified. But it is easy to see how it arose, and we can hardly wonder at its prevalence. It was due to various causes, which, though they had been long in operation, were then first beginning to make themselves generally felt. One of these was a multitude of social and political reforms, designed to ameliorate the mental and material condition of the masses: another was the enormous commercial and industrial development of the country, which, having made many of these reforms necessary, helped to render them possible; and a third was the development of the physical sciences, especially those that bear on the origin of the earth and man. All these causes tended to produce in this country an optimism of a peculiar kind. It was less violent, more definite, and more systematic, than that of the age of Byron. It was more concrete than what found expression in Wordsworth. It was the optimism of evolution, as distinguished from the optimism of revolution on the one hand and the optimism of reaction or quietism on the other. It was an optimism which saw in industrial progress the promise of universal peace; which saw in political freedom the promise of universal happiness; and which saw in the physical sciences the handmaids of Christianity generally, and especially of Christianity as interpreted by the English Church. War was to cease; all classes were to live in harmony; the church bells were to ring in 'the Christ that is to be'; and in the midst of these happy conditions the domestic affections were to develope themselves with a fulness unequalled in any previous period. Such was the optimism which nourished the genius of Tennyson with 'the fairy tales of science, and the long result of Time,' and enabled him to find inspiration in the spectacle of the world 'spinning for ever down the ringing grooves of change,' and for ever getting nearer and nearer to 'the wonder that would be.' The same diffused optimism, though assimilated in a different manner, nourished the genius of Browning. Browning was less affected than Tennyson by the scientific spirit of his time; and he was more exclusively, though not more deeply, touched by its religious spirit. The elements of his religion were compounded in different manner from those of

Tennyson ; but they were none the less supplied by the mental atmosphere which surrounded him. The religion of Browning contained an element of the Positivist worship of humanity : it regarded man as a constantly erring but in no sense as a fallen being : it attributed a kind of divinity even to many of his coarsest instincts. But, unlike the religion of Comte, and indeed unlike that of Tennyson, it laid no stress on the prospect of any social progress which should make life a thousand years hence superior to what it is now. If man, his nature, his conduct, his feelings, his experiences, are worth anything, they are worth as much to-day as they ever have been or ever will be. On this side of the grave they always have been and always will be incomplete ; but life on this side of the grave is merely the first act of a drama which owes its hope and its meaning to a prescience of other acts that are to follow. Such was the religion which animated Browning's poetry. It was a religion whose feet were Positivism, and whose head was a semi-Christian mysticism ; and both these elements belonged to the world of which he formed a part. Of Mr. Swinburne too the same thing may be said. Mr. Swinburne's poetry, in its earliest vigour, was an impassioned expression of the Positivist conception of human nature. It was the protest of man, as a being who has no other life but this, against the creeds ' that refuse and restrain '—that would shut him out from the full fruition of his faculties, and would call the fairest part of this sole inheritance unclean ; and this purely sensual protest was elevated or reinforced by association with the hope of some transfiguration of the human lot, which was somehow or other to result from revolutionary progress, and of which a redeemed and unified Italy was to offer the world a sample.

But now, one after the other, all these movements, these quickenings of thought and hope, have exhausted themselves. Byron, Shelley, and Keats died too early to outlive the sources from which their genius derived its nutriment ; and therefore we cannot accurately estimate how much in their poetry was due to their own rare individual faculties, and how much to the influence of the conditions which surrounded them. But the fate of Tennyson, of Browning, and of Mr. Swinburne, has been different. They all lived long enough to experience a change in the mental atmosphere whose oxygen they inhaled when composing their greatest works ; and we are able to note how, though to all appearance their personal faculties remained as vigorous as ever, the quality of their work underwent a change, and lost much of the vigour and inspiration that originally made them great. The nature and the operation of this change can be seen most clearly in the later works of Tennyson. We can trace in many of these the increasingly saddening impression made on his mind by the recent developments of science, and by the sinister transformation of a kind of knowledge which he had once welcomed as the handmaid of the religion of Christ into an enemy which threatened to be fatal to all religion whatsoever. In one of his later poems we find him writing thus :—

'Many a hearth upon our dark globe sighs after many a vanish'd face,
Many a planet by many a sun may roll with the dust of a vanish'd race.

*   *   *   *   *

'What is it all, if we all of us end but in being our own corpse-coffins at last,
Swallow'd in Vastness, lost in Silence, drown'd in the deep of a meaningless Past?'

He does not yield to such thoughts : on the contrary, to the last he protests against them. But no longer, as in his earlier days, is he the spokesman of a faith that is triumphant; he is as one who is doing all he can to sustain the desperate courage of a faith that, with its utmost efforts, can but just keep itself alive. And as in the sphere of science, so has it been in the sphere of politics. The world, as it went 'spinning down the ringing grooves of change,' no doubt brought many improvements to the general condition of mankind ; but the worst characteristics of human nature did not seem appreciably to decrease. If one kind of evil subsided, another kind of evil took its place ; the reign of universal blessedness seemed as far off as ever ; and freedom, though it 'broadened down from precedent to precedent' a great deal faster than Tennyson himself had anticipated, instead of realising his vision of an united national wisdom, seemed only to result, as he himself puts it, in—

'Lies upon this side, lies upon that side, truthless violence mourn'd by the Wise,
Thousands of voices drowning his own in a popular torrent of lies upon lies.'

In other words, the optimism which had been dominant whilst his genius was developing itself, had been gradually dissipated by the dispassionate logic of events; and with its dissipation there set in a decline, not indeed in Tennyson's mental powers, but in his practical ability any longer to produce poetry equal to that which had first raised him to eminence. The case of Mr. Swinburne is no less instructive. His early beliefs in the advent of some democratic millennium, with Mazzini for its John the Baptist, and a united Italy and a republican France as examples of it, have not survived the disenchantments of experience ; and though his singing voice has, perhaps, as much volume and melody as ever, there seems to be little left for him to sing about with any real enthusiasm.

Now the same causes which thus affected the genius of Tennyson, and are still affecting the genius of Mr. Swinburne, are having a similar effect on our contemporary poets generally, and afford at all events a partial explanation of the fact that we have no living poet who can reasonably be called great. Whatever may be thought of personal faculties, the general conditions that go to produce great poetry are for the moment wanting. The faiths, the hopes, and the aspirations of the present generation are not in a state of sufficient, or sufficiently definite, excitement to generate the emotional atmosphere which great poetry requires. To the truth of this observation we have only one poet who offers even the semblance of an exception. That poet is Mr. Kipling. His genius to-day has found itself in its proper element; and he has in a very remarkable manner embodied in his poetry the one element in our national life which is, for the time being, in a state of exceptional vitality. He is the poet of the Imperial idea, of the sense of Imperial responsibilities, of the romance of Imperial expansion. He has indeed done more than any other poet to make his countrymen vividly conscious of the variety of peoples and civilisations which make up the British Empire, as it extends itself across all the seas and continents, and throughout all the zones and climates of the globe. But Mr. Kipling's poetic genius has many limitations. It certainly expresses the Imperial idea, but in its more vigorous manifestations it is altogether confined to the expression of it. It expresses, moreover, the mere fact of Imperialism. It does not express, as did the genius of Virgil and Horace, any of the deeper effects which Imperialism may have upon life and character. With the exception of Mr. Kipling, there is no one amongst the present generation of poets whose work even suggests greatness.

Amongst these poets there are two who, though less known, perhaps, as poets than some writers far inferior to them, illustrate better than any others the truth which we are now anxious to enforce. These are Mr. George Meredith and Mr. Wilfrid Blunt. Their best poems, it is true, were produced some time ago; but so far as they depend on any conditions independent of the poets themselves, they might have been written yesterday. The poems we refer to are

Mr. Meredith's ' Modern Love ' and Mr. Blunt's ' Love Sonnets of Proteus.' ' Modern Love ' is unfortunately disfigured by something of that fantastic obscurity which Mr. Meredith has deliberately cultivated in his novels, thereby doing himself an incalculably greater injustice than could possibly have been inflicted on him by the most malignant critic, while Mr. Blunt's sonnets are as perfect in their lucidity as profound in their thought and feeling. But in Mr. Meredith's work, no less than in Mr. Blunt's, we have love-poetry of a very high order. We still recollect with pleasure that a critic in one of the most thoughtful of our weekly Reviews compared Mr. Blunt's sonnets with those of Shakespeare. Mr. Meredith's ' Modern Love ' is worthy of the same comparison. A fact of this kind may seem to militate against our present contention that one of the elements essential to the production of great poetry consists in certain general conditions independent of the poet himself, which at the present time are lacking. The work of these poets does not, however, in reality, even form an exception to our rule; but for the moment let us treat it as though it did, and as such let us consider the explanation of it. Love-poetry such as that of Mr. Meredith and Mr. Blunt expresses love under its most exclusively subjective aspect— love as felt by the lover in isolation from all circumstances except those involved in his own direct experience of it; and though love takes its colour in different ages from different conceptions of itself, there is no reason why, as a personally experienced passion, it should not be as intense in one age as in another. At all events, as a stimulus to poetry, its power from age to age varies much less than that of emotions of other kinds. And the same thing may be said of all the primary affections, taken singly, and regarded merely as the experience of such and such individuals. But a poetic expression of the affections, taken singly, though it may make beautiful poetry, profound poetry, and enduring poetry, does not, as we will explain presently, make great poetry; and the main point on which we are here insisting is, not that exceptional conditions of national or intellectual life are essential to the production of all good poetry, or even of all perfect poetry, but that they are essential to the production of poetry that is really great.

To beautiful poetry of a minor or less comprehensive kind, the absence of these conditions may be more favourable than their presence; as it is easy to see by a study of the later Roman poets. In these poets, from Statius downwards, we may trace, for example, the gradual development of something nearly resembling the modern feeling for nature. In the charming

poem in which Statius describes the villa of Vopiscus there is
a more intimate and imaginative association of natural scenes
and sounds—of the glimmer of leaves, the gleam of still water,
the murmur of the waterfall—with feelings and moods of mind
than is to be found in the Augustan poets; and a yet more
remarkable development of this modern mood is to be found in
a poet almost unknown to the general reader, who belonged to a
period when Roman literature generally is supposed to have
entered on its final stage of decay.   This poet is Ausonius.   In
two of his poems, 'The River Moselle' and 'Roses,' we have a
most startling anticipation of Wordsworth's delight in nature ;
and in a third poem, 'Cupid Crucified,' we have an anticipation,
equally startling, of the sentiment and the style of Keats.
Ausonius lacks the vigour and mental grasp of Wordsworth
and the enthusiasm of Keats, but these poems have something
of the peculiar beauty of both—a beauty beyond the reach of
the great classical age.   So, too, we, in the poets of the present
moment, may find frequent expressions of delicate and poignant
feeling, great command over the metrical resources of our
language, and a keen sense of the most elusive niceties of
style ; whilst two of our poets at least, Mr. Meredith and
Mr. Blunt, have given us examples of the poetry of personal
passion which have hardly been excelled by the poets of any
period.

    We have said, however, that none of this poetry is great.
The fundamental difference between poetry that is great and
poetry that is not great lies partly in the volume and quality
of the emotion expressed and partly in the fact that great poets
are masters of even the strongest emotion expressed by them,
while smaller poets are mastered by it.   More is implied in
both these points of difference than may at first sight appear.
Let us illustrate them by a few examples.   Mr. Austin Dobson
is a complete master of the emotions with which he deals.
He is as complete a master of them as Shakespeare was of the
emotions of Macbeth or of Othello.   But Mr. Dobson's emotions
are toys, exquisite playthings, which only suggest anything
great or serious by exhaling a faint aroma of a seriousness
which has passed away.   His mastery of emotion, therefore,
cannot possibly make him great.   Let us take a converse case.
We shall find one in the love-poetry of Mr. Meredith.   Here
the emotion expressed is really intense and serious; but the
emotion masters the poet : he is not master of it.   The really
great poet stands in a double relation to emotion : he not only
feels it, but he feels about it.   The poetic expression, however vivid and beautiful, of a mere personal experience, however

intense, will never make a great poem. If the poem which expresses it is to be great, any personal experience on which it may be founded must have been first universalised by the poet, and apprehended in a multitude of relations to things outside itself. The poet must feel the passion not only as his own, but as the passion of all other lovers as well; and he must, moreover, have considered it as something which forms part of life as a whole, which elevates life, or illuminates it, rather than as something which hides from view every factor in the human destiny but itself. For this reason 'Faust' is a great poem, whilst 'The Sorrows of Werther' is not a great romance. When Goethe wrote 'The Sorrows of Werther' he was the servant of passion: when he wrote 'Faust' he was its master. The fact is that no love-poetry can be great so long as it is merely love-poetry; and the same observation applies to the poetry of all the affections, taken singly. If they are to form the material of great poetry, they must be enlarged and elevated by being connected with the whole of life, or the whole of life must be exhibited as elevated or irradiated by them. It is this universal quality, this grasp of life as a whole, that our contemporary poetry lacks—not only such love-poetry as that of Mr. Blunt and Mr. Meredith, but also the poetry of Imperialism, which has made Mr. Kipling famous.

And now let us pursue our analysis of great poetry farther; and in doing this we must ask ourselves the old question, the question what poetry, whether great or not great, is. The fundamental answer to this question relates, not to the means by which the poet expresses himself, but to the distinguishing, the generic, character of what it is his mission to express: and this, described in the briefest and most general manner, is emotion. Emotion indeed, as Count Tolstoi in a recent volume has shown, with a temperance of argument which does not always distinguish him, is the special something the representation of which is the generic function, not of poetry only, but of all art. Art, he says, is essentially a means by which emotion felt by the artist is externalised and expressed in such a way that the emotion is communicated to and reproduced in others. But though this definition shows us what is the essence of all genuine art, it affords us no criterion by which to distinguish high and healthy art from art that is low or morbid, or great art from art that is not great. We shall endeavour here to remedy this deficiency, confining ourselves to the art of poetry.

The quality of poetry, then, as distinct from the fact of its genuineness, and distinct also from the technical adequacy of its form, depends on the quality of the emotion which it expresses. But first we must pause to observe that not its quality only but even its genuineness depends on one condition which Count Tolstoi does not mention. It depends on the fact of the emotion having a certain degree of intensity, or a certain degree of concentration. There are some kinds of emotion which are by no means strong, but may nevertheless inspire poetry of an exquisite though slight kind: such, for example, is the volatile and elusive sentiment captured and concentrated in the verse of Mr. Austin Dobson. But poetry as a rule differs from prose, not only in the fact that it expresses emotion rhythmically, but in the further fact, which alone makes the use of rhythm appropriate, that the emotion expressed possesses some exceptional strength. Poetry, says Wordsworth, is the natural language of all strong feeling; but it is certainly not the natural language of the mild preferences, dislikes, regrets, hopes, and disappointments which make up the every-day life of most people, though these are all emotion at a certain degree of temperature. To attempt to express them as poetry would be to make them ridiculous. In Kensington Gardens, on any fine Sunday morning, the ordinary observer may see any number of humble lovers 'keeping company,' and, if he be a good-natured observer, with some gift of kindly sympathy, he will be pleased rather than annoyed by the spectacle; but if he referred in a letter to the fact of his having chanced to notice it, he would hardly be moved to break into rhyme or into blank verse. If, however, the observer be one who is more than ordinary, if he have the insight which Arthur Hugh Clough had when this very spectacle was witnessed by him, his emotions would be intensified as Clough's were, and the natural expression of them would be poetry, as it was in the case of Clough, when he wrote the beautiful poem whose last stanza runs thus :—

> ' Ah, years may come, and years may bring
>   The truth that is not bliss :
> But will they bring another thing
>   That will compare with this ? '

Poetry, then, described in the most comprehensive way, is the expression—we need not here insist on its being rhythmical, it is enough to say adequate—the adequate expression in language, not of all emotion, but of emotion raised to a certain pitch of intensity. We may observe also that by the phrase 'adequate expression' is to be understood language which is capable of reproducing in the

reader the emotion felt by the writer. And now follows a
question to which the foregoing remarks are preparatory. By
what means, and under what conditions, is emotion raised to
that particular pitch at which the adequate expression of it is,
from the nature of the case, poetic, and rises inevitably above
the common level of prose ? Emotion is raised to such a pitch
firstly by intense personal experience, or by vivid imaginative
experience, and secondly by reflection on the facts which such
experience offers to the mind. The mere emotional experience
in itself is not enough. People, as we all know, may be very
deeply in love ; they may know all the joys and tortures which
originate in that passion, and they may yet be unable to write
even a tolerable love-poem. The language in which they
express their feelings, if it be quite spontaneous and unaffected,
will, no doubt, in accordance with Wordsworth's principle,
tend to have something poetic in it; but they would be
altogether unable to express them in any shape which an
impartial critic would recognise as a poem. They would
—to put their case in the light of Count Tolstoi's formula—
be unable to express their emotions in a form of words
calculated to reproduce the same emotions in the reader.
Nor is this inability accounted for by mere absence of
literary skill, or deficient command of language. To explain
the matter thus is to put the cart before the horse. The
truth is that a deficient command of the language of poetry
is due to an underlying deficiency in mental and imaginative
capacity.

This important critical truth is very clearly illustrated by
the single stanza which has just been quoted from Clough,
which refers to the prentice and the maid 'keeping company'
in Kensington Gardens. Nothing can, at first sight, seem
simpler than the sentiment there expressed ; but if we examine
the lines closely we shall see that the sentiment has been lifted
into poetry by the action of thought eminently comprehensive
in its character, and is fused with the sentiment by a rare power
of imagination.

> ' Ah, years may come, and years may bring
> The truth that is not bliss.'

In these words we have concentrated a whole philosophy of
life—of the relations of thought and knowledge to happiness,
and to the meaning of man's existence ; and in the two last
lines of the stanza this philosophy is applied to the affection of
the prentice and the maid, which is transfigured into a
universal symbol. Let us take one more example, equally

short, a complete poem of four lines only, by Walter Savage
Landor:—

> ' Stand close around, ye Stygian set,
>   With Dirce in one boat conveyed,
> Lest Charon seeing may forget
>   That he is old, and she a shade.'

The emotion here expressed is, in its origin, purely dramatic
and imaginative. It is, taken by itself, fainter than a half-
heard echo. But thought, through the vehicle of imagination,
has lifted it to the poetic pitch, and has impregnated it with
suggestions of all the dreams of youth and all the lost opportunities of age, with man's longing for the ideal, with man's
failure to realise it; and has made of this one small stanza a
shell whispering with ' all regret.'

Now, beautiful as this poem of Landor's is, it is not a great
poem. No one could compare it, for instance, with the
' Inferno,' or with ' Hamlet.' It bears the same relation to a
great poem that a gem bears to a picture; and in the foregoing
analysis of the reasons that make it beautiful we shall find an
explanation of the reason why it is not great, and also an
explanation of what the greatness of great poetry is. Poetry is
great, or the contrary, in proportion to two things: firstly, the
variety, the importance, and the representative character of the
facts or experiences which it exhibits to us as the subject of
emotion; and secondly, the extent to which the emotion in
question is intensified, interpreted, and impregnated with
significance by thought. The truth of the matter may be
expressed accordingly in a statement which to some will seem
a heresy and to others a paradox—that poetry is great in
proportion as it is something more than poetry, and that poets
are great in proportion as they are something more than poets.
To say this is really not more than to say that no faculty can
fulfil its highest functions when it works singly, and without
the assistance of others. That such is the case can be very
easily seen by a brief reference to the great poets and their
works. The essence of poetry being, as we have seen,
emotional, we shall find that in the production of the greatest
poems there has always been involved the exercise of various
faculties, judgments, and kinds of mental application which
intrinsically are outside the domain of emotion altogether.

Consider the characters of the following five poets: Dante,
Shakespeare, Goethe, Tennyson, and Browning. These all
were men of high and commanding intellect, of profound and
various knowledge. Dante was a scholar, a theologian, a
philosopher, a philosophical politician. Shakespeare, in spite

of his want of ordinary educational opportunities, has astonished and perplexed the world by the intimate acquaintance evinced by him with the technicalities of law, with the medical science of his time, with the pursuits which occupy men and the sports and amusements which distract them; by his keen insight into the nature of the bonds which unite classes, and of the false theories and prejudices that cause division between them; and by his grasp of some of the deepest truths of moral and metaphysical philosophy. He sums up for us in a few pregnant words the practical teaching of Aristotle's ' Ethics '; and no poet who was not also a philosopher could possibly have written the passage in the ' Tempest ' which begins with the words 'And like the baseless fabric of this vision.' Goethe's knowledge and mental activity were similarly comprehensive. Not only was he a philosopher, a scholar, a student of history, a keen and dispassionate critic, but he was a man of affairs, a man of the world, and a man of science as well. Browning was an indefatigable scholar, a historical and theological student, and his restless critical intellect was ceaselessly at work upon his knowledge; whilst Tennyson, though he lived secluded from society and from public affairs, and, as we venture to think, suffered from this seclusion, grasped the tendencies of the scientific discoveries of his time, and the nature of the difficulties and the changes which they were introducing into our conception of life, with an intellect which in point of masculine vigour and perspicacity was not excelled by that of any of his contemporaries. Portions of ' In Memoriam ' concentrate in a few stanzas the essence of scientific volumes, and the applied results of the scientific thought of a generation. Could we abstract from the works of any one of these great poets the elements contributed by faculties other than the poetic their poems would no doubt not cease to be poetry; but the greatness which has given them their hold on the world would go. The mere emotional gift of poetry will no more make a man a great poet than the mere emotion of patriotism will make a soldier a great general.

The production, then, of great poetry is a process of the following kind. It is not the expression in beautiful and adequate language of any personal and private emotion as directly experienced by the poet. Logically it begins with the selection of some fact or incident, or some nexus of facts or incidents, which represent human life under an important and significant aspect. Some of these facts may have been supplied him by his own experience; but he will deal even with these as though they were the experiences of another person, as though they were facts of human nature rather than of his own history. His selection of his materials will be made in accordance with some principle, some knowledge of life consciously or unconsciously organised, in the light of which such and such facts and incidents seem to be more significant and more representative than others ; and as his intellect and imagination continue to concentrate themselves on these their significance will become greater, more various, more profound. In thus employing his intellect he will, as the case may be, employ it as a theologian, a man of science, a philosopher : he will not be employing it as a poet. Even if we take into consideration, at this stage of our analysis, the act of arranging his materials in some artistic order, he will not be engaged in a work that is itself specifically poetic : he will merely be doing what must be done by any great novelist. Indeed the point now before us may be partially indicated by the question of how a great poem differs from a great novel. For one thing, the poem differs from the novel in the fact that it represents emotion at a higher degree of intensity ; but we must first consider where, in the production of a great poem, emotion makes its appearance, and what is its precise function. In the logical order of events, emotion makes its appearance after experience, observation, and philosophy have got together the poet's materials for him, and provided him with certain significant and typical facts of life, which he is ultimately to transform into a poem ; and it is the specific function of emotion to effect this transformation. The poet's emotion fuses these materials by its heat ; it irradiates them by its light. In proportion as this process is complete, the result is a true poem ; in proportion to the amount, the value, the general significance of the materials, the poem is a great poem.

That the emotion in question shall reach a certain degree of intensity we assume. It is difficult to measure this intensity by any definite standard ; but one sufficiently intelligible for our present purpose is afforded us by the degree of intensity which it reaches in a fine love-poem. We may say, then, that a great poem is a poem which does for life, or for life in its larger relations, what a love-poem does for one of life's elements. It presents to us what George Eliot called 'the human lot' as the one object of impassioned clairvoyance and overwhelming interest, similar to that with which a lover regards his mistress.

Now the capacity for emotion in the poet being taken for granted, for what reasons, and under what conditions, does the human lot, as distinct from his own experience of it, rouse his emotion into life? 'What's Hecuba to him, or he to Hecuba?'

What is Faust to Goethe? What is Goethe to Faust? The reason why the poet regards the human lot with emotion is that he sees it in the light of some unifying principle, and refers all its phenomena to some conviction, religious or philosophic, by which consciously or unconsciously he is dominated, and which invests all the facts of existence with some universal meaning. It is to these convictions that the emotion of the poet is due. And this observation brings us back to another, which has been made already. It is essential that the convictions in question, if the requisite emotion is to be roused by them, shall be not only intense in the mind of the poet himself, but shall also be prevalent amongst those whom the poet addresses. It is only on this condition that the force of his own emotion will be available for the production of poetry. He may have these convictions himself, but, if they are not shared by his contemporaries, the emotion which they excite in him will urge him not to exhibit life in the light which such convictions throw on it, but to prove that they are the convictions by which life ought to be interpreted. He will, as has been already said, be urged to address the world, not as a poet, but as a missionary or a controversialist. Here, then, we have the explanation of the intimate connexion which exists between great poetry and the general conditions of the age in which the poet lives. The poet need not always be conscious of the fact of their influence. Still less need he be able consciously to analyse the nature of it; or to say whether the vitality of the convictions which are the oxygen of his mental atmosphere is due to the prevalence of some definite religious faith or of certain intellectual principles, or to the sanguine and practical meaning imparted to either or both of these by some general quickening and development of national life. Shakespeare would certainly have been unable to describe the sources of his inspiration; but to us, viewing them from a distance, their character is sufficiently apparent. They lay partly, let us repeat, in the national development of England: they lay partly in that movement, full of restless hope, commonly called the Renaissance, by which Europe was still agitated; but behind all these, and bearing the same relation to them that the body of a violin bears to its strings, were the ethics of the old Catholicism, with its judgments of conduct and character, almost as fixed and vivid for Shakespeare as they were for Dante. Now, while conditions more or less analogous to those that surrounded Shakespeare have succeeded each other, as we have seen, during three quarters of the nineteenth century, it might be easily shown that during the last quarter they have sunk gradually into abeyance. The optimisms of the middle of the century have, in recent times, exhausted themselves; and although they have given place to a number of new ideas, new hopes, and new enthusiasms, none of these, except the idea of Imperialism, has acquired sufficient coherence, and become sufficiently prevalent, to impart any distinct and general character to the emotional conditions of the time. Even the Imperial idea itself, in spite of its vitality, is as yet but half developed; and its influence is calculated, as Mr. Kipling's work shows us, to produce stirring and spirited poems rather than great poetry.

It may be observed, however, that the period in question, though not favourable to poetry, has witnessed an unusual activity in the production of novels; and many of these have been of high, if not of the highest, excellence. The reason of this is to be found in a fact which has been already noticed. The novelist, like the poet, represents life as apprehended through the medium of emotion; but the emotion is less intense, nor does it fuse, pervade, and transmute the whole of the materials so completely as is requisite for the production of a great poem. Consequently, the novel may well flourish amid conditions which are not favourable to the production of great poetry; and we may even ask whether the mere fact that at any given period the novel becomes the most important kind of imaginative literature is not itself a sign that the conditions favourable to the production of great poetry are wanting.

It remains, however, to consider once more the other factor in the case, namely, the personal faculties of the poet, as distinct from the conditions under which they are exercised; and, whilst fully admitting that under unfavourable conditions the genius even of a Shakespeare would not produce Shakespeare's poetry, we must admit also that there may be periods in the life of the world or of a nation when the conditions seem unfavourable to great poetry only because there is no one with the genius of a Shakespeare to take advantage of them. This may be true to a certain extent of our own country to-day. We do not think that it is so, but it is difficult to prove a negative. One thing, however, we may venture to say with confidence, that were the conditions of the moment more favourable to great poetry than they are, we have many poets amongst us whose poetry would possess qualities greater beyond comparison than any which, as matters stand, the most partial flattery, unless it be the flattery of the poets themselves, can attribute to it. Could Mr. Meredith or Mr. Blunt treat life as a whole with a clearness of vision, with a genuine intensity of emotion, similar to that with which they have treated one of its passions, they would have produced poetry as much above their existing love-poems as their poetry on any other subject actually falls below them. Mr. Blunt's latest poem, 'Satan Absolved,' supports us in this conjecture. It is a sort of mystical drama. The scene of it is laid in Heaven, but the subject of it in reality is the life and destiny of mankind. It exhibits Mr. Blunt as possessing the personal faculties of a poet of a high order; it shows him to us as gifted with a style at once delicate, vigorous, and incisive, a vivid imagination, and great capacity of emotion; but he has nothing on which to exercise these faculties that is in any degree worthy of them. His drama in Heaven, despite all its technical excellencies, is nothing but a querulous lampoon on the Anglo-Saxon race, the language of which is, in many places, so exaggerated that, the stronger the writer's emotion, and the greater his success in expressing it, the more completely does he fail to attain the impressiveness at which he aims. A poet of his capacity, setting himself to deal emotionally with a really great subject, could not have missed so completely any ideas with regard to it which were really great and profound, and calculated to give to it sane emotional unity, had ideas of the requisite kind been prevalent in the world around him. A similar judgment must be passed on the rest of our latter-day poets, among whom a high place must be given to Mr. Davidson. Mr. Davidson's ballad of the nun who left her convent, a poem deservedly well known, is the work of a man endowed with remarkable poetic gifts. No one but a man with a high poetic faculty could have described, as he has done, the cities which 'smouldered and glittered on the plain,' or the subtle influences of the external world which troubled the nun's being :—

> ' Sometimes it was a wandering wind,
>   Sometimes the fragrance of the pine,
>   Sometimes the thought how others sinned,
>   That turned her sweet blood into wine.'

But with all these technical gifts for producing poetry that might be great, this poem as a whole has nothing great in it whatsoever. The genuine poetic emotion, which is beyond doubt present in it, is inspired by, and ministers to the expression of, no great, no definite, no unifying belief with regard to human life, and no clear insight into it. And the same may be said of all our contemporary poets who are really poets at all—of Mr. Yeats, of Mr. Watson, of Mr. Symons, of Mr. Phillips, and others. The poetic impulse, the poetic imagination, the sense of form, the command of language, are there.   Everything is ready for the great poetic sacrifice, with the exception of a worthy offering; and of this fact a partial, if not complete, explanation is to be found, not in a deficiency of faculty in the poets themselves, but in certain peculiarities in the general conditions of the time, which, whilst eminently favourable to certain forms of mental activity, are not favourable to the development of that high emotion which, born as it is of some strenuous, some general optimism, intellectual or religious, is favourable, and indeed essential, to the production of great poetry.

The lovers of the English muse need not, however, despair. Sooner or later, in one form or another, the desired conditions will once more make their appearance.   We may even now see them being slowly prepared around us, in the ferment of these unsettled opinions, and in the battle of these disunited enthusiasms, which seem, when taken singly, so exaggerated, so grotesque, so impracticable, or so unconvincing, but which will in time, with greater or less completion, coalesce into beliefs and hopes greater, more sane, and more moving than any one of them, and will unite instead of dividing and disintegrating the emotions of men.   When that event takes place, the conditions which make great poetry possible will once more be present; nor do the accomplishments and character of the present generation of poets give us any reason to fear that, when poetry of a greater kind than theirs becomes possible, the personal genius will be wanting that shall convert the possible into the actual.

TITLES IN THIS SERIES

Criticism: General, Poetic, and Dramatic

Parody, Satire, Literary Controversy, and Curiosa

22. James Carnegie. JONAS FISHER: A POEM IN BROWN AND WHITE. 1875. with [A. C. Swinburne.] THE DEVIL'S DUE: A LETTER TO THE EDITOR OF "THE EXAMINER." BY THOMAS MAITLAND. 1875

23. Philip James Bailey. THE AGE; A COLLOQUIAL SATIRE. 1858

24. [W. C. Bennett.] ANTI-MAUD. 1865. with [Eustace Clare Grenville Murray.] THE COMING K———. 1873. with [W. H. Mallock.] EVERY MAN HIS OWN POET. 1877

25. [John Burley Waring.] POEMS INSPIRED BY CERTAIN PICTURES AT THE ART TREASURES EXHIBITION, MANCHESTER. 1857. with [Anon.] THE LAUGHTER OF THE MUSES. 1869

26. Robert Buchanan. THE FLESHLY SCHOOL OF POETRY AND OTHER PHENOMENA OF THE DAY. 1872. with Algernon Charles Swinburne. UNDER THE MICROSCOPE. 1872

27. J. Rutter. THE NINETEENTH CENTURY, A POEM, IN TWENTY-NINE CANTOS. 1900

Collections of Critical Essays

28. William E. Fredeman, editor. VICTORIAN PREFACES AND INTRODUCTIONS: A FACSIMILE COLLECTION. 1986

29. Ira Bruce Nadel, editor. VICTORIAN FICTION: A COLLECTION OF ESSAYS FROM THE PERIOD. 1986

30. Ira Bruce Nadel, editor. VICTORIAN BIOGRAPHY: A COLLECTION OF ESSAYS FROM THE PERIOD. 1986

31. John F. Stasny, editor. VICTORIAN POETRY: A COLLECTION OF ESSAYS FROM THE PERIOD. 1986

32. William E. Fredeman, editor. THE VICTORIAN POETS: AN ALPHABETICAL COMPILATION OF THE BIO-CRITICAL INTRODUCTIONS TO THE VICTORIAN POETS FROM A. H. MILES'S "THE POETS AND POETRY OF THE NINETEENTH CENTURY." 1986